W9-CQE-421

Praise for previous editions

"Ott and Dicke should be applauded for their outstanding efforts, which bridge the macro and micro levels of the nonprofit sector for the first time and consequentially enrich the intellectual understanding of the field."

—*Public Administration Review*, Vol. 73, Issue 1, January/February, 2013

"The editors have done the work for you—if you want to understand the theories behind the nonprofit sector, this is the book to read."

—Joanne Carman, University of North Carolina, Charlotte

"[A] wonderful collection of readings, eminently suitable for introductory courses as well as great starting point for more advanced students and scholars. Theory and practice, national and international, and current and historical perspectives are all embraced in this valuable book."

—Dennis R. Young, Case Western Reserve University

The Nature of the Nonprofit Sector

The Nature of the Nonprofit Sector is a collection of insightful and influential classic and recent readings on the existence, forms, and functions of the nonprofit sector—the sector that sits between the market and government. The readings encompass a wide variety of perspectives and disciplines and cover everything from Andrew Carnegie's turn-of-the-century philosophy of philanthropy to the most recent writings of current scholars and practitioners. Each of the text's ten parts opens with a framing essay by the editors that provides an overview of the central themes and issues, as well as sometimes competing points of view.

The fourth edition of this comprehensive volume includes both new and classic readings, as well as two new sections on the international NGO sector and theories about intersectoral relations. *The Nature of the Nonprofit Sector, Fourth Edition* is therefore an impressively up-to-date reader designed to provide students of nonprofit and public management with a thorough overview of this growing field.

J. Steven Ott is Professor of Political Science and Public Administration at the University of Utah, USA.

Lisa A. Dicke is Professor of Public Administration at the University of North Texas, USA.

The Nature of the Nonprofit Sector

Fourth Edition

Edited by

J. STEVEN OTT

AND LISA A. DICKE

Routledge
Taylor & Francis Group

NEW YORK AND LONDON

Fourth edition published 2021
by Routledge
605 Third Avenue, New York, NY 10158

and by Routledge
2 Park Square, Milton Park, Abingdon, Oxon, OX14 4RN

Routledge is an imprint of the Taylor & Francis Group, an informa business

© 2021 Taylor & Francis

The right of J. Steven Ott and Lisa A. Dicke to be identified as the authors of the editorial material, and of the authors for their individual chapters, has been asserted in accordance with sections 77 and 78 of the Copyright, Designs and Patents Act 1988.

First edition published by Westview Press 2000
Third edition published by Westview Press 2015

Library of Congress Cataloging-in-Publication Data
A catalog record for this book has been requested

ISBN: 978-0-367-69652-8 (hbk)
ISBN: 978-0-367-69648-1 (pbk)
ISBN: 978-0-367-69655-9 (ebk)

DOI: 10.4324/9780367696559

Typeset in Garamond

Contents

I Introduction to the Nonprofit Sector   1

II The History, Values, and Activities of Nonprofit Organizations in the United States   63

III   The Nonprofit Sector Internationally: The Global Context   111

IV   Tax Exemption and Tax Deduction   181

V   Economic Theories of the Nonprofit Sector   215

IX Theories of Relations and Collaboration Within and Between Sectors **421**

X The Nongovernmental (NGO) Sector in Other Countries **491**

Figures and Tables

Figures

Tables

Foreword

In 2000, when I wrote the Foreword to the first edition of this volume, I noted that the field of nonprofit studies had exploded during the prior decade. Now more than 20 years later, the explosion continues and our understanding of the nonprofit sector has improved correspondingly. I am therefore very happy to welcome this fourth edition of *The Nature of the Nonprofit Sector* with its mix of important classics in the field and new selections.

Research on the sector continues to develop, partly because of the growing number of individual scholars now specializing in the field. During the past two decades, the number of Ph.D. dissertations on topics related to philanthropy and the nonprofit sector shows rapid growth. A search of titles and abstracts that include variants on "nonprofit" or "philanthropy"[1] shows a cumulative total of more than 53,500 dissertations and theses in the field as of December 31, 2019. More than a quarter of these (26 percent) were accepted between January 2010 and December 2019, another 23 percent during the first decade of the 21st century, and another quarter (28 percent during the previous two decades combined (see Figure 1).

Publication of books has also increased, although the number has slowed considerably in recent years. A ProQuest search of books in English that include variants on "nonprofit" or "philanthropy" shows a total of more than 24,400 books published.[2] The number published per year increased from less than 50 between 1980 and 1985 to about 700 from 1993 to 2003 and reached 1,100 in 2011 and 2012 before declining rapidly to 180 in 2018 and only 78 in 2019.

FIGURE 1. Number of Dissertations and Theses on Nonprofit and Philanthropy Related Topics, by Period of Completion as of December 31, 2019

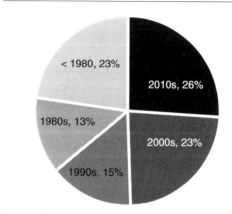

Source: See note 1

By contrast, the number of articles published in scholarly, peer-reviewed journals continues to grow rapidly, with more than 313,200 published as of December 31, 2019, including a total of 310,300 between January 1, 1980 and December 31, 2019.[3] As Figure 2 shows, the number of articles published in peer-reviewed scholarly journals increased from less than 300 per year in 1980–83 to more than 1,000 in 1993, about 6,200 in 2000, 12,200 in 2010, and almost 31,200 in 2019. The count is probably incomplete for the last several years, since some journals are late in publishing issues. The growth *reflects most likely an increase in the number of scholarly journals as well as the spread of these topics to a broader array of journals.*

Also significant have been efforts by several key institutions to make important sources of data on the sector available to

FIGURE 2. **Number of Articles Published in Peer-Reviewed Scholarly Journals on Nonprofit and Philanthropy Related Topics, January 1, 1980 through December 31, 2019, by Year of Publication**

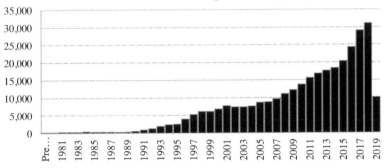

Source: See note 2

nonprofit scholars and policy analysts. While several of these efforts began prior to 2000, they have become more fully institutionalized and widely used, undoubtedly contributing to the growth in scholarly journal articles. They include:

- Candid (www.candid.org), representing the merger of GuideStar (www.guidestar.org), which provides scanned images of Form 990s available for all IRS-registered entities, and the Foundation Center (www.foundationcenter.org), which provides data on foundation and corporation grants.

- The National Center for Charitable Statistics Data Archive (https://nccs-data.urban.org/), housed in the Center for Philanthropy and Nonprofits at the Urban Institute, which provides access to electronic data files from the full scope of IRS-registered tax-exempt entities. NCCS no longer provides technical assistance or customized data extracts but does undertake some data checking procedures.

- The Corporation for National and Community Service (www.nationalservice.gov/),

which has produced annual data on volunteering in the U.S. from 2002 to 2016 in collaboration with the Bureau of Labor Statistics (see www.bls.gov/opub/ted/volunteer-work.htm). The sequence and phrasing of questions changed in 2017 to reflect more focus on civic engagement. The new series is now available at www.nationalservice.gov/serve/via. The data are collected annually as part of the Current Population Survey, a very large (60,000 households) and high-quality survey (participation is mandatory).

- The Lilly Family School of Philanthropy (www.philanthropy.iupui.edu, formerly the Center on Philanthropy) at Indiana University, which since 2001 has developed a national biennial supplement on giving and volunteering to the long-running Panel Study of Income Dynamics.

- The Giving USA Foundation (https://givingusa.org/), which sponsors Giving USA (first compiled in 1956, now produced by the Lilly Family School of Philanthropy), a comprehensive annual analysis of philanthropy in the U.S.

- The Center for Civil Society Studies (www. ccss.jhu.edu), housed at Johns Hopkins University, which has developed systematic data on the size and composition of nonprofit/civil society organizations for almost 50 nations as well as comprehensive information on paid employment in the sector for a number of U.S. states.
- Global Philanthropy Indices (https://global indices.iupui.edu/), developed by the Hudson Institute, now housed at the Lilly Family School of Philanthropy, which has compiled systematic data on the philanthropic environment and philanthropy resource flows for 79 economies.

Similarly, the number of universities that offer at least three graduate-level courses in the nonprofit sector has also grown, from 17 in 1990 and 82 in 1996 to 126 in 2006 and 218 in 2016.[4] Indeed, 651 colleges and universities offered at least one course in the field in 2016, up from 426 in 2006 and 284 in 1996. These programs are located in a variety of academic homes, from freestanding programs and institutes, to traditional academic disciplines in the social sciences and humanities, to those that have become areas of specialization within existing professional degrees, most notably the MPA (Masters of Public Affairs/Administration), but also the MPP (Masters of Public Policy), MBA (Masters of Business Administration), and MSW (Master of Social Work) degrees.

Detailed guidelines for nonprofit management education[5] were first developed in the late 1990s and have been updated several times under the auspices of NASPAA—the Network of Schools of Public Policy, Affairs, and Administration, formerly the National Association of Schools of Public Affairs and Administration (the major accrediting body for MPA programs)—as well as the Nonprofit Academic Centers Council (NACC).[6] The continued inclusion of nonprofit management in MPA/MPP and MBA degree specializations ranked by *U.S. News and*

World Report is another indicator of the extent to which the field of nonprofit studies has grown, matured, and become institutionalized.

These trends reflect a number of underlying forces, perhaps most obviously the growth of the sector itself, up from just over a million in 1995 to more than 1.6 million in 2010 and almost 1.7 million in 2018 according to IRS registration data on tax-exempt entities.[7] The count dropped briefly to about 1.4 million in 2013, reflecting new regulations implemented in 2008 that removed exempt entities that had failed to file newly required annual reports for three consecutive years.[8] The sector has also significantly increased its share of paid employment. For example, data for Indiana show that nonprofit paid employment increased from 6.9 percent of total paid employees in 1995 to 9.6 percent in 2018. Its share of total payroll increased from 5.8 percent to 9.9 percent.[9]

Indeed, the sector is increasingly recognized as an economic, political, and social force in U.S. society. Government budget cuts, devolution, and privatization have encouraged policymakers to look to nonprofit service agencies as alternatives to direct government provision and have highlighted the role of service networks (in which nonprofits often play prominent roles). At the same time, other types of nonprofits—traditional membership and civic organizations that promote social capital and civic engagement—are thought by some observers to have declined, raising questions about the future of these key functions in democratic society.

The task of understanding the sector is indeed of major proportions, as this volume makes clear. Although the sector has grown and become more visible as indicated previously, it is surprisingly difficult to comprehend how pervasive, ubiquitous, and complex the sector is. As a test, try reading your own local newspaper carefully from front to back, including announcements, obituaries, and want ads—everything in the paper. (Of course, that's assuming you still have a local newspaper.) If your experience is like mine and that of my students, you will most likely be surprised to find that nonprofits surface everywhere—in 90 percent of the obituaries, in about one-quarter of reports on national and international news (albeit depending on the events of the day), and in the majority of items on local developments and events. Nonprofits appear both as the subject matter of newspaper reports, as the home base of experts or commentators on specific issues, and as participants in or the site of events that are listed in the paper.

But you need to know something about the sector to take this test—that all associations and churches are nonprofit, that the majority of social service agencies are nonprofit as are some health or arts and culture organizations (but not all), and so forth. That means you also need to know how to determine whether a particular organization is indeed nonprofit. But that is no simple matter. Although online lists of those registered with the IRS are available from several sources (the IRS, Guidestar.org, and NCCS), our data for Indiana suggests that may only cover about 60 percent of nonprofits. And some government institutions are also registered as tax-exempt organizations.

Developing a cognitive map of the sector is difficult—but essential if we are to understand its capacities as well as its limitations. How are we to accomplish this? By analyzing the underlying puzzles of why people give money, goods, and time to strangers, of how such giving is structured and institutionalized, or what accounts for variations in these dimensions across social groups, time, and space? By examining the sector's functions and the variety of tasks it performs for the overall society (enhancing innovation, pluralism, integration, and preservation), the policy process (providing negative feedback, societal support, latent resources, obscuring the size of government), or the individual (experiencing play, mystery/the sacred, and personal development)? By looking at the major fields of activities in the sector (by

economic function or by primary purpose) and how these fields relate to the political economy? By applying disciplinary perspective, primarily from among the social sciences and humanities and related professional fields? By comparing it and the roles it plays to those of the other sectors: business, government, and private households and how boundaries between the sectors shift over time? By comparing the sector with those in other societies or in other time periods?

These questions get to one of the key issues addressed in this volume: What is distinctive about the nonprofit sector? I would emphasize five major elements—all addressed by the readings in one way or the other. First, the sector operates under private, not public, auspices. That has important implications for how accountability and authority are structured and carried out—there is no easy way for concerned citizens or voters to "throw the rascals out."

Second, the sector operates under a particular ownership structure in which there are no formal ownership rights, with corresponding implications for the exercise of property rights and lack of access to equity finance. The latter is compensated for in part by access to broad variety of non-market revenue streams, such as charitable donations. The lack of formal owners in particular creates complex principal-agent relations and corresponding difficulties in sorting among and prioritizing multiple constituency groups.

Third, the sector is rooted in voluntarism. That means that the sector is inextricably intertwined with all the complexities associated with diverse values, motivations, incentives, and the vagaries of human behavior. It also means that the sector is centrally involved in confrontations, negotiations, and dispute resolutions.

Fourth, the sector's purpose involves substantive rationality—the achievement of particular missions and substantive goals—not just profit for the sake of profit or reelection to political office for the sake of power. But substantive goals change over time and reflect environmental conditions, such as the state of technology, but also the state of the political economy, particularly the structure of social, economic, and political opportunities. What is a problem today may not be a problem 50 years from now or even ten years from now, because problems reflect not only actual conditions, but the values and experiences of particular stakeholders along with their abilities to mobilize networks and cultural capital at a particular point in time.

Finally, the nonprofit sector operates with a particular type of technology. By and large, it does not produce things or process cases or transactions but seeks to change people—their views, values, behaviors, and/or knowledge. Thus, the nonprofit sector finds itself deeply immersed in uncertain causal structures—what, after all, does cause people to change their behavior or values, at least in the absence of coercive institutions? How do we transmit knowledge effectively so that it sticks and is used? Indeed, changing people is difficult because it interrupts their routines and therefore is painful or inconvenient for them and their surroundings. The nonprofit sector is composed of millions of organizations that experiment with those five sets of challenges on a daily basis.

I have emphasized these five elements because I believe they convey both the complexity and the importance of understanding the nonprofit sector. This volume of essential readings on the nonprofit sector—carefully edited to be accessible to students, professionals, and scholars alike—both reflects the important developments that the sector has seen in recent years and is a major contribution in its own right. J. Steven Ott and Lisa A. Dicke have succeeded in identifying, selecting, and editing a set of readings that takes us a long way toward making sense of the sector's complexity and recognizing its distinctive roles in the U.S. society. Although many scholars in the field will have a favorite selection that did not make it into the volume or got dropped from the previous edition (indeed, I have my own candidates),

everyone—whether specialist scholar, beginning student, or seasoned professional—will benefit from a careful reading of the selections that are included. The introductory sections to the various parts of the book are of enormous help.

As someone who has taught both graduate and undergraduate courses in the field, I am painfully aware of the difficulty of developing a list of engaging readings that covers the major concepts and theories in the field. We owe the editors and the publisher a major debt of gratitude once again for having produced this updated volume.

June 2020
Kirsten A. Grønbjerg

O'Neill School of Public and Environmental Affairs
Indiana University Bloomington

Notes

1. I used the advanced search option of www.proquest.com to search titles and abstracts of doctoral dissertation and theses, using various date range specifications and the search terms (philanthrop*) OR (charit*) OR (nonprofit*) OR ("third sector") OR ("voluntary sector") OR ("civil society") OR ("not-for-profit") OR ("independent sector") OR ("tax-exempt"). The count is most likely incomplete for the period prior to 1980 when only titles are searchable. The count may fail to incorporate themes related to nonprofit social enterprise and related topics. The database covers doctoral dissertations and selected master's theses accepted by U.S. institutions of higher education since 1853. The search term "tax-exempt" was added this year and the results therefore differ from what was included in previous editions of this volume.

2. I used the advanced search option of www.proquest.com to search English language books, using various date range specifications and the search terms (philanthrop*) OR (charit*) OR (nonprofit*) OR ("third sector") OR ("voluntary sector") OR ("civil society") OR ("not-for-profit") OR ("independent

3. I used the advanced search option of www. proquest.com to peer-reviewed scholarly journals, using various date range specifications and the search terms (philanthrop*) OR (charit*) OR (nonprofit*) OR ("third sector") OR ("voluntary sector") OR ("civil society") OR ("not-for-profit") OR ("independent sector") OR ("tax-exempt"). The count may fail to incorporate themes related to nonprofit social enterprise and related topics. The search term "tax-exempt" was added this year and the results therefore differ from what was included in previous editions of this volume.

4. Mirabella, Roseanne M. (2015). "Nonprofit Management Education and Philanthropic Studies." In Melvin J. Dubnick and Domonic A. Bearfield (editors), *Encyclopedia of Public Administration & Public Policy* (EPAP3), 3rd Edition. Taylor and Francis, CRC Press. Mirabella, Roseanne; Hoffman, Timothy; and Teo, Terence K. (2019). "The Evolution of Nonprofit Management and Philanthropic Studies in the United States: Are We Now a Disciplinary Field?" *Journal of Nonprofit Education and Leadership* 9, No. 1:63–84.

5. See NASPAA's "Guidelines for Graduate Professional Education in Nonprofit Organizations, Management and Leadership," Revised October 2006. Available online at www.naspaa.org/accreditation/NS/document/GuidelinesForNonprofit.pdf (retrieved August 24, 2014).

6. The latter now offers interested programs the opportunity to have their curriculum reviewed in terms of how well it aligns with the NACC Curricular Guidelines. As of 2019, ten programs had done so. NACC refers to this process as "accreditation" although NACC itself is not recognized as an accrediting body by the Council for Higher Education Accreditation.

7. See Internal Revenue Service (IRS) Data Book (www.irs.gov/statistics/soi-tax-stats-irs-data-book). The 2018 edition is the most recent available.

8. Religious organizations are not required to register with the U.S., so the count of tax-exempt organizations excludes most of the estimated 350,000 religious congregations in the U.S. Many other nonprofits are also not registered with the IRS for a variety of reasons. See Grønbjerg, Kirsten A.; Liu, Helen K.; and Pollak, Thomas H. (2010). "Incorporated but Not IRS-Registered: Exploring the (Dark) Grey Fringes of the Nonprofit Universe" *Nonprofit and Voluntary Sector Quarterly* 39 (5, October): *925–45.*

9. Unpublished data from Indiana Nonprofits Project, see https://nonprofit.indiana.edu/.

Preface

People in many countries conduct almost all of their formally organized religious activity and many cultural and arts, human service, educational and research activities through private nonprofit organizations.[1] Nonprofits in the United States have always received substantial support from local, state, and federal governments, and from fees paid by those who use their services, but they have also always relied on donations and voluntary service. How did countries everywhere come to rely so heavily on nonprofits or nongovernmental organizations? Why have they continued to do so? What are the consequences?[2]

The Nature of the Nonprofit Sector is designed to answer these and similar questions by helping people understand and appreciate the theories, concepts, perspectives, and themes that define or frame the nonprofit sector in the United States and around the globe. Each part introduction and the previously published readings in the chapters use influential theories about the NGO sector to describe and explain how and why the sector has developed and operates as it does in different contexts.

This book is about the sector whose organizations engage in a surprisingly wide array of activities and provide an enormous range of services, mostly for the purpose of improving aspects of people's quality of life or preventing its deterioration. As Kirsten Grønbjerg notes in the Foreword to this 4th edition, although the sector has changed enormously over the past several decades, it continues to include some of the most interesting and useful organizations in

society. Likewise, this volume attempts to present an informative mix of readings about the sector's nature, scope, history, roles, and theories, as well as some of the greatest challenges it faces in the United States and around the world. All of the introductory essays and readings provide partial answers to the four questions that shape and define this volume:

- What is distinctive about the nonprofit sector, and why?
- What has caused the nonprofit sector to be distinctive?
- What are the important implications of the nonprofit sector's distinctiveness?
- Why, and in what ways, do the NGO sectors differ in their functions, size, and degree of independence in countries around the world?

In short, all of the introductory essays and readings in this volume help answer foundational questions of "why?". For example: Why is the sector structured as it is? Why does it do what it does—instead of government or for-profit businesses? Why is it not allowed to distribute profits (or surpluses)? Why do people give to and volunteer in it? Why does it receive favorable tax treatment in most countries? Why does the sector differ among countries but also share many commonalities? Theories and research allow us to formulate answers to questions such as these.

Several significant changes have been made from the 3rd edition that we believe are essential, including

- The nongovernmental sector has expanded dramatically in countries outside of the U.S. We believe it essential to expose readers in the U.S. and in other countries to theories about the sector that are not specific to the U.S. Therefore, instead of one part on the sector outside the U.S. as in the 3rd edition, there are now two. Part III examines NGOs from a global perspective, particularly the roles and functions of international nongovernmental sector (INGOs). Part X examines why the NGO sectors in countries outside of the U.S. exist as they are, and why they differ from each other.

- As a result, several of the parts of this 4th edition have been changed in important ways. Part I now introduces the sector irrespective of geography. Part II focuses on the history and contributions of the nonprofit sector in the U.S. As mentioned, Part III examines NGOs from a global perspective, particularly the roles and functions of INGOs, and Part X focuses on the NGO sectors within countries. We hope these changes make it easy for course instructors to choose the perspectives they want to emphasize.

- In recent years, many countries have moved toward "shared governance" or "new public governance." This is a significant development for countries and for NGO sectors. Under shared governance, nongovernmental organizations "sit at the table" when decisions are being made about the delivery of government services and how to allocate funding for services that used to be delivered by government employees. These shared governance programs and services often are required to be delivered and coordinated through "partnerships" among organizations outside of government. The implications of shared governance and multi-sector partnerships for nonprofit organizations are enormous, especially in the human services. Therefore, Part IX that was titled "The Blending and Blurring of the Sectors" in previous editions has been reframed and is now titled "Theories of Relations and Collaboration Within and Between Sectors."

- We are also pleased that so many newer insightful theories and concepts have become available since the 3rd edition went to press. Therefore, many readings from the 3rd edition have been replaced.

The Nature of the Nonprofit Sector deals only with macro-level concepts and theories. It examines macro-level theories about the existence, form, and functions of the sector and groupings of organizations in the sector. In contrast, micro-level theories have as their unit of analysis the behavior of individuals and groups inside organizations. Micro-level issues are the focus of the 4th edition of our companion book, *Understanding Nonprofit Organizations: Governance, Leadership, and Management*, also published in 2021 by Routledge.[3]

In attempting to provide rich answers to its central questions, *The Nature of the Nonprofit Sector* frames the nonprofit sector from widely diverse perspectives and from foundational concepts found in older classics up to newer and sometimes more controversial perspectives found in current literature. Each part approaches the sector from a different slant and emphasizes distinctive variables, factors, concepts, and theories as well as causes and implications.

- Part I, "Introduction to the Nonprofit Sector," introduces the sector's place in societies generally, including its scope, subsectors, revenue sources, and strikingly divergent purposes and roles, and the implications of its underlying values and features—the public good, individualism, philanthropy, and voluntarism.

- Part II, "The History, Values, and Activities of Nonprofit Organizations in the United States," introduces the nonprofit sector in the United States by addressing the book's basic questions about the sector in the United States: How and why has the sector evolved into its current form and status? What is distinctive about the sector, and why? And how and why does the nonprofit sector differ from the public (government) and private (business) sectors in its foundational values and its place in and contributions to the socio-political-economic system of the United States?

- Part III, "The Nonprofit[4] Sector Internationally: The Global Context," attempts to answer similar questions about the NGO sector in countries outside the U.S., especially NGOs that operate across national boundaries that are commonly known as "International Nongovernmental Organizations," or simply INGOs.

- Part IV, "Tax Exemption and Tax Deduction," explores the reasons why government extends favorable tax treatment to organizations in the nonprofit sector and the influences of tax policy in the U.S. and selected other countries on the distinctiveness of organizations in the sector. Favorable tax treatment is a result of both the sector's purposes and roles, and it plays a vital role in the strength and shape of the sector.

- Parts V through IX present many important theories of the nonprofit sector. These theories help explain the sector's existence, roles, forms, structures, values, functions, and distinctiveness, including economic theories (Part V), political theories (Part VI), community/civil society theories (Part VII), and theories of giving and philanthropy (Part VIII).

- Part IX, "Theories of Relations and Collaboration Within and Between Sectors," addresses issues involving the nonprofit sector's increasing participation in governance—one of the most dramatic changes in the governance function over the last decade. Often, participation in governance is through "partnerships" (not always voluntary partnerships) with government agencies, private businesses, and other nonprofits.

- Part X, "The Nongovernmental (NGO) Sector in Other Countries," concludes this book with an exploration of how and why NGO sectors and organizations in countries around the world differ, with an emphasis on the effects of governments' policies on the roles and functions NGOs perform.

First, however, we briefly introduce theories in general.

Theories of the Nonprofit Sector: Diverse Perspectives Addressing Diverse Issues

For many readers, *theory* is an ugly, intimidating term that suggests irrelevance and impracticality.

—ROGER A. LOHMANN[5]

The word *theory* has such a mystique about it. We tend to talk about theory as researchers much like our forebears would have discussed theology: with a mixture of awe, fascination, and cynicism.

—JACQUELYN THAYER SCOTT[6]

It is necessary to appreciate that there is no such thing as *the* theory of the nonprofit sector—there cannot be and should not be. Rather, there are many different types of theories that attempt to explain why the sector exists in its current form, how nonprofit organizations and the people in and around them behave in different circumstances, and why government provides them with special treatment. As mentioned earlier, the macro-level theories in this volume try to explain and predict the existence, form, and functions of the sector and groupings of organizations in the sector. In contrast, micro-level theories have as their unit of analysis the behavior of individuals and groups within organizations.[7]

Most theories of the sector can be grouped by the aspects of the sector or organizations they emphasize; their assumptions about the sector, the organizations, and the societal environment of which they are a part; and the methods used to study the sector and its organizations. These groupings of theories and theorists tend to be associated with fields of study, particularly economics, sociology, social psychology, cultural and social anthropology, philosophy and ethics, political science, religion, history, public administration, and business administration. Social work, public health, and a few theories from applied mathematics, statistics, and systems theory also are represented. None of these groupings of theories is the "right approach." Each wrestles with different questions and issues, incorporates different variables, and approaches the sector and its organizations from a different perspective. Although these different theories represent loosely knit communities of diverse approaches and perspectives, collectively they form the intellectual base for the sector.

Theories of the nonprofit sector are also important for decision-making in practice. They are frequently used to justify public policy decisions that affect, for example, the tax-exempt status of organizations and the tax deductibility of gifts, favorable treatment for government contracts, and restrictions on commercial activities by nonprofits that compete with for-profit businesses. Remember Kurt Lewin's astute observation: "There is nothing so practical as a good theory."[8]

We have tried to bring a sense of cohesion to these multiple perspectives and approaches by grouping the theories in Parts V through X:

- *Part V, "Economic Theories of the Nonprofit Sector":* Almost all economic theories of the nonprofit sector are concerned with issues such as the place of—or the roles of—nonprofit organizations in a three-sector political economy; the types of revenue-generating activities that nonprofits tend to engage in; the nature of relationships between nonprofit-sector organizations and their revenue sources, particularly government agencies and businesses (including transactions); and the effects of these relationships on organizations in all three sectors—and thus on the political economy of a society.
- *Part VI, "Political Theories of the Nonprofit Sector":* Political theories seek to identify political implications of the nonprofit sector, with particular emphasis on its role in advancing the interests of groups that are underrepresented in society and the sector's role in developing leaders for a democracy.

- *Part VII, "Community and Civil Society Theories of the Nonprofit Sector":* Community theories and civil society theories help explain the "place" of nonprofits in communities; the niches they fill; the complexity of the relationships among nonprofit organizations; the relationships among nonprofits and democratic institutions; and the interactions among their stakeholders, community networks, and other institutions.
- *Part VIII, "Theories of Giving and Philanthropy":* Why do people give their money, time, and effort? Why do they give to certain causes and organizations but not others? Why do some people give more than others? To what extent is giving driven or influenced by sympathy, empathy, altruism, a sense of justice, a need to alleviate guilt, a desire for public recognition, or rational calculation of personal utility? Is giving an inherited drive or learned from others? How and why do giving patterns differ among people from different national backgrounds and at various life stages?
- *Part IX, "Theories of Relations and Collaboration Within and Between Sectors":* This part introduces theories, research, and issues about interdependence among organizations in the nonprofit sector and in different sectors (for example, "partnerships"), social entrepreneurialism, and newer forms of organizations that exist in more than one sector (for example, "hybrid organizations"). The NGO sector has always needed to position itself between the business sector and the government sector, and this positioning has become more complex in recent years. Nonprofits increasingly must include business-like and government-like approaches in order to survive and grow while still living by their values and meeting social needs. The implications of the shifts are not clear for the business, nonprofit, and public sectors—nor, indeed, for democratic governance and civil society.
- *Part X, "The Nongovernmental (NGO) Sector in Other Countries":* Whereas Part III explores

effects of different economic systems, political systems, and governments' policies on NGO sectors.

Criteria for Selection of Readings

When we have looked back at earlier editions of this book, we have been impressed at how greatly the quality and quantity of literature on the sector has expanded in recent years. For this edition, we had to choose among a much wider array of excellent articles and book chapters. Therefore, we applied our criteria for deciding which readings to include and exclude more than in earlier editions.

The first criterion that any reading had to satisfy was a three-part substantive test:

- Should the serious student of the NGO sector be expected to be able to identify the author(s) of the reading, the reading's basic themes, and the crux of its arguments?
- Does the reading provide a reason or reasons why the nonprofit sector exists in its current form? Does it explain why organizations in the sector engage in (or refrain from engaging in) particular types of activities?
- Does the reading help to explain how the sector developed and how it fits into the sociopolitical-economic systems of a society? Does it explain the sector's distinctive characteristics and contributions or the paramount challenges that it faces?

Second, the reading had to be readable. Students who have already had reason to peruse the literature of nonprofit organizations will appreciate the importance of this criterion. Some theories can be very dense.

Finally, the reading had to fit the purposes of this volume. It had to address issues or ideas that are important to the sector and discuss either the organizations that comprise the sector or organizations as elements in networks,

systems, or societies. Because this book is about macro concepts and theories—not micro issues and theories—many interesting readings about the internal structures and workings of nonprofit organizations are not included here. They are reprinted in the 4th edition of our companion book, *Understanding Nonprofit Organizations: Governance, Leadership, and Management.*

Placing the readings into specific parts was not always an easy task. For example, philanthropy is an integral component of the sector's historical values-base, and the history of philanthropy is inexorably intertwined with the history of the sector. Therefore, for example, Andrew Carnegie's treatise on "The Gospel of Wealth" belongs in Part II—but also could fit well in Part VIII—and Nuno Themudo's "A Cross-National Philanthropic Puzzle" easily could fit in Parts V or VIII.

The readings reprinted in this book range from old classics to recent contributions. We readily admit that we had to exclude many significant contributors and contributions. There are simply too many to fit into one book. We doubt that many will criticize us for the readings we have included, but we can easily be criticized for important readings we did not include. We accept full responsibility for our decisions.

Lisa A. Dicke   *J. Steven Ott*
University of North Texas   University of Utah

Notes

1. Most of the world uses the term "nongovernmental organization" or simply "NGO." In the United States, however, "nonprofit organization" or simply "nonprofit" is used. Throughout most of this book, we use "nongovernmental" and "nonprofit" interchangeably. The exceptions are: "nongovernmental" in Parts III and X, which are about the sector outside the U.S., and "nonprofit" in Part II, which is about the sector in the U.S.

2. Hammack, David C. (1988). "Introduction: The Growth of the Nonprofit Sector in the United States." In David C. Hammack (editor), *Making the Nonprofit Sector in the United States*. Bloomington and Indianapolis, Indiana University Press, xv.

3. J. Steven Ott and Lisa A. Dicke, eds., *Understanding Nonprofit Organizations: Governance, Leadership, and Management*, 4th ed. (New York: Routledge, 2022).

4. The term "nonprofit" or "nonprofit organization" is preferred in the United States. In other countries, the term "nongovernmental organization" or simply "NGO" is preferred. In this volume, we tend to use "non-profit" and "NGO" interchangeably, but lean toward "nonprofit" when discussing the United States and "NGO" when discussing other countries.

5. Roger A. Lohmann, *The Commons* (San Francisco: Jossey-Bass/Wiley, 1992), vi.

6. Scott, Jacquelyn Thayer (1995). "Some Thoughts on Theory Development in the Voluntary and Non-profit Sector," *Nonprofit and Voluntary Sector Quarterly* 24: 31–40.

7. See our companion volume, *Understanding Nonprofit Organizations: Governance, Leadership and Management*, 4th ed.

8. Alfred J. Marrow, *The Practical Theorist: The Life and Works of Kurt Lewin* (New York: Basic Books, 1969).

Acknowledgments

We wish that we could acknowledge everyone who has contributed ideas, insights, support, challenges, and constructive criticisms, but we must limit our words of appreciation to those who played the most central roles in shaping our vision and refining our ideas into a cohesive fourth edition of this anthology. Among those whose intellectual contributions absolutely must be acknowledged are Kirsten Grønbjerg, Indiana University—Bloomington, who made major updates to her informative Foreword for this 4th edition. Pitima Boonyarak at the City of Calgary, Alberta, Canada restructured Part IV and rewrote the part introduction. Jesus Valero, University of Utah, offered numerous valuable suggestions and co-authored the insert about INGOs that is included in Part III. Hee Soun Jang and Christopher Byrd at the University of North Texas along with Georgina Griffith-Yates at the University of Utah provided ideas, support, and assistance. Brigham Daniels, a former University of Utah graduate student and now on the faculty of the J. Reuben Clark School of Law at Brigham Young University, wrote most of the introduction to what is now Part V, "Economic Theories of the Nonprofit Sector."

The Routledge/Taylor & Francis staff has been wonderful to work with. Laura Varley and Katie Horsfall have been responsive, thorough, and persistent in securing permissions to reprint previously published articles and chapters, and have steered us artfully through the development and production of this book.

We owe debts of gratitude to David Gies and Jay Shafritz, who collaborated with Steven Ott in compiling *The Nonprofit Organization: Essential Readings* (Pacific Grove, CA: Brooks/Cole, 1990). Their ahead-of-the-time ideas and insights helped shape our thinking about the sector and thus unknowingly contributed substantially to this volume.

And finally, special thanks to Floyd Rosencrantz and Pat Ott for putting up with us as we prepared this 4th edition while working mostly under foot at home during the pandemic.

Permissions credits

Extract 4, Chapter II. Reprinted with permission of Melvin & Leigh, Publishers. All rights reserved. This chapter originally appeared in Reframing Nonprofit Organizations: Democracy, Inclusion, and Social Change (2019), edited by Angela Eikenberry, Roseanne Mirabella, and Billie Sandberg.

Extract 1, Chapter VII. From BOWLING ALONE: The Collapse & Revival of American Community by Robert D. Putnam. Copyright © 2000 Robert D. Putnam. Reprinted with the permission of Simon & Schuster, Inc. All rights reserved.

Extract 4, Chapter VII. Originally published as To Empower People: The Role of Mediating Structures in Public Policy. Washington, DC: American Enterprise Institute for Public Policy Research, 1977. Reprinted with permission of the American Enterprise Institute.

PART I

INTRODUCTION TO THE NONPROFIT SECTOR[a]

Defining the Nonprofit Sector[b]

Most definitions of the nonprofit sector begin by stating what nonprofit organizations *are not* and *what they cannot do.* For example, they cannot distribute profits to "owners" or "shareholders" — they cannot even have owners or shareholders. Articulating what the nonprofit sector *is* and *does* and why in positive terms is more difficult and requires more words, but is far more rewarding. Positives can express the spirit and values of the sector — *its essence* — while negatives cannot.

What the nonprofit sector encourages and enables — what it allows people of all standings to engage themselves in, to try to accomplish and how — is what distinguishes the nonprofit sector from government agencies and businesses. The essence of the NGO sector is a blend of *personal* passion and *voluntary action for the public good* — however *the public good* may be defined. Therefore, the nonprofit sector is a *civil society* — it is the "realm of independent citizen activity outside both government and business,"[1] or, stated more completely, it is:

> The contested arena between the state and the market where public and private concerns meet and where individual and social efforts are united. Nonprofit and voluntary action expresses a complex and at times conflicting desire to defend the pursuit of private individual aspirations, while at the same time affirming the idea of a public sphere shaped by shared goals and values.[2]

Usually, similar ideas and concepts are used to describe and define the *nonprofit sector* (or *NGO sector*) and *civil society.* Both are conceived of as the space between the market and government where people come together by their own choice, out of mutual caring, to respond to problems or to enact what is important in their lives, for their family, or to improve their neighborhood, their community, or the world.[3] No government agency requires them to act, defines the public good for them, chooses what cause they are (or should be) passionate about, or how they operationally define *family, neighborhood,* or *community.* For example, *community* might be a village in southern France or Haikou, Hainan, China, a couple of benches around a checkerboard in a park in Vienna, a café in Dubai, or a group of individuals scattered around the globe with shared interests who are connected through social media and who will never meet each other face to face.

Nonprofits are also where people initiate activities and programs to ameliorate, remedy, or "pick up the pieces" behind society's most grievous problems and nature's disasters without necessarily waiting for government to act. Poverty, ignorance, homelessness, chemical spills, illiteracy, child and

DOI: 10.4324/9780367696559-1

spousal abuse, birth defects, genetic defects, war, racism and white nationalism, chronic physical and mental illnesses, hurricanes and typhoons, tornadoes, earthquakes, floods, mine cave-ins—the list is endless. NGOs employ different strategies to deal with these cases and their root causes. Many nonprofit organizations provide direct services to individuals or groups in need, others seek to eliminate the causes of the needs, some attempt to do both, and some raise funds to distribute to other organizations that are helping to get things done.

People also come together in civil society's nonprofit organizations for uplifting reasons, including, for example, to worship together, for personal growth and development, and to create and share art, history, music, literature, and poetry. Still others gather to preserve a part of their history or culture, to advance the standing of their profession or industry, or simply to enjoy themselves.

It is important to understand that the NGO sector and what it does in a country is partially a product of the socio-political-economic systems that have evolved and emerged in the particular countries. From this view, the sector provides a means for reacting to marketplace failures and the failure of government to adequately serve citizens in need by filling these voids with volunteered time and charitable contributions[4]—as well as a means to fulfill peoples' passions.

Defining the NGO Sector by What It Is Not and What It Does Not Do

The tendency to define the sector by what it is not caused Roger Lohmann to write the poignantly titled article, "And Lettuce Is Nonanimal," in which he muses:

> Virtually all nonprofit management theories explicitly or implicitly begin with this negative accent and contribute to the paradoxical consensus position that nonprofit action has no independent basis. Nonprofits arise only from the failures of other institutions but are themselves inefficient, unproductive, poorly managed or mismanaged, and inadequately controlled.[5]

Although it is relatively easy to define the nonprofit sector by what it is not and what it cannot do, this is neither very useful nor satisfying. The sector's distinctive aspects and its invaluable contributions to society cannot be captured by defining it only in negatives. For example, making money *is not* the primary purpose for nonprofits. It isn't that money is unimportant for NGOs—quite the contrary—it is extremely important. Nonprofit organizations must make money and manage it well in order to survive and grow. It is the *relative importance* of money that distinguishes the nonprofit sector from the private business sector. In the private business sector, making money, or more precisely making profits, comes first. Profit is *the reason* why business firms are created and continue to exist. In contrast, making money in the NGO sector is vitally necessary but *not* primary. Revenue is a necessary resource for accomplishing substantive ends, but it is *not* the reason for existence or the end purpose.[6]

Making money is not the primary purpose for organizations in the public sector (government agencies) either. Revenue is a resource used by government to advance the public good—not an end in itself. The most important factor that separates the nonprofit sector from the public sector, quite obviously, is that government raises revenue primarily through taxes that are imposed on individuals and businesses while nonprofits *do not* have taxing power. Nonprofits raise revenue from a variety of sources. The largest sources of revenue for the nonprofit sector vary among countries. Until the 1980s in the United States, the largest sources were the millions of individuals, corporations, and private foundations who decided voluntarily to support the mission and activities of nonprofits through donations of their time, effort, and money.[7] In many other countries, the largest sources have been government grants and contracts—which are now also the largest sources in the United

States. Although advancement of the public good usually is the central purpose for both nonprofit and public sector organizations, nonprofits are not government and, until recent decades, had not been "government-like."

Tax exempt organizations in the nonprofit sector do not pay taxes. For *tax deductible organizations*, individuals and corporations who give money (or other assets) may deduct the gift from their income taxes—and thus they do not pay taxes on that amount of their income. Nonprofits that are tax deductible in most countries are not permitted to participate in political campaigns and must carefully limit the time, effort, and money they expend on lobbying activities.[8] Invaluable contributions to society cannot be captured by defining it only in negatives. Therefore, trying to define the nonprofit sector by what it is not is neither very useful nor satisfying.

THE U.S.'S TAX REFORM ACT OF 2018

In 2017, the United States enacted income tax reforms that went into effect in 2018. This act significantly raised the standard deduction for individuals and persons filing jointly, making it much less likely that filers can offset some tax burden by donating to tax deductible organizations and itemizing the gift as a deduction.

To determine taxable income, a taxpayer's Adjusted Gross Income (AGI) is reduced by either the standard deduction or the sum of itemized deductions. Prior to 2018, the standard deduction amounts, indexed to inflation, were to have been: $6,500 for single individuals and married individuals filing separately, $9,550 for heads of household, and $13,000 for married individuals filing jointly (including surviving spouses). Under the New Act through December 31, 2025 the standard deduction is increased to $24,000 for married individuals filing a joint return, $18,000 for head-of-households, and $12,000 for all other taxpayers, adjusted for inflation in tax years beginning after 2018. No changes were made to the current-law additional standard deduction for the elderly and blind (Geoffrey Gallo, December 30, 2017. "New Tax Reform Act Summary and Details").

Voluntary action for the public good begins with individuals taking the initiative to improve the lives of others. Since the Reformation, two predominant forms of giving and assisting for the benefit of others have been evident in Western civilizations: *individual* and *associational*. This volume focuses on *associational philanthropy*—the NGO sector that enables and supports philanthropy—including voluntarism.

Philanthropy

It can be argued that the study of the nonprofit sector begins with philanthropy, an area of applied ethics or applied moral philosophy. *Philanthropy*, including giving and volunteering, collectively organized and enabled through nonprofit organizations, is the primary means for individuals to make their individual policy choices among value preferences. First, though, several key definitions.

Philanthropy, perhaps the nonprofit sector's most distinctive pillar, is "voluntary giving, voluntary serving, and voluntary association to achieve some vision of the public good [and] includes charity, patronage, and civil society."[9] Thus, *philanthropy* is a broader term than *charity*, which means "relieving or alleviating specific instances of suffering—aiding the individual victims of specific social ills." With philanthropy, a return is expected from the donation in some form of improvement in the public's welfare or general benefit. *Philanthropy* attempts to eliminate the causes of problems that *charity* seeks to alleviate. *Voluntarism* is "actions undertaken freely by individuals, groups, or organizations that are not compelled by government, or directed principally at financial or economic gain, regarded as beneficial by participants or the larger society."[10]

Although many good things happen when individuals volunteer to give time or money to people in need or to causes, many more good things happen for longer periods of time when individuals join together, form associations, and collectively attack social or environmental ills or aid their victims. *Associational philanthropy* thus is the essence of *social capital formation*, "those bonds of trust and reciprocity that seem to be pivotal for a democratic society and a market economy to function effectively."[11] And giving—of time, energy, and money—is the "fuel" that energizes associational philanthropy.

Not all nonprofit organizations are recipients of or conduits for philanthropy. Many nonprofits rely on fees-for-services and government contracts for most of their income and many do not utilize volunteers. Yet a huge number of others do rely on philanthropy, particularly in the subsectors of religion, the arts and humanities, advocacy, private education, environmental protection, and to a lesser extent but still substantially, in health and human services. Although many government agencies also are recipients of philanthropy, including for example, volunteer fire departments, elementary schools, public libraries, and even occasionally the Internal Revenue Service, these exceptions do not detract from the distinctiveness of philanthropy in the nonprofit sector.

The Subsectors: The Nonprofit Sector's Fields of Interest

The United States Internal Revenue Service Codes identify and define about 30 types of nonprofit organizations. The IRS Codes provide a glimpse of the great variety of purposes and activities that are characteristic of nonprofit organizations. For example, they include qualified pension and profit-sharing trusts; individual retirement accounts (IRAs); publicly supported charitable organizations (501[c][3]s), including religious, scientific, educational organizations, and private foundations; political organizations including PACs, "super PACs," and 527 501(c)(4)s; homeowners' associations, civic leagues, and social welfare organizations; labor, agricultural, and horticultural organizations; business leagues, chambers of commerce, and boards of trade; fraternal beneficiary societies; benevolent life insurance associations; cemetery companies; state-chartered credit unions and mutual reserve funds; cooperative crop financing organizations; veterans' organizations; black lung benefit trusts; cooperative hospital services organizations; farmers' cooperatives; and charitable remainder trusts.

Lester Salamon has proposed categories of subsectors that provide an excellent overview of the main subsectors in which nonprofit organizations are active:[12]

- Health care
- Education and training
- Social services (or human services)
- Arts and culture
- Housing and community development
- Environmental organizations
- International assistance
- Religious congregations

- Civic participation and advocacy
- Infrastructure organizations
- Foundations and corporate philanthropy

These subsectors are, in effect, *fields of interest*. They identify the substantive reasons why organizations in the nonprofit sector exist, their purposes, and what they do. These are the clusters of causes and cases that engage the attention and the emotions of volunteers, donors, boards of directors, and grantors. They are the sources of energy, the purposes that activate individuals and groups to form or join nonprofit associations and to be engaged and give of themselves and their money—to *do something*.

Defining the Sector Positively

Nonprofit Organizations Exist to Improve the Quality of Life—Or to Prevent Things From Becoming Worse

Nonprofits and the people who work in them are legally and ethically allowed to make money. Personal gain, however, is not the primary purpose for nonprofits—it is not an adequate reason for a nonprofit to exist and should not be the primary reason why individuals choose employment in the sector. The most basic reason why the nonprofit sector exists is to encourage and enable the benevolent donation of money, property, time, and effort to provide services to people in need and/or to eliminate causes of or to prevent social, economic, and environmental problems and injustices; to ameliorate the consequences of these problems and injustices; and, to improve the overall quality of life around us. This is true whether the organization exists primarily to promote the arts and humanities, to help terminally ill persons die with dignity, to advocate for environmental protection or LGBTQ+ rights, to conduct research on cancer, or to advance a set of religious beliefs.

In recent decades, the NGO sectors in many countries have become the object of high expectations among elected officials and a large segment of the general public. They are expected to serve as "safety nets" for individuals and families who have exhausted their access to public supports but are not self-sufficient. The sector is expected to solve (not merely ameliorate) deep social problems by rebuilding "community" through its ability to generate *social capital*. For example, U.S. President George H. W. Bush espoused the importance of the "thousand points of light" as voluntary solutions to societal problems. His son, the 41st president, was a strong proponent of enabling "faith-based" nonprofit organizations to solve social problems. Thus, we have come to expect our nonprofit sector to right myriad societal wrongs and to "pick up the pieces" when society and "the system" fail.

The Sector Defines "The Public Good" Through Its Core Values of Individualism and Pluralism

Equity and *justice* are the foundational values of democratic governments, and government's overriding concern for equity and justice has caused a well-publicized and often scorned proliferation of policies, procedures, and rules (and inflexibility) that attempt to ensure that everyone receives equal treatment. The four-decades-old era of government downsizing, devolution, outsourcing, reinvention, and unwavering government concern for equity and justice has been declared inadequate.[13] Flexible responsiveness to individual client needs, circumstances, and preferences has replaced equity and justice as the values we assert we want emphasized when responding to social problems. "One size does not fit all."[14]

The values of *individualism* and *pluralism* have moved to the center of the justification for the existence and the essence of the nonprofit sector as well as justification for favorable tax treatment. The sector has a long-standing record of "championing"—leading the way with voluntary giving for—causes and cases that appeal to people individually and through voluntary associations. Philanthropy and voluntarism, collectively organized and enabled through nonprofit sector organizations, are the primary means societies are using to make individual choices among value preferences.

The nonprofit sector shares its core values of individualism and pluralism with the for-profit business sector because these values are essential to the functioning of a market economy. Thus, although these values are an essential part of the nonprofit sector's distinctiveness, they are not unique to this sector.

Many of us have our own personal visions of *the public good*, visions that we believe are compelling enough that others should share them—particularly elected officials and candidates for public office. *The public good* is an elusive concept, however, because it is a socially constructed reality—a subjective and individualistic point of view and set of preferences.[15] Implementation of any vision of the public good requires collective action and an allocation of resources, however. Thus, *some* collective definition of the public good is needed in order to advance a vision into solution strategies and action. Otherwise a vision remains nothing more than a dream.

Governments define the public good through legislative actions and executive orders that apply essentially to people equally. The core of the public policy-making process lies in legislatures allocating tax revenues among competing values, priorities, and projects. In contrast, the NGO sector defines the public good by the extent of the willingness of individuals, families, corporations, foundations, and the government to donate, volunteer, or contract with nonprofit organizations to support the accomplishment of their particular vision. Therefore, although organizations in the nonprofit sector may advocate for universal definitions of the public good, such universal definitions are rarely achieved. Instead, operational definitions of the public good evolve piecemeal from the voluntary individual and associational philanthropy, charity, volunteering—giving—of people and organizations in all three sectors.

Nonprofits as "Pathways to Participation"

Nonprofit organizations are the means for enactment—the "vehicles"—that individuals, families, and neighbors use to become active participants in their communities. Few problems can be solved or opportunities capitalized upon by people working alone. Nonprofits are the voluntary associations of people who *decide individually* to *work collectively* to achieve ends that are important to them. If the ends are not important to them, they will not participate for very long.

> In no country in the world has the principle of association been more successfully used or applied to a greater multitude of objects than in America. . . . A vast number [of associations] . . . are formed and maintained by the agency of private individuals.[16]

Nonprofits as "Manifestations of Community"

As a nonprofit organization works to help alleviate causes of poverty or a theater group practices for a performance, other long-term and often unplanned and unintended benefits are achieved at the same time. First, the organization provides outlets for individuals to develop and express their creativity—while they solve community housing problems or provide new learning or recreational opportunities in their neighborhoods.[17]

Second, community leadership capability is developed among individuals, which can be applied in organizations in all three sectors. Future government officials, business executives, and nonprofit organizations' board members develop leadership, political, networking, and managerial skills and values by participating in nonprofit organizations.

Third, while individuals are working together on problems, community "networks" are built, used, and "banked" for future use on different issues. This creates a pool of latent talent that can be mobilized at a later date and can serve as an important community resource in emergencies and when other needs for action arise. *Social capital* is the term used to describe the established linkages among people who share common cares and concerns. These linkages or networks are themselves "capital assets" of a community. When caring people share common concerns, a capacity is created or expanded to prevent or resolve a variety of social problems.

And fourth, if enough individuals give enough time or money to the problem or opportunity, the need for government funding may be reduced.

Therefore, as "manifestations of community,"[18] nonprofits serve at least five distinctive public benefit ends: The situation that was the cause for the participation is improved; individuals find outlets for their creativity and desire to participate; community leadership is developed; social capital is created; and reliance on government may be diminished. As Alexis de Tocqueville observed in 1834,

> when an association is allowed to establish centers of action at certain important points in the country, its activity is increased and its influence extended. Men have the opportunity of seeing one another; means of execution are combined; and opinions are maintained with a warmth and energy that written language can never attain.[19]

Summary—The Sector's Distinctive Contributions to Better Societies

Helmut Anheier identifies three major trends wherein NGOs are playing increasingly important roles in improving the quality of life in developing societies and in developed nations alike.[20] He expects these trends to continue and expand. First, NGOs have become the central players in *New Public Management* and *New Public Governance*[21] approaches to the delivery of human services in countries around the world. They deliver services to vulnerable populations under contract to a government.[22] These two trends have made NGOs essential elements in the worldwide movement away from direct service delivery by government agencies that are often seen as inefficient and ineffective bureaucracies.[23] Second, nonprofit organizations facilitate civic engagement that results in the creation of *social capital*.

> Economic growth and democratic government depend critically on the presence of social capital—the existence of bonds of trust and norms of reciprocity that can facilitate social interaction. . . . Without such norms, contracts cannot be enforced nor compromises sustained. Hence, markets and democratic institutions cannot develop or flourish. . . . Thus, nonprofits form the social infrastructure of civil society and create, as well as facilitate, a sense of trust and social inclusion.[24]

Third, from a social accountability perspective, individuals and civil society organizations are increasingly becoming active in "affirming and operationalizing direct accountability relationships between (a) citizens and the state, (b) citizens and businesses, (c) businesses and the state, and (d) NGOs and relevant stakeholders."[25]

Although identifying truly distinctive contributions that the nonprofit sector makes may be difficult, Anheier has made the task easier. Nonprofit organizations have become key components in improving communities, democracies, governance, and economies—the quality of life—in many societies worldwide.

But the sector is not independent. Until a few decades ago, many of us liked to think of the nonprofit sector as *the independent sector*, a sector whose organizations are free to pursue missions and purposes unfettered by legislatively and bureaucratically imposed mandates and restrictions, and free from the need to chase profits. Unquestionably, the nonprofit sector has been an independent voice for progressive solutions to an enormous number of social ills and an independent source of creative approaches to dealing with complex problems. NGOs have always been largely dependent on others for their revenue, however, and it is difficult for financially dependent organizations to remain functionally independent. Further, as the boundaries among the three sectors have continued to grow increasingly blurry over the past three decades, the independence of organizations in the nonprofit sector has diminished.

Readings Reprinted in Part I

The readings reprinted in Part I introduce the nonprofit sector from three quite different perspectives.

In the first reading, "Roles and Responsibilities of Nonprofit Organizations in a Democracy," Elizabeth Boris, Brice McKeever, and Béatrice Leydier argue that the basic role of nonprofit organizations is "as enablers of civic engagement and promoters of the common good [which] is the cornerstone of a pluralistic democracy." NGOs differ widely in their purposes, activities, and impacts but all are "self-governing, may not distribute profits, and serve public purposes or the common goals of their members." Like governments, nonprofits promote the public good, but, in the spirit of pluralism, they are free to define "the public good" as they see fit (within some legal and IRS limits), and one NGO's definition of the public good may well conflict with others' notions of the public good.

"Many countries have long-standing expansive nonprofit sectors that play economic, social, and political roles similar to those in the United States, but with variations reflecting the different cultural, historical and economic contexts." Nonprofit organizations are defined and regulated primarily under statutes and the tax code. As Boris and her colleagues explain, the laws and rules that regulate NGOs in different countries vary widely because the legal framework and tax code are products of cultural, political, and economic factors. The legal framework in turn influences the culture, politics, and economy of a nation. This reading introduces the concept of "social capital" that we will return to many times throughout this volume. "Nonprofit organizations, regardless of origin, create networks and relationships that connect people to each other and to institutions quite apart from the organization's primary purposes." These "community associations build the trust and cooperation that is essential for the effective functioning of society, politics, and economy." (See Part VII for more about "social capital.")

Meghan Elizabeth Kallman and Terry Nichols Clark examine reasons for the differences in size, resilience, and influence on society among NGO sectors in different countries, including the United States.

> The countries examined [here] fall into one of two categories: those with a strong central state and—we argue, consequently—a weaker involvement of third sector organizations in some regards, and those comparatively 'weak' national governments with historically strong third sector organizations.

Many of the original nonprofit organizations in the U.S. were Protestant churches where parishioners provided "food, clothing, and basic necessities" as well as worshiped, but did not become engaged in "systematic political advocacy or agitation." But, even in non-democratic countries, the end of communism in 1989 brought out a drastic drop in the hierarchy of the state, and neoliberalization processes have brought about a new political emphasis on third sector organizations as the central state shrinks, and policy work is 'rescaled' to municipal governments and civil society organizations.

These transformations led political philosopher Jürgen Habermas to "theorize how the potential of this sort of discursive, 'coffee house model' of associationalism could serve as the basis for extrastate democratic engagement and participation in general."

Kallman and Clark identify and explain "five basic institutional logics operating simultaneously in the third sector" that together "create tensions, synergies, and unevenness" "in civil societies across the globe": clientelism, paternalism, bureaucracy, activism, and professionalism. These factors are causing the role of activism and engagement to change. The changes, however, are "often with doubts, complex adaptations, and challenges."

"The Idea of a Nonprofit and Voluntary Sector," a chapter from Peter Frumkin's 2002 book, *On Being Nonprofit: A Conceptual and Policy Primer*, identifies three underlying principles that link organizations in the nonprofit sector: "(1) they do not coerce participation; (2) they operate without distributing profits to stakeholders; and (3) they exist without simple and clear lines of ownership and accountability." These features "give these entities [nonprofit organizations] a set of unique advantages that position them to perform important societal functions neither government nor the market is able to match."

The nonprofit and voluntary sector can be thought of as a "tent covering public-serving charities, member-serving organizations, and a range of informal organizations, including voluntary and grassroots associations." The "tent" "occupies an ambiguous and at times contentious position in the current American political scene. . . . Today, for quite different reasons, nonprofit and voluntary organizations are embraced by both conservatives and liberals." "The politics of nonprofit and voluntary action can take on many different meanings."

Frumkin introduces two broad conceptual distinctions for understanding the core functions of nonprofit organizations.

> The first critical distinction concerns how the sector is explained: the question is whether nonprofit and voluntary activity is driven primarily by *demand or by supply*. . . . The second distinction concerns how the sector is justified: here the issue is whether the value of nonprofit and voluntary action is seen as residing in *the instrumental character of the outcomes* that are generated for society or in *the inherently expressive quality of the activities themselves* that reward those who undertake them (emphasis added).

These conceptual distinctions intersect to create a matrix "that depicts, on one side, the nature of the value produced by the sector (instrumental versus expressive) and, on the other side, the underlying animus or force (demand versus supply)."

Notes

a. Portions of this introduction were written by David L. Gies and were published originally in David L. Gies, J. Steven Ott, and Jay M. Shafritz, eds., *The Nonprofit Sector: Essential Readings* (Pacific Grove, CA: Brooks/Cole, 1990), pp. xxiii–xxv.

b. Most of the world uses "nongovernmental organization" (or simply "NGO"). In the United States and Canada, "nonprofit organization" or simply "nonprofit" is used. We use "nongovernmental" and "nonprofit" interchangeably throughout this chapter and most of this book with the following exceptions. We use "nongovernmental" in Parts III and X, which are about the sector outside the U.S., and "nonprofit" in Part II, which is about the sector in the U.S.

1. Elizabeth T. Boris, "The Nonprofit Sector in the 1990s," in Charles Clotfelter and Thomas Erlich (eds.), *Philanthropy and the Nonprofit Sector in a Changing America.* (Bloomington and Indianapolis, IN: Indiana University Press, 1999).

2. Peter Frumkin, *On Being Nonprofit: A Conceptual and Policy Primer* (Cambridge, MA: Harvard University Press, 2002), p. 1. (Reprinted in this part).

3. For more extensive discussions of civil society, see Part VII, "Community and Civil Society Theories of the Nonprofit Sector"; Michael Edwards, *Civil Society*, 4th ed. (Cambridge, UK: Polity, 2020); and Michael Edwards, *The Oxford Handbook of Civil Society* (Oxford, UK: Oxford University Press, 2013).

4. See Part III, "The Nonprofit Sector Internationally: The Global Context," Part V, "Economic Theories of the Nonprofit Sector," Part VI, "Political Theories of the Nonprofit Sector," and Part X, "The Nongovernmental (NGO Sector in Other Countries."

5. Roger A. Lohmann, "And Lettuce Is Nonanimal: Toward a Positive Economics of Voluntary Action," *Nonprofit and Voluntary Sector Quarterly 18* (1989): 368.

6. See the *Foreword* to this volume by Kirsten Grønbjerg.

7. Brice McKeever, *The Nonprofit Sector in Brief 2015: Public Charities, Giving, and Volunteering* (Washington, DC: The Urban Institute, 2015).

c. This ability to deduct contributions was limited by the U.S. Tax Reform Act of 2018. See the Insert Box immediately following.

8. Bruce R. Hopkins, *The Law of Tax-Exempt Organizations*, 12th ed. (New York: Wiley, 2019).

9. Warren F. Ilchman, "Philanthropy," in Jay M. Shafritz (ed.), *International Encyclopedia of Public Policy and Administration* (Boulder: Westview, 1998), p. 1654.

10. Jeffrey L. Brudney, "Voluntarism," in Jay M. Shafritz (ed.), *International Encyclopedia of Public Policy and Administration* (Boulder: Westview, 1998), p. 2343.

11. See "Bowling Alone: Thinking About Social Change in America," a 2001 chapter by Robert Putnam reprinted in Part VII of this volume; Robert Putnam, *Bowling Alone: Revised and Updated: The Collapse and Revival of American Community* (New York: Simon & Schuster, 2020); David Halpern, *Social Capital* (Cambridge, UK: Polity, 2004); and Michael Edwards, *The Oxford Handbook of Civil Society* (Oxford, UK: Oxford University Press, 2013); Lester M. Salamon, ed., *The State of Nonprofit America*, 2nd ed. (Washington, DC: Brookings Institution Press, 2012).

12. Lester M. Salamon, ed., *The State of Nonprofit America*, 2nd ed. (Washington, DC: Brookings Institution Press, 2012).

13. J. Steven Ott and Lisa A. Dicke, "Challenges Facing Public Sector Management in an Era of Downsizing, Devolution, Diffusion, Empowerment—and Accountability?," *Public Organization Review 1* (2002): 321–339.

14. See, for example David Osborne and Ted Gaebler's classic, *Reinventing Government* (Reading, MA: Addison-Wesley, 1992), Chapter 1.

15. Peter L. Berger and T. Luckmann, *The Social Construction of Reality* (Garden City, NY: Doubleday, 1966).

16. Alexis de Tocqueville, "Political Associations in the United States," in *Democracy in America*, Vol. 1 (The Henry Reeve text as revised by Francis Bowen, now further corrected and edited by Phillips Bradley) (New York: Vintage Books, 1945), 198.

17. Peter Frumkin, *On Being Nonprofit: A Conceptual and Policy Primer* (Cambridge, MA: Harvard University Press, 2002).

18. Chapter 4 in Steven Rathgeb Smith and Michael Lipsky, *Nonprofits for Hire: The Welfare State in the Age of Contracting* (Cambridge, MA: Harvard University Press, 1992).

19. Tocqueville, "Political Associations," p. 199.

20. Helmut K. Anheier, *Nonprofit Organizations: Theory, Management, Policy*, 2nd ed. (London: Routledge, 2014).

21. For example, Douglas F. Morgan and Brian J. Cook, eds., *New Public Governance: A Regime-Centered Perspective* (New York: Routledge, 2014).

22. See, for example, Josephine Barraket, Robyn Keast, and Craig Furneaux, *Social Procurement and New Public Governance* (New York: Routledge, 2016); Victor Pestoff, Taco Brandsen, and Bram Verschuere, eds., *New Public Governance, the Third Sector, and Co-Production* (New York: Routledge, 2012); Kjell A. Eliassen and Nick Sitter, *Understanding Public Management* (London: Sage, 2008); and David E. McNabb, *The New Face of Government: How Public Managers are Forging a New Approach to Governance* (Boca Raton, FL: Auerbach, 2009).

23. See the publications in Note 21, and Donald F. Kettl, *The Global Public Management Revolution: A Report on the Transference of Governance* (Washington, DC: The Brookings Institution, 2005); for comparative perspectives, Christopher Pollitt, Sandra Van Thiel, and Vincent Homburg, eds., *The New Public Management in Europe: Adaptation and Alternatives* (New York: Palgrave Macmillan, 2007); and, *A Profile of the Public Service of Australia: Current Good Practices and New Developments in Public Service Management*, written and published by the Commonwealth Secretariat (Canberra, Australia, 2004).

24. Helmut K. Anheier, "What Kind of Nonprofit Sector, What Kind of Society? Comparative Policy Reflections," *American Behavioral Scientist 52* (2009): 1085–1086.

25. Anheier, "What Kind of Nonprofit Sector, What Kind of Society? Comparative Policy Reflections."

Bibliography

Anheier, Helmut K., *Nonprofit Organizations: Theory, Management, Policy*, 2nd ed. (London: Routledge, 2014).
——, "What Kind of Nonprofit Sector, What Kind of Society? Comparative Policy Reflections." *American Behavioral Scientist 52* (2009): 1082–1094.
——, and Jeremy Kendall, *Third Sector Policy at the Crossroads: An International Non-profit Analysis* (London: Routledge, 2013).
Barraket, Josephine, Robyn Keast, and Craig Furneaux, *Social Procurement and New Public Governance* (New York: Routledge, 2016).
Beck, Tammy E., Cynthia A. Lengnick-Hall, and Mark L. Lengnick-Hall, "Solutions Out of Context: Examining the Transfer of Business Concepts to Nonprofit Organizations." *Nonprofit Management & Leadership 19* (2008): 153–171.
Berger, Peter L., and Thomas Luckmann, *The Social Construction of Reality* (Garden City, NY: Doubleday, 1966).
Boris, Elizabeth T., Brice McKeever, and Béatrice Leydier, "Roles and Responsibilities of Nonprofit Organizations in a Democracy." In Elizabeth T. Boris and C. Eugene Steuerle, eds., *Nonprofits and Government: Collaboration and Conflict*, 3rd ed., pp. 1–36 (Lanham, MD: Rowman & Littlefield. 2017).
Casey, John, *The Nonprofit World: Civil Society and the Rise of the Nonprofit Sector* (West Hartford, CT: Kumarian, 2015).
Clotfelter, Charles, and Thomas Erlich, eds., *Philanthropy and the Nonprofit Sector in a Changing America* (Bloomington and Indianapolis, IN: Indiana University Press, 1999).
Coles, Robert, *The Call of Service: A Witness to Idealism* (Boston: Houghton Mifflin, 1993).
Corry, Olaf, "Defining and Theorizing the Third Sector." In Rupert Taylor, ed., *Third Sector Research*, pp. 11–19 (New York: Springer, 2010).
Drucker, Peter F., Sheryl K. Sandberg, Muhammad Yunus, and Arthur C. Brooks, eds., *On Nonprofits and the Social Sectors* (Boston, MA: Harvard Business Review Press, 2019).
Edwards, Michael, *Civil Society*, 4th ed. (Cambridge, UK: Polity, 2020).
——, *The Oxford Handbook of Civil Society* (Oxford, UK: Oxford University Press, 2013).
Eikenberry, Angela M., Roseanne M. Mirabella, and Billie Sandberg, *Reframing Nonprofit Organizations: Democracy, Inclusion, and Social Change* (Irvine, CA: Melvin & Leigh, 2019).

Eliassen, Kjell A., and Nick Sitter, *Understanding Public Management* (London: Sage, 2008).

Farazmand, Ali, ed., *Global Encyclopedia of Public Administration, Policy, and Governance* (New York: Springer, 2018).

Frumkin, Peter, *On Being Nonprofit: A Conceptual and Policy Primer* (Cambridge, MA: Harvard University Press, 2002).

———, and Jonathan B. Imber, eds., *In Search of the Nonprofit Sector* (Piscataway, NJ: Transaction Publishers, 2004). Republished in hardback (New York: Routledge, 2017).

Gallo, Geoffrey, "New Tax Reform Act: Summary and Details." Posted in *Grennan Fender Company News.* https://orlandoaccounting.com/new-tax-reform-act-summary-and-details/ (December 30, 2017).

Gies, David L., J. Steven Ott, and Jay M. Shafritz, eds., *The Nonprofit Sector: Essential Readings* (Pacific Grove, CA: Brooks/Cole, 1990).

Halpern, David, *Social Capital* (Cambridge, UK: Polity, 2004).

Hansmann, Henry, *The Ownership of Enterprise* (Cambridge, MA: Belknap Press, 1996).

Hopkins, Bruce R., *The Law of Tax-Exempt Organizations*, 12th ed. (New York: Wiley, 2019).

Kallman, Meghan Elizabeth, and Terry Nichols Clark, *The Third Sector: Community Organizations, NGOs, and Nonprofits* (Urbana, Chicago, and Springfield, IL: University of Illinois Press, 2016).

Kettl, Donald F., *The Global Public Management Revolution: A Report on the Transference of Governance* (Washington, DC: The Brookings Institution, 2005).

Lohmann, Roger A., "And Lettuce Is Nonanimal: Toward a Positive Economics of Voluntary Action." *Nonprofit and Voluntary Sector Quarterly* 18 (1989): 367–383.

Land, Sabine, *NGOs, Civil Society, and the Public Sphere* (Cambridge, UK: Cambridge University Press, 2013).

McKeever, Brice, *The Nonprofit Sector in Brief 2015: Public Charities, Giving, and Volunteering* (Washington, DC: The Urban Institute, 2015).

McNabb, David E., *The New Face of Government: How Public Managers are Forging a New Approach to Governance* (Boca Raton, FL: Auerbach, 2009).

Mirabella, Roseanne M., "University-Based Educational Programs in Nonprofit Management and Philanthropic Studies: A 10-Year Review and Projections of Future Trends." *Nonprofit and Voluntary Sector Quarterly 36* (2007): 11S–27S.

Morgan, Douglas F., and Brian J. Cook, eds., *New Public Governance: A Regime-Centered Perspective.* New York: Routledge, 2014).

Muukkonen, Martti, "Framing the Field: Civil Society and Related Concepts." *Nonprofit and Voluntary Sector Quarterly 38* (2009): 684–700.

Osborne, David, and Ted Gaebler, *Reinventing Government* (Reading, MA: Addison-Wesley, 1992).

Pestoff, Victor, Taco Brandsen, and Bram Verschuere, eds., *New Public Governance, the Third Sector, and Co-Production* (New York: Routledge, 2012).

Pollitt, Christopher, Sandra Van Thiel, and Vincent Homburg, eds., *The New Public Management in Europe: Adaptation and Alternatives* (New York: Palgrave Macmillan, 2007).

Powell, Walter W., "What is the Nonprofit Sector?" In Walter Powell and Patricia Bromley, eds., *The Nonprofit Sector: A Research Handbook*, 3rd ed., pp. 3–22 (Palo Alto, CA: Stanford University Press, 2020).

Putnam, Robert D., *Bowling Alone: Revised and Updated: The Collapse and Revival of American Community* (New York: Simon & Schuster, 2020).

———, *Bowling Alone* (New York: Simon and Schuster, 2000).

Salamon, Lester M., *New Frontiers of Philanthropy: A Guide to the New Tools and New Actors that Are Reshaping Global Philanthropy and Social Investing* (New York: Oxford University Press, 2014).

———, *The Resilient Sector Revisited*, 2nd ed. (Washington, DC: Brookings Institution Press, 2015).

———, S. Wojciech Sokolowski, and Megan A. Haddock, *Explaining Civil Society Development: A Social Origins Approach* (Baltimore: Johns Hopkins University Press, 2017).

Shafritz, Jay M., ed., *International Encyclopedia of Public Policy and Administration* (Boulder, CO: Westview Press, 1998).

Silber, Norman I., *A Corporate Form of Freedom* (Boulder, CO: Westview, 2001). Reprinted in hardback (New York: Routledge, 2019).

Smith, David Horton, *Voluntary Action Research* (Lexington, MA: Lexington, 1973).

Smith, Steven R., and Michael Lipsky, *Nonprofits for Hire* (Cambridge, MA: Harvard University Press, 1993).

Tocqueville, Alexis de, "Political Associations in the United States." In *Democracy in America*, Vol. 1 (The Henry Reeve text as revised by Francis Bowen, now further corrected and edited by Phillips Bradley) (New York: Vintage Books, 1945).

United States Government Accountability Office, U. S. (GAO), *Nonprofit Sector: Increasing Numbers and Key Role in Delivering Federal Services* (Washington, DC: United States Government Accountability Office, 2007, GAO-07-1084T).

Van Til, John, *Growing Civil Society: From Nonprofit Sector to Third Space* (Bloomington and Indianapolis, IN: Indiana University Press, 2000).

Vaughn, Shannon K., and Shelly Arsneault, *Managing Nonprofit Organizations in a Policy World*, 2nd ed. (Irvine, CA: Melving & Leigh, 2021).

Weisbrod, Burton A., ed., *To Profit or Not to Profit: The Commercial Transformation of the Nonprofit Sector* (Cambridge, UK: Cambridge University Press, 1998).

CHAPTER 1

Roles and Responsibilities of Nonprofit Organizations in a Democracy

Elizabeth T. Boris, Brice McKeever, and Béatrice Leydier

In Elizabeth T. Boris and C. Eugene Steuerle, eds. (2017). *Nonprofits and Government: Collaboration and Conflict*. Lanham, MD: Rowman & Littlefield.

Nonprofit Organizations of Civil Society

Nonprofit organizations are a vital force of civil society, distinct from both government and business, although they display elements of both. Their basic role as enablers of civic engagement and promoters of the common good is the cornerstone of our pluralistic democracy. Nonprofits and government interact in many fascinating ways, yet we must understand the variety of roles played by nonprofit organizations before we can thoroughly explore these relationships. Because their spheres of activity intersect in so many ways, the nature, scope, and impacts of nonprofit organizations are sensitive to changes in public policy and vice versa. Simplistic assumptions about what nonprofit organizations do, their finances, and how they affect society may lead to public policies that are ineffective or have unintended negative consequences both for the organizations and for society. At the same time, there has been significant growth in the nonprofit sector of civil society over the past decade, with major changes in types of institutions, financing

mechanisms, and interactions with government, politics, and business, which we will document in this reading.

"Nonprofit" is the generic term used in this chapter and in this volume to describe organizations that make up the "nonprofit" sector, in contrast to the government and business sectors. The nonprofit sector includes philanthropic foundations, religious congregations, universities, hospitals, environmental groups, art museums, youth recreation associations, civil rights groups, community development organizations, labor unions, political parties, social clubs, and many more. These organizations are even more diverse than the terms typically associated with them: charities, nongovernmental organizations, civil society, philanthropic sector, tax exempt organizations, voluntary associations, civic sector organizations, third sector organizations, independent sector organizations, nonprofit organizations, and social sector organizations.

Nonprofits exhibit a wide diversity of missions, activities, reach, and impacts, but what they have in common is that they all are voluntary and self-governing, may not distribute profits, and serve public purposes or the common

DOI: 10.4324/9780367696559-2

goals of their members. Nonprofits promote and defend values and competing visions of the public good, and many harness altruism and public and private resources to serve those who need assistance. All of these activities require the freedom to associate, deliberate, and act in the public sphere—freedoms guaranteed by the United States Constitution and Bill of Rights. Inevitably, however, competing values and interests often produce conflict. Also inevitably, where public resources are directly or indirectly involved, government regulation and oversight follow.

Like government, nonprofits generally promote the common good or public benefit, but in contrast to government, they are not bound by majority preferences. They embody democratic pluralism, promoting individual or particularistic conceptions of the public good that may conflict with others' notions of the public good. Through both collaboration and conflict, however, nonprofits shape and are shaped by government policies and funding.

Like businesses, nonprofits must obtain revenues to cover the costs of services they provide, as well as capital to scale up or branch out. Revenues can be from individual, corporate or foundation donors, volunteer labor (including labor at below market wages), fees for services or products, government grants and contracts, earnings on endowments or other assets, and special events. Capital can come from individuals, foundations, and government bonds and increasingly from social and impact investors that may include a mix of nonprofit, government, and business resources. Unlike businesses, nonprofits may not have owners or shareholders to whom they distribute profits; any surplus revenues must be used for the organization's mission.

Nonprofit organizations play prominent social, economic, and political roles in society as service providers, but many are also employers and advocates. Their numbers and economic impact have grown significantly as they increasingly earn fees and contract with government to deliver a variety of services, particularly health care and social services. These relationships are usually collaborative, or, in economic terms, complementary or supplementary to government, although the scale of nonprofit resources are dwarfed by those of government. In their civic role, they are often advocates; they provide a voice for their constituents, and may lobby for or against government policies that affect their constituencies or interests, often invoking conflict and adversarial relationships with government, businesses, and other nonprofits.

Less visible but vital nonprofit roles are captured under the rubric of "civil society": fostering community engagement and civic participation, and promoting and preserving civic, cultural, and religious values. Scholars are exploring the central role that formal and informal nonprofit organizations play in creating the glue that holds communities together and the avenues they provide for civic participation and a robust civil society (O'Connell 1997; Putnam 2000; Sievers 2010; Skocpol and Fiorina 1999; Verba, Schlozman, and Brady 1995; Zuckerman 2014). These roles are usually financed through giving and volunteering rather than by fees and contracts, and they can involve either collaboration or conflict with government, although these types of activities typically fall outside of direct government purview.

The interaction between government and nonprofit organizations in civil society is complex and dynamic, ebbing and flowing with shifts in social and economic policy, political administrations, and social norms. Because nonprofits are heterogeneous, they reflect sharp differences as well as common aspirations. Their impacts can be positive or negative and antagonistic or conciliatory, depending on their activities as well as the perspective of the analyst. Of course, speaking about nonprofits in the aggregate invites overgeneralization—obscuring huge variation and diversity of nonprofit roles, contributions, and interactions with government, subjects to which we will turn.

Regulation of Nonprofit Organizations

Nonprofit organizations in the United States are defined and regulated primarily under the federal tax code. They are exempt from federal income taxes by virtue of being organized for public purposes. Regulation of nonprofits is fragmented; there is no central US government agency that focuses solely on oversight of nonprofit organizations. At the national level, the Internal Revenue Service (IRS) is the primary regulator of nonprofit organizations and is charged with determining their legitimacy as tax exempt entities and overseeing that their activities are tax exempt and that charitable deductions are used for charitable purposes. State governments oversee and regulate nonprofits that operate in their jurisdictions, though usually more from a consumer protection standpoint. The Federal Election Commission regulates nonprofits engaged in federal elections. Regulatory frameworks in other countries are varied but also generally involve tax incentives and greater or lesser limitation of political activity. They have in common with the United States the lack of an overarching philosophy or approach to nonprofit-government relationships.

All US nonprofit organizations with annual gross receipts of $5,000 or more, except religious groups, are required to register with the IRS. Organizations with revenues (gross receipts) of more than $50,000 are required to complete and file an annual information form, IRS Form 990; all private foundations must file IRS Form 990-PF. These forms are public documents that provide the basis for federal and state oversight of nonprofits and the only financial data on nonprofit organizations required to be publicly available.[1]

Those nonprofit organizations that serve broad public purposes and are organized for educational, religious, scientific, literary, poverty relief, and other activities for the public benefit are eligible to apply for charitable status under section 501(c)(3) of the tax code. Charitable status permits organizations to receive tax-deductible contributions, an important incentive to encourage donations. Religious congregations, however, do not have to apply for charitable status; they are, by definition, charities. Charitable nonprofits serving broad public purposes account for the majority of tax exempt organizations.

Even within the charitable portion of the nonprofit sector, the organizations are extremely diverse. They vary greatly in mission, origin, structure, size, sources of revenues, and financial means and are accountable to multiple constituencies—board and staff, members, donors, clients, volunteers, funders, and the public.[2] Public confidence and trust are crucial to their success, yet the public has limited understanding of the scope and operations of nonprofits. Lack of transparency, particularly about the use of donated money, and scandals of any type negatively affect the whole sector, often leading to public outcry, congressional inquiries, and new regulatory proposals.[3]

Types of Organizations

Nonprofits' diversity confounds attempts to explain them through some overarching theory. Researchers have made progress in categorizing and measuring the scope of formal organizations (McKeever 2015), but less has been accomplished in measuring the informal groups, coalitions, and religious organizations (Smith et al. 2010).

The National Taxonomy of Exempt Entities (NTEE), developed by the National Center for Charitable Statistics,[4] classifies all nonprofit organizations into over 400 categories, demonstrating their diversity (Stevenson 1997). The basic divisions are as follows:

- Arts, culture, and humanities (e.g., art museums, theater companies, historical societies)
- Education (e.g., private schools and universities, parent-teacher groups)
- Environment and animals (e.g., Humane Societies, the Chesapeake Bay Foundation)
- Health, hospitals (e.g., nonprofit hospitals and clinics, the American Lung Association)
- Human services (e.g., Girl Scouts, YMCA, food banks, homeless shelters)
- International, foreign affairs (e.g., CARE, the Asia Society, International Committee of the Red Cross)
- Public and societal benefit (private and public foundations, e.g., Rockefeller Foundation, the Cleveland Foundation, the Urban Institute, civil rights groups, United Ways)
- Religion related (e.g., interfaith coalitions, religious societies, congregations)

NTEE classifications permit researchers to track the growth of different types of nonprofits as in table I.1 which covers operating public charities.

Nonprofit Activities

The variety of nonprofit organizations is matched by a great diversity of activities. Among others, they produce and display art, culture, and music; generate knowledge through research and education; protect consumers, the environment, and animals; promote health; prevent and treat diseases; provide basic social services—housing, food and clothing; promote international understanding; provide international aid and relief; create community social and economic infrastructure; advocate for and against public policies; provide services and funding to other nonprofit groups; transmit religious values and traditions; provide solidarity, recreation, and services to members and others; and educate and register voters.

TABLE I.I Growth in Nonprofit Organizations [in the US] by Type of Service, 2003–2013

Type	2003	2008	2013	2003–2013 # Change	% Change
Arts and culture	29,203	36,145	38,083	8,880	30.4
Education	38,872	48,644	48,287	9,415	24.2
Environment and animals	10,313	14,103	16,838	6,525	63.3
Health	31,263	35,436	37,440	6,177	19.8
Human service	91,546	110,743	120,241	28,695	31.3
International	4,749	6,202	7,877	3,128	65.9
Public and societal benefit	19,937	25,074	27,512	7,575	38.0
Religion related	15,114	20,608	23,758	8,644	57.2
Not classified	25	280	579	554	2216.0
Total	**241,022**	**297,235**	**320,615**	**79,593**	**33.0**

Source: The Urban Institute, NCCS Core Files, Public Charities, 2003, 2008, 2013

Note: Only operating public charities are included.

This laundry list gives some sense of the difficulty of defining and describing the nonprofit sector. It also makes it clear that voluntary organizations do many things that are also done by governments and businesses. There are no sharp boundaries among the sectors; in fact, there is increasing blurring of the boundaries, particularly with regard to commercial activities. There are, however, some activities (such as religious worship, membership activities, and monitoring of government) that are almost exclusively accomplished in the nonprofit sector and other activities (such as museums, botanical gardens, and zoos) that are more likely to be undertaken by nonprofits than by either government or business. Some activities are more evenly divided between government and nonprofits (such as providing social services), while others (such as primary education) are largely a government activity. Business and government also sometimes collaborate or cooperate with nonprofits in providing, for example, low-income housing and disaster relief.

Nonprofits have a long history of pioneering programs that were subsequently taken over by the other sectors. Primary education, kindergartens, and disease control were popularized by nonprofits and taken over by government when demand outpaced the ability of nonprofit providers to supply services. Recreation programs pioneered by nonprofits were picked up by businesses and developed into profit-making enterprises. Nonprofits are often lauded for being flexible and innovative, a source of discoveries for improving society with breakthroughs that transcend sectors.

Collaboration with government, however, is often difficult for both partners. Experiences with disaster relief in large-scale tragedies, such as the attacks of September 11, 2001, Hurricane Katrina in 2010, Hurricane Sandy in 2012, and the earthquake in Haiti in 2010, reveal the strengths and weaknesses of nonprofits in their collaboration with government. Nonprofits are quick to respond and galvanize volunteers and donations, but their capacity varies in different regions of this country and around the world. They are flexible problem solvers, but often weak on coordination and long-term logistics and follow-through (Morley and De Vita 2007). But, importantly, given their relative size, they cannot compensate for weak government leadership or inadequate government resources for large-scale disasters.

Some nonprofits have the characteristics of business corporations or of government programs, and a small proportion of organizations change from one type of organization to another (Goddeeris and Weisbrod 2006). Governments set up nonprofit corporations to carry out some public programs; for example, the Corporation for Public Broadcasting and the National Trust for Historic Preservation. Nonprofits may create profit-making subsidiaries to subsidize their charitable activities. Even though it has a charitable owner, such a subsidiary's income would generally be taxable unless it independently qualified as an exempt organization. They also engage in social enterprises that directly use market activities as part of their missions (Cordes and Steuerle 2009; Dees 1998; Kerlin 2005; Young, Salamon, and Grinsfelder 2012). DC Central Kitchen, for example, picks up and distributes surplus food to hungry people and trains unemployed workers in culinary skills, preparing food that is sold to stores and schools (Moore 2014).

The interaction of nonprofits with the business sector affects their relationships with government. A few nonprofits give up their tax exempt status when their missions can be accomplished more effectively as business corporations, or when economic incentives, government policies, or the need for capital make it profitable for them to become businesses. The conversion of nonprofit hospitals to for-profit businesses is one example. Conversions raise questions about whether it is in the public interest for businesses to take over hospitals and certain other types of services, but as long as the assets are reserved for charitable purposes, usually in a foundation, the current barriers to conversion seem to be minimal.

The sometimes overlapping and complementary nature of the three sectors may at times seem inefficient, but it provides flexibility and adaptability. Public-serving activities are not restricted to government but can be undertaken through multiple avenues. Diverse populations with different tastes and requirements can create entities to meet their perceived needs. Government can contract with nonprofits to provide social and health services without expanding the government workforce. Social entrepreneurs can implement their visions through nonprofit organizations, and the alternatives they develop sometimes find their way into the public or business sectors. This complementarity can be leveraged when actors work together.

Finances of Nonprofit Organizations

Nonprofits vary tremendously in resources and capacity. Almost all nonprofits, however, benefit financially from their tax exempt status, and charities additionally benefit from the incentives that charitable income tax deductions provide for the approximately 2 percent of personal income that individuals give to charities.[5] Most nonprofits are extremely small entities with meager resources that operate locally with modest budgets and volunteer labor. Some organizations, however, are large and professional, with hundreds of employees and many millions of dollars in expenditures; nonprofit resources are concentrated in these large organizations, mostly in hospitals, universities, and multipurpose service organizations.

Nonprofit revenue sources include fees for service, government and foundation grants, individual and corporate donations, income from special events, member dues, investments, revenues from commercial ventures, and miscellaneous other sources. Direct government grants are less important than fee-for-service income,

which is the dominant source of revenue for the sector in aggregate terms. Government provides significant amounts of fee income, both directly and indirectly, although there is significant variation by type of organization. Fees involve payments for services provided (including, e.g., individual payments for tuition), government contracts through Medicare and Medicaid, and government or private vouchers for job training or childcare.

Health and educational institutions dominate the finances of the nonprofit sector. About three-fifths of the total revenue and expenses of public charities [in the US] are in health-related organizations. Hospitals make up about 1.1 percent of organizations, but 43.2 percent of expenditures and 36.5 percent of assets. Private higher education accounts for about 0.7 percent of organizations, but for 12 percent of expenses and 24.6 percent of assets. Human service organizations, in contrast, account for 37.5 percent of operating charities but less than 14 percent of expenses and just under 12 percent of assets. They tend to be smaller, and their financial status is often quite weak.

Private and public foundations hold significant nonprofit assets in endowments that generate revenues used to make grants to nonprofit organizations. Private grantmaking foundations are 501(c)(3) organizations created by an individual or a family or by a corporation to fund other, mostly nonprofit, entities over time. Public foundations, including community foundations and similar funds, are endowed public charities that raise money from individuals to benefit a city, other geographic area, or specific set of causes. Together these organizations hold approximately one-fifth of the assets of the charitable sector (excluding religious congregations).[6] Donor-advised funds established by national providers, such as Fidelity Charitable, Vanguard Charitable, and others, are a rapidly growing vehicle for philanthropic giving.

While hospitals and higher education have long relied on fees, commercial fee-for-service income is increasingly important for other types of charities. Recent analyses show that it had grown to approximately 58 percent (Kerlin and Pollak 2011). Increasing reliance on fee-for-service income from government and other sources inevitably affects the character and operations of many nonprofits. With the increase in contracting between government and nonprofits, competition for clients and for government contracts—among nonprofits and between nonprofits and businesses—has increased and has led to more businesslike marketing strategies and management practices.

Opportunities for commercial ventures and social enterprises have increased as social entrepreneurs start new organizations: nonprofits, for-profits, and hybrids. Concerned with lack of capital for scaling programs as well as sustainability of financial resources, some foundations are also using private sector models to finance nonprofits, shifting from almost exclusive reliance on grantmaking to making loans and using assets to make impact investments. These market-like investments require greater concern for efficiency, the financial bottom line, performance measurement, and outcome evaluation.

Roles of Nonprofit Organizations

Why do nonprofits exist? Scholars answer this question in different ways, depending on their disciplines and orientations. Economic theories include the notions of "market failure," "government failure," and "nonprofit failure" as ways of explaining the public services delivered by nonprofits and the partnership of the government with the nonprofit sector in financing a variety of public services.

Market failure is based on the concept that there are desired services or collective "goods" that do not have sufficient potential for profit to attract business providers. Market failure is also precipitated by insufficient information on the quality of services, which may lead consumers to turn to nonprofit providers that are perceived as trustworthy because they do not have a profit motive. Similarly, government failure implies that there are public services that government will not provide for reasons that may include the cost or the limited constituency that desires the service (Hansman 1987; Weisbrod 1988). "Nonprofit failure" explains the nonprofit-government partnership as a consequence of the public demanding services best met by nonprofit provision but requiring government financing. In this theory, nonprofits are the preferred providers of services, and government action becomes necessary because nonprofits are unable to meet perceived needs (Salamon 1995) and raise the necessary revenues.

In contrast to economists, political scientists tend to stress the role of the nonprofit sector in terms of providing avenues of civic participation and representation of interests in the pluralistic political system of a heterogeneous society. Diverse values and interests are aggregated through associations and represented to the political system through political advocacy and lobbying of the government by many nonprofit groups (Berry 1984; Berry and Arons 2003; Boris and Krehely 2002; Boris and Maronick 2012; Clemens 2006; Sievers 2010; Verba, Schlozman, and Brady 1995; Warren 2002). Roger Lohmann builds on the idea of the commons as the civic arena in his book on the nonprofit sector (Lohmann 1992, 2003; Sievers 2010). While there is no agreement on the effectiveness of their representation of disadvantaged interests, there is an acknowledgment that, however imperfect, nonprofit advocacy provides some counterbalance to the interest advocacy of business institutions (Jenkins 2006).

The government-nonprofit relationship in the political sphere is delineated in part by the constitutionally guaranteed rights of free speech and association and in part by the limits on using dollars subsidized by the charitable tax deduction for advocacy, lobbying, and, particularly, political activity (Colinvaux 2014; Fremont-Smith 2004; Reid 2003). Conflict occurs when government and nonprofits disagree on the boundaries of permissible efforts to influence government policies and engage in political activities.[7]

Interdisciplinary approaches to studying nonprofits provide valuable alternative perspectives. Communitarians view voluntary associations in organic terms, as the precursors of government and the market and, thus, among the most basic of social relationships that connect people and create communities. These relationships became more complex over time and evolved into the state and the market (Etzioni 1993). Robert Putnam and others use the concepts of social capital and civil society in a basically communitarian framework (Putnam 1993; Walzer 1995).

Scholars also look to the civic history of the United States—the suffrage, antislavery, and child welfare movements, for example—and to the religious roots of charity, altruism, and social justice to explain the giving and volunteering that characterize involvement in nonprofit organizations and rights-oriented social movements (Hess 2003; McCarthy 2003; O'Connell 1997; Payton 1988; Skocpol 1995; Wuthnow 1991).

Each of these approaches reveals a different aspect of nonprofits' roles and, thus, their relationship with government. A civil society approach examines the role of nonprofits in generating the social capital that links people to their communities and to others. A political analysis highlights efforts to influence the political process and create social change. An economic perspective looks at resources, at the creation of income, jobs, and knowledge, at service provision, and at economic development, often in collaboration with government. A value perspective helps explain the role of nonprofits in alleviating poverty and promoting and maintaining religious, ideological, cultural,

and artistic values and beliefs, activities that sometimes lead to conflict with government. The chapters in this volume reflect the richness of these approaches.

Social Capital

Nonprofit organizations, regardless of origin, create networks and relationships that connect people to each other and to institutions quite apart from the organization's primary purposes. Research by Robert Putnam and others suggests that relationships such as those fostered by choral societies, bowling leagues, and other community associations build the trust and cooperation that is essential for the effective functioning of society, politics, and economy (Brown and Ferris 2007; Perks and Haan 2011; Putnam 1993).

Despite growing professionalism in the nonprofit arena, most nonprofits still facilitate relationships and connect people to each other and to the constituencies they serve. Members and volunteers are critical to the success of many nonprofits. Volunteers serve in governance capacities on boards of directors, in staff management and service positions, as fundraisers, and in many other ways. Volunteers bring expertise from business, government, and the community to bear on local, national, and international problems. Volunteers enhance civic engagement and spread expertise: people of various backgrounds learn about the needs of their communities and others and act together to solve them. Volunteering also harnesses the enthusiasm of young and old and adds meaning to their lives. People who are involved in youth groups, churches, and other voluntary activities when young are more likely to give, volunteer, and be engaged in civic life in adulthood (Brown and Ferris 2007; Hodgkinson and Weitzman 1993; Perks and Haan 2011). Those who are involved in their communities are also more likely to be healthy and happy (Post 2011; Seligman 1991).

Civic Roles

Civic activities carried out by nonprofits include getting out the vote for elections, informing people about voting dates, times, and venues, conducting nonpartisan forums for discussing issues, and providing civic education classes for young people and new citizens. Indirectly, nonprofits are training grounds where people learn and use skills critical for civic participation. Members learn how to organize, lead, negotiate differences, adopt, and implement goals within organizations. These skills are transferable to civic activism and may also be employed in direct and indirect activities designed to influence attitudes, behavior, public policies, legislation, and elections.

Public education is a critical tool of civic life. Many nonprofits inform and influence domestic social and economic policies as well as international affairs through nonpartisan research, writing, evaluation, and demonstration projects. Expertise may be provided to inform and influence executive agencies or the legislative branch. Think tanks and universities conduct research and evaluations and make that information available to policymakers through publications, news media, forums, and individual conversations (Boris 1999; Boris and Maronick 2012). The role of the nonprofit policy expert is changing, however, as some think tanks have become advocates with ideological agendas, calling into question their expertise, credibility, and ability to conduct disinterested research (Rich 2004, 2005).

Grantmaking foundations and other nonprofits try to influence public policy by demonstrating the efficacy of alternative approaches to economic development, population issues, or hunger (Anheier and Hammack 2010; Fleishman 2007; Kania, Kramer, and Russell 2014). They may conduct experimental programs, evaluate the results, and communicate them to public authorities. Foundations may also promote policy agendas indirectly, for example the foundations that financed conservative think tanks that provided much of the intellectual capital for the Reagan and Bush administrations (Covington 1997; Mayer 2016; Rich 2004) and the liberal foundations that helped to finance the marriage equality movement, which resulted in the Supreme Court decision in the *Obergefell v. Hodges* case that legalized same-sex marriages in June 2015.

Advocacy, Lobbying, and Political Roles

Nonprofit advocacy groups try to educate the public and encourage individuals to contact their representatives directly or to sign petitions for or against certain positions; they may also try to influence public policy through demonstrations, sit-ins, parades, and boycotts. Jeffrey Berry maintains that public interest citizen groups have been very effective at setting and influencing the congressional agenda (Berry 1999). The National Committee for Responsive Philanthropy found that investments in advocacy leveraged significant state policy changes in Minnesota, resulting in measurable benefits of over $2 billion for residents (Gulati-Partee and Ranghelli 2009).

Certain nonprofits are involved more directly in politics, and some develop multiple organizational structures to permit them to do so in a variety of ways. They might have a 501(c)(3) charity, entitled to receive tax-deductible contributions, which permits them to provide services, and advocate and conduct limited lobbying for or against legislation. Such charities may be affiliated with a 501(c)(4) social welfare organization which can conduct unlimited lobbying for (or against) policies that affect their constituencies without revealing its donors. They may also be related to a 527 organization that is permitted to engage in issue advocacy during electoral campaigns. Some even have related political action committees (PACs) so they can be involved in partisan political campaigns, endorsing and supporting political candidates for office. These structures are a direct result of the different ways government regulates the various types of political activities, trying not to hinder free speech on the one hand while avoiding government subsidy of political activities on the other (Colinvaux 2014; Pekkanen, Smith, and Tsujinaka 2014; Reid and Kerlin 2003; Reid 2006).

Some of the most profound social changes of this century have been promoted through a combination of research, public education, advocacy, legislation, and litigation fostered by nonprofit organizations. These nonprofits usually work in coalitions, sometimes in collaboration with government and business interests, and sometimes in conflict with them and with other nonprofits (Boris and Maronick 2012). Civil rights groups, working with religious and other organizations, attacked racial segregation in this country through direct action, lobbying, advocacy, litigation, and public education. Environmental groups used research, public education, advocacy, and litigation in their pioneering efforts to reduce air and water pollution and protect the environment and wildlife. Currently, they are using public education to disseminate research and promote policies to curb global warming. Antismoking groups joined insurance companies, foundations, and government agencies to foster research and use the results to educate the public about the negative impacts of tobacco smoking on health. David Cole, in *Engines of Liberty: The Power of Citizen Activists to Make Constitutional Law* (2016), profiles three issues: marriage equality, right to bear arms, and human rights in the war on terror, in which advocacy organizations over time managed to change constitutional law.

Not all advocacy is designed to introduce change. Groups all along the political spectrum may aim to conserve or protect values that they espouse or may try to prevent the erosion of values they cherish or advantages they enjoy. The National Rifle Association, for example, promotes gun ownership and lobbies against

legislation that would limit an individual's right to own guns. The American Civil Liberties Union defends individual rights and litigates against legislation that it believes threatens freedom of speech and other liberties guaranteed in the Constitution and the Bill of Rights. Tea Party groups advocate for conservative values in a countrywide movement (Skocpol and Williamson 2012).

Religious, Cultural, and Artistic Roles

The most deeply felt controversies over values are played out in the nonprofit sector—around religious beliefs, artistic expression, personal responsibility, individual rights, and the separation of church and state. Nonprofits express conflicts over competing values long before they reach the political system. These conflicts may be positive when they promote the dialogue and deliberation that are healthy for democracy. In extremely divisive cases like racial segregation and access to abortions, conflicts can involve legislative and judicial battles at the national, state, and local levels over long periods of time.

Religious organizations serve the spiritual needs of their members and promote and preserve the group's religious doctrines and values. Sacramental activities and membership-serving activities such as childcare and counseling may be supplemented by social and health services, crisis care, and advocacy activities (Chaves 2002; Cnaan 1997; Hodgkinson and Weitzman 1993; Printz 1997; Wuthnow 2004). Religious congregations also impart civic skills to members who learn to organize and collaborate for common ends. Black churches, for example, are well known for their efforts to mobilize their members to vote and for their political work, particularly around ending segregation and promoting civil rights (Harris 1994). The IRS, however, in very limited ways has scrutinized political speech in religious organizations to determine if they are engaging in prohibited partisan campaign activities by using taxpayer-subsidized charitable contributions to endorse candidates who share their values.[8]

The separation of church and state in the United States involves an ongoing debate with a long evolution (Crimm and Winer 2011). Historically, however, the religious charities' receipt of government revenues for services provided to the general public is well established (Hall 1982). Government-funded social service provision by nonprofits affiliated with Catholic, Lutheran, and Jewish faiths, for example, has been widespread. When providing government-funded services, such groups have usually accepted limitations on proselytizing and on providing preferential services to their members.

Most religious entities fall outside of the government regulatory framework for nonprofit organizations. Houses of worship and closely aligned entities enjoy the benefits of tax exemption and deductible contributions but are not required to register or report to the IRS; many do report however, and the number is increasing, partially in an effort to create a formal structure to qualify for faith-based funding initiatives. Government funding requires accountability, and some fear that monitoring contracts and performance will involve the government too deeply in the affairs of religious bodies. Congregations that desire government funding often set up separate charities to segregate finances, avoid potential conflicts, and protect their sacramental activities from government involvement.

The implementation of the Affordable Care Act, which requires employers to provide female employees access to insurance that covers contraception costs, still reveals the tension that arises from government regulation. Some businesses and religious organizations claim that even enabling such coverage operates as a mandate that violates their religious beliefs. Litigation has reached the Supreme Court.

Other values conversations are ongoing and are at times mediated by nonprofit organizations themselves. Government support of the arts raises a host of questions about the types of art that deserve public support, given that different standards of morality and decency may offend some people but not others (Wuthnow 2006). Arts and culture are embedded in community life and are reflected in worship, education, celebrations, and much more. Through arts and culture, we transmit group memory, celebrate ethnic and national identity, and interpret the past. The arts enhance our quality of life and generate economic benefits and much more for communities (Jackson 1998).

Service Roles

Nonprofits of all types provide services that may be offered to the whole community, to special populations, to members only, to governments, to businesses, and to other nonprofits. As service providers, nonprofits often overlap with business and government, for example, in education and medical care. They may be contractors for governments and businesses (providing preschool programs or drug abuse treatment), collaborators with governments (maintaining national and regional parks or preventing diseases), or act in lieu of government (accreditation or consumer protection). As the contracting out of government services has increased dramatically, the nonprofit share of the workforce has increased by roughly the amount that government employment has decreased.

With more government money at stake, it is not surprising that nonprofits find themselves in competition with for-profit providers (U.S. Congress 1996).[9] The effects, including the adoption of business practices, are felt not just internally but also by donors and clients. Nonprofits often find that competition means that they must market, actively attract clients, and report on their outcomes and impacts. These changes can be positive, but may affect the way nonprofits are viewed by donors and experienced by clients. A pervasive bottom-line orientation may inadvertently affect even nonprofits that do not have government contracts or commercial revenues; the effort may increase efficiency and, at the same time, undermine charitable service missions and public trust.

Government may turn to nonprofits to undertake activities that require reaching local populations with culturally sensitive materials or to avoid hiring permanent staff for temporary projects. Nonprofits provide a way for governments to devolve programs either directly or through state and local authorities and provide services without incurring government salary scales and bureaucratic red tape, although nonprofits must then deal with government-imposed red tape and inefficiencies (Pettijohn and Boris 2013).

The use of nonprofits by governments to deliver services may separate governments from accepting responsibility for services funded, thus undermining popular support for public financing of programs or promoting cynicism toward nonprofits if programs fail. Nonprofits can provide a "cop out" for political leaders who wish to curtail government responsibilities. Nonprofits can also be used by wealthy communities to provide for their own needs, while neglecting to provide tax revenues for public education and other public health and human services for low-income residents.

Nonprofits also interact with and provide a variety of services directly and indirectly to the business sector (Cordes and Steuerle 2009). They collaborate with businesses in promoting quality of life in areas where firms operate. Donations to and contracts with cultural organizations and with childcare and recreation groups underwrite amenity services that attract and hold corporate employees, thereby helping to maintain the community's tax base. Environmental groups help to level the playing field for socially responsible behavior by demanding, for example, that all competitors within an industry clean up pollutants.

Nonprofit business associations provide information, research, and advocacy services for member corporations. They monitor the health of industries and the impact of legislation and regulation on corporate activities. They may provide low-cost insurance or cooperative buying opportunities. Nonprofit associations may provide similar types of services for groups of nonprofits, health-related nonprofits, philanthropic foundations, colleges and universities, symphonies, museums, and others.

State and local governments directly and indirectly fund nonprofits to provide services and also oversee the activities of nonprofits and their fundraising to ensure that the public is given accurate information and not misled by false claims and illegal operators (see chapter 5 by Lott and Fremont-Smith).

Economic Impacts

As mentioned earlier, nonprofits make significant contributions to the economy as employers and service providers. Millions of people serve as volunteers, further expanding nonprofit resources. This economic role, however, is disproportionately concentrated in the largest organizations and in certain sectors, especially in hospitals, private universities, and multipurpose organizations like the American Red Cross, Catholic Charities, and others; over 40 percent of nonprofit employees work in hospitals.

Nonprofits provide the entry point into the labor force for many women and minorities. About two out of three workers in the nonprofit sector are women. Employment in the smaller nonprofits is often at lower-than-market wages and without health and retirement benefits. Major nonprofit hospitals and universities anchor whole inner-city neighborhoods or small towns with employment opportunities, services, and amenities like arts, culture, and recreation opportunities. They contribute to public coffers by paying payroll taxes, while employees pay both income and payroll taxes.

Because nonprofits generally do not pay property taxes or sales taxes, they may be perceived as a drain on the local economy (Brody 2002, 2010; Brody, Marquez, and Toran 2012). Some local governments seek payments in lieu of taxes (PILOTs) and services in lieu of taxes (SILOTS) from nonprofits in their communities to help cover costs of services (Brody et al. 2012). These are generally not systematic efforts; they target the largest nonprofits and foundations. They are controversial but are becoming more prevalent.

To counter the view that nonprofits are a drain on communities, nonprofit associations and others have conducted or commissioned reports on the economic contributions of nonprofits. These economic impact studies are being used to grab the attention of policymakers as nonprofits attempt to negotiate for policy influence and revenues and deflect efforts to deny them tax benefits.

International Trends

Many countries have long-standing, expansive nonprofit sectors that play economic, social, and political roles similar to those in the United States, but with variations reflecting the different cultural, historical, and economic contexts. Governments often provide extensive resources to nonprofits in their countries and may permit more or less advocacy than in the United States, or none at all. In many countries, the source of funds for most nonprofits, even churches, is government. Private contributions are almost universally a lower share of personal income than in the United States. The extensive scope of activities, giving, volunteering, and economic impact of nonprofit sectors around the world is being illuminated by increasing numbers of scholars, and notably through the Comparative Nonprofit Sector Program at Johns Hopkins University (Salamon 2006, 2014).

The US foundations and nonprofits that operate across national borders, as well as nonprofits that work within other countries, are growing both in numbers and influence. International nongovernmental organizations (INGOs) are active in human rights, economic development, disaster relief, disease prevention and treatment, environmental protection, conflict resolution, and many other fields. They often act in concert with national governments, and multinational and international institutions, although conflicts are also common. Contracts with governments are becoming more prevalent, and disaster relief and recovery have become high-profile issues. The Internet has transformed the ability of INGOs to collaborate, advocate, and raise money. They are linked in global networks that have huge potential to monitor and affect public policies.

As in the United States, social enterprises and hybrid organizational forms are growing in numbers and influence. So too is impact investing, involving governments, foundations, nonprofits, and businesses. In 2011, for example, the US Agency for International Development partnered with three foundations, Rockefeller, Gates, and Gatsby in the United Kingdom, as well as the investment bank JP Morgan Social Finance and a Uganda-based consultancy, Pearl Capital Partners, to create, fund, and manage a $25 million African Agriculture Capital Fund. This private investment fund, one example among many, is applying impact-investing techniques to spur agricultural development in Africa (Shah and Pease 2012; Salamon 2014).

Regulation and oversight of nonprofits and foundations around the world reflect many of the same concerns and tensions that we find in the United States, although issues of control differ because of the typically higher share of revenues from government, while repression is generally more intense in countries with weak or nonexistent democratic institutions.

Conclusion

The nonprofit sector continues to play critical roles in society both in collaboration and in conflict with government. Over time, changes within society and the nonprofit sector inevitably alter the dynamics of those relationships. New philanthropic forms, investment vehicles, and hybrid structures arise, while demands for transparency and measurable impacts increase. Nonprofit organizations today are more visible than in the past. They are more likely to communicate and advocate online and via social media, and many operate locally, nationally, and globally. They are more likely to have diversified revenue streams that include fees for services, often from government, as well as businesslike enterprises. Financing relationships with government and business take new forms through joint investing and pay-for-success efforts. Donors have more choices in the ways they give and the vehicles and institutions they support, while many high net worth donors actively engage in philanthropic activities at younger ages, making significant gifts during their lifetimes rather than through their estates at death.

This dynamic picture contrasts with the more static nature of government oversight, which remains necessary for protecting donors and ensuring that dollars given for charitable purposes are spent for such purposes. Given their very limited resources, federal and state regulators are limited in their ability to coordinate activities, monitor nonprofit organizations, and keep up with the changes in the sector. More than ever, public oversight relies upon nonprofits and foundations to uphold the public trust; such efforts go well beyond deterring malfeasance to producing better outcomes and advancing society through charitable efforts. This oversight role requires both collaboration with and sometimes conflict between the sectors. The adequacy of this approach will be tested in the coming years.

Acknowledgments

The author is indebted to Gene Steuerle for his thoughtful comments. Collaborating with Gene is a joy. Thanks also to Brice McKeever and Béatrice Leydier for contributions to and suggestions, and to Ellen Steele for assistance.

Note on Data Sources

The data used [here] are compiled by the National Center for Charitable Statistics (NCCS) at the Urban Institute from government and private sources and are reported in annual updates (*Nonprofit Sector in Brief*) and in periodic editions of the *Nonprofit Almanac*.

Notes

1. Forms 990 are public documents that provide financial data—assets, revenues, expenses, and so on. They are available for inspection on the websites of the National Center for Charitable Statistics (NCCS), GuideStar, and the Foundation Center. Research databases with financial information based on Forms 990 are available at NCCS.

2. For a thorough discussion of nonprofit accountability, see Kevin Kearns's "Accountability in the Nonprofit Sector" (Kearns 2012) and Evelyn Brody's "Sunshine and Shadows on Charity Governance: Public Disclosure as a Regulatory Tool" (Brody 2012).

3. See for example, Senate Finance Committee white paper: "Senate Finance Committee Staff Discussion Draft, Tax Exempt Governance Proposals." June 22, 2004. The proposals in this document led to a sector-wide effort to address the proposals and develop recommendations that nonprofits could live with. The Panel on the Nonprofit Sector, convened by the Independent Sector, formed working groups to draft and discuss recommendations for strengthening nonprofit transparency and governance. The results were published in *Strengthening Transparency, Governance, and Accountability of*

Charitable Organizations (Panel on the Nonprofit Sector 2005).

4. The National Taxonomy of Exempt Entities (NTEE) was developed by the National Center for Charitable Statistics (NCCS) and is currently used by the IRS and by many researchers to classify nonprofit organizations. See www.urban.nccs.org for a description of the categories.

5. Each of these tax benefits has a cost to government of revenues foregone, in effect a subsidy that in tight financial times may become a source of controversy. For example the Senate Finance Committee actions to limit the deductibility of car donations to the actual revenue realized by charities will cut government costs. Measuring the cost to the government and the benefit to nonprofits is possible; more difficult to measure is the benefit to society.

6. See the Foundation Center's "Foundation Stats" (2014) accessible at http://data.foundation center.org/#/foundations/all/nationwide/total/list/2014.

7. Nonprofit tax exemption may be an attempt by government to respect the sovereignty of the nonprofit sector: government takes a hands-off approach to taxing, and nonprofits are required to be hands off in terms of advocating for government subvention.

8. To counter this limitation, Representative Walter Jones introduced a bill in the US House called the Houses of Worship Free Speech Restoration Act of 2005.

9. Todd J. Gillman. "Health Clubs Hit YMCAs' Tax Breaks," *Washington Post*, June 30, 1987.

References

Anheier, Helmut K., and David C. Hammack, eds. 2010. *American Foundations: Roles and Contributions*. Washington, DC: Brookings Institution Press.

Berry, Jeffrey M. 1984. *The Interest Group Society*. Boston: Little, Brown.

———. 1999. *The New Liberalism: The Rising Power of Citizen Groups*. Washington, DC: Brookings Institution Press.

Berry, Jeffrey M., and David F. Arons. 2003. *A Voice for Nonprofits*. Washington, DC: Brookings Institute Press.

Boris, Elizabeth T. 1999. "The Nonprofit Sector in the 1990s." *The Future of Philanthropy in a Changing America*, Charles Clotfelter and Thomas Erlich, eds. (pp. 1–33). New York, NY: The American Assembly, Columbia University.

Boris, Elizabeth T., and Jeff Krehely. 2002. "Civic Participation and Advocacy." *The State of Nonprofit America*, Lester M. Salamon, ed. (pp. 299–330). Washington, DC: Brookings Institute Press.

Boris, Elizabeth T., and Matthew Maronick. 2012. "Civic Participation and Advocacy." *The State of Nonprofit America*, 2nd ed., Lester M. Salamon, ed. (pp. 394–422). Washington, DC: Brookings Institution Press.

Brody, Evelyn. 2010. "All Charities are Property-tax Exempt, but Some Charities are More Exempt than Others." *New England Law Review* 44(3): 621.

———, ed. 2002. *Property Tax Exemption for Charities*. Washington, DC: Urban Institute Press.

———. 2012. "Sunshine and Shadows on Charity Governance: Public Disclosure as a Regulatory Tool." *Florida Tax Review* 12(4): 183.

Brody, Evelyn, Mayra Marquez, and Katherine Toran. 2012. *The Charitable Property-Tax Exemption and PILOTs*. Washington, DC: Urban Institute.

Brown, Eleanor, and James Ferris. 2007. "Social Capital and Philanthropy: An Analysis of the Impact of Social Capital on Individual Giving and Volunteering." *Nonprofit and Voluntary Sector Quarterly* 36(March): 85–99.

Chaves, Mark. 2002. "Religious Congregations." *The State of Nonprofit America*, Lester M. Salamon, ed. Washington, DC: Brookings Institution Press.

Clemens, Elisabeth. 2006. "The Constitution of Citizens: Political Theories of Nonprofit Organizations." *The Nonprofit Sector: A Research Handbook*, 2nd ed., Walter W. Powell and Richard Steinberg, eds. New Haven: Yale University Press.

Cnaan, Ram. 1997. "Social and Community Involvement of Local Religious Congregations: Findings from a Six-City Study." Paper presented at annual meeting of ARNOVA, Indianapolis, IN, December 4–6.

Cole, David. 2016. *Engines of Liberty: The Power of Citizen Activists to Make Constitutional Law.* New York, NY: Basic Books.

Colinvaux, Roger. 2014. "Political Activity Limits and Tax Exemption: A Gordian's Knot." *Virginia Tax Review* 34(1).

Cordes, Joseph, and C. Eugene Steuerle. 2009. "The Changing Economy and the Scope of Nonprofit-Like Activities." *Nonprofits and Business*, Joseph Cordes and C. Eugene Steuerle, eds. Washington, DC: Urban Institute.

Covington, Sally. 1997. *Moving A Public Policy Agenda: The Strategic Philanthropy of Conservative Foundations.* Washington, DC: National Committee for Responsive Philanthropy.

Crimm, Nina J. 1952, and Laurence H. Winer. 2011. *Politics, Taxes, and the Pulpit: Provocative First Amendment Conflicts.* New York, NY: Oxford University Press.

Dees, Gregory J. 1998. "Enterprising Nonprofits." *Harvard Business Review* (January–February): 55–67.

Etzioni, Amitai. 1993. *The Spirit of Community: Rights, Responsibilities, and the Communitarian Agenda.* New York, NY: Crown Publishers, Inc.

Fleishman, Joel L. 2007. *The Foundation: A Great American Secret: How Private Wealth is Changing the World.* New York, NY: Public Affairs.

Fremont-Smith, Marion. 2004. *Governing Nonprofit Organizations.* Cambridge, MA: President and Fellows of Harvard College.

The Foundation Center. 2014. *Key Facts on U.S. Foundations*, 2014 ed. New York, NY: The Foundation Center.

Gillman, Todd J. 1987. "Health Clubs Hit YMCAs' Tax Breaks." *Washington Post*, June 30.

Goddeeris, John H., and Burton A. Weisbrod. 2006. "Ownership Forms, Conversions, and Public Policy." *Nonprofits & Government: Collaboration & Conflict*, 2nd ed., Elizabeth T. Boris and C. Eugene Steuerle, eds. (pp. 277–310). Washington, DC Urban Institute Press.

Gulati-Partee, Gita, and Lisa Ranghelli. 2009. *Strengthening Democracy, Increasing Opportunities: Impacts of Advocacy, Organizing, and Civic Engagement in Minnesota.* Washington,

DC: National Committee for Responsive Philanthropy.

Hall, Peter Dobkin. 1982. "Institutions, Autonomy, and National Networks." *Making the Nonprofit Sector in the United States*, David C. Hammack, ed. Bloomington: Indiana University Press.

Hansman, Henry. 1987. "Economic Theories of Nonprofit Organization." *The Nonprofit Sector: A Research Handbook*, Walter W. Powell, ed. New Haven: Yale University Press.

Harris, Frederick C. 1994. "Something Within: Religion as a Mobilizer of African-American Political Activism." *Journal of Politics* 56: 42–68.

Hess, Gary. 2003. "Waging the Cold War in the Third World: The Foundations and the Challenges of Development." *Charity, Philanthropy, and Civility in American History*, Lawrence J. Friedman and Mark D. McGarve, eds. New York, NY: Cambridge University Press.

Hodgkinson, Virginia, and Murray Weitzman. 1993. *From Belief to Commitment: The Community Service Activities and Finances of Religious Congregations in the United States.* Washington, DC: Independent Sector.

Jackson, Maria-Rosario. 1998. "Arts and Culture Indicators in Community Building: Project Update." *Journal of Arts Management, Law and Society* 28(3): 201–205.

Jenkins, Craig J. 2006. "Nonprofit Organizations and Political Advocacy." *The Nonprofit Sector: A Research Handbook*, 2nd ed. Walter W. Powell and Richard Steinberg, eds. New Haven: Yale University Press.

Kania, John, Mark Kramer, and Patty Russell. 2014. "Strategic Philanthropy for a Complex World." *Stanford Social Innovation Review* 12(3): 26–37.

Kearns, Kevin P. 2012. "Accountability in the Nonprofit Sector." *The State of Nonprofit America*, 2nd ed., Lester M. Salamon, ed. (pp. 587–615). Washington, DC: Brookings Institution Press.

Kerlin, Janelle A. 2005. "Social Enterprise in the United States and Abroad: Learning from Our Differences." *Researching Social Entrepreneurship*, M. Mosher-Williams, ed. ARNOVA Occasional Paper Series, 1(3).

Kerlin, Janelle A., and Tom H. Pollak. 2011. "Nonprofit Commercial Revenue: A Replacement for

Declining Government Grants and Private Contributions?" *The American Review of Public Administration* 41(6): 686–704.

Lohmann, Roger. 1992. *The Commons.* San Francisco, CA: Jossey-Bass Publishers.

———. 2003. "The Commons: Our Mission if We Choose to Accept It." *Nonprofit and Voluntary Sector Quarterly* 10(Summer): 6–10.

Mayer, Jane. 2016. *Dark Money: The Hidden History of the Billionaires behind the Rise of the Radical Right.* New York, NY: Doubleday.

McCarthy, Kathleen. 2003. *American Creed: Philanthropy and the Rise of Civil Society 1700–1865.* Chicago: The University of Chicago Press.

McKeever, Brice. 2015. *The Nonprofit Sector in Brief 2015: Public Charities, Giving and Volunteering.* Washington, DC: Urban Institute.

Morley, Elaine, and Carol J. De Vita. 2007. *Providing Long-Term Services after Major Disasters.* Washington, DC: Urban Institute.

Moore, Alexander J. 2014. *The Food Fighters: DC Central Kitchen's First Twenty-Five Years on the Front Lines of Hunger and Poverty.* Bloomington, IN: iUniverse.

National Center for Charitable Statistics. 2016. *Profiles of Individual Charitable Contributions by State, 2013.* Washington, DC: Urban Institute.

O'Connell, Brian. 1997. *Powered By Coalition: The Story of Independent Sector.* San Francisco, CA: Jossey-Bass Publishers.

Payton, Robert L. 1988. *Philanthropy: Voluntary Action for the Public Good.* New York, NY: American Council on Education/Macmillan Publishing Company.

Panel on the Nonprofit Sector. 2005. *Strengthening Transparency, Governance, Accountability of Charitable Organizations: A Final Report to Congress and the Nonprofit Sector.* Washington, DC: Independent Sector.

Pekkanen, Robert, Steven Rathgeb Smith, and Yutaka Tsujinaka, eds. 2014. *Nonprofits and Advocacy: Engaging Communities and Government in an Era of Retrenchment.* Baltimore: Johns Hopkins University Press.

Perks, Thomas, and Michael Haan. 2011. "Youth Religious Involvement and Adult Community Participation: Do Levels of Youth Religious Involvement Matter?" *Nonprofit and Voluntary Sector Quarterly* 40(February): 107–129.

Pettijohn, Sarah L., and Elizabeth Boris. 2013. *Contracts and Grants between Nonprofits and Government.* Washington, DC: Urban Institute.

Post, Stephen G. 2011. *The Hidden Gifts of Helping: How the Power of Giving, Compassion, and Hope Can Get Us through Hard Times.* San Francisco, CA: Jossey-Bass.

Printz, Tobi J. 1997. "Services and Capacity of Faith-Based Organizations in the Washington, DC, Metropolitan Area." Paper presented at annual meeting of ARNOVA, Indianapolis, IN, December 4–6.

Putnam, Robert D. 1993. *Making Democracy Work: Civic Traditions in Modern Italy.* Princeton: Princeton University Press.

———. 2000. *Bowling Alone: The Collapse and Revival of American Community.* New York, NY: Simon and Shuster.

Reid, Elizabeth J. 2003. *In the States, Across the Nation, and Beyond: Democratic and Constitutional Perspectives on Nonprofit Advocacy.* Washington, DC: Urban Institute Press.

———. 2006. "Advocacy and the Challenges. It Presents for Nonprofits." *Nonprofits & Government: Collaboration & Conflict,* 2nd ed., Elizabeth T. Boris and C. Eugene Steuerle, eds. (pp. 343–372). Washington, DC: Urban Institute Press.

Reid, Elizabeth J., and Janelle Kerlin. 2003. "More than Meets the Eye: Structuring and Financing Nonprofit Advocacy." A paper delivered at the American Political Science Association, Annual Conference, Philadelphia, Pennsylvania.

Rich, Andrew. 2004. *Think Tanks, Public Policy, and the Politics of Expertise.* Cambridge, UK: Cambridge University Press.

———. 2005. "War of Ideas." *Stanford Social Innovation Review* 3: 18–25.

Salamon, Lester M. 1995. *Partners in Public Service: Government-Nonprofit Relations in the Modern Welfare State.* Baltimore: Johns Hopkins University Press.

———. 2006. *Nonprofits & Government: Collaboration & Conflict,* 2nd ed., Elizabeth T. Boris and

C. Eugene Steuerle, eds. Washington, DC: Urban Institute Press.

———. 2014. *Leverage for Good: An Introduction to the New Frontier of Philanthropy and Social Investment.* Oxford University Press.

Seligman, Martin E. P. 1991. *Learned Optimism: How to Change Your Mind and Your Life.* New York, NY: A. A. Knopf.

Shah, Sapna, and Min Pease. 2012. "Diverse Perspectives, Shared Objective: Collaborating to Form the African Agricultural Capital Fund." Global Impact Investing Network, Case Studies.

Sievers, Bruce R. 2010. *Civil Society, Philanthropy, and the Fate of the Commons.* Medford, MA: Tufts University Press.

Skocpol, Theda. 1995. *Protecting Mothers and Soldiers: The Political Origins of Social Policy in the United States.* Cambridge, MA: Harvard University Press.

Skocpol, Theda, and Morris P. Fiorina. 1999. *Civic Engagement in American Democracy.* Washington, DC: Brookings Institution Press.

Skocpol, Theda, and Vanessa Williamson. 2012. *The Tea Party and the Remaking of Republican Conservatism.* New York, NY: Oxford University Press.

Smith, David H., Helmut K. Anheier, Stefan Toepler, and Regina List. 2010. "Grassroots Associations." *International Encyclopedia of Civil Society* (pp. 804–810). New York, NY: Springer.

Stevenson, David R. 1997. *The National Taxonomy of Exempt Entities Manual.* Washington, DC and New York, NY: National Center for Charitable Statistics and Foundation Center.

U.S. Congress. 1996. "House Committee on Small Business. Government-Supported Unfair Competition with Small Business." 104th Cong, 2d scss., July 19.

Verba, Sidney, Kay Lehman Schlozman, and Henry E. Brady. 1995. *Voice and Equality: Civic Voluntarism in American Politics.* Cambridge, MA: Harvard University Press.

Walzer, Michael, ed. 1995. *Toward A Global Civil Society.* Providence, Rhode Island: Berghahn Books.

Warren, Mark. 2002. *Democracy and Association.* Princeton: Princeton University Press.

Weisbrod, Burton A. 1988. *The Nonprofit Economy.* Cambridge, MA: Harvard University Press.

Wuthnow, Robert, ed. 1991. *Between States and Markets: The Voluntary Sector in Comparative Perspective.* New Jersey, NJ: Princeton University Press.

Wuthnow, Robert. 2006. "Clash of Values: Government Funding for the Arts and Religion." *Nonprofits & Government: Collaboration & Conflict,* 2nd ed., Elizabeth T. Boris and C. Eugene Steuerle, eds. (pp. 311–342). Washington, DC: Urban Institute Press.

———. 2004. *Saving America.* New Jersey, NJ: Princeton University Press.

Young, Dennis R., Lester M. Salamon, and Mary Clark Grinsfelder. 2012. "Commercialization, Social Ventures, and For-profit Competition." *The State of Nonprofit America,* 2nd ed., Lester M. Salamon, ed. (pp. 521–548). Washington, DC: Brookings Institution Press.

Zuckerman, Ethan. 2014. "New Media, New Civics?" *Policy & Internet* 6(2): 151–168.

CHAPTER 2

Democratic Governance and Institutional Logics Within the Third Sector (or, How Habermas Discovered the Coffee House)

Meghan Elizabeth Kallman and Terry Nichols Clark*

Kallman, Meghan Elizabeth, and Terry Nichols Clark, *The Third Sector: Community Organizations, NGOs, and Nonprofits.* (Urbana, Chicago, and Springfield, Ill.: University of Illinois Press, 2016).

It would be well to infuse political life into each portion of the territory, in order to multiply to an infinite extent opportunities of acting in concert for all the members of the community, and to make them constantly feel their mutual dependence on each other . . . if the object be to have the local affairs of a district conducted by the men who reside there, the same persons are always in contact, and they are, in a manner, forced to be acquainted, and to adapt themselves to one another.

—ALEXIS DE TOCQUEVILLE

CSOs (civil society organizations), NPOs (nonprofit organizations), NGOs (nongovernmental organizations), INGOS (international nongovernmental organizations), and formal and informal associations are part of an important, relatively new sector that is now a world political force. Though the components of this "third sector" vary by country, their net effect is increasingly important across the globe.

This third sector plays a critical role in creating values worldwide, through its work in service delivery, advocacy, cultural programs, and social movements. The third sector includes different types of relief and welfare organizations, innovation organizations, public service organizations, economic development organizations, grassroots mobilization groups, advocacy groups, and social networks (J. Clark 1991:40–41).

Foundational differences in religious and political tradition across different countries create different types of meanings for third sector organizations. Contexts shift drastically, internationally and over time. A children's art group, for example, means something very different in a wealthy Los Angeles suburb than in a poor Lima neighborhood. Chinese civic organizations, for example, follow the predominantly Asian model of being funded largely by government and are linked to goals of national politics. This contrasts with Western experience of the third sector, which has often explicitly challenged government objectives.

DOI: 10.4324/9780367696559-3

Generally speaking, the countries examined here fall into one of two categories: those with a strong central state and—we argue, consequently—a weaker involvement of third sector organizations in some regards, and those comparatively "weak" national governments with historically strong third sector organizations. These differences have important implications for current policy debate and changes of the third sector in each country. Countries with historically weak state involvement (like the United States) often have a third sector that began as an independent sector and more recently has moved closer to government. Countries with strong state traditions (like China and Japan) generally have had a government-linked third sector and more recently diversified to include more advocacy-oriented activities. As these two categories move toward one another, participants can learn from one another, if one recognizes these broad policy shifts and looks for cross-national lessons.

Five crucial features of third sector organizations have been widely identified in the literature (see Salamon, Hems, and Chinnock 2000:8). Fundamentally, the third sector can be conceptualized as a set of entities that is composed of *organizations that are self-governing, do not distribute profit, are primarily private and nongovernmental* in basic structure, and are *meaningfully voluntary*, thus likely to engage constituents on the basis of shared interest. This definition we follow throughout the reading.[1]

How the state interacts with other, nonstate actors in the third sector, how social movements become institutionalized into NGOs, and how governments use associations either to bolster their own images or to accomplish goals—are very new animals in most of the world. They are classically undertheorized by political philosophers. The third sector as it is commonly known has its roots in an Anglo-Saxon tradition that only arrived on the general theoretical map with the publication of Alexis de Tocqueville's seminal *Democracy in America*.

Some recent work, however, has taken up these relationships between third sector organizations and the state. Da Silva's (2010) book on the rise of the welfare state theorized the United States as normatively "behind" the rest of the Western world because it lacked a welfare state—in the United States, the third sector has always been an excuse to neither more fully develop nor continue centralized welfare policies, particularly since the decline of Keynesianism. The political right has classically invoked civic groups as a reason *not* to fund state agencies. The end of communism in 1989 brought out a drastic drop in the hierarchy of the state, and neoliberalization processes have brought about a new political emphasis on third sector organizations as the central state shrinks, and policy work is "rescaled" (Brenner 2009) to municipal governments and civil society organizations (Castree 2008, 2010).

And these transformations have been powerful. Jürgen Habermas himself, a political philosopher most famous for his work on the public sphere, began to theorize how the potential of this sort of discursive, "coffee house model" of associationalism could serve as the basis for extra-state democratic engagement and participation in general. His work on the public sphere expanded to include theories of a "post-national constellation" (Habermas 2001)—a public sphere for the globalized world, or an international civil society.

Deep Structures of the Third Sector: Religious Traditions, Organizational Impulses

The classic starting point for discussions of organizations and associations is Alexis de Tocqueville's *Democracy in America*, first published in 1835. He and other French leaders were then fearful of what the impending French democracy might entail, and a leading French advisory group sent Tocqueville to investigate crime in the

United States, which broadened into a study of how democracy functioned. The United States was chosen as a young society wherein democracy had started recently after colonization, and where there was minimal tradition associated with older Western economic and political arrangements. Tocqueville spent several months traveling around the United States talking to citizens about their society and civic activities, seeking commentary on a broad range of social, economic, and political practices. The result was *Democracy in America*, a project that intended to find lessons on associationalism and democracy in general to bring back to Europe and France.

Tocqueville's original conclusion was that local organized groups were one of the most critical building blocks of the entire US society. These organizations were one of the most distinctively non-European aspects of America, important primarily because they and their participants were separate and autonomous from the state and from higher-level political officials. Tocqueville stressed how, in the United States, the "engaged citizen" was really quite an average person in most instances. In the process of participating in these small civic groups, average citizens created new services, new social arrangements, and during that process, *they themselves were transformed*. As they planned the construction of churches or worked together on projects, citizens learned to trust their neighbors more; they learned to serve as leaders themselves, temporarily or for long periods of time. Neighborhood groups brought together average persons, fostering feelings of pride and commitment for having completed a specific task jointly and successfully. Consider this passage from *Democracy in America*:

> The legislators of America did not suppose that a general representation of the whole nation would suffice to ward off a disaster [despotism] at once so natural to the frame of democratic society, and so fatal: they also thought that it would be well to infuse political life into each portion of the territory, in order to multiply to an infinite extent opportunities of acting in concert for all the members of the community, and to make them constantly feel their mutual dependence on each other . . . if the object be to have the local affairs of a district conducted by the men who reside there, the same persons are always in contact, and they are, in a manner, forced to be acquainted, and to adapt themselves to one another.
>
> (1969:126)

Importantly, in the United States, some of the most salient of these original third sector groups were small churches, representative of the many branches of Protestantism that split apart during the early years of US history as a formally independent nation. Protestantism's influence on poverty and civic life generally emerged in both Europe and the United States in local-level organizations (Kahl 2005), with their focus on providing food, clothing, and basic necessities, rather than with systemic political advocacy or agitation. By contrast, the southern United States had a comparatively hierarchical social structure, and its civic groups were much less visible.

In addition to Protestantism, there are several fundamental traditions that have helped structure the development of organizational life (and consequently the third sector) in the United States and in Western Europe. These traditions come from the European context and deserve separate consideration; these religious roots affect the third sector across the globe today.

One tradition is Lutheranism (the sect following the sixteenth-century German Protestant reformer Martin Luther). Luther broke with the Roman Catholic Church in the early sixteenth century but nevertheless managed to find converts in many of the central European countries that had been Roman Catholic for centuries. Under Luther, the idea of the "undeserving" poor emerged—those who were able-bodied but unwilling to work—and notions of individual responsibility took hold (Kahl 2005:103). He trod a delicate line between dissent and cooperation—one could see parallels between this approach and contemporary third sector organizations working in a close and politically cooperative relationship with strong state leaders. Many of these current third sector organizations are highly attuned to the (sometimes conflicting) demands of their governing bodies, the state, and their constituents; they embody an institutional logic of activism, operate within certain domains, and choose their political battles carefully. The success of Martin Luther is certainly worth attending to, as Lutheranism's spread had tremendous subsequent impacts not only on religious, but also on cultural development throughout both Western Europe and North America.

Calvinism is the other major European religious tradition that has had powerful effects on traditions of associationalism. John Calvin broke with the overwhelmingly hierarchical tradition of French Roman Catholicism as a young priest. He migrated to Switzerland, where he found many followers, who in turn spread Calvinism to the Netherlands, Scotland, parts of Scandinavia, and New England. Calvinists were critically different from the Lutherans and the Roman Catholics in their organizational structure; they employed a bottom-up rather than a top-down principle of organization and governance, captured in the principle of "sovereignty in one's own social circles" (Cox 1993:64), and the role of the state in this sort of framework was to encourage spontaneity in private life by affording private groups sufficient space in which to operate. According to Calvin, poor relief should be part of the Church's purview rather than the state's, and therefore Calvinism encouraged a great deal of private charity (Kahl 2005). The average Calvinist church member was a direct participant in church leadership, because congregations selected church leaders. The "aldermen"—as they were termed in the Netherlands, for instance, and as they are known in the United States today—were responsible to their parishioners in a manner

that is much more like contemporary democracy than like the vertical relationship between a Roman Catholic priest and his "flock."[2] Indeed, contemporary democracy has strong Calvinist components, which have increased in visibility and salience in the last years of the twentieth century.[3] The Calvinist Church was the classic bottom-up model of the organized group in Western society, that of the active citizen, and many activist third sector organizations.

This Calvinist tendency toward bottom-up organization manifested itself in many ways. For instance, in the unequal society of Europe from the Middle Ages onward, it was generally expected that the poor would steal from the rich. The general answer to such a problem was to deal with the poor as criminals, looking them into prisons or poorhouses. The Calvinist Dutch, by contrast, consistent with their principles of sovereignty, dealt with their poor differently: each was assigned a family and adopted as an extended family member.

In the eighteenth and early nineteenth centuries in regions of England, the churches and associated civic groups, similarly to the Dutch, sought to address the problems confronting the poor and new industrial workers who had recently left their farms. Farmers had driven peasants off the land in an era when selling wool brought a better return, and vast farm areas of Scotland and England were thus transformed into market-oriented industrial farming regions. This in turn drove peasants to the new manufacturing towns of Manchester and Glasgow. There was great concern, of course, about crime and possible revolution in these newly industrializing areas. But serious uprisings were minimal, in part due to this tradition of civic and political participation. By contrast, similar social and economic problems were found in continental Europe, including in Germany, Italy, and France; in those cases peasants revolted, crime was rampant, and there was more commonly talk of class warfare. The patterns of conflict and accommodation that were reached by these groups are interesting to briefly consider: these examples suggest that local-level associations can potentially serve as integrating mechanisms for dangerous or dislocated individuals.

Even today we can see the impact of this sort of Calvinist approach to governance and participation. This story of bottom-up accountability and associational structure is essentially what Tocqueville observed with respect to New England civic life. Associationalism has been labeled American; however, later work has shown that it was more fundamentally Calvinist and not uniquely or even most powerfully American (Gorski 2003)—Tocqueville could have found a more pure version of his democracy story if he had gone to parts of Switzerland and the Netherlands and probed the workings of Calvinist institutions and churches there.

Neoliberalism and the New Political Culture

The conservative turn in the West took hold in the early 1970s and spurred the transformation of centralized state social services to an intersectoral social service design such as that which we know today. There are two components of liberalism: the fiscal and the social.

Neoliberalism refers broadly to the set of policies originally enacted in the United States and the UK (and subsequently adopted throughout the world) since the late 1970s and the decline of Keynesianism. In the last two decades neoliberalism has come to suggest a market fundamentalism that embodies laissez-faire principles. The term "neoliberalism" has been used by scholars as a means of denaturalizing globalization processes and simultaneously calling attention to their associated ideological and political implications (Peck, Theodore, and Brenner 2010:97).

In particular, we stress the ways that classic fiscal conservatives (like Reagan or Thatcher) differ profoundly from Bill Clinton or Tony Blair. Both Clinton and Blair were more socially liberal, even though their fiscal policies were conservative compared to those advocated by the left. Clinton and Blair illustrate the unique blend of fiscal conservatism and social liberalism, sometimes dubbed the "New Political Culture" (T. Clark and Hoffmann-Martinot 1998). We note here simply that when one shifts from government to third sector organizations, the "purity" of ideology and distinctive types of institutional logics can grow more salient and differentiated as there are far more organizations than governments. Third sector organizations, like local governments, can thus contribute to deeper understandings of national and global processes by virtue of the greater range and diversity they illustrate. Third sector analysis can correspondingly build on related insights about political and cultural transformations, national and especially local. This New Political Culture created a new set of social and economic conditions that helped spark the global rise of nonprofits, which has been analyzed with data for thousands of local governments and neighborhoods (Silver and Clark 2016; T. Clark et al. 2014) in related work to date.

The nonprofit sector across the world grew rapidly after the 1980s, and inevitably, it bears the markings of a combination of factors that have helped engender that growth. Some are shared globally. But there are also important national institutional components that shifted how the third sector took shape. A variety of pressures stemming from government, civil, and other kinds of social configurations all act on the third sector.

Institutional Logics in the Third Sector

We think about these pressures in terms of institutional logics. Institutional logics (Alford and Friedland 1985; Friedland and Alford 1991; Fligstein 1987) are an organizational-sociological concept that illustrates how socially constructed belief systems shape people's cognition and behavior in a given environment. Thornton and Ocasio (1999:804) define them as "the socially constructed, historical patterns of practices, assumptions, values, beliefs, and rules by which individuals produce and reproduce their material subsistence, organize time and space, and provide meaning to their social reality." They are important organizational characteristics, defining the "desirable," setting up norms and values, and mediating meaning within an organization. Institutional logics are intertwined with the construction of social identities; those identities then reinforce participants' positions as stakeholders and their associated discourse (Creed, Scully, and Austin 2002).

This project has unearthed five basic institutional logics operating simultaneously within the third sector. Their combined presences create tensions, synergies, and unevenness that can be seen in different proportions in civil societies across the globe. These logics are present to different degrees in different places, but are present in all the countries we have studied here. The five institutional logics are:

- Clientelism
- Paternalism
- Bureaucracy
- Activism
- Professionalism

At times, some of these logics emerge into a hybrid sort of approach that we examine on a case-by-case basis. Here we take each logic one by one to outline its components and its theoretical contours.

Clientelism

The first institutional logic present within the third sector is *clientelism*. Clientelism and patronage refer to the "trade of votes and other types of partisan support in exchange for public decisions with divisible benefits" (Piattoni 2001:4). Clientelist polities are those in which particular interests are promoted at the expense of the general interest. In other words,

clientelism is a strategy for acquiring or increasing political power on the part of the patrons and for protecting and promoting interests on the part of the clients; the incentives and disincentives to engage in clientelism are structural. In other words, clientelism is a structural feature of a given political setup, shaped by political institutions and historical circumstances (Piattoni 2001:2).

Clientelism emerges in the third sector primarily in terms of financial support that is exchanged for political favors. As a Chicago alderman, for example, one might give money to an influential person's pet charity, thereby hoping to win that person's support, especially for reelection. Clientelism has long been the foundation of most politics globally, but it has come under attack in recent decades as globalization processes and social movements have brought about new emphases on transparency. Critics have used the media and international organizations to bring out scandals and variously seek to change the clientelist rules of the game that have long governed political relationships across the world.

Paternalism

The second institutional logic that is widely identifiable within the third sector we term *paternalism*. Paternalism is behavior that limits the autonomy or decision-making power of individuals or entities for their own good; it describes a relationship in which one entity's choice is insufficiently voluntary to be genuinely considered her own. Paternalism, unlike clientelism, is not a relationship that is meant to produce material or power benefits for a certain group, but rather an approach that emphasizes the condescending nature of interactions between the powerful and the powerless.

Dynamics of paternalism are deeply implicated in charity historically. Indeed, the very notion of noblesse oblige suggests that privilege entails responsibility; those who are fortunate are required to aid those who are understood as less so. Individual paternalistic support could be leveraged though charitable organizations. And it was often upper-status persons, especially women, who showed their personal kindness on a one-to-one basis with the poor by volunteering in hospitals, churches, and social agencies. Interestingly, Tocqueville characterized the organizations providing such services as distinctly democratic when he saw them in America in the 1830s, but not in his native France.

The nineteenth- and early twentieth-century British and American models of such paternalism spread globally in the late twentieth century. Paternalism moved beyond the individual, expanded though benevolent or charity organizations, and gave distinctive character to locations where they were more widespread, like British and American cities in the late nineteenth century. Charity was attached to social prestige, but the self-defined driver was not prestige but "doing good." Critics have long pointed out that more is involved in charity than simply "doing good," building on ideas such as the classic Marxist concept of "false consciousness."

The institutional logic of paternalism appears contemporarily in private practices of philanthropy, particularly in small family foundations that are managed by individuals or family members of wealthy individuals who create and manage the foundations themselves. In many cases these foundations continue to be administered by people with no expertise other than their own wealth. The accountability structures for this kind of third sector work were historically few, and family foundations in the United States served as both tax havens and as sites of social prestige among wealthy individuals.

Bureaucracy

The third institutional logic that we identify is *bureaucracy*. Especially in the European and Asian contexts, the national state incarnates centralized bureaucratic power. The central state in many places traditionally resisted the "private" initiatives of the third sector, as it often sought monopolistic control of fundamental social policies. Some trace this emphasis on a unified central state to the desire for military preparedness. However, in the globally important French case, the monopolistic state bureaucracy was legitimated by a combination of principles of liberty, equality, and fraternity after the 1789 Revolution. Its republican logic drove the state to impose limits against its classic enemies (in this case the Church and the royal/aristocratic legacy). This fraternal impulse that created the state, ironically, left no space for a third sector, which was legally prohibited in much of nineteenth-century France and was similarly weak in Asia. But as education and incomes have risen, unskilled labor declined, and media and travel increased, the hierarchy of the central state in France has come under attack. After the political uprisings of 1968, demands for more democracy by average citizens rose, leading to the subsequent logic of activism.

An institutional logic of bureaucracy continues to articulate within the third sector as these organizations learn to negotiate power sharing and responsibilities in conjunction with local or national arms of government around the world.

Activism

A fourth institutional logic in the third sector we call *activism*, primarily seen among the grassroots organizations and volunteers who are impatient with the bureaucratic constraints of their institutional contexts and who are more open to using contentious practices to further their goals. Those operating under this kind of institutional logic often call on the language and tactics of social movements to make sense of their own participation. If clientelism and paternalism are centuries old, activism enters seriously after the 1968 student uprisings in the West, which subsequently spread globally. This activist logic typically shows up in smaller or more grassroots organizations, formal and informal.

The institutional logic of activism matches easily with a small, fluid organization of volunteers, where the entire organization feels itself to be part of an ongoing social movement, rather than organizational employees. But it can also penetrate the staff and programs of churches, foundations, big social agencies, and even some government agencies where some staff may be appointed—or understand themselves—as trying to make traditional institutions less bureaucratic and more activist. They may seek allies with others outside the organization. For example in China after 2000, some Beijing ministry staff encouraged local protests, even if these were opposed by other national ministries.

Amateurs' activism is often contrasted with a professional side of management. The activists are often more amateur in the sense that they may be volunteers, working without pay. What, then, drives them? It is often their commitment to values, particularly egalitarianism, manifesting through such specific concerns as human rights, feminism, environmentalism, and anti-poverty efforts. They are often driven to advance these values in opposition to those who resist them (Capital, The State, The Man, The Establishment, or Neoliberalism). The distinction between amateurs and professionals has been used to interpret many past political battles (see, for example, *The Amateur Democrat* [Wilson 1962] or Trounstine [2008] on professional political monopolies). We stress the critical role of volunteers in responding to natural disasters in China, Korea, and Taiwan, where there has been a huge increase in voluntarism since the end of the twentieth century. Voluntarism in Asian countries has often been less explicitly linked to movements than in the West, but it does share a broad and strong commitment to humanistic values and helping those most in need.

These volunteers illustrate the distinct characteristics shared by many activists within the third sector. They are by-and-large youthful, well-educated, idealistic, and value-driven liberal/left persons who bring a serious commitment to third sector issues. This demographic group takes on more importance as democracy, education, human rights, individualism, and related social and political values are codified internationally (T. Clark and Hoffmann-Martinot 1998). The new technologies widely available in the last sixty years, ranging from television to cell phones to social media and Internet calls, have helped this kind of activist organize more quickly and fluidly and evade some of the constraints that states imposed.

Professionalization

The fifth and most novel institutional logic that appears within the third sector is *professionalization*. The process of professionalization involves transforming a job into a skilled profession, typically implying the establishment of accepted qualifications, professional norms, industry standards, professional bodies, and training programs. Professionalization as a term, first explored in depth by Carr-Saunders and Parsons in the 1930s, later Wilensky (1964), refers to a technical, systematic knowledge of something, as well as the presence of professional norms within any given occupation. These norms are defined by professional associations, not the state or the foundation leadership. This professionalization, within the field of foundations and funding, is a relatively new phenomenon and has increased dramatically in recent decades, generating a "program professional," who is an expert in a particular field of social policy, moving between government agencies, community organizations, foundations, and universities (McCarthy and Zald 1977; Wilensky 1964). The development of the foundation "program professional" has been encouraged by the institutionalization of dissent within mainstream US society: "as a result of the massive growth in funding, it has become possible for a larger number of professionals to earn a respectable income committing themselves full-time to activities related to social movements" (McCarthy and Zald 1977:15). Two different dynamics, both rooted in bureaucracy, can be credited with its emergence.

First, professionalization can be a reaction against both central state control and the clientelist approach that earlier characterized philanthropy in places as diverse as Chicago and Japan. Ostensibly meritocratic structures, clear programmatic goals and designations, bureaucratic organizational structures, progress indicators, evaluative terms, and an infrastructure supporting philanthropy can provide common standards against which to measure organizational behavior. Professionalization suggests that philanthropic programs and their supporters need to justify their behavior using more "universalistic," accepted standards of the third sector, seeking to reduce the subjectivity associated with paternalistic or clientelist charity.

The second reason for the emergence of professionalization is structural and pertains to the increasingly important role that the central state has played in funding the third sector worldwide in the last forty years—ironically in some ways, given the difficulties that the third sector had in breaking free of that very state in places like France. When private organizations accept money from state entities, particularly in places like the United States and France, they become accountable for its use. These questions of accountability have engendered the growth of whole industries devoted to monitoring, compliance, and program evaluation.

Professionalization can have both normatively positive and negative impacts for the organizations that sustain it. Clearly, transparency has a plethora of benefits for a democratic society, and the benefits of systems of accountability in the third sector have been widely documented by academics and policymakers (DeHoog and Salamon 2002; Salamon 2003).

But professionalization has shortcomings too; many nonprofit workers and activists complain that it creates yet another instantiation of Weber's iron cage, at worst ensnaring participants in endless red tape, and at best functioning as a short-sighted approach to nonprofit programming (see Ebrahim 2005).

In the United States and throughout the world, these multiple institutional logics have led to some mini culture wars within individual organizations, organizational fields, and third sectors in general. While this diversity is by no means a new theme, our project has sought to identify the major components of this diversity and to show how the broader context has specifically contributed to its development.

In China, South Korea, Japan, and Taiwan, third sector organizations are spinning off of state agencies and have often, through that very professionalization, become *more* independent than the state agencies that birthed them. The transition from authoritarian clientelism in the East to respect for associational autonomy is an important dimension of democratization, unfolding unevenly through iterative cycles of conflict among authoritarian rulers, reformist elites, and autonomous social movements (Fox 1994). The high degrees of professionalization and institutionalization in the United States, by contrast, make the historically fractious third sector start to look much less radical. This movement toward "joining the establishment" is a central theme of self-criticism by more activist commentators on third sector developments in, for example, France and the United States. Yet simultaneously, some national governments have explicitly opposed or limited activities of third sector activists in areas like China and Japan. Themes of openness and closure, as they stand in relation to each other, become salient as third sector participants jockey for position and, in the process, create new rules among the competing institutional logics within the field. Two illustrations from different parts of the world elucidate these points.

SUSAN G. KOMEN FOR THE CURE AND PLANNED PARENTHOOD

In late December 2011, the world's largest breast cancer foundation, Susan G. Komen for the Cure, announced that it would be halting its funding to health and education programs run by Planned Parenthood and its affiliates, who also perform abortion services. The move stopped a flow of nearly $700,000 in healthcare support to low-income women. Though a spokeswoman for the Komen foundation claimed that the main factor in the decision was a new rule that prohibits grants to organizations being investigated by local, state, or federal authorities, the Komen foundation's decision was widely understood as yielding to longstanding pressure from anti-abortion groups.

Cecile Richards, Planned Parenthood's leader, said that the decision "came so abruptly in the face of a long, good, working relationship with Komen" and that the change in financing criteria "was written specifically to address the political pressure that they've been under[. . . .] Until really recently, the Komen foundation had been praising [Planned Parenthood's] breast health programs as essential," Richards said. "This really abrupt about-face was very surprising. I think that the Komen foundation has been bullied by right-wing groups" (Belluck 2012).

A barrage of popular support for Planned Parenthood—including more than $3 million for its breast cancer program from private donations in the space of a week (Khan 2012)—led the Komen foundation to reverse its course. The organization apologized, stating that only those organizations under "criminal" investigation will be barred from receiving funding. Planned Parenthood was once again deemed eligible to apply for support. Several days later, in February 2012, Karen Handel, a Susan G. Komen executive, resigned from her post. Popular donations to the Komen foundation dropped in 2012.

UPPER-LEVEL JAPANESE OFFICIALS FIRED IN WAKE OF POLITICAL BRAWL

Makiko Tanaka, foreign minister, was relieved of her post in 2002 in the wake of a battle over who caused two NGOs to be barred from an Afghanistan Reconstruction conference. Tanaka's arch-rival in the NGO dispute, Administrative Vice Foreign Minister Yoshiji Nogami, was also fired, and a chairman of the lower house steering committee, Muneo Suzuki, voluntarily resigned.

The clash erupted over the issue of whether political pressure played a role in the ministry's decision to bar two Japanese nongovernmental organizations—Peace Winds Japan and Japan Platform—from the conference. The groups attended the second day of the conference as observers after Tanaka intervened. Prime Minister Koizumi hastily called a news conference early Wednesday morning and explained that the ousters were necessary to have the budget enacted as swiftly as possible amid the stalling economy (*Japan Times* 2002). Tanaka and Vice Foreign Minister Yoshiji Nogami gave contradictory testimonies at the Diet on whether Muneo Suzuki, a senior Liberal Democratic Party lawmaker with strong influence at the Foreign Ministry, was involved in the Foreign Ministry decision to bar the two NGOs from participation.

Tanaka quoted Nogami as telling her that influential LDP lawmaker Muneo Suzuki had pressured the ministry to bar the groups from the event. Nogami later flatly denied making any such statement, and still later Chief Cabinet Secretary Yasuo Fukuda told reporters he believed the vice minister had said nothing of this nature to Tanaka. Suzuki denied the allegation, telling reporters, "The foreign minister lied. I am quite displeased." Suzuki had considerable influence over foreign policy decisions despite the fact he did not hold any administrative post within the ministry.

Tanaka's dismissal was the culmination of a turbulent nine-month alliance in which two of Japan's most popular politicians tried to balance their reformist tactics within the same government. Tanaka, Japan's first female foreign minister and highly activist by standards of the Foreign Ministry, had won followers by criticizing Japan's conservative old guard and their clientelist political policies. But her constant feuding with bureaucrats made her a liability for an administration burdened by a poor economy and economic challenges. Both political analysts and voters saw her dismissal as a sign that Koizumi was giving in to the conservative old guard in an effort to stabilize his weakening government (Brooke 2002a, 2002b).

In both these vignettes, popular support stood in tension with administrative decisions made within the organizations themselves, and ex post facto mobilization of the organizations' supporters led to a reconfiguration of the organization's administrative boards, as well as a reversal of the contentious decisions themselves.

In the Japanese case, political pressures and clientelism backfired when an activist (and female) minister challenged entrenched power; the state bureaucracy then clamped down on both parties, causing all involved to lose their positions. Similarly, the Komen case illustrates the ways that activists organized to challenge what they

perceived as clientelist funding decisions, calling on both Planned Parenthood's professional comportment and legions of individual donors and activists to contest and repeal a decision.

These similar cases illustrate some of the ways that these five logics interarticulate within the third sector. They show the importance of articulating the separate institutional logics that drove specific conflicts.

Social Movements Within the Third Sector: From Radical to Establishment

The New Social Movements that are most commonly discussed today are those that emerged in the 1970s. New Social Movements generally emerged around issues of environmentalism, human rights, women's issues, peace, antinuclear protest, and the like—they were nonmaterial movements focusing on more abstract ideas and postmaterialist values. As close studies of these have shown, many of them did not seek to be anti-establishment.

The environmental movements pressed on independently of party affiliation, but they were so small and had so little visible impact on elected officials that they became frustrated. There were no means of effective communication with elected officials, and the media marginalized them. They then embraced a dramatically new style of activism: they became terrorists. They dynamited railroad trains, they took hostages and kidnapped high-level political officials, and they assassinated professors and engaged in many highly visible, media-oriented activities that clearly brought them to public attention. This continued for several years in both Italy and Germany.

In the next decades, however, it became clear that environmental issues were popular with a wide part of the general public. The leading political parties, especially those on the left, began to engage with environmental issues. There were also efforts to create Green political parties, and these have had a significant competitive impact on the large established parties, especially in Europe. This change has been termed "reframing" (Snow 2007); it has transformed the political opportunity structure within which the environmental movement could operate, creating a far more hospitable environment for issues of environmentalism. As the opportunity structure opened up and they were welcomed into the established political parties, the radical terrorist groups suddenly became quite conventional in their style of operation. Environmentalism was added to the socialist program, and many cities and regions elected combinations of candidates who became labeled "Red-Green," referring to this new combination of socialism and environmentalism. Cities like Freiburg, Germany, were governed by Red-Green coalitions for many years and implemented some of the most active and comprehensive environmental socialists plans and programs (see Sellers 2002).

Many related issues (those of women, moralism, etc.), which were launched in the 1970s as New Social Movements, have since been incorporated into various political party programs. As the numbers of citizens who support these issues have risen, especially for questions of issues like human rights, the notion of the social movement organization as the "extreme outsider" is much less relevant. The social movements have been institutionalized and, in many cases, professionalized.

For a country such as China, whose third sector is tightly regulated, these concepts of the political opportunity structure and the transformation of social movements, (termed "framing" in social movement language), are quite illuminating. Framing has to do with the language in which an idea is discussed—it can be considered as the process of attaching meaning to something and situating it within a relevant cultural discourse. In the example of European environmental movements, the same

issue (environmentalism) was framed several ways—first as an outside movement, then as a terrorist movement, and finally as a standard part of the governmental and party fare.

Another perspective would label this transition of the environmental movement "cooptation"; that is, the leaders of the European environmental movement were brought into the establishment, and some critics accuse them of abandoning their earlier perspectives and constituents. This type of critique would see the radical quasi-terrorist style as having been "sold out" or abandoned in favor of joining "the establishment." The establishment, by definition, implies more established rules of the game, which includes formalized guidance on everything from seeking members to fundraising.

Nevertheless, these examples are mainly from Western Europe and the United States, as we do not have as clear, detailed data on other countries. In parts of Korea and Eastern Europe, more participation may lead to less trust, in a manner that refutes the classic Tocquevillian model.

The Internet has markedly changed the sphere of influence in which activists operate. When even social mechanisms such as Facebook, Twitter, and MySpace act as players in larger-scale movements, from the Korean beef ban to the 2009 Green Revolt in Iran, it is obvious that action via technology is rapidly expanding.

This Internet-oriented, "invisible" style of public engagement has spread worldwide since 2000 and can be a very powerful force. We could interpret this as illustrating a new form of New New Social Movement (NNSM) political engagement. The difference between New Social Movements (NSMs) and NNSMs is that the NNSMs do not have any formal organization—they lack a president, a board, a budget, formalized membership cards, a fundraising program, or other similar activities. Rather, they permit individuals to be much more anonymously engaged and only to the degree that they choose. Larger activities and meetings have been described in these terms as well, such as the protests against the World Trade Organization and international financial agencies that occurred in cities where these organizations meet. People travel, individually or through organizational coordination, to places like Seattle or Genoa, making substantial commitments of time and money to fly often halfway around the world in order to participate in street-like activities.[4] The Occupy movement included protests in 951 cities across 82 countries in just 2011 (Thompson 2011). Quite unlike earlier protests over race or the environment or human rights, many of these NNSMs have been highly disorganized, dispersed, uncoordinated, and filled with dozens and dozens of individual small organizations and many individuals who do not identify with any organization.

Looking Forward: Associational Politics and Political Life

We lay out three ways of looking at the role of associational politics and how they might fit into the large picture of political life. The first is the Tocquevillian discourse, which is often seen as linking citizens to government through civic participation. Although the goals and activities of the citizens—and associations that they create and energize—are not independent of government, they nevertheless keep citizens engaged in part of a legitimating process. This participation incorporates citizens and their groups into public decision making in important ways.

We can see the impacts of associationalism when contrasting associational politics with the second, highly individualized approach to participation that relies on preexisting networks, kinship groups, and the like. We see this, for example, in places like southern Italy, where voluntary associations are either absent or mistrusted.

A third approach is to consider organizations as quite explicitly opposed to the "establishment," openly critical, seeking sometimes to consciously undermine the legitimacy and the stability of government. The extreme version would be terrorist organizations, but such organizations are not generally included in the broader conversation about the third sector. However, it may be worth considering them in such context—they are organizations sometimes explicitly linked to the Calvinist tradition of being bottom-up, engaging citizens in issues that are important to them, but also overtly challenging general authority and leadership.

For us, the point is not so much which is the correct interpretation, but rather that all three interpretations have offered important insights into associative life and the third sector generally at different times and in different places.

Even if traditions of these sorts help explain the background against which third sector organizations have developed around the world, we should not assume them to be unchanging. The dramatic transformations in China in the last few decades, for instance, are one of the most powerful testimonies as to how rapidly change can occur. From the strong political model of egalitarianism to the spread of market principles, and then the global integration with other economies, China has shown the world how forcefully a nation can craft such a change. With other transformations underway around the globe, increasingly since the fall of the Berlin wall in 1989, the concepts of capitalism and socialism as competing worldviews are no longer such helpful guides to interpret many specific policies. More specific elements, like those debated around Tocqueville or Calvinism, grow more salient.

A clear shift in the contemporary iteration of this third sector development, however, is that it is no longer solely Calvinist, nor even religious. Many of these social organizations are secular; many have no concern with religion, explicitly or otherwise, and yet they bear the markings of the political and social dynamics that birthed them. Some of the participants and members still carry on a fervent moralistic concern to make the world a better place, to improve the lot of the disadvantaged, to help the poor, or to help women or endangered species; they are identifiable as activists and working within an institutional logic of activism. Clearly, not all nonprofit organizations are moralistic even in this sense; many are technical, non-ideological, and highly professionalized. Nevertheless it would be shortsighted to ignore the moral agenda driving many of these nonprofits, especially those with Western roots and affiliations—Amnesty International, the Sierra Club, Doctors Without Borders, and others—all organizations with no formal religious affiliation, but with a strong sense of social commitment regardless.

This moralistic agenda is visible—increasingly so—throughout third sectors globally, although it remains secular in its terminology, reflecting, perhaps, the sense that moralism is an effective motivator of social change, even when not explicitly linked to a faith tradition. Recent movements seeking to combat climate change, for instance, have explicitly charged their adversaries with the responsibility to be on the morally "right" side of history.

A third factor that may be contributing to the reconfiguration of third sector activities is educational achievement. Worldwide, educational levels have been rising, helping to create a new group of people who have high school diplomas or some college education, making potential supporters (literate, informed citizens) of NNSMs much larger.

Participants are able to challenge the establishment in new and specific ways. For instance, the "Twitter revolutions" everywhere from Moldova in 2009 to Tunisia in 2010–2011 (and across the world) are dependent not only on technology but also on literacy: increasing numbers of literate, informed people, coupled with increasing availability of technology, create a new class of potential participants in civic and social movement behavior.

Likewise, there has been a mushrooming of third sector organizations internationally within the last several decades. Some suggest this is because citizens and their economic systems have performed so well that they can now "afford" to pay attention to these new kinds of issues, such as environmentalism and women's movements—the pressing concerns in their hierarchy of needs are met, and citizens now have "time" to devote to such causes. The ongoing international crisis of the financial system certainly suggests that such arguments are debatable, and in any case, they do not account for the healthy development of the third sector in, say, Bolivia, which as of 2015 still retains the dubious honor of being the second-poorest country in the Western Hemisphere.

Social challenges, taking contemporary forms in the likes of air pollution, traffic, crime, theft, family conflicts, and so forth, become more visible and challenging as the traditional family structure weakens in the context of a metropolis, particularly a modern metropolis. Whereas grandmothers and neighbors may have assisted young families in a traditional village, a city (especially a globalized city) ruptures accommodations previously made on the basis of kinship ties and spatial proximity. In this new context, the third sector is seen as providing an assertive new version of such social cohesion and community; community organizations can move in to replace the neighbor who enforced sidewalk etiquette among the children in the village, and the after-school youth groups can be a good proxy for the grandmother who used to supervise homework.

The major difference between continental Europe in general and the Calvinist areas of the Netherlands, Switzerland, and parts of England was that there was a greater open concern to help the disadvantaged, to act charitably, to found hospitals, to set up schools for the illiterate— following the Bible *but using participation and civic acts as a mechanism.* Thus, nonconformist Calvinists brought new members into their churches, teaching them about participation through religion. They developed the rhetoric of helping and assistance that one still finds today, inside and outside churches.

By contrast, most of continental Europe has strong central states that took responsibility for the poor and the criminals and sought to provide welfare through the major state institutions. They either prohibited or discouraged the development of separate charitable civic groups such as emerged in the Calvinist regions of Europe and later in New England. Recently, similar developments have been more visible in Asia, Africa, and Latin America: strong control followed by a recent rise in third sector activities.

All this is to say that the role of activism has been changing, and in some cases taking on more symbolic, emotional, and theatrical elements in conversing with this new constituency. Contemporary Chinese leaders, for example, have made direct linkages to the traditional Chinese past, referencing clothing, history, religion, art, and music that both enhance these past traditions and join them definitively with ongoing cultural, artistic, and political concerns. The French Ministry of Culture has employed this approach as well: it has taken as an objective the enhancement of the "national patrimony" by investing in museums, statues, national theaters, and so on, but has linked that initiative with an ongoing effort to support innovation and artistic creativity in new forms.

Conclusion

Internationally, the third sector is widely celebrated (Salamon 2003, 1995), sometimes uncritically. It is also growing. Such a form of political participation resonates deeply with advocates of and for democracy in development, policy, and international relations fields. Watching leaders throughout the world grapple with political legitimacy through decentralization and associationalism is instructive. This leads us to a central question: can organized third sector groups help governance? If so, where, why, and in what contexts?

The following are some general points to consider on organizational life and guide our analysis of the development of associational life and the institutional logics that contour it:

- The rapid rise of third sector organizations has been particularly dramatic and sometimes disruptive in more traditional and more isolated societies. International communication between these organizations has brought newer issues, such as gender equality, into the spotlight.
- The third sector has become a major economic force in the past twenty years, and is currently the seventh largest economy in the world, responsible for $1.3 trillion in expenditures in the late 1990s (Salamon and Sokolowski 2004:15).

  Many political systems, in areas like Eastern Europe and the former Soviet Union, as well as much of Latin America and parts of Asia and Africa, previously had strong hierarchical political systems that either closely contained or prohibited many organized groups from becoming politically engaged. This is changing, but often with doubts, complex adaptations, and challenges. We examine several cases to try to understand some of these dynamics.
- In areas such as continental Europe, civic and third sector organization work has been traditionally weak. Political parties were generally much stronger than third sector organizations and tended to subordinate them. Countries like France, Germany, and Italy, as well as Japan and China, have changed profoundly in this regard in recent years, having created new legal and administrative provisions that provide more autonomy for organized groups. The main point here is that this transformation is not an issue of one country, but a global

occurrence. Worldwide, countries' embrace of the third sector is often so rapid, and conflictual, that it is useful to look comparatively to see what mechanisms can yield solutions among the emerging third sector groups.

- Increased income and wider diversity of citizen preferences makes it harder for governments and their agencies to satisfy all citizens. That is, demand is diversifying. The variability and volatility of citizen/consumer preferences is especially challenging for leaders of large organizations and high-level political officials. A common solution has been decentralization: to delegate responsibilities to third sector organizations, families, or citizens. This same sort of decentralization holds for everything from choosing and producing clothing styles, types of coffee, designing a sensitive retirement facility, or providing health services.

- The challenge of providing services or products to a diverse population has been heightened by the fact that the types and qualities of services and products have changed. Notably, these new products or services may involve average citizens in more of their provision. The term "coproduction" has been introduced to describe such activities as citizens engaged in recycling efforts. The term is meant to designate a transformation among citizens from passive subject to more active, engaged participant.

- These new sectoral projects are international, creating new kinds of relationships, flows of resources, and discourses that can generate both development and pathologies. They are participating in a kind of international linkage that the world has never seen before. (Santos 2002) suggests that transnational NGOs (TNGOS) are civil society's answer to multinational corporations, and that the third sector can answer to neoliberal globalization in kind. Others disagree, claiming that the very nature of the current political economy necessitates a rethinking of civil society as we know it.

Notes

* With assistance from Cary Wu and Jean Yen-Chun Lin

1. The idea of a "tax-exempt organization" does not capture the huge array of informal organizations that comprises the nonprofit sector. The third sector continues to this day in its search for identity; today, the term "nongovernmental organization" (NGO) remains popular around the world. An interesting element of the term "nongovernmental" is that it defines these independent organizations in opposition to the government, rather than in opposition to private sector firms; the sector is thus defined as that which is not part of the state, rather than that which is not oriented toward profit making (Frumkin 2005:11–12). Defourny (2001) suggests that third sector activities can be classified along two lines: legal-institutional definitions would entail grouping associations by the characteristics of their formal organizational structures (such as by tax-exempt or legal status, by 501(c) designation, etc.), and a normative or ethical definition of the third sector would group organizations by the principles that they have in common (such as the aim of serving members of the community rather than generating profit, etc.). We often refer to the "third sector," as the term reflects both the institutional and ethical components of the kind of work that the sector performs.

2. The Catholic Church in the early post-Reformation period was highly isolationist, but still highly hierarchical. Historical events, including the Schism of Utrecht, helped reinforce the introverted nature of the Dutch Catholic Church. Though it operated in some ways independently of Rome, its clergy still "maintained a high degree of control over their flocks" (Bakvis 1981:23).

3. A "moralism" was added to the public culture/media discussion of many continental European and some Asian countries in these years. This is part of the general rise of the New Political Culture, especially the populist egalitarianism wherein political leaders were increasingly treated as if the morality of the average citizen should apply to them as well. The most dramatic historical shift was after the 1968 student disturbances, from Paris to California, compounded by the rise of "advocacy journalism," i.e., the critical style of younger journalists in interviewing and

commenting on established leaders. See T. Clark and Hoffmann-Martinot (1998:2–3).

4. Clark (2004) has explored these themes.

References

Alford, Robert R., and Roger Friedland. 1985. *Powers of Theory: Capitalism, the State, and Democracy*. Cambridge, UK: Cambridge University Press.

Bakvis, Herman. 1981. *Catholic Power in the Netherlands*. Kingston, ON: McGill-Queen's University Press.

Belluck, Pam. 2012. "Cancer Group Halts Financing to Planned Parenthood." *New York Times*, January 31. Retrieved May 8, 2013 (www.nytimes.com/2012/02/01/us/cancer-group-halts-financing-to-planned-parenthood.html).

Brenner, Neil. 2009. "Open Questions on State Rescaling." *Cambridge Journal of Regions, Economy and Society* 2(1): 123–139.

Brooke, James. 2002a. "Japan Premier Taking Heat over Firing of Minister." *New York Times,* January 31. Retrieved May 10, 2013 (http//www.nytimes.com/2002/01/31/world/japan-premier-taking-heat-over-firing-of-minister.html).

———. 2002b. "Japan's Foreign Minister Is Fired after Months of Feuding." *New York Times*, January 30. Retrieved May 10, 2013 (http//www.nytimes.com/2002/01/30/world/japan-s-foreign-minister-is-fired-after-months-of-feuding.html).

Castree, Noel. 2008. "Neoliberalising Nature: The Logics of Deregulation and Reregulation." *Environment and Planning A* 40(1): 131–152.

———. 2010. "Neoliberalism and the Biophysical Environment 1: What 'Neoliberalism' Is, and What Difference Nature Makes to It." *Geography Compass* 4(12): 1725–1733.

Clark, John. 1991. *Democratizing Development: The Role of Voluntary Organizations*. West Hartford, CT: Kumarian Press.

Clark, Terry Nichols, ed. 2004. *The City as an Entertainment Machine*. Bingley, UK: Emerald Group.

Clark, Terry Nicholas, et al. 2014. *Can Tocqueville Karaoke? Global Contrasts of Citizen Participation, the Arts, and Development*. Bingley, UK: Emerald Group.

Clark, Terry Nichols, and Vincent Hoffmann-Martinot. 1998. *The New Political Culture*. Boulder, CO: Westview Press.

Cox, Robert Henry. 1993. *The Development of the Dutch Welfare State: From Workers' Insurance to Universal Entitlement*. Pittsburgh: University of Pittsburgh Press.

Creed, W. E. Douglas, Maureen A. Scully, and John R. Austin. 2002. "Clothes Make the Person? The Tailoring of Legitimating Accounts and the Social Construction of Identity." *Organization Science* 13(5): 475–496.

Defourny, Jacques. 2001. "Introduction: From Third Sector to Social Enterprise." In *The Emergence of Social Enterprise*, edited by Carlo Borzaga and Jacques Defourny, 1–28. London: Routledge. Retrieved July 31, 2012 (http://orbi.ulg.ac.be/handle/2268/90501).

DeHoog, Ruth Hoogland, and Lester M. Salamon. 2002. "Purchase-of-Service Contracting." In *Tools of Government: A Guide to the New Governance*, edited by Lester M. Salamon, 319–339. New York: Oxford University Press.

Ebrahim, Alnoor. 2005. "Accountability Myopia: Losing Sight of Organizational Learning." *Nonprofit and Voluntary Sector Quarterly* 34(1): 56–87.

Fligstein, Neil. 1987. "The Intraorganizational Power Struggle: Rise of Finance Personnel to Top Leadership in Large Corporations, 1919–1979." *American Sociological Review* 52(1): 44–58.

Fox, Jonathan. 1994. "The Difficult Transition from Clientelism to Citizenship: Lessons from Mexico." *World Politics* 46(2): 151–184.

Friedland, Roger, and Robert K. Alford. 1991. "Bringing Society Back In: Symbols, Practices, and Institutional Contradictions." In *The New Institutionalism in Organizational Analysis*, edited by Walter W. Powell and Paul DiMaggio, 232–263. Chicago: University of Chicago Press.

Frumkin, Peter. 2005. *On Being Nonprofit: A Conceptual and Policy Primer*. Cambridge, MA: Harvard University Press.

Gorski, Philip S. 2003. *The Disciplinary Revolution: Calvinism and the Rise of the State in Early Modern Europe*. Chicago: University of Chicago Press.

Habermas, Jürgen. 2001. *The Postnational Constellation: Political Essays*. Cambridge, MA: MIT Press.

Japan Times. 2002. "Koizumi Sacks Tanaka, Nogami; Suzuki Also Walks Following Row." *Japan Times*, January 31. Retrieved May 10, 2013 (http://archive.is/PGZM).

Kahl, Sigrun. 2005. "The Religious Roots of Modern Poverty Policy: Catholic, Lutheran, and Reformed Protestant Traditions Compared." *European Journal of Sociology* 46(1): 91–126.

Khan, Huma. 2012. "Susan G. Komen Apologizes for Cutting Off Planned Parenthood Funding." *ABC News Blogs*, February 3. Retrieved May 8, 2013 (http://abcnews.go.com/blogs/politics/2012/02/susan-g-komen-apologizes-for-cutting-off-planned-parenthood-funding/).

McCarthy, John D., and Mayer N. Zald. 1977. "The Trend of Social Movements in America: Professionalization and Resource Mobilization." Center for Research on Social Organization. CRSO Working Paper no. 164 (http://hdl.handle.net/2027.42/50939).

Peck, Jamie, Nik Theodore, and Neil Brenner. 2010. "Postneoliberalism and Its Malcontents." *Antipode* 41: 94–116.

Piattoni, Simona. 2001. *Clientelism, Interests, and Democratic Representation: The European Experience in Historical and Comparative Perspective*. Cambridge, UK: Cambridge University Press.

Salamon, Lester M. 1995. *Partners in Public Service: Government-Nonprofit Relations in the Modern Welfare State*. Baltimore: Johns Hopkins University Press.

———. 2003. *The Resilient Sector: The State of Nonprofit America*. Washington, DC: Brookings Institution Press.

Salamon, Lester, Leslie C. Hems, and Kathryn Chinnock. 2000. "The Nonprofit Sector: For What and for Whom?" Working Papers of the Johns Hopkins Comparative Nonprofit Sector Project, no. 37. Baltimore: Johns Hopkins Center for Civil Society Studies.

Salamon, Lester M., and S. Wojciech Sokolowski. 2004. *Global Civil Society: Dimensions of the Nonprofit Sector*. Baltimore: Kumarian Press.

Santos, Boaventura de Sousa. 2002. *Toward a New Legal Common Sense: Law, Globalization, and Emancipation*. 2nd ed. London: Butterworths LexisNexis.

Sellers, Jefferey M. 2002. *Governing from Below: Urban Regions and the Global Economy*. Cambridge, UK: Cambridge University Press.

Silva, Filipe Carreira da. 2010. *Mead and Modernity: Science, Selfhood, and Democratic Politics*. Lanham, MD: Lexington Books.

Silver, Daniel, and Terry Nichols Clark. 2016. *Scenescapes: How Qualities of Place Shape Social Life*. Chicago: University of Chicago Press.

Snow, David A. 2007. "Framing Processes, Ideology, and Discursive Fields." In *The Blackwell Companion to Social Movements*, edited by David A. Snow, Sarah A. Soule, and Hanspeter Kriesi, 380–412. Malden, MA: Blackwell.

Thompson, Derek. 2011. "Occupy the World: The '99 Percent' Movement Goes Global." *Atlantic*, October 15. Retrieved October 15, 2011 (www.theatlantic.com/business/archive/2011/10/occupy-the-world-the-99-percent-movement-goes-global/246957/).

Thornton, Patricia H., and William Ocasio. 1999. "Institutional Logics and the Historical Contingency of Power in Organizations: Executive Succession in the Higher Education Publishing Industry, 1958–1990." *American Journal of Sociology* 105(3): 801–843.

Tocqueville, Alexis de. [1835] 1969. *Democracy in America*. Reprint, Garden City, NY: Doubleday.

Trounstine, Jessica. 2008. *Political Monopolies in American Cities: The Rise and Fall of Bosses and Reformers*. Chicago: University of Chicago Press.

Wilensky, Harold L. 1964. "The Professionalization of Everyone?" *American Journal of Sociology* 70(2): 137–158.

Wilson, James Q. 1962. *The Amateur Democrat: Club Politics in Three Cities*. Chicago: University of Chicago Press.

CHAPTER 3

The Idea of a Nonprofit and Voluntary Sector

Peter Frumkin

The nonprofit and voluntary sector is the contested arena between the state and the market where public and private concerns meet and where individual and social efforts are united. Nonprofit and voluntary action expresses a complex and at times conflicting desire to defend the pursuit of private individual aspirations while at the same time affirming the idea of a public sphere shaped by shared goals and values. For this difficult balancing act to work, participation in the sector demands a commitment to, among other things, expression, engagement, entrepreneurship, and service. Constituted by both legally chartered nonprofit organizations and myriad informal groups and voluntary associations, this sector occupies an increasingly critical and visible position in our political, social, and economic life.[1]

Thus, the nonprofit and voluntary sector is at once a visible and compelling force in society and an elusive mass of contradictions. On the one hand, the rise of nonprofits is thought to have contributed to democratization around the world, opening up societies and giving people a voice and a mode of collective expression that has in too many cases been suppressed.[2] In the United States nonprofit and voluntary organizations are seen as playing a central role in generating, organizing, and emboldening political opposition, working through national networks and building international linkages. Nonprofit and voluntary organizations have also acted as practical vehicles for the delivery of a broad spectrum of community services, ranging from affordable housing to theater performances to vocational training to health care. The nonprofit sector appears, therefore, to be a real and identifiable group of tax-exempt "organizations" that encourage political engagement and produce services. The sector is in fact a documented economic powerhouse that employs millions of people and accounts for a significant portion of the nation's gross domestic product, all of which makes the nonprofit sector a strong and compelling concept that appears grounded in economic, political, and legal reality.

On the other hand, the nonprofit and voluntary sector is home to such a wide range of organizations that grouping them together into one entity is highly problematic. From the

 DOI: 10.4324/9780367696559-4

largest hospitals and universities (which fund their operations by collecting fees or tuition) to small mentoring programs and avant-garde arts organizations (which survive on charitable contributions), nonprofits span a tremendous range of organizational forms. Many of these forms are stable and lasting, while others are fragile and transient. Some of the organizations that are considered part of the nonprofit sector, such as religious congregations and private membership organizations, operate without government funding. Other nonprofit organizations, particularly those that service the elderly and poor, could not survive without the steady flow of funds from federal, state, and local government. Beyond differences in funding, the organizations within the sector are balkanized by legal status, level of professionalization, and underlying purpose.

Thus, any exploration of the nonprofit and voluntary sector would do well to begin by acknowledging its fundamentally contested nature.

Three Features of Nonprofit and Voluntary Organizations

Attempting to define the fundamental features of the disparate entities that constitute the nonprofit and voluntary sector is a complex and daunting task. Yet there are at least three features that connect these widely divergent entities: (1) they do not coerce participation, (2) they operate without distributing profits to stakeholders, and (3) they exist without simple and clear lines of ownership and accountability. These structural features give these entities a set of unique advantages that position them to perform important societal functions neither government nor the market is able to match.

Perhaps the most fundamental of the three features is the sector's noncoercive nature. Citizens cannot be compelled by nonprofit organizations to give their time or money in support of any collective goal. This means that, in principle at least, nonprofits must draw on a large reservoir of good will. Free choice is the coin of the realm: Donors give because they choose to do so. Volunteers work of their own volition. Staff actively seek employment in these organizations, often at lower wages than they might secure elsewhere. Clients make up their own minds that these organizations have something valuable to offer. Though they stand ready to receive, nonprofit and voluntary organizations demand nothing. As a consequence, nonprofits occupy a moral high ground of sorts when compared to public-sector organizations that have the ability to compel action and coerce those who resist.

In some ways, the noncoercive character of the nonprofit and voluntary sector situates it closer to the market than to government. The sector makes choices available rather than deciding for others. The flow of resources to a nonprofit depends entirely on the quality and relevance of its mission and its capacity to deliver value.

The second feature of nonprofit and voluntary organizations sharply differentiates them from business firms, however. While corporations are able to distribute earnings to shareholders, nonprofit and voluntary organizations cannot make such distributions to outside parties. Rather, they must use all residual funds for the advancement of the organization's mission.[3] By retaining residuals rather than passing them on to investors, nonprofit organizations seek to reassure clients and donors that their mission takes precedence over the financial remuneration of any interested parties. Since there are certain services, such as child care and health care, that some consumers feel uncomfortable receiving if the provider is profit driven, nonprofits are able to step in and meet this demand by promising that no investors will benefit by cutting corners or by delivering unnecessary services.

While the noncoercive feature of nonprofits brings nonprofits closer to business and separates them from government, the nondistribution constraint pushes nonprofits closer to the public sector and away from the private sector. Government's inability to pay out profits from the sale of goods or services is related to its need to be perceived as impartial and equitable.[4] With nonprofits, the nondistribution constraint also builds legitimacy and public confidence. In both sectors the nondistribution constraint strongly reinforces the perception that these entities are acting for the good of the public.

The third feature of nonprofit and voluntary organizations is that they have unclear lines of ownership and accountability.[5] This trait separates these entities from both business and government. Nonprofit and voluntary organizations must serve many masters, none of which is ultimately able to exert complete control over these organizations. Donors, clients, board members, workers, and local communities all have stakes, claims, or interests in nonprofit and voluntary organizations. Yet none of these parties can be clearly identified as the key ownership group. The relative strength of these ownership claims depends on how an organization is funded and on its chosen mission.[6] Nonprofit organizations that depend heavily on charitable contributions are often held closely accountable by their donors, some of whom believe that as social investors, they have a real stake in the organizations to which they contribute. Nonprofits that are largely driven by service fees or commercial revenues are in a different position. While these more commercial organizations do not have donors asserting claims over them, social entrepreneurs and professional staff may view themselves as the key stakeholders in these more businesslike organizations.

Often, however, the lines of ownership and accountability are rendered more complex by the fact that many nonprofit organizations combine funding from multiple sources—foundations, corporations, and government—with earned income, making it hard to point to any particular party as the key stakeholder to whom

these special institutions must answer.[7] One might be tempted to point out that nonprofit and voluntary organizations are almost always governed by boards, and to propose this as a solution to the ownership and accountability issue. Unfortunately, board members are not owners. They are stewards who are held responsible for the actions of their organization.

These three features of nonprofit organizations are not without controversy and contention. In fact, each has been called into question in recent years. First, the noncoercive nature of the sector has been challenged by the growing tendency to mandate community service or volunteer work. Within professional associations, licenses to practice medicine, law, and other callings are granted and denied by nonprofit entities.[8] Within many religions, the behavior of adherents is severely constrained by doctrine. In some neighborhoods, independent community groups have been granted the power to plan and constrain future development by residents. The exercise of power may be subtle in some cases. For example, many private funders exercise considerable influence over the recipients of their grants. This influence can take the form of a gentle suggestion or a condition of support that programs be revamped.[9]

Second, the nondistribution constraint of nonprofit organizations has likewise been under assault from a number of different directions. In recent years increased scrutiny of the high salary levels of many nonprofit executives has led some to ask whether the "profits"—or, more accurately, the increased program revenues—are not in fact being routinely distributed to staff in the form of generous compensation and benefit packages.[10] In the area of capitalization, large nonprofit organizations have been aggressive in raising funds through bond offerings, which do not offer investors the ownership stake that stock offerings do but have the effect of opening up major capital flows into the nonprofit sector. The accumulation of capital in the form of large endowments has also called into question the boundary between business and nonprofit organizations: Endowment funds, by their nature, are not used to fulfill an organization's immediate needs. Instead, they are invested in stocks, real estate, and other speculative investments designed in the long run to maximize financial return. This is a strategic move that some have characterized as contrary to the public purposes of nonprofit organizations.[11]

Third, the ownerless character of nonprofit and voluntary organizations has come under fire as the legal claims of nonprofit stakeholders have evolved. The courts have held that only members (in the case of a membership organization), trustees or directors, and the attorney general in the state where the nonprofit is located have legal standing to contest the action of a charitable corporation. Over the years, however, the power of trustees and directors has grown substantially, not to the point where they can claim ownership of the assets of a nonprofit but to the point where boards now have tremendous leeway in the way they operate a charitable organization.[12]

Composition of the Nonprofit and Voluntary Sector

In the United States today, there are more than one and a half million registered nonprofit organizations as well as several million informally organized community groups. The formally registered organizations fall into two broad and porous categories: those that serve the public and those that serve members. The public-serving organizations, classified under section 501(c) (3) of the IRS code, operate in almost every imaginable field of human endeavor and include, among countless others, social service agencies helping children, the elderly, and the poor; independent schools and private colleges; community clinics and hospitals; think tanks; environmental organizations; cultural groups such as museums, theaters, and historical societies; and a range of international assistance organizations. They are the most visible and recognizable part of this organizational universe. But substantial resources are concentrated in the member-serving or mutual-benefit organizations, which include credit unions, business leagues, service clubs, veterans' organizations, and trade associations. They tackle problems ranging from the most complex issues of business policy to the most prosaic challenges of small-town life. Also included in the sector (though not filing forms annually with the IRS) is a vast array of churches, synagogues, and mosques that form the foundation of the nation's religious life. While we tend to think of congregations as membership organizations, they are treated differently by government and are not subject to the same forms of oversight as other member-serving nonprofits.

The sector can thus be conceived as a tent covering public-serving charities, member-serving organizations, and a range of informal organizations, including voluntary and grassroots associations.

This diverse and at times contradictory group of entities comprises organizations and associations that are neither part of the state nor fully engaged in the market. Using charitable contributions, many nonprofit and voluntary organizations can deliver services to clients who are unable to pay. At other times, nonprofit and voluntary action represents an attempt to move beyond government action to find solutions to public problems that a majority of citizens are unable or unwilling to support. In some fields of activity within the sector, intense commercialism has eroded the moral high ground of these organizations and transformed nonprofits into shadow businesses that compete actively for clients able to pay for the services they offer. In other fields nonprofits have lost their autonomy from government and have come to serve as dutiful implementers of public-sector programs and priorities.

The Politics of the Nonprofit and Voluntary Sector

The nonprofit and voluntary sector occupies an ambiguous and at times contentious position in the current American political scene.

Just as few people agree on the right name to use to describe these organizations, Americans are likewise engaged in heated debate about the sector's underlying politics. Today, for quite different reasons, nonprofit and voluntary organizations are embraced by both conservatives and liberals.

For at least three reasons, nonprofit and voluntary organizations have, particularly from the 1960s forward, represented a tremendous resource and ally to liberals. First, a natural affinity between liberals and nonprofit workers quickly became apparent, since those willing to toil in often low-paying or voluntary positions—and frequently in difficult circumstances—constitute a self-selected group of socially committed individuals dedicated to the idea of making a difference and initiating change. Not only could nonprofit organizations serve as new channels through which social programs could be delivered, but they also represented a new and important space in which potential supporters of progressive policies might well be located.[13]

The second reason liberals were attracted to the sector as a whole was more operational. Nonprofit organizations were seen as an ideal and untainted partner to government, one that could most effectively deliver needed services to the most disadvantaged populations. As concern over the impact of Great Society programs grew and as distrust of government increased, nonprofits came to be seen as neutral and legitimizing forces with the capacity to give large

human service initiatives a more diverse, pluralistic face.[14] The funding crunch that most nonprofit organizations face on a continuing basis appeared to put government in a position to use its substantial resources, in the form of contracts and grants, to gain control over a whole new range of community actors and problems. At the same time, nonprofits represented an ideal "bottom-up" approach to implementation, one that empowered the grassroots level and that gave government tremendous leverage for each dollar spent.

Third and finally, liberals were attracted by the political activity of many nonprofits and their ability to mobilize groups around issues and concerns in a distinctive way. This flexibility lends itself well, in principle, to the pursuit of progressive, alternative agendas. Moreover, since many advocacy nonprofits seek to give voice to populations that have long been excluded from the political debate, liberals continue to view the broader nonprofit sector as a means to exert pressure for social change and justice.[15]

Conservatives were attracted by three completely different features of nonprofits. First, they believed that nonprofit organizations might well represent an appealing alternative to direct public expenditures on social programs that conservatives believed had not produced results.[16] Compared to taxation and national spending, private charity and volunteerism were seen as preferred means of solving social problems because they permitted greater individual freedom and choice. A strong and vital nonprofit and voluntary sector fit well with the emerging ideas of both devolution and privatization, two mantras of the conservative movement. As government functions were pushed "down" from the federal level to the state and local levels, and transferred "out" of government to private providers through contracting, nonprofits were ideally situated to deliver services that once had been the province of bureaucrats in the nation's capital.[17]

Second, conservatives also argued that nonprofits, particularly faith-based nonprofits, were in a position to bring to social programs something that public entitlements had long lacked—namely, a moral or spiritual component.[18] Faith-based nonprofits were seen as willing to make demands on the recipients of charity and require a change of character and behavior in exchange for assistance. At the same time, given that many nonprofits are fueled by volunteer labor and private contributions, conservatives were attracted to the idea of nonprofits because they represented the ideal of self-help and independence. This was a powerful feature that, conservatives argued, was perilously missing from public assistance programs.[19] For those who believed that public entitlements bred dependence and complacency, the idea of delivering not only a check but also a moral and spiritual message was a very strong attraction.

Finally, for conservatives, nonprofit organizations were also a potential wellspring of innovation, representing a plurality of local solutions to social problems and a powerful alternative to the ongoing search for uniform national solutions to public problems. Grounded in an ethos of self-help and respecting regional cultural variations, voluntary action fit well with a growing sense among conservatives that a broad range of alternatives to an expanding state needed to be actively cultivated. By giving local organizations a chance to try their hand at program implementation, conservatives believed that good ideas would percolate up from communities. Nonprofit organizations thus represented a way of breaking through the red tape of Washington to find new approaches to longstanding problems. Nonprofits, conservatives maintained, could serve as a battering ram for policy innovation.[20]

Because it simultaneously supports the autonomy of the private individual actor while affirming the importance of shared and public purposes, the politics of nonprofit and voluntary action can take on many different meanings.

The ability to speak across, or rather above, traditional political boundaries has become one of the most powerful features of the sector, and this trait has led to its growth and popularity, particularly among young people.

The Two Dimensions of Nonprofit and Voluntary Action

I organize my exposition of the central functions of voluntary and nonprofit organizations along two broad conceptual distinctions. The first critical distinction concerns how the sector is explained. The question is whether nonprofit and voluntary activity is driven primarily by demand or by supply—that is, whether it can best be understood as a response to unmet demands or whether it is taken to be an important supply function that creates its own demand. The second distinction concerns how the sector is justified. Here the issue is whether the value of nonprofit and voluntary action is seen as residing in the instrumental character of the outcomes that are generated for society or in the inherently expressive quality of the activities themselves that reward those who undertake them.

Starting with the distinction between demand and supply, it is easy to see nonprofit and voluntary action as responding to two quite different but important forces.[21] The demand-side perspective starts with the premise that the sector exists by virtue of the broader social context within which it is embedded and that its activities are responsive to the demands of the public or its members. Thus, nonprofits exist because they are able to meet important social needs. Urgent public problems such as illiteracy, drug addiction, and violence demand solutions, and the nonprofit sector exists to respond to the powerful pull of such issues.

On a more normative level, the demand-side approach to nonprofit organizations has spawned a literature focusing on the social and political responsibilities of nonprofit organizations, defined in relation to the demands of the neediest members of society. Starting with the claim that the tax exemption accorded these institutions conveys an obligation to help, many people have made the normative argument that nonprofit organizations should seek to assist the most disadvantaged and empower the most disenfranchised members of society. Accordingly, the success or failure of the sector can and should be judged by how well or how poorly it meets society's needs. The demand for nonprofit and voluntary action leads neatly to a set of prescribed activities, including greater advocacy work within the sector and the empowerment and mobilization of those left out of the political process. The demand for nonprofit activity thus brings with it the expectation that these institutions will help give voice and opportunity to those who have been marginalized by the market economy and the political process.

An alternative, supply-side position argues that the sector is impelled by the resources and ideas that flow into it—resources and ideas that come from social entrepreneurs, donors, and volunteers.[22] Rejecting many of the preceding arguments about the needs that pull on the sector, the supply-side perspective holds that nonprofit and voluntary organizations are really all about the people with resources and commitment who fire the engine of nonprofit and voluntary action. Drawn to the sector by visions and commitments, social entrepreneurs bring forward agendas that often operate independently of immediately obvious and enduring community needs. This supply-side theory of nonprofits, like the demand-side approach, has both descriptive and normative elements.

On the descriptive side, this approach emphasizes the entrepreneurial quality of nonprofit activity. Instead of starting with the demand of clients, positive supply-side theories of the nonprofit sector draw attention to the way various forms of entrepreneurship fuel innovation within the sector and how an emerging

class of new social enterprises—increasingly led by a new generation of social entrepreneurs—is challenging old models of nonprofit management. Seen from the supply side, nonprofit organizations have a logic that is far more complex than a simple response to a gap in government service or the failure of the market to meet a particular demand. The entrepreneur, donor, and volunteer take on a much greater role in this model, since it is the supply of new ideas, charitable dollars, and volunteer commitments that is the real driving force behind the sector.

The supply-side approach has an important normative component, which holds that we must reassess the moral claims that needy clients have on nonprofit programs. Instead of asking that a nonprofit meet a test of moral stewardship that is ultimately decided by the level and quality of service provided to those in need, the supply-side approach advises that society should look to and protect the private interests and values of the critical actors who are fueling nonprofit and voluntary action, including philanthropic donors, volunteers, and social entrepreneurs. In order to ensure the continued flow of charitable inputs, the interests and values of these actors should be the first priority of those who seek an enlarged role for nonprofits. This means recognizing that the satisfaction of donors and the preservation of their intent constitute a critical normative task for the sector.

We must also develop a second dimension for our conceptual framework. As soon as we begin to consider the broad number of important projects and causes to which the sector is dedicated, it becomes clear that nonprofit and voluntary organizations rest on two different ideas about what justifies and gives meaning to the work that is carried out in the sector.

First, nonprofit and voluntary action is an important instrument for the accomplishment of tasks that communities view as important. Nonprofit service agencies and volunteer helping organizations play an important role in the delivery of critical services in a broad array of fields. The sector's instrumental value is measured in terms of its concrete outcomes. In the search for validation and learning, the programmatic outcomes of nonprofit and voluntary action are increasingly being measured and evaluated using metrics borrowed from the business and public sectors. The idea that nonprofit and voluntary organizations are valuable because they can be useful tools for the accomplishment of public purposes constitutes the core of what I will term the "instrumental dimension" of the nonprofit and voluntary sector.

Second, the sector can be seen as valuable because it allows individuals to express their values and commitment through work, volunteer activities, and donations. By committing to broad causes that are close to the heart or by giving to an effort that speaks directly to the needs of the community, nonprofit and voluntary action answers a powerful expressive urge. For donors, volunteers, and particularly staff, the very act of attempting to address a need or fight for a cause can be a satisfying end in itself, regardless of the ultimate outcome. The value that is created may be entirely psychic and may arise simply from the act of expressing commitment, caring, and belief. This is what I will refer

to as the "expressive dimension" of nonprofit and voluntary action.[23] The managerial challenge, of course, is to bring the expressive and instrumental dimensions into alignment.

The contrast between the supply and demand sides and the opposition of the expressive and instrumental dimensions give us a basis for thinking systematically about the functions of nonprofit and voluntary action. We can construct a matrix that depicts, on one side, the nature of the value produced by the sector (instrumental versus expressive) and, on the other side, the underlying animus or force (demand versus supply). This book [*On Being Nonprofit: A Conceptual and Policy Primer*] is organized around the four cells generated by this matrix (see Figure 3.1), which have come to represent the four underlying functions of the nonprofit and voluntary sector: encouraging civic and political engagement, delivering needed services, enacting private values and religious convictions, and providing a channel for social entrepreneurship.

At a time when nonprofit and voluntary activity has been the subject of increasing public attention and academic study, the breadth and depth of our understanding of this phenomenon

FIGURE 3.1 The Four Functions of Nonprofit and Voluntary Action

	Demand-side orientation	Supply-side orientation
Instrumental rationale	*Service delivery* Provides needed services and responds to government and market failure	*Social entrepreneurship* Provides a vehicle for entrepreneurship and creates social enterprises that combine commercial and charitable goals
Expressive rationale	*Civic and political engagement* Mobilizes citizens for politics, advocates for causes, and builds social capital within communities	*Values and faith* Allows volunteers, staff, and donors to express values, commitments, and faith through work

has been severely constrained by the lack of a clear statement of the sector's core activities, rationales, and dimensions. This chapter strives to respond to this need by presenting four critical functions that the sector performs. Many of the most essential conceptual and policy problems within the sector can be usefully captured with this framework. The normative argument is simply that the sector cannot survive and garner financial, political, and volunteer support if it swings too far in the direction of any particular function. In the long run, balance, achieved through the fulfillment of a diversity of functions, is ultimately essential within the vast range of nonprofit organizations and across the sector as a whole.

Nonprofit and voluntary action can be a powerful force for good in society. Ultimately, it is the diversity of purposes and rationales embodied in nonprofit and voluntary organizations that make them increasingly visible and exciting vehicles for the pursuit of common social goals. And it is the sector's diversity and flexibility that may well help nonprofit organizations solve some of the pressing challenges they now confront.

Notes

1. The literature on the nonprofit and voluntary sector has burgeoned over the past two decades. One of the early attempts to bring the sector's many competing research agendas together can be found in Walter W. Powell, *The Nonprofit Sector: A Research Handbook* (New Haven, CT: Yale University Press, 1987). Other overviews of the sector that have provided basic data on the dimensions of nonprofit and voluntary activity include Lester M. Salamon, *America's Nonprofit Sector: A Primer*, 2nd ed. (New York: Foundation Center, 1999); William G. Bowen et al., *The Charitable Nonprofits: An Analysis of Institutional Dynamics and Characteristics* (San Francisco: Jossey-Bass, 1994); and Jon Van Til, *Growing Civil Society* (Bloomington: Indiana University Press, 2000). For the most detailed statistical profile of

nonprofit activity, see the most recent version of the *Nonprofit Almanac: Dimensions of the Independent Sector* (San Francisco: Jossey-Bass, 1996), which is updated periodically.

2. On the growth of nonprofit and voluntary organizations around the world, see John Burbidge, ed., *Beyond Prince and Merchant: Citizen Participation and the Rise of Civil Society* (New York: Pact Publications, 1997); John Keane, *Civil Society: Old Images, New Visions* (Stanford, CA: Stanford University Press, 1998); Victor M. Perez-Diaz, *The Return of Civil Society: The Emergence of Democratic Spain* (Cambridge, MA: Harvard University Press, 1993); Lester M. Salamon and Helmut K. Anheier, *Defining the Nonprofit Sector: A Cross-National Analysis* (New York: Manchester University Press, 1997); and Robert I. Rotberg, ed., *Vigilance and Vengeance: NGOs Preventing Ethnic Conflict in Divided Societies* (Washington, DC: Brookings Institution Press, 1996).

3. The idea of nondistribution constraint is clearly outlined in Henry B. Hansmann, "The Role of Nonprofit Enterprise," in *The Economics of Nonprofit Institutions: Studies in Structure and Policy*, edited by Susan Rose-Ackerman (New York: Oxford University Press, 1986), 57–84.

4. The literature on the management of public-sector organizations provides insights into some of the challenges of sustaining and leading a nonprofit organization. Some of the best studies of public management include Michael Barzelay, *Breaking Through Bureaucracy: A New Vision for Managing in Government* (Berkeley: University of California Press, 1992); Sanford Borins, *Innovating with Integrity: How Local Heroes Are Transforming American Government* (Washington, DC: Georgetown University Press, 1998); Laurence E. Lynn, Jr., *Public Management as Art, Science and Profession* (Chatham, NJ: Chatham House, 1996); Mark H. Moore, *Creating Public Value: Strategic Management in Government* (Cambridge, MA: Harvard University Press, 1996); David Osborne and Ted Gaebler, *Reinventing Government: How the Entrepreneurial Spirit Is Transforming the Public Sector* (New York: Plume, 1992).

5. A good discussion of the legal framework guiding accountability in the nonprofit sector can be found in Laura Chisolm, "Accountability of Nonprofit Organizations and Those Who Control Them:

The Legal Framework," *Nonprofit Management and Leadership* 6, no. 2 (Winter 1995): 141–156.

6. Henry Hansmann, *The Ownership of Enterprise* (Cambridge, MA: Harvard University Press, 1996).

7. Kirsten A. Grønbjerg, *Understanding Nonprofit Funding: Managing Revenues in Social Services and Community Development Organizations* (San Francisco: Jossey-Bass, 1993).

8. Thomas Haskell, ed., *The Authority of Experts: Studies in History and Theory* (Bloomington: Indiana University Press, 1984).

9. One critique of philanthropy has emphasized that some funders have channeled social protest and deradicalized grassroots social movements by imposing constraints and attempting to shape these efforts. See J. Craig Jenkins, "Channeling Social Protest: Foundation Patronage of Contemporary Social Movements," in *Private Action and the Public Good*, edited by Walter W. Powell and Elisabeth S. Clemens (New Haven, CT: Yale University Press, 1998), 206–216; and Rosa Proietto, "The Ford Foundation and Women's Studies in American Higher Education: Seeds of Change?," in *Philanthropic Foundations: New Scholarship, New Possibilities*, edited by Ellen Condliffe Lagemann (Bloomington: Indiana University Press, 1999), 271–286.

10. The issue of how much nonprofit workers earn and the need for complete public disclosure that compensation decisions create is taken up in Peter Frumkin, "Transparent Nonprofits," *The Public Interest* 142 (Winter 2001): 83–94. See also Peter Frumkin and Alice Andre-Clark, "Nonprofit Compensation and the Market," *University of Hawaii Law Review* 21, no. 2 (Winter 1999): 425–485.

11. See Henry Hansmann, "Why Do Universities Have Endowments?" *Journal of Legal Studies* 19, no. 1 (January 1990): 3–42.

12. Most states' adoption of the American Bar Association's Model Nonprofit Corporation Statute had a significant impact on accountability and ownership issues in nonprofit organizations. Among other things, the statute shifted the fiduciary standard toward a business judgment standard and away from that traditionally applied to trusts. In so doing, it enabled nonprofit boards to use proxy voting, change by-laws without membership approval, and delegate powers to executive committees. The main effect of these changes was to empower boards and to weaken the role of members (in membership organizations). For a detailed account of this shift, see Michael C. Hone, "Aristotle and Lyndon Baines Johnson: Thirteen Ways of Looking at Blackbirds and Nonprofit Corporations: The American Bar Association's Revised Model Nonprofit Corporation Act," *Case Western University Law Review* 39, no. 3 (1989): 751–762; and Peter Dobkin Hall, "Law, Politics, and Charities in the Post-Liberal Era," in *Serving the Public Trust: Insights into Fundraising Research and Practice*, edited by Paul Pribbenow (San Francisco: Jossey-Bass, 2000), 5–31.

13. Lee Staples, *Roots to Power: A Manual for Grassroots Organizing* (New York: Praeger, 1984).

14. The desire to find new ways to argue for social initiatives has been part of a broader trend toward a politics of moderation and centrism. Rather than arguing for additional federal spending measures, much of the liberal agenda has been translated into the simple preservation of existing entitlement programs and the funding of local— often nonprofit—initiatives aimed at solving discrete community problems.

15. One attempt to examine the broad array of nonprofit activities for new insights about "what works" is Lisbeth B. Schorr, *Common Purpose: Strengthening Families and Neighborhoods to Rebuild America* (New York: Anchor Books, 1997).

16. Critiques of Great Society social programs proliferated in the early 1980s, but few were as influential as Charles Murray, *Losing Ground: American Social Policy, 1950–1980* (New York: Basic Books, 1984).

17. Many of the core conservative themes were articulated in Charles Heatherly, ed., *Mandate for Leadership* (Washington, DC: Heritage Foundation, 1981); and again in Newt Gingrich, *To Renew America* (New York: HarperCollins, 1995).

18. Marvin Olasky, *The Tragedy of American Compassion* (Washington, DC: Regency Publishing, 1992). Of course, long before the conservative revolution embraced faith-based approaches, the government had in various ways assisted religiously affiliated organizations. See Amos Warner, *American Charities* (New York: Thomas Cromwell, 1908).

19. Great Society programs provided extensive financial support to community empowerment programs, many of which were affiliated with inner-city congregations. Catholic Charities, the Salvation Army, and Lutheran Social Services have long been the recipients of some of the largest social service grants from the government. What made the conservative approach distinctive was the active involvement of theologically conservative religious bodies that had traditionally avoided commitment to social service delivery.

20. Richard C. Cornuelle, *Reclaiming the American Dream: The Role of Private Individuals and Voluntary Associations* (New Brunswick, NJ: Transaction Publishers, 1993).

21. Avner Ben-Ner and Theresa Van Hoomissen, "Nonprofit Organizations in the Mixed Economy: A Demand and Supply Analysis," in *The Nonprofit Sector in the Mixed Economy*, edited by Avner Ben-Ner and Benedetto Gui (Ann Arbor: University of Michigan Press, 1993), 27–58.

22. Dennis Young, *If Not for Profit, for What? A Behavioral Theory of the Nonprofit Sector Based on Entrepreneurship* (Lexington, MA: Lexington Books, 1983).

23. For a good discussion of the challenges of managing a nonprofit in a way that allows workers to express their values and commitments, see David E. Mason, *Leading and Managing the Expressive Dimension: Harnessing the Hidden Power Source of the Nonprofit Sector* (San Francisco: Jossey-Bass, 1996).

PART II

The History, Values, and Activities of Nonprofit Organizations in the United States

As was mentioned in Part I, a country's nonprofit sector is partially a product of the democratic-capitalistic, socio-political-economic systems that have evolved over the years. From this perspective, the sector provides a means for reacting to marketplace failures and the failure of government to adequately serve citizens in need by filling these voids with volunteered time and charitable contributions.[1]

> In few countries is the system of aid [for persons in need] more complicated and confusing, however, than in the United States. Reflecting a deep-seated tradition of individualism and an ingrained hostility to centralized institutions, Americans have resisted the worldwide movement toward predominantly governmental approaches to social welfare provision, adding new governmental protections only with great reluctance, and then structuring them in ways that preserve a substantial private life.[2]

The nonprofit sector's evolution in the United States has been neither consciously planned nor linear. It has evolved in response to events, changing patterns and norms in the public and for-profit sectors, shifting cultural values, and societal changes at points in time. Patterns in its development are reflections of the richness of the political, social, demographic, economic, and cultural histories of the United States—and therefore the rationale for Peter Dobkin Hall's claim that nonprofit organizations pose "almost insuperable problems for anyone who would presume to relate their history."[3]

Several historical themes or dimensions are easily identifiable by reviewing the evolution of the nonprofit sector in the United States, including its earliest roots; its philosophical history; and, the history of choices among democratic values, associational philanthropy, and major changes in the relationships between nonprofits and the government. These are the topics of the next several sections. Interestingly, many of the sector's most important features and functions did not develop until the last three to four decades of the 20th century.

 DOI: 10.4324/9780367696559-5

Unquestionably, the nonprofit sector in the United States has been heavily influenced by the nation's distinctive early history—the colonial era—a time and set of circumstances when survival was possible only if neighbors readily banded together into voluntary associations for mutual assistance. Government did not exist or did not have the resources to put out fires in barns, to protect against hostile intruders, or to help build houses. In this aspect of the sector's distinctiveness, voluntarism, voluntary associations, and serving others have emerged as defining forces.[4]

Early Colonial History: Associational Philanthropy and Alexis de Tocqueville

During the first half of the 19th century, Alexis de Tocqueville, the astute French observer of American life, traveled through the colonies documenting his impressions of this nation's approach to shared control and responsibility for efforts to meet community needs. He observed the potent contributions that voluntary associations made to political and intellectual life in the United States:

> An association consists simply in the public assent which a number of individuals give to certain doctrines and in the engagement which they contract to promote in a certain manner the spread of those doctrines. . . . An association unites into one channel the efforts of divergent minds and urges them vigorously toward the one end that it clearly points out. . . . The second degree in the exercise of the right of association is the power of meeting.[5]

Tocqueville was amazed at the degree of shared responsibility for efforts to meet community needs that existed in the United States. He observed that in contrast with the U.S. experience, throughout Europe the "secondary power"—the ability of the nobility, cities, and provincial bodies to represent local affairs—had been relinquished to the centralized authorities. Such centralization eliminated the need for the development of philanthropy in Europe. Tocqueville wrote:

> All these various rights which have been successively wrested, in our time, from classes, guilds, and individuals have not served to raise new secondary powers on a more democratic basis, but have uniformly been concentrated in the hands of the sovereign. Everywhere the state acquires more and more direct control over the humblest members of the community and a more exclusive power of governing each of them in his smallest concerns.[6]

Almost all charitable establishments in Europe were formerly in the hands of private persons or of guilds. Today, they continue to be dependent on the state and in many countries the state almost exclusively delivers the services directly. It undertakes to supply bread to the hungry, assistance and shelter to the sick, work to the idle, and to act as the sole reliever of all kinds of misery—or controls the management and operations of the nonprofit that delivers the services. Tocqueville's "secondary power"—the ability of the nobility, cities, and provincial bodies to represent local affairs—had been relinquished to the centralized authority. His secondary power is what we refer to today as activities that serve the public good, and Tocqueville's discussion continues today about concepts of the *public good*, *common goods*, and *private goods*. It also continues about the concept of *social capital*—networks of mutual trust, goodwill, and obligations that are created as by-products of people working together to achieve an end and that can be called upon in the future to achieve other ends. (See particularly Part VII for more about social capital.)

Tocqueville noted that the sharing of power and responsibilities across Europe had taken a markedly different form. In the early 1800s in the United States, social welfare needs often were met through the actions of voluntary associations, which in turn created the civic life that is the wellspring of democratic community life. Tocqueville's issues are as timely now as they were then. Once again as a nation, we are engaged in similar debates about public and private goods, and the extent of individuals' and governments' responsibilities for citizens versus the extent of citizens' responsibilities for helping others through voluntary associations.[7]

Philosophical History

The Western tradition of voluntarism has its roots in two diverse ideological streams:[8]

- The Greco-Roman heritage of emphasis on community, citizenry, and social responsibility. The Greco-Roman ideology rests on a foundation of social reform to relieve community social problems, or in other words, to improve the quality of life for all in the community.
- The Judeo-Christian belief that relationships with a higher power affect our choices and thus our decision-making. Our purpose is not to change people's lot in life but rather to alleviate the "preordained" suffering of others, particularly the poor. Under the Judeo-Christian tradition, we do not help others solely from concern for ourselves or our neighbors, but first and foremost because a deity has given us instructions to do so. We are told to love our neighbors as we love ourselves. We love our neighbor because we love God first and thus seek to obey.

The influence of these two distinct, historical ideologies has been replayed countless times and in countless ways through the history of the American nonprofit sector, and it is reflected in the following definitions of two types of voluntarism:

- *Philanthropy*, the giving of money or self to solve social problems. Philanthropy is developmental, an investment in the future, an effort to prevent future occurrences or recurrences of social ills.
- *Charity*, relieving or alleviating specific instances of suffering—aiding the individual victims of specific social ills. Charity is acts of mercy and compassion.

These two forms of voluntary action are complementary dimensions of the nonprofit sector. We need philanthropy, and we need charity. This interdependence has not always been recognized, however. For example, Andrew Carnegie, the ardent philanthropist, abhorred charity.[9]

It were better for mankind that the millions of the rich were thrown into the sea than so spent as to encourage the slothful, the drunken, the unworthy . . . so spent, indeed, as to produce the very evils which it hopes to mitigate or cure.[10]

Yet from the Judeo-Christian charitable tradition, almshouses, charitable hospitals, orphan homes, and charitable organizations such as Catholic Charities, the Little Sisters of the Poor, the Salvation Army, the International Red Cross, and countless others have helped relieve untold instances of human suffering in the United States.

The Nonprofit Sector's Distinctive Values and Contributions to Society

Distinctive Values

Many of the nonprofit sector's values and contributions to society are truly distinctive. Yet, the wide range in organizational sizes, purposes, functions, sources of income, levels of hierarchy, structural formality, managerial sophistication, degree of commercialization and social entrepreneurialism,[11] and reliance on volunteers makes it difficult to speak in generalities about the distinctiveness of the nonprofit sector. Thus, the term *distinctive* is approached with caution in this book, and the term *unique* has been avoided completely.

Despite these caveats and cautions, most organizations in the nonprofit sector can claim some degree of distinctiveness in most of the following respects:[12]

1. Their origins and histories are based on the values and practices of *philanthropy*—defined broadly to include *volunteerism, charity,* and *altruism*.
2. Unlike government organizations, they do not coerce participation. "Citizens cannot be compelled by nonprofit organizations to give their time or money in support of any collective goal."[13]
3. Unlike for-profit businesses, they cannot distribute earnings or surpluses to owners or shareholders.
4. They exist primarily for the purpose of making some aspects of their communities or environments better—or preventing them from becoming worse.
5. Historically, organizations in the nonprofit sector have been financed largely through a *charitable* or *grants economy* rather than a *market economy* or *compulsory economy*.
6. They share a commitment to the values of *individualism* and *pluralism* with for-profit businesses probably more than they share the values of *equity* and *justice* that are the foundation values of governments in the U.S.
7. Their perception of the *public good* is defined through *individualism* and *pluralism* rather than through official *public decision-making* as in government.
8. They are *pathways to participation*, the means people use to gain access to, to participate in, and to establish links within their communities.[14]
9. Indeed, nonprofit organizations are the essence of community.[15]

Several of these areas of distinctiveness are discussed in the next pages.

The History of Difficult Choices Among Democratic Values

In Part I, we introduced *individualism* and *pluralism* as two foundational values of the nonprofit sector, values that are as much a part of the democratic ideal in the United States as are the foundational values of government, namely *equity, justice,* and *fairness*. Since the 1980s, the basic approach in the U.S. has changed for alleviating domestic social problems, such as poverty, homelessness, opioid overdoses, youth gangs, mental illness, intellectual challenges, and lack of access to healthcare and employment. The approach for dealing with these types of social problems had developed from individual and family responsibility in the 18th and 19th centuries, to community problem solving as the nation urbanized in the 19th century, and to massive state and national government intervention in the 20th century. Since the early years of the 1980s, however, this trend has reversed through a movement labeled *devolution*—the shifting of money and decision-making authority away from national and state action back toward community problem solving. Nonprofit organizations have reemerged as the primary foci of "on the ground" solution strategies for social ills. State governments (often with federal government support) are still the primary source of funding for social programs, but moral and practical responsibility—and quite a bit of the financial burden—for problem solutions and the direct delivery of services has moved to community nonprofit organizations.[16]

What the Nonprofit Sector in the U.S. Does: Provide Services and Advocate

Throughout the history of the United States, individual citizens have recognized a need or a problem, joined with others who share their concern, and built a voluntary constituency committed to ameliorating, solving, or eliminating it. This has been true even when the issue or the people associated with it were *stigmatized*—were socially undesirable. In instance after instance, this voluntary process has been used to influence changes in public policy and government support—or tolerance—for what was originally an unacceptable cause, case, or issue—politically, socially, morally, and/or religiously.

Provide Services. Since well before American independence from Great Britain, most colonists distrusted governments and their intrusion into private lives, a sentiment that continues today. U.S. citizens tend to trust themselves and their neighbors more than they do government. This reflects the long-standing and widespread U.S. spirit of individualism and small-group collectivism. And churches provide resources and supports for people in need. So we have a long history of helping one another, especially those in need. The sentiment continues today: communities will rally to advocate for, serve, and protect its residents—keep the government out of things. Nonprofits thereby continue to help define the tradition and culture of shared concern for others.

The provision of services to people with intellectual challenges and chronic mental illness is a prime example of nonprofits providing services when governments would not. Prior to the 1960s, very little was done for people with chronic mental illness or intellectual challenges beyond the efforts of parents and relatives who struggled through mazes of limited, disconnected, and segregated services. Large state institutions—or warehouses, depending on one's point of view—were the dubious exceptions. The few community services that existed typically had been established by or through organizations established and operated voluntarily by parents, other relatives, and friends. Over time, those who shared concerns about the lack of services and access to them established organizations for mutual support, services, advocacy, and public information. Eventually, many succeeded in securing services and resources from government. The history of efforts to obtain services and supports for people with HIV/AIDS in the 1980s and 1990s, for opioid overdoses in the 2010s, and for people infected by and who lost their businesses to the Coronavirus in the 2020s has been quite similar.

Across time and place, voluntary grassroots civil society organizations have given members the strength, support, and power needed to speak their views about "the general welfare" and to seek out the "domestic tranquility" needs of their children and themselves. The list of these organizations is endless and always changing. You have heard or read about many of these examples: AIDS.org, AIDS Children in Africa, Alliance for the Mentally Ill, Alzheimer's Association, The Arc, Big Brothers/Big Sisters, Child Abuse Prevention Center, Rape Abuse & Incest National Network, Tapestry Against Polygamy, Parkinson's Disease Foundation, Citizens Against Physical and Mental Abuse, Community Treatment Alternatives, Disabilities Law Center, Gay and Lesbian Alliance Against Defamation, Brain Injury Recovery Network, American Leprosy Missions, Help for Kids, Homeless Children's Foundation, Independent Living Center, Society for the Prevention of Cruelty to Animals, Intermountain Therapy Animals, Make-a-Wish Foundation, National MS Society, and Literacy Action Center, as well as numerous art appreciation programs, symphony orchestras, dance troupes, museums, zoos, aviaries, humanities societies, and botanical gardens. Many programs such as these were initiated by faith-based organizations, often in response to pleas from their members to meet social needs, such as Catholic Community Services, Lutheran Social Services, Jewish Social Services Agency, Islamic Social Services, and American Hindu Social Services. Many others resulted from groups of family members and friends organizing to create and provide needed services.

No single government agency is responsible for providing services to homeless people or individuals with HIV/AIDS. Services to people with HIV/AIDS became a national topic only after local groups, often church-related, recognized the need and organized to do something—despite angry opposition and threats from neighbors, many churches, and politicians. The same was true as the opioid crisis began killing people by the thousands in the decade of the 2010s. As the means to meet new needs become apparent, volunteers organize under the auspices of nonprofit organizations;

grant applications are submitted to private foundations and government agencies; "special events" are sponsored to raise funds; programs develop and community awareness of the problem expands; and, communities eventually respond with new or adapted public social programs. Often, the need is redefined and articulated as communities gain experience in dealing with it. In time, new patterns of services are created. In some cases, the unpopular cause and the people affected directly by it begin to gain public acceptance. If so, government may step forward with financial assistance. Secondary power thereby affects the community and national consciousness, philosophy, and programs. This is pluralism at its best—freedom to help meet needs and to preserve social order.

Advocate. Many nonprofits that provide services also advocate for their causes with legislatures and agencies at all levels of government. Advocacy may be for almost any cause including, for example, increased funding, funding for new services, changes in restrictive legislation, and changes in administrative rules and regulations. For example, all state legislatures in the U.S. passed laws in the 1960s creating and funding systems of services for persons with intellectual challenges primarily because of grassroots campaigns conducted by parents of persons with challenges. In most states, community-based nonprofit organizations became the leading providers of direct services, working in the seams between government agencies, for-profit enterprises, and families. Similar sagas could be told about advocacy that led to services for people with, for example, chronic mental illness, Alzheimer's disease, opioid addictions, muscular dystrophy, multiple sclerosis, and cystic fibrosis; individuals who suffered strokes or physical, psychological, and/or sexual abuse; those who live in poverty and are homeless.

The saga is often the same for organizations that advocate for a cause but do not provide direct services, for example, organizations that advocate for clean air or clean water, sustainability, the "#MeToo movement," and recovery from opioid addictions. Each of these community assets was started by individuals coming together voluntarily in nonprofit associations to advocate for a perceived need and to advance their cause.

The Sector's Distinctive Contributions to Our Society

In 1973, David Horton Smith made an eloquent statement about the nonprofit sector's distinctive contributions to our society. Although others have added to Smith's list since "The Impact of the Voluntary Sector on Society" was published,[17] Smith's list remains perhaps the richest and most comprehensive. He emphasizes the nonprofit sector's ability to provide social risk capital, ideological innovation, social buffering, social integration, and preservation of cultures and traditions. Smith explains individual motivations for involvement with nonprofits and their activities—for example, nonprofits are "safe havens for change and reform" and "keepers of valued traditions." Smith's list of distinctive contributions follows with comments and a few contributions of our own added, and Smith's original chapter is reprinted in this chapter. Note that not all nonprofit organizations make all of these contributions.

Nonprofit organizations:

1. *Provide a variety of partially tested social innovations.*

   The nonprofit sector provides the risk capital of human society free from the types of constraints that private businesses and governments face.

2. *Provide perspectives and world-views that challenge prevailing assumptions.*

   Organizations in the nonprofit sector publicly advocate for changes in policy—for causes that start social movements. They are often the first to publicly proclaim that "the emperor (government or business) has no clothes."

3. *Provide the play element in society.*

   The play element in our society is neither trivial nor unimportant as the pace and complexity of our society continues to rise. Nonprofit organizations provide a variety of opportunities to gain intrinsic satisfactions in, for example, the visual and performing arts and sports.

4. *Assist with social integration.*

   This is accomplished through, for example, groups that provide supports, fellowship, sociability, and companionship that help satisfy human needs for self-sufficiency, belonging, and acceptance.

5. *Help buffer social adjustments.*

   For example, they help individuals adjust to new settings and ease the shock of social dislocations whether the adjustments are for immigrants and refugees, individuals released from prisons or rehabilitation programs, or persons escaping spousal abuse.

6. *Link together people, groups, and institutions that otherwise would be in greater conflict or competition with each other.*

   Nonprofits' volunteers and directors, for example, often bring together people from different backgrounds who would not ordinarily know or spend time together—who build social capital as they work collaboratively toward common purposes.

7. *Preserve values, ways of life, ideas, beliefs, and artifacts.*

   Historical societies, museums, libraries, and voluntary groups preserve the values of cultures or subcultures.

8. *Pass along bodies of beliefs and values;* and
9. *Embody and represent the sense of mystery, wonder, and the sacred.*

   These organizations include organized religions, historical societies, and cultural societies.

10. *Help people grow, develop and realize their personal potential.*

    There are endless numbers of self-help groups, such as Toastmasters, groups that develop personal and family financial skills, study groups, and groups that support recovery.

11. *Serve as a source of social criticism.*

    Similar to (2), nonprofits are vital to the continuing development of society, pointing out to businesses and governments the need to change.

12. *Supporting the economic system.*

    We seldom pause to think about how nonprofits support and advance our economic system through, for example, professional, industrial, trade, and labor associations.

13. *Provide a reservoir of potential energy for future mobilizations.*

    No society can maintain the resources needed to deal with future needs such as disasters. Some nonprofits serve as "latent resources" by providing the means to mobilize people and needed resources when confronted by special purposes, such as volunteer fire departments, the Red Cross, and search and rescue teams.

14. *Strengthen the sense of community and individual responsibility for self and others.*

    Without places to volunteer, there would be fewer ways to maintain a sense of community or to advocate for social issues. The process of working together toward better communities creates *social capital*—the "glue" that helps hold communities together.

15. *Help others to heal and/or recover.*

    Nonprofit hospitals, community health and mental health centers, and self-help groups not only provide services but also provide ways for individuals to help others improve their lives.

16. *Create and maintain a civil society and strengthen democracy.*

    Without nonprofits, how would we build a caring civil society or provide opportunities for individuals to prepare themselves for future leadership in government and businesses?

17. *Provide opportunities for people to express their hopes, dreams, values and passions.*

Collectively, David Horton Smith's list of nonprofits' contributions to society paints an impressive rationale for maintaining a strong nonprofit sector in our society and for awarding nonprofits preferential tax treatment.

Corporatized Nonprofits—Nonprofits That Look and Act More Like Businesses

Many nonprofit organizations do not look, feel, or act very much like the mental images that most of us have of nonprofits. Most large nonprofits in, for example, health care (including hospitals), PACs, insurance, trade associations, and financial services do not begin to resemble voluntary associations.[18] Often, these commercial or *corporatized nonprofits* originated as grassroots associations but evolved into large businesslike organizations. The Blue Cross/Blue Shield insurance organizations, large credit unions, the National Association of Manufacturers, labor unions, the American Association for Retired Persons (AARP)—even the National Basketball Association and the National Hockey League—are only a few examples. Corporatized nonprofits can be difficult to distinguish from for-profit firms. Likewise, nonprofits that depend extensively on government contracts to fund the services they provide can be difficult to recognize as "nonprofit organizations" in the sense or spirit of voluntary civil society organizations.

   Although corporatized nonprofits are in the nonprofit sector, they are on the edge of it. An organization is legally a nonprofit if it meets criteria set forth in the tax laws and tax codes. They can make it difficult, however, to explain the sector in positive terms. The legalistic approach to defining nonprofits also opens the door for Congress and state legislatures to restrict their scope of activities or to alter the tax codes to stiffen eligibility requirements for tax exemption.

Political Nonprofits

Political nonprofits are the subject of Part VI, but they warrant a brief introduction here because they are in the news frequently. Most nonprofits are permitted to engage in political activities but only to a limited, "not significant" extent. Two U.S. Internal Revenue Service (IRS) categories of nonprofit organizations, however, allow certain nonprofits to engage actively in political activities, including contributing funds to political campaigns. When you see or hear, for example, about a "nonprofit PAC" (Political Action Committee) or "nonprofit Super Pac" contributing large sums to a political campaign for a candidate or a ballot issue, remember that this is a different kind of non-profit organization than the *501(c)(3) charitable nonprofits* that most of us think about as "nonprofit organizations." But these types of political nonprofits are authorized by the Congress and therefore also by the IRS. As we discuss in Part IV, these types of nonprofits do not receive the same level of favorable tax treatment as 501(c)(3)s.

Changes in the U.S. Nonprofit Sector in Recent Decades

Toward the end of the 20th century, the historical barn-raising spirit of neighbors helping neighbors in good times and in bad began to reemerge as the foundation for domestic public policy. In the short span from about 1960 to 1980, the underlying philosophy—or ideology—of programs for people in need moved a great distance from what they had been throughout most of that century. Several streams of events and philosophical currents led to this radical redefinition of U.S. social policy. This nation had been committed to and believed it could win the "War on Poverty" through "Great Society" programs in the 1960s and 1970s. During the decades starting from the 1980s, however, two different beliefs or understandings emerged as public policy "self-evident truths": social needs are endless, and government programs seldom can solve social problems. Governments wanted to "wash their hands" of problems and turn services over to nongovernmental organizations.

As a vivid example of this shift, the primary source of revenue for nonprofits in the U.S. until the early 1980s was donations—charitable gifts and grants made to nonprofits by individuals, private foundations, and corporations. Starting in the 1980s, however, the U.S. government went into a "paradigm shift." Presidents Jimmy Carter through George H. W. Bush worked to persuade Executive Branch agencies and Congress to reduce direct services, turning instead to the delivery of services by nongovernmental organizations ("outsourcing"), especially in the human services sub-sector. As is discussed in Part III, even large segments of U.S. foreign aid programs have been outsourced to international nongovernmental organizations (INGOs) for implementation. The outsourcing trend continued into the 1990s, through initiatives such as Vice President Al Gore's "National Performance Review," Congressman Newt Gingrich's "Contract with America," and the widely adopted government organizational philosophy of Osborne and Gaebler's "Reinventing Government."[19] Today, the largest source of revenue into the nonprofit sector is government grants and contracts—no longer individual donations. With this shift in revenue sources have come increased rules, policies, regulation, and performance measurement/accountability reporting requirements. Nonprofit staff must have the knowledge and skills needed to secure and retain contracts with government agencies. In short, nonprofits that contract with government agencies have been "professionalized." Professionalization of the sector has yielded many advantages, but as we will examine later in this volume, there are also downsides.

Readings Reprinted in Part II

In the first reading reprinted here, Thomas P. Holland and Roger A. Ritvo explore the key developments in the history of nonprofit organizations in the United States from the early colonial period to the first decade of the 21st century. They write,

> The United States has a long and diverse history of local groups of volunteers coming together to address social, cultural, educational, and human needs. . . . Furthermore, the Americans see

themselves as benevolent people who care for one another, especially the needy, and are ready to work as a community to take care of problems.

Local initiative by individuals and in association with others—but without government involvement—was a core value of the early settlers that continues to affect communities and nonprofit organizations today.

Holland and Ritvo cite Alexis de Tocqueville's well-documented surprise at the extent and importance of associational life in the United States while touring the country in 1831. They also relate Tocqueville's observations of economic theory, including particularly *government failure theory.* (See also Part V, "Economic Theories of the Nonprofit Sector.")

Organizations in the nonprofit sector—particularly in the human services—experienced major declines in government funding during the 1980s and early 1990s, as the political winds changed quickly. Holland and Ritvo observe that "Nonprofit organizations are . . . being asked to do more in absolute terms and to do so with private contributions" and less from government contracts and grants. Entrepreneurship, especially through partnerships with government agencies, businesses, and other nonprofits is the current trend in the nonprofit sector. (Also see Part IX, "Theories of Relations and Collaboration Within and Between Sectors.")

Although written almost 50 years ago, David Horton Smith's "The Impact of the Volunteer Sector on Society," makes an eloquent statement about the nonprofit sector's distinctive contributions to society. Others have documented the sector's contributions since, but his list remains perhaps the richest and most comprehensive.[20] Smith emphasizes the nonprofit sector's ability to provide social risk capital, ideological innovation, social buffering, social integration, and preservation of traditions and ideas. Smith also explains individual motivations for involvement with nonprofit organizations and their activities; for example nonprofits became "safe havens" for change and reform in the volatile post-1960s years and, at the same time, keepers of valued traditions.

"The Gospel of Wealth" by Andrew Carnegie, the turn-of-the-20th-century steel baron whose personal saga is one of the greatest rags-to-riches models of industrial opportunity in the new world, was originally published in two 1889 journal articles under the simpler title "Wealth." It was renamed and republished as "The Gospel of Wealth" in 1900 and became the first compelling justification for a philosophy of philanthropy in the United States. "The Gospel of Wealth" was highly influential in establishing an early conceptual basis for philanthropy and a bias against charity. Carnegie himself was a premier philanthropist who gave away most of his wealth to colleges and community libraries.

Concerned about the spread of communism into the United States, Carnegie believed that the democratic ideals of individualism, the right to hold private property, and the right to accumulate wealth are essential for humankind and this nation to evolve into a higher form. Carnegie was both pragmatic and philosophical. He advocated for maintaining a spirit of competition and the higher result of human experience. He sought to prevent the spread of communism in the United States by word and deed: (1) Redistribute wealth by those who achieved it, (2) live a moderate lifestyle, and (3) do not leave large sums to heirs and thereby spoil them. Carnegie insisted that money should be used to help people help themselves. Money should not be wasted on a passing beggar to encourage "slothful behavior." Carnegie was truly concerned about possible struggles between the "haves" and the "have-nots." The rich, he believed, bore the obligation to "even things out." Carnegie's "Wealth" presents an important but controversial point of view that is still alive and influential today.

As the title of Billie Sandberg's reading, "Critical Perspectives on the History and Development of the Nonprofit Sector in the United States" informs, it presents a contrasting perspective on the history of the U.S. nonprofit sector. We believe it presents an important alternative to the prevailing more traditional history as presented, for example, by Holland and Ritvo, and P. D. Hall.[21] Sandberg "interrogates [understandings of the American nonprofit sector] to understand how the current historical narrative of the American nonprofit sector came to be authoritative and powerful." Sandberg frames her historical analysis using Foucault's postmodern philosophy "in which nothing is inherently good or bad, only dangerous." Prevailing assumptions about the sector

This includes prevailing understandings of the nature of nonprofit work and workers (including volunteers), the place nonprofit and voluntary organizations hold in communities, and the role the nonprofit sector plays in the fabric of American society.

How we structure and organize nonprofits, use volunteers and manage the business of nonprofits is not predetermined by the sector's history.

Notes

1. Peter D. Hall, "Historical Perspectives on Nonprofit Organizations in the United States," in *The Jossey-Bass Handbook of Nonprofit Leadership and Management*, 3rd ed., edited by David O. Renz, 3–41 (San Francisco: Jossey-Bass/Wiley, 2010).

2. Lester M. Salamon, *America's Nonprofit Sector: A Primer*, 2nd ed. (New York: Foundation Center, 1999), 1.

3. Hall, "Historical Perspectives on Nonprofit Organizations in the United States."

4. Alexis de Tocqueville, *Democracy in America* (New York: Knopf, 1840).

5. Tocqueville, *Democracy in America*, vol. 1: 199.

6. Tocqueville, *Democracy in America*, vol. 2 (1840, reprint, New York: Knopf, 1945), 303–304.

7. Michael Edwards, *Civil Society*, 3rd ed. (Cambridge, UK: Polity, 2014).

8. See for example Stephen R. Block, "A History of the Discipline," Chapter 8 in the first edition of this volume (Boulder, CO: Westview Press, 2001).

9. Carnegie's philosophy of philanthropy is articulated in the "Gospel of Wealth" which is reprinted in this part. It is from Carnegie's *The Gospel of Wealth: And Other Timely Essays* (New York: Century, 1900).

10. Andrew Carnegie, *The Gospel of Wealth: And Other Timely Essays* (New York: Century, 1900), 26.

11. See J. Gregory Dees, *Social Entrepreneurship: Harnessing Private Initiative, Ingenuity, and Investment for the Common Good* (New York: Columbia University Press, 2001); Guo Chao and Wolfgang Bielefeld, *Social Entrepreneurship: An Evidence-Based Approach to Creating Social Value* (San Francisco: Jossey-Bass/Wiley, 2014); Georgia Levenson Keohane, *Social Entrepreneurship for the 21st Century: Innovation Across the Nonprofit, Private, and Public Sectors* (New York: McGraw-Hill Education, 2013); David Bornstein and Susan Davis, *Social Entrepreneurship: What Everyone Needs to Know* (Oxford, UK and New York: Oxford University Press, 2010); Paul C. Light, *The Search for Social Entrepreneurship* (Washington, DC: Brookings Institution Press, 2008); Alex Nichols, ed., *Social Entrepreneurship: New Models of Sustainable Social Change* (Oxford, UK: Oxford University Press, 2006); and Johanna Mair, Jeffrey Robinson, and Kai Hockerts, eds., *Social Entrepreneurship* (New York: Palgrave Macmillan, 2006).

12. Lester Salamon, Wojciech Sokolowski, and Megan Haddock, building on earlier work by the Johns Hopkins Comparative Nonprofit Sector Project, identify five features that any entity must possess to be considered within the civil society sector: formal or informal organization, private, nonprofit-distributing, self-governing, and non-compulsory. They refer to these characteristics as "a consensus structural operational definition of the civil society sector." Lester Salamon, Wojciech Sokolowski, and Megan Haddock, *Explaining Civil Society Development: A Social Origins Approach* (Baltimore, MD: Johns Hopkins University Press, 2017), 23.

13. Peter Frumkin, *On Being Nonprofit* (Cambridge, MA: Harvard University Press, 2002), 3, reprinted in this volume as Chapter 3 in Part I.

14. See Steven Rathgeb Smith and Michael Lipsky, "Nonprofit Organizations and Community," in *Nonprofits for Hire*, edited by Steven R. Smith, and M. Lipsky (Cambridge, MA: Harvard University Press, 1993).

15. Steven Rathgeb Smith and Michael Lipsky, "Nonprofit Organizations and Community."

16. J. Steven Ott and Lisa A. Dicke, "Important but Largely Unanswered Questions about Accountability in Contracted Public Human Services," *International Journal of Organization Theory and Behavior 3* (2000): 283–317.

17. David Horton Smith, "The Impact of the Volunteer Sector on Society," in *Voluntary Action Research*, edited by David H. Smith (Lexington, MA: Lexington Books, 1973).

18. There are differences, but they can be difficult to identify and are not always viewed as important enough to warrant favorable tax treatment. See Parts IV and IX.

19. See David Osborne and Ted Gaebler, *Reinventing Government: How the Entrepreneurial Spirit is Transforming the Public Sector* (New York: Penguin Books, 1992).

20. See Rober Putnam, "Bowling Alone" and Sabine Lang, "Civil Society as a Public Sphere," both reprinted in Part VII of this volume.

21. Peter Dobkin Hall, *Inventing the Nonprofit Sector* (Baltimore: Johns Hopkins University Press, 1992).

Bibliography

Anheier, Helmut K., *Nonprofit Organizations: Theory, Management, Policy*, 2nd ed. (London: Routledge, 2014).

——, "What Kind of Nonprofit Sector, What Kind of Society? Comparative Policy Reflections." *American Behavioral Scientist 52* (2009): 1082–1094.

——, and Jeremy Kendall, *Third Sector Policy at the Crossroads: An International Non-profit Analysis* (London: Routledge, 2013).

Boris, Elizabeth T., and C. Eugene Steuerle, eds., *Nonprofits and Government: Collaboration and Conflict*, 3rd ed. (Lanham, MD: Urban Institute Press/Rowman & Littlefield, 2017).

——, "Scope and Dimensions of the Nonprofit Sector." In *The Nonprofit Sector: A Research Handbook*, 2nd ed., eds., Walter W. Powell and Richard Steinberg (New Haven, CT: Yale University Press, 2006): 66–88.

Bornstein, David, and Susan Davis, *Social Entrepreneurship: What Everyone Needs to Know* (Oxford, UK and New York: Oxford University Press, 2010).

Carnegie, Andrew, *The Gospel of Wealth: And Other Timely Essays* (New York: Century, 1990).

Casey, John, *The Nonprofit World: Civil Society and the Rise of the Nonprofit Sector* (West Hartford, CT: Kumarian Press, 2016).

Chao, Guo, and Wolfgang Bielefeld, *Social Entrepreneurship: An Evidence-Based Approach to Creating Social Value* (San Francisco: Jossey-Bass/Wiley, 2014).

Corry, Olaf, "Defining and Theorizing the Third Sector." In *Third Sector Research*, ed., Rupert Taylor (New York: Springer, 2010): 11–19.

Dees, J. Gregory, *Social Entrepreneurship: Harnessing Private Initiative, Ingenuity, and Investment for the Common Good* (New York: Columbia University Press, 2001).

Edwards, Michael, *Civil Society*, 3rd ed. (Cambridge, UK: Polity, 2014).

Frumkin, Peter, *On Being Nonprofit: A Conceptual and Policy Primer* (Cambridge, MA: Harvard University Press, 2002).

——, and Jonathan B. Imber, eds., *In Search of the Nonprofit Sector* (London and New York: Routledge, 2018).

Hansmann, Henry, *The Ownership of Enterprise* (Cambridge, MA: Belknap Press, 1996).

Holland, Thomas P., and Roger A. Ritvo, *Nonprofit Organizations: Principles and Practices* (New York: Columbia University Press, 2008).

Hopkins, Bruce R., *The Law of Tax-Exempt Organizations*, 12th ed. (New York: Wiley, 2019).

Hunter, Albert, and Carl Milofsky, *Pragmatic Liberalism: Constructing a Civil Society* (New York: Palgrave Macmillan, 2007).

Husock, Howard A., *Who Killed Civil Society? The Rise of Big Government and Decline of Bourgeois Norms* (New York: Encounter Books, 2019).

Keohane, Georgia Levenson, *Social Entrepreneurship for the 21st Century: Innovation Across the Nonprofit, Private, and Public* Sectors (New York: McGraw-Hill Education, 2013).

Lang, Sabine, *NGOs, Civil Society, and the Public Sphere* (New York: Cambridge University Press. 2014).

LeRoux, Kelly, and Mary K. Feeney, *Nonprofit Organizations and Civil Society in the United States* (New York: Routledge, 2015).

Light, Paul C., *The Search for Social Entrepreneurship* (Washington, DC: Brookings Institution Press, 2008).

Mair, Johanna, Jeffrey Robinson, and Kai Hockerts, eds., *Social Entrepreneurship* (New York: Palgrave Macmillan, 2006).

Milofsky, Carl, *Smallville: Institutionalizing Community in Twenty-First-Century America* (Medford, MA: Tufts University Press, 2008).

Musick, Marc A., and John Wilson, *Volunteers: A Social Profile* (Bloomington and Indianapolis, IN: Indiana University Press, 2008).

Muukkonen, Martti, "Framing the Field: Civil Society and Related Concepts." *Nonprofit and Voluntary Sector Quarterly* 38 (2009): 684–700.

Nichols, Alex, ed., *Social Entrepreneurship: New Models of Sustainable Social Change* (Oxford, UK: Oxford University Press, 2006).

Powell, Walter W., and Patricia Bromley, eds., *The Nonprofit Sector: A Research Handbook* (Palo Alto, CA: Stanford University Press, 2020).

——, and Richard Steinberg, eds., *The Nonprofit Sector: A Research Handbook*, 2nd ed. (New Haven, CT: Yale University Press, 2006).

Putnam, Robert D., *Bowling Alone: Revised and Updated: The Collapse and Revival of American Community* (New York: Simon and Schuster, 2020).

——, *The Upswing: How America Came Together a Century Ago and How We Can Do It Again* (New York: Simon and Schuster, 2020).

Salamon, Lester M., *America's Nonprofit Sector: A Primer*, 2nd ed. (New York: Foundation Center, 1999).

——, *New Frontiers of Philanthropy: A Guide to the New Tools and New Actors that Are Reshaping Global Philanthropy and Social Investing* (New York: Oxford University Press, 2014).

——, *The Resilient Sector Revisited* (Washington, DC: Brookings Institution Press, 2015).

——, *State of Nonprofit America*, 2nd ed. (Washington, DC: Brookings Institution Press, 2012).

——, and Megan A. Haddock, *Explaining Civil Society Development: A Social Origins Approach* (Baltimore, MD: Johns Hopkins University Press, 2017).

——, and S. Wojciech Sokolowski, eds., *Global Civil Society: Dimensions of the Nonprofit Sector*, Vol. 2 (Bloomfield, CT: Kumarian Press, 2004).

Sandberg, Billie, "Critical Perspectives on the History and Development of the Nonprofit Sector in the United States." In *Reframing Nonprofit Organizations: Democracy, Inclusion, and Social Change*, eds. Angela M. Eikenberry, Roseanne M. Mirabella, and Billie Sandberg (Irvine, CA: Melvin & Leigh, 2019): 26–37.

Silber, Norman, *A Corporate Form of Freedom: The Emergence of the Modern Nonprofit Sector* (London and New York: Routledge, 2018).

Smith, David Horton, *Voluntary Action Research* (Lexington, MA: Lexington, 1973).

Smith, Steven R., and Michael Lipsky, *Nonprofits for Hire* (Cambridge, MA: Harvard University Press, 1993).

Soskis, Benjamin, "A History of Associational Life and the Nonprofit Sector in the United States." In *The Nonprofit Sector: A Research Handbook*, 3rd ed., eds. Walter Powell and Patricia Bromley (Palo Alto, CA: Stanford University Press, 2020): 23–80.

Taylor, Rupert, ed., *Third Sector Research* (New York: Springer, 2011).

Tocqueville, Alexis de, *Democracy in America* (New York: Knopf, 1840).

Van Til, John, *Growing Civil Society: From Nonprofit Sector to Third Space* (Bloomington and Indianapolis, IN: Indiana University Press, 2000).

Vaughn, Shannon K., and Shelly Arsneault, *Managing Nonprofit Organizations in a Policy World*, 2nd ed. (Irvine, CA: Melving & Leigh, 2021).

Wall, Joseph F., *Andrew Carnegie* (New York: Oxford University Press, 1970).

► CHAPTER 4

History and Theories of Nonprofit Organizations

THOMAS P. HOLLAND AND ROGER A. RITVO

Beginning With Many Roots

Nonprofit organizations enable people to work together to address a community's needs when multiple interests exist without widespread consensus on the best course of action.[1] This perspective is called *pluralistic theory* and refers to several agencies trying to fulfill a particular need. Sometimes coordinated, often not, each organization carves out a specific area of activity. From a macrocommunity perspective, the hope is that needs are addressed by all the activities together. The early history of nonprofit organizations documents this pluralism in action.

The United States has a long and diverse history of local groups of volunteers coming together to address social, cultural, educational, and human needs. The early colonists saw themselves as a self-organizing and self-governing nation. In reaction to the eighteenth-century European monarchies, state-established religions, and inherited status hierarchies, the newly arrived immigrants emphasized voluntary initiatives, local government, separation of church and state, and egalitarian relationships.[2]

Well before the United States' war for independence from Great Britain, Americans distrusted governmental involvement in many aspects of their lives, an attitude that continues to shape many of their political views. Americans believe that needs are best understood by the people in the community and that they are the best ones to address it. Furthermore, Americans see themselves as benevolent people who care for one another, especially the needy, and are ready to work as a community to take care of problems.

Organizations to help the needy originated in the early days of our colonies, in which less formal approaches were used to resolve civic concerns. The first English settlements in the New World emphasized the practice of charity; indeed, the Puritans in New England saw it as a religious duty. This compassion took many forms, but at its core was caring for one another. Inequalities were accepted as given parts of the natural order, driving people to depend on one another to thrive.

Poverty therefore was seldom seen as a problem, as neighbors expected to help one another. The next line of support was to turn to relatives

DOI: 10.4324/9780367696559-6

for help. If they were not available, people in need were understood to have a claim on the community for aid, which often was disbursed through local congregations. Since the communities were so small, their leaders often wore several hats in local government, business, and as "overseers of the poor."

The designated overseers sought gifts of food, clothes, firewood, and other necessities to enable those in need to get through their temporary distress. Most people lived in families, either with their own or in the houses of others, exchanging labor for food and shelter.

In those days few people worried that aiding people in distress might lead to idleness and dependence; rather, people saw the charitable support of those in need as a virtue to be cultivated. Those rare individuals who seemed to be exploiting or abusing such support were simply refused more help, a practice that later led to the distinction between the "worthy" and the "unworthy" poor. Moreover, there was a recognized distinction between neighbors and strangers. Strangers, or transients, had no claim on the community for help.

Many churches designated a portion of their collections for local people in need, and some towns established funds from which the overseers could draw to purchase needed supplies. In other areas pooled funds were used to establish programs that were widely seen as needed by the whole community. One of the first needs was for an educated clergy, which led groups of wealthy citizens to found Harvard and Yale Colleges, both of which soon received legislative grants. In New England some larger towns levied taxes to support local schools, while education elsewhere in the colonies tended to be offered on a limited basis by churches and private tutors. Gifts from wealthy benefactors provided most of the financial resources for these early organizations, although a few began soliciting wider support.

Benjamin Franklin was an early advocate of mutual aid groups that would strengthen the capabilities of members to become hardworking, thrifty, and self-reliant. Indeed, Americans value local initiatives to address community concerns, believing that government at all levels is inefficient and ineffective as a means of meeting local needs or solving problems. The freedom to form voluntary associations is thus prized.

One view of nonprofits sees them as *mediating structures*, as smaller social agencies linking individuals to larger organizations and systems such as government and large businesses. Mediating structures include the family, religious organizations, civic clubs, and other such associations that contribute to positive social values and community engagement. They draw our attention beyond our own self-interests to the well-being of other people.

The Commons

Drawing on the old practice of having an open space in or near a village for everyone's use, the theory of the commons emphasizes our mutual responsibilities and shared values for life together. Beyond the individual market transactions of buying and selling, communities are held together by a shared language, culture, values, and resources that enrich the lives of everyone in them. The commons refers to practices of religious worship, artistic expression, recreation, and other forms of voluntary activity that contribute to the well-being of everyone in the community.

Lohmann identified several important dimensions of the commons: Every culture has forms of collective activity through which people demonstrate values beyond their individual interests.[3] These activities are grounded in shared, subjective meanings and are intended to produce something for the good of others, not for individual profit.

The practice of having young men become apprentices to successful people in business or the trades struck Benjamin Franklin as forcing them to be dependent on the largess of the privileged. He therefore set up mutual aid groups that provided the knowledge, skills, and habits that its members needed to become successful in their own enterprises and, in so doing, would benefit the whole community and not just the members. Franklin applied similar reasoning to the problem of poverty. Rather than just giving poor people money, which they would soon spend, Franklin's approach was to form educational groups in which people would learn the basic skills they needed to become self-supporting.[4]

This emphasis on individual and community improvement through local initiatives was central to the values of those who formed the new nation of the United States.

The Pre-Civil War Period

When the Frenchman Alexis de Tocqueville toured the United States in 1831, he documented its "immense assemblage of associations" and made this community development the highlight of his *Democracy in America*. Such organized, collaborative efforts illustrated how Americans expressed their freedom and democracy, a tradition that continues today.

> Americans of all ages, all stations in life, and all types of disposition are forever forming associations in the U.S. and in many other societies. There are not only commercial and industrial in which all take part, but others of a thousand different types—religious, moral, serious, futile, very general and very limited, immensely large and very minute. Americans combine to give fetes, found seminaries, build churches, distribute books, and send missionaries to the antipodes. Hospitals, prisons, and schools take shape in that way. Finally, if they want to proclaim a truth or propagate some feeling by the encouragement of a great

example, they form an association. In every case, at the head of any new undertaking, where in France you would find the government or in England some territorial magnate, in the United States you are sure to find an association.[5]

Economic theory helps explain this early history. Weisbrod proposed that nonprofit associations and organizations formed because the government had failed to offer these services.[6] In democratic countries governments tend to address the interests and needs of the average voter and to ignore those of people at the margins of society, such as the wealthy and the poor or members of a particular region. Those people may respond in several ways. Citizens may choose to work together voluntarily to supply a resource that they value, such as establishing a museum or a shelter for the homeless. According to this perspective, a greater number of nonprofit organizations can be found in communities whose population is more diverse.

Nonetheless, the public sector and government still figure in this history, for the next step was obtaining legislative approval for such programs to incorporate and acquire the rights of other business organizations. These programs were permitted to own property, make contracts, and continue to exist beyond the participation of their current members. In some states they were exempted from taxes and were allowed to raise money through such efforts as fairs and lotteries.

The Reconstruction Period

After the Civil War the federal government established the Freedmens Bureau, which oversaw a variety of reconstruction programs intended to help newly freed slaves become established as full members of society.[7] Among these efforts was the establishment of schools, some funded publicly and many through the work of volunteer missionaries and educators from religious organizations in the northern states. Self-help groups made up of former slaves were numerous, including ones offering food, job skills, and help in finding employment. In the face of pervasive southern racism, however, these efforts fell far short of the needs. Land reform to enable people to establish their own small farms never worked out as promised, and subsistence tenant farming thus soon became the norm for freedmen.

In the next decades nonprofit organizations in the northern states accelerated the pattern of coming together to form national associations that addressed a wide range of community needs. But the rapid growth of such national organizations was not welcomed by everyone, especially those in more rural areas. Critics saw them as bureaucracies that were undermining the traditional links of personal charity, in which givers and receivers knew each other. Because they had hired staff, larger associations were seen as self-serving, as raising money to support themselves as well as delegating impersonal services.

The Post-Depression Era

Well into the twentieth century private donations by wealthy individuals and grants from foundations provided the main sources of revenue for most nonprofit organizations. Then, when the nation entered the Great Depression in the 1930s, the federal government took several steps to help the needy, including the establishment of the Social Security system to benefit aged persons, Aid to Dependent Children, and public works programs to provide employment to the unemployed. Although such programs helped many people regain their independence, they brought criticism from those who believed that such expenditures undermined self-reliance.

After the Depression, the distinctions among the public, corporate, and nonprofit sectors were

clarified, even though many programs still were administered by hybrid organizational forms, as they are now. Citizens often joined many different voluntary associations, with these overlapping memberships reaching across social boundaries and discouraging the emergence of dominating class structures.[8]

Some nonprofits are established to address externalities. Addressing a negative externality may take the form of advocacy against locating a landfill near a neighborhood or efforts to require a power company to reduce its emissions. Promoting positive externalities may be establishing after-school programs for low-income children, with the long-term objective of improving the quality of life for both them and those around them as well as reducing delinquency rates in the community.

Private foundations have often been a source of funds to address these unexpected consequences, and they have enlarged and extended their efforts to improve particular aspects of the nation as a whole. But in the mid-twentieth century questions were raised about these foundations' rapidly growing endowments as well as questions about the nonprofit organizations that benefited from the gifts from those foundations and from wealthy benefactors. There was little public regulation of these organizations, and critics saw them as amassing enormous sums of money free from both taxes and public scrutiny. Congressional hearings led to the passage of the Tax Reform Act of 1969, which instituted two new regulations: Foundations were required to distribute at least 5 percent of their assets every year, and nonprofits were required to report their income and expenses annually, using the new 990 tax form.

Public support for community services came to a peak with President Lyndon Johnson's "Great Society" legislation directing money to numerous local projects designed to help individuals gain greater skills and resources as well as become more active participants in local governments.

THE CHILDREN'S DEFENSE FUND

Marian Wright Edelman founded the Children's Defense Fund (CDF) in 1973, which today is recognized for its effective advocacy for children and families. Its mission is to ensure that every child has a healthy and well-prepared start in life (see www.childrensdefense.org/about). A private, nonprofit organization, the CDF accepts support from foundations, corporations, and individuals. It does not accept government funds. The fund adopted the popular slogan "Leave no child behind" and continues to advocate for children.

Edelman, a graduate of both Spelman College and Yale Law School, first directed the Jackson, Mississippi, office of the NAACP Legal Defense and Educational Fund. In 1968 she moved to Washington, DC, as the legal counsel for Dr. Martin Luther King Jr.'s Poor People's Campaign. Then, after serving for two years as the director of the Center for Law and Education at Harvard University, she started the CDF, which she still directs.

The Children's Defense Fund has had documented success in improving the lives of children through its research, public education programs, budget and policy advocacy, and coalition building. Edelman notes that "service was as much a part of my upbringing as eating breakfast." She is well on her way to fulfilling her desire that "the legacy I want to leave is a child care system that says no kid is going to be left alone or feel unsafe."[9]

The Reagan Revolution

Despite these efforts, public dissatisfaction grew over the huge federal expenditures for local community services, especially when some of them included activities to increase the political influence of the poor. Accordingly, the Reagan administration (1981–1989) began withdrawing federal support from programs serving low-income people, thereby leaving them to local nonprofit organizations, which soon became overwhelmed with the widespread needs and the scarcity of resources. In response, these organizations began allocating more staff time to fund-raising, which led eventually to the creation of a new profession, that of nonprofit fund-raiser (for more information about this profession, see www.afpnet.org). Some nonprofits began charging or raising user fees for their services, and special events to attract local donors soon became common in most communities. Continuing to the present is this trend of declining federal support for social services and increasing efforts by nonprofits to raise the funds they need. The growing competition among nonprofits for contributions has led to turbulence in the field and to the rise of public demands for accountability regarding how the nonprofits raise and use their funds.

The Contract for America

The challenges of assessing the quality, efficiency, and effectiveness of nonprofit and governmental services opened the door to conservatives' questions about the role of the federal government in funding these megaprograms. Dissatisfaction with federal expenditures for community programs led to political victories in the 1990s for candidates espousing two basic assumptions:

1. The federal government is wasteful and ineffective in producing results. Some candidates argued that President Johnson's Great Society programs were more rhetoric than accomplishment.

2. Social welfare programs are more harmful than helpful to the people they claim to be serving. A better approach would be one in which governmental policies emphasize self-sufficiency

through individual responsibility rather than dependence on public support (see Payton Papers).

Often referred to as the Republican Party's Contract for America, these efforts led to steep reductions in both the federal bureaucracy and federal spending for public welfare programs; cultural, arts, and humanities organizations; and research in all fields. If individuals or organizations want to support any of these endeavors, they should do so on their own.

As we have noted, the emphasis on individualism is a deeply held American value, and personal responsibility and self-help are matters of ethics as well as economics. We live in networks of memberships that provide mutual aid, starting with the family and extending to civic and religious organizations and professional associations. We have long assumed that some services should be public responsibilities, such as defense, police, highways, emergency disaster assistance, and foreign policy. This is communitarian ethics. Beyond those areas, though, we are unsure about the appropriate role of the federal government in meeting community needs.

The most visible target of reduced spending is welfare, especially when it seems to be supporting people who are able-bodied but unemployed—in other words, what some have called the "undeserving poor." Unfortunately, attacks on such expenditures also threaten children, the elderly, persons with disabilities, and other vulnerable populations. Nonetheless, many people expect private philanthropy to deal with such issues without public support.

By the last decade of the twentieth century, those concerned with the credibility of nonprofit organizations began establishing several national programs to monitor their performance and make their evaluations publicly available. The national Better Business Bureau instituted its Wise Giving Alliance, which formulates standards of accountability

for nonprofits, periodically surveys nonprofits on key aspects of their performance, and then reports their findings on www.give.org. Another organization began collecting IRS 990 forms, which report the financial performance of all nonprofits, and making them publicly available at www.guidestar.org.

In addition, many states began requiring nonprofits engaging in fund-raising campaigns to register with the state attorney general's or the secretary of state's office and then report annually on the amounts raised and the proportion of that sum spent on the fund-raising effort itself. The state office that controls this usually posts the annual fund-raising results, allowing the public to find out how much money a specific nonprofit raised and how much of that went to the nonprofit's programs and how much to the fund-raisers.

Paradigm Shifts

Both history and economic theory illustrate that nonprofit organizations have grown, developed, adapted, changed, altered, and adjusted their purposes, missions, and aspirations to meet emerging needs. Nonprofits help define the United States' ethos of caring and represent its effective response to shifting national political views and changing local needs.

Indeed, change, or paradigm shift, has become a constant idea in management circles, television talk shows, and educational seminars. When accepted patterns undergo a fundamental, usually irrevocable, change, it is called a paradigm shift.

The role of the federal government in the past fifty years has undergone two major paradigm shifts. The first occurred in the 1960s under President Lyndon Johnson and the Great Society. In this paradigm the shift was away from the relaxed post–World War II society in which the government stayed out of its citizens' personal lives to one that wanted and supported federal, state, and local governments helping those in need. Medicare, Medicaid, the Voting Rights Act, and the civil rights movements all were part of this effort.

The next big change came in the 1980s. Two decades after the Great Society programs were enacted, the Reagan revolution began. The term revolution itself is a clue that the shift was of major proportions. In the 1980s the paradigm shifted power from the federal government to the state and local governments. The goal was to let local authorities assess local needs and use local funds to meet them. The federal government was the last resort for only rare cases and national emergencies. The results of this shift remain with us into the twenty-first century.

One of the paradigm shifts that may be occurring as this book [*Nonprofit Organizations: Principles and Practices*] is being written is the growing need for nonprofit partnerships. Partly in response to the declining funds and partly in response to a general feeling that nonprofit organizations should not compete because this leads to duplication, the number of mergers and partnerships is increasing.

The United States is estimated to have about two million nonprofit organizations. According to Peter Drucker, more than 70 percent of these were established since the mid-1960s.[10] Thus, this explosive growth occurred during the expansion of social change in the 1960s and later helped fill the gaps in health, human services,

the arts, and other social concerns created by the Reagan revolution.

Notes

1. L. M. Salamon, *The Resilient Sector: The State of Nonprofit America* (Washington, DC: Brookings Institution Press, 2002).

2. H. K. Anheier, *Nonprofit Organizations: Theory, Management, Policy* (New York: Routledge, 2005).

3. R. A. Lohmann, *The Commons: New Perspectives on Nonprofit Organizations and Voluntary Action* (San Francisco: Jossey-Bass, 1992).

4. R. A. Gross, "Giving in America: From Charity to Philanthropy," in *Charity, Philanthropy, and Civility in American History*, edited by L. J. Friedman (Cambridge: Cambridge University Press, 2003), 29–48.

5. Alexis de Tocqueville, "On the Use Which the Americans Make of Associations in Civil Life," in *Democracy in America*, edited by Alexis de Tocqueville, vol. 2 (New York: Doubleday/Anchor, 1969), 513.

6. B. A. Weisbrod, *The Voluntary Nonprofit Sector: An Economic Analysis* (Lexington, MA: Lexington, 1977).

7. Eric Foner, *Forever Free: The Story of Emancipation and Reconstruction* (New York: Knopf, 2005).

8. L. Coser, *The Functions of Social Conflict* (Glencoe, IL: The Free Press, 1956).

9. B. Lanker and M. W. Edelman, *I Dream a World: Portraits of Black Women Who Changed America* (New York: Stewart, Tabori, and Chang, 1989), 121.

10. Peter Drucker, *The Age of Social Transformation* (Glencoe, IL: The Free Press, 1994).

CHAPTER 5

The Impact of the Voluntary Sector on Society

David Horton Smith

Originally published as "Impact of Voluntary Sector on Society," in *Voluntary Action Research*, edited Lexington Books, 1973). Reprinted with the permission of the author.

Having now looked at a few facets of the impact of voluntary action from the level of the individual up to the level of social movements, let us take a final step up to the highest currently applicable level of impact of voluntarism—on society as a whole. In looking at impact on all of the previous system levels, it is all too easy to get lost among the "trees," thus losing sight of the "forest." In our view, the forest is the larger context of social meaning that voluntary action has in human society. By *social* we mean to include all aspects of social structure and culture here, and by society we mean to include not just American society or any other particular society but all of mankind, past, present, and (hopefully) future.

The *voluntary sector* refers to all those persons, groups, roles, organizations, and institutions in society whose goals involve primarily voluntary action. Roughly speaking, it includes what one is neither made to nor paid to do but rather what one does out of some kind of expectation of psychic benefits or commitment to some value, ideal, or common interest. The voluntary sector may be roughly delineated in

a negative way by contrasting it with the commercial or business sector (sometimes called the private sector) and with the government or public sector. Another way of describing the voluntary sector is by saying that it is the total persisting social embodiment (in the form of norms, expectations, customs, and ways of behaving) of voluntary action in society.

Our question here is, simply, What impact does the voluntary sector as a whole have on society? There is not sufficient research information to permit one to do an aggregate analysis, building up a picture of the whole by systematically combining the parts—the kinds of impacts of voluntary action at different system levels we have been examining in part in prior chapters [of *Voluntary Action Research*]. Instead, we can only do the very sketchiest global analysis based on a loose inductive logic and general theoretical considerations. In making this very brief and simplistic analysis, we are again more interested in suggesting some lines of possible future research and theory than in being exhaustive or thorough.

Another way of looking at what we are calling the impacts of the voluntary sector is to see

DOI: 10.4324/9780367696559-7

the processes behind these impacts and to term them the "functions" or "roles" of the voluntary sector. These processes are not necessary features of the voluntary sector in any given nation, let alone in all nations. But they do represent what the voluntary sector can do and often has done in the past in particular societies at particular times. This is an attempt to help delineate more clearly why there is a voluntary sector in society, much as one might elsewhere discuss the role of government institutions or business or even the family in society. Like all of the latter, of course, the role of the voluntary sector changes over time in a given society and even in human society as a whole. The impacts of the voluntary sector we discuss briefly below are suggested as very general aspects of the voluntary sector in human society, and, hence, they are present to at least some degree as long as there is a voluntary sector.

First, one of the most central impacts of the voluntary sector is to provide society with a large variety of partially tested social innovations, from which business, government, and other institutions can select and institutionalize those innovations that seem most promising. The independent voluntary sector is thus the prototyping test bed of many, perhaps most, new social forms and modes of human relations. Where business and government, science and technology are active in the creation and testing of technological innovations, the independent voluntary sector specializes in the practical testing of social ideas. Nearly every function currently performed by governments at various levels was once a new social idea and the experiment of some voluntary group, formal or informal; this is true of education, welfare, care for the aged, building roads, and even fighting wars (volunteer citizen militias).

In sum, the voluntary sector has tended to provide the social risk capital of human society. It has been sufficiently free of the kinds of constraints that bind business (the constant need to show a profit) and government (the need to

maintain control and, in societies with effective democracies, the need to act in accord with a broad consensus) so that its component elements (particular voluntary groups or even individuals) can act simply out of commitment to some value or idea without needing to wait until the payoffs for that kind of activity can be justified in terms appropriate to mobilizing economic or governmental institutions. It is thus the most "error-embracing" and experimental component of society (see Smith with Dixon 1973).

Second, another central impact of the voluntary sector on society has been the provision of countervailing definitions of reality and morality: ideologies, perspectives, and worldviews that frequently challenge the prevailing assumptions about what exists and what is good and what should be done in society. The voluntary sector is that part of society that, collectively, is most likely to say that "the emperor has no clothes." Voluntary groups of various kinds are distinctive among human groups in the extent to which they develop their own ideologies and value systems. If these definitions of reality and morality are sufficiently compelling to people, voluntary groups grow into huge social movements and can change the course of history, both within a given nation (e.g., the abolitionist movement in the early and middle nineteenth century of the United States) and across human society as a whole (e.g., Christianity, Buddhism, democracy, communism).

This kind of impact of the voluntary sector is related to the previous one, but where the former kind of impact emphasized experimentation with social innovation in practice, the present impact emphasizes instead ideological and moral innovation. Where the previous point focused on the social risk capital role of the voluntary sector in society, the present point focuses on the role of the voluntary sector as a gadfly, dreamer, and moral leader in society. Voluntary groups of various kinds are concerned with the generation and allocation of human commitment in the deepest sense. In the process of doing this, the voluntary sector as a whole provides moral and ideological leadership to the majority of human society and often calls into question the existing legitimacy structures and accepted social definitions of reality of particular societies.

A third major impact of the voluntary sector on society is to provide the play element in society, especially as the search for novelty, beauty, recreation, and fun for their own sake may be collectively organized. Again, because the voluntary sector is not constrained generally by such values as profit, control, and broad social consensus, voluntary groups can form in terms of literally thousands of different kinds of common interests. A full array of common interest groups (especially expressive rather than instrumental ones) in an elaborated but still evolving voluntary sector permits (in principle) nearly all individuals to find at least one group that will be satisfying to them. If there is no such group, one or more individuals may form one, if they wish, to reflect their own needs and vision of the play element. Such a group may be formal or informal, large or small, permanent or transient, open or closed, and so forth.

To speak of the play element here is not to speak of something trivial and unimportant. As society becomes increasingly complex and work activity is increasingly structured in terms of large bureaucracies, people's unsatisfied needs for play, novelty, new experience, and all manner of recreation tend to increase. The kind of easy interchange and blending of play and work that could be present in more traditional economies tends to be lost. Under such circumstances, voluntary groups often provide a window of variety and intrinsic satisfaction in an otherwise rather boring or at least psychically fatiguing world of work and responsibility.

Fourth, the voluntary sector also has a major impact on the level of social integration in society. Partly through directly expressive groups, whose aims are explicitly to provide fellowship, sociability, and mutual companionship, and partly through the sociability aspects of all other kinds of collective and interpersonal forms of voluntary action, the voluntary sector helps in a very basic way to satisfy some of the human needs for affiliation, approval, and so on. In advanced industrial and urbanized societies, where the family and kinship as well as the local community and neighborhood play a markedly reduced role in providing social integration, affiliations based on common interests can become very important to the individual. Indeed, without the latter kind of voluntary, sector-based, common-interest affiliations, the resulting rates of individual social isolation in society would lead to even more anomie, alienation, and a variety of attendant social and psychological problems than are now the case. Obviously, the voluntary sector has not been the whole solution to the root problem of social isolation in modern society, yet voluntary groups do play a demonstrable and important part in the solution. And with the feeling of being accepted as a person that the voluntary sector provides (or can provide) to a significant proportion of the population in modern societies goes the correlative provision of positive affect, a major component of human happiness and the quality of human life.

Another aspect of the role of the voluntary sector in providing social integration is the social adjustment "buffering" function that many kinds of voluntary groups provide. When numerous individuals of a certain social and cultural background are for some reason uprooted from their customary societal niches, new voluntary groups frequently emerge to provide these individuals with an insulated or "buffered" special environment for part of their time. Typical examples would be the numerous immigrant associations that sprang up in the United States as a result of successive waves of immigration from various countries (Handlin 1951) or the kinship-oriented voluntary associations that emerged to ease the adjustment of rural West Africans to life in large cities (Little 1965).

These kinds of social adjustment–oriented voluntary groups do not, however, emerge only in the case of physical/geographical changes on a large scale. The voluntary sector also provides a social adjustment mechanism to ease the shocks of social dislocations and rapid social changes of all sorts. The voluntary groups involved may cater to a former elite that has been disenfranchised or deprived of its former holdings (e.g., the association of maharajahs of India, which arose to fight for "maharajahs rights" when the Indian Congress stripped them of their traditional privileges and land, substituting a moderate annual stipend). Or the voluntary groups involved may represent a deprived category of persons who are attempting to adjust to changed social conditions that are more conducive to their sharing equitably in the good life as lived in their society (e.g., the early labor unions or black power groups, striving for recognition of their right to exist and to fight for the betterment of the conditions of their constituencies).

On another level, the voluntary sector plays an important integrative role by linking together individuals, groups, institutions and even nations that otherwise would be in greater conflict, or at least competition, with each other. (This and other impacts of voluntary groups are discussed further in Smith 1966.) At the community level, a variety of voluntary associations will each tend to have as members a set of two or more individuals representing differing and often opposing political, religious, cultural, or social perspectives and backgrounds. The coparticipation of this set of individuals in the same voluntary association can have significant moderating effects on the relationships among these individuals. Similar integrative effects can be found at national levels, where several groups from different parts of the country and/or different social and cultural perspectives participate together in a common federation or other national voluntary organization. And at the international level, the joint participation of voluntary groups from otherwise conflicting nations in some transnational federative organization may well have important long-range effects on the relations between the countries involved and on the possibilities of peace in the world.

A fifth kind of general impact of the voluntary sector involves the opposite of the first one, which dealt with the social innovation role of voluntarism. In addition to providing a wide variety of *new* ideas about social behavior, the voluntary sector also is active in preserving numerous old ideas. Voluntary action and voluntary organizations have played a major role in history in preserving values, ways of life, ideas, beliefs, artifacts, and other productions of the mind, heart, and hand of man from earlier times so that this great variety of human culture is not lost to future generations. For example, there are in the United States numerous local historical societies that specialize in preserving the history of particular towns and areas. There are nonprofit voluntary organizations that run local museums, libraries, and historical sites. And there are a number of voluntary organizations whose primary function is to preserve the values of cultures or subcultures that no longer have any substantial power or importance in American society but that nevertheless represent a way of life of significant numbers of people at some period in history or somewhere around the world (e.g., American Indian groups, in some instances, or immigrant ethnic associations that persist long after the ethnic group involved has been thoroughly assimilated into American culture). The role of municipal, state, and national governments in supporting museums and historical sites grows from the roots of earlier nonprofit, nongovernmental support of such "islands of culture."

Another aspect of the belief/value preservation role of the voluntary sector involves voluntary associations as educational experiences, especially where these associations are attempting to pass on to their members or to the public at large some body of beliefs and values originating in the past. In part this would include many of the activities of most religious sects and denominations, especially insofar as one focuses on their socialization and indoctrination activities (e.g., catechism classes, "Sunday schools," Hebrew day schools, etc.). In part this function also includes all manner of more strictly educational voluntary organizations, from Plato's Academy (see Peterson and Peterson 1973) to modern Great Books Discussion Groups and so-called "Free Universities."

The various levels of government in the contemporary world have largely taken over the task of education on a broad scale, yet voluntary organizations still are active in supplementing government-run educational systems by filling in the gaps and by prodding these systems to improve or take on responsibility for the preservation of additional knowledge or values. For instance, voluntary civil rights and black liberation organizations have taken the lead in educating both blacks and whites in the United States regarding black history and accomplishments. Gradually, under the pressure of such voluntary associations in the past several years, the public educational system in the United States has been changing to accommodate a more accurate and complete picture of black history, although the process is by no means finished yet. Similar examples could be given with regard to other content areas as well (e.g., women's history, American Indian history, etc.).

A sixth major impact of the voluntary sector is its embodiment and representation in society of the sense of mystery, wonder, and the sacred. Neither the business nor government sectors in modern society have much tendency to be concerned with such matters. Many would say that religion today is very much a big business, and both business and government support science in a substantial way. Yet precisely in those areas where religion and science almost meet, where the borders of religion are receding under the pressure of an ever-expanding science, the business and government sectors are often least

involved. Voluntary associations and nonprofit foundations/research organizations are the only groups experimenting seriously with new forms of worship, non-drug-induced "consciousness expansion" and the "religious experience," the occult, investigation of flying saucers, extrasensory perception, etc.

The "heretics" of both science and religion are seldom supported in their work directly and consciously by the business or government sectors. Only through voluntary action and the support of the voluntary sector have the major changes in man's view of the supernatural and its relation to the natural tended to come about in the past. The same has also been true, by and large, for major changes in man's view of himself and of the natural universe in the past. The dominant economic and political (and religious) systems of any given epoch are seldom very receptive to the really new visions of either the natural or supernatural world (e.g., Galileo and Copernicus, Jesus). Voluntary action is thus the principal manner in which a sense of the sacred, the mysterious, and the weird can be preserved and permitted some measure of expression in our otherwise hyper-rational contemporary society.

A seventh impact of the voluntary sector results from its ability to liberate the individual and permit him or her the fullest possible measure of expression of personal capacities and potentialities within an otherwise constraining social environment. All societies have their systems of laws, customs, roles, and organizations that box people in and limit their opportunities for personal expression and personal development. The full extent of societal limitations on people has just begun to be realized in recent decades, spurred in part by the "liberation" movements of women, blacks, the poor, the "Third World," and other disadvantaged or disenfranchised groups. The primary embodiments of these societal barriers and boxes have generally been the economic and governmental systems, although other major institutions of society have played a role as well (e.g., education, the family, religion, etc.).

Voluntary associations and groups, on the other hand, have long been a primary means of at least partially escaping these barriers and boxes. Through participation in voluntary action, a wide variety of people have been able to find or create special social groups that would permit them to grow as individuals. This kind of personal growth has many relevant aspects but can be summed up generally as "self-actualization," to use a term from Maslow (1954). For some this means intellectual development, the process of becoming increasingly analytical, informed, and self-conscious about the nature of one's life situation and problems. When this occurs for a whole category or group of people, the process is often referred to as "group conscienticization" or "consciousness raising" (e.g., among blacks, women, the poor). Seldom does such special personal growth occur on a broad scale outside voluntary groups and movements.

For others, self-actualization through voluntary action takes the form of developing otherwise unused capacities, talents, skills, or potentials of a more active and practical sort. For many kinds of people, depending on the stage of social, economic, and political development of a society, voluntary associations and voluntary action offer the only feasible opportunity for leadership, for learning to speak in public, for practicing the fine art of management, for exercising analytical judgment, etc. Until very recently in American society, for instance, neither blacks nor women nor the members of certain other disadvantaged groups could hope to develop fully their capacities through the occupational system of the economic or government sectors. Only in voluntary groups of their own making could they seek any kind of fulfillment and self-expression, bound as they were (and in part continue to be) by the prejudices and discrimination of the dominant white, male, Anglo-Saxon Protestants in our

society. However, this situation is not unique to the United States. There are similar and even different forms of prejudice and discrimination in all other societies, varying only in degree and the particular social groups singled out for attention. And in all societies voluntary associations also offer the disadvantaged some chance of enhanced self-development, though these associations must sometimes meet in secret as underground groups if the society in which they are operating is oppressive and does not respect the right of free association.

Voluntary action potentially offers unique opportunities for personal growth and realization of personal potentials not only for those people whom society otherwise deprives but also for all the members of society in certain directions. No matter how free, open, egalitarian, and highly developed the society, there are always limitations of some sort placed on the development of each person by his particular social environment. Any major decision to follow a certain line of personal, occupational, or educational development, for instance, automatically forecloses a number of other alternatives, or at least makes them highly unlikely. Voluntary associations, however, exist (or can exist) in such profusion and variety that they can provide otherwise missed personal development opportunities to almost any person at almost any stage of life. This is as true for the school teacher who always wanted to learn to fly (and who can join a flying club to do so even at age 60), as it is for the airline pilot who always wanted to write novels (and who can join a writer's club to work toward this end).

Of course, not every person will find the appropriate voluntary association for his or her personal growth needs to be available at the time it is needed. But the voluntary sector as a whole, nevertheless, still serves in some significant degree this general role of providing substantial numbers of individuals in society with otherwise unavailable opportunities for self-actualization and self-fulfillment.

An eighth major impact of the voluntary sector in society is one of overriding importance, relating directly to the first and second impacts discussed above. We are referring to the impact of the voluntary sector as a source of "negative feedback" for society as a whole, especially with regard to the directions taken by the major institutions of society such as government and business. Without "negative feedback," any system is dangerously vulnerable to destroying itself through excesses in one direction or another. Thus, however uncomfortable and irritating they may be at times, voluntary associations and the voluntary sector are absolutely vital to the continuing development of a society.

This systemic corrective role of the voluntary sector is, of course, not carried out by all voluntary associations, any more than all voluntary associations are concerned with the play element, value preservation, or the sacred. Yet the small cutting edge of the voluntary sector that does perform the role of social critic is extremely important, usually bearing the responsibility for the continued existence and future growth of the rest of the voluntary sector. In societies where a sufficient number and variety of voluntary groups are unable to play effectively their roles as social critics, the dominant governmental and economic institutions may well take over and suppress the entire voluntary sector (e.g., Allen 1965).

In the contemporary United States there are numerous examples of voluntary associations and groups playing this systemic corrective role. All of the cause-oriented, advocacy, and issue-oriented groups tend to fall into this category, from the environmental movement to the civil rights movement and women's liberation. The tactics and strategies of such groups cover a broad range, from rather traditional lobbying through demonstrations and "be-ins" to direct remedial action such as "ecotage" (sabotage of notable corporate polluters and other "environmental undesirables").

Some of the more imaginative and innovative approaches have been developed in an attempt to modify the business sector rather than focusing solely on the government sector. For instance, there have been in-depth investigations by Ralph Nader and his associates of particular companies' practices and their relationship to the public interest (e.g., for First National City Bank of New York and for DuPont), counter-management stockholder activity in the public interest (e.g., Project G.M.), dissenting annual reports written to present a full public accounting of a corporation's activities harmful to the general public interest and welfare, class action suits brought by voluntary groups against manufacturers and developers, etc.

When looked at in the particular, such activities (which vary markedly in their success) often seem fruitless and doomed to failure given the power of the organizations and systems being challenged. Yet when we see these activities of voluntary groups in a larger context, when we sum up these numerous activities attempting to modify and improve the dominant systems and organizations of our society, they take on a very important general meaning. Even if many or most of such system-correction attempts by voluntary groups should fail, the continual and expanding pressure being brought to bear by the voluntary sector on the central institutions of society is still likely to have a salutary long-term modifying influence. When the leaders of the business and governmental sectors know that "someone is watching," that they will eventually have to account to the public interest for their actions, this awareness encourages greater attention to the public interest rather than merely to narrow, private interests.

When for one reason or another the voluntary sector is not able to operate effectively as a systemic corrective (either because of its own inadequacies or the failure of the leaders of dominant institutions to listen and change accordingly), the usual result in human history has been a broad social revolution (not just a palace revolution or simple coup). When the dominant institutions of any society have ignored for too long or too often the voices of the public interest as expressed by elements of the voluntary sector, revolutionary and usually underground voluntary groups arise and make concrete plans to overthrow the existing system completely. The American, French, Russian, Chinese, Cuban, and other revolutions all attest to this pattern.

Thus, when the voluntary sector cannot make itself heard adequately through the permissible communication and influence channels in a society, certain voluntary groups and movements tend to arise to revamp the whole system, establishing whole new institutional arrangements with their corresponding new channels of influence and communication. Not surprisingly, these new channels generally favor those kinds of persons and groups who were unable to be heard previously (although the kinds of people formerly dominant often end up in as bad a position or worse than that faced by the formerly disadvantaged prior to the revolution). This cycle will tend to repeat itself until a society reaches a point where it is effectively and continuously self-correcting through the activities of a strong and social change-oriented voluntary sector and where its major institutions are basically operating primarily in the public interest of all of its citizens (not just its white, male, Anglo-Saxon Protestants, or their equivalents in some other societies than the United States and the British Commonwealth).

The ninth major impact of the voluntary sector worth mentioning here is the support given by the voluntary sector specifically to the economic system of a society, especially a modern industrial society. Voluntary associations of many kinds provide crucial kinds of social, intellectual, and technical linkages among workers in numerous occupations: Professional associations increase the effectiveness of most kinds of scientists, engineers, technicians, etc., just as manufacturers' and trade associations support the growth of whole industries. And various kinds of labor unions play their part as well, although many businessmen would question the degree to which they "support" the economic system. But labor unions only seem nonsupportive of the economic system when the latter is viewed narrowly from the point of view of an employer interested solely in profit maximization. Labor unions ultimately have to be deeply concerned with the viability of the economic system and the productivity of their own members if they are to survive.

This economic support role of the voluntary sector is usually lost sight of because so many people tend to view all kinds of economic self-interest and occupationally related voluntary associations as integral parts of the business sector. In fact, these kinds of voluntary organizations are quite distinct from the business sector itself, however close their relationship might be to business corporations and occupational activities. The primary purpose of business corporations is to make a profit for their owners, whether they are actually involved in running the corporation or not. On the other hand, economic self-interest voluntary associations have as their primary purpose the enhancement of the long-term occupational and economic interests of their member-participants. While corporation employees and professionals are paid in salaries, wages, or fees for their participation, the members of economic self-interest voluntary associations themselves pay for the privilege of belonging to and benefiting from these associations.

The tenth major impact of the voluntary sector we shall note is a rather subtle one: The voluntary sector constitutes an important latent resource for all kinds of goal attainment in the interests of the society as a whole. Put another way, the voluntary sector represents a tremendous reservoir of potential energy that can be mobilized under appropriate circumstances for broad societal goals. The role of the voluntary sector in revolutionary situations is but one example of this latent potential. The activity of voluntary association networks in more limited disaster situations is a more common example (Barton 1970). The voluntary sector and its component associations, groups, and channels of communication and influence make possible the mobilization of large numbers of people on relatively short notice for special purposes (usually in the common interest) without resorting to economic rewards or legal coercion as activating forces. Such a latent potential in the voluntary sector is especially important when neither economic nor political-legal forces can feasibly be brought to bear to resolve some widespread problem situation.

The latent potential of the voluntary sector can be viewed in another way as well. Voluntarism is based on a charitable grants economy (donations of time, money, etc.) as contrasted with the coercive grants economy (taxation) on which the government sector operates or the market economy on which the business sector operates. Both of the latter types of economy work well for certain kinds of purposes, but neither works well for the accomplishment of all kinds of purposes in society. In the same way, there are many kinds of purposes and activities (several of which are implicit in the nine major impacts of the voluntary sector reviewed above) for which the charitable grants economy tends to work best.

Now the important latent potential of the voluntary sector is that, under appropriately compelling circumstances (i.e., for the "right" value, goal, or ideal), the money, goods, real property, and services mobilized by the voluntary sector through the charitable grants economy can completely overwhelm all considerations of the coercive grants economy and the market economy. For certain goals and ideals, a large majority of society can be induced to "give their all" and to do so gladly, willingly, and voluntarily. This does not occur very often, to be sure, nor does it last very long. But the latent potential is there in any society at any time. With the right spark—usually a charismatic

leader with an idea and an ideal—the course of history can be changed in these brief, rare periods of almost total societal mobilization through the leadership of the voluntary sector.

The Negative Side

In describing the foregoing ten types of impact that the voluntary sector tends to have in some degree in any society, we have emphasized the positive contributions that voluntary action makes to society. However, as with any form of human group or activity, voluntary action and the voluntary sector are by no means always positive in their impacts. For every one of the ten types of impact we have noted, there can be negative consequences in certain circumstances and with regard to certain values. Thus, when voluntary associations experiment with new social forms, the failures can often be harmful to specific people and organizations. When alternative definitions of reality and morality are offered, these can be evil, as in the case of Nazi Germany and its ideology as generated by the Nazi party, a voluntary association. When voluntary groups focus on the play element, their fun can become mischievous, as in the case of a boys' gang that wrecks a school "just for kicks." When social clubs provide a warm and close sense of belonging to their members, they can also create deep dissatisfaction in people who would dearly like to belong but are excluded from a particular club or kind of club.

In the same way, voluntary groups striving to preserve some beliefs or values from the past may be holding on to anachronisms that would be better left to the pages of history books. Clubs whose members chase around seeking flying saucers and little green men from Mars might more profitably spend their time and energy elsewhere with more satisfying results. Organizations that arouse the full potentials of black people—who must then go out into the real world and face a harsh reality of bigotry and discrimination—may or may not be doing them a favor. The kinds of systemic corrections being suggested by cause-oriented and advocacy groups may not be conducive to the greatest good of the greatest number. Economic self-interest voluntary groups often tend to ignore the public interest in favor of an exclusive and selfish private interest. And the latent potentials of the voluntary sector can be mobilized to do evil as well as to do good for one's fellow man.

References

Allen, William Sheridan. 1965. *The Nazi Seizure of Power*. Chicago: Quadrangle Books.

Barton, Allen H. 1970. *Communities in Disaster*. Garden City, NY: Anchor Books, Doubleday and Company.

Handlin, Oscar. 1951. *The Uprooted*. New York: Grosset and Dunlap.

Little, Kenneth. 1965. *West African Urbanization: A Study of Voluntary Associations in Social Change*. Cambridge, England: Cambridge University Press.

Maslow, Abraham H. 1954. *Motivation and Personality* New York: Harper and Row.

Peterson, Sophia, and Virgil Peterson. 1973. "Voluntary Associations in Ancient Greece." *Journal of Voluntary Action Research* 2, no. 1: 2–16.

Smith, David Horton. 1966. "The Importance of Formal Voluntary Organizations for Society." *Sociology and Social Research* 50: 483–492.

Smith, David Horton, with John Dixon. 1973. "The Voluntary Sector." Chapter 7 in Edward Bursk, ed., *Challenge to Leadership: Managing in a Changing World*. New York: The Free Press, Macmillan and Co.

CHAPTER 6

The Gospel of Wealth

Andrew Carnegie

Andrew Carnegie, "The Gospel of Wealth" (published originally as "Wealth"), *North American Review* 147 (June 1889): 653–664, and 149 (December 1889): 682–698.

The problem of our age is the proper administration of wealth, so that the ties of brotherhood may still bind together the rich and poor in harmonious relationship. The conditions of human life have not only been changed, but revolutionized, within the past few hundred years. In former days there was little difference between the dwelling, dress, food, and environment of the chief and those of his retainers. The Indians are to-day where civilized man then was. When visiting the Sioux, I was led to the wigwam of the chief. It was just like the others in external appearance, and even within the difference was trifling between it and those of the poorest of his braves. The contrast between the palace of the millionaire and the cottage of the laborer with us to-day measures the change which has come with civilization.

This change, however, is not to be deplored, but welcomed as highly beneficial. It is well, nay, essential for the progress of the race, that the houses of some should be homes for all that is highest and best in literature and the arts, and for all the refinements of civilization, rather than that none should be so. Much better this great irregularity than universal squalor. Without wealth there can be no Maecenas. The "good old times" were not good old times. Neither master nor servant was as well situated then as to-day. A relapse to old conditions would be disastrous to both—not the least so to him who serves—and would sweep away civilization with it. But whether the change be for good or ill, it is upon us, beyond our power to alter, and therefore to be accepted and made the best of. It is a waste of time to criticise the inevitable.

To-day the world obtains commodities of excellent quality at prices which even the generation preceding this would have deemed incredible. In the commercial world similar causes have produced similar results, and the race is benefited thereby. The poor enjoy what the rich could not before afford. What were the luxuries have become the necessaries of life. The laborer has now more comforts than the farmer had a few generations ago. The farmer has more luxuries than the landlord had, and is more richly clad and better housed. The landlord has books and pictures rarer, and appointments more artistic, than the King could then obtain.

The price we pay for this salutary change is, no doubt, great. We assemble thousands of operatives in the factory, in the mine, and in the counting-house, of whom the employer can know little or nothing, and to whom the employer is little better than a myth. All

DOI: 10.4324/9780367696559-8

intercourse between them is at an end. Rigid Castes are formed, and, as usual, mutual ignorance breeds mutual distrust. Each Caste is without sympathy for the other, and ready to credit anything disparaging in regard to it. Under the law of competition, the employer of thousands is forced into the strictest economies, among which the rates paid to labor figure prominently, and often there is friction between the employer and the employed, between capital and labor, between rich and poor. Human society loses homogeneity.

The price which society pays for the law of competition, like the price it pays for cheap comforts and luxuries, is also great; but the advantages of this law are also greater still, for it is to this law that we owe our wonderful material development, which brings improved conditions in its train. But, whether the law be benign or not, we must say of it, as we say of the change in the conditions of men to which we have referred: It is here; we cannot evade it; no substitutes for it have been found; and while the law may be sometimes hard for the individual, it is best for the race, because it insures the survival of the fittest in every department. Having accepted these, it follows that there must be great scope for the exercise of special ability in the merchant and in the manufacturer who has to conduct affairs upon a great scale. That this talent for organization and management is rare among men is proved by the fact that it invariably secures for its possessor enormous rewards, no matter where or under what laws or conditions. The experienced in affairs always rate the man whose services can be obtained as a partner as not only the first consideration, but such as to render the question of his capital scarcely worth considering, for such men soon create capital; while, without the special talent required, capital soon takes wings. Such men become interested in firms or corporations using millions; and estimating only simple interest to be made upon the capital invested, it is inevitable that their income must exceed their expenditures, and that they

must accumulate wealth. It is a law, as certain as any of the others named, that men possessed of this peculiar talent for affairs, under the free play of economic forces, must, of necessity, soon be in receipt of more revenue than can be judiciously expended upon themselves; and this law is as beneficial for the race as the others.

Objections to the foundations upon which society is based are not in order, because the condition of the race is better with these than it has been with any others which have been tried. Of the effect of any new substitutes proposed we cannot be sure. The Socialist or Anarchist who seeks to overturn present conditions is to be regarded as attacking the foundation upon which civilization itself rests, for civilization took its start from the day that the capable, industrious workman said to his incompetent and lazy fellow, "If thou dost not sow, thou shalt not reap," and thus ended primitive Communism by separating the drones from the bees. One who studies this subject will soon be brought face to face with the conclusion that upon the sacredness of property civilization itself depends—the right of the laborer to his hundred dollars in the savings bank, and equally the legal right of the millionaire to his millions. To those who propose to substitute Communism for this intense Individualism the answer, therefore, is: The race has tried that. All progress from that barbarous day to the present time has resulted from its displacement. Not evil, but good, has come to the race from the accumulation of wealth by those who have the ability and energy that produce it. But even if we admit for a moment that it might be better for the race to discard its present foundation, Individualism,—that it is a nobler ideal that man should labor, not for himself alone, but in and for a brotherhood of his fellows, and share with them all in common, realizing Swedenborg's idea of Heaven, where, as he says, the angels derive their happiness, not from laboring for self, but for each other,—even admit all this, and a sufficient answer is, This is not evolution, but revolution. It necessitates the changing of human nature itself—a work of aeons, even if it were good to change it, which we cannot know. We might as well urge the destruction of the highest existing type of man because he failed to reach our ideal as to favor the destruction of Individualism, Private Property, the Law of Accumulation of Wealth, and the Law of Competition; for these are the highest results of human experience, the soil in which society so far has produced the best fruit.

We start, then, with a condition of affairs under which the best interests of the race are promoted, but which inevitably gives wealth to the few. Thus far, accepting conditions as they exist, the situation can be surveyed and pronounced good. The question then arises,—and, if the foregoing be correct, it is the only question with which we have to deal,—What is the proper mode of administering wealth after the laws upon which civilization is founded have thrown it into the hands of the few? And it is of this great question that I believe I offer the true solution. It will be understood that *fortunes* are here spoken of, not moderate sums saved by many years of effort, the returns from which are required for the comfortable maintenance and education of families. This is not wealth, but only competence, which it should be the aim of all to acquire.

There are but three modes in which surplus wealth can be disposed of. It can be left to the families of the decedents; or it can be bequeathed for public purposes; or, finally, it can be administered during their lives by its possessors. Under the first and second modes most of the wealth of the world that has reached the few has hitherto been applied. Let us in turn consider each of these modes. The first is the most injudicious. In monarchical countries, the estates and the greatest portion of the wealth are left to the first son, that the vanity of the parent may be gratified by the thought that his name and title are to descend to succeeding generations unimpaired. Even in Great Britain the strict law of entail has

been found inadequate to maintain the status of an hereditary class. Its soil is rapidly passing into the hands of the stranger. Under republican institutions the division of property among the children is much fairer, but the question which forces itself upon thoughtful men in all lands is: Why should men leave great fortunes to their children? If this is done from affection, is it not misguided affection? Observation teaches that, generally speaking, it is not well for the children that they should be so burdened. Neither is it well for the state. Beyond providing for the wife and daughters moderate sources of income, and very moderate allowances indeed, if any, for the sons, men may well hesitate, for it is no longer questionable that great sums bequeathed oftener work more for the injury than for the good of the recipients. Wise men will soon conclude that, for the best interests of the members of their families and of the state, such bequests are an improper use of their means.

It is not suggested that men who have failed to educate their sons to earn a livelihood shall cast them adrift in poverty. If any man has seen fit to rear his sons with a view to their living idle lives, or, what is highly commendable, has instilled in them the sentiment that they are in a position to labor for public ends without reference to pecuniary considerations, then, of course, the duty of the parent is to see that such are provided for in moderation. There are instances of millionaires' sons unspoiled by wealth, who, being rich, still perform great services in the community. Such are the very salt of the earth, as valuable as, unfortunately, they are rare; still it is not the exception, but the rule, that men must regard, and, looking at the usual result of enormous sums conferred upon legatees, the thoughtful man must shortly say, "I would as soon leave to my son a curse as the almighty dollar," and admit to himself that it is not the welfare of the children, but family pride, which inspires these enormous legacies.

As to the second mode, that of leaving wealth at death for public uses, it may be said that this is only a means for the disposal of wealth, provided a man is content to wait until he is dead before it becomes of much good in the world. Knowledge of the results of legacies bequeathed is not calculated to inspire the brightest hopes of much posthumous good being accomplished. The cases are not few in which the real object sought by the testator is not attained, nor are they few in which his real wishes are thwarted. In many cases the bequests are so used as to become only monuments of his folly. It is well to remember that it requires the exercise of not less ability than that which acquired the wealth to use it so as to be really beneficial to the community. Besides this, it may fairly be said that no man is to be extolled for doing what he cannot help doing, nor is he to be thanked by the community to which he only leaves wealth at death. Men who leave vast sums in this way may fairly be thought men who would not have left it at all, had they been able to take it with them. The memories of such cannot be held in grateful remembrance, for there is no grace in their gifts. It is not to be wondered at that such bequests seem so generally to lack the blessing.

The growing disposition to tax more and more heavily large estates left at death is a cheering indication of the growth of a salutary change in public opinion. Men who continue hoarding great sums all their lives, the proper use of which for public ends would work good to the community, should be made to feel that the community, in the form of the state, cannot thus be deprived of its proper share. By taxing estates heavily at death the state marks its condemnation of the selfish millionaire's unworthy life.

It is desirable that nations should go much further in this direction. Indeed, it is difficult to set bounds to the share of a rich man's estate which should go at his death to the public through the agency of the state, and by all means such taxes should be graduated, beginning at nothing upon moderate sums to dependents, and increasing rapidly as the amounts swell,

until of the millionaire's hoard, as of Shy-lock's, at least

> "—The other half Comes to the privy coffer of the state."

This policy would work powerfully to induce the rich man to attend to the administration of wealth during his life, which is the end that society should always have in view, as being that by far most fruitful for the people.

There remains, then, only one mode of using great fortunes; but in this we have the true antidote for the temporary unequal distribution of wealth, the reconciliation of the rich and the poor—a reign of harmony—another ideal, differing, indeed, from that of the Communist in requiring only the further evolution of existing conditions, not the total overthrow of our civilization. Even the poorest can be made to see this, and to agree that great sums gathered by some of their fellow-citizens and spent for public purposes, from which the masses reap the principal benefit, are more valuable to them than if scattered among them through the course of many years in trifling amounts.

If we consider what results flow from the Cooper Institute, for instance, to the best portion of the race in New York not possessed of means, and compare these with those which would have arisen for the good of the masses from an equal sum distributed by Mr. Cooper in his lifetime in the form of wages, which is the highest form of distribution, being for work done and not for charity, we can form some estimate of the possibilities for the improvement of the race which lie embedded in the present law of the accumulation of wealth. Let the advocate of violent or radical change ponder well this thought.

We might even go so far as to take another instance, that of Mr. Tilden's bequest of five millions of dollars for a free library in the city of New York, but in referring to this one cannot help saying involuntarily, How much better if

Mr. Tilden had devoted the last years of his own life to the proper administration of this immense sum; in which case neither legal contest nor any other cause of delay could have interfered with his aims. But let us assume that Mr. Tilden's millions finally become the means of giving to this city a noble public library, where the treasures of the world contained in books will be open to all forever, without money and without price. Considering the good of that part of the race which congregates in and around Manhattan Island, would its permanent benefit have been better promoted had these millions been allowed to circulate in small sums through the hands of the masses? Even the most strenuous advocate of Communism must entertain a doubt upon this subject. Most of those who think will probably entertain no doubt whatever.

Poor and restricted are our opportunities in this life; narrow our horizon; our best work most imperfect; but rich men should be thankful for one inestimable boon. They have it in their power during their lives to busy themselves in organizing benefactions from which the masses of their fellows will derive lasting advantage, and thus dignify their own lives. The highest life is probably to be reached, not by such imitation of the life of Christ as Count Tolstoï gives us, but, while animated by Christ's spirit, by recognizing the changed conditions of this age, and adopting modes of expressing this spirit suitable to the changed conditions under which we live; still laboring for the good of our fellows, which was the essence of his life and teaching, but laboring in a different manner.

This, then, is held to be the duty of the man of Wealth: First, to set an example of modest, unostentatious living, shunning display or extravagance; to provide moderately for the legitimate wants of those dependent upon him; and after doing so to consider all surplus revenues which come to him simply as trust funds, which he is called upon to administer, and strictly bound as a matter of duty to administer in the manner which, in his judgment, is best calculated to produce the most beneficial results for the community—the man of wealth thus becoming the mere agent and trustee for his poorer brethren, bringing to their service his superior wisdom, experience, and ability to administer, doing for them better than they would or could do for themselves.

The best uses to which surplus wealth can be put have already been indicated. Those who would administer wisely must, indeed, be wise, for one of the serious obstacles to the improvement of our race is indiscriminate charity. It were better for mankind that the millions of the rich were thrown into the sea than so spent as to encourage the slothful, the drunken, the unworthy. Of every thousand dollars spent in so called charity to-day, it is probable that $950 is unwisely spent; so spent, indeed, as to produce the very evils which it proposes to mitigate or cure. A well-known writer of philosophic books admitted the other day that he had given a quarter of a dollar to a man who approached him as he was coming to visit the house of his friend. He knew nothing of the habits of this beggar; knew not the use that would be made of this money, although he had every reason to suspect that it would be spent improperly. This man professed to be a disciple of Herbert Spencer; yet the quarter-dollar given that night will probably work more injury than all the money which its thoughtless donor will ever be able to give in true charity will do good. He only gratified his own feelings, saved himself from annoyance,—and this was probably one of the most selfish and very worst actions of his life, for in all respects he is most worthy.

In bestowing charity, the main consideration should be to help those who will help themselves; to provide part of the means by which those who desire to improve may do so; to give those who desire to rise the aids by which they may rise; to assist, but rarely or never to do all. Neither the individual nor the race is improved by alms-giving. Those worthy of assistance, except in rare cases, seldom require assistance.

The really valuable men of the race never do, except in cases of accident or sudden change. Every one has, of course, cases of individuals brought to his own knowledge where temporary assistance can do genuine good, and these he will not overlook. But the amount which can be wisely given by the individual for individuals is necessarily limited by his lack of knowledge of the circumstances connected with each. He is the only true reformer who is as careful and as anxious not to aid the unworthy as he is to aid the worthy, and, perhaps, even more so, for in alms-giving more injury is probably done by rewarding vice than by relieving virtue.

The rich man is thus almost restricted to following the examples of Peter Cooper, Enoch Pratt of Baltimore, Mr. Pratt of Brooklyn, Senator Stanford, and others, who know that the best means of benefiting the community is to place within its reach the ladders upon which the aspiring can rise—parks, and means of recreation, by which men are helped in body and mind; works of art, certain to give pleasure and improve the public taste, and public institutions of various kinds, which will improve the general condition of the people;—in this manner returning their surplus wealth to the mass of their fellows in the forms best calculated to do them lasting good.

Thus is the problem of Rich and Poor to be solved. The laws of accumulation will be left free; the laws of distribution free. Individualism will continue, but the millionaire will be but a trustee for the poor; intrusted for a season with a great part of the increased wealth of the community, but administering it for the community far better than it could or would have done for itself. The best minds will thus have reached a stage in the development of the race in which it is clearly seen that there is no mode of disposing of surplus wealth creditable to thoughtful and earnest men into whose hands it flows save by using it year by year for the general good. This day already dawns. But a little while, and although, without incurring the pity of their fellows, men may die sharers in great business enterprises from which their capital cannot be or has not been withdrawn, and is left chiefly at death for public uses, yet the man who dies leaving behind him millions of available wealth, which was his to administer during life, will pass away "unwept, unhonored, and unsung," no matter to what uses he leaves the dross which he cannot take with him. Of such as these the public verdict will then be: "The man who dies thus rich dies disgraced."

Such, in my opinion, is the true Gospel concerning Wealth, obedience to which is destined some day to solve the problem of the Rich and the Poor, and to bring "Peace on earth, among men Good-Will."

CHAPTER 7

Critical Perspectives on the History and Development of the Nonprofit Sector in the United States

BILLIE SANDBERG

Sandberg, Billie, "Critical Perspectives on the History and Development of the Nonprofit Sector in the United States. In *Reframing Nonprofit Organizations: Democracy, Inclusion, and Social Change*, eds. Angela M. Eikenberry, Roseanne M. Mirabella, and Billie Sandberg (Irvine, Calif.: Melvin & Leigh, 2019) 26–37.

The focus of this chapter is the history and development of one country's non-profit and voluntary sector: that of the United States. As John Casey (2016) recently noted, "each country is unique, subject to the path dependency generated [in part] by its [own] historical baggage [and] by contemporary institutional transformations" (132). If the nonprofit or voluntary sector of another country is of interest to students, I encourage the application of the critical frame posed in this chapter to the contemporary understanding of the nonprofit or voluntary sector in that country, and its history.

Traditional histories of the American non-profit sector generally provide an accounting of the evolution of the sector by detailing its development from the establishment of voluntary associations in colonial times, to the rapidly growing sector American students know today. This chapter does not present a traditional history of the American nonprofit sector, but rather a critical one. The events, occurrences, and facts discussed in traditional histories are not disputed here. What makes this chapter and the accounting of the history of the U.S. nonprofit sector that it presents critical lies in its questioning of the depiction of the nonprofit sector that traditional histories present and take for granted as "the truth" of the sector. Traditional histories not only present events and occurrences through time, but they also knit them together into a coherent narrative that constitutes our understanding of how things have come to be as they are.

The traditional historical narrative of the American nonprofit sector goes something like this: Greatly informed by a Puritanical ethic, English legal tradition, and full of democratic spirit, citizens of the new republic formed voluntary associations to express their individual and collective interests. Over time and influenced by changing social, economic, juridical, and population dynamics, the country came to rely on these voluntary associations to help run many aspects of daily life. Through the nineteenth and twentieth centuries, voluntary associations and other community and civic organizations became defined legally, socially, and economically as *nonprofit* organizations and as a part of a distinct sector that acts as an alternative to the marketplace and government when they fail to function for all people. The nonprofit sector, now veritably booming, is an essential part of the landscape of **civil society** and necessary for the provision of vital services for scores of people every year. It is now a sector that is organized, professionalized, and rapidly evolving to meet growing demand.

The narrative presented is clearly a gross oversimplification of numerous well-written, well-documented histories of the American nonprofit sector. At the same time, it captures the essence traditional histories have taken: The American nonprofit sector evolved from humble democratic beginnings to become an essential part of the American social, economic, and political landscape such that it holds a legitimate place alongside the market and government sectors. The narrative is a rather glorious one and provides a strong basis for the legitimacy of the nonprofit sector and the functions it carries out. It also supports and reinforces the commonly held notion that nonprofit and voluntary organizations and the American nonprofit sector are necessary and inherently good for society. It is not a particularly critical stance.[1] When we simply assume and take for granted that nonprofit and voluntary organizations, the place they hold in society, and the nature of their work are *inherently* legitimate and good for society, we ignore the fallibility of nonprofit and voluntary organizations and the people that occupy them. We also ignore larger forces that shape these organizations and the nature of their work. Furthermore, we risk oversimplifying the role that nonprofit organizations play in serving the public. Nonprofit and voluntary organizations can open spaces for creating social change, while at the same time constraining individual freedoms. Erica Kohl-Arenas' (2011) study of the Farm Worker Movement in California's Central

Valley provides an excellent example of this. Her study concluded that social movement and philanthropic organizations' efforts to organize poor migrant workers in California provided the workers with opportunities to participate in regional alliances aimed at improving their lot, but at the same time failed to address any of the systemic political–economic relationships that laid the groundwork for their poverty in the first place. These include historically low wages, substandard educational opportunities, and disincentives to organize for political action.

By way of contrast, this chapter does not take for granted understandings of the American nonprofit sector. Instead, it interrogates them to understand *how* the current historical narrative of the American nonprofit sector came to be authoritative and powerful and, in doing so, create space for nonprofit scholars, practitioners, and students to identify alternate stories to define the nonprofit sector and nonprofit work. To do so, the chapter draws on the work of postmodernist historian and philosopher, Michel Foucault, and operates from his viewpoint that nothing is inherently good or bad, only dangerous (Foucault 1997, 256; cited in Dean 1999, 40);[2] which is to say that everything carries risks and the potential for having adverse consequences. This includes assumptions about the nonprofit sector. That is, all powerful, authoritative narratives have real, concrete consequences, and should be examined with a correspondingly critical eye. This includes prevailing understandings of the nature of nonprofit work and workers (including volunteers), the place nonprofit and voluntary organizations hold in communities, and the role the nonprofit sector plays in the fabric of American society.

Writing "Effective History"

This chapter draws on Foucault's genealogical method or "effective history." This approach describes how things come to be, as with a typical historical narrative, but it also affords possibilities for action by demonstrating that histories are not predestined (Flyvbjerg 1998). Foucault argued that traditional histories operate from the notion that time is linear and one historical event flows logically and causally into the next, forming a pattern that holds inherent meaning (McNay 1994). As historical events occur or are studied, historians place them into the appropriate pattern so that the overall unity of history is maintained. This is a unity Foucault (1984) argues is false, suggesting the world is messy and not neat, tidy, and so easily understood. Traditional histories also tend to privilege their own accountings of events and actively seek to affirm them—so much so that alternate explanations often are suppressed. We can see this tendency in what has been called the "white washing" of American history.

In contrast, Foucault's genealogical approach does not rely on a linear conception of time and does not privilege a particular accounting of events. Instead, a historian using this critical framework approaches the study of history by **problematizing** a contemporary issue confronting society and then examines its contingent historical and political emergence (Howarth 2000, 73). A genealogy "opposes itself to the search for 'origins'" (Foucault 1984, 77) because such a task is a fool's errand; one that is a fanciful and abstract "attempt to capture the exact essence of things, their purest possibilities, and their carefully protected identities" (78), despite the fact that events have no *inherent* meaning or identity.

The genealogist seeks to uncover the methods by which historical events and our current understanding of them become imbued with a particular meaning over time. The genealogist interrogates the present through an examination of the historical past to chart *the development of meaning*. Camilla Stivers' (2000) *Bureau Men, Settlement Women* is one example of this concept. In this study, Stivers unsettles common conceptions of Public Administration by uncovering the significant contributions women made to the development of the administrative state in the twentieth century. These contributions had largely been ignored in a field traditionally dominated and defined by rationality and masculinity.

Recognition of the role power plays in the production of discourses through the course of time strips traditional histories of their constants—no longer can one declare that events in history are marching toward an ultimate destiny from a categorical origin. Observers of the present, who produce traditional histories, risk reinforcing society's dominant discourses (Foucault 1980). The ultimate pursuit of genealogies is to *counteract* this process, and "to emancipate historical knowledges from that subjection, to render them, that is, capable of opposition and of struggle against the coercion of a theoretical, unitary, formal and scientific discourse" (Foucault 1991, 85).

Problematizing the Business of Nonprofits

A genealogy begins with a "question about the present" and examines history to offer some explanations for "how present-day phenomena arose, through their historical derivation and constitution" (Nilson 1998; as quoted in Burnier 2008, 400). So, what questions do we have about the present state of America's nonprofit sector? No doubt there are many, but one question that is increasingly occupying the minds of nonprofit scholars in recent years has been: *How and why has the nonprofit sector become so "businesslike?"* While there is no definitional consensus on the term "businesslike" itself, it is generally accepted that it involves the **professionalization**, **rationalization**, **commercialization**, and **marketization** of nonprofit and voluntary organizations and their functions. Traditional histories of the American nonprofit sector and its theoretical base tell us the nonprofit sector is, in part, an alternative to the marketplace (Sandberg 2012). So, this leads us to ask questions such as, why are nonprofits being incited to act like businesses? Why is "good" nonprofit management and leadership now being framed in language we once reserved for for-profit businesses? What tacit assumptions underlie this framing of "good" nonprofit management?

When we examine the historical record, we find that what constitutes the "right" way to care for others in society through voluntary action and through service in nonprofit and voluntary organizations has evolved. In the early history of the United States, charity was accepted and commonplace. Over time, however, charity fell into disfavor, and a philanthropic mode of service ascended, a development that coincided with increased reliance on nonprofit and voluntary organizations. Philanthropy dominated for much of the twentieth century, but now its tenets are being twisted such that nonprofit and voluntary organizations are incited to "act like businesses." To make sense of this phenomenon, we must understand how a philanthropic frame for voluntary service and nonprofit organizing suits the sensibilities of **neoliberalism**, the **governing rationality** that has dominated the globe since the late twentieth century and that seeks to remake all aspects of life in the image of the marketplace.

Philanthropy's Turn Toward Professionalization

During the course of the twentieth century, three significant events helped lay the foundation for philanthropy's eventual cooptation by neoliberalism to facilitate the adoption of "businesslike" discourses as authoritative and powerful for the nonprofit sector. These events are: 1) the passage of the Tax Reform Act of 1969, 2) the reformation of the American tax code to create the 501(c) tax designation for nonprofit organizations, and 3) the creation of the Filer Commission. Traditional histories tell us these events served to usher in the era of a professionalized nonprofit sector and organize nonprofit and voluntary organizations into a definable sector. Using a critical lens, however, these events take on an additional meaning in that they served to homogenize the landscape of nonprofit and voluntary organizations

around a philanthropic norm, making the sector and its activities more legible, governable, and, ultimately, amenable to the aims of neoliberalism.

Tax Reform and the "End of Methodless Enthusiasm"

As early as 1915, drumbeats of discontent could be heard as the public began scrutinizing the activities of foundations and other nonprofit and voluntary organizations. According to Peter Dobkin Hall (1992, 2003), this scrutiny lasted into the 1960s, coming from all sides and for various reasons, but all questioning the loyalty of nonprofit and voluntary organizations and their purpose in American life. During the latter half of the nineteenth century and continuing through both world wars, the United States witnessed not only an unprecedented proliferation of foundations and other tax-exempt organizations, but also the reliance upon these organizations by the federal government to provide much needed social services. Congress passed key pieces of legislation to better enable individuals and corporations to receive tax breaks in return for contributing to tax-exempt organizations. This—coupled with legislators' inability to streamline the tax code so that wealthy individuals could not take advantage of every loophole therein to funnel their personal wealth into tax-exempt foundations—led to the establishment of some tax-exempt institutions whose public purpose was dubious, at best. In addition, the federal government funneled increasing amounts of responsibility and public dollars to these organizations to achieve programmatic objectives.[3] At the same time, very few regulatory mechanisms were established by which the public could monitor how these funds and opportunities were being used in everyday life. As a result, many saw the tax privileges enjoyed by those who could afford to make monetary contributions and the growing wealth of nonprofit and voluntary organizations as unfair and unreasonable. In a straightforward *quid pro quo* relationship, the public trusted that the organizations to which tax-exemption was granted were providing a service that in some way benefited society at large.

There were legislative fits and starts throughout the twentieth century aimed at increased regulation of tax-exempt entities, but no law passed until President Richard Nixon signed the Tax Reform Act of 1969. While it set forth myriad reforms encompassing income tax law, it held special provisions pertaining to foundations' activities. Specifically, the Tax Reform Act of 1969 remedied purported abuses of tax exempt status by private foundations by clearly defining the limits and obligations of their activities. Critics had alleged private foundations abused their status in several ways, namely through 1) self-dealing between foundations and private donors, 2) inadequate distribution of funds to other nonprofit organizations, 3) ownership and control of for-profit enterprises, 4) market speculation, and 5) misuse of foundation funds for nontax-exempt activities (Smith and Chiechi 1974, 44–45). Accordingly, the Tax Reform Act of 1969 prohibited self-dealing between contributors and foundations, set a standard for the minimum amount of income a foundation must distribute to other nonprofit organizations, limited foundations' holdings in private businesses, and taxed foundations' activities that might jeopardize its tax-exempt activities, including lobbying or any other related political activity. In addition, the law explicitly required that private foundations implement administrative procedures for governing organizational and personal conduct related to the successful execution of the provisions set forth in the law. These include maintaining appropriate financial documentation and filing it with the Internal Revenue Service (IRS) on an annual basis.

While the measures laid out in the Tax Reform Act of 1969 specifically dealt with private foundations and not all nonprofit and voluntary organizations, prominent historians and scholars of the sector, such as Peter Dobkin Hall (1992) and Peter Frumkin (1998), view the passage and implementation of the law as the commencement of a period of enhanced professionalization of the nonprofit sector (cf., Popple and Reid 1999; Skocpol 2004).[4] Indeed, Smith and Chiechi (1974) report that nonprofit and voluntary organizations were alarmed at the law's imposition of administrative rules and the corresponding demands these posed. At the time, few organizations engaged paid employees, only volunteers. Ultimately the Tax Reform Act of 1969 served to dial up the level of vigilance with which the IRS regarded nonprofit and voluntary organizations of all types, especially as it relates to the granting of tax-exemption and the oversight of financial administration. In response, all nonprofit and voluntary organizations were forced to raise their own **managerial** standards. As Hall (1992) notes, no longer would "methodless enthusiasm" suffice to keep nonprofit and voluntary organizations going in the face of increasingly complex reporting requirements and funding restrictions. Now more formality, complexity, and rationality—indeed, more professionalization of staff and of standards—was required to demonstrate financial responsibility to both the IRS and the American public. The professionalization of an occupation has a profound effect on the personnel and institutions that comprise it.

That is, professionalization of an occupation serves to define what is considered accepted or normal practice for those who are engaged in it. In this case, the professionalization of the nonprofit sector helped to normalize a philanthropic mode for caring for, and serving others, in society.

Normalizing Philanthropy

Norms are a method by which a group (or an organization, nation, or society) can "provide itself with a common denominator in accordance with a rigorous principle of **self-referentiality**, with no recourse to any kind of external reference point . . . [by] which everyone can measure, evaluate, and identify himself or herself" (Ewald 1990, 154). Norms act as both a measurement and a form of judgment by which individuals within a group can be ordered. Put simply, they establish the rules for behavior and the consequences for deviating from those rules. Group members will adhere to the rules of the norm or pay a price: They will be branded as *abnormal*. According to Foucault (2008), the law has become increasingly associated with the processes of **normalization**. The law serves to support and reinforce the normalization process in that it represents both a codified set of norms and the means by which they can be coercively enforced. The Tax Reform Act of 1969 can be viewed as one way in which the law has established a *norm of professionalization* for nonprofit and voluntary organizations. That is, it is normal to act professionally and rationally in terms of organizational leadership and management.

In the twentieth century, we can also view two other legal proceedings that served to outline and define a *philanthropic norm* for the American nonprofit sector: The establishment of the 501(c) section of the tax code and the proceedings of the Filer Commission. First, the government codified philanthropy as a norm for nonprofit and voluntary organizations by literally establishing it as the measurement by which all nonprofit and voluntary organizations should be judged, albeit in an oblique way. In 1954, the U.S. Congress reformed the tax code to establish a section strictly for the classification of tax-exempt organizations: the 501(c) section of the tax code. Prior to the passage of these sweeping changes, the IRS classified all organizations that had some sort of special dispensation regarding the payment of taxes under one section (Section 101) without a demarcation of their purpose (Hall 2006). Section 101 included organizations ranging from foundations to insurance companies. By contrast, the 501(c) section of the tax code classifies organizations of an exclusively benevolent nature into one

of twenty-eight categories with twenty-eight specific purposes, ranging from the religious to charitable to educational (501(c)3) to workers' compensation (501(c)27). The requirements for meeting the designations of each category are spelled out in a seventy-two-page Department of the Treasury (2010) document.

For the federal government to designate a nonprofit or voluntary organization as a lawful member of one of these twenty-eight categories and for the organization to receive all the benefits that accompany one of these designations (e.g., tax-exemption, legitimacy, ability to fundraise, etc.), it must make an application to the federal government. The application consists of a twenty-seven-page questionnaire in which an organization must indicate the purpose of its organization, its goals for service, and the methods (i.e., its financial, human, and physical capital) by which it expects to achieve those goals (Department of the Treasury 2006). A nonprofit or voluntary organization cannot successfully complete the application process unless it establishes a goal that benefits society, develops a plan for achieving that societal goal, and then orients itself and its resources toward enacting that plan in the most efficient and effective manner possible. In this way, a philanthropic norm is married effectively with a norm of professionalization.

It should be recognized that although few nonprofit or voluntary organizations can survive (particularly financially) outside the government's twin blessings of legitimacy and tax-exemption, nonprofit or voluntary organizations can still exercise their freedom of choice. They can *choose* to apply for 501(c) status. Of course, if an organization does choose to seek 501(c) status, it must adhere to the legal and social norms that accompany that designation.

In the mid-1970s, the Commission on Private Philanthropy and Public Needs (commonly known as the Filer Commission) further served to delineate an "in" versus "out" group for nonprofit or voluntary organizations and embed philanthropic and professionalized norms for the sector. Organized at the behest of John D. Rockefeller III, the Commission spent two years studying nonprofit or voluntary organizations and the role that private giving played in them. The Commission's findings determined that nonprofit and voluntary organizations play an important role in American society and that private giving is vital for their maintenance and should be encouraged through legislative action (e.g., tax deductions for donors) (Brilliant 2000). This is probably unsurprising given the Commission was comprised primarily of private philanthropists and members of prominent nonprofit or voluntary organizations. Most noteworthy is the Commission's unprecedented recognition of legally sanctioned nonprofit or voluntary organizations *as a sector* that is distinct from the market and government sectors. In doing so, it placed the heretofore unheard of "nonprofit and voluntary sector" in the same abstract space as the marketplace and government sectors and further defined the boundaries that had been placed around it through the development of the 501(c) section of the tax code thus solidifying legally sanctioned nonprofits as the norm for the United States.

Neoliberalizing Philanthropy and the Business of Nonprofits

In his later writings, Foucault argued that large scale societal changes—such as shifts from a charitable mode of caring for and serving others in society to a philanthropic mode and, now, to a "businesslike" mode—do not occur in a vacuum but rather within a larger container of activities that he dubbed governing rationalities, or governmentalities. Government is a form of power, specifically the means by which we understand "the **conduct of conduct**" (Gordon 1991, 2): how we seek to conduct ourselves and inform the conduct of others, both at an interpersonal level and at an institutional level. During the course of the development and evolution of the American nonprofit sector, the centuries

witnessed a shift from a **liberal** governmentality to a neoliberal one.

The guiding *ethos* of liberalism can be summed up as "one should always suspect that one governs too much" (Foucault 2008, 319). That is, liberalism is skeptical of any benefits wrought by the exercise of too much government. Rather, a *laissez-faire* approach is preferred in that we seek to balance the larger interests of the state and society with individual rights by seeking only to *shape* individuals' interests as much as possible to ensure the predictability of individual and collective choices in the interest of maintaining society and the state (Burchell 1991). This is where a shift from charity to philanthropy in the seventeenth and eighteenth centuries proved helpful. Rather than focus on simply caring for individuals, philanthropy seeks to *reform* them through the application of knowledge so that they can better contribute to the maintenance of the country and to society. If individuals know better, then they will do better; they will become better citizens, better neighbors, and better consumers.

Liberalism ultimately came to be viewed as a failure, however, because it proved unable to produce satisfactory economic and social norms (Rose 1996). Liberalism proved ill-equipped to contend with issues, for its *laissez-faire* nature disallowed involvement in the lives of the individuals, only in their interests. So, in terms of finding a "better" governmentality, the question became one of how to intervene in individual lives so that the poor, for example, were successfully incorporated into society, especially as they pertain to participation in the marketplace and adherence to economic norms. Ultimately, a solution presented itself in the form of neoliberalism, a governmentality that emerged in the late twentieth century. Neoliberalism, which is now the dominant governmentality worldwide (Dardot and Laval 2016), argues that over time liberalism betrayed its own *ethos* of "not governing too much," resulting in a welfare state run amok, replete with rigid bureaucracy, a proliferation of top-heavy state institutions, professionals whose authority was unchecked, and a distorted marketplace.

The ultimate aim of neoliberalism is to produce satisfactory economic and social norms by extending the economic model of supply and demand and competition to all areas of life by making individual behavior completely calculable and predictable (Burchell 1996). Its primary vehicle for actualizing this aim is the enterprise model. For neoliberalism, promoting the enterprise model at the individual level involves a particular way of behaving: the individual-as-enterprise competes. Not only this, but she begins to view not only herself but also all of her relationships through the lens of competition. As such, competition becomes the model for social and interpersonal relations, which in turn serves to extend economic rationality into the whole of society (Foucault 2008). With the enterprise as the model for human behavior and competition the basis of interpersonal relations, government of oneself becomes highly "**responsibilized**" (Burchell 1996, 29). That is, individuals actively seek to mitigate the negative impact their behavior has on the marketplace and on society through a responsible practice of freedom and individual choice. The successful promotion and maintenance of the responsibly autonomous, self-governing individual is integral to neoliberalism (Dean 1999), and it requires a network of discourses, institutions, and knowledges to organize and support it.

A nonprofit sector that has normalized philanthropy throughout its discourses, institutions, and knowledges suits the aims of neoliberalism. Philanthropy seeks to reform individuals so that they better contribute to the larger aims of society through the application of knowledge. But what constitutes the knowledge that is applied to the individual? In a neoliberal governmentality, it is the knowledge of the enterprise and of competition. In a formalized, professionalized nonprofit sector that has been organized around a norm of philanthropy, neoliberalism has a homogenized container of organizations, people, and activities through

and by which individuals can learn to responsibly exercise their freedom by reforming their behavior to align with market values like entrepreneurialism and competition. This is what it means to become "businesslike."

So, when you hear claims like "we need to operate more like a business" or "we need more business savvy to be successful" in your nonprofit or voluntary organization or out in the philanthropic community, remember that nonprofits operating like businesses is not just about adopting tactics and strategies that have helped corporations, for example, meet their profit margins. It is about creating spaces and practices within nonprofit and voluntary organizations that help the marketplace to generate better, more competitive consumers who are less of a burden to both the state and society. Is that your nonprofit organization's goal? Is that the aim of the nonprofit and voluntary sector? Was that your vision when you chose nonprofit work as your vocation?

Conclusion and Key Takeaways

This chapter began with an implicit assumption that if we changed the method by which we analyze the nature of events, then we might be afforded the opportunity to change what is possible to say about those events. Not only this, but also to create an opportunity to change "what is possible to do, to think, or to be" in relation to those events (Cruikshank 1999, 21). To that end, this chapter used a critical frame to examine the prevailing narrative that constitutes our understanding of the history and development of the American nonprofit sector. In doing so, this chapter laid bare some of the historical and political forces that have worked to transform our understanding of voluntary action and service through nonprofit and voluntary organizations over time. As a result, this chapter also stimulated understanding of how professionalized, philanthropic, and "businesslike" forms of voluntary action and voluntary and nonprofit organizations have become normalized and taken for granted as the "right" way to manage and lead the nonprofit sector.

On a more fundamental level, this chapter demonstrated that our understandings of what we consider to be "right" voluntary action and voluntary and nonprofit management is *changeable*. Over the course of several centuries, our understanding of these concepts transformed from charity to philanthropy, and from philanthropy to "acting like a business." Each of these modes of voluntary action and organizational management has in turn been deemed the "right" way to care for others and to serve society. Collectively, what these transformations demonstrate is that our understanding of what it means to care for others and to serve society is not "natural" and "self-evident," nor is it "indispensable" (Foucault 1991, 75). Thus, the manner in which we engage in voluntary action and in managing nonprofit and voluntary organizations is not predetermined.

Notes

1. There have been other critiques of the American nonprofit sector and its development. See, for example, the work of Wagner (2000), Roelofs (2003), and INCITE! (2017). The purpose of this chapter is to problematize and critique the prevailing narrative that constitutes the history of the American nonprofit sector.

2. The full quotation is,

> My point is not that everything is bad, but that everything is dangerous, which is not exactly the same as bad. If everything is dangerous, then we always have something to do. So my position leads not to apathy but to hyper- and pessimistic activism.

3. Of paramount importance is legislation associated with the New Deal (Hall 2006), but also the GI Bill, which spurred growth in new institutions of higher learning, and legislation establishing the National Institutes of Health and National Science Foundation, and expanding Social Security and public social and health insurance, all of which provided funds for the establishment and growth of private organizations with a public purpose and their programs (Hall 2003).

4. Note that some scholars tend to distinguish between the professionalization of the nonprofit sector and the professionalization of charitable work. For instance, while Hall (1992) contends that the professionalization of the sector commenced with the Tax Reform Act of 1969, Wagner (2000) notes that the professionalization of charitable giving occurred in the early twentieth century with the formation of several professions (e.g., social work and public administration) and the increased rationalization of charitable work through the establishment of foundations and community chests.

References

Brilliant, E. 2000. *Private Charity and Public Inquiry: A History of the Filer and Peterson Commissions.* Bloomington, IN: Indiana University Press.

Burchell, G. 1991. "Peculiar Interests: Civil Society and Governing 'The System of Natural Liberty'." In *The Foucault Effect: Studies in Governmentality*, ed. G. Burchell, C. Gordon and P. Miller, 119–150. Chicago: University of Chicago Press.

Burchell, G. 1996. "Liberal Government and Techniques of the Self." In *Foucault and Political Reason: Liberalism, Neo-liberalism and Rationalities of Government*, ed. A. Barry, T. Osborne and N. Rose, 19–36. London: UCL Press.

Burnier, D. 2008. "Frances Perkins' Disappearance from American Public Administration: A Genealogy of Marginalization." *Administrative Theory & Praxis* 30(4): 398–423.

Casey, J. 2016. *The Nonprofit World: Civil Society and the Rise of the Nonprofit Sector.* Boulder, CO: Kumarian Press.

Cruikshank, B. 1999. *The Will to Empower: Democratic Citizens and Other Subjects.* Ithaca, NY: Cornell University Press.

Dardot, P., and C. Laval. 2016. *The New Way of the World: On Neoliberal Society.* London: Verso.

Dean, M. 1999. *Governmentality: Power and Rule in Modern Society.* London: Sage.

Department of the Treasury. 2006, June. *Application for Recognition of Exemption Under 501(c)3 of the Internal Revenue Code.* Available from www.irs.gov/pub/irs-pdf/f1023.pdf.

Department of the Treasury. 2010, October. *Tax-Exempt Status for Your Organization.* Available from www.irs.gov/pub/irs-pdf/p557.pdf.

Ewald, F. 1990. "Norms, Discipline, and the Law." *Representations* 30: 138–161.

Flyvbjerg, B. 1998. "Habermas and Foucault: Thinkers for Civil Society?" *British Journal of Sociology* 49(2): 210–233.

Foucault, M. 1980. "Truth and Power." In *Power/Knowledge: Selected Interviews and Other Writings 1972–1977,* ed. C. Gordon, 109–133. New York: Pantheon Books.

Foucault, M. 1984. "Nietzsche, Genealogy, History." In *The Foucault Reader,* ed. P. Rabinow, 76–100. New York: Pantheon Books.

Foucault, M. 1991. "Questions of Method." In *The Foucault Effect: Studies in Governmentality,* ed. G. Burchell, C. Gordon and P. Miller, 73–86. Chicago: University of Chicago Press.

Foucault, M. 2008. *The Birth of Biopolitics: Lectures at the College de France, 1978–1979.* Translated by G. Burchell. New York: Palgrave MacMillan.

Frumkin, P. 1998. "The Long Recoil from Regulation: Private Philanthropic Foundations and the Tax Reform Act of 1969." *American Review of Public Administration* 28(3): 266–286.

Gordon, C. 1991. "Governmental Rationality: An Introduction." In *The Foucault Effect: Studies in Governmentality,* ed. G. Burchell, C. Gordon, and P. Miller, 1–51. Chicago: University of Chicago Press.

Hall, P.D. 1992. *Inventing the Nonprofit Sector and Other Essays on Philanthropy, Voluntarism, and Nonprofit Organizations.* Baltimore, MD: Johns Hopkins University Press.

Hall, P.D. 2003. "The Welfare State and the Careers of Public and Private Institutions Since 1945." In *Charity, Philanthropy, and Civility in American History,* ed. L.J. Friedman, and M.D. McGarvie, 363–383. Cambridge, UK: Cambridge University Press.

Hall, P.D. 2006. "A Historical Overview of Philanthropy, Voluntary Associations, and Nonprofit Organizations in the United States, 1600–2000." In *The Nonprofit Sector: A Research Handbook,* 2nd ed., ed. W.W. Powell, and R. Steinberg, 32–65. New Haven, CT: Yale University Press.

Howarth, D. 2000. *Discourse.* Buckingham, UK: Open University Press.

INCITE! 2017. *The Revolution Will Not Be Funded: Beyond the Non-profit Industrial Complex.* Durham, NC: Duke University Press.

Kohl-Arenas, E. 2011. "Governing Poverty Amidst Plenty: Participatory Development and Private Philanthropy." *Geography Compass* 5(11): 1–14.

McNay, L. 1994. *Foucault: A Critical Introduction.* Cambridge, UK: Polity Press.

Popple, P., and P.N. Reid. 1999. "A Profession for the Poor? A History of Social Work in the United States." In *The Professionalization of Poverty,* ed. G.R. Lowe and N.P. Reid, 9–28. New York: Aldine de Gruyter.

Roelofs, J. 2003. *Foundations and Public Policy: The Mask of Pluralism.* Albany, NY: State University of New York Press.

Rose, N. 1996. "Governing 'Advanced' Liberal Democracies." In *Foucault and Political Reason: Liberalism, Neo-liberalism and Rationalities of Government,* ed. A. Barry, T. Osborne, and N. Rose, 37–64. London: UCL Press.

Sandberg, B. 2012. "Constructing Society's Aide." *Administration & Society* 44(8): 935–960.

Skocpol, T. 2004. "Voice and Inequality: The Transformation of American Civic Democracy." *Perspectives on Politics* 2(1): 3–20.

Smith, W.H., and C.P. Chiechi. 1974. *Private Foundations Before and After the Tax Reform Act of 1969.* Washington, DC: American Enterprise Institute for Public Policy Research.

Stivers, C. 2000. *Bureau Men, Settlement Women: Constructing Public Administration in the Progressive Era.* Lawrence, KS: University of Kansas Press.

Wagner, D. 2000. *What's Love Got to Do with It? A Critical Look at American Charity.* New York: New Press.

PART III

The Nonprofit Sector Internationally: The Global Context

CSOs (civil society organizations), NPOs (nonprofit organizations), NGOs (nongovernmental organizations), INGOs (international nongovernmental organizations), and formal and formal associations are part of an important, relatively new sector that is now a world political force. . . . This third sector plays a critical role in creating values worldwide, through its work in service delivery, advocacy, cultural programs, and social movements.[1]

In Part I, we provided an overview of the nonprofit sector (or NGO sector) irrespective of geography. We also explained that we use the terms "civil society" and "nonprofit sector" essentially to mean similar things.[2] In Part II, we introduced the nonprofit sector in the United States. Here in Part III, we present a picture of the NGO sector globally with an emphasis on international nonprofit organizations (or INGOs) that organize and facilitate the flow of resources and influence across national boundaries. It is not possible to understand the nongovernmental sector globally, however, without some knowledge about domestic NGOs in different countries. Therefore, Part X completes our introduction to the nonprofit sector internationally by focusing on domestic nongovernment organizations (NGOs) in selected countries around the globe and their roles in nations with widely varying government structures and governing philosophies and strategies.

First, though, a reminder:

The difference between nonprofit organizations (NPOs) and NGOs is slim. However, the term "NGO" is not typically applied to U.S.-based nonprofit organizations. Generally, the NGO label is given to organizations operating on an international level although some countries classify their own civil society groups as NGOs.

NGO activities include, but are not limited to, environmental, social, advocacy and human rights work. They can work to promote social or political change on a broad scale or very locally. NGOs play a critical part in developing society, improving communities, and promoting citizen participation.[3]

DOI: 10.4324/9780367696559-10

In other words, *NGOs* are essentially the same entities as nonprofit organizations and civil society organizations—that *operate outside of the North America*. For some reason, the United States and Canada prefer the term "nonprofit" whereas the rest of the world prefers "nongovernmental."

Defining the NGO Sector Globally

As Alexis de Tocqueville wrote in 1840, almost all charitable establishments in Europe at that time were once in the hands of private persons or guilds, but eventually charitable efforts came to be dependent on the state. In many European countries to this day, the state delivers most services directly and undertakes to supply bread to the hungry, assistance and shelter to the sick, and work for the idle.[4] With services that the state does not deliver, the state often controls the management and operations of the NGOs that deliver the services. Yet, the NGO sector outside of the United States is much larger and healthier in most parts of the world than we in the U.S. tend to assume. But, it has only been since the 1990s that anyone could make this assertion.

> The structure, governance, financing, permitted activities, and public acceptance of domestic NGOs varies greatly among countries. The roles they play in any given nation depend mostly on the government's views about its own purposes and its institutions. For example, to the degree that a government views its role as a servant of the people, voluntary organizations (NGOs) are likely to be vibrant actors. In contrast, a government that seeks to control its population through the use of power usually will not permit robust NGOs.[5]

Unfortunately, defining what an NGO is and is not globally is a difficult task—many would argue an impossible task. Laws, traditions, tax codes, and practices vary. Therefore, although scholars may wish to assess the strength of the NGO sector in a specific country or to compare the strengths of the sector in more than one country, it is necessary to determine the "boundaries" of the NGO sector—to define which organizations are included and which are not.

In 1991, a team of researchers at the Johns Hopkins University Center for Civil Society Studies' Comparative Nonprofit Sector Project (CNP) began research on civil society (or NGO sectors) in countries around the globe. Under the leadership of Lester M. Salamon, the Center created, developed, and pilot tested a "Global Civil Society Index" to assess the strength of NGO sectors in about 40 nations. At the conceptual level:

> There seems to be a reasonable consensus about its [civil society's] central core. That core consists of the basic private associational life of a society—the private associations and organizations that operate more or less outside the confines of the state and business as well as of the family, though they may receive aid and support from all of these. Such "intermediary" institutions function as the social glue of society. They bring people together for joint activity without the need for official auspices. They thus provide vehicles for the individual initiative for the common good, or at least for the common good as perceived by some reasonable segment of the community.[6]

Although the Johns Hopkins CNP team appears to have backed away from its early attempts to quantitatively measure the conceptual, structural, and operational features of civil society organizations, their factors (or criteria) that define inclusion in the NGO sector (or global civil society) globally have been widely accepted. They are:

The set of (1) formal or informal organizations or structured relationships among people that are (2) private (i.e., not part of the apparatus of the state), (3) not profit-distributing, (4) self-governing, and (5) voluntarily constituted and supported.

This definition has proven to be useful. For example, it has allowed the Johns Hopkins CNP team and others to conclude that the NGO sector outside of the United States is much larger and healthier in many parts of the world than we in the U.S. have tended to assume. The criteria also make it apparent why many totalitarian states place restrictions on the formation and operations of civil society organizations. They could easily become breeding grounds, support systems, and collective voices for people who hold views that are contrary to the state and its policies. As a specific example, the massive migration from rural western provinces to the industrialized eastern provinces in China overwhelmed the government's ability to provide services. Therefore, despite pervasive governmental distrust of civil society organizations, the Chinese government reportedly has permitted civil society organizations in areas such as the Pearl River Delta to provide service functions—but never expressive functions or mobilization of significant voluntary efforts that might lead to civil unrest.[7]

International Nongovernmental Organizations (INGOs)

Citing data from the World Bank and the *Economist*, the Global Development Research Center has estimated that the number of INGOs operating around the globe increased from approximately 6,000 in 1990 to 26,000 in 1999 and to about 29,000 in 2016.[8] Most INGOs exist to transfer resources from more developed countries ("northern countries") to less developed countries ("southern countries") for humanitarian assistance, development assistance, and/or recovery and rehabilitation purposes; or to advocate for causes. Many INGOs provide financial support, technical assistance, and other forms of resources to NGOs in order to advance society, strengthen communities, and enable citizen participation. Therefore, it is not unusual for INGOs to receive funding from government agencies whose services are aligned with governments' foreign aid programs.

INTERNATIONAL NONGOVERNMENTAL ORGANIZATION (INGO)[a]

J. Steven Ott and Jesus N. Valero[9]

During the 19th and early 20th century, a government's primary responsibility was to protect citizens against external threats and internal disorder.

Other aspects of public life could be left to the family or to organized groups not directly under governmental control. . . . As governments increased their involvement in building the foundations of an international society with rules and norms for activities such as trade and commerce, travel and transport, health services and even warfare, so the potential arose for international nongovernmental organizations (INGOs). These bodies represented nongovernmental organizations working across frontiers to particular ends.

The primary functions of most INGOs are to transfer resources from more developed countries to less developed countries for humanitarian assistance, development assistance, and/or recovery and rehabilitation purposes; or to advocate. A few well-known examples of assistance-type INGOs include Save the Children International, Oxfam International, Médecins San

Frontières, and CARE International. Examples of INGOs that are predominantly dedicated to advocacy include Amnesty International, Greenpeace, and World Wildlife Federation. Some INGOs engage in both assistance and advocacy.

The number and activities of INGOs burst onto the global scene in the 1970s and 1980s largely because the governments of the United States and a few other developed countries decided to use INGOs as their intermediaries in delivering foreign aid, development assistance, and humanitarian relief particularly in less developed nations. For instance, INGOs permitted the U.S. government to have "clean hands" as they attempted to keep newly emerging nations from opting for alliance with the then-Soviet Union. The use of private institutions to alleviate poverty and stimulate popular participation in the civic life of these societies became a major objective of U.S. foreign policy.[10]

In addition to governments' foreign aid policies, other factors that have influenced INGOs in their assistance efforts include: the post 9/11 security environment, pressure from funders to increase staff professionalism and accountability, increasing political influence and advocacy by INGOs, the effects and after-effects of the great recession of 2008, ongoing conflicts in Afghanistan and other countries in the Middle East, state failures in, for example, Cambodia and Africa, and many weakened legal, financial and cultural barriers to INGOS.

> INGOs themselves, have accounted for between $60 billion and $65 billion in aid to developing countries annually for about the past decade. . . . An OECD [Organization for Economic Cooperation and Development] estimate for 1994 is that $5.7 billion in aid to developing countries passes through NGOs.[11]

Helmut Anheier has identified a cluster of factors and trends that together help to explain the explosive growth and influence of INGOs up into the second decade of the twenty-first century although at a lower rate in the most recent years. They include:[12]

- INGOs are rapidly gaining favor with individual, foundation, and corporate donors around the globe;
- High profile humanitarian disasters, such as the devastating 2009 earthquake in Haiti and floods in Pakistan in 2010 with heavy publicity due to the development of international media, including the Internet, which provided nearly instantaneous information about international disasters and emergencies worldwide[13];
- The end of the Cold War and many regional conflicts that had been fueled by the Cold War opened doors for INGOs into countries that had been closed;
- New opportunities for INGOS in the global governance system including, for example, INGOs gaining access to United Nations-organized conferences and summits and the growing influence of "parallel summits" for civil society organizations since the 1992 Earth Summit in Rio de Janeiro;
- The ability of international support networks to apply pressure on antagonistic repressive governments and help local NGOs fight for national and local causes and policies;
- The development of legal systems and regulatory structures and processes within countries that permit, support, and legitimize INGOs and indigenous NGOs;
- Technological progress, especially in information and communication by email and internet, has dramatically facilitated cooperation across borders. For example, "dot causes" . . . such as . . . social networks that mobilize support for particular policy campaigns primarily . . . through a website"[14];
- The emergence of a "world culture" or "world society" as a powerful force behind internationalization of the nonprofit sector.

Abby Stoddard reports that the number of U.S.-based NGOs engaged in international relief and development grew from 52 in 1970 to over four hundred in 1994. There were 584 U.S.-based NGO funding partners with the U.S. Agency for International Development (USAID) at the end of 2008.[15]

Although *globalization* is obviously interwoven among Anheier's factors, we are more direct in addressing it as a factor. *Globalization* is the interconnectedness of the world-wide economy, the interweaving of international and domestic organizations, governance systems, and communication capabilities that ignore boundaries of time and space. Transnational connectedness is the reason why most INGOs exist.

Typically, INGOs are based in "northern," more developed countries. They advocate and/or distribute goods and services mostly in "southern," lesser developed countries. Many nonprofits actively reach out across national boundaries to find new sources of funding and to operate programs and provide services in new territories often in partnership with domestic or indigenous nonprofits (variously known as "nongovernmental organizations," "local NGOs," or simply "NGOs"). Some of the international nongovernmental organizations (INGOs) serve primarily as global advocates while many others are agents that transfer resources and expertise across borders.[16] Therefore, two primary types of organizations had moved to the forefront of international nonprofit activities by the 1990s: "humanitarian relief and private-development assistance organizations, and interest associations."[17]

INGOs—working with their domestic NGO partners—have become important social, economic, and in some instances political actors in many lesser developed emerging nations as well as in developed nations.[18] As defined originally by United Nations ECOSOC resolution 288[X], Article 71, 1950, a nongovernmental organization or NGO is: "Any international organization which is not established by intergovernmental agreement shall be considered as a nongovernmental organization."[19] A more useful definition is offered by Archer:

A group brought together by common aims and with a basic organizational structure; it does not rely upon governments for its formation or for most of the resources of its continued existence, and it is not profit-making in its aim.[20]

It is not possible to know how many nonprofit organizations are engaged in international activities or their operating budgets.[21] Estimates about their magnitude usually are extrapolated from reports of government agencies and international organizations such as the United Nations, the World Bank, and the Organization of Economic Cooperation and Development (OECD). Dichter, for example, uses reports produced by governments of developed nations and organizations such as the World Bank and USAID.[22]

Understanding the concept of "civil society" or "global civil society" is helpful for grasping the scope and functions of INGOs.[23] The efforts by a team at Johns Hopkins University to develop and refine a "Global Civil Society Index" provides a useful starting point. It is impossible to develop a Global Society Index without first defining what is—and is not—included in a "civil society."

INGOs emerged on the global scene in the 1970s and 1980s aided by the U.S. government and a few other countries that decided to use nonprofit organizations as their "nonpolitical" hands and arms for delivering foreign aid, development assistance, and humanitarian relief. "As the Cold War continued, the U.S. government and a host of private citizens shared an interest in keeping newly emerging nations from opting for alliances with the Soviet Union. Accordingly, the creation of private institutions to alleviate poverty and stimulate popular participation in the civic life of these societies became a major objective of U.S. foreign policy."[24] The major impetus behind the expansion of nonprofit organizations' international activities during the 1980s and 1990s, therefore, was increased government financing—not private philanthropy.

Anheier's cluster of factors and trends has helped to explain the explosive growth and influence of INGOs up into the second decade of the 21st century although at a lower rate in the most recent years.

Thus, as globalization has become a reality, many political, legal, financial, and cultural barriers to INGOs have been weakened or have fallen in countries around the globe, INGOs are expanding rapidly while their indigenous NGO partners in lesser developed and emerging nations also are often benefiting from the relationships.

Readings Reprinted in Part III

The readings included in this part begin with "International Trends in Government-Nonprofit Relations: Constancy, Change, and Contradictions" by Susan D. Phillips and Mark Blumberg. In this reading about international policy trends, Phillips and Blumberg remind us that

> while growth of this sector is a global phenomenon, the patterns of government-nonprofit relationships vary considerably across locales. In some countries, governments have been adaptive in responding to an evolving nonprofit sector and proactive in creating an enabling environment for its work, but in other places the story is one of policy drift.

Factors that have led to the differences among countries include changing demographics, heightened public expectations of transparency by NGOs and proof of their impacts, the globalization of philanthropy, and therefore the internationalization of what had been a domestic phenomenon.

Phillips and Blumberg emphasize four public policy tools affecting the governance of nonprofits: government oversight, tax incentives, restrictions on political and business activities, and the relationship between the state and the sector. The authors conclude that "surprisingly few countries have an overarching philosophy or meta-policy to guide development of this relationship," and as would be expected, policy contradictions exist in most countries. On the other hand, increased regulatory oversight over nonprofits and their fundraising activities is nearly universal.

Phillips and Blumberg[25] examines how "foundational differences in religious and political tradition across different countries create different types of meanings for third sector organizations. Contexts shift drastically, internationally and over time" (p. 2). As Read and Pekkanen note in a reading in Part X, countries with a strong central state tend to have weaker third sector organizations that tend to operate "close" to the government, whereas countries with less authoritarian governments tend to have stronger third sectors.

John Casey's "The Internationalization of the Nonprofit Sector"[26] provides a comprehensive overview of the expansion of the INGO sector especially since the decade of the 1970s and identifies the primary drivers of its meteoric growth. Casey includes such factors as

> the opening of political spaces [particularly with the end of the Cold War], the reconceptualization of the obligations of the international community, the growing demands of the more educated and prosperous citizens in the developing world, and the increasing availability of resources have all contributed to the expansion of the international activities of nonprofits.
>
> (Casey 2016, p. 179)

In this reading, Casey explores the dynamic relationships between INGOs and "global civil society" and identifies the largest and most reputable operating INGOs.

Abby Stoddard's reading, "International Assistance" that is reprinted here, traces the rapid development of the role of nonprofits in international assistance since the period between World Wars I and II up through the first decade of the 21st century. She particularly notes the "unprecedented levels of humanitarian crisis" in the 1990s, including "state fragmentation and violent civil conflicts" as well as natural disasters as contributing factors in the growth. "Africa in particular has been bested by the twin phenomena of 'failed states' and 'complex emergencies,' where long-standing environmental and food security problems are exacerbated by fighting or by the outright collapse of central authority."

Stoddard identifies three principal program areas where NGOs have been active in the international assistance field: development assistance, humanitarian assistance, and recovery and rehabilitation. The nature of the NGO assistance provided in these areas has been affected by a number of factors and forces including, for example, the post 9/11 security environment and problems with, for example, staff security; dramatic growth in U.S. Foreign Disaster Assistance funding (the USAID relief arm); pressure from funders to increase staff professionalism and accountability; increasing political influence and advocacy by NGOs with Congress as well as with agencies; economic globalization including the effects and after-effects of the great recession of 2008; ongoing conflict in Afghanistan and parts of the Middle East; and, state failures. Stoddard also predicts likely future roles for INGOs in the field of development assistance but acknowledges that "the uncertainty of the global economic environment . . . makes the immediate future of international nonprofit relief and development organizations hard to predict." Stoddard concludes:

> The world of well-meaning amateurs [in international development and relief] has given way to an epistemic community of well-trained professionals. . . . Development, and to a lesser degree, relief assistance is being increasingly devolved—though arguably not fast enough—into global networks of international affiliates and locally based capacities.

Notes

1. Meghan Elizabeth Kallman and Terry Nichols Clark, "Democratic Governance and Institutional Logics Within the Third Sector (or, How Habermas Discovered the Coffee House)." In The Third Sector: Community Organizations, NGOs, and Nonprofits, eds. Meghan Elizabeth Kallman and Terry Nichols Clark (Urbana, Chicago, and Springfield, IL: University of Illinois Press, 2016), 1, 1–35.

2. See Parts I and VII for more about civil society.

3. Grantspace, a service of the Foundation Center, New York, NY. http://grantspace.org/tools/knowledge-base/Resources-for-Non-U.S.-Grantseekers/ngo-definition-and-role. Retrieved 12/01/2019.

4. Alexis de Tocqueville, Democracy in America, Vol. 2 (1840; reprint, New York: Knopf, 1945).

5. J. Steven Ott and Jesus N. Valero, "Nongovernmental Organization (NGO) and International Nongovernmental Organization (INGO)." In Global Encyclopedia of Public Administration, Public Policy and Governance, ed., A. Farazmand (New York: Springer, 2017). First published 03 March 2017 online. DOI 10.1007/978-3-319-31816-5_3197-1.

6. Lester M. Salamon and S. Wojciech Sokolowski, eds., Global Civil Society: Dimensions of the Nonprofit Sector, Vols. 2–3 (Bloomfield, CT: Kumarian, 2004).

7. Qiusha Ma, Non-Governmental Organizations in Contemporary China: Paving the Way to Civil Society? (London and New York: Routledge, 2006). Benjamin Read and Robert Pekkanen explain why civil society organizations have varying types and degrees of freedom in different East and Southeast Asia countries, in Local Organizations and Urban Governance in East and Southeast Asia: Straddling State and Society (London and New York: Routledge, 2009); Qiusha Ma, "The Governance of NGOs in China since 1978: How Much Autonomy?" Nonprofit and Voluntary Sector Quarterly 31 (2002): 305–328; and Chien-Chung Huang,

Guosheng Deng, Zhenyao Wang, and Richard L. Edwards (Eds.), China's Nonprofit Sector: Progress and Challenges (New York: Routledge, 2014).

8. Rephael Harel Ben-Ari, The Legal Status of International Non-Governmental Organizations: Analysis of Past and Present Initiatives (1912–2012) (Leiden: Martinus Nijhoff Publishers, 2013).

a. Adapted from Op. cit., Ott and Valero.

9. Op. cit., Ott and Valero.

10. Helmut K. Anheier, "International Aspects of Globalization." In Nonprofit Organizations: Theory, Management, Policy, 2nd ed., ed. Helmut K. Anheier (Abington, Oxford, Oxon, UK and New York: Routledge, 2014).

11. Ibid., 40. Dichter cites D. Hulme and M. Edwards, Beyond the Magic Bullet (Bloomfield, CT: Kumarian, 1996).

12. Helmut K. Anheier, Chapter 17, "International Aspects and Globalization." In Nonprofit Organizations: Theory, Management, Policy, 2nd ed., ed. H. K. Anheier (Abington, Oxford, Oxon, UK and New York: Routledge, 2014).

13. Ibid., 471.

14. Ibid., 472.

15. Abby Stoddard, "International Assistance." In The State of Nonprofit America, 2nd ed., ed. Lester M. Salamon (Washington, DC: Brookings Institution Press, 2012), 332. Reprinted in this part.

16. William E. DeMars, NGOs and Transnational Networks: Wild Cards in World Politics (London, UK: Pluto Press, 2005).

17. Helmut K. Anheier and Kusuma Cunningham, "Internationalization of the Nonprofit Sector." In The Jossey-Bass Handbook of Nonprofit Leadership and Management, ed., Robert D. Herman (San Francisco: Jossey-Bass, 1994), 102.

18. For examples, see: Jie Chen, Transnational Civil Society in China: Intrusion and Impact (Cheltenham, UK: Edward Elgar, 2013); Julie Hearn, "African NGOs: The New Compradors?" Development and Change 38 (2007): 1095–1110; Mary Kay Gugerty, "The Emergence of Nonprofit Self-Regulation in Africa." Nonprofit and Voluntary Sector Quarterly 39 (2010): 1087–1112; Qiusha Ma, "The Governance of NGOs in China since 1978: How Much Autonomy?" Nonprofit and Voluntary Sector Quarterly 31 (2002): 305–328; Roseanne M. Mirabella, Giuliana Gemelli, Margy-Jean Malcolm, and Gabriel Berger, "Nonprofit and Philanthropic Studies: International Overview of the Field in Africa, Canada, Latin America, Asia, the Pacific, and Europe." Nonprofit and Voluntary Sector Quarterly 36 (2007): 110S–135S.

19. United Nations ECOSOC resolution 288[X], Article 71, 1950.

20. Clive Archer, "Nongovernmental Organization." In International Encyclopedia of Public Policy and Administration, ed., Jay M. Shafritz (Boulder, CO: Westview, 1998), 1504.

21. Comparisons among estimates about the size and magnitude of the nonprofit sector's international presence should be made only with considerable caution. There is not widespread agreement on terms or what should be included. See for example, op. cit. Salamon and Sokolowski, vol. 2.

22. Thomas W. Dichter, "Globalization and Its Effects on NGOs: Efflorescence or a Blurring of Roles and Relevance?" Nonprofit and Voluntary Sector Quarterly 28 Supplement (1999): 38–58.

23. Op. cit. Ott and Valero.

24. Brian H. Smith, "Nonprofit Organizations in International Development: Agents of Empowerment or Preservers of Stability?" In Private Action and the Public Good, eds., Walter W. Powell and Elisabeth S. Clemens (New Haven, CT: Yale University Press, 1998), 218.

25. Susan D. Phillips and Mark Blumberg, "International Trends in Government-Nonprofit Relations: Constancy, Change, and Contradictions." In Nonprofits and Government: Collaboration and Conflict, eds., Elizabeth T. Boris and C. Eugene Steuerle (Lanham, MD: Rowman & Littlefield), 313–342.

26. John Casey, "The Internationalization of the Nonprofit Sector." In The Nonprofit World: Civil Society and the Rise of the Nonprofit Sector, ed. John Casey (Boulder, CO: Kumarian Press/Lynn Riemer Publisher, 2016), 167–199. Reprinted in this part.

Bibliography

Anheier, Helmut K., *Nonprofit Organizations: Theory, Management, Policy*, 2nd ed. (Abington, Oxford, Oxon, UK and New York: Routledge, 2014).

——, "What Kind of Nonprofit Sector, What Kind of Society? Comparative Policy Reflections." *American Behavioral Scientist 52* (2009): 1082–1094.

——, and Kusuma Cunningham, "Internationalization of the Nonprofit Sector." In *The Jossey-Bass Handbook of Nonprofit Leadership and Management*, ed., Robert D. Herman (San Francisco: Jossey-Bass, 1994): 100–116.

——, and Jeremy Kendall (Eds.), *Third Sector Policy at the Crossroads: An International Non-profit Analysis* (New York and London: Routledge, 2013).

Barkdull, John, and Lisa A. Dicke, "Globalization, Civil Society, and Democracy? An Organizational Assessment." *Seton Hall Journal of Diplomacy and International Relations 5* (2004): 33–50.

Ben-Ari, Rephael Harel, *The Legal Status of International Non-Governmental Organizations: Analysis of Past and Present Initiatives (1912–2012)* (Leiden: Martinus Nijhoff Publishers, 2013).

Boris, Elizabeth T., and C. Eugene Steuerle (Eds.), *Nonprofits and Government: Collaboration and Conflict* (Lanham, MD: Rowman & Littlefield, 2017).

Brown, Rajeswary Ampalavanar, and Justin Pierce (Eds.), *Charities in the Non-Western World: The Development and Regulation of Indigenous and Islamic Charities* (New York: Routledge, 2013).

Casey, John, "The Internationalization of the Nonprofit Sector." In *The Nonprofit World: Civil Society and the Rise of the Nonprofit Sector*, ed. J. Casey (Boulder, CO: Kumarian Press/Lynn Riemer, 2016): 167–199.

Chen, Jie, *Transnational Civil Society in China: Intrusion and Impact* (Cheltenham, UK: Edward Elgar, 2013).

DeMars, William E., *NGOs and Transnational Networks: Wild Cards in World Politics* (London, UK: Pluto Press, 2005).

Dichter, Thomas W., "Globalization and Its Effects on NGOs: Efflorescence or a Blurring of Roles and Relevance?" *Nonprofit and Voluntary Sector Quarterly 28* (1999): 38–58.

Dupuy, Kendra, and Aseem Prakash, "Global Backlash against Foreign Funding to Domestic Nongovernmental Organizations." In *The Nonprofit Sector: A Research Handbook*, 3rd ed., eds., Walter W. Powell and Patricia Bromley (Stanford, CA: Stanford University Press, 2020): 618–630.

Edwards, Michael, *Civil Society*, 3rd ed. (Cambridge, MA: Polity Press, 2015).

Gugerty, Mary Kay, "The Emergence of Nonprofit Self-Regulation in Africa." *Nonprofit and Voluntary Sector Quarterly 39* (2010): 1087–1112.

Hammack, David C., and Steven Heydemann (Eds.), *Globalization, Philanthropy, and Civil Society: Projecting Institutional Logics Abroad* (Bloomington and Indianapolis, IN: Indiana University Press, 2009).

Hearn, Julie, "African NGOs: The New Compradors?" *Development and Change 38* (2007): 1095–1110.

Huang, Chien-Chung, Guosheng Deng, Zhenyao Wang, and Richard L. Edwards (Eds.), *China's Nonprofit Sector: Progress and Challenges* (New York: Routledge, 2014).

Iriye, Akira, "Nongovernmental Organizations and the Making of the International Community." In *Globalization, Philanthropy, and Civil Society: Projecting Institutional Logics Abroad*, eds., David C. Hammack and Steven Heydemann (Bloomington and Indianapolis, IN: Indiana University Press, 2009): 32–46.

Kallman, Meghan Elizabeth, and Terry Nichols Clark, *The Third Sector: Community Organizations, NGOs, and Nonprofits* (Urbana, Chicago, and Springfield, IL: University of Illinois Press, 2016): 1–35.

Kerlin, Janelle, "U.S.-Based International NGOs and Federal Government Foreign Assistance: Out of Alignment?" In *Nonprofits and Government: Collaboration & Conflict*, 2nd ed., eds., Elizabeth T. Boris and C. Eugene Steuerle (Washington, DC: Urban Institute, 2006): 373–398.

Lindenberg, Marc, and J. Patrick Dobel, "The Challenges of Globalization for Northern International Relief and Development NGOs." *Nonprofit and Voluntary Sector Quarterly 28* (1999): 4–24.

Ma, Qiusha, "The Governance of NGOs in China since 1978: How Much Autonomy?" *Nonprofit and Voluntary Sector Quarterly 31* (2002): 305–328.

——, *Non-Governmental Organizations in Contemporary China: Paving the Way to Civil Society?* (London and New York: Routledge, 2006).

Mascarenhas, Michael, *New Humanitarianism and the Crisis of Charity: Good Intentions on the Road to Help* (Bloomington, IN: Indiana University Press, 2017).

Mirabella, Roseanne M., Giuliana Gemelli, Margy-Jean Malcolm, and Gabriel Berger, "Nonprofit and Philanthropic Studies: International Overview of the Field in Africa, Canada, Latin America, Asia, the Pacific, and Europe." *Nonprofit and Voluntary Sector Quarterly 36* (2007): 110S–135S.

Ott, J. Steven, and Jesus N. Valero, "Nongovernmental Organization (NGO) and International Nongovernmental Organization (INGO)." In *Global Encyclopedia of Public Administration, Public Policy and Governance*, ed., A. Farazmand (New York: Springer). First published 03 March 2017 online. DOI 10.1007/978-3-319-31816-5_3197-1.

Park, Susan, "The Role of Transnational Advocacy Networks in Reconstituting International Organization Identities." *Seton Hall Journal of Diplomacy and International Relations 5* (2004): 79–92.

Petric, Boris (Ed.), *Democracy at Large: NGOs, Political Foundations, Think Tanks and International Organizations* (New York: Palgrave Macmillan, 2013).

Phillips, Susan D., and Steven Rathgeb Smith (Eds.), *Governance and Regulation in the Third Sector: International Perspectives* (New York: Routledge, 2011).

Powell, Walter W., and Patricia Bromley, *The Nonprofit Sector: A Research Handbook*, 3rd ed. (Palo Alto, CA: Stanford University Press, 2020).

Read, Benjamin L., with Robert Pekkanen, eds., *Local Organizations and Urban Governance in East and Southeast Asia: Straddling State and Society* (London and New York: Routledge, 2009).

Salamon, Lester M., "Government-Nonprofit Relations from an International Perspective." In *Nonprofits and Government: Collaboration & Conflict*, 2nd ed., eds., Elizabeth T. Boris and C. Eugene Steuerle (Washington, DC: Urban Institute, 2006): 399–435.

——, *New Frontiers of Philanthropy: A Guide to the New Tools and New Actors that Are Reshaping Global Philanthropy and Social Investing* (New York: Oxford University Press, 2014).

——, and Megan A. Haddock, *Explaining Civil Society Development: A Social Origins Approach* (Baltimore, MD: Johns Hopkins University Press, 2017).

——, Regina List, *Global Civil Society: An Overview* (Baltimore, MD: Center for Civil Society Studies, Institute for Policy Studies, Johns Hopkins University Press, 2003).

——, and S. Wojciech Sokolowski, eds., *Global Civil Society: Dimensions of the Nonprofit Sector*, Vol. 2 (Bloomfield, CT: Kumarian, 2004).

Schofer, Evan, and Wesley Longhofer, "The Global Rise of Nongovernmental Organizations." In Walter W. Powell and Patricia Bromley, eds., *The Nonprofit Sector: A: Research Handbook*, 3rd ed. (Stanford, CA: Stanford University Press, 2020): 603–617.

Smith, Brian H., "Nonprofit Organizations in International Development: Agents of Empowerment or Preservers of Stability?" In *Private Action and the Public Good*, eds., Walter W. Powell and Elisabeth S. Clemens (New Haven, CT: Yale University Press, 1998): 217–227.

Smith, Jackie, "Globalization and Transnational Social Movement Organizations." In *Social Movements and Organization Theory*, eds., Gerald F. Davis, Doug McAdam, W. Richard Scott and Mayer N. Zald (Cambridge, UK: Cambridge University Press, 2005).

Sokolowski, Wojciech (Ed.), *Global Civil Society: Dimensions of the Nonprofit Sector*, Vol. 2 (Bloomfield, CT: Kumarian Press, 2004).

Stoddard, Abby, "International Assistance." In *The State of Nonprofit America*, 2nd ed., ed., Lester M. Salamon (Washington, DC: Brookings Institution Press, 2012): 329–361.

Stroup, Sarah S., *Borders among Activists: International NGOs in the United States, Britain, and France* (Ithaca, NY: Cornell University Press, 2012).

Taylor, Rupert (Ed.), *Third Sector Research* (New York: Springer, 2011).

Themudo, Nuno S., *Nonprofits in Crisis: Economic Development, Risk, and the Philanthropic Kuznets Curve* (Bloomington and Indianapolis: Indiana University Press, 2013).

Willetts, Peter, *Non-governmental Organizations in World Politics: The Construction of Global Governance* (New York: Routledge, 2011).

CHAPTER 8

International Trends in Government-Nonprofit Relations: Constancy, Change, and Contradictions

SUSAN D. PHILLIPS AND MARK BLUMBERG

Susan D. Phillips, and Mark Blumberg. (2017). "International trends in Government-Nonprofit Relations: Constancy, Change, and Contradictions." In Elizabeth T. Boris & C. Eugene Steuerle (Eds.), *Nonprofits and government: Collaboration and conflict* (pp. 313–342). Lanham, MD: Rowman & Littlefield.

The worldwide expansion of numbers of nonprofits over the past decade suggests that we are living in an era in which "civil society's time has come" (World Economic Forum 2013). Nonprofits are not only delivering a wide and expanding range of services, but serving as vehicles for the expression of cultural identities and sources of social innovation and taking activist roles in social and policy change.[1] While growth of this sector is a global phenomenon, the patterns of government-nonprofit relationships vary considerably across locales. In some countries, governments have been adaptive in responding to an evolving nonprofit sector and proactive in creating an enabling environment for its work, but in other places the story is one of policy drift in the absence of political incentives and pressure from the sector for constructive reform. In a substantial number of countries, governments have intentionally closed the space in which civil society organizations (CSOs) operate, particularly limiting their ability to advocate, and in more extreme cases are exercising outright repression of them (Rutzen 2015; Carothers and Brechenmacher 2014). The conditions that led to this divergence in government-nonprofit relationships are changing quite rapidly under the pressures of several trends: changing demographics; heightened public expectations of transparency and demonstration of impacts; diversification and hybridization of this sector; and the globalization of philanthropy and nonprofit activities, making once mainly domestic phenomena transnational in scope. Can we expect these emerging trends to produce new models of government-nonprofit relationships and greater convergence of public policies for the nonprofit sector across countries?

This chapter assesses the implications of these trends on approaches to public policy and regulation for the third and emerging "fourth" sector (Sabeti 2009) across a wide range of countries. We focus on developments in four aspects of public policy governing nonprofits: registration, oversight, and promotion of transparency; tax incentives; regulation of political and business activities; and "meta-policy"—the ideational policy framework that articulates a vision for the relationship between the state and nonprofit sector and gives rise to governmental machinery and programs to implement this vision (Phillips and Smith 2014).

DOI: 10.4324/9780367696559-11

The State of the Nonprofit Sector: An International Overview

Internationally, the nonprofit sector is larger and more significant than is often perceived (Salamon et al. 1999). According to the Johns Hopkins Comparative Nonprofit Sector Project (JHCNSP), if the operating expenditures of nonprofits across the 40 countries it studied were aggregated, it would rank as the world's seventh largest economy, only slightly smaller than France (Salamon et al. 2013). In terms of employment, the nonprofit sector constitutes, on average, 7.4 percent of the workforce (including the contributions of volunteers for 13 countries for which reliable data are available), placing it ahead of other major industries such as transportation and finance (Salamon et al. 2013). Globally, this sector has been growing, in both number of organizations and economic contributions to gross domestic product (GDP), with an annual growth rate from the late 1990s to the mid-2000s estimated to be 5.8 percent, compared to 5.2 percent for the economies as a whole (Salamon et al. 2013). These economic measures, however, do not capture the contributions of the nonprofit sector to the social, cultural, and democratic life of citizens through both service delivery and expressive activities (Frumkin 2002; Salamon et al. 2003). In general, service functions dominate expressive ones (with little difference between developed and developing countries): 63 percent of the sector's paid and volunteer personnel is dedicated primarily to services and 32 percent to expressive activities, as measured across thirty-two countries (Salamon et al. 2003). The range of services provided is diverse, although education (23 percent of the workforce), social services (19 percent), and health (14 percent) dominate; among expressive functions, 19 percent of nonprofit personnel are engaged in cultural activities, 7 percent in professional, and 4 percent in civic and advocacy roles (Salamon et al. 2003).

The revenues for the sector come from three main sources: the sale of goods and services (which, on average, account for 50 percent of income), governments (36 percent), and philanthropy (14 percent) (Salamon et al. 2013). An international trend is the growing reliance on fees due to the marketization of services, even in social democratic countries (Bode 2011), the shrinking availability of government grants, and the growing preference for social entrepreneurship as business models. As Salamon (2010) note, governments remain critical of the financial sustainability of the sector, and nowhere are nonprofits supported primarily by philanthropy. The significance of donations varies greatly across subsectors, however, and may be more important for the "typical" mid-sized nonprofit than averages suggest (Lasby 2011).

While aggregate figures are impressive, there are significant variations in the size, composition, and revenue sources of the nonprofit sector across regions. For countries with national satellite account data, the economic contributions as a percentage of GDP range from 8 percent in Canada to 0.8 percent in Thailand (Casey 2016). Although the United States has the largest number of nonprofits, the relative size of its sector, compared to the economically active population, is actually smaller than in many European countries (Salamon 2010). The countries with the largest nonprofit sector, constituting more than 10 percent of paid employment, are the Netherlands, Canada, Belgium, Israel, the United Kingdom, and Ireland (the United States constitutes 9.2 percent); those in which the nonprofit sector is less than 1 percent include Slovakia, Pakistan, Poland, and Romania (Salamon 2010). The common perception that a large welfare state crowds out nonprofits and philanthropy is, in fact, not supported as the Scandinavian countries have both large welfare states and nonprofit sectors. One explanation is that in Scandinavian countries a large number of nonprofits are engaged in sports and expressive activities, including advocacy, rather than the provision of quasi-public services. Further, in testing the "social origins" (Salamon and Anheier 1998) hypothesis that charitable giving is highest in liberal democracies, Einolf (2015) finds the opposite—that people are more likely to give in countries with larger public sectors. Across developed countries, however, philanthropy has become increasingly concentrated with fewer numbers of people carrying the bulk of giving and volunteering. The overall percentage that households donate has remained unchanged for decades (Cowly et al. 2011), and overall giving levels have remained stable only as a result of larger gifts by high net worth (HNW) individuals.

Transition and developing countries tend to have the least developed nonprofit sectors, although, as Casey notes (2016; see Themudo 2013), the relationship between economic development and size of the sector is "not necessarily linear," given that economic stability, as opposed to mere size, and a philanthropic culture are important factors. Although comparative research emphasizes consistent regional variations, for instance, a Nordic, industrialized Asian or African model (Salamon et al. 2003), significant intraregional differences are evident, and at critical junctures governments have taken quite different routes to supporting (or restricting) the growth of nonprofits. China and Vietnam, for example, have fostered substantial nonprofit sectors while keeping them under state control (Wang et al. 2015). By comparison, when South Korea, with virtually no domestic giving or organized civil society under the period of dictatorship, began its path of rapid growth in the mid-1980s, the government adopted a corporatist, collaborative approach that promoted a very vibrant nonprofit sector (Einolf 2015; Kang et al. 2015). Similarly, the nonprofit sectors in Eastern Europe and Eur-Asia are evolving in quite different ways. With a population of only 1.3 million, Estonia supports more than 30,000 CSOs and ranks highest on the USAID (2012) CSO Sustainability Index,

in large part due to its supportive legal environment and sector infrastructure. Belarus and Turkmenistan, in contrast, have, respectively, only 2,600 and 106 registered CSOs, and they operate in a legal environment that is highly restrictive with very limited access to funding and little space for advocacy (USAID 2012). On top of these differences, the military conflict and humanitarian crisis in Ukraine following Russia's annexation of Crimea in 2014 had a "spillover effect" on the region with some following Russia to exert tighter controls over civil society and others consolidating a commitment to "democratic values," accentuating two very different trajectories of government-nonprofit relations in the region (USAID 2012).

Comparative analysis must acknowledge that measurement methods may not consistently capture civil society activity across societies. Use of a uniform definition of "nonprofit" and consideration of engagement only through these formal organizations, as done in the JHCNSP, may overlook a large portion of more informal activity that is not captured by notions of philanthropy, volunteerism, or nonprofit. An example is the South African philosophy and practice of *ubuntu*, which has pan-African versions and equivalents in indigenous philanthropy elsewhere. Based on "principles of reciprocity and co-operation grounded in unwritten, but widely understood, behaviours of giving" (Mottiar and Ngcoya 2016), *ubuntu* has its own formalized traditions and structures, but in many studies these would not be counted as part of the nonprofit sector. In the context of Latin America, Oxhorn (2011; see also Butcher and de Tagtachian 2015) argues that Western analytical conceptions of civil society, nongovernmental organizations (NGOs), and nonprofits are inadequate for understanding the more collectivist components of its social structures and cultures. In addition, the blunt division between service and expressive activities may miss important dynamics of this sector. Comparing Mexico and Brazil, Lavalle and

Bueno (2011) observe that a "modernization" and "functional diversification" of this sector in recent years has introduced new organizations, including new kinds of social movements, coordinating bodies and church-inspired issue-oriented "pastorals," that are working alongside more traditional neighborhood associations and service nonprofits. Collectively, they are enhancing the capacity for influencing public policy, but do not fit into tidy definitional categories or functions.

In sum, the nonprofit sector is large, diverse in its functions—including service delivery and expressive and advocacy activities—and growing in most countries. Similar cultural frames (Casey 2016) and welfare regimes (Salamon and Anheier 1998) have generated regional similarities in nonprofit sectors, albeit with significant country-specific variations. While deeply embedded cultural factors and historical patterns of government-nonprofit relationships tend to carve path-dependent channels that produce mainly incremental change, quite rapid disruption also occurs, for instance through the effects of natural disasters on giving, as occurred in China and Japan in recent years, and through uprisings and widespread dissent, as happened with the "colored revolutions" in the Balkans in the early 2000s and the "Arab Spring" beginning in 2010 (Civicus 2014). In addition to these sudden disruptions, government-nonprofit relationships are also being influenced—in gradual but more predictable ways—by changes in demographics and the geographies of wealth, heightened expectations of transparency, diversification of the sector, and transnationalism.

Changing Demographics

Engagement in philanthropy and nonprofits is being reshaped by two demographics: women and Millennials (those born between 1980 and 2000). A growing number of women are able to make substantial gifts in their own right (TD and Investor Economics 2015; US Trust and Lilly Family School 2014), and their patterns for engagement are different from their male counterparts, including being more internationally oriented (Mesch and Pactor 2016; Micklewright and Schnepf 2009). Women are leading new forms of collective philanthropy, such as giving circles, through which they seek to transform communities or address causes "from the bottom up" (Eikenberry 2016) and have assumed highly effective roles—as leaders not just clients—in microfinance and financial inclusion across many developing countries (Cosgrove 2010). The Millennial generation is the largest, most diverse cohort in history, currently representing almost a third of the global population, and by 2025 it will constitute about 75 percent of the global workforce (Deloitte 2014). As digital natives, they are highly networked, less religious than their parents, and entrepreneurial; they value authenticity, want to "solve real problems" with systemic solutions (Johnson Center 2013), and volunteer at higher rates than their parents or the Boomer generation, preferring to support causes in various ways rather being loyal to specific organizations (Achieve 2014; Nielsen 2014).

Religious affiliation and attendance at faith services has been a strong predictor of giving and volunteering, and religion is still the primary destination of philanthropy in many countries. However, religious attachment (particularly among Christians) is declining rapidly in many European and North and South American countries, and the composition of religions among once quite homogenous populations is changing due to immigration. Globally, Islam is significant for its growth (Hackett et al. 2015); in addition, its culturally embedded but largely informal charitable practices are increasingly relying on the formal tools of philanthropy (Wagner 2016), and a wide range of associated new nonprofits, including community foundations, are being registered and assuming active roles in community development (Herrold 2015; Kuttab et al. 2015).

Changing Expectations of Transparency and Impact

Public trust is the currency of the nonprofit sector. A variety of surveys indicate that public trust in nonprofits remains high compared to other sectors, but there is evidence of a decline in recent years. Two messages are clear from these surveys. First, the public is concerned about waste and wants to know more about where the money goes; second, people increasingly want evidence of impact, which is that nonprofit programs are effective in achieving results (Muttart 2013). Expectations of transparency increase the need for both a credible state regulator and more effective self-regulation.[2]

In an era of big data and "the network effect of the internet" (Bria 2015), transparency no longer means just access to standardized information such as nonprofit Internal Revenue Service (IRS) information returns, but entails coproducing meaningful information that is used to mobilize public good. A rapidly expanding movement of digital social innovation is working with governments and nonprofits to open up and cocreate data, produce more meaningful data, and increase their capacity to use this information more effectively (see Bria 2015).

Diversification of the Sector

Hybridity—the embodiment of more than one institutional logic in an organization (Skelcher and Smith 2015)—has long characterized the nonprofit sector, as evidenced by charity shops, community economic development corporations, cooperatives, and quasi-public institutions such as universities and museums. Hybridity has become more extensive and more complex in recent years as nonprofits and charities pursue new revenue sources, private investors seek both financial and social returns on impact investments, foundations look to put their endowments to work through program-related investments (PRIs), and for-profits value a triple bottom line. In some cases, business and social purposes are intertwined in a single organization, often called "social enterprises"; in others, new ownership chains and relationships are created when nonprofits own for-profit entities, create affiliated foundations, or participate in joint ventures. Although the rhetoric of hybridization has outpaced practice, the public policy challenge is that historically, at least in common law countries, regulation has been organized to cover three discrete categories: (1) charities and foundations; (2) other nonprofits that meet a non-distribution constraint but are absent charitable purposes; and (3) for-profits. The development of a mixed "fourth" sector raises questions of whether new legal forms are needed, what should be regulated and how? The Zuckerberg-Chan "gift" put a spotlight on these legal forms because they, like many wealthy young entrepreneurs, prefer using vehicles over which they retain control; in this case, putting the $45 billion in Facebook shares the couple will ultimately contribute into a limited liability company rather than a philanthropic vehicle (Levine 2015).

Transnationalism

Like hybridity, cross-border philanthropy and nonprofit activity are not new: for instance, more money flows as remittances through diasporas than as official government aid (Schmid and Nissim 2016). International influences and funding have been instrumental in building civil society in many countries as diverse as Israel, South Korea, and Lebanon (see Wiepking and Handy 2015). International-scale NGO federations such as World Vision and Oxfam have been engaged in humanitarian assistance and development for sixty years, with the seven largest having a combined income of over $7 billion, and still growing. The global reach of philanthropy and nonprofit action has assumed a new scale, however, with new implications for public policy.

The geographies of wealth are undergoing significant change due to the spread of the hyper-wealthy and the rise of the middle class in the Global South. Described as akin to a "billionaire social movement" (Smith 2013), more than 142 of the world's richest people, including 25 from outside the United States, have signed on to the Giving Pledge initiated by Bill Gates and Warren Buffet, committing to give away a total of $708 billion of their personal wealth. These philanthropists tend to be hands-on and purport to seek the "best innovations and the most effective institutions wherever they find them" (CAF 2014) while potentially maintaining cultural affinities with their countries of origin. The Bill and Melinda Gates Foundation was the "tipping point" of such internationalization as it operates in over 100 countries and has become the largest funder of global health programs other than the US and UK governments, spending more than the World Health Organisation (McGregor-Lowndes 2016).[3] Although at first this American brand of strategic philanthropy did not export well due to differing cultural perspectives and legal regimes restrictive of nonprofits, the interest is growing, particularly in Asia, where it may be an impetus for policy change that is more enabling of nonprofits. The geographic redistribution of wealth is occurring not only at the very high end, but through a growing middle class in the Global South.

On the darker side of transnationalism are money laundering and financing of terrorist organizations which may, albeit acknowledged as rarely, involve nonprofits as complicit in raising and transferring funds illegally or as victims in having legitimate funding diverted or their interconnections and work exploited, particularly in conflict zones (van der Does de Willebois 2010). A fundamental tension is that the existing policy regimes were built on assumptions that philanthropy and the work of nonprofits are strictly domestic affairs, and they are now grappling with the challenge of how to support, or control, cross-border monetary flows and nonprofit activities.

Our argument is that collectively these factors are transforming, in both quiet and bold ways, the policy approaches and instruments for nonprofit policy.

The Nonprofit Policy Toolkit

Public policy for the nonprofit sector takes many forms, although four primary rationales form a common core for purposes of comparative analysis: promoting transparency and providing oversight to prevent abuse and maintain public trust; providing exemptions from taxation and tax incentives to encourage giving; regulating political and business activities to ensure spending primarily on charitable and "public benefit" purposes; and creating an overall ethos and framework by which to manage relationships between governments and nonprofits.[4] The four goals with their associated policy instruments and issues of implementation are presented in table 11.1. This should be thought of as a *conceptual* toolkit, implemented in different ways, with some tools not used at all, in different countries.

Art of the State-Nonprofit Relations: International Trends

In this section, we examine contemporary patterns and recent developments for each of the four aspects of government-nonprofit relationships.

Transparency and Oversight

A virtually universal trend in recent years has been toward increased accountability and regulation of nonprofits, but this movement has taken two markedly different paths based on disparate motivations: one is to enhance transparency and trust in nonprofits and the other to retain

TABLE 8.1 Policy Goals and Instruments

Policy Goal	Primary Policy Instruments	Issues of Implementation
Promote transparency, good practices and trust; provide government oversight for accountability; prevent abuse	• Basic human and civil rights • Forms to establish legal identities • Registration with government regulator • Annual reporting on finances and activities (and public benefit) • Self-regulation	• Auspices of the regulator: in the tax agency, independent commission or line department • Information to be reported: usefulness and accuracy; administrative burden of reporting • Coverage: whether organizations other than those with charitable purposes require registration and oversight; availability of alternative corporate and legal forms
Provide tax exemption on income that is nonprofit; create incentives for charitable giving; build a broad culture of philanthropy; protect the integrity of the tax system	• Determination of eligible organizations, through legislation, common law, or tax code • Exemptions on income, property, and value-added taxes • Tax incentives for charitable giving • Regulations on cross-border giving; antiterrorism regulations • Education and moral suasion to promote giving and volunteering	• Eligibility: does eligibility for tax exempt status fit the contemporary nature of the sector and policy goals; does it enable or repress nonprofits? • Harmonization: whether eligibility for tax exemptions and ability to offer tax incentives and registration are automatic or different • Size and basis of tax incentives: what can be donated (including tax relief on social investments); whether a tax deduction or credit • Distribution of donations: whether differential incentives should be given to different causes, or donor choice should determine distribution • Strings attached: appropriate restrictions on nonprofit activities related to tax exemption • Domestic vs. international: extent to which cross-border giving (with tax receipts) and foreign funding are allowed

(Continues)

TABLE 8.1 Policy Goals and Instruments (continued)

Policy Goal	Primary Policy Instruments	Issues of Implementation
Ensure charities and tax exempt organizations spend primarily on charitable purposes; maintain fair treatment relative to business; restrict political activities	• Regulation of political and business activities, fundraising, and administrative costs • Corporate entities for social enterprises and social purpose businesses	• Degree of restrictiveness: whether restrictions are appropriate or intended to contain or repress, regardless of tax exemption • Enabling and regulating social enterprise: provision of different corporate forms and regulations for the "fourth" sector
Establish a guiding framework ("meta-policy") with which to provide political leadership and manage relationships with nonprofits and public expectations	• Political philosophy and policy frameworks or "compacts" • Government machinery for relationship management • Partnerships and engagement of the sector in policy and co-production of services • Financing sector infrastructure and capacity and supporting the ability to innovate • Regulations and support for transnational work and organizations	• Independence of sector: respecting autonomy • Scope and relevance: managing a government and sector-wide framework when each is diverse and changing; stance toward international and transnational operations • Monitoring and compliance for both government and the sector

state control over their creation and operations. Aligned with the first track, a number of
common law jurisdictions—notably Australia,
New Zealand, Ireland, Scotland, and Northern
Ireland—have established new regulators[5] with
mandatory registration and reporting systems for
"charities." Across Europe, sixty-five government
initiatives designed to increase transparency and
accountability have been undertaken in recent
years, motivated by a recognition of the social,
economic, and policy importance of this sector
and the need to reinforce public confidence and
safeguard nonprofits from abuse related to terrorist financing and other illegal activity (ECNL
2009).[6] Many of Europe's civil law countries
(e.g., Bulgaria, Hungary, Italy, Netherlands,
and Poland) have enacted a new status of "public
benefit organization" that unifies accountability
requirements across different legal forms and
are accompanied by new national registries or
requirements that make existing information
on nonprofits more publicly accessible (ECNL
2009; Bullain and Toftisova 2005).[7]

In addition to providing greater transparency of finances, two new dimensions are being
added to accountability: reporting on public
benefit and on internal governance. England
has not only legislated a statutory definition of
charity, which includes a public benefit requirement, but with 2011 revisions to its legislation,
now requires that charities demonstrate in their
annual reports how they are meeting a public
benefit test. The established regulators, notably
in the United States, England, and Canada, are
increasingly seeing good governance as a key
means to regulatory compliance, and are requiring more information on governance and fundraising practices (House of Commons 2016;
McGregor-Lowndes 2016; Phillips 2013). How
far government regulators will go with intensive
monitoring of nonprofit governance is an open
question because such oversight would be enormously resource intensive and, like reporting on
results, would require the regulator to provide
education and guidance regarding good practice

rather than simply relying on standard setting,
auditing, and sanctions.

State regulation seems to be moving away
from this kind of "responsive" regulation
based on education first, however, with state
regulators more narrowly focused on preventing
abuse, and the enhancement of good practices
left to self-regulation. In part, this narrowing
of regulatory focus has occurred as a reaction
to significant cases of abuse, for instance, the
use of charities as tax shelters in Canada where
over $6.3 billion CDN was claimed by donors
on these fraudulent schemes (CRA 2015), and
the public outcry and exposure of questionable
practices (e.g., selling of donor lists and lack of
protection of privacy) that followed the 2015
suicide of the ninety-two-year-old "poppy lady"
in England, who was said to be "hounded to
death" by charities (Birkwood 2015). This has
led to the replacement of the sector-led voluntary system of fundraising regulation by a
more independent model. A number of other
countries (Finland, Austria, Bulgaria, and Ireland) have similarly introduced more stringent
regulations on fundraising with strengthened
reporting requirements (ECNL 2009).

No matter the scope of its mandate, the
credibility of the regulator is key to effective
oversight: that of several of the well-established
"model" regulators has recently been seriously
challenged, albeit in different ways. Cuts of
almost one-half to the budget of England's
Charity Commission greatly undermined its
work (Morgan 2015), leading to a parliamentary
review declaring it "not fit for purpose" (Public
Accounts Committee, House of Commons,
UK 2014) and recommending it to refocus on
catching abuses rather than providing guidance.
Only a year after the creation of Australia's not-
for-profit commission, the Abbott government
slashed its budget and announced it would be
dismantled, although a change in government
has reversed this plan. Similarly, in Canada, the
allocation by the former Conservative government of major new funding directed to political

activity audits resulted in the tax agency being perceived politicized; recognizing the damage of such perceptions, the new Liberal government has asserted its desire to protect "the independence of the Charity Directorate's oversight role for charities" (Blumberg 2016). With a larger, more diverse sector and public expectations of enhanced transparency, nonprofit regulators cannot be allowed to simply limp along, and thus an important task in the government-nonprofit relationship is to (re)define and support their responsibilities and restore their legitimacy.

In many other countries, governments are on a different trajectory where the intended destination is not a well-functioning, pluralistic nonprofit sector, but a more contained and controlled one. Since 2012, more than 100 laws have been proposed or enacted in a wide range of countries to restrict the registration, activities, or funding of nonprofits (Rutzen 2015; see also Breen 2015; Carothers and Brechenmacher 2014; Civicus 2014). With the perception that CSOs provoke opposition to the government (see Ibrahim 2015 on Egypt; Wood 2016 on Kenya), such restrictions are achieved in a variety of ways, including burdensome registration and reporting requirements, tight restrictions on activities, limits or bans on foreign funding, overzealous application of counterterrorism and money-laundering rules, and limits on freedom of assembly and the media (Civicus 2014; Rutzen 2015). The majority of recently legislated constraints on nonprofits are in the former Soviet countries and sub-Saharan Africa (Civicus 2014), where, in addition to more general restrictions, targeted measures (in Russia, Uganda, and Nigeria) have been taken to silence LGBT activists.

Controls on foreign funding have become one of the most common means of diminishing the capacity of nonprofits to engage in advocacy. As Breen (2015) notes, the breadth of such restrictions shows that nonprofits are being viewed as "troublesome adversaries more than

as supportive allies." Resistance to foreign funding is also being felt in Israel where proposed legislation would require nonprofits to receive a majority funding from foreign governments to be "foreign agents" and declare foreign funding on all official documents a measure most likely to stigmatize groups on the political left that are involved with human rights work (Gancman 2015). The emerging industrialized countries[8] are characterized by an ambivalence toward non-profits involving an interest in legitimizing them "but only if they can control them carefully" (Spero 2014). For instance, India has recently strengthened restrictions on foreign funding (and political activities), which have been emulated by other governments in the region (Sidel 2016). The direction that China takes (which ranks 133 of 135 countries on the World Giving Index and has low levels of trust for nonprofits, but where philanthropy is growing very quickly) will be particularly consequential. China has significantly strengthened the environment for charitable organizations providing social services, including drafting new charity legislation that would provide a registration system and more coherence to its fragmented system of separate regulations for social organizations, foundations, and "private non-enterprise units" (Sidel 2016; China Development Brief 2016). At the same time, tighter government controls over foreign nonprofits are proposed, requiring them to have government sponsors and giving wide latitude to police to oversee their funding and activities, a measure that is widely criticized internationally and is currently being reconsidered (*Straits Times* 2016).

Tax Incentives

Exemptions for nonprofits from income, property, value-added and inheritance taxes, as well tax incentives to donors for charitable gifts have become "almost universal policy across market economies," albeit with different rationales, means, and conditions attached (Carmichael 2016; CAF 2006). In recent years, many countries have increased the scope of these tax privileges (CAF 2006; Dehne et al. 2008), both as a means to create a broadly based culture of philanthropy and to substitute private capital for reduced public spending. Following the 2008 recession, for example, Spain significantly increased the amount of the tax benefit as the government looked to private giving to replace some of the public funding that was cutback as part of its austerity measures (Hudson Institute 2015). The effects of tax incentives on individual giving is debated: evidence suggests that they tend to "nudge" but are not the determining factor in promoting philanthropy (Layton 2015), although there is no definitive comparative research (CAF 2006). On one hand, only about a third of tax filers claim the benefit (Government of Canada 2014); on the other hand, tax incentives may be of greater significance to HNW donors making substantial gifts which, given that philanthropy has become more reliant on such donors, need to be encouraged. Three issues are currently affecting the application of tax incentives.

The first issue is which organizations should qualify to be tax exempt and whether the determination of such status automatically awards the privilege of being able to issue tax-deductible receipts to donors.

Second, a hint of a new debate—the clash of tax incentives with concerns over inequality—is emerging, with the United States serving as the proverbial canary. Tax incentives, particularly if they are deductions rather than credits, disproportionately benefit the wealthy making large donations (Reich 2005; Layton 2015). Under the logic of creating greater equity across tax brackets, the Obama administration has seven times proposed a cap on the charitable deduction for the highest tax bracket (which would affect individuals with incomes over $200,000). This proposal has met vigorous opposition among organized philanthropy predicting it

would reduce giving by $9.4 billion in one year (Brooks 2013); due to the stalemate in Congress, it has not passed. Whether this debate is an example of American exceptionalism or likely to be felt elsewhere is an open question. When the idea of reducing the tax incentives was floated in the United Kingdom and Mexico, opposition led to its quick dispatch, and Canada has moved in the opposite direction of significantly increasing for income earners its already very generous tax credits.

The third issue reflects the increasing cross-border flows of philanthropic capital and nonprofit activity, and is playing out as restrictions on inflows of foreign funding noted earlier and as attempts to facilitate transnationalism. How tax systems, even in more facilitating countries, accommodate transborder giving varies greatly, as illustrated by Australia and the United Kingdom (McGregor-Lowndes 2016): Australia has adopted a restrictive (and opaque) policy, while the United Kingdom has extended tax relief for donations to organizations outside the country, with controls on illegal activities (McGregor-Lowndes 2016).

In sum, tax incentives have been one of the most stable components of public policy for nonprofits, but they have been rooted in an assumption that philanthropy is domestic, and that absent regulatory competition, countries will not "outbid" each other to attract contributions and nonprofits from other places. Like business capital, however, philanthropy capital is increasingly footloose, and countries now need to determine whether they will embrace and facilitate this, recognizing it might produce outflows as well as inflows of giving, and manage it against oversight of transnational money laundering and financing of terrorist activities.

Political and Business Activities

The strings attached to tax exempt status generally include limitations on political and business activities, the former often reinforced by concerns over criticism of government and the latter by preventing unfair advantage relative to business. Among countries that accept nonprofits as part of democratic life, there is substantial variation—and growing divergence—in how political and business activities are treated (Carmichael 2016).

The ability to advocate (in nonpartisan ways) is seen as a criterion for the independence of the nonprofit sector in (Panel on the Independence of the Voluntary Sector 2015), but there is a very lively debate over how unconstrained this should be, especially relative to the common law doctrine of political purposes which makes nonprofits that have politically oriented missions ineligible to be considered "charitable" (Parachin 2015). In both common and civil law countries, the interpretations of eligibility and limits on advocacy vary widely, even among the relatively homogenous OECD countries (Bloodgood 2010), and recent court cases have widened the gap of legal interpretations.[9] Sweden and Norway are among the most permissive as political purposes are considered an aspect of public benefit and are eligible for registration (Carmichael 2016). Although there is considerable talk in democratic countries of a "chill" on advocacy because regulation unduly circumscribes it, evidence indicates that charities are undertaking only a fraction of the amount of political activities that they can legally do under current rules (Blumberg 2013; Bass et al. 2014), likely due to lack of expertise or interest in investing in advocacy, a desire to focus on services or concern over stakeholder backlash.

Business activities already account for 50 percent of the revenues of nonprofit sectors; and, with growing interest in social enterprise, they are being pursued even more actively with more creative ways of blending the commercial with social good. When business activities are undertaken by nonprofits recognized as charitable or public benefit, they may be regulated under three distinctive models. In only a very few cases are they prohibited from carrying on business activities, although this is the case in Turkey where nonprofits need to establish a separate legal entity which is treated for tax purposes like any other for-profit (ECNL 2015). At the other extreme is a permissive model, allowing nonprofits to undertake economic activities without limitation, as long as it is not the primary purpose of the organization and does not distribute the profits, which applies in France, Germany, and other countries of Western Europe. The revenues may be taxed as in the United States, fully tax exempt as in France, or exempt as long as they their destination is the charitable purpose. The third model permits business activity only if it is "related" and "incidental" to the organization's charitable purposes, as in India, Canada, and most of Eastern Europe.

Current regulatory approaches thus provide very differing degrees of flexibility when social entrepreneurs try to meld business and social good into one organizational form. The trend across Europe and Asia is to allow more scope for economic activities (Sidel and Moore n.d.), although approaches vary considerably. A means of facilitating social enterprise in England and several US states, now being emulated elsewhere, has been to create new hybrid corporate forms, Community Interest Companies (CICs) in the United Kingdom and low-profit limited liability companies (L3Cs) in the United States, to legitimate dual purposes and allow greater flexibility in raising capital, pursuing activities, and using revenues and assets (Manwaring and Valentine 2011). In spite of the hype about social enterprise, the use of CICs and L3Cs is still very limited (Pearse and Hopkins 2014). What seems to be occurring instead, although almost invisibly, are more complicated chains of ownership: charities and nonprofits owning for-profits, or being controlled by for-profits, raising new challenges for accountability and transparency.

Meta-Policies

Meta-policy reflects an overarching philosophy—explicit or implicit—about the appropriate roles of the state and the nonprofit sector (and the market), which gives rise to specific policies, programs, and governmental machinery, and guides reform. In the 1990s and early 2000s, several governments adopted such public philosophies. A popular policy instrument was the "compact," a negotiated framework agreement setting out the expectations and terms of engagement between government and the sector. These began in the United Kingdom and were transferred widely, including to Estonia, France, Spain, Sweden, Canada, and several Australian states (Casey et al. 2010; Reuter et al. 2012; Bullain and Toftisova 2005). As governments changed and priorities shifted to addressing austerity measures, however, most of these enabling frameworks quietly faded away. In recent years, a few nonprofit sectors have been successful in obtaining new strategies for collaboration. In general, however, coherent, publicly articulated meta-policies are strikingly absent.

Most meta-policies for this sector are not so explicit, nor do they arise from a base of mutual agreement. For many governments, particularly those favoring a smaller state or dealing with tight financial constraints, the policy is a quiet one of privatized services in which "charity" is supported by private philanthropy and social investment. Tax incentives for charitable giving are sizable; social investment is embraced; regulations restrict advocacy; the main role of the regulator is to prevent abuse and waste; umbrella and peak associations are intentionally weakened; and discussions in the public sphere about government-nonprofit relationships are lacking. Canada under a Conservative government from 2006 to 2015 and Australia under its neoliberal governments (Lyons and Dalton 2011; Ronalds 2015) are prime examples.

A third model is one in which government is openly adversarial to non-profits (Young 1999), restricting their activity in a variety of ways and isolating the sector from international funding and influences, as discussed above (Rutzen 2015; Civicus 2014; Carothers and Brechenmacher 2014). Several large economies, notably China and possibly India (Sidel 2016; China

Development Brief 2016), seem to be drifting from more restrictive models toward more supportive policies for nonprofits and more openness to internationalization. Where they land over the next few years will have important implications for other countries.

Finally, depending on how the current enchantment with social investment unfolds, particularly pay-for-success contracting (also called social impact bonds), a model of privatized charity may be reinforced, only with greater access to private capital, or a new approach germinated. The central issue of social investment is no longer the ability to attract capital but to build sufficient capacity on the demand side, including removing regulatory barriers.

Conclusion

Has civil society's time come in terms of building more constructive relationships with governments? Patterns of government-nonprofit relationships show considerable consistency across regions and over time, but they also demonstrate marked differences, even among subsectors within specific countries, depending on the policy goals and strategies pursued by both governments and nonprofits. How advocacy groups are treated may be very different from social service organizations, and in many places, environmental and LGBT organizations are singled out for even tighter controls. Surprisingly few countries have an overarching philosophy or meta-policy to guide development of this relationship that is visibly and coherently directed toward enabling a vibrant, pluralist nonprofit sector that contributes to policy making and citizenship, as well as service provision. Indeed, the troubling development of recent years has been the shrinking spaces for civil society and cross-border philanthropy, which have been declared priority concerns by the UN, EU, the Obama administration, and a variety of other governments and international organizations (Rutzen 2015).

TABLE 8.2 Models of Government-Nonprofit Relationships

Model	Basis	Features
Enabling	Relationship based	Well-articulated, mutually supported policy for the government-nonprofit relationship and divisions of labor across sectors; capable public and nonprofit sectors; extensive collaboration; enabling regulation and credible regulator; transparency; tax incentives support a broad culture of philanthropy; respect for independence of the nonprofit sector and advocacy; adaptable to evolving needs of the relationship
Charity	Tax-incentivized provision of services	Sizeable tax incentives to encourage private giving; interest in social investment; nonprofit services substitute for public services; limits on advocacy; main role of state regulation is to prevent abuse; few policy debates about the role of nonprofits
Restrictive	State control	Legislative and regulatory restrictions on formation, registration and activities of nonprofits; intolerance for advocacy; limits on foreign funding and influence; lack of transparency; no investment in capacity building; may be outright repression and conflict
Drifting and transition	Mixed elements; lack of political incentives for change	Ambivalence between developing a pluralistic nonprofit sector and controlling it; still an emphasis on service roles of nonprofits; mixed signals regarding legitimacy of advocacy and internationalization

Even in places that see a positive role for this sector, a variety of contradictions are pulling the government-nonprofit relationship in opposing directions. Philanthropy's increased reliance on HNW donors favors expanded tax incentives, which is countered by concerns over inequality, the policy influence of wealth, and the cost in tax expenditures. While tax privileges have been granted only to eligible categories of charitable or registered organizations, the entrepreneurial super rich and Millennials tend to be "sector agnostic" (Smith 2013), caring little if the organization they support is officially charitable, a hybrid social enterprise, or a social purpose business. The interest in accommodating the hybridization arising from new ways of blending economic activities and social must grapple with unforeseen issues of accountability and transparency. Although acknowledging the autonomy of the sector, regulators are increasingly interested in oversight of nonprofit governance and fundraising. Countries feel a sense of ownership over their domestic regulatory regimes; at the same time, increased cross-border philanthropy and nonprofit activity are creating pressures to liberalize and harmonize their approaches. The convention of a sharp divide between charity and political activity and current attempts to restrict nonprofit advocacy do not sit well with the Millennial generation's activism.

How these tensions will be worked out in different places is what will make analysis of government-nonprofit relationships so fascinating in coming years. The one outcome that is quite certain is that greater transparency will be the norm, and more meaningful data will be co-created and put to work for public benefit through digital social innovation. And, such transparency may create the political incentives for positive reform of government-nonprofit relations that are currently lacking.

Notes

1. In many contexts, the term "civil society organization (CSO)" is preferred over that of "nonprofit" because it emphasizes that the primary function may be engagement in citizenship and civic life rather than service delivery, and that many are not as highly institutionalized as they are in the United States and other developed countries.

2. Although charity regulators are not the most high profile institutions, public confidence in them matters, as demonstrated by an Australian survey which found that public confidence in charities increased significantly among those who were aware of and understood the role of the newly created not-for-profit commission (ACNC 2013).

3. The pledge of $3 billion by Jack Ma, one of China's richest people, to aid causes related to health care and environmental protection could have a significant influence on how nonprofits and governments address these issues (*Economist* 2014; Soskis 2014).

4. Direct government financing, through grants and contracts is of course also important, providing operational support and purchasing public services from nonprofits and indirectly regulating their activities. Such financing is difficult to assess without a deep dive into government data, a task beyond the scope of this chapter.

5. Following the model of the Charity Commission of England and Wales (created in 1853), all were established as independent commissions, although New Zealand's commission has been moved into a line department. The US and Canada have long-standing regulators, both housed in the tax agency.

6. In most countries, sector self-regulation goes hand-in-hand with state regulation, and ranges from voluntary codes of standards to a rigorous (albeit voluntary) certification system recently established by the sector in Canada. Although participation in and effectiveness of self-regulation varies considerably, it is an important component of the evolving co-regulatory relationship with governments, but also beyond the scope of this chapter.

7. In common law countries, the legal concept of charity, defined by centuries of case law, focuses on purposes and activities; if they meet eligibility criteria of purposes and activities, organizations are registered and receive associated tax benefits. In most cases (e.g., UK and Canada), registered charities automatically qualify for tax exemptions and receipting privileges, whereas in Australia, registered charities need to apply separately to the tax office to become eligible as Designated Gift Recipients. This means that while religion is considered charitable and exempt from income tax, unless a religious charity can demonstrate it provides some other public benefit it will not be able to issue tax receipts for donations. In civil law countries, the legal form determines the treatment of nonprofits, and "registration" refers to acquiring this legal form. There is often much greater variety of legal forms within civil law countries, and many recent reforms have aimed at greater harmonization of treatment among them. While a number of common law countries (except the US and Canada) have created independent charity commissions, the tendency for civil law countries is to house primary regulatory functions in the tax agency.

8. These fast growing industrializing countries are often referred to as the "BRICS"—Brazil, Russia, India, China, and South Africa—although their booming economic conditions have changed significantly since the term was first coined in 2001.

9. The Australian High Court determined that advocacy related to a charitable purpose can itself be considered charitable, while a New Zealand court decided in favour of Greenpeace being considered a charity as political purposes can be charitable, and in 2014 a UK tribunal went even further to reason that human rights based advocacy can be "immune to the rules restricting political advocacy" (Parachin 2015).

References

Achieve. (2014). *2014 Millennial Impact Report: Millennial Usability Testing*. Indianapolis, IN: Achieve Inc.

ACNC—Australian Charities and Not-for-Profits Commission. (2013). *Public Trust and Confidence in Australian Charities*. Sydney: ACNC.

Bass, Gary D., Abramson, Alan J., and Dewey, E. (2014). "Effective Advocacy: Lessons for Nonprofit Leaders from Research and Practice." In R. J. Pekkanen, S. R. Smith, and Y. Tsujinaka (Eds.), *Nonprofits and Advocacy: Engaging Community and Government in an Era of Retrenchment* (pp. 254–294). Baltimore, MD: Johns Hopkins University Press.

Birkwood, S. (2015). "Fundraising Standards Board to Investigate Death of Poppy Seller Olive Cooke, Says Chief Executive Alistair McLean." *Third Sector*, May 18. Retrieved from www.thirdsector.co.uk/fundraising-standards-board-investigate-death-poppy-seller-olive-cooke-says-chief-executive-alistair-mclean/fundraising/article/1347535.

Bloodgood, E. (2010). "Institutional Environment and the Organization of Advocacy NGOs in the OECD." In A. Prakash and M. K. Gugerty (Eds.), *Advocacy Organizations and Collective Action*. Cambridge UK: Cambridge University Press.

Blumberg, M. (2013). *Initial T3010 Descriptions of Political Activities by Canadian Charities*. Retrieved from www.globalphilanthropy.ca/images/uploads/Initial_T3010_Descriptions_of_Political_Activities_by_Canadian_Charities.pdf.

Blumberg, M. (2016). *Increasing the Productivity of the Charity and Non-profit Sector through Greater Transparency and Accountability Submission to the House of Commons Standing Committee on Finance*. Toronto, ON: Blumberg Segal LLP. Retrieved from www.globalphilanthropy.ca/images/uploads/Submission_to_Finance_Committee_by_Mark_Blumberg_of_Blumberg_Segal_LLP_January_2016_docx.pdf.

Bode, In. (2011). "Creeping Marketization and Postcorporatist Governance: The Transformation of State-Nonprofit Relations in Continental Europe." In S. D. Phillips and S. R. Smith (Eds.), *Governance and Regulation in the Third Sector: International Perspective* (pp. 115–141). London: Routledge.

Breen, O. (2015). "Allies or Adversaries? Foundation Responses to Government Policing of Cross-Border Charity." *International Journal of Not-for-Profit Law*, 7(1), 45–71.

Bria, F. (2015). *Growing a Digital Innovation System for Europe*. Brussels: Digital Social Innovation. Retrieved from https://issuu.com/digitalsocial innovation/docs/disreport-forwebsite-print.

Brooks, A. C. (2013). *The Great Recession, Tax Policy, and the Future of Charity in America*. Washington, DC: American Enterprise Institute.

Bullain, N., and Toftisova, R. (2005). "A Comparative Analysis of European Policies and Practices of NGO-Government Cooperation." *International Journal of Not-for-Profit Law*, 7(4), 64–112.

Butcher, J., and de Tagtachian, B. B. (2015). "Latin America and the Caribbean Revisited: Pathways for Research." *Voluntas*, 27(1), 1–18.

CAF. (2006). *International Comparisons of Charitable Giving*. Charities Aid Foundation Briefing Paper, November. London: CAF.

CAF. (2013). *Future World Giving: Unlocking the Potential of Global Philanthropy*. London: CAF.

CAF. (2014). *Philanthropy: A Gift or Investment? How Young, Socially-Conscious Investors are Balancing Approaches to Philanthropy*. London: CAF.

Carmichael, C. (2016). "The Fiscal Treatment of Philanthropy from a Comparative Perspective." In T. Jung, S. D. Phillips, and J. Harrow (Eds.), *The Routledge Companion to Philanthropy* (pp. 244–259). London: Routledge.

Carothers, Thomas, and Brechenmacher, S. (2014). *Closing Spaces: Democracy and Human Rights Support under Fire*. Washington, DC: Carnegie Endowment for International Peace.

Casey, J. (2016). *The Nonprofit World: Civil Society and the Rise of the Nonprofit Sector*. Boulder and London: Kumarian Press.

Casey, J., Bronwen, D., Melville, R., and Onyx, J. (2010). "Strengthening Government-Nonprofit Relations: International Experiences with Compacts." *Voluntary Sector Review*, 1(1), 56–76.

China Development Brief. (2016, February 23). *An Interview with Mark Sidel: Engaging with Chinese Philanthropy from a Global Perspective*. Retrieved from http://chinadevelopmentbrief.cn/articles/an-interview-with-mark-sidel-engaging-with-chinese-philanthropy-from-a-global-perspective/.

Civicus. (2014). *State of Civil Society Report: Reimaging Global Governance*. Johannesburg: Civicus.

Cosgrove, S. (2010). *Leadership From the Margins Women and Civil Society Organizations in*

Argentina, Chile, and El Salvador. New Brunswick, NJ: Rutgers University Press.

Cowly, E., McKenzie, T., Pharoah, C., and Smith, S. (2011). *The New State of Donation: Three Decades of Household Giving to Charity 1978–2008.* Centre for Charitable Giving and Philanthropy. London: Cass Business School.

CRA—Canada Revenue Agency. (2015). *The Canada Revenue Agency Revokes the Registration of the Canadian Friends of Pearl Children.* Ottawa, ON: CRA. Retrieved from http://news.gc.ca/web/article-en.do?nid=1002989.

Dehne, A., Friedrich, P., Nam, C. W., and Parsche, R. (2008). "Taxation of Nonprofit Associations in an International Comparison." *Nonprofit and Voluntary Sector Quarterly*, 37(4), 709–729.

Deloitte. (2014). *Big Demands and High Expectations: The Deloitte Millennial Study.* London: Deloitte Touche Tohmatsu Limited.

Economist. (2014). "China's Carnegie." *The Economist*, May 3. Retrieved from www.economist.com/news/leaders/21601510-jack-mas-establishment-new-charitable-foundation-offers-his-country-important.

Eikenberry, A. (2016). "Could Giving Circles Rebuild Philanthropy from the Bottom Up?" *Nonprofit Quarterly*, February 4. Retrieved from https://nonprofitquarterly.org/2016/02/04/could-giving-circles-rebuild-philanthropy-from-the-bottom-up/.

Einolf, C. J. (2015). "The Social Origins of the Nonprofit Sector and Charitable Giving." In P. Wiepking and F. Handy (Eds.), *Palgrave Handbook of Global Philanthropy* (pp. 509–529). Basingstoke, UK: Palgrave Macmillan.

ECNL—European Center for Not-for-Profit Law. (2009). *Study on Recent Public and Self-Regulatory Initiatives Improving Transparency and Accountability of Non-Profit Organisations in the European Union.* Budapest: ECNL.

ECNL—European Center for Not-for-Profit Law. (2015). *Legal Regulation of Economic Activities of Civil Society Organizations.* Budapest: ECNL.

Frumkin, P. (2002). *On Being Nonprofit: A Conceptual and Policy Primer.* Cambridge, MA: Harvard University Press.

Gancman, L. (2015). "Cabinet Moves to Force NGOs to Declare Foreign Government Funding." *Times of Israel*, December 27. Jerusalem. Retrieved from www.timeso-fisrael.com/cabinet-moves-to-force-ngos-to-declare-foreign-government-funding/.

Government of Canada, Department of Finance. (2014) *Tax Expenditures and Evaluations.* Ottawa: Department of Finance.

Hackett, C., Cooperman, A., and Ritchey, K. (2015). *The Future of World Religions: Population Growth Projections, 2010–2050.* Philadelphia, PA: Pew Research Center.

Herrold, C. (2015). "Giving in Egypt: Evolving Charitable Traditions in a Changing Political Economy." In P. Wiepking and F. Handy (Eds.), *Palgrave Handbook of Global Philanthropy* (pp. 307–315). London: Palgrave Macmillan.

House of Commons Public Administration Select Committee—UK. (2016). *The 2015 Charity Fundraising Controversy: Lessons for Trustees, the Charity Commission, and Regulators.* London: PAC.

Hudson Institute. (2015). *The Index of Philanthropic Freedom 2015.* Washington, DC: Hudson Institute.

Ibrahim, B. (2015). "States, Public Space, and Cross-border Philanthropy: Observations from the Arab Transitions." *International Journal of Not-for-Profit Law*, 17(1), 72–85.

Johnson Center on Philanthropy. (2013). *#Nextgen Donors, Respecting Legacy, Revolutionizing Philanthropy.* Grand Rapids, MI: Johnson Center on Philanthropy at Grand Valley State University.

Kang, C., Auh, Yoonkyung, E., and Hur, Y. (2015). "Giving in South Korea: A Nation of Givers for the Population under Public Assistance." In P. Wiepking and F. Handy (Eds.), *Palgrave Handbook of Global Philanthropy* (pp. 426–454). Basingstoke, UK: Palgrave Macmillan.

Kuttab, A., Matic, N., and ElMikawy, N. (2015). "Arab Philanthropy: From Social Giving to Social Change." *Alliance Magazine*, 20(3), 22–24.

Lasby, D. (2011). "What T3010 Data tell Us about Charity Financing." *The Philanthropist*, 24(2), 155–160.

Lavalle, A. G., and Bueno, N. S. (2011). "Waves of Change Within Civil Society in Latin America Mexico City and São Paulo." *Politics & Society*, 39(3), 415–450.

Layton, M. D. (2015). "The Influence of Fiscal Incentives on Philanthropy across Nations." In P. Wiepking and F. Handy (Eds.), *Palgrave Handbook of Global Philanthropy* (pp. 540–557). Basingstoke, UK: Palgrave Macmillan.

Levine, M. (2015). "Chan Zuckerberg LLC: No Tax Breaks + No Accountability – What Exactly?" *Nonprofit Quarterly*, December 7. Retrieved from http://nonprofit-quarterly.org/2015/12/07chan-zuckerberg-llc-are-no-tax-breaks-plus-no-accountability-good for-the-public/.

Lyons, Mark, and Dalton, B. (2011). "Australia: A Continuing Love Affair with New Public Management." In S. D. Phillips and S. R. Smith (Eds.), *Governance and Regulation in the Third Sector: International Perspective* (pp. 238–259). London: Routledge.

Manwaring, Susan, and Valentine, A. (2011). *Social Enterprise in Canada: Structural Options.* Toronto, ON: MaRS.

McGregor-Lowndes, M., Tarr, J.-A., and Silver, N. (2016). "The Fisc and the Frontier: Approaches to Cross-border Charity in Australia and the UK." *The Philanthropist*, May.

Mesch, D., and Pactor, A. (2016). "Women and Philanthropy." In T. Jung, S. D. Phillips, and J. Harrow (Eds.), *The Routledge Companion to Philanthropy* (pp. 88–101). London: Routledge.

Micklewright, J., and Schnepf, S. V. (2009). "Who Gives Charitable Donations for Overseas Development?" *Journal of Social Policy*, 38, 317–341.

Morgan, G. (2015). "The End of Charity?" *Valedictory Lecture*. Sheffield: Sheffield Hallam University. Retrieved from www.shu.ac.uk/_assets/pdf/the-end-of-charity-morgan.pdf.

Mottiar, S., and Ngcoya, M. (2016). "Indigenous Philanthropy: Challenging Western Preconceptions." In T. Jung, S. D. Phillips, and J. Harrow (Eds.), *The Routledge Companion to Philanthropy*. London: Routledge.

Muttart Foundation. (2013). *Talking about Charities 2013.* Edmonton, AB: Muttart Foundation.

Nielsen. (2014). *Millennials-Breaking the Myths.* New York: Nielsen.

Oxhorn, P. (2011). *Sustaining Civil Society Economic Change, Democracy, and the Social Construction of Citizenship in Latin America.* University Park, PA: Penn State University Press.

Panel on the Independence of the Voluntary Sector. (2015). *An Independent Mission: The Voluntary Sector in 2015.* London: Baring Foundation. Retrieved from www.independencepanel.org.uk/wp-content/uploads/2015/02/Independence-Panel-Report_An-Independent-Mission-PR.pdf.

Parachin, A. (2015). *Charitable Foundations and Advocacy; Reimagining the Doctrine of Political Purposes.* Montreal: Montreal Research Laboratory on Canadian Philanthropy.

Pearse, J. A., and Hopkins, J. P. (2014). "Regulation of L3Cs for Social Enterprise: A Prerequisite to Increased Utilization." *Nebraska Law Review*, 92(2), 259–288.

Phillips, S. D. (2013). "Shining Light on Charities or Looking in the Wrong Place? Regulation-by-Transparency in Canada." *Voluntas*, 24(3), 881–905.

Phillips, S. D., and Smith, S. R. (2014). "A Dawn of Convergence?: Third Sector Policy Regimes in the 'Anglo-Saxon' Cluster." *Public Management Review*, 16(8), 1141–1163.

Public Accounts Committee, House of Commons, UK. (2014). *The Charity Commission.* London: PAC. Retrieved from http://www.publications.parliament.uk/pa/cm201314/cmselect/cmpubacc/792/792.pdf.

Reich, R. (2005). "A Failure of Philanthropy: American Charity Shortchanges the Poor, and Public Policy is Partly to Blame." *Stanford Social Innovation Review*, Winter, 25–33.

Reuter, M., Wijkström, F., and von Essen, J. (2012). "Policy Tools or Mirrors of Politics. Government-Voluntary Sector Compacts in the Post-Welfare State Age." *Nonprofit Policy Forum*, 3(2).

Ronalds, P. (2015). "Australia: Federal Government and Nonprofit Relations in Australia." In J. Brothers (Ed.), *Rebalancing Public Partnership*. London and New York: Routledge.

Rutzen, D. (2015). "Aid Barriers and the Rise of Philanthropic Protectionism." *International Journal of Not-for-Profit Law*, 17(5), 5–44.

Sabeti, H. (2009). *The Emerging Fourth Sector: A New Sector of Organizations at the Intersection of the Public, Private and Social Sectors.* Washington, DC: Aspen Institute. Retrieved from www.fourthsector.net.

Salamon, L. M. (2010). "Putting Civil Society Sector on the Economic Map." *Annals of Public and Cooperative Economics*, *81*(2), 167–210.

Salamon, L. M., and Anheier, H. K. (1998). "Social Origins of Civil Society: Explaining the Nonprofit Sector Cross-Nationally." *Voluntas*, *9*(3), 213–248.

Salamon, L. M., Anheier, H. K., List, R., Toepler, S., and Wojciech Sokolowski, S. (1999). *Global Civil Society: Dimensions of the Nonprofit Sector*. Baltimore, MD: The Johns Hopkins Center for Civil Society Studies.

Salamon, L. M., Sokolowski, S.-W., and List, R. (2003). *Global Civil Society: An Overview*. Baltimore, MD: Johns Hopkins University Press.

Salamon, L. M., Sokolowski, S. W., Megan, A., and Tice, H. S. (2013). "The State of Global Civil Society and Volunteering: Latest Findings from the Implementation of the UN Nonprofit Handbook." *Working Papers of the John Hopkins Comparative Nonprofit Sector Project*, *49*, 18.

Schmid, H., and bar Nissim, H. S. (2016). "The Globalization of Philanthropy: Trends and Channels of Giving." In T. Jung, S. D. Phillips, and J. Harrow (Eds.), *The Routledge Companion to Philanthropy* (pp. 162–177). London: Routledge.

Sidel, M. (2016). "Philanthropy in Asia: Evolving Public Policy." In T. Jung, S. D. Phillips, and J. Harrow (Eds.), *The Routledge Companion to Philanthropy* (pp. 260–272). London: Routledge.

Sidel, Mark, and Moore, D. (n.d.). *The Law Affecting Civil Society in Asia: Developments and Challenges for Nonprofit and Civil Society Organizations: Report prepared by the International Center for Not-for-Profit Law (ICNL)*. Retrieved from https://media.law.wisc.edu/m/fjfgn/SidelMoore-ICNLAsiaLawAug2015.pdf.

Skelcher, C., and Smith, S. R. (2015). "Theorizing Hybridity: Institutional Logics, Complex Organizations, and Actor Identities: The Case of Nonprofits." *Public Administration*, *93*(2), 433–448.

Smith, B. K. (2013). *Version 2.0: The Giving Pledge Globalizes*. New York, NY: The Foundation Center. Retrieved from http://blog.glasspockets.org/2013/02/smith-20130221.html?_ga=1.214 95932.674833088.1456840336.

Soskis, B. (2014). "How the Giving Pledge is Inspiring Foreigners to Give." *The Atlantic*, May 15. Retrieved from www.theatlantic.com/business/archive/2014/05/how-us-philanthropy-is-inspiring-foreigners-to-give/370889/.

Spero, J. E. (2014). *Charity and Philanthropy in Russia, China, India and Brazil*. New York: The Foundation Center.

The Straits Times. (2016). "China Defends NGO Law, Says Still Being Revised." *The Straits Times*, March 4. Retrieved from www.straitstimes.com/asia/east-asia/china-defends-foreign-ngo-law-says-still-being-revised.

TD Bank and Investor Economics. (2015). *Time, Treasure, Talent: Canadian Women and Philanthropy*. Toronto, ON: TD Bank.

Themudo, N. S. (2013). *Nonprofits in Crisis: Economic Development, Risk and the Philanthropic Kuznets Curve*. Bloomington, IN: Indiana University Press.

USAID. (2012). *The 2012 CSO Sustainability Index for Central and Eastern Europe and Eurasia*. Washington, DC: USAid.

US Trust and Lilly Family School of Philanthropy. (2014). *The 2014 US Trust Study of High Net Worth Philanthropy*. Boston, MA, and Indianapolis, IN: US Trust and Lilly Family School of Philanthropy.

Wang, X., Liu, F., Nan, F., Xiaoping, Z., and Xiulan, Z. (2015). "Giving in China: An Emerging Nonprofit Sector Embedded within a Strong State." In P. Wiepking and F. Handy (Eds.), *Palgrave Handbook of Global Philanthropy* (pp. 354–368). Basingstoke, UK: Palgrave Macmillan.

Wagner. I. (2016). *Diversity and Philanthropy: Expanding the Circle of Giving*. Santa Barbara, CA: Praeger.

Wiepking, P., and Handy, F. (Eds.). (2015). *The Palgrave Handbook of Global Philanthropy*. London: Palgrave Macmillan.

Willebois, E. V. D. D. De. (2010). *Nonprofit Organizations and the Combatting of Terrorism Financing: A Proportionate Response*. Washington, DC: World Bank Publications.

Wood, J. (2016). *Regulatory Waves and a Rising Tide: CSO Regulation and Self-Regulation*. Unpublished Paper. Ottawa, ON: Carleton University, School of Public Policy and Administration.

World Economic Forum. (2013). *The Future Role of Civil Society*. Geneva: World Economic Forum.

Young, D. R. (1999). "Complementary, Supplementary, or Adversarial? A Theoretical and Historical Examination of Nonprofit-Government Relations in the United States." In E. T. and S. Boris (Eds.), *Nonprofits and Government: Collaboration and Conflict* (pp. 31–70). Washington, DC: The Urban Institute Press.

CHAPTER 9

The Internationalization of the Nonprofit Sector

John Casey

Casey, John. "The Internationalization of the Nonprofit Sector," in *The Nonprofit World: Civil Society and the Rise of the Nonprofit Sector*, J. Casey (Boulder, Colo: Kumarian Press/Lynn Riemer, 2016: 167–199).

Just as nonprofits have become increasingly influential at national levels, the activities of the international dimensions of a nonprofit sector that operates between the expanding intergovernmental structures and the global marketplace for transnational and multinational businesses have correspondingly escalated (Anheier 2014; Batliwala and Brown 2006; Boli 2006; Schechter 2010). The current wave of globalization and deterritorialization has engendered denser networks of cross-border connections in almost every sphere of modern life, and the nonprofit sector is no exception.

The international work of the nonprofit sector encompasses all aspects of the operations and impact of nonprofit organizations that transcend national borders. Formerly domestic, nonprofits are "going international" at the same time as increasing numbers of deliberately international nonprofits are being established (Anheier 2014; Boli 2006; Lewis 2007). The following discussion is focused on organizations that are autonomous, nongovernmental entities that comply with the structural-functional definition of nonprofits. Excluded are the purely intergovernmental international organizations—the bilateral or multilateral institutions created through treaties or other agreements that have national governments as their primary membership, including global organizations such as the United Nations, the World Bank, and the World Trade Organization and regional institutions such as the European Union and the African Union.

Many hybrid organizations straddle definitions, either in themselves or through their affiliated organizations. The UN Children's Fund (UNICEF) is a UN agency with an executive board comprising representatives of member nations, and as such it is clearly an intergovernmental organization. To support its work, UNICEF has fostered the creation of a network of UNICEF national committees, which are incorporated as independent local nonprofit organizations in their countries of operations. Currently thirty-seven such nonprofit UNICEF national committees are in operation, all in industrialized wealthy countries, which raise funds on behalf of UNICEF and advocate in support of its programs.

Given the considerable national variations in political regimes and service delivery models, the nonprofit legal structure has become a "flag of convenience" for international dialogues in a wide range of fields. The nonprofit form sidesteps many of the constraints imposed on intergovernmental structures by sovereignty and geopolitical tensions.

DOI: 10.4324/9780367696559-12

The Rise of the International Nonprofit Sector

Since 1907, the Union of International Associations has documented the growth of intergovernmental and international nongovernmental organizations. The database of the union includes only "prominent" organizations and so does not count the thousands of smaller international nonprofits or the primarily domestic nonprofits around the world that also have an international dimension to their work. In the database, international nonprofits now outnumber intergovernmental organizations by a factor of 10, and their growth rate since the 1970s has been significantly larger.

The organizations that from a contemporary lens would now be considered international nonprofits have a long history. Faith-based institutions have long fomented contact and exchange between the far-flung corners of their influence and have actively proselytized and fought wars to extend their range. The colonial structures of the European powers in the sixteenth to twentieth centuries often went accompanied by philanthropic outreach to indigenous populations and indigent colonialists (generally through faith-based organizations).

In the database of the union is recorded the years of founding for international nongovernmental organizations. The first entry is for the Sovereign Constantinian Order, a monastic order founded in 312; the second is the Order of Saint Basil in 358. A steady trickle of organizations were founded in the fourth to eighteenth centuries, almost exclusively religious, including Muslim Sufi tariqas after the ninth century. Early fraternal organizations, universities, scientific and academic associations, mercantile organizations, and performing arts groups were also founded around this time, but not until the mid-1800s did secular international nonprofits—advocacy, social welfare, professional, and sports—begin to appear in greater numbers than faith-based organizations.

The secular independent international nonprofit sector began to emerge in significant numbers through social movements focused on humanitarianism and human rights, including antislavery and women's suffrage. Although avowedly secular, many of these new organizations had identifiably faith-related roots, particularly in Quaker communities. A number of now emblematic international nonprofits appeared in the mid-1800s, albeit in original forms that do not necessarily correspond with their current focus—the Young Men's Christian Association (YMCA) was founded in London in 1844 as an evangelical organization, and the Red Cross was formed in Geneva in 1863 to minister to soldiers wounded on European battlefields.

The globalization of the labor movement and radical left also date from this period—the Universal League for the Material Elevation of the Industrious Classes was an English political organization established in 1863 primarily to agitate for the right to assembly, labor rights, and suffrage of English workers, but its founding mandate also sought to increase recreational and educational opportunities and to promote international fraternity.

Even though some of the earliest organizations continued to exist, the early 1900s saw the first surge of truly modern international nonprofits, instantly identifiable as such to contemporary observers. Save the Children was founded in the United Kingdom in early 1919 by two Quaker social activist sisters, Eglantyne Jebb and Dorothy Buxton, in response to the aftermath of World War I and the Russian Revolution. The organization was controversial, as it sought to aid children in Germany and Austria, the enemies in the war. However, the concept of children's rights quickly found support around the world, particularly from women who were also campaigning for their own suffrage.

Also established in the first decades of the twentieth century were the US service clubs such as the Rotary (1905), the Kiwanis (1915), the Lions (1917), and Toastmasters (1924), as well as the large foundations associated with the US barons of industry, the Carnegie Corporation of New York (1911) and the Rockefeller Foundation (1913) (the foundations were originally chartered by legislation but later converted to nonprofits).

The importance of the work of international nonprofits was acknowledged in the 1945 Charter of the United Nations. The term *nongovernmental organization* (NGO) is commonly regarded as having come into widespread use through its inclusion in Article 71 of Chapter 10 of the Charter, which established a formal consultative status for organizations that were not agencies of member states. In the first years of the United Nations, only some fifty NGOs had consultative status (there are currently 3,800). The earliest NGOs with this status reflected both the primarily European, UK, and US origins of the first international nonprofits and the diversity of what constitutes the nongovernmental sector.

A considerable uptick can be seen in the international sector since the 1970s as part of the same associational revolution evident at domestic levels. The combination of the comparative advantage of the nonprofit sector in service delivery and policymaking, along with the globalization of professional and epistemic communities, has resulted in an explosion of the international nonprofit sector in numbers and salience. The expansion of the sector has been both a consequence and driver of globalization. It is a key part of the humanitarian aid industry but also of the environmental, peace, and justice movements. It also includes academic, professional, and cultural exchanges in areas as diverse as sport, gourmet cooking, and a range of commercial interests. In the past the focus of the work of international nonprofits had primarily been on issues of "low politics" of the environment, development assistance, human rights, and disaster relief, and on "Track II" international relations between professionals and civil servants. International nonprofits now increasingly also work directly with the "high politics" of international affairs and security and help manage "Track 1" state-level

relations (Ahmed and Potter 2006; Carey 2012; Schechter 2010).

Religious faith continues to be an important impetus in international nonprofits. The modern nonprofit sector may be more secular and universalist than earlier iterations, but religion is still a key part of the sector. Large historic faith-based entities, such as the Salvation Army, Islamic Relief, and American Jewish World Service, as well as networks such as the Association of World Council of Churches Related Development Organisations in Europe (APRODEV), continue to be major players in the international nonprofit scene, and the foundation story of a significant percentage of contemporary organizations includes narratives of faith-based inspirations. The YMCA evolved its focus and mission from the "aggressive evangelism" of its origins to its current focus on "social responsibility for human beings" (Muukkonen 2002), and a similar description could be applied to many of the historic nonprofits.

Currently, no figures have been consolidated on the broader international nonprofit sector beyond the some 30,000 active organizations identified in the Union of International Associations database.

The number of international nonprofits is hard to estimate due to varying opinions on what qualifies an organization to be included in the count. Where national statistics formally identify international nonprofits as a separate category from domestic organizations, they appear to be around only 1 percent to 2 percent of the total number of nonprofits in any country (Anheier 2014), and within that figure, only a minority are large enough to be included in international databases. However, many more organizations, although not formally classified as international, are still doing international work. In the United States, for example, of the 1.6 million nonprofits registered with the IRS, only around 20,000 (1.3 percent) register under the National Taxonomy of Exempt Entities (NTEE) Category Q, "international, foreign affairs, and national security" (the NTEE classification is self-designated by the organizations, and it allows for multiple classifications). Of these 20,000 organizations, 75 percent have an income of less than $100,000 per annum or do not report their income, and only 2.5 percent have an income of more than $5 million (National Center for Charitable Statistics 2012). However, any count based only on NTEE Category Q does not include the many organizations that clearly do international work but do not use that designation when registering. Olympic sports organizations, including the US Olympic Committee (with revenues of $140 million), are in a separate code, N71, "Olympics." While international nonprofits are only a small minority of the sector in the United States, they are well represented among the largest nonprofits in the country.

In contrast to the small number of organizations classified as Category Q in the NTEE database, a keyword search of the some 1.8 million US organizations in the database of GuideStar, the nonprofit transparency website, identifies 163,000 organizations (9 percent) that use the word *international* as part of their name, mission statement, or program description. In the United Kingdom, a similar keyword search of the 180,000 charities registered with the Charity Commission identifies only some 6,800 organizations (3.7 percent) that use the descriptor *international.*

In addition, an extensive network of international nonprofit activity is not formally constituted or is operating under the legal and fiscal sponsorship of other organizations. These informal organizations and the smaller formal organizations appear to be part of a rising number of "boutique" international nonprofits, which include numerous immigrant hometown associations. Many all-volunteer efforts are created to support specific foreign institutions (most often schools, orphanages, or medical clinics) or localities with which the principals have a particular bond either because their ancestral roots are there or because they feel some particular affinity after traveling, volunteering, or working in that area.

As globalization drives fundamental changes in economic, political, and social relations, organizations in the public and for-profit sectors are becoming more international and complex, and the nonprofit sector is keeping pace, driven by the same imperatives to scale-up in response to global concerns and facilitated by innovations in communications technology and the reduced transaction costs of the movement of information, capital, and personnel. The nonprofit sector has been able to act akin to the for-profit sector, without the sovereignty constraints that limit collaborations between governments. Nonprofits can construct multinational identities and operations, and parallels are evident between international nonprofits and multinational corporations in their search for new markets, brand promotion at the worldwide level, the internationalization of personnel, and the deterritorialization of the organizations (Siméant 2005). The growth of Oxfam, for example, exhibits many of the processes of partnerships and mergers more commonly associated with the for-profit sector.

In the following sections, I look at three forms, or degrees, of the internationalization of nonprofits: international cooperation between primarily domestic nonprofits, the increasing international reach of the work of formerly domestic nonprofits, and purposely created international nonprofits. They can be considered stages of internationalization (Anheier 2014), but they can also be seen as a series of coexisting ecologies of international connectivity. Overlaps and transitions can be found as existing domestic organizations become increasingly internationalized and new organizations are created with specific international intent, sometimes as the direct consequences of the increased connections between domestic nonprofits.

The Drivers of International Growth

The growth of the sector has been bolstered at the international level by the same debates unfolding at the domestic level about the inefficiencies of governmental institutions and the need to engage a wider range of partners in policymaking and service delivery. The growth in intergovernmental cooperation has helped drive a parallel expansion of "bottom-up multilateralism," as Michael Schechter (2010) called it, built on the connections between stronger activity "nodes" created by the expanding domestic nonprofit sectors (Florini 2000). The international versions of new public management, governance, and third-party agency approaches are the justifications for reducing government footprints and working with organizations that are seen as more flexible and innovative than public bureaucracies. Just as nonprofits have been seen as the answer to domestic service delivery and policymaking conundrums, they also became an international "magic bullet" (Edwards and Hulme 1996; Lindenberg and Dobel 1999). As state capacity wanes around the world in the face of economic constraints and eroding trust, the international nonprofit sector plays an ever-escalating role in delivering and regulating transnational public goods. The nonprofits' work is embraced by a wide range of ideologies and commercial interests.

Perhaps the most visible and most commonly identified driving force for the globalization of the nonprofit sector is the impact of new communication technologies. The Internet, social media, and other elements of new communication technologies have immeasurably reduced the transaction costs of managerial tasks, long-distance operations, and cross-border collaborations. Technology has also facilitated the creation of a new class of digital nonprofits that operate almost entirely in the ether of the Internet. Decolonization and nationalist liberation movements in the 1950s and 1960s created new sovereign countries, many of which were underdeveloped and fertile ground for the expansion of the activities of humanitarian nonprofits. Development assistance to these new countries was at first primarily channeled through official government-to-government aid, particularly as part of the client relationships of the Cold War superpowers, but the international nonprofits

that had previously focused their work on war relief in Europe then began to take on a wider developmental role around the globe.

During the Cold War, the battle of the two superpowers was the primary global backdrop for conflicts between and within nations. The end of the Cold War has opened up new political and programmatic space for a wider range of nonstate actors (Florini 2000; Götz 2010). It has shifted the focus of international aid from client states to an even broader development agenda by shining a harsh light on previous official aid projects in which the funds ended up in the pockets of corrupt elites. The broader agenda, as exemplified by the adoption by the United Nations of the Millennium Development Goals, has facilitated the emergence of the new interventionist principles such as the "Responsibility to Protect" (often referred to as R2P), which argues that the international community has the responsibility to intervene to protect threatened populations.

The opening of political spaces, the reconceptualization of the obligations of the international community, the growing demands of the more educated and prosperous citizens in the developing world, and the increasing availability of resources have all contributed to the expansion of the international activities of nonprofits. Those who may have been hesitant to act under previous nonintervention doctrines have left such reluctance behind, and many regimes that in the past resisted the work of nonprofits have come to accept that they can play a useful role.

More prosaically, nonprofit approaches to service delivery are also disseminated globally by the increasing numbers of people from around the world who have studied or worked in the United States and other industrialized countries with strong nonprofit sectors. Nonprofit globalization also has a substantial individual dimension. International workers, expatriates, students, and volunteers are circulating more freely around the globe and becoming key carriers of nonprofit mind-sets and the agents of cross-border linkages. The flow of individuals and ideas is facilitated by a number of key inter-national networks.

The evolving dynamics that have driven the expansion of the international nonprofit sector have also led to its greater politicization. As international nonprofits take on more respon-sibility for providing disaster relief, delivering aid, and managing international cultural and professional exchanges, some inevitably become more embroiled in the policymaking process and political conflicts. As a result, these orga-nizations increasingly find themselves the target of ideological critiques, as well as of physical attacks by armed groups (Ronalds 2010).

An important feature of the recent growth of the sector has been the increasing numbers of indigenous, South-based organizations that are emerging as a consequence of a growing skill base and the greater availability of funds in developing countries. These new organiza-tions often work in partnership with nonprofits from the North, but they are increasingly form-ing their own regional networks. Although resources and know-how have in the past flowed primarily from the North to the South, increasingly South-South collaborations and knowledge networks are forming. A nascent "reverse imperialism" can be identified. Many Northern international aid nonprofits now also operate "at home," working to address domestic social justice issues using strategies they have

learned in the developing world (Lewis 2014), and organizations from the South are setting up branches in the North.

International Nomenclature

Civil society (particularly when rendered as the more specific *civil society organizations*) is the more generic term that perhaps better embraces the broad range of organizations addressed in this reading. CIVICUS (2012), for example, described civil society as

> the arena, outside of the family, the State and the market, which is created by individual and collective actions, organizations and institutions to advance shared interests. Civil society therefore encompasses civil society organizations and the actions of less formal-ized groups and individuals (8).

Some commentators assert that because the term *NGO* deliberately purports to be apolitical, attaching that label and its associated logics to organizations that have sprung from grassroots or oppositional movements depoliticizes them and decouples them from their roots (Banks and Hulme 2012). In this framework, NGOs are seen as the domain of educated professionals

TABLE 9.1 Population and Consultative Status by Continent

Continent	Population, 2010 (Percentage of World Total)	NGOs With Consultative Status, 2007 (Percentage of Total)
Africa	14.95	11
Asia	60.31	16
Europe	10.61	37
Latin America/Caribbean	8.52	6
North America	5.09	29
Oceania	0.52	1

Source: Global Policy Forum (2012)

and are driven by the agendas of foreign or local elite donors. Organizations that seek to maintain a more grassroots identity instead prefer labels such as *social movement, civil society, community based,* or *right-holder.* Progressive feminists decry the "NGOization" of the women's movement (Bernal and Grewal 2014; Jad 2007; Lang 2013), which they claim has eviscerated it by reframing the struggle of women as a technical process instead of a political movement. Their concerns are primarily about the impact of professionalization and the role played by international sponsors of the movement, but the critique also focuses on the label *NGO* itself and the impact it has on the discourse around the movement.

The use of the concept of civil society in the international context goes beyond the mere identification of organizational forms as it raises the question of whether or not speaking of an emerging international, transnational, cosmopolitan, or global civil society (all of these descriptors have been used by different authors) is legitimate. International civil society transcends the aggregation of the work of individual organizations and so projects to the international polis the role that civil society is said to play in national contexts.

International Nonprofits and Global Civil Society

No global government or executive body legislates and regulates affairs or exercises the coercive powers equivalent to states. Yet public and private affairs are increasingly global, so regulation is effected through international governance "regimes" (Abbott and Snidal 2009; Karns and Mingst 2004), "systems" (Willetts 2011), "webs" (Zadek 2011), or "triangles" (Abbott and Snidal 2009) constructed by a patchwork of processes and institutions that include intergovernmental institutions, for-profit industry self-regulation, and international nonprofits. The treaties and conventions that emerge from the United Nations and the dozens of other multilateral and regional agreements, combined with the protocols and agreements from global summit meetings and conferences, constitute the dense networks of regulation and oversight that are the basis of international law. But the powers of these various instruments fall far short of those exercised by sovereign states within their own borders, particularly in matters of enforcement. The global governance organizations that develop and administer the patchwork are continually negotiating their legitimacy and authority (Koppell 2008), and in doing so, they are potentially conferring considerable political space to nonstate actors.

Scholars continue to debate whether globalization is leaving nation-states behind as the highest legitimate level of democratic power, a position they have held since the modern concepts of national sovereignty emerged from the Westphalia peace treaties of the 1640s (Chandhoke 2005; Clark 2008; Kaldor 2000; Keane 2003; Sparke 2013; Walzer 1998). For much of the twentieth century, the debates focused largely on interstate relations and the possible emergence and merits of a global government. More recently, however, the focus has broadened to include analyses of the multilayered and multifaceted governance of international rule making and the processes of global governmentality. Nonprofits are seen as an integral element of the construction of global governance "from below," as intergovernmental and multilateral institutions increasingly incorporate a broader range of nonstate actors into the processes for policy development and legitimation (Jonsson and Tallberg 2010; Karns and Mingst 2004; Sparke 2013; Willetts 2011).

Are international nonprofits part of an emerging global civil society that constitutes a truly new institutional realm with an increasingly autonomous role in global governance, as the "authentic" voice of world public opinion? Or are they unrepresentative artifacts, bound to the donor elites, narrow interests, or national governments that created them and facilitated their growth? John Keane (2003) argued that a global civil society is emerging, and it is a new "society of societies," but it is still evolving, and its salience will depend on its ability to become more democratic, better integrated into governance institutions, and more invested with universal values. However, others argue that international nonprofits continue to primarily represent the interests of their donors and sponsor states over those of their putative constituencies or beneficiaries.

In fact, their authority to represent anyone is often called into question. The mandate of international nonprofits is ambiguous at best given that their combined claimed membership is less than the population of a small state, and the internal governance processes of most organizations are less than democratic (Archibugi 2008).

The debates around the existence of an autonomous global civil society focus particularly on the role of nonprofits as opinion makers and as rule makers through their work in promoting, developing, and supervising international norms, standards, and regulations. They perform in these roles in fields as diverse as environmental issues, human rights, the empowerment of women, corporate social responsibility, election monitoring, prison reform, and post-transitional justice. Even though they have limited formal legal standing in the international arena (Lindblom 2013), nonprofits can be advocates for new standards and watchdogs for their implementation and oversight. L. David Brown and Fox (2000) noted that nonprofits help shape international events by identifying problems that might otherwise be ignored, articulating new values and norms to guide international practice, building transnational alliances, disseminating social innovations, helping negotiate resolutions to transnational disagreements, and mobilizing resources to intervene directly to address problems.

After the post-World War II period, in which nonprofits "underachieved" (Charnovitz 1997), the policy role of international nonprofits reemerged post-Cold War in the late twentieth century with high-profile campaigns such as the International Campaign to Ban Landmines and the continuing advocacy of the numerous environmental organizations. Perhaps the most durable contributions to global governance structures are the oversight and accreditation functions of dozens of international nonprofit professional and trade associations. At national levels, professional associations and advocacy groups may operate in effect as "private authorities" (Green 2014), regulating individuals and organizations that must, or voluntarily agree to, meet their standards. Some are chartered by their governments to steward the third-party accreditation or certification needed to exercise professions or to meet production standards, whereas others simply adopt this role through entrepreneurial accreditation or "seal of approval" schemes (Evetts 1995; Green 2014). Their international equivalents play similar roles in filling the voids of global regulation. The International Air Transport Association (IATA) is the successor organization to the International Air Traffic Association, was one of the original NGOs given consultative status by the United Nations. It is the trade association for the world's airlines and is a key player in formulating industry policy on aviation issues and representing the industry in negotiations with the International Civil Aviation Organization, an agency established by the United Nations in 1947 to codify international air navigation.

The question of whether true global "governing without government" is built on the relationships between multilateral institutions, nonprofits, and other nonstate actors, and how sustainable it can be, is an increasing preoccupation of international relations discourses (Karns and Mingst 2004; Reinicke 1998). International nonprofits are often not "at the table" when final rule making takes place, as that is generally the preserve of international civil servants and diplomats designated by their governments, but they may have been instrumental in shaping public perceptions and in pressuring for changes, and they are likely to help ensure that new rules are implemented and adhered to.

Within the international nonprofit sector, relationships are often strained between the various factions that lay claim to the title of the "true" civil society, given the chasm between those that have the resources to organize and project their voice, and the grassroots movements that see themselves as the authentic disenfranchised (Bond 2008). A civil society debate that focuses primarily on the role of larger, more established international nonprofits is regarded by some critics as a top-down institutional version divorced from its roots and should be contrasted, or contested, by a more bottom-up version.

Classifying International Nonprofits

International nonprofits are most commonly classified by their subject or field of work. The US NTEE Category Q subcodes present a more typical field-based taxonomy:

- Q01: Alliances and Advocacy
- Q02: Management and Technical Assistance
- Q03: Professional Societies and Associations
- Q05: Research Institutes and Public Policy Analysis
- Q11: Single Organization Support
- Q12: Fund-raising and Fund Distribution
- Q19: Support Not Elsewhere Classified
- Q20: Promotion of International Understanding
- Q21: International Cultural Exchange
- Q22: International Academic Exchange
- Q23: International Exchange Not Elsewhere Classified
- Q30: International Development
- Q31: International Agricultural Development
- Q32: International Economic Development

- Q33: International Relief
- Q35: Democracy and Civil Society Development
- Q40: International Peace and Security
- Q41: Arms Control and Peace
- Q42: United Nations Associations
- Q43: National Security
- Q50: International Affairs, Foreign Policy, and Globalization
- Q51: International Economic and Trade Policy
- Q70: International Human Rights
- Q71: International Migration and Refugee Issues
- Q99: International, Foreign Affairs, and National Security Not Elsewhere Classified

Other taxonomies of international nonprofits focus on key structural markers such as the geographic reach of organizations, the nature of the membership, and the relationship between the various international units.

International nonprofits generally have multilevel structures with international, national, and local elements. The articulation between headquarters and the units scattered around the world varies considerably according to how each organization manages the centrifugal-centripetal dynamics that push it toward decentralization or centralization. What the public identifies as a single organization may in fact be a conglomerate of linked international and national organizations.

Researchers (L. D. Brown, Ebrahim, and Batliwala 2012; Lindenberg and Bryant 2001; Young et al. 1999) who focus on such intraorganizational relationships have identified clusters along a continuum of the centralization-decentralization of governance structures and accountabilities that typically include the following:

- Networks: Are created by fully independent organizations that form loose connections to exchange information about strategies and advocacy campaigns.
- Weak umbrellas: Seek to coordinate strategies and collaborate on advocacy campaigns through stable coalitions but do not delegate any powers to a central secretariat (which may

be rotating or housed in the offices of a wealthier member).

- Confederations: Delegate a central office or secretariat with limited responsibilities for coordination and standard setting, but leave significant powers with affiliates. Larger and wealthier affiliates often dominate the confederation dynamics.
- Federations: Have strong centralized powers for standard setting and resource acquisition. Members retain separate boards and some operational independence, but the federation structure requires joint decisions for core operating principles and strategies.
- Unitary organizations: Have a single, central board and strong hierarchy. Local structures are branch offices, controlled directly from headquarters, with only limited distributed powers of independent action (although field operations may require some form of local registration).

This continuum is a bit misleading as the extremes generally describe different sets of organizations that in all likelihood cannot, or will not, migrate too far along the spectrum. Independent organizations in a network may seek to deepen their coordination and to harmonize their activities, and occasionally two or more may even choose to merge, but as a network they are unlikely to move beyond the federation stage (although some federations such as Oxfam have built such a strong brand identity that many outsiders assume they are a unitary organization). Equally, a unitary organization is unlikely to devolve to the point that its former units become independent organizations, although the increasingly common practice of Northern organizations partnering with existing local Southern organizations, or sponsoring the establishment of new affiliates, is in effect the process of a unitary organization creating its own federation that may spin off increasingly independent organizations.

Any analysis of the tensions between centralization and decentralization is contingent on whether it focuses on a single organization or on the relationships between multiple organizations. Also pertinent is whether the focus is on bottom-up network building by like-minded organizations seeking to coordinate their activities or on top-down outreach by organizations seeking partnerships or fostering the creation of local affiliates. The international "franchising" of organizational models such as Teach for America (corps of young teachers working in poverty zones) and the Repair Cafés (clubs of volunteer retirees, primarily men, who run community repair shops) generally create linkages that are somewhere between federations and confederations (the Repair Cafés also have a parallel in the Men's Sheds, popular in Ireland and Australia).

The structures of international nonprofits and their networks are inherently unstable (Foreman 1999; Lindenberg and Bryant 2001). Organizations that form part of a weak umbrella structure find that competition for resources, duplication of efforts, and donor confusion create pressures to strengthen the linkages between members; confederations face the challenge of noncompliant members so they often seek to strengthen the mechanisms of centralized control; and strong federations and unitary organizations must deal with demands for increased local autonomy. Different aspects of the work of an organization may operate in different structural modes. Wendy Wong (2012) suggested that human rights advocacy nonprofits that centralize agenda setting and decentralize the implementation of that agenda will be more successful in influencing public policy.

Continued tension can be found over the trade-off when balancing centralized coordination and efficiency in decisionmaking and resource allocation against decentralized local autonomy and buy-in by disparate units (Young et al. 1999). Unitary organizations decentralize to strengthen local ownership, at the same time as alliances, networks, and confederations move to greater centralization to improve harmonization while retaining the diversity and independence of members (Johnston 2012). Organizations are continually seeking the holy grail of the optimal equilibrium point in the intricate interactions and power relationships between affiliates and the central office. Some commentators suggest that the optimal configuration is a "bumblebee" federation of interdependent organizations that can flexibly adapt to the flurries of activity (Foreman 1999; Lindenberg and Bryant 2001; Lindenberg and Dobel 1999).

Marc Lindenberg and Coralie Bryant (2001) documented how the prominent international nonprofits Médecins Sans Frontières (Doctors Without Borders), Save the Children, and Plan International have moved through different structural configurations in response to changing organizational and political pressures. Many international organizations, including World Vision International and Habitat for Humanity, have adapted their international governance structure to allow for a range of relationships with the central office, based on the level of stability and strength of local affiliates. Some are branch offices, whereas others are federated independent organizations.

The Largest International Nonprofits

Which are the largest international nonprofit organizations? The question is difficult to answer given the different conceptualizations of the category and the ambiguities of what constitutes an organization for such calculations. Does the term *international nonprofit organization* refer to only a single legal entity, or does it also include all affiliates of conglomerates, federations, subsidiaries, and brands? Separating the eleemosynary activities of organizations from their faith-based or commercial work or separating their international work from domestic activities can also be difficult.

Added to the definitional and jurisdictional complications are differences in transparency regulations and in the enforcement of accounting standards between countries, as well as idiosyncrasies in accounting practices regarding contributions. Regulators in the United States

have recently alleged that some international nonprofits are overvaluing noncash contributions (supplies, logistic support, etc.) to raise their profile and to inflate perceptions of their effectiveness.

Notwithstanding these challenges in documenting income and assets, the organizations below can still be identified as among the largest international nonprofits. Almost all of the organizations have some type of federated structure with semiautonomous affiliates around the world. The figures quoted below are from the organizations' own annual reports or tax returns, [and] are not necessarily definitive appraisals of their full wealth or reach.

Arguably, at the top of the list of the largest international nonprofits should be the *faith-based organizations* that also have a social service and aid mission, including the Salvation Army, St. Vincent de Paul, the Anglican Mission societies, Jewish Communal Fund, and Islamic Relief.

Operating as international nonprofits (see discussion later in this chapter), the largest *sports associations* move billions of dollars through multiple legal entities. The International Olympic Committee (IOC) and the Fédération Internationale de Football Association (FIFA, the governing body for football-soccer) are Switzerland-based nonprofits, but both are also registered in the United States as 501(c)(4) organizations. In 2012, the IOC declared to the US tax authorities an annual income of $3.4 billion and FIFA $1.1 billion. Both have substantial additional income through numerous affiliated nonprofit and for-profit legal entities, and their national associations move many billions more.

Given that the United States is by far the largest contributor to both official development aid and global philanthropy, international aid organizations headquartered (or with a substantial presence) in the United States dominate the list of the largest *aid and relief organizations*. Seventeen international aid and relief organizations are among the fifty largest non-profits in the United States (see Table 9.2).

TABLE 9.2 Largest US International Aid and Relief Organizations

Name	Activities (Summary From the Organization's Website)	Income, 2012 (US$ Millions)
American Red Cross	Providing humanitarian aid and social services	$3,154.5
Habitat for Humanity International	Providing affordable housing	$1,492.3
World Vision	Providing relief, development, and advocacy organization (Christian nonprofit)	$1,009.7
Food for the Poor	Providing food, medicine, and shelter (ecumenical Christian nonprofit)	$900.1
Catholic Relief Services	Providing humanitarian aid (international Catholic nonprofit)	$699.5
Feed the Children	Providing food, clothing, educational supplies, medical equipment, and other necessities to needy individuals (international Christian nonprofit)	$617.8
Compassion International	Providing for the development of children living in poverty around the world (Christian child sponsorship organization)	$598.8
Save the Children USA	Promoting of children's rights, providing relief and support for children in developing countries	$576.5
CARE (Cooperative for Assistance and Relief Everywhere)	Fighting global poverty, with a special focus on empowering women and girls	$557.5
AmeriCares	Providing disaster relief and humanitarian medical aid	$526.1
US Fund for UNICEF	Supporting UNICEF work	$501.8
International Rescue Committee	Supporting refugees and displaced persons	$386.5
Samaritan's Purse	Providing medical aid (Christian nonprofit)	$376.1
Kingsway Charities	Providing medical aid	$331.4
American Jewish Joint Distribution Committee	Providing humanitarian assistance (Jewish nonprofit organization)	$315.8

(continued)

Direct Relief	Improving the health and lives of people affected by poverty, disaster, and civil unrest	$299.7
Good360/Gifts in Kind International	Fostering corporate donations to nonprofits	$298.4

Source: "America's Top 50 Charities in 2013 Ranked by Total Income," *Christian Science Monitor*, www.csmonitor.com/Business/Guide-to-Giving/America-s-Top-50-charities-in-2013-ranked-by-total-income

Notes: These figures are from the *Christian Science Monitor* annual review of US nonprofits. A similar review by *Forbes* gives a somewhat different ranking, even though both indicate that they are based on Form 990 tax returns. Neither of the two rankings includes Family Health International (now known as FHI360) or Partnership for Supply Chain Management, two nonprofits that appear on the list of the largest USAID vendors and appear to have incomes that qualify them for this list.

The incomes reported in Table 9.2 are for the US branches only, but organizations such as Habitat for Humanity, World Vision, Save the Children, and the US Fund for UNICEF have dozens of federated affiliates around the world. The US affiliates generally contribute 30 percent to 50 percent of the worldwide income of their organizations or federations. World Vision, for example, reported a worldwide income of $2.67 billion, some 2.5 times its US income. Other large aid organizations and federations include the following (the incomes quoted are worldwide figures from annual reports):

- BRAC: $4.2 billion
- International Committee of the Red Cross: $1.2 billion
- Oxfam: $1.1 billion
- Plan International: $960 million
- Médecins Sans Frontières: $568 million
- Danish Refugee Council (officially an umbrella organization of over thirty Danish refugee organizations): $300 million

Calculations of the size of *foundations* are based on their endowments and do not necessarily reflect their disbursements or their impact. Some of the foundations listed below (see Table 9.3) have recently come under criticism for providing comparatively few grants relative to their size.

The Rotary, Lions, Kiwanis, and other *service clubs* each have hundreds of affiliates around the world, which raise funds for local and international projects. Rotary claims a worldwide membership of 1.22 million in over 34,000 clubs.

Only two *environmental organizations* appear among the largest international nonprofits: the World Wildlife Fund ($720 million) and Greenpeace ($320 million).

A grab bag of dozens of *other large entities with nonprofit legal status* also exists. They include organizations as diverse as the ISO, which has a core funding of $36 million for the Swiss secretariat and estimates that some $140 million is spent by member organizations to support the individual standards secretariats, and the British

Council, the UK cultural relations and development organization created by royal charter in 1934, which is now, according to its website, "a public corporation, a charity and an executive non-departmental public body with operational independence from the U.K. government." The British Council reports an income of $1.2 billion and has over 100 federated councils around the world, many of which operate under the nonprofit legislation of their host countries.

The "Top 100" Nonprofits

Another dimension of "internationalness" is the global reputation a nonprofit garners regardless of the scope of its activities. In 2012, the *Global Journal*, a Swiss magazine focusing on global governance, published its first ranking of the global top 100 NGOs and now publishes an annual list. The rankings are based on reputation surveys that ask key informants to rate nonprofits based on their perceived impact, innovation, and sustainability. Reputation surveys have their evident limits: the lists are heavily weighted to a newer generation of "popular" organizations. However, the lists provide a noteworthy snapshot of nonprofits around the world. The NGOs that head the ranking are, according to the *Global Journal* (2013),

- BRAC (Bangladesh, international development)
- Wikimedia Foundation (United States, parent organization of Wikipedia)
- Acumen (United States, fund for social innovation)
- Danish Refugee Council (Denmark, international humanitarian work)
- Partners in Health (United States, international health)
- Ceres (United States, corporate social responsibility)
- CARE International (Switzerland, poverty reduction)
- Médecins Sans Frontières (Switzerland, medical assistance)
- Cure Violence (United States, community-based antiviolence)

TABLE 9.3 Foundations With Endowments of More Than $7 Billion, 2012

Organization	Country	Headquarters	Endowment (US$ Billions)
Bill and Melinda Gates Foundation	US	Seattle, WA	$37.1
Stichting INGKA Foundation (associated with IKEA)	Netherlands	Leiden	$36.0
Wellcome Trust	UK	London	$22.1
Howard Hughes Medical Institute	US	Chevy Chase, MD	$16.1
Ford Foundation	US	New York City	$11.2
J. Paul Getty Trust	US	Los Angeles	$10.5
Mohammed bin Rashid Al Maktoum Foundation	United Arab Emirates	Dubai	$10.0
Robert Wood Johnson Foundation	US	Princeton, NJ	$9.0
Li Ka Shing Foundation	China	Hong Kong	$8.3
W. K. Kellogg Foundation	US	Battle Creek, MI	$8.2
Church Commissioners, Church of England	UK	London	v$8.1
William and Flora Hewlett Foundation	US	Menlo Park, CA	$7.4
Kamehameha Schools	US	Honolulu, HI	$7.3
Lilly Endowment	US	Indianapolis, IN	$7.28

Sources: "Top Funders," Foundation Center, http://foundationcenter.org/findfunders/topfunders/top100assets.html; "List of Wealthiest Charitable Foundations," Wikipedia, http://en.wikipedia.org/wiki/List_of_wealthiest_charitable_foundations.

- Mercy Corps (United States, international relief and recovery)

The remainder of the top 100 demonstrates the diversity of origins and of fields of interests. Although most are among the largest international nonprofits, a number of small organizations are also represented, such as Krousar Thmey, a Cambodian foundation for children. Many are nominally domestic organizations, but they almost all have an international dimension, either because they receive a substantial portion of their funding from outside the country and work closely with international partners or because they have extended their domestic work globally. Common Ground, a US organization on the list, works with the homeless in New York City and through its affiliated organization, Community Solutions, is replicating the model nationally and internationally. The ranking also demonstrates the dominance of the United States in the nonprofit sector, with one-third of the organizations headquartered there.

Bibliography

Abbott, Kenneth W., and Duncan Snidal. 2009. "The Governance Triangle: Regulatory Institutions and the Shadow of the State." In *The Politics of Global Regulation*, edited by Walter Mattli and Ngaire Woods, 44–88. Princeton, NJ: Princeton University Press.

Ahmed, Shamima, and David M. Potter. 2006. *NGOs in International Politics.* Bloomfield, CT: Kumarian.

Anheier, Helmut. 2014. *Nonprofit Organizations: Theory, Management, Policy.* 2nd ed. London: Routledge.

Archibugi, Daniele. 2008. *The Global Commonwealth of Citizens Toward Cosmopolitan Democracy.* Princeton, NJ: Princeton University Press. http://public.eblib.com/EBLPublic/PublicView.do?ptiID=457744.

Banks, Nicola, and David Hulme. 2012. *The Role of NGOs and Civil Society in Development and Poverty Reduction.* Brooks World Poverty Institute Working Paper no. 171. Manchester University. http://papers.ssrn.com/sol3/papers.cfm?abstract_id=2072157.

Batliwala, Srilatha, and L. David Brown. 2006. *Transnational Civil Society: An Introduction.* Bloomfield, CT: Kumarian.

Bernal, Victoria, and Inderpal Grewal, eds. 2014. *Theorizing NGOs: States, Feminisms, and Neoliberalism.* Next Wave: New Directions in Women's Studies. Durham, NC: Duke University Press.

———. 2006. "International Nongovernmental Organizations." In *The Nonprofit Sector: A Research Handbook,* 2nd ed., edited by Walter W. Powell and Richard Steinberg, 333–351. New Haven, CT: Yale University Press.

Bond, Patrick. 2008. "Reformist Reforms, Non-Reformist Reforms and Global Justice: Activist, NGO and Intellectual Challenges in the World Social Forum." *Societies Without Borders* 3: 4–19.

Brown, David L., Alnoor Ebrahim, and Srilatha Batliwala. 2012. "Governing International Advocacy NGOs." *World Development* 40 (6): 1098–1108.

Brown, David L., and Jonathan Fox. 2000. *Transnational Civil Society Coalitions and the World Bank: Lessons from Project and Policy Influence Campaigns.* Working Paper no. 3. Cambridge, MA: Hauser Center for Nonprofit Organizations, Kennedy School of Government, Harvard University.

Carey, Henry F. 2012. *Privatizing the Democratic Peace: Policy Dilemmas of NGO Peacebuilding.* Basingstoke, UK: Palgrave Macmillan.

Chandhoke, Neera. 2005. "How Global Is Global Civil Society?" *Journal of World-Systems Research* 11 (2): 354–371.

Charnovitz, Steven. 1997. "Two Centuries of Participation: NGOs and International Governance." *Michigan Journal of International Law* 18 (2): 183–286.

CIVICUS. 2012. *State of Civil Society 2011.* Johannesburg, South Africa. http://socs.civicus.org/2011/wp-content/uploads/2012/04/State-of-Civil-Society-2011.pdf.

Clark, John D. 2008. "The Globalization of Civil Society." In *Critical Mass: The Emergence of Global Civil Society,* edited by James W. St. G. Walker and Andrew S. Thompson. Waterloo, ON: Wilfrid Laurier University Press.

Edwards, Michael, and David Hulme. 1996. *Beyond the Magic Bullet: NGO Performance and Accountability in the Post-Cold War World.* West Hartford, CT: Kumarian.

Evetts, Julia. 1995. "International Professional Associations: The New Context for Professional Projects." *Work, Employment and Society* 9 (4): 763–772.

Florini, Ann, ed. 2000. *The Third Force: The Rise of Transnational Civil Society.* Washington, DC: Carnegie Endowment for International Peace.

Foreman, Karen. 1999. "Evolving Global Structures and the Challenges Facing International Relief and Development Organizations." *Nonprofit and Voluntary Sector Quarterly* 28 (4): 178–197.

Global Journal. 2012. "The Top 100 NGOs 2012," vol. 9. http://theglobaljournal.net/2012/Top100NGOs/.

———. 2013. "The Top 100 NGOs 2013," vol. 15 (special edition). www.theglobaljournal.net/group/top-100-ngos/.

Global Policy Forum. 2012. "Tables and Charts on NGOs." www.globalpolicy.org/ngos/tables-and-charts-on-ngos.html.

———. 2010. "Civil Society and NGO: Far from Unproblematic Concepts." In *Third Sector Research,* edited by Rupert Taylor, 185–196. New York: Springer.

Green, Jessica F. 2014. *Rethinking Private Authority: Agents and Entrepreneurs in Global Environmental Governance.* Princeton, NJ: Princeton University Press.

Jad, Islah. 2007. "NGOs: Between Buzzwords and Social Movements." *Development in Practice* 17 (4–5): 622–629.

Johnston, Keith. 2012. "Acting Globally—Thinking Globally: Stepping Up to Govern an International

NGO." Cultivating Leadership. www.cultivating leadership.co.nz/wordpress/wp-content/uploads/2012/01/Acting-Globally-Thinking-Globally-January-29-2012-CL.pdf.

Jonsson, Christer, and Jonas Tallberg, eds. 2010. *Transnational Actors in Global Governance: Patterns, Explanations, and Implications.* New York: Palgrave Macmillan.

Kaldor, Mary. 2000. "'Civilising' Globalisation? The Implications of the 'Battle in Seattle'." *Millennium—Journal of International Studies* 29 (1): 105–114.

Karns, Margaret P., and Karen A. Mingst. 2004. *International Organizations: The Politics and Processes of Global Governance.* Boulder, CO: Lynne Rienner.

Keane, John. 2003. *Global Civil Society?* Cambridge, UK: Cambridge University Press.

Koppell, Jonathan G. S. 2008. "Global Governance Organizations: Legitimacy and Authority in Conflict." *Journal of Public Administration Research and Theory* 18 (2): 177–203.

Lang, Sabine. 2013. *NGOs, Civil Society, and the Public Sphere.* New York: Cambridge University Press.

Lewis, David. 2007. *The Management of Non-Governmental Development Organizations.* 2nd ed. London: Routledge.

———. 2014. "Heading South: Time to Abandon the 'Parallel Worlds' of International Non-Governmental Organization (NGO) and Domestic Third Sector Scholarship?" *Voluntas* 25 (5): 1132–1150.

Lindblom, Anna-Karin. 2013. *Non-Governmental Organisations in International Law.* Cambridge, UK: Cambridge University Press.

Lindenberg, Marc, and Coralie Bryant. 2001. *Going Global: Transforming Relief and Development NGOs.* Bloomfield, CT: Kumarian.

Lindenberg, Marc, and J. Patrick Dobel. 1999. "The Challenges of Globalization for Northern International Relief and Development NGOs." *Nonprofit and Voluntary Sector Quarterly* 28 (4): 4–24.

Muukkonen, Martti. 2002. *Ecumenism of the Laity: Continuity and Change in the Mission View of the World's Alliance of Young Men's Christian Associations, 1855–1955.* Joensuun Yliopiston Teologisia Julkaisuja, no. 7. Joensuu, Finland: University of Joensuu.

National Center for Charitable Statistics. 2012. "Registered International Nonprofit Organizations by Level of Total Revenue." http://nccsdataweb.urban.org/NCCS/V1Pub/index.php.

Reinicke, Wolfgang H. 1998. *Global Public Policy: Governing Without Government?* Washington, DC: Brookings Institution Press.

Ronalds, Paul. 2010. *The Change Imperative: Creating the Next Generation NGO.* Boulder, CO: Kumarian.

Schechter, Michael G. 2010. *Historical Dictionary of International Organizations.* Lanham, MD: Scarecrow.

Siméant, Johanna. 2005. "What Is Going Global? The Internationalization of French NGOs 'Without Borders'." *Review of International Political Economy* 12 (5): 851–883.

Sparke, Matthew. 2013. *Introducing Globalization: Ties, Tension, and Uneven Integration.* Malden, MA: Wiley-Blackwell.

———. 1998. *Toward a Global Civil Society.* Providence, RI: Berghahn.

Willetts, Peter. 2011. *Non-Governmental Organizations in World Politics: The Construction of Global Governance.* Routledge Global Institutions Series No. 49. New York: Routledge.

Wong, Wendy H. 2012. *Internal Affairs: How the Structure of NGOs Transforms Human Rights.* Ithaca, NY: Cornell University Press.

Young, Dennis R., Bonnie L. Koenig, Adil Najam, and Julie Fisher. 1999. "Strategy and Structure in Managing Global Associations." *Voluntas* 10 (4): 323–343.

Zadek, Simon. 2011. "Civil Society and the Market." In *The Oxford Handbook of Civil Society,* edited by Michael Edwards, 428–440. New York: Oxford University Press.

▶ CHAPTER 10

International Assistance

ABBY STODDARD

Abby Stoddard, "International Assistance," in *The State of Nonprofit America,* 2nd. ed., Lester M. Salamon (Washington, DC: Brookings Institution Press, 2012): 332. Reprinted in this Part.

In the provision of aid to foreign populations suffering the effects of war, natural disasters, or chronic poverty, private nonprofit organizations play a crucial operational and advocacy role. Commonly referred to in the international aid field as nongovernmental organizations (NGOs), these entities not only undertake independent charitable activities but also serve as the main implementers of governments' foreign assistance programs. Over the past four decades, NGOs have matured and professionalized, earning a reputation for speed, flexibility, deployment capacity, and programming innovation beyond the reach of most governmental actors. In addition, their grassroots orientation and their staffs' firsthand knowledge of local conditions have earned them the stamp of credibility and a measure of influence in national and international policymaking circles.

The proliferation of complex humanitarian emergencies and the widespread shrinking of the public sector role that characterized the post–Cold War period increased the need for and the growth of international assistance organizations. These organizations have increasingly ventured into environments of active conflict or catastrophic state failure, and as a result have found themselves literally and figuratively under fire. New forms of intrastate conflict, characterized by self-perpetuating illicit economies and heavy civilian tolls, have created hazardous working conditions and wrenching moral dilemmas for humanitarian organizations. They have also inflicted enormous damage on family livelihoods and national development efforts, most notably in Africa. In addition to these politically rooted crises, the AIDS pandemic, the global food crisis, and the proliferation of small-to-medium-scale natural disasters associated with climate change have also increased the need for, and the challenges to, international assistance providers. Heightened visibility of NGOs, combined with inflated expectations as to what they can and should attempt to accomplish, has at times provoked criticism from both practitioners and outside observers about the performance, transparency, and accountability of these organizations. This in turn has spurred far-reaching reforms in the field. The tension between voluntarism and professionalism seen in other parts of the nonprofit sector is continually evident in the international aid subsector as well, as organizations strive to improve performance with data-driven and results-oriented programming while at the same time attempting to remain true to the altruistic ethos and independent spirit of international aid that bridles

DOI: 10.4324/9780367696559-13

against regimentation and bureaucratization. Civic activism, or advocacy, as it is termed in the international assistance parlance, has grown in importance to NGOs as evidenced by the proliferating policy and advocacy departments among organizations and their campaigns for public outreach and political change. This is countered and complicated by certain commercialist trends in the NGO community. In particular, the rise in large-scale government contracts taken on by some NGOs (particularly in the reconstruction settings of Afghanistan and Iraq) has led some organizations to assume roles and relationships to the donor government (a government that funds foreign aid implemented through NGOs) very much resembling those of sector government contractors. For NGOs operating in foreign aid contexts, the general blurring of the lines between assistance and commercial or military activities remains a source of concern and internal debate.

In this chapter we will describe the basic characteristics of the nonprofit international relief and development subsector and explore the features of the international context that have shaped its important role in developing world crises. In the process, we will identify the external events and internal pressures that over the past four decades have transformed much of the subsector from an arena of well-meaning amateurs into a professionalized network of technical experts, dominated by a small number of very large and influential agencies.

The Key Role of Nonprofits in the International Assistance Field

The first internationally oriented assistance organizations in the United States appeared during the interwar period, and the field continued to grow slowly after World War II. The aim of these early organizations was to provide emergency relief supplies to war victims in Europe. This changed with decolonization after World War II,

as the emergence of many newly independent, and underdeveloped, nations triggered a movement for economic development assistance, so that throughout the 1960s and '70s the focus of NGOs shifted to poverty reduction efforts in the third world. Widespread disappointment with the initial government-to-government approach to development, which had resulted in high-profile, wasteful projects or outright diversion of aid monies by corrupt governments, shone a light on NGOs as an alternative vehicle for progress.[1] Using a bottom-up approach, international NGOs working at the village level represented a strategy for development upward from the local communities, which many donors embraced.

By the late 1970s a boom had begun in the relief and development field, likely fueled in part by amendments to the U.S. Foreign Assistance Act in 1973, which created the mechanisms and policy impetus for increased government funding of private voluntary organizations through small-scale assistance grants rather than large-scale government-to-government transfers. The growth in the number of NGOs gained increased momentum over the next twenty years as a consequence.[2]

The last decade of the twentieth century witnessed unprecedented levels of humanitarian crisis. Not only were there three times as many natural disasters in the 1990s as there were in the 1960s, but the 1990s also marked a high point for state fragmentation and violent civil conflicts.[3] Only two of the world's twenty-seven major armed conflicts in 1999 were wars between nations.[4] Although the number of intrastate conflicts has decreased in more recent years, chronic and regionally based conflicts continue to thwart development and keep populations on the brink of humanitarian catastrophe. Africa in particular has been beset by the twin phenomena of "failed states" and "complex emergencies," where long-standing environmental and food security problems are exacerbated by fighting or by the outright collapse of central authority. The modus operandi of combatants in such conflicts has been to inflict damage and exert control on civilian areas and populations rather than on opposing military forces, resulting in unprecedented numbers of civilian casualties, refugees, and internally displaced persons. Finally, global climate change has contributed to an upsurge of floods, droughts, storms and other moderate-scale natural disasters, which do not receive the attention that massive calamities such as 2005's Indian Ocean tsunami do but which, combined, cause billions of dollars' worth of damage and disrupt vast numbers of lives.[5] After both natural and man-made disasters, the burden of post-crisis recovery sets back years of development progress in the countries where the disasters occurred.

Along with burgeoning humanitarian need, the 1990s saw greatly increased access by independent relief agencies to victims. The end of the Cold War ushered in a new era of cooperation on the Security Council and a willingness to take action on humanitarian grounds. By essentially loosening the principle of national sovereignty and promoting international "humanitarian intervention" to safeguard stability and individual human rights, the council's actions helped to further legitimize the work of private relief agencies.[6] In addition, these NGOs were now accorded the freedom to operate in formerly "closed" societies transitioning from communism.

The increased need and opportunity for humanitarian aid stimulated a doubling of relief funding from industrialized countries, and an explosion of new NGOs in the late 1980s and '90s. Organizations already doing development work in the field found that their existing infrastructures and local knowledge made them well placed to respond to emergent needs as they arose, while scores of new organizations were created in the wake of each new humanitarian disaster for the express purpose of launching a rapid response delivery of relief aid. The number of international relief and development organizations based in the United States grew from fifty-two organizations in 1970 to over four hundred by 1994.[7] By the end of 2008, the United

States Agency for International Development (USAID) registered 584 U.S.-based NGOs as funding partners, up from 439 in 2000,[8] the largest number of such organizations in any OECD nation. The combined revenue and in-kind support from public and private sources for these 584 organizations totaled over $27 billion in 2007—more than the total amount of U.S. official development assistance.[9]

The U.S.-based NGOs represented on the USAID registry range widely in organizational size and scope of work, with the smallest operating on budgets of under $10,000, and the largest having budgets in the hundreds of millions. Some of these organizations focus on issues peripheral to development assistance, such as environmental conservation or political democratization, and others have chosen a single issue or activity, such as adoption, or a specific country or region. An untold number of other small NGOs exist outside the USAID partnership, and it is common for many to spring up around a particular emergency and then dissolve or reappear in a different institutional form. The largest U.S. consortium of relief and development organizations, the Washington D.C.-based NGO consortium InterAction, narrows the field somewhat by requiring membership dues and entry criteria, and counts 190 members, still a sizable number. Yet even with proliferating aid organizations in the 1990s, the bulk of global aid dollars and materials continue to be channeled through a small group of large and long-standing NGOs. Of a roughly estimated four thousand NGOs based in the global North at the turn of the current century, the ten largest accounted for an estimated 20 percent of combined NGO revenue.[10] Among these giants are four of the largest American relief and development NGOs: CARE USA, Catholic Relief Services, Save the Children USA, and World Vision. These four organizations—two of them religious in orientation and two secular—are examples of broad-based, "multisectoral" relief and development agencies that undertake a wide range of program activities in which they are joined by the larger community of NGOs, some of which also do work across a variety of program areas and others of which specialize in one or two.

Principal Program Areas Within International Assistance

There are three principal—and somewhat interrelated—program areas in the international assistance field: development assistance, humanitarian assistance, and recovery and rehabilitation.

Development Assistance

The aim of development assistance, geared toward long-term poverty reduction, is to build local capacities, support livelihoods, and create sustainable improvements in quality of life. Such projects include technical assistance in agriculture, education, small business development and micro-credit initiatives, primary health care with an emphasis on maternal and child health, nutrition, and food security. In attempting to understand and eliminate the root causes of poverty and underdevelopment, the development assistance portion of the development field has also come to focus on civil society strengthening, democratization, and press freedom, reproductive health and family planning, and human rights. Issues of gender inequality, environmental degradation, and HIV/AIDS, critical "cross-cutting" issues whose impacts must be considered and integrated into all aspects of programming, are given varying levels of attention and resources by NGOs.

Increasingly, the major international NGOs working in development assistance are nationalizing their country offices and devolving their programming to local partner organizations. The growing self-sufficiency of global South development organizations in mounting their own development efforts has their international counterparts doing less direct implementation of assistance and more technical assistance and resource provision.[11]

Humanitarian Assistance

Humanitarian assistance refers to relief efforts to save lives and mitigate damage caused by natural disasters and complex political emergencies, including armed conflict. Often this takes place within the context of refugee movements or large-scale internal displacement of populations, where rapid provision of basic goods and services is required. The major subsectors of this field are emergency food aid, health care interventions, shelter, and water and sanitation services.

Most of the larger United States–based NGOs that undertake emergency humanitarian response are also involved in long-term poverty reduction activities in their areas of operation, including a wide range of assistance activities focusing on the development of food resources, shelter, health, sanitation, agriculture, micro-enterprise, and infrastructure. These multi-mandate organizations have discovered the strategic and cost advantages to launching emergency response in areas where they already maintain an operational presence, logistical infrastructure, networks of contacts, and partnerships in the community. Furthermore there is now widespread recognition that the two sets of activities are functionally and conceptually interdependent. Poverty, overpopulation, and environmental degradation can increase a country's vulnerabilities to disaster, and, conversely, disasters have an antithetical effect on development. Thus development seeks to reduce a country's vulnerability to disasters, and relief aid, appropriately targeted, can help provide a solid foundation for rehabilitation and ongoing development.

Recovery and Rehabilitation

During the 1990s the relief and development communities recognized a third set of needs to be met besides the urgent, life-saving activities of acute humanitarian crises and the long-term poverty fighting: post-crisis recovery and rehabilitation programs, undertaken in "stable development contexts." This large, somewhat gray, area of international assistance encompasses elements of both types of programming as well as activities specific to early recovery and reconstruction assistance such as infrastructure repair, peaceful reintegration of displaced populations, property rights mediation, and support for the recurrent costs of maintaining the public sector, such as civil servants' salaries. Research has shown the critical importance of the post-crisis period, particularly after armed conflict, when populations need to see tangible evidence of improvements in their lives to avoid the very real risk of backsliding into instability and violence.[12] Governments and international organizations have for years grappled with a de facto gap during the recovery period between acute crisis relief and development aid in terms of funding and institutional mandates, with the result that the critical activities of early recovery have been under-resourced. Although most large donors continue to categorize activities into "relief," "recovery," and "development," this distinction has been challenged by most practitioners as outmoded and counterproductive. Since relief, recovery, and development activities are in reality all interrelated and overlapping, treating them as separate stages along a continuum results in funding and service gaps, and the threat of backsliding into renewed crisis.[13]

Characteristics of the Relief and Development Nonprofit Subsector

The international relief and development organizations represent a unique subsector of U.S. nonprofits. Although a few also engage in some domestic programming, the bulk of their work is carried out overseas, in poor or war-torn countries. The majority of their employees (between 85 and 95 percent in most cases) are developing-country nationals. To operate effectively these organizations and their employees must navigate relationships with host country governments and local authorities, occasionally with warring parties, and with a range of international bodies and political actors. Also unlike other nonprofits, these organizations, especially those engaged in humanitarian relief efforts in conflict situations, face serious security risks and have suffered increasing casualties to their personnel. In recent years NGOs have had to grapple with such matters as hostage taking, and the effects of psychological stress and burnout of field staff.

There are unique dynamics within the relief and development community as well. U.S. international relief and development organizations exist as part of a complex transnational community of NGOs and other international actors. The NGOs are essentially private organizations, each following its own distinctive normative mandate in a highly politicized environment. Some observers make the argument that the diversity and independence of the members of this community is a thing to be valued, as the key to NGOs' operational advantage in the field. As a senior staffer of InterAction put it, "Civil society is by nature diverse, and the last thing we want is to make it monolithic. Varied opinions help make us innovative, and challenge us to perform better."[14] At the same time, however, aid organizations have recognized that their objectives are too large to accomplish independently, and that if they truly want to have a positive effect on the lives of their beneficiaries, their work will have to be strategically and operationally coordinated with that of their counterparts. For this reason aid practitioners have made efforts to identify the common core principles of humanitarian assistance and to promote constructive cooperation in the field and at the headquarters level.[15] This is no easy task, as cultural differences abound among the NGOs, along both organizational and regional lines.

Factors Shaping the NGO Position in the Field

At the dawn of the twenty-first century, the international environment was characterized by both economic globalization and conflict and state failure. This combination of factors thrust aid NGOs into unaccustomed prominent roles, some for which they were never intended or adequately prepared. The 9/11 attacks and the transformations in the U.S. global military security agenda that followed created a further set of conditions in the form of a subset of aid environments (specifically Afghanistan and parts of the Middle East) where NGOs are marginalized and buffeted by competing political forces. Aid funding on the whole has continued to increase, but with new contribution modalities, and with sources and recipients that do not always favor the mission and interests of the NGO community. The lingering effects of the 2008 banking crisis and resulting economic recession are further disrupting NGO budgets and program planning. Security of personnel has deteriorated in many areas, and violent attacks on aid workers have proliferated over the past several years.

Globalization and the Shrinking Public Sector

On the development side, globalization has had both direct and indirect effects on the work of NGOs. It has opened new doors for fundraising and private sector partnerships. New technology that has suddenly become available and affordable to NGOs, such as portable satellite communications systems, has helped increase NGO access to victims and improved their logistical capacity to provide assistance. And of course the Internet has revolutionized fundraising. To give just one example, CARE USA generated upwards of $5 million in small online donations from private citizens in the first ten days after the Indian Ocean tsunami.[16] At the same time, while globalization has been hailed as a boon to developing countries, creating new jobs and educational opportunities, raising the standard of living and building bridges to the modern industrialized world, it also seems to have increased rather than decreased inequities within states, creating new forms of poverty and social tensions just as it creates new forms of wealth. In the post–Cold War period fundamentalist free market economic theories ruled the day, proponents of the "Washington consensus" argued for rapid privatization of national economies, and states undergoing fiscal crisis found an enabling philosophy for cutting back on social services. The shrinking of the public sector and fraying of the social safety net occurred all over the world, including in many nominally socialist countries. National governments and the United Nations have increasingly called on international aid agencies and local NGOs to meet the resulting social needs, and are faced with ever-widening gaps to fill in places where they have been working for decades.[17]

The global economic recession that began in 2008 is exacerbating these problems. The recession is anticipated to have particularly devastating effects on developing countries, particularly coming as it has on the heels of a global crisis of rising food prices.

Post–Cold War Conflict Patterns and the Post-9/11 Security Environment

New challenges have also confronted the international assistance organizations as a result of the end of the Cold War and the attacks of September 11, 2001. During the 1990s, relief agencies found themselves in the unenviable position of representing the *primary* response of the international community to many of the emergencies resulting from the violent civil conflicts that emerged in the aftermath of the Cold War. The breakup of the USSR ended the Security Council's long-standing deadlock between the veto powers of the United States and the Soviet Union, resulting in a spate of new peacekeeping activity. More than triple the amount of UN peacekeeping operations were approved after 1988 than had been mandated in the prior forty years of the UN's existence. However, these missions suffered from persistent underfunding and disputes over command and control. Absent the geostrategic contest between the superpowers, governments had little by way of a compelling national interest in the outcome of most of these conflicts, and the United States in particular was loath to run the risk of troop losses after the early experience with humanitarian intervention in Somalia. Despite the passage in 2006 of the UN resolution enshrining the "Responsibility to Protect," Russia, the People's Republic of China, and a number of developing countries on the Security Council continue in various ways to oppose the idea of forceful "humanitarian intervention" on the grounds that it violates the principle of sovereignty.[18] The tendency of the Western democracies to support humanitarian aid operations while eschewing deeper political or military commitments prompted accusations that they were using aid as a "humanitarian fig leaf" to conceal their inaction. In Bosnia, Rwanda, and Somalia it became clear that without resolute political action, including security measures as necessary, relief work could become both dangerous and futile.

Since 9/11, however, NGOs in some settings have faced the opposite problem. Political and military interests are paramount for the United States in the protracted conflict settings of Afghanistan and Iraq (and in certain short-term emergencies such as Lebanon in 2006) and aid actors must take pains to dissociate themselves from the political agendas that would compromise their core principles of independence and neutrality. It has been especially difficult for U.S.-based NGOs to project independence and neutrality when the majority of their funding comes from the U.S. government. The U.S. government not only has been a party to the conflict in Afghanistan and Iraq but also has made it a point of policy in recent years to use aid as an integral component of its hearts-and-minds strategy, and to consider the NGO providers as "force multipliers."[19]

Funding and Partnerships

Equally significant developments confront U.S.-based NGOs in the area of finance. NGOs require substantial funding for large-scale assistance projects. For example, even a short-term three-to-six-month project grant from the Office of U.S. Foreign Disaster Assistance (USAID's relief wing) can easily top $1 million. The United States government, by far the largest aid donor among governments in absolute terms, contributed $21.8 billion worth of international relief and development assistance in 2007.[20] Roughly a quarter of this official development assistance (ODA) was channeled through NGOs.[21] This reflects in part the credibility and legitimacy that has accrued over the past few decades to these nonprofit, nonstate actors operating in the international sphere.

Unlike the major European NGOs, until recently most of the U.S. relief and development organizations have traditionally relied heavily on the U.S. government for the bulk of their resources. At the beginning of the decade, the four largest and most prominent U.S. relief and development NGOs listed earlier (CARE, Catholic Relief Services, Save the Children, and World Vision) accounted for nearly 47 percent of total U.S. government annual support to NGOs, and all but one of the four, World Vision, relied on U.S. government sources for more than 50 percent of their funding.[22]

The proportion of official government assistance that is channeled through NGOs is in fact understated, since a large percentage of what is given as a direct grant to an international agency such as the UN High Commissioner for Refugees is typically then distributed to NGOs in the form of subgrants and implementing partnerships. These international agencies represent another important source of funding for NGOs and provide a locus of coordination for aid efforts. And UN agencies, like national governments, depend on NGOs to carry out much of the end-stage service delivery and to move quickly to identify and access populations in need.

Overall aid funding from governments has trended upward over the past several years, with a spike in 2005 owing to the tsunami response. Combined official development assistance (ODA) from the government donors reached $109 billion in 2007, with the U.S. contribution accounting for roughly 20 percent of the total.[23] Only a handful of governments have met or exceeded the ODA target of 0.7 percent of national budgets (the United States, which never committed to the target, has never gotten higher than 0.23 percent and is now at 0.16 percent) but this movement has already served to help raise the tide of international assistance funding. For NGOs, the increases in government funding have been more evident in humanitarian relief, as opposed to the development side.

On the humanitarian relief side (typically about 10 percent of overall aid), new international financing mechanisms such as the UN's expanded Central Emergency Relief Fund (CERF) and the country-level Common Humanitarian Funds (CHFs) have allowed donor governments to pool their contributions in a single fund that is allocated by UN officials to their aid agencies and NGO partners. What these humanitarian funding mechanisms provide for donors, apart from facilitating coordination of planning and allocation on the part of the operational agencies, is a convenient vehicle to funnel larger volumes of aid with fewer transaction costs on the part of the donor agency. In other words, they are able to make fewer large contributions instead of multiple

individual grants, each of which requires processing and administrative oversight. Although the new mechanisms have been credited with raising humanitarian funding levels for NGOs, they have been an even greater boon to the UN agencies, which act as the pass-through or umbrella grantors to the NGOs—thus gaining both administrative overhead funds from the grant and an important coordinating role in the aid programming—who then do the actual implementation of aid projects. For NGOs this has meant adjusting to receiving a larger share of their humanitarian funding through UN subgrants, and in some cases coping with delays and inefficiencies that result, including the phenomenon of multiplying overheads, as the money passes through the intermediary levels, as opposed to going to the end user directly.[24] With such large sums coming from government donors, the autonomy of the recipient organization may also understandably be called into question. Similarly, political advocacy by an NGO arguably becomes problematic when the government that is being lobbied is also the organization's single largest donor, though as we will see later, many NGOs seem to have circumvented this dilemma.

In the face of these challenges associated with government funding, recent years have seen NGO efforts to diversify their resource base by taking advantage of new fund-raising technologies as well as of the emergence of significant new private donors for development, such as Bill Gates and Warren Buffett. These efforts have clearly begun to pay off, as can be seen in table 10.1, which shows the growth of the private share of support for some of the largest U.S. NGOs. These changes have also helped boost the development side of the funding equation for NGOs. The majority of development funds for the U.S.-based NGOs now derive from these private sources.

The global financial crisis that unfolded in 2008 has clearly threatened some of these gains, however, since the major private contributors to

TABLE 10.1 Funding Sources of American NGOs[a]

Organization	FY2003		FY2006	
	Income (US$ Millions)	Percent From Private Sources	Income (US$ Millions)	Percent From Private Sources
World Vision	686	71	944	74
CARE USA	523	25	656	23
Catholic Relief Services	484	22	562	38
Save the Children (U.S.)	241	44	355	55

Source: USAID, Report of Voluntary Agencies, 2003 and 2006

[a] Includes U.S. government–donated food and freight costs.

NGOs had most of their resources invested in the stock market. The crisis has also diminished the endowments and other investment assets of nonprofits.

Finally, a long-standing financing concern for all but the very largest organizations is the general lack of endowments and reserve funds. This problem is particularly acute in the area of emergency humanitarian relief, where the nature of donor-agency financing results in costly and less effective outcomes.[25] The basic dilemma is that most emergency grants are negotiated and awarded only after the onset of a disaster. NGOs wishing to respond in the critical early days and weeks of the emergency are forced to use their own funds, but most have inadequate reserves. The dearth of unrestricted advance funding has also prevented NGOS from establishing organizational preparedness capacities such as standby personnel and relief supply stockpiles. Certain partnership framework funding mechanisms do exist between NGOs and donors to provide the necessary upfront funding to overcome this dilemma, but they are few, ad hoc, and underutilized.[26]

For U.S.-based NGOs, government partnerships encompass not only the donor relationship with the United States government but also with the national governments in the countries of operation, and with the "international public sector," meaning the United Nations and other multilateral, regional, and subregional organizations that exist to provide what can be thought of as transnational public goods. NGOs have historically had a complex relationship with local authorities. Designed to serve the people directly at the local community level, they have long been seen by some national governments as a threat to sovereignty. At times NGOs have been accused of being covers for spies, or simply pawns for furthering the Cold War agendas of their own national donors. Conversely, some governments nowadays may lean too heavily on NGOs to provide the services that governments no longer provide. Whether in socialist countries transitioning to a market economy or failing states with weak or corrupt governments, there is a global trend of weakened state capacity and political will to provide public goods.[27] NGOs have had to ask themselves whether they are providing a necessary stopgap or merely letting governments in recipient countries get a free ride with their services, creating greater dependencies on external assistance.[28] In extreme cases involving the complete collapse of central authority, such as in Somalia and Haiti, NGOs and international agencies have had to step in to form a virtually new public sector, providing everything from infrastructure maintenance to education and health care services.

Security

Staff security has become another issue of vital importance to NGOs over the past two decades. A decisive juncture came during the Somalia crisis in the early 1990s, when NGOs were forced to "militarize" themselves by traveling in armored vehicles or under the escort of heavily armed local mercenaries. (A sobering discovery made around this time was that the insurance policies that NGOs had heretofore used for their overseas staff covered only accidents and medical conditions, not "acts of war" such as sniper fire or mine explosions.) The murder of the Red Cross workers in Chechnya in 1996 was also seen as a turning point in the operational reality of relief agencies. A 2006 study on aid worker violence undertaken by the Humanitarian Policy Group revealed that the rate of violent attacks against aid workers had increased 20 percent since 1997.[29] In the ten years since 2000 over 1,700 aid workers have been the victims of armed attacks, and there have been over 700 fatalities.[30] International aid work is among the most hazardous of civilian occupations, coming in at fifth place, after such professions as loggers and fishermen. Unlike these other professions, however, much of the risk to aid workers comes in the form of intentional violence.[31]

Far from being protected by their neutral humanitarian status, aid workers have increasingly become targets for violence in conflict settings, and a growing body of literature on the "war economies" in modern-day conflicts suggests that such risks will not abate as long as there are parties to the conflict who benefit politically and economically from continued mayhem.[32] Newly globalized threats, such as that embodied by Al Qaeda, have targeted the international aid system, which is disproportionately populated by Western organizations and donor governments, and is accused of pursuing Western political agendas and cultural values. The threat is enhanced by the fact that in many remote locations aid workers represent the sole international presence and are a soft target. In addition, aid operations involve cash and resources for the taking, so that in Afghanistan, Darfur, and Somalia, the criminal element has colluded with political actors in kidnappings and armed robberies of aid workers.

These escalating risks of assassination, kidnapping, armed raids, bombing, harassment or arrest by local authorities, and road banditry have come on top of the familiar threats of robbery, rape, traffic accidents, and health dangers such as malaria and HIV. There is also risk inherent in the nature of field work in underdeveloped areas, such as dealing with large sums of cash, transporting food or other material supplies, and hiring and firing local staff.

Beginning in the mid-1990s NGOs began looking seriously at their security status, and designed field security protocols and awareness-raising events for staff. Many have hired in-house security professionals to oversee organizational training or as adjuncts to country offices. Additionally, over the past few years a growing, and highly controversial, trend has emerged in the form of NGOs' contracting with private sector security companies for protective and security consulting services.[33] Without question the level of professionalism and expertise in security matters has risen within the community, as has the sophistication of available tools. However, the NGOs walk a difficult line in their security planning and management, particularly in terms of their security coordination with other organizations. Many remain reluctant to communicate security information and concerns for fear of damaging their public image or scaring off scarce recruits.[34]

Security risk management—and the considerable costs thereof—will continue to be a critical area for NGOs. Security issues also compound the tension between voluntarism and professionalism in the humanitarian arena—the subject of the subsequent section. The informal, independent, even adventurous, image of the aid worker roughing it in dangerous conditions has not always yielded easily to the changes seen in organizations' security stances. While a few organizations have opted for a protective response to "harden the target," including in some cases the use of armed guards, armored vehicles, and the like, many others have tried very different styles of adaptation, opting instead to take an ultra-low-profile approach, where all branding is removed from offices and vehicles and programming takes place in an almost covert fashion. Still others have relied on the principle of fostering acceptance with the local community and reaching out to all actors as the best way to ensure security for their staffs. Each of the approaches and adaptations entails potential drawbacks and dangers, so in highly insecure environments NGOs are forced to weigh short- and long-term risks to their personnel against the needs of beneficiary populations.

Performance, Professionalism, and Accountability

In security management, and in most other areas of activity, international aid organizations have increasingly professionalized and formalized their operational practice, following the trend toward professionalization that characterizes the nonprofit sector as a whole. As organizations age and grow they move from a voluntaristic, do-gooder spirit to one embodying expertise and experience. Like their domestic counterparts, therefore, NGOs have in the past several years put renewed emphasis on improving the quality, integrity, and measurable outputs of their programming. These changes unfolded in response to both self-assessment and external criticism. Indeed the nonprofit international assistance community found itself exposed to a variety of often scathing accusations, which peaked in volume in the 1990s: of overdependence on large government grants; of being donor-driven as opposed to need-based in programming; of using poor accounting and evaluation practices;

of lacking objective measures and quantifiable data on progress; and of under-investing in organizational learning and operations research.[35]

These critiques led to the current growing emphasis on impact measurement and evidence-based planning and analysis in international aid work. The Paris Declaration on Aid Effectiveness, of March 2, 2005, adopted by senior officials of thirty donor countries and sixty recipient countries as well as international aid agencies and the World Bank, lays out commitments by governments and their partner organizations to monitor the effectiveness of aid programs and measure progress and results against specific indicators.[36] Most large donors now insist that results-oriented program design, illustrated by logical framework matrices, be clearly demonstrated in grant proposals. Inter-agency working groups on evaluation share empirical methodologies and develop software and other tools for field use. Increased attention to gender dynamics, cultural and religious factors, and community participation has also characterized the evolution of relief and development programming in the past two decades. Organizations such as CARE, Oxfam, and others have adopted a "rights-based approach" to relief and development, and have developed programming frameworks that focus on food and income security at the level of the individual household, and these have had significant impact on the entire field.

On the humanitarian side, the movement to improve performance standards was kick-started after the Rwandan refugee crisis of 1994. The humanitarian efforts in the camps in Zaire (now Democratic Republic of the Congo) saw some significant achievements by aid organizations in containing a cholera outbreak and providing food and shelter to approximately 2 million refugees. At the same time, it witnessed a veritable "relief circus," with literally hundreds of NGOs scrambling for a piece of the action and competing for funds and air time, legions of inexperienced and untrained international volunteers, and several examples of unsound health practices. Leaving aside the later controversy involving the takeover of the camps by individuals responsible for the Rwandan genocide, many practitioners felt the initial response amounted to an operational and ethical failure on the part of the aid community.

On a basic level, the U.S. NGO consortium InterAction established early on a set of written standards for its members—a "financial, operational and ethical code of conduct" under which its NGO members are required to self-certify each year.[37] This process is meant to encourage compliance and self-evaluation to identify areas for improvement.[38] Such standard setting has a great deal to do with "enhancing the public trust" of relief and development agencies, which has been unquestionably damaged by recent scandals exposed in the press.[39] These include the lucrative but controversial practice of child sponsorship; in 1998 a series in the *Chicago Tribune* uncovered widespread accounting discrepancies and misrepresentation to donors. Ethical objections to child sponsorship, raised both within and outside the aid community, are that it exploits children through graphic depictions of suffering and hopelessness, and panders to a paternalistic desire for gratitude on the part of the donor. Another blow to NGOs came when some agencies were charged with abetting the corporate "dumping" of expired pharmaceuticals and otherwise inappropriate aid commodities onto disaster victims.

For NGOs accountability once meant simply telling their donors how their aid dollars were spent. Increasingly, relief and development NGOs are attempting to be equally accountable to their "customers" or "clients" in developing countries, in other words, the people they are there to assist. An independent office or ombudsman for humanitarian accountability was at one time proposed as a way to encourage NGO compliance with best practices in programming and adherence to humanitarian assistance principles.[40] The body

that was ultimately established in 2003 is called the Humanitarian Accountability Partnership, whose members voluntarily commit to "meeting the highest standards of accountability and quality management."[41]

In some of their personnel concerns, the international NGOs probably do not differ much from other U.S. nonprofits. For instance, there is the eternal question of how to attract and retain qualified individuals at salary scales considerably lower than those in the private sector. Yet there are also many issues unique to internationally oriented organizations; one of them is the inherent difficulty of managing field staff from great distances. Different NGOs have struck their own balance between "supervision" and "support" in the headquarters-field relationship, depending on how centralized they require their decision-making process to be. Another problem posed by maintaining expatriate staff in overseas missions is in trying to govern aspects of a staff member's private life, which in the domestic setting would be considered strictly off limits. In the field, staff members are never truly off-duty, and must be cognizant that their public behavior and romantic relationships, and even privately expressed opinions, may have an impact on the safety or success of their mission.

A host of issues revolves around the employment of locally hired professionals and support staff. Indigenous national staffers are the backbone of NGO operations in almost every country, and in the majority of missions they now fill all the positions, or all but the most senior. The disparity between national and international staff pay scales and benefits has long been a subject of debate. On the whole, NGOs pay their national staff at levels consistent with local salary levels—those at the upper end of the scale, in order to attract skilled workers, which may be in short supply, and to remain competitive with other NGOs and UN agencies. Yet the ethically questionable result is that a local and an international staff member may be paid vastly different salaries for doing very similar jobs. The NGO community has yet to confront this issue head on. The *NGO Field Coordination Protocol* deals with salary issues, but more with the purpose of preventing competitive outbidding of local staff among NGOs than addressing questions of equity between expatriates and locals. Health and life insurance benefits for local staff are also problematic, since many carriers that cover international staff will not offer policies for local hires, or only at prohibitive rates. NGOs have dealt with the insurance problem through a variety of jury-rigged solutions, depending on the local circumstance.

More generally, as NGOs have grown and taken on more corporate-like structures and bureaucratic procedures, a culture clash of sorts has developed between the values of voluntarism and professionalism in the relief and development community. To lose the voluntarism element, some say, would be robbing the NGOs of their unique role and motivation. NGOs worry about losing their organizational soul and succumbing to the global "commercial zeitgeist," the creeping "corporatization" of culture.[42] But it could also be argued, conversely, that professionalization is not simply a by-product of the inevitable bureaucracy and standardization that accompany organizational growth, but rather a moral imperative. If NGOs are truly to be accountable to their beneficiaries, then they are ethically obligated to provide the highest-quality, most cost-effective services possible. In circumstances where promoting the voluntaristic spirit is at odds with that obligation (for instance, sending volunteers on missions where their presence will be more of a logistical burden than a value), ethics dictates that voluntarism be sacrificed in favor of a professionalized operation. In international health programming this conflict can take the form of a clash between the divergent values of *public health* (raising the overall health status of the population) on the one hand, and *medicine* (treating individual patients with the highest level of care available) on the other.[43]

The increased security risk to NGO personnel has also contributed to the professionalization movement. In addition to the moral responsibility that NGOs feel for the safety of their staff, and therefore insist that they be well-trained professionals, now liability issues resulting from injuries and deaths have created a legal responsibility around the issue of duty of care (the legal obligation of employers to protect employees from harm), particularly for NGOs based in the highly litigious United States.

Political Influence and Advocacy

The professionalization phenomenon, which saw the evolution of NGOs from intrepid charity workers to expert practitioners, has also affected how NGOs relate to governments, and vice versa. NGOs engage in a variety of advocacy efforts on behalf of their beneficiaries and of their own ability to gain access to and serve people in need. Vis-à-vis the U.S. government NGO advocacy ranges from public statements and lobbying of Congress to behind-the-scenes briefings and informal communications with government officials. The most important asset NGOs have to leverage in their advocacy efforts is their firsthand field-level information and contextual knowledge of the aid settings. This is particularly important in crisis contexts where security conditions often make it impossible for diplomatic personnel and other international political actors to move freely outside the capital city, and the humanitarian aid workers frequently become the eyes and ears on the ground for governments and the United Nations.[44] The power of this information, and the reputations many organizations have gained as technical experts, have given the operational assistance NGOs a measure of influence among policymakers that is well beyond that of most other international nonprofits.

Although the direct policy impact is less clear, NGOs also consider public outreach and education to be a crucial element of their advocacy efforts. This generally requires a more complex and nuanced discussion of poverty and development issues than is possible in sound bites or "tear-jerker" appeals for contributions. Avoiding the easy but exploitative ploys has become for some organizations a measure of their integrity. (One NGO has even promised on its direct mail envelopes that the reader will not be subjected to pictures of starving children within.)

Despite international criticism over the large portion of their funding that comes from U.S. government sources, and the expectation that this would inevitably hinder independence in programming and policy stance, U.S.-based NGOs have acted in concerted opposition to the U.S. government on a number of issues: the deliberate targeting of humanitarian aid to favor one side of a conflict (Sudan and Bosnia); the U.S. Export-Import Bank's lending program to African nations to support the sale of U.S.-manufactured AIDS drugs, which even at the reduced rate are much more expensive than locally produced generic products; and the use of military personnel, armed but not in uniform, to deliver humanitarian assistance in Afghanistan Provincial Reconstruction Teams.

However, there remains some confusion among U.S. NGOs as to what the law allows when it comes to advocacy and lobbying.

Advocacy directed at a developing country government on behalf of its own citizens is a trickier matter, for NGOs essentially operate at the pleasure of the host government or local authorities. When faced with evidence of grievous government neglect or outright human rights abuses, NGOs must decide whether to remain silent and continue to work, or to speak out and potentially jeopardize their programs and personnel. As a partial solution, many relief and development NGOs have established formal and informal partnerships with local and international human rights organizations whereby any information impugning the local government can be passed along discreetly to

a local human rights organization for public action.

Challenges in Relating to Political and Military Actors

Political relationships become especially problematic for NGOs operating in conflict situations. In the camps for Rwandan refugees in Zaire from 1992 to 1994, it became increasingly evident that interspersed with innocent civilians were a large number of ex-army and militiamen responsible for perpetrating the genocidal massacres in Rwanda that preceded the overthrow of the state and the refugee exodus. The NGOs working in the camps became aware that these men were still armed and were using the camps as a safe haven to regroup and to launch periodic cross-border attacks into Rwanda. The *génocidaires* were exercising control over the other refugees who served as their human shield, terrorizing them against returning to Rwanda, redistributing the food rations, and generally dictating daily life in the camp. As acts of violence inside the camp became commonplace, the NGOs appealed to the international community to provide military protection to disarm and separate the *génocidaires* from the general population. When this was not forthcoming, the aid organizations had to decide whether their presence in the camps and their continued provision of material aid was doing more harm than good. Finally, the NGO Médecins Sans Frontières, after much internal debate, took the difficult decision to halt operations and withdraw from the camps. They were later followed by a few other large NGOs, such as the International Rescue Committee, Oxfam, and CARE. Other organizations remained, concerned that the innocents in the camps would be left helpless if they withdrew.

Such are the agonizing dilemmas that can confront NGOs providing humanitarian assistance in complex emergencies. Over the past several years much organizational soul searching has gone on in an attempt to clarify mission principles and political stances, and find ways to incorporate themes of justice and human rights in relief work.

To be sure, humanitarian organizations have always operated within a highly political environment while espousing a normative value system intended to transcend politics.

Owing to its unique history, structure and legal status, the Red Cross is a different sort of organizational entity than an NGO. Yet at least four of the Red Cross's seven "fundamental principles" of humanitarian assistance are all seen, with varying degrees of emphasis, in the mission statements and practices of NGOs working in humanitarian assistance. Those four concepts, sometimes referred to as "core" principles of humanitarian aid, are *humanity* (prevention and relief of suffering), *neutrality* (not taking sides), *impartiality* (providing aid indiscriminately, based on need alone), and *independence* (freedom from influence of a foreign government and not pursuing a political or religious agenda). With these criteria satisfied, the reasoning once went, an agency could expect to deliver aid without interference by combatants. Naturally, any humanitarian action will in some way affect the course of conflict so cannot be said to be truly neutral, yet the banner of completely neutral apolitical humanitarianism was a convenient "fiction" that allowed NGOs to operate.[45]

The reality of modern conflict confounds these principles. Now the combatants are less likely to be opposing national armies and more often are loosely organized armed bands or paramilitaries. The belligerents flout the rules of war by deliberately targeting civilians (and occasionally aid workers), and manipulate assistance for strategic advantage or even as an end in itself. The fiction of neutrality has largely unraveled, and NGOs have been forced to rethink their position. Many organizations have adopted the "do no harm" approach, which acknowledges aid's potential for negative impacts in conflicts and

seeks to minimize it, while maintaining as neutral a stance as possible. Others have abandoned the concept of neutrality altogether, adopting a stance of solidarity with the victims. This is the approach most commonly associated with organizations belonging to the "French Doctors' Movement" such as Médecins Sans Frontières and Médecins du Monde. A third or middleway course attempts to straddle the two, in that it strives to target the root causes of conflict and to use humanitarian aid move toward peaceful outcomes, yet "resists taking sides." The talk is now more about "complementarity"—finding ways to coordinate effectively with political and military actors while maintaining independence and staying true to principles.

In conflict settings where there is no great power interest at stake, the NGOs, along with the humanitarian agencies of the UN, have been effectively thrown into the breach left open by the international political community, expected to function without adequate protection for their workers or the populations they serve, and are then often blamed for undesirable outcomes. Conversely, in areas considered strategically important to the United States and its allies in the fight against "global terror" in the post-9/11 era, international assistance has been overridden by political and military objectives, and NGOs must take pains to avoid being used or appearing to be used as political tools. Aid workers have also expressed concern about the U.S. military's taking on aid roles of its own, further reducing the neutral "humanitarian space" in which NGOs try to operate. The latest U.S. National Security Strategy names development assistance as one of the "three pillars" of U.S. foreign policy, along with diplomacy and defense.[46] An unwelcome (to the aid community) manifestation of this policy framework has been the increase in Department of Defense funding resources allocated for "humanitarian assistance." Although the volume of U.S. assistance funding managed by USAID has not decreased, the Defense Department's percentage of U.S.

official development assistance rose from 5.6 percent in 2002 to over 20 percent in 2005.[47]

Faith Based Versus Secular Aid Traditions

One of the impacts of the Bush administration on the character of U.S. foreign aid was the emphasis it placed on religious charitable organizations, particularly evangelical Christian NGOs.

Although religious and secular aid organizations have a long history of working well together in the field, the proselytizing mission of the evangelical movement has created tensions with the secular NGO community, which maintains as a primary principle that aid must be given to those in need regardless of religious, political, or other considerations. Although it is a far less frequent occurrence nowadays, occasionally complaints still surface about an organization that combined proselytizing with aid work in a way that placed conditions on receipt of aid by needy people.

The Likely Future Role of International Nonprofits in the Field

Against this backdrop, the uncertainty of the global economic environment at the time of this writing makes the immediate future of international nonprofit relief and development organizations hard to predict. Many fear that foreign aid funding may be among the first government budget cutbacks, and private charitable giving may suffer as well in the short term because of the economic crisis. Looking to the longer term, however, it is reasonable to expect a continuation of a few key trends.

Slowing of Growth of the NGO Sector

The growth in numbers of new NGOs, after slowing down in the 1980s and '90s, will likely slow further in the next few years.[48] Rising start-up costs and dwindling share of funding for new organizations effectively deterred any significant further expansion during the recent combination of major complex emergencies like Darfur and a massive natural disaster like the Indian Ocean tsunami. The virtual oligopoly of the dozen or so largest NGOs has solidified and accounts for an ever greater proportion of the international resources for assistance. Many major donors, such as USAID, exhibit a preference for NGOs with which they have prior working relationships and in which they have confidence. An additional barrier to entry for new NGOs may be the perception of heightened security risks to personnel in the field.

Continued Standardization, Professionalization, and Homogenization

The tide of professionalization, performance enhancement, and coordination of operations and standards across the aid community seems likely to continue and gain strength, as NGOs increasingly feel pressured to conform to international performance standards. For smaller, younger NGOs especially, the desire for legitimacy and credibility with donors and counterparts will push them toward adherence to such norms. Although many hail this evolution as necessary and desirable, others have raised alarms that increasing homogenization threatens the vitality, innovative capacity, and flexibility for which NGOs first made their mark.

Increasing Role of the Private Sector in International Assistance

The importance of private sector actors, particularly corporations, to international assistance has surged and seems poised to grow further. Many corporations are starting their own foundations, or contributing technical or in-kind assistance to relief and development efforts. But already for years large multinationals have explored opportunities for assisting populations in the developing world, where new markets for their products are emerging or anticipated. This movement, dubbed "global corporate citizenship," brings societal needs and concern for the public good within a firm's overall business strategy. Participating in development projects helps large firms stay attuned to local cultures and conditions as a matter of good business sense, since in many cases "the company may be multinational but its approach is multilocal."[49]

Acknowledging their lack of expertise in the area of development assistance, the corporations are partnering with UN agencies and NGOs. BP Amoco in Angola, Chevron in Kazakhstan, and many others have used such development partnerships to increase their standing with local governments, burnish their public image, and nurture growing markets. The head of AT&T's foundation, Reynold Levy, formerly the president of the International Rescue Committee, predicts, "More companies will join the early pioneers of overseas giving. To do otherwise isn't just uncharitable; it would deprive these companies of an important business asset."[50]

NGOs are approaching these new relationships thoughtfully and cautiously, with an eye toward the potential pitfalls as well as the benefits. A number of complex and strategic "cross sector alliances" have sprung up in recent years, such as those between CARE and Starbucks, and ACCION International and Citibank, where both parties identify and exploit complementarities of mission and values, with an eye to maximizing the interests of both the aid partners and aid recipients.

A bigger challenge for NGOs than such private-public alliances is corporate contractors' stepping into post-crisis or reconstruction settings and taking on aid functions themselves. The U.S. government's reconstruction efforts in Afghanistan and Iraq ushered in a wave of for-profit contractors operating alongside, and at times in competition with, NGOs. The vast amounts of money flowing through contracts for the post-9/11 post-conflict reconstruction campaigns have taken private sector participation to a new level. For instance, in the first year of the Iraq war, the U.S. government contracted with for-profit firms to undertake reconstruction activities to the tune of more than $1 billion—in contrast to $0.3 billion slated for nonprofit grants.

NGO representatives hope that political and military actors will draw the lines more clearly between the domains of assistance, politics, and soldiering, and the military will end its forays into aid delivery. NGOs would also like to see USAID's staffing increased to its level prior to Clinton era personnel cutbacks, and its director given cabinet-level status.

In terms of changes to their own organizations and community, the international assistance NGOs would do well to keep attention focused on a few key areas:

—*Evidence-based and results-driven planning, programming, and evaluation.* NGOs in all aid sectors have acknowledged they must improve their performance in the areas of needs assessment, program monitoring, and evaluation. These are performed reasonably well at the individual project level, but they are done poorly or not at all at the organization, national, and sector levels. To strengthen NGOs' capacities in this area—a goal recognized by both governments and their grantees in the Paris Declaration—the NGOs will need to work together to establish and flesh out common criteria for performance and specific indicators to measure their progress.

—*Staff care and local staff security.* Typically the most complex and dangerous NGO missions, such as Darfur, are staffed primarily by younger, less-experienced personnel. The senior international NGO staffers have earned the right to choose non-hardship posts, and the more junior hires have an interest in paying their dues to move up the ladder. Unfortunately this situation is inherently prone to mishaps, high turnover, and a good deal of staff stress and burnout. The threats to and risk factors facing local, national staff must be more carefully assessed and care taken to give these personnel security resources comparable to those of international staff.

—*Long-term, strategic devolution of responsibility to local actors.* As a long-term goal, the future of the international system for relief and development lies not with the NGO sector of the advanced, industrialized countries of the global North, which for the moment has maximized its capacity for growth (though not for effectiveness and quality), but rather with the global South. Nationalization or localization of relief and development assistance has been happening piecemeal throughout the NGO sector. Whether this is done through training individual professionals, mentoring existing local organizations, or spinning off former country offices into independent NGOs, the goal is to transfer responsibility and "ownership" of the assistance from international agencies to local authorities and organizations. Successful devolution will not happen by itself, but requires the leap from reactive action to long-term strategic planning and capacity building.

Indeed, scarce resources and inefficient funding arrangements make serious long-term planning practically impossible for all but the most well-endowed NGOs. However, if these organizations genuinely support the idea of a lower-cost, locally based response capacity, they need to adopt a forward-looking, proactive approach. A fundamental first step is the realignment of the governance structures so that the organization may draw on diverse national, as well as regional and global, perspectives.

Conclusions

The past decade has been by turns elevating, solidifying, and humbling for the international assistance NGOs. David Rieff and other observers of the field have alluded to the "hubris" of humanitarian practitioners, who refuse to recognize the limitations of their organizations in the face of the tremendously complicated situations in which they now operate. More realistic expectations of the proper roles and potential impact of NGOs are required of both policymakers and the NGOs themselves. This is especially true in complex emergencies, where humanitarian action without political action has proved ineffectual at best, disastrous at worst.

Fortunately, international relief and development has always been a highly introspective and self-critical field, with its NGO members capable of innovative and adaptable response to new challenges. And unfortunately, the persistence of poverty and violent conflict in the developing world means there is no shortage of opportunities for experiential learning and operations research at the field level. Indeed, the most far-reaching analyses of the issues of relief and development assistance tend to emanate from individuals directly involved in its implementation. The world of well-meaning amateurs has given way to an epistemic community of well-trained professionals. Gone, too, is the old model of relief and development as charity from the global North to recipients in the South. Development and, to a lesser degree, relief assistance is being increasingly devolved—though arguably not fast enough—into global networks of international affiliates and locally based capacities.

Notes

1. Vernon Ruttan, *United States Development Assistance Policy: The Domestic Politics of Foreign Economic Aid* (Baltimore, MD: Johns Hopkins University Press, 1996), pp. 476–477.

2. Marc Lindenberg and J. Patrick Dobel, "The Challenges of Globalization for Northern International Relief and Development NGOs," *Nonprofit and Voluntary Sector Quarterly* 28, no. 4 (1999): 4–24.

3. Kofi Annan, *Facing the Humanitarian Challenge: Towards a Culture of Prevention* (New York: UN Department of Public Information, 1999), p. 2.

4. Taylor Seybolt, "Major Armed Conflicts," in *SIPRI Yearbook 2000: Armaments, Disarmament and International Security* (Oxford and Stockholm: Oxford University Press and Stockholm International Peace Research Institute, 2000).

5. For specific figures, see data available at Centre for Research on Epidemiology of Disasters, International Disaster Database (www.emdat.be/database).

6. Security Council resolutions 688 and 794, pertaining to humanitarian intervention in northern Iraq and Somalia, have been seen as precedent-setting decisions, essentially eroding the principle of nonintervention in sovereign states in the interest of humanitarianism and human rights.

7. Marc Lindenberg, "Declining State Capacity, Voluntarism, and the Globalization of the Not-for-Profit Sector," *Nonprofit and Voluntary Sector Quarterly* 28, no. 4 (1999): 147–167.

8. USAID, "Private Voluntary Organizations" (www.pvo.net/usaid); USAID, *Report of Voluntary Agencies* (VOLAG Reports), 2000–08; Thomas Dichter, "Globalization and Its Effects on NGOs: Efflorescence or a Blurring of Roles and Relevance?" *Nonprofit and Voluntary Sector Quarterly* 28, no. 4 (1999): 40.

9. Organization for Economic Cooperation and Development, International Development Assistance Committee (OECD-DAC), development statistics (www.oecd.org/dac/stats); USAID, "2008 VOLAG: Report of Voluntary Agencies" (http://pdf.usaid.gov/pdf_docs/PNADN444.pdf).

10. Janet Salm, "Coping with Globalization: A Profile of the Northern NGO Sector," *Nonprofit and Voluntary Sector Quarterly* 28, no. 4 (1999): 83–103.

11. For instance the Grameen Bank, established in the late 1970s as a microcredit program for the poorest of the poor, is now the largest rural lending institution in Bangladesh, with more than 7.6 million loan recipients, primarily women.

12. Shepard Forman and Stewart Patrick, eds., *Good Intentions: Pledges of Aid in Post-Conflict Recovery* (Boulder: Lynne Rienner, 2000).

13. Shepard Forman, Stewart Patrick, and Dirk Salomons, *Recovering from Conflict: Strategy for an International Response* (New York: New York University, Center on International Cooperation, 2000).

14. Linda Poteat, senior program manager for disaster response at InterAction, author interview, December 18, 2008.

15. See Nicholas Leader, "The Politics of Principle: The Principles of Humanitarian Action in Practice," report prepared for the Overseas Development Institute's Humanitarian Policy Group (London: ODI, March 2000). The report cites examples of NGO cooperation around principles of engagement, including the Code of Conduct for the International Red Cross and Red Crescent Movement and NGOs in Disaster Relief (1992), the Principles and Protocols of Humanitarian Operation (Liberia, 1995), and the Agreement on Ground Rules in South Sudan (1994).

16. Abby Stoddard, *Humanitarian Alert: NGO Information and Its Impact on US Foreign Policy* (Bloomfield, CT: Kumarian Press, 2006), p. ix.

17. Lindenberg, "Declining State Capacity, Voluntarism, and the Globalization of the Not-for-Profit Sector."

18. Security Council Resolution 1674, April 28, 2006.

19. U.S. Department of State and U.S. Agency for International Development, *Security, Democracy, Prosperity: Strategic Plan Fiscal Years 2004–2009, Aligning Diplomacy and Development Assistance* (Washington, 2003); Secretary of State Colin Powell, "Remarks to the National Foreign Policy Conference for Leaders of Nongovernmental Organizations," Loy Henderson Conference Room, U.S. Department of State, Washington, October 26, 2001.

20. OECD, Development Co-operation Directorate (DCD-DAC), "Aid Statistics" (www.oecd.org/dac/stats).

21. U.S.-based NGOs registered with USAID received $2.6 billion in USAID grants, contracts, and material assistance, and $5.2 billion in grants from other U.S. government agencies as well as other governments and international organizations. See USAID, "2008 Report of Voluntary Agencies" (http://pdf.usaid.gov/pdf_docs/PNADN444.pdf).

22. Ibid.

23. OECD, Development Co-operation Directorate (DCD-DAC), "Aid Statistics."

24. Abby Stoddard, "International Humanitarian Financing: Review and Comparative Assessment of Instruments," final report of a study for the Good Humanitarian Donorship Initiative, commissioned by the Office of U.S. Foreign Disaster Assistance

(Washington, DC: Humanitarian Outcomes, July 2008).

25. Lester Salamon and Associates, "The Preparedness Challenge in Humanitarian Assistance," unpublished background paper prepared for the Center on International Cooperation (New York: New York University, 1999) (www.nyu.edu/pages/cic/projects/humanassist/publication.html).

26. Examples include prearranged rapid-response consortia such as the Indefinite Quantities Contract signed between the Office of U.S. Foreign Disaster Assistance and the NGOs CARE, International Medical Corps, and International Rescue Committee and earmarked advance funds for emergencies such as the State Department Bureau for Population, Refugees and Migration's memorandum of Understanding with IRC. Salamon and Associates, "Preparedness Challenge."

27. Lindenberg and Dobel, "Challenges of Globalization for Northern International Relief and Development NGOs."

28. Alex de Waal, *Famine Crimes: Politics and the Disaster Relief Industry in Africa* (Bloomington, IN: Indiana University Press, 1997).

29. Abby Stoddard, Adele Harmer, and Katherine Haver, *Providing Aid in Insecure Environments: Trends in Policy and Operations* (London: Overseas Development Institute, Humanitarian Policy Group, September 2006).

30. Humanitarian Outcomes, *Aid Worker Security Database*, "AWSD Summary Table of Incidents as of 17 Sep 2010" (www.aidworkersecurity.org/resources/AWSDsummarytableofincidents17Sep2010.pdf).

31. Stoddard, Harmer, and Haver, *Providing Aid in Insecure Environments*, p. 4.

32. See Mats Berdal and David Keen, "Violence and Economic Agendas in Civil Wars," *Millennium* 26, no. 3 (1997): 715–818; William Reno, *Warlord Politics and African States* (Boulder, CO: Lynne Rienner, 1998).

33. Abby Stoddard, Adele Harmer, and Victoria DiDomenico, "The Use of Private Security Providers and Services in Humanitarian Operations," HPG Policy Brief 33 (London: Overseas Development Institute, Humanitarian Policy Group, September 2008).

34. Koenraad Van Brabant, "Security Training: Where Are We Now?" Report (London: Overseas Development Institute, 1999).

35. Michael Edwards and David Hulme, *Making a Difference—NGOs and Development in a Changing World* (London: Earthscan, 1992).

36. OECD, "Paris Declaration on Aid Effectiveness: Ownership, Harmonisation, Alignment, Results and Mutual Accountability," endorsed at the High Level Forum, Paris, February 28–March 2, 2005 (www.oecd.org/dataoecd/11/41/34428351.pdf).

37. See InterAction, "PVO [Private Voluntary Organizations] Standards" (www.gdrc.org/ngo/pvo-stand.html).

38. Barkley Calkins, "Improving InterAction's PVO Standards through the Pursuit of Excellence," *Monday Developments* 18, no. 19 (2000): 4.

39. Ibid.

40. Humanitarian Ombudsman Project, "An Ombudsman for Humanitarian Assistance?" *Disasters* 23, no. 2 (June 1999): 115–124.

41. For more information on the Humanitarian Accountability Partnership (HAP International) see their website (www.hapinternational.org/default.aspx).

42. Dichter, "Globalization and Its Effects on NGOs," p. 52.

43. Bradford Gray, "World Blindness and the Medical Profession: Conflicting Medical Cultures and the Ethical Dilemmas of Helping," *Milbank Quarterly* 70, no. 3 (1992): 535–556.

44. Abby Stoddard, *Humanitarian Alert: NGO Information and US Foreign Policy* (Bloomfield, CT: Kumarian Press, 2006).

45. Leader, *Politics of Principle*.

46. U.S. Department of State and U.S. Agency for International Development, *Security, Democracy, Prosperity: Strategic Plan Fiscal Years 2004–2009, Aligning Diplomacy and Development Assistance* (Washington, 2003).

47. Organization for Economic Cooperation and Development, "The United States: Development Assistance Committee (DAC) Peer Review" (2006), pp. 12–13.

48. Lindenberg, "Declining State Capacity, Voluntarism, and the Globalization of the Not-for-Profit Sector," p. 155.

49. D. Logan and M. Tuffrey, "Striking a Balance between McStandardization and Local Autonomy," *@lliance* 5, no. 2 (2000): 6.

50. Reynold Levy, *Give and Take: A Candid Account of Corporate Philanthropy* (Allston: Harvard Business School Press, 1999), p. 187.

PART IV

Tax Exemption and Tax Deduction

Pitima Boonyarak, Ph.D. [a]

What Are Tax Exemptions and Tax Deductions?

Tax exemptions and tax deductions are defining features of nonprofit organizations almost everywhere. In many developed countries, including for example, the United States, the United Kingdom, Australia, and Canada, governments allow nonprofit organizations exemptions from having to pay taxes on their business transactions and operations. In Canada, under the Income Tax Act, a nonprofit organization can apply for tax-exempt status with the Canadian Revenue Agency (CRA), and publicly supported charitable nonprofit organizations are required to register with the CRA before receiving *tax-exempt* status. In most states in the United States, tax-exempt organizations are free from paying corporate income tax. They also do not pay state or local taxes, which include property, sales, user, and franchise taxes.[1] In Canada, these financial privileges also include exemption from capital gains tax and VAT or GST.[2]

Tax-deductibility allows corporations or individuals to deduct donations made to tax-deductible nonprofit organizations from their taxable income. Many publicly supported charitable tax-exempt organizations are eligible for tax deductions. In the United States, individuals and corporations who donate money and other items of value to 501(c)(3) publicly supported charitable nonprofit organizations are entitled to deduct the value of their gifts from their federal income taxes and in most states also from state income taxes. In Canada and the UK, only registered charitable nonprofit organizations can issue tax receipts to individuals and corporate donors to be used for personal and corporate income tax deductions.

Why Do Governments Give Nonprofits Favorable Tax Treatment?

Granting tax exempt and/or tax deductible status to nonprofit organizations means loss of revenue for governments. Tax exempt organizations cost local, state, and the United States government tax

 DOI: 10.4324/9780367696559-14

revenue every year.[3] It was estimated in 2001 that state and local governments lost $2 billion in uncollected sales tax revenue and $400 million in exempted sales tax revenue. The amount of lost revenue from *property tax* was estimated to be from $9–$15 billion—and this amount does not include church-owned properties. The loss of state *income tax* was estimated from $3.8–$4 billion.[4] Why then are governments in these countries willing to grant favorable tax treatment to nonprofit organizations? Why are they willing to forgo revenue they could otherwise earn? Why are they willing, in effect, to subsidize nonprofit organizations?

There are several reasons why federal, state, and local governments are willing to provide tax benefits to nonprofit organizations. First, nonprofit organizations relieve government burden by providing *public goods* or *public benefit goods*, and *public benefit services*. Typically, government agencies would need to provide these *goods* and *services* themselves. Without nonprofit organizations, governments would be forced to provide more goods and services than they currently do. For example, these organizations provide shelter for the homeless population, settlement services for new immigrants, help families find affordable services for children with disabilities. They provide basic healthcare for low income populations, better public access to healthcare within their communities,[5] and deliver free meals to seniors, along with a host of other tangible benefits. Nonprofit organizations receive preferential tax treatment in exchange for providing these types of public benefit goods.[6]

Secondly, nonprofit organizations are often sources of positive energy. They help connect individuals and build social networks within a community (see Part VII). Alexis de Tocqueville documented his first-hand witness of the voluntary, self-help spirit when he traveled across America (see Part II). In the United States, governments at all levels recognize the presence of nonprofit organizations in sustaining the *self-help* attitudes in American society. This is why the U.S. Congress authorized tax deductions for charitable donations in the Revenue Act of 1917, four years after the 16th Amendment to the Constitution established the personal income tax.[7]

Likewise, governments around the globe subsidize activities of nonprofit organizations to assist them in advancing the well-being of their communities. In the 1800s in the UK, most educational institutions were nonprofit organizations that provided literacy and generated social and scientific innovations for society. In the early 1900s, nonprofit organizations in Canada led moral and social reforms, including women's education, public health, and recreational opportunities.[8]

How Do Tax Exemptions and Deductions Work?

To be eligible for both tax exemption and tax deduction, a nonprofit organization operating in these countries must meet broad criteria set by tax laws and revenue service code requirements.

Typical Criteria for Being Tax Exempt and/or Deductible

A nonprofit organization must be organized for charitable or mutually beneficial purposes to be eligible for tax deductibility and tax exemption. For U.S. nonprofit organizations to be eligible for tax exemption and tax deductions as 501(c)(3) organizations under Internal Revenue Service (IRS) code, they must meet criteria defined by the IRS. In the UK and Canada, a nonprofit organization must meet the description of a "charity" as defined by common law[9] and must also meet public benefit requirements. In these three countries—and many others—their missions must be charitable and must serve public interests as defined by the deciding authorities. Examples of common charitable purposes include religious, charitable, scientific, educational, and prevention of cruelty to children or animals or similar.

Earning Criteria

Nonprofit organizations also must be *non-distributive* with their earnings. None of their net earnings ("profit" also known as "surplus") may be distributed to benefit any shareholders or individual. Henry Hansmann originated the term *non-distribution constraint* for this—which he considers the defining feature of nonprofits.[10] It is widely but erroneously believed that nonprofit organizations are not permitted to make a profit. In the United States and Canada, tax-exempt nonprofit organizations are permitted to make and retain profit. Tax-exempt organizations, however, are severely restricted in what they can do with surpluses. Most importantly, nonprofits do not have owners or shareholders who might receive distributed surpluses as dividends—as for-profit businesses routinely do.[11] With tax-exempt nonprofit organizations, *private inurement* is not permitted.[12] Surpluses may be used for many purposes, including to acquire new equipment, hire more staff, or rent a larger office, but only if these acquisitions advance the nonprofit's charitable, religious, scientific, educational, literary, or other Tax Code-permitted purposes. When a nonprofit organization goes out of existence, its assets must be distributed to other tax-exempt organizations or government agencies.

In the United States, if a 501(c)(3) nonprofit organization earns too much revenue from business-like activities unrelated to the organization's charitable mission or which have a mutual benefit purpose claimed when applying for tax exempt status, it must pay[13] *Unrelated Business Income Tax* (*UBI*). Canada takes an "all or nothing" approach. Registered charitable nonprofit organizations, known as 149(1)(f) organizations under the Canadian Revenue Agency (CRA) code, cannot engage in commercial activities unrelated to their charitable purposes. Punishment for noncompliance ranges from a 5–100 percent sanction on profits or the revoking of the organization's charitable status.[14]

Political Activity Criteria

Countries may restrict certain political activities of nonprofit organizations that enjoy the tax-exempt status and tax deduction benefits. In the United States, 501(c)(3) organizations are restricted from participating in activities that attempt to influence legislation, nor can they participate in campaigns for political candidates. They may devote an *unsubstantial* portion of their assets to political activities, but lobbying is not permitted.[15] 149(1)(f) organizations in Canada have somewhat more freedom. They can engage in nonpartisan political activities, such as influencing public policy if a policy aligns with their charitable purpose. They are, however, prohibited from partisan political activities involving political campaigns and in supporting political candidates.

To receive favorable tax treatment, nonprofit organizations are subject to regulations and scrutiny. As mentioned in the previous paragraph, in the United States, publicly supported charitable nonprofit 501(c)(3)s have tight restrictions on engaging in political activity and lobbying. Conversely, the 501(c)(4)—*Civic Leagues and Social Welfare Organizations*—are free to actively engage in political campaigns and may attempt to directly influence legislation. The *price* the 501(c)(4) organizations *pay* for the right to be politically active is ineligibility for tax-deductible contributions.

Until 2018, charitable nonprofit organizations, 149(1)(f) organizations in Canada faced heavy regulations and scrutiny from the federal government. The "Ten Percent Rule" that restricts nonpartisan political activities to account for no more than 10 percent of the charitable nonprofit organizations' budget was applied to all registered charitable nonprofit organizations.[16] Organizations that were viewed as carrying a political agenda were subject to possible federal audits.[17] The federal government, however, recently loosened its restrictions on registered charity organizations due to rising political pressure which resulted in the 2018 court decision *Canada Without Poverty versus AG Canada*. The Court's opinion declared that the government's restriction on political activities infringes upon charities' rights to free expression protected under the *Canadian Charter of Rights and Freedom.* Also in 2018, the federal government passed Bill C-86 (*Budget Implementation Act*) allowing charitable organizations to engage in unlimited nonpartisan political activities under the *Income Tax Act.*[18] Canadian charitable organizations, 149(1)(f) organizations, can now participate in *Public Policy Dialogue and Development Activities* (PPDDAs) such as policy advocacy and political mobilization to advance their stated charitable purposes. However, activities that directly support a political party or a candidate to a political office are still prohibited.[19]

The UK government has a less restrictive policy on the political activities of charitable nonprofit organizations than Canada or the US. The *Charity Commission* permits a registered charitable nonprofit organization to participate in both political campaigning and political activity if the participation supports the organization's charitable purposes[20] and the participation is not the sole purpose for the organization. This is due to a long-held British tradition of charitable nonprofit organizations engaging in political activities that advance their causes.

Readings Reprinted in Part IV

The three readings included here present overviews of the rationale for granting favorable tax treatment in the United States. They are not in-depth analyses of tax laws or IRS codes.

Christopher Hoyt defines a "Tax-Exempt Organization" as an organization exempt from income taxation because it operates to provide broad social benefits to the public or mutual benefits to its members. Most tax-exempt organizations are also exempt from state and local income and property taxes, although the exemptions vary across jurisdictions. Hoyt explains the justifications and legal requirements for tax exemption, provides an overview of the economic activities of tax-exempt organizations, and presents a comprehensive list (with short descriptions) of the various types of tax-exempt organizations. He notes that many other nations have followed the United States' lead in establishing tax-exempt policies for social welfare and mutual benefit organizations.

In "Why Are Nonprofits Exempt From the Corporate Income Tax?", Michael Rushton analyzes the general structure of the corporate tax treatment of nonprofit organizations with a focus on efficiency. His analysis offers an alternative rationales for why nonprofit organizations are exempt from Corporate Income Tax and for the existence of Unrelated Business Income Tax (UBIT).

There are three primary reasons why governments grant nonprofit organizations tax-exempt status. First, the net income of nonprofit organizations cannot be clearly defined in the traditional sense of profit-making because nonprofit organizations do not exist to generate profits. Profits are made to advance their missions. Second, nonprofit organizations are subsidized by governments to deliver services that government would have to otherwise provide. Subsidies are also granted for other reasons including the altruistic nature of nonprofits, volunteerism, and innovation. Third, nonprofit organizations have traditionally been excluded from government's tax base due to their historically independent nature which precludes state interference into their affairs. Rushton concludes that these rationales focus on the special characteristics of nonprofit organizations—lack of profit distribution, public interest focus, and their independent nature. He asserts that they do not provide adequate reasons for exemption.

The alternative rationale offered by Rushton focuses on the lack of efficiency in the current structure of Corporate Income Tax (CIT). CIT exists to ensure that profits distributed to individuals are taxed. Nonprofit organizations are exempt not because they deserve the subsidy but instead because their profits are mandated to be reinvested in the organizations—not to be distributed to individual shareholders or members of the organizations.

> If there were an effective means for attributing and taxing at the individual shareholder level all net profits earned through corporations, there would be no need for the CIT, and the apparent subsidy to nonprofits from the CIT exemption would disappear.

The Unrelated Business Income Tax (UBIT) ensures that a nonprofit's investment in unrelated business activities is treated in a similar manner as for-profit businesses in order to avoid malpractices where for-profit firms register themselves under a nonprofit veil to reduce economic cost or nonprofit organizations engage in unrelated activities simply to take advantage of the lower tax-free cost.

Rob Reich questions why governments impose restrictions on philanthropic giving in liberal democratic countries where individuals should have freedom to give away their money to whomever or whatever they please, in "A Political Theory of Philanthropy." Moreover, why do governments provide tax incentives to individuals to exercise their liberty to make charitable contributions?

Reich focuses his answers to these questions on tax deductions as a mechanism used by governments to provide incentives to individuals to make charitable donations. Reich proposes and assesses three justifications for tax incentives for individual charitable contributions: *the tax base rationale*, *the efficiency rationale*, and *the pluralism rationale*. The justification for the *tax base rationale* claims that deductions are not subsidies. Instead, they are needed to account for the proper base for taxable income. The justification for the *efficiency rationale* is that tax deductions are a form of subsidy. Governments forego revenue in exchange for something of great social value. Tax incentives function as a stimulus to generate public benefit services that are in undersupply in the society. The justification for the *pluralism rationale* links tax incentives to the stimulus of pluralistic, associational life, civic engagement, and decentralization of authority—*civil society*. The benefits are the civil society itself which is fundamental to democratic societies (see Part VII). Reich concludes that although the efficiency and pluralism rationales offer plausible justifications for providing tax incentives to encourage charitable giving, they are not helpful in the design of tax-subsidized giving.

Notes

a. Business and Policy Strategist, City of Calgary, Alberta, Canada.

1. Bruce R. Hopkins, *The Law of Tax-Exempt Organizations*, 12th ed. (Hoboken, NJ: Wiley, 2019).

2. Callum M. Carmichael, "Dispensing Charity: The Deficiencies of an All-or-Nothing Fiscal Concept." *Voluntas* 23 (2012): 392–414. DOI:10.1007/s11266-011-9207-3

3. In the field of public finance, these lost tax revenues are known as "opportunity costs" or, more commonly, "tax expenditures." See Marcia L. Whicker, "Tax Expenditure." In *International Encyclopedia of Public Policy and Administration*, edited by Jay M. Shafritz (pp. 2217–2219) (Boulder, CO: Westview Press, 1998).

4. Woods Bowman, M. Marion, and R. Freemont-Smith, "Nonprofits and State and Local Government." In *Nonprofits & Government: Collaboration and Conflict*, edited by E. T. Boris and C. E. Steuerle (pp. 181–213) (Washington, DC: The Urban Institute Press, 2006).

5. Young Joo Park and Shuyang Peng, "Advancing Public Health Through Tax-Exempt Hospitals: Nonprofits' Revenue Streams and Provision of Collective Goods." *Nonprofit and Voluntary Sector Quarterly* 49(2) (2020): 357–379.

6. Melissa A. Walker and Linsey F. Sipult, "Nonprofit Sales Tax Exemption: Where Do States Draw the Line?" *Nonprofit and Voluntary Sector Quarterly* 40(6) (2011): 1005–1019.

7. Paul Arnsberger, Melissa Ludlum, Margaret Riley, and Mark Stanton, "A History of the Tax-Exempt Sector: An SOI Perspective." In *Statistics of Income Bulletin 2007–2008* (Washington, DC: U.S. Internal Revenue Service, 2008).

8. Peter R. Elson, "The Origin of the Species Charity Regulation: Why Charity Regulations in Canada and England Continue to Reflect Their Origins." *International Journal of Not-for-Profit Law* 12(3) (2010): 75–89.

9. Callum M. Carmichael, "Dispensing Charity: The Deficiencies of an All-or-Nothing Fiscal Concept." *Voluntas* 23 (2012): 392–414. DOI:10.1007/s11266-011-9207-3

10. Henry Hansmann, "The Role of Non-profit Enterprise." *Yale Law Review* 89(5): 835–901.

11. Bruce R. Hopkins, *The Law of Tax-Exempt Organizations*, 12th ed. (Hoboken, NJ: Wiley, 2019).

12. James J. Fishman and Stephen Schwarz, *Nonprofit Organizations: Cases and Materials*, 4th ed. (New York: Foundation Press, 2010); and Bruce R. Hopkins, *The Law of Tax-Exempt Organizations*, 12th ed. (Hoboken, NJ: John Wiley & Sons, 2019).

13. Bruce R. Hopkins, *The Law of Unrelated Business for Nonprofit Organizations*, 12th ed. (Hoboken, NJ: Wiley, 2019).

14. Tamara Larre, "Allowing Charities to 'Do More Good' by Carrying Through Carrying on Unrelated Business." *Canadian Journal of Nonprofit and Social Economy Research* 7(1) (2016): 29–45.

15. Internal Revenue Service 2020, "Exemption Requirements 501 C (3)—Exempt Organizations, the United States," viewed 6 May 2020, <www.irs.gov/charities-non-profits/charitable-organizations/exemption-requirements-501c3-organizations>.

16. Nazita Lajevardi, Mirle Rabinowitz Bussell, James Stauch, and Nicole Rigillo, "Room to Flourish: Lessons for Canadian Grantmaking Foundations from Sweden, Germany, and the Netherlands." *Canadian Journal of Nonprofit and Social Economy Research* 8(2) (2017): 80–96.

17. Tamara Larre, "Allowing Charities to 'Do More Good' by Carrying Through on Unrelated Business." *Canadian Journal of Nonprofit and Social Economy Research* 7(1) (2016): 29–45.

18. Peter R. Elson, "The Origin of the Species Charity Regulation: Why Charity Regulations in Canada and England Continue to Reflect Their Origins." *International Journal of Not-for-Profit Law* 12(3) (2010): 75–89.

19. Government of Canada 2019, "Public Policy Dialogue and Development Activities by Charities, Canada," viewed 28 May 2020, <www.canada.ca/en/revenue-agency/services/charities-giving/charities/policies-guidance/public-policy-dialogue-development-activities.html>.

20. The United Kingdom Government 2008, "Campaigning and Political Activity Guidance for Charities (CC9)," viewed 29 May 2020, <www.gov.uk/government/publications/speaking-out-guidance-on-campaigning-and-political-activity-by-charities-cc9/speaking-out-guidance-on-campaigning-and-political-activity-by-charities>.

Bibliography

Abramson, Alan J., Lester M. Salamon, and C. Eugene Steuerle, "Federal Spending and Tax Policies: Their Implications for the Nonprofit Sector." In *Nonprofits & Government: Collaboration & Conflict*, edited by Elizabeth T. Boris and C. Eugene Steuerle (pp. 107–140) (Washington, DC: Urban Institute Press, 2006).

Arnsberger, Paul, Melissa Ludlum, Margaret Riley, and Mark Stanton, "A History of the Tax-Exempt Sector: An SOI Perspective." In *Statistics of Income Bulletin 2007–2008* (pp. 105–135) (Washington, DC: US Internal Revenue Service, 2008).

Blazek, Jody, *Tax Planning and Compliance for Tax-Exempt Organizations* (Hoboken, NJ: John Wiley & Sons, 2009).

Bowman, Woods, M. Marion, and R. Freemont-Smith, "Nonprofits and State and Local Government." In *Nonprofits & Government: Collaboration and Conflict*, edited by E. T. Boris and C. E. Steuerle (pp. 181–213) (Washington, DC: The Urban Institute Press, 2006).

Brody, Evelyn, and Joseph J. Cordes, "Tax Treatment of Nonprofit Organizations: A Two-Edged Sword?" In *Nonprofits & Government: Collaboration & Conflict*, edited by Elizabeth T. Boris and C. Eugene Steuerle (pp. 141–180) (Washington, DC: Urban Institute Press, 2006).

Cafardi, Nicholas P., and Jaclyn Fabean Cherry, *Tax Exempt Organizations: Cases and Materials* (3rd ed.) (Newark, NJ: Matthew Bender & Company, 2015).

Clotfelter, Charles T., ed., *Who Benefits from the Nonprofit Sector?* (Chicago: University of Chicago Press, 1992).

Fishman, James J., and Stephen Schwarz, *Nonprofit Organizations: Cases and Materials* (4th ed.) (New York: Foundation Press, 2010).

——, *Nonprofit Organizations: Statutes, Regulations, and Forms* (New York: Foundation Press, 2007).

Hansmann, Henry, *The Ownership of Enterprise* (Cambridge, MA: Belknap Press of Harvard University Press, 1996).

——, "The Role of Nonprofit Enterprise." *Yale Law Journal* 89 (1980): 835–901.

Hopkins, Bruce R., *The Law of Tax-Exempt Organizations* (12th ed.) (Hoboken, NJ: John Wiley & Sons, 2019).

——, *The Law of Unrelated Business for Nonprofit Organizations* (Hoboken, NJ: John Wiley & Sons, 2010).

Hoyt, Christopher, "Tax-Exempt Organization." In *International Encyclopedia of Public Policy and Administration*, edited by Jay M. Shafritz (pp. 2214–2217) (Boulder, CO: Westview Press, 1998).

Lajevardi, Nazita, Mirle Rabinowitz Bussell, James Stauch, and Nicole Rigillo, "Room to Flourish: Lessons for Canadian Grantmaking Foundations from Sweden, Germany, and the Netherlands." *Canadian Journal of Nonprofit and Social Economy Research* 8(2) (2017): 80–96.

Park, Young Joo, and Shuyang Peng, "Advancing Public Health Through Tax-Exempt Hospitals: Nonprofits' Revenue Streams and Provision of Collective Goods." *Nonprofit and Voluntary Sector Quarterly* 49 (2020): 357–379.

Rushton, Michael, "Why Are Nonprofits Exempt from the Corporate Income Tax?" *Nonprofit and Voluntary Sector Quarterly* 36 (2007): 662–675.

Salamon, Lester A., *America's Nonprofit Sector: A Primer* (New York: Foundation Center, 1992).

——, *The State of Nonprofit America* (2nd ed.) (Washington, DC: The Brookings Institution, 2012).

Scrivner, Gary N., "A Brief History of Tax Policy Changes Affecting Charitable Organizations." In *The Nature of the Nonprofit Sector* (1st ed.), edited by J. Steven Ott (pp. 126–142) (Boulder, CO: Westview Press, 2001).

Simpson, Steven D., *Tax Compliance for Tax-Exempt Organizations* (Chicago: Commerce Clearing House, 2018).

United States Master Tax Guide (Chicago: Commerce Clearing House, yearly).

US Internal Revenue Service. *IRS Statistics of Income Bulletin* (Washington, DC: IRS, yearly).

Walker, Melissa A., and Linsey F. Sipult, "Nonprofit Sales Tax Exemption: Where Do States Draw the Line?" *Nonprofit and Voluntary Sector Quarterly* 40 (2010): 1005–1019.

Weisbrod, Burton A., *The Nonprofit Economy* (Cambridge, MA: Harvard University Press, 1988).

CHAPTER 11

Tax-Exempt Organization

Christopher Hoyt

From *The International Encyclopedia of Public Policy and Administration*, edited by Jay M. Shafritz. Copyright © 1998 by Jay M. Shafritz. Reprinted by permission of Westview Press, a member of the Taylor & Francis Group.

A tax-exempt organization is an] organization exempt from income taxation because it operates to provide either broad social benefits to the public or mutual benefits to its members. Many organizations are also exempt from state and local income and property taxes, although the exemptions vary with each local jurisdiction.

Reason for Exemption

In the United States, Congress determined that two categories of nonprofit organizations qualified for exemption from income taxation: social benefit organizations and mutual benefit organizations. Social benefit organizations operate to improve the quality of life in a community. Examples include charitable organizations and social welfare organizations. Mutual benefit organizations operate to promote the welfare of the members of the organization rather than the public at large. Examples include labor unions, trade associations, and social clubs.

An essential feature of both types of organizations is that they must not be organized to enrich investors. For example, a music school that is owned by a few teachers and investors will not qualify as a charity, whereas a similar school that is part of a college will. A privately owned restaurant cannot qualify for tax-exemption, whereas a private social club that restricts its dining facilities to its members can. Similarly, a privately owned business that gathers statistics about industry sales and sells it to purchasers will not qualify as a tax-exempt organization, whereas a nonprofit trade association that gathers and distributes similar information to its members will. Although the purpose of many mutual benefit organizations is to improve the economic vitality of their members, that is not considered a form of private benefit that will prohibit tax-exempt status.

Despite a general exemption from income tax, a tax-exempt organization will generally be liable for income tax on profits from unrelated business activities. This can arise from fundraising activities, such as selling holiday cards, or from certain investments, such as being a partner in a mining operation.

    DOI: 10.4324/9780367696559-15

Economic Activity

The number of tax-exempt organizations in the United States has significantly increased in recent years, according to the Internal Revenue Service (IRS) *Statistics of Income Bulletin* issued August 1995. In 1990, there were 1,022,223 tax-exempt organizations, which is a 27 percent increase over the 806,375 organizations that existed in 1978. Over that time period, the assets of tax-exempt organizations increased by 150 percent to over US$1 trillion and their revenues increased by 225 percent to US$560 billion, whereas the nation's gross domestic product (GDP) increased by only 52 percent. In 1990, the revenue of tax-exempt organizations constituted nearly 10 percent of the nation's GDP, an increase from 6 percent in 1975. Charities alone accounted for more than 7 percent of GDP in 1990.

Charitable organizations comprise the largest category of tax-exempt organizations (48 percent of all tax-exempt organizations described in Section 501 [c]), followed by social welfare organizations (14 percent), fraternal organizations (10 percent), labor and agricultural organizations (7 percent), business leagues (6 percent), and social clubs (6 percent). Certain segments of the tax-exempt sector are growing faster than others. Whereas the number of tax-exempt organizations grew by 27 percent from 1978 to 1990, the greatest growth was in the number of charities (67 percent), business leagues (45 percent), and social welfare organizations (14 percent). By comparison, the number of labor and agricultural organizations decreased by 18 percent.

Overview of Legal Requirements

Most state statutes specify procedures to establish a nonprofit corporation or some other form of nonprofit organization, such as a cooperative or a benevolent association. Many statutes require the organization to specify in its organization documents (e.g., articles of incorporation, bylaws) whether it is a social benefit or a mutual benefit organization. Complying with these state laws does not ensure that an organization will be tax-exempt under the federal income tax laws. Instead, each organization's governing documents must also contain specific provisions that comply with the federal laws that grant tax-exemption. Most organizations must apply to the IRS for tax-exempt status before they will be treated as tax-exempt, although churches are a notable exception.

Section 501(c) Organizations

The most important statute that grants tax-exemption is Section 501(c) of the Internal Revenue Code. It lists 25 types of tax-exempt organizations in relatively random order. In order to obtain tax-exemption, most organizations structure their legal documents and limit their operations to comply with the appropriate exemption. Many organizations can describe their operations to outsiders by simply referring to the appropriate paragraph of the statute.

The different types of tax-exempt organizations are listed here in the order that they appear in Section 501(c). For example, number (3) on the list corresponds to Section 501(c)(3). The number in brackets represents the number of that type of organization that existed in the United States in 1991, according to IRS records. The following types of organizations are exempt from federal income tax under Section 501(c):

1. A tax-exempt corporation organized by an act of Congress that is an instrumentality of the United States. Examples include the Federal Deposit Insurance Corporation (FDIC) and the Pension Benefit Guarantee Corporation (PBGC). [9]
2. A corporation organized for the exclusive purpose of holding title to property, collecting income therefrom and turning over the entire amount, less expenses, to another tax-exempt organization. [6,408]

3. A charitable organization that engages primarily in charitable activities. [516,554 plus an estimated 340,000 churches for a total of 856,554]

4. A social welfare organization that promotes the general welfare of a community by bringing about civic betterments and social improvements. The statute also exempts certain local associations of employees, such as a local police relief association. [142,811]

5. A labor union, agricultural, or horticultural organization. A labor organization is an association of workers who have combined to promote their interests by bargaining collectively with their employers to secure better working conditions, wages, and similar benefits. An example is the United Auto Workers. An agricultural or horticultural organization operates to improve the economic conditions of agriculture or horticulture workers, the grade of their products, and the efficiency of production. [72,009]

6. A trade association, business league, chamber of commerce, real-estate board, board of trade, or professional football league. Examples include the American Medical Association and a city's Chamber of Commerce. [68,442]

7. A social club organized for pleasure, recreation, and other nonprofit purposes, provided that substantially all of its activities are restricted for such purposes. Although revenue paid by members as dues, service fees, and charges for meals will generally be tax-exempt, a social club will pay tax on its investment income. [63,922]

8. A fraternal benefit society, order, or association that operates under the lodge system or for the exclusive benefit of its members and provides for the payment of life, sickness, accident, or other benefits to its members and their dependents (compare with [10] below). [98,840]

9. A voluntary employees' beneficiary association (VEBA) that provides for the payment of life, sick, accident, or other benefits to the employee members of such association or their dependents. [14,708]

10. A fraternity, sorority, domestic fraternal society, order, or association that operates under the lodge system and devotes its net earnings exclusively to religious, charitable, scientific, literary, educational, and fraternal purposes and that does not pay life, sick, accident, or other benefits to its members and their dependents (compare with [8] above). [18,360]

11. A local teachers' retirement fund whose income consists solely of amounts received from public taxation, assessments on the teaching salaries of members, and income from investments. [10]

12. A mutual ditch or irrigation company, mutual or cooperative telephone company, or a local benevolent life insurance association; but only if 85 percent or more of the income consists of amounts collected from members for the sole purpose of meeting losses and expenses. [5,984]

13. A cemetery association or company that is owned and operated exclusively for the benefit of its members or is operated not for profit. [8,781]

14. Certain types of nonprofit credit unions that are organized and operated for mutual purposes and certain types of mutual associations (organized before 1958) that provide reserve funds and insure deposits at banks and savings and loan associations. [6,219]

15. Certain types of insurance company (other than a life insurance company) whose net premiums do not exceed US$350,000 in a year. [1,147]

16. A corporation to finance the ordinary crop operations of its members. [20]

17. A trust that provides supplemental unemployment benefits to employees. [644]

18. A trust created before June 25, 1959, that is part of a pension plan that is funded only by contributions of employees. [8]

19. A post or organization that has at least 75 percent of its members comprised of past or present members of the US Armed Forces. [27,962]

20. An organization that is part of a qualified group legal services plan. [206]

21. A trust established to pay claims to miners and other victims of black lung disease. [23]

22. A trust established by sponsors of a multi-employer plan (usually a union-administered retirement plan) to pay certain pension plan withdrawal liabilities. [None]

23. An association to provide insurance and other benefits to veterans associations, but only if the association was established before 1880. [2]

24. A trust to pay certain types of retirement income obligations. [None]

25. A corporation or trust that holds title to buildings and other real property for certain retirement plans, charities, or governmental subdivisions (maximum 35 beneficiaries of each organization). [181]

Other Tax-Exempt Organizations

1. A qualified retirement, pension, profit-sharing, and stock bonus plan is tax-exempt. Such a retirement plan will not pay tax on revenue from contributions from employers or from investment income, but it will be liable for tax on unrelated business income (Sections 401[a] and 501[a]). [Unknown]

2. A charitable remainder trust that distributes amounts annually to a person for life, or for a fixed number of years, and then terminates and distributes its assets to a charity. In 1995, the Tax Court concluded that a charitable remainder trust will lose its tax-exempt status in any year that it has unrelated business taxable income. [16,000]

3. A farmers' cooperative is tax-exempt (Section 521). Most cooperatives merely share costs among their members rather than operate a business for profit, and they are therefore generally exempt from taxation under Subchapter T of the Internal Revenue Code. [2,129; by comparison there were 3,219 taxable farmers' cooperatives]

4. Special rules apply to cooperative service organizations of hospitals (Section 501[e] [72 in existence]) and for a pooled investment fund of educational organizations (Section 501[f] [Only 1 in existence, "The Common Fund"]).

5. A political organization (political party, election committee, etc.) is tax-exempt with respect to the amounts it receives from contributions, member dues, and proceeds from fund-raising events. However, it must pay income tax at the highest corporate rate (currently 35 percent) on its net investment income. In addition, a political candidate will be liable for income tax if any amounts are diverted for his or her personal use (Section 527).

6. A homeowners' association (an organization that manages a subdivision development or a condominium) is tax-exempt with respect to the amounts it receives as membership dues, fees, or assessments from owners of the managed property. However, it must pay a 30 percent income tax on its net investment income (Section 528).

Many nations have adopted similar policies to those of the United States and have exempted social welfare and mutual organizations from income, sales, and property taxes. Of course, the laws vary from nation to nation.

Reference

Internal Revenue Service. 1995. *IRS Statistics of Income Bulletin* (Summer). Washington, DC.

CHAPTER 12

A Political Theory of Philanthropy

ROB REICH

Reich, Rob, *Just Giving: Why Philanthropy is Failing Democracy and How It Can Do Better* (Princeton, NJ: Princeton University Press, 2018).

People have been giving away their money, property, and time to others for millennia. In the liturgical system in classical Athens, the institutional design of the waqf in Islam, and the foundations in France and England vigorously criticized by Turgot and Mill, practices of philanthropy are embedded within social and religious custom, civic norms, and the law. Political and social arrangements facilitate and structure the practice of philanthropy.

In the United States and many other countries, the tax code provides incentives, in the form of tax advantages, to people to give away their money and property (though not their time).

The charitable contributions deduction in the United States is barely a century old, created by the U.S. Congress in 1917 shortly after the institution of a system of federal income taxation. Similar incentives built into tax systems exist in most developed and many developing democracies. Most countries, not only democracies, use some kind of deduction scheme, including Australia, Egypt, France, Germany, India, Japan, Mexico, the Netherlands, Russia, South Africa, Spain, and Thailand. To the best of my knowledge, only Sweden provides no subsidy structure at all for charitable giving.[1]

Beyond the tax deduction for charitable giving, legal rules govern the creation of nonprofit organizations and various kinds of endowments, such as private foundations and community trusts. These policies spell out the rules under which these organizations may incorporate and operate, sometimes setting limits on permissible activities (for example, whether nonprofits may engage in electioneering, partisan political communication, or lobbying). Other laws set up special tax exemptions for nonprofit organizations and philanthropic foundations, and they frequently permit tax concessions for individual and corporate donations of money and property. Still other laws protect and enforce donor intent, even beyond death. The effects of these laws are significant: they define and regulate the philanthropic sector, confer the state's imprimatur on what counts as an official charity or foundation, and articulate the range of state-sanctioned charitable purposes. The legal regime promotes and shapes the sector, and in so doing the state and by extension all citizens forgo considerable tax revenue.

Contemporary practice, in which philanthropy is structured by a regulatory framework of incentives, of forgone tax revenue, is not the norm but the historical anomaly. Governments

    DOI: 10.4324/9780367696559-16

have often respected the liberty of people to make donations of money and property, and might even have encouraged the practice by providing civic recognition and honor for them to do so, as in classical Athens. Yet I am unaware of cases prior to the twentieth century in which states attempted to stimulate the exercise of a person's liberty to give money away via fiscal incentives such as tax subsidies. Two questions arise: why have such incentives, and what is their justification in a liberal democracy?[2]

The historical practice of philanthropy is littered with instances in which the relevant question that presented itself to the state was how vigorously it should *constrain* the liberty of people to give money away. Donors did not possess something akin to a property right over their charitable assets, neither in life and certainly not after death; the assets belonged, thought Mill, to their intended beneficiaries. The principle of social utility is what provided the grounds to justify limits on the liberty of would-be philanthropists.

These are not the only grounds, however. Public influence obtained through private wealth might be injurious to the state by, for example, threatening the authority of the ruling class. Aristocratic elites have often been considered public threats, dangerous because they could seek to translate private munificence into political power. In the *Discourses*, Machiavelli tells the following story about ancient Rome:

> When the city of Rome was overburdened with hunger, and public provisions were not enough to stop it, one Spurius Maelius, who was very rich for those times, had the intent to make provision of grain privately, and to feed the plebs with it, gaining its favor for him. Because of this affair he had such a crowd of people in his favor that the Senate, thinking of the inconvenience that could arise from that liberality of his, so as to crush it before it could pick up more strength, created a dictator over him and had him killed.

The question about constraining the liberty of people to give away money and property remains with us today. We need only consider debates about inheritance taxation and campaign finance contributions to realize that states may have good reasons—reasons founded on justice—to limit the liberty of people to give money away.

We might also point to the U.S. Constitution itself for reasons that in some circumstances individuals should not merely *not* receive a tax concession for a charitable donation but should be entirely blocked from making the donation. The Appropriations Clause of the Constitution—"no money shall be drawn from the Treasury, but in Consequence of Appropriations made by law"[3]—or the so-called power of the purse, can be construed to prohibit private donations to federal agencies. "As a consequence of the appropriations requirement," Kate Stith argues, "all 'production' of government must be pursuant to legislative authority, even where the additional production is financed with donations and thus appears costless to the Treasury."[4]

In the United States and elsewhere there have been, and continue to be, reasons to limit the liberty of people to give money away for charitable purposes.

So here, then, is a simple question of first principle: what attitude should a liberal democratic state have toward the preference of individuals to make donations of money or property for a philanthropic purpose? More generally, what rules should govern philanthropic giving in a liberal democracy? I suggest we consider an answer to the question by starting with a few assumptions that will assist in posing the question in the widest or most general form for liberal democratic theory.

A Simple Framework

Consider this simple framework to motivate the question. Assume first that there is a private property regime of some type and that individuals have duly come into possession of resources over which they have legitimate title. People have property, and they properly own it. All the framework requires is a system in which individuals legitimately acquire some property, have possession rights over the property, and are subject to taxation, of some kind, on that property. After being taxed, they have resources that they wish to give away for a charitable purpose. This, I suggest, is a universal phenomenon in any society. What now? How should the state treat the prospective philanthropic donor?

Before proceeding further, two comments about what motivates these assumptions. First, why the assumption about property? I want entirely to set aside for the purposes of this analysis a complaint sometimes made about philanthropy, namely that the money donated by an individual isn't properly or legitimately hers to give in the first place. Kant captures the concern aptly: individuals should not deceive themselves that they are practicing praiseworthy beneficence when their wealth is the product of distributional injustice.

> Having the resources to practice such beneficence as depends on the goods of fortune is, for the most part, a result of certain human beings being favored through the injustice of government, which introduces an inequality of wealth that makes others need their beneficence. Under such circumstances, does a rich man's help to the needy, on which he so readily prides himself as something meritorious, really deserve to be called beneficence at all?[5]

Kant's obvious answer is no. The appropriate understanding of philanthropy under these circumstances is that it should serve reparative aims, to redress the background wrongs of the unjust system that produced the unfair distribution of resources in the first place.[6]

A parallel worry I hope to dismiss with the assumption about property is what is sometimes called the problem of dirty money or blood money: wealth obtained through illicit means. Here the problem is not that circumstances of

back ground justice do not hold but that income itself has been generated illegally, via, for example, criminal activity, exploitation, or oppression. When a person whose possessions have been acquired illicitly announces an intention to make philanthropic donations of his wealth, we rightly complain that the money should not be considered his to give at all. If I steal your wallet and announce a plan to donate its contents rather than purchase something for myself, my philanthropic aim does not excuse the initial theft. For the purposes of my motivating framework, I assume lawful and just possession of resources.

Second, why the assumption about taxation? Different theories of justice lead to various views about taxation. I stipulate only that people have property, that they have been taxed on it in whatever manner is taken to be consistent with justice, and that they have money or property after taxation that they wish to give away. How the state should treat this preference is a question that will now arise for each variant of a liberal democratic theory of justice.

With the framework set up in this manner, here is the question I pose: what attitude should the liberal democratic state have toward the preference of an individual to make a philanthropic donation of her money or property? It is, I think, a fundamental question in that it will arise in any society, liberal democratic or otherwise, and a political theory should provide the resources to answer it.

A liberal democratic state is committed, in virtue of its liberal commitments, to a limited state and robust protection of individual rights and liberties. From the framework I describe, therefore, one plausible starting point in a liberal democratic state regarding philanthropy, it seems to me, is that individuals should possess the liberty to give their money or property away to whomever or whatever they please. The state bears the burden of showing why such restrictions are necessary or permissible. In parallel form, I suggest that incentives for people to exercise their liberty to give their money away also stand in need of justification; the state bears the burden of showing why such incentives are desirable and consistent with justice.

Justifications for Tax Incentives

This returns us to my original question: what is the justification for the current practice in the United States and elsewhere of providing tax incentives for citizens to make charitable contributions? Because the tax incentive constitutes a subsidy—the loss of federal tax revenue—it is no exaggeration to say that the United States and other countries currently subsidize the liberty of people to give money away, forgoing tax revenue for an activity that for millennia has gone unsubsidized by the state. What justification for this practice could there be?

The remainder of this chapter lays out and assesses three possible justifications for the existence of tax incentives for charitable giving.[7] I focus special attention on the incentive mechanism currently used in the United States and in many other countries: the charitable contributions deduction, a deduction of charitable gifts from a citizen's taxable income.[8] The first justification is that the deduction is necessary in order to account for the proper base of taxable income; the deduction, in other words, is no subsidy at all. The second justification is that the deduction efficiently stimulates the production of public goods and services that would otherwise be undersupplied by the state. The third justification links the incentive to the desirable effort to decentralize authority, to some degree, in the definition and production of public benefits and, in the process, to support a pluralistic civil society that is itself an important component of a flourishing democracy.

Tax Base Rationale

The first justification rejects entirely the claim that the deduction is a subsidy. The deduction constitutes, instead, the fair or appropriate way to treat the donor; deductibility is *intrinsic* to the tax system. First offered by William Andrews, the basic argument is that deducting philanthropic contributions is necessary in order to properly define an individual's taxable income. Charity cannot be equated with personal consumption since charitable gifts redirect resources from private and preclusive consumption to public and non-preclusive consumption. Tax scholar Boris Bittker offers a similar argument, concluding that charitable donations ought not count as consumption because in making a voluntary donation the donor is made worse off (with respect to others at the same income who do not make a donation), relinquishing use of resources that could have been directed to personal benefit.[9]

Unlike subsidy justifications, the tax base justification focuses on the fair treatment of the donor; it does not inquire into the goods produced with the donation or the efficiency with which these goods are produced. There are four obvious and strong criticisms to make of the tax base rationale.

First, and commonsensically, if a person has legitimate ownership of resources and can rightfully decide how to dispose of those resources, then whatever a person decides to do with those resources—spend it on luxury goods or give it to charity—is by definition, tautologically, a kind of consumption. Some people have a taste for spending, others for donating; each brings apparent satisfaction to the respective person.

Second, there are obvious benefits that some, perhaps many or even all, donors receive in making a philanthropic contribution. Philanthropy may be motivated by a prosocial or altruistic aim, yet it can simultaneously deliver benefits to the donor. Economists have attempted to model and measure the motivation of receiving a "warm glow" or psychological benefit in acting altruistically.[10] In making a charitable contribution, the donor experiences pleasure in giving and receives in return for the gift a "warm glow," consuming the benefit of her own altruism.

Other economists have demonstrated how much charitable giving, especially to elite institutions such as universities, hospitals, and cultural organizations, is motivated by status signaling.[11] Here the motivation to give is status seeking and self-interested, not altruistic, to maintain position or move up the social hierarchy. Status is zero sum, after all, and only so many names can appear on a donated building. Regardless of motive—altruistic or self-interested—there are returns to the donor that make it impossible to describe donors as engaging in behavior that is public and non-preclusive or that necessarily makes them worse off. We need not be incorrigible cynics to believe that donors are purchasing something for themselves when they make a charitable contribution.[12]

Third, Andrews's theory has perverse implications about the permissible recipients of charity according to current law in the United States and elsewhere. If for Andrews anything that is not personal consumption or accumulation should be deductible from the donor's tax base, then a billionaire's gift of a million dollars to Walmart, a for-profit company, to encourage its efforts in union busting, ought to be deductible. (Assume the billionaire holds no stock in Walmart.) Similarly, a donation to a foreign country or foreign charity where the donor has no connection and is motivated simply, say, to alleviate poverty ought to be deductible. But U.S. tax law—like the tax regimes of most of other countries—excludes donations of both kinds.

Finally, and moving from theoretical conceptualization to empirical fact, even the briefest reflection on philanthropy in the real world reveals how donors quite frequently purchase with their charitable dollars rival and excludable material or intangible goods for which they are among the primary consumers. Contributions to one's religious congregation are an obvious example; churches provide something more like club goods than public goods. Or to put it differently, they are more like *mutual benefit*

rather than *public benefit* organizations.[13] Donations to arts organizations or university sports teams for which one receives in return premium seats, special access, private tours, and so on are another example. Gifts to construct buildings, fund university chairs, or lay bricks in a public library, school, or park that bear the name of the donor are still another example. Charitable gifts to one's child's public school may also deliver improved educational opportunities or outcomes for one's child, not to mention boosting the value of one's house due to the fact that public school quality and real estate values are correlated.

On top of these criticisms can be added yet another that is more fundamental. I refer to the argument by Liam Murphy and Thomas Nagel that the choice of a tax base cannot be assessed in the absence of the larger normative consideration of what constitutes social and economic justice.[14] The tax system [is] just a mechanism for pursuing larger social aims. As a result, there is for Murphy and Nagel no such thing as the intrinsic fairness of the tax system or tax base but only taxation that is an instrument in realizing or pursuing the aims of a larger theory of social and economic justice.

Their argument is built on the claim that private property is a convention of the legal system. Property rights are not preinstitutional or prepolitical but rather a consequence of a set of laws that form a part of a broader theory of justice. Consequently, a person's pretax income does not count automatically as a person's own money, though what Murphy and Nagel call everyday libertarianism suggests as much to many people.

> Since there are no property rights independent of the tax system, taxes cannot violate those rights. There is no prima facie objection to overcome, and the tax structure, which forms part of the definition of property rights, along with laws governing contract, gift, inheritance, and so forth, must be

evaluated by reference to its effectiveness in promoting legitimate societal goals, including those of distributive justice.[15]

It is nonsense, then, to argue that charitable contributions ought to be deducted from one's taxable income because such deductions logically belong to the identification of the appropriate tax base.

I accept the Murphy and Nagel thesis but do not attempt here to defend it. Tax incentives for giving, if they are to be justified, find their justification in a larger account of justice for which the tax system is just an instrument.

Efficiency Rationale

The more typical defense of the charitable contributions deduction—and one that does, even if sometimes only implicitly, take into account a broader theory of social and economic justice—is that the state accomplishes something of important social value by providing subsidies for citizens to be charitable. The state provides incentives for charity because it is believed that the incentives stimulate the production of something of greater social value than what the state could have produced on its own, had it not offered the incentives.

The subsidy therefore counts as a tax expenditure, the fiscal equivalent of a direct spending program.[16] When the state allows citizens to deduct their charitable contributions from their taxable income, the state forgoes tax revenue, which is to say that all citizens are affected. They are affected in (at least) two important ways. First, they stand to lose some portion of the benefit they would receive from direct governmental expenditures. Second, citizens lose in democratic accountability, for the forgone funds are not accountable, or even traceable, in the way that direct government expenditures are. To give an obvious example, citizens can unelect their representatives if they are dissatisfied with the spending programs of the state; the Gates

Foundation also has a domestic and global spending program, partly supported through tax subsidies, but its leaders and trustees cannot be unelected.

Thus the success of the efficiency rationale depends on whether the benefits brought about by the subsidy exceed the costs of the lost tax revenue. Consistent with the Murphy and Nagel thesis, the subsidy is but a mechanism for realizing larger social aims. If these aims are realized, then the subsidy may be defensible.

What's obvious about the efficiency rationale is that it shifts attention from the fair treatment of the donor to the recipient of the donation and the good that is done with the gift. First, the deduction is available only to itemizing taxpayers, and thus the subsidy is capricious, for its availability depends on a characteristic, one's status as an itemizer, that has nothing whatsoever to do with the value of giving. If the subsidy is justified because it produces some social good, then why should two donors who make identical donations to identical organizations, ostensibly producing the identical social good, be treated differently by the tax code?

Second, in a system of progressive taxation the deduction is tied by definition to marginal tax brackets. The richer you are, the less a charitable contribution actually costs you. The deduction functions as an increasingly greater subsidy and incentive with every higher step in the income tax bracket. Those at the highest tax bracket receive the largest deduction, those in the lowest tax bracket the lowest.

But these concerns are criticisms of the mechanism, currently in use in the United States and in many other countries, to deliver the subsidy, the deduction of charitable donations from taxable income. Reform of the subsidy mechanism could eliminate or mitigate the problems. For example, the deduction could be extended to all taxpayers regardless of itemizer status; or the deduction could be eliminated in favor of a partial or total tax credit; or the incentive could come, as in the United Kingdom, in the form of so-called "gift aid," where the state matches some portion of an individual's charitable donation to an eligible organization without reducing the taxes owed by the individual donor.

How then might we assess the efficiency rationale as a whole? One obvious way to evaluate the rationale, rather than just the mechanism currently in use, is to look to the social good the subsidy produces and the efficiency with which it is produced.

Supposing that the goods produced by charitable recipients were of social value, we might ask, for instance, whether the subsidy is so-called treasury efficient. Does the subsidy shake out more in donations than it costs in federal tax revenue? If so, the subsidy is treasury efficient. Economists will then argue about the optimal rate of the subsidy, or how to stimulate the most giving at the least cost to the treasury.

Empirical analyses of the tax deduction in the United States show that the deduction is indeed treasury efficient, though significantly less so than initially was thought.[17] Some evidence shows, however, that the deduction has no effect on giving—is treasury inefficient—for particular kinds of donations, such as contributions to one's religious congregation (because, it is suggested, such gifts are experienced as religious obligations to be undertaken independent of whether the obligation qualifies as a tax event). Few donors, one might think (or at least hope), are engaging in tax optimization or avoidance strategies when the Sunday basket is passed around in church.[18]

When we inquire into the social good produced by charitable donations, rather than focusing squarely on questions of treasury efficiency, three problems present themselves, at least in the U.S. context.

First, U.S. law permits a truly kaleidoscopic landscape of public charities to receive tax-deductible charitable contributions.[19] Some and perhaps many of the social goods produced by charities will be of no value whatsoever to certain citizens. Because churches are eligible to give tax deductions to donors (i.e., congregants) for contributions, atheists are vicarious donors to churches through the tax subsidy. By contrast, Catholics are vicarious donors to Planned Parenthood and its support for abortion rights. The basic point is that the subsidy cannot be justified as a Pareto improvement, where some benefit and no one is made worse off.[20] At best, the subsidy is a Kaldor-Hicks improvement, where the gains for those who consume the particular social good produced by charity offset the losses to those with no interest in that social good.

But relying on a Kaldor-Hicks improvement as the standard for justifying the efficiency rationale raises a second set of problems. For obvious reasons, the beneficiaries of the deduction are highly skewed toward upper income earners. The result is a decidedly *plutocratic bias* in the subsidy, where the favored beneficiaries of the wealthy receive the lion's share of the subsidy.

The plutocratic bias is troubling, for systematic overattention in the policy tool itself to the interests and preferences of the wealthy against those of the middle-class and poor seems a strange, indeed unjustifiable, basis for social policy.

This trouble might be undercut if the product of charitable giving were pure public goods, in the economic sense, namely goods that are nonexcludable and nonrivalrous. If wealthy people donate to produce goods that no one can be prevented from enjoying and that no person's consumption reduces the amount available to others, then the plutocratic bias nevertheless redounds to the advantage of all citizens. But the vast majority of public charities do not produce pure public goods. Hospitals and universities, for instance, together account for more than half of the revenue of all nonprofits organizations in the United States. Both hospitals and universities can easily exclude persons who cannot pay for their services. The same is true for cultural and artistic organizations.

Despite the ability of hospitals, universities, and museums to exclude people who cannot pay for services, a funder of such organizations might point to evidence of positive spillover effects of hospitals in their communities and to the public benefits of basic research and an intellectual and artistic culture that are the products of research universities and museums.

Leaving aside the strict conditions of pure public goods, the concern about plutocratic bias might be mitigated if the favored beneficiaries of philanthropic donors, and of the wealthy especially, were charities engaged in social welfare or services for the poor. That is, plutocratic bias might be tolerable when charity provides for the basic needs of all citizens and thereby realizes an important aim of distributive justice. At the very least, then, the effect of charitable giving would be to some degree redistributive. Yet this is also not the case, at least in the United States. And this is the third problem with the efficiency rationale. Recall that more than half of all individual giving in the United States goes to religion, and none of this giving goes to the faith-based social-service charities associated with religious groups (e.g., the Salvation Army, Mercy Corps). Those offshoots of religious organizations have been counted in the relevant category of public/social benefit organizations, which receive less than 6 percent of all charitable giving.[21] If we focus squarely on the favored beneficiaries of the wealthy, we see that cultural organizations, hospitals, and universities are the usual recipients. Sometimes these gifts have redistributive benefits (e.g., scholarships for the poor); sometimes not. The best economic analyses of the redistributional nature of the charitable sector conclude that, at best, no strong conclusions about distributional impact can be made but that plenty of evidence shows "that relatively few nonprofit institutions serve the poor as a primary clientele."[22]

Moreover, the higher up the income ladder, *the less likely donors are to direct their giving to the poor.*

One final and important point. Suppose now that charitable donations were redistributive in the sense that gifts from the relatively wealthy flowed to the relatively poor. Granting this, we may nevertheless not yet conclude that nonprofit organizations and foundations are in fact redistributive all things considered because we must still account for the tax concessions to philanthropy and the counterfactual scenario in which the money flowing into nonprofit organizations and foundations would have been taxed and become public revenue. The relevant question is not merely, "Is philanthropy redistributive?" but rather, "Do philanthropic dollars flow more sharply downward than government spending does?" In order for the return, so to speak, on the public's investment in philanthropy to be worthwhile, philanthropy must do better than the state would do had it taxed the philanthropic assets.

Answering this counterfactual question is difficult. We are forced to speculate about how the state might spend the tax revenue it could have collected if it hadn't extended the tax concessions to philanthropists for their gifts.[23] We are also forced to speculate whether, if denied a tax incentive for giving, donors would or could successfully find alternative mechanisms to shelter their assets from taxation.

Anyone who seeks to ground the special tax treatment of philanthropy in the United States on the sector's redistributive outcomes must confront at least three reasons to be suspicious that any such redistribution actually occurs. There is the first and obvious difficulty that a motley assortment of nonprofit groups all qualify for 501(c)(3) status, puppet theaters and soup kitchens alike. There is the second difficulty that religious groups dominate as the beneficiaries of individual charitable dollars. And there is the third difficulty that the burden on the sector's advocate is to show not merely that philanthropy is redistributive but that it is *more redistributive* than would be government spending. In short, we have some good prima facie reasons to doubt that philanthropy is redistributive in effect or eleemosynary in aim.

These problems once again target the mechanism in the United States and elsewhere to deliver the subsidy: the tax deduction. The plutocratic bias in the subsidy and the lack of redistribution could be altered by both changing the mechanism of the subsidy (change to a capped tax credit, for instance) and limiting the kinds of organizations that are permitted to receive tax-deductible donations (eliminating churches and elite cultural organizations, for instance). Whatever the remedy, the expectation would be that the subsidy must still be *efficient*. To be justified, the subsidy must cost less to the treasury than it produces in social benefits.

I turn now to an alternative rationale that does not displace the idea of a subsidy but drops the necessity that it be an efficient use of tax dollars in producing certain public benefits.

Pluralism Rationale

The pluralism rationale comes in several stripes and cannot be called a unified theory. The basic idea is that a tax incentive to make charitable donations should not be justified on the basis of assessing the discrete social goods, or outputs, of the various nonprofit organizations funded through these donations. Instead, a tax incentive is justified for its role in stimulating or amplifying the voice of citizens in the production of a diverse, decentralized, and pluralistic associational sector, which is itself normatively desirable because it is considered to be a bedrock of a flourishing liberal democracy. If nonprofit organizations constitute, to a significant degree, the institutional matrix of associational life, then stimulating charitable donations to a wide array of nonprofits might amplify the voice of citizens and enhance civil society to the overall benefit of liberal democracy. The public good or social benefit being produced is civil society itself, not the catalogue of public goods or benefits

produced by the roster of organizations that constitute civil society.

Even if there is a net loss to the treasury in the production of the social goods generated by nonprofit organizations—if the state could more efficiently deliver these goods itself—the pluralism rationale holds that the subsidy is nevertheless worthwhile. The pluralism rationale does not demand efficiency for the success of the argument. The state might justifiably forgo tax revenue for the sake of fostering citizens' voices and the sustenance of pluralistic associational life.

Before developing the pluralism rationale in greater detail, consider a few worries. First, vigorous safeguarding of liberty is typically thought to be the institutional guarantee for associational life. Is it really necessary to subsidize the exercise of liberty to produce a vibrant civil society? After all, there was no charitable contributions tax deduction when Tocqueville toured the United States.

Second, the defender of the pluralism rationale has to answer to a disturbing feature of the historical record about associational life over the last century. It is no exaggeration to say that the rise of nonprofit organizations in the United States and the use of the charitable contributions deduction coincides with the *decline* of civic engagement and associational life, at least if the Robert Putnam literature is credible. The post–World War II rise of professionally run nonprofit organizations may have contributed to the calcification of civil society, diminished civic engagement, and a decline in social capital production.[24]

So what, then, is the case for the pluralism rationale in support of subsidizing philanthropy? There are two main and connected ideas: decentralizing the process of producing social goods and promoting the pluralism of associational life by diminishing state orthodoxy in defining its contours.

These ideas are given partial expression in a U.S. Supreme Court opinion from Justice Lewis

Powell, where he takes issue with the notion that the purpose of the nonprofit sector is efficiently to deliver or supplement services or social goods that the government would otherwise supply through direct expenditures.

> In my opinion, such a view of 501(c)(3) ignores the important role played by tax exemptions in encouraging diverse, indeed often sharply conflicting, activities and viewpoints. As Justice Brennan has observed, private, nonprofit groups receive tax exemptions because "each group contributes to the diversity of association, viewpoint, and enterprise essential to a vigorous, pluralistic society."

In a diverse society, there will be heterogeneous preferences about what kinds of social goods to supply through direct expenditures of tax dollars. Democratic mechanisms for deciding how to allocate these dollars are of course one fundamental means of dealing with heterogeneous preferences. But another potentially important means is to decentralize the authority for deciding what kinds of public benefits are produced and to permit, indeed to enhance, citizen voice in this process by providing a stimulus for that voice. Tax incentives for charitable giving represent, on this view, an effort to stimulate all citizens to cast their own preferences, in the form of dollars, about their favored social goods into civil society, where the resulting funding stream is partly private (from the donor) and partly public (from the tax subsidy).

The result is that citizen groups that cannot muster a majority consensus about a particular public benefit provision through the regular democratic political process will still have a tax-supported means to pursue their minority or eccentric goals. Philanthropy becomes a means of voting for one's favored civil society projects with dollars partially private and partially public.[25]

Note here that concerns about the redistributive nature of charitable dollars recede from view. When the justification for tax incentives for philanthropy runs along the pluralist line, philanthropy is not, at least in the first instance, about assisting the poor or disadvantaged; it is instead about protecting and promoting a flourishing and pluralistic civil society.[26] Moreover, the tax incentive, now equally available to every citizen, might provide a stimulus for individuals to take a greater interest in social problems, local organizations, and so on. It might help promote civic agency, association, and engagement.

As described earlier, a tax deduction for charitable contributions, when there is a progressive income tax, establishes a plutocratic element in the public policy. The deduction supplies a greater subsidy to the wealthy, who are, of course, already likely to possess a more powerful voice in associational life and the political arena without any subsidy whatsoever. We get not egalitarian citizen voice in civil society but plutocratic citizen voice, underwritten and promoted by tax policy.[27]

Here, then, in the pluralism rationale is where an egalitarian norm can and should inform the legal rules that structure philanthropy. Many possible mechanisms track the pluralism rationale, but for the sake of illustration, consider two possible designs. First is a flat and capped nonrefundable tax credit for charitable donations. By offering an equivalent tax credit to all donors (say 25 percent of any donation) with the total annual credit capped at some level (say $1,000), the mechanism avoids the upside-down structure of the deduction, offers an equal credit to all donors, and affords donors the liberty to continue to give money away after the cap has been reached, but no longer with any state subsidy to do so. The policy proposal bears a resemblance to a stakeholding grant or a campaign finance voucher scheme for each citizen, though rather than directing the use of the stakeholding grant for investment in one's own projects or a voucher for expressing political voice, the tax credit could be directed only toward eligible civil society organizations.[28] Call it a civil society stakeholding grant, assigned on an equal basis to every citizen in the form of a nonrefundable tax credit, Bill Gates receiving the same-sized credit as every other citizen. Second, consider the practice of so-called percentage philanthropy, which has arisen recently in several Central and Eastern European countries. In Hungary, for instance, a law passed in 1996 permits citizens to allocate 1 percent of their income taxes to a qualifying nongovernmental organization. This is not a tax credit, as in the previous example, because citizens here do not pay less tax. Citizens redirect what would otherwise be state revenue in the form of income taxes to the civil society organizations of their choice.

Conclusion

Though people have engaged in philanthropy for millennia, the practice of giving money away has only recently become a tax-subsidized activity. Philanthropy is now embedded within a framework of public policies, many centered on the tax regime, that structures its practice and alters its shape from what it would otherwise be without the state's intervention. I have canvassed three distinct justifications for providing tax incentives for philanthropy: a tax base rationale, an efficiency rationale, and a pluralism rationale. While I find nothing to recommend the tax base rationale, the efficiency and pluralism rationales do offer potentially good reasons to support subsidies for philanthropy. Neither of these latter two justifications, however, provides support for the actual design of most tax-subsidized giving, where a wide array of eligible recipient organizations and a tax deduction for giving are the favored mechanisms. A political theory of philanthropy might offer a defense, or several distinct defenses, of state incentives for giving money away, but the current practice of

state-supported philanthropy, especially in the United States, is indefensible.

Notes

1. For an overview of tax incentives for charitable giving across twenty-one countries, see Lester M. Salamon and Stefan Toepler, *The International Guide to Nonprofit Law* (New York: John Wiley, 1997).

2. Ruth W. Grant's *Strings Attached: Untangling the Ethics of Incentives* (Princeton, NJ: Princeton University Press, 2011) provides an excellent analysis of the ethical dimensions of the general use of incentives. She views them as an exercise of power that stands in need of political and moral justification. She neglects, however, a golden opportunity to employ her framework to analyze philanthropy, and this in two respects: first, in the use of tax incentives for charitable contributions and, second, in the strings that donors routinely attach to their contributions.

3. U.S. Constitution, article I, section 9, clause 7.

4. The history of the Smithsonian Institution is fascinating. James Smithson, a ne'er-do-well Scotsman who had never set foot in the country, bequeathed his considerable fortune in 1838 to the United States to establish, he prescribed in his will, the Smithsonian Institution to increase the diffusion of knowledge among men. Many in Congress were opposed to accepting the gift, worried about the corrupting influence of private, especially foreign, money in democratic politics. Senator James Calhoun argued that "it was beneath the dignity of the United States to receive presents of this kind from *anyone*."

5. Immanuel Kant, "The Metaphysics of Morals," in *Practical Philosophy: The Cambridge Edition of the Works of Immanuel Kant*, edited by Allen Wood, translated by Mary Gregor (Cambridge: Cambridge University Press, 1996), 573.

6. This is the argument of Chiara Cordelli, "Reparative Justice and the Moral Limits of Discretionary Philanthropy," in *Philanthropy in Democratic Societies*, edited by Rob Reich, Chiara Cordelli, and Lucy Bernholz (Chicago: University of Chicago Press).

7. In this chapter I draw from a modest literature on the charitable deduction, which is unwieldy and narrow, resting almost entirely within tax law and, to a lesser extent, economics journals. What's

remarkable about this literature is how little it engages with normative argument. Most theories about the deductions, comments David Pozen, "lack a coherent normative basis" (David Pozen, "Remapping the Charitable Deduction," *Connecticut Law Review* 39 [2006]: 547).

8. As explained earlier, the mechanism of an income tax deduction for a charitable donation works by creating a subsidy at the rate at which the donor is taxed. So a person who occupies the top tax bracket—currently 39 percent in the United States—would find that a $1,000 donation actually "cost" her only $610. The government effectively pays $390 of her donation, subtracting this amount from her tax burden. Similar incentives exist for the creation of private and family foundations and for contributions to community foundations, where donations and bequests to a foundation are deducted from estate and gift taxation. In permitting these tax incentives, federal and state treasuries forgo tax revenue. Had there been no tax deduction on the $1,000 contribution, the state would have collected another $390 in tax revenue.

9. Boris I. Bittker, "Charitable Contributions: Tax Deductions or Matching Grants?" *Tax Law Review* 28 (1972): 37.

10. James Andreoni, "Impure Altruism and Donations to Public Goods: A Theory of Warm-Glow Giving," *Economic Journal* 100 (1990): 464–477.

11. Amihai Glazer and Kai A. Konrad, "A Signaling Explanation for Charity," *American Economic Review* 86 (1996): 1019–1028; William T. Harbaugh, "The Prestige Motive for Making Charitable Transfers," *American Economic Review* 88 (1998): 277–282; William T. Harbaugh, "What Do Donations Buy? A Model of Philanthropy Based on Prestige and Warm Glow," *Journal of Public Economics* 67 (1998): 269–284.

12. Recent studies in neuroscience claim to show that helping others boosts happiness in the giver. Philanthropy is allegedly a win-win: good for the recipient, good for the donor.

13. Some people mistakenly believe that gifts to religious organizations do in fact provide public goods because many congregations are thought to provide extensive social services. The best available evidence about the use of donations to churches does not bear this out. Sociologist Robert Wuthnow, who writes admiringly of faith-based social service providers, observes that "the amount spent on local service activities is a relatively small proportion of total giving, probably on the order of 5 percent" (Robert Wuthnow, *Saving America? Faith-Based Services and the Future of Civil Society* [Princeton, NJ: Princeton University Press, 2004], 49).

14. Liam Murphy and Thomas Nagel, *The Myth of Ownership: Taxes and Justice* (Oxford: Oxford University Press, 2002).

15. Ibid., 58–59.

16. On the concept of a tax expenditure, see Stanley S. Surrey and Paul R. McDaniel, *Tax Expenditures* (Cambridge, MA: Harvard University Press, 1985). On the ubiquity and scope of their use in official state policy, see Suzanne Mettler, *The Submerged State: How Invisible Government Policies Undermine American Democracy* (Chicago: University of Chicago Press, 2011), and Christopher Howard, *The Hidden Welfare State: Tax Expenditures and Social Policy in the United States* (Princeton, NJ: Princeton University Press, 1997). Howard examines nearly all the major tax expenditures, the home mortgage interest deduction, employer pensions, the earned income tax credit, and targeted jobs tax credits, and his book is framed as an examination of the hidden welfare state, but he curiously provides no discussion of the charitable contributions deduction, one of the costliest of all tax expenditures.

17. Newer studies that take long-term effects into account generally find lower price elasticities than earlier studies, ranging from –0.47 to –1.26 rather than –1.09 to –2.54. The decision to make a charitable donation is not made solely with reference to the availability of a deduction in any given year; people are likely to look to the year ahead and the year behind in deciding how much to give. Because previous studies have focused on short-term effects of changes in tax incentives, they have often exaggerated the impact of incentives. When tax benefits for charitable contributions decreased one year, short-term studies documented a significant decrease in giving for that year. But these studies missed the longer term reactions of donors, who would eventually increase their giving again once they became accustomed to the changes in tax incentives. The overall picture is that incentives are significantly less important than was initially thought. In explaining why people make

charitable contributions, Evelyn Brody concludes, "Apparently tax considerations are not paramount. After all, philanthropy long preceded the enactment of the federal income tax, and no income-tax subsidy is available to the 70% of individual taxpayers who claim the standard deduction" (Evelyn Brody, "Charities in Tax Reform: Threats to Subsidies Overt and Covert," *Tennessee Law Review* 66 [1998]: 714).

18. Fack and Landais argue that wealthy donors across many countries frequently use philanthropy as a tax cheating strategy. Their results show, for example, that in the United States "a very significant fraction (around 30%) of contributions reported by the very wealthy before 1969 were driven by tax avoidance or tax cheating purposes." See Gabrielle Fack and Camille Landais, "Philanthropy, Tax Policy, and Tax Cheating: A Long-Run Perspective on US Data," in *Charitable Giving and Tax Policy: A Historical and Comparative Perspective*, edited by Gabrielle Fack and Camille Landais (Oxford: Oxford University Press, 2016), 61–114.

19. U.S. law permits tax-deductible donations to organizations "operated exclusively for religious, charitable, scientific, testing for public safety, literary, or educational purposes, to foster national or international amateur sports competition, or for the prevention of cruelty to children or animals" (Internal Revenue Code sec. 501(c)(3)). In 2012, not including churches or religious groups, these numbered in excess of 1.3 million organizations. Counting churches and religious groups, which do not need to register as nonprofit organizations with the state but receive all the tax benefits that attach to the legal status of a public charity, the number of tax-exempt organizations balloons quickly to nearly 2 million. The IRS also approves more than 50,000 new 501(c)(3) nonprofits every year, with an approval rate of applicants (those for which a decision is rendered) at over 99 percent. See Reich, Dorn, Sutton, *Anything Goes: Approval of Nonprofit Status by the IRS*. Stanford, CA: Stanford University Center on Philanthropy and Civil Society.

20. This is Mark Gergen's argument in "The Case for a Charitable Contributions Deduction," *Virginia Law Review* 74 (1988): 1393–1450.

21. Giving USA publishes an annual data book on charitable giving, from which I have drawn these figures. Recall here that donations to religion (i.e.,

to one's own congregation) do not fund more than trivial amounts of service provision; these donations predominantly fund operating expenses of the congregation (e.g., utilities, salaries, facilities, etc.).

22. Charles T. Clotfelter, ed., *Who Benefits from the Nonprofit Sector?* (Chicago: University of Chicago Press, 1992), 22.

23. Western European governments have been historically more redistributive than the United States. The counterfactual question presented here has correspondingly greater bite the more redistributive a government is with its taxpayers' money.

24. See Robert D. Putnam, *Bowling Alone: The Collapse and Revival of American Community* (New York: Simon & Schuster, 2000), and Skocpol, *Diminished Democracy* (Norman, OK: University of Oklahoma Press, 2003), on the rise of bureaucratic civil society.

25. Saul Levmore nicely articulates this view, adding that the mechanism might also encourage volunteering for and oversight of nonprofits by "develop[ing] a sense of commitment to chosen charities." See Levmore, "Taxes as Ballots," *University of Chicago Law Review* 65 (1998): 406. For a similar proposal in the domain of campaign finance, see Bruce Ackerman and Ian Ayres, *Voting with Dollars* (New Haven, CT: Yale University Press, 2002).

26. Liam Murphy and Thomas Nagel write,

The word charity suggests that [the charitable contribution] deduction is a means of decentralizing the process by which a community discharges its collective responsibility to alleviate the worst aspects of life at the bottom of the socioeconomic ladder. Since there is disagreement about what the exact nature of that responsibility is, and about which are the most efficient agencies, it is arguably a good idea for the state to subsidize individuals' contributions to agencies of their choice rather than itself making all the decisions about the use of public funds for this purpose.

27. For a similar argument, see Emma Saunders-Hastings, "Plutocratic Philanthropy," *Journal of Politics* 80, no. 1 (2018): 149–161.

28. See Bruce Ackerman and Anne Alstott, *The Stakeholder Society* (New Haven, CT: Yale University

Press, 2000) and Ackerman and Ayres, *Voting with Dollars*. For a similar proposal in the charitable sector, see Ryan Pevnick, "Democratizing the Nonprofit Sector," *Journal of Political Philosophy* 21 (2013): 260–282.

Bibliography

Ackerman, Bruce, and Anne Alstott. *The Stakeholder Society*. New Haven, CT: Yale University Press, 2000.

Ackerman, Bruce, and Ian Ayres. *Voting with Dollars*. New Haven, CT: Yale University Press, 2002.

Andreoni, James. "Impure Altruism and Donations to Public Goods: A Theory of Warm-Glow Giving." *Economic Journal* 100 (1990): 464–477.

Bittker, Boris I. "Charitable Contributions: Tax Deductions or Matching Grants?" *Tax Law Review* 28 (1972): 37–63.

Brody, Evelyn. "Charities in Tax Reform: Threats to Subsidies Overt and Covert." *Tennessee Law Review* 66 (1998): 687–763.

Clotfelter, Charles T. "Tax-Induced Distortions in the Voluntary Sector." *Case Western Reserve Law Review* 39 (1988): 663–694.

———, ed. *Who Benefits from the Nonprofit Sector?* Chicago: University of Chicago Press, 1992.

Cordelli, Chiara. "Justice as Fairness and Relational Resources." *Journal of Political Philosophy* 23 (2015): 86–110.

Fack, Gabrielle, and Camille Landais. "Philanthropy, Tax Policy, and Tax Cheating: A Long-Run Perspective on US Data." In *Charitable Giving and Tax Policy: A Historical and Comparative Perspective*, edited by Gabrielle Fack and Camille Landais, 61–114. Oxford: Oxford University Press, 2016.

Gergen, Mark P. "The Case for a Charitable Contributions Deduction." *Virginia Law Review* 74 (1988): 1393–1450.

Glazer, Amihai, and Kai A. Konrad. "A Signaling Explanation for Charity." *American Economic Review* 86 (1996): 1019–1028.

Grant, Ruth W. *Strings Attached: Untangling the Ethics of Incentives*. Princeton, NJ: Princeton University Press, 2011.

Harbaugh, William T. "The Prestige Motive for Making Charitable Transfers." *American Economic Review* 88 (1998): 277–282.

———. "What Do Donations Buy? A Model of Philanthropy Based on Prestige and Warm Glow." *Journal of Public Economics* 67 (1998): 269–284.

Howard, Christopher. *The Hidden Welfare State: Tax Expenditures and Social Policy in the United States*. Princeton, NJ: Princeton University Press, 1999.

Kant, Immanuel. "The Metaphysics of Morals." In *Practical Philosophy: The Cambridge Edition of the Works of Immanuel Kant*, edited by Allen Wood, translated by Mary Gregor, 353–604. Cambridge: Cambridge University Press, 1996.

Levmore, Saul. "Taxes as Ballots." *University of Chicago Law Review* 65 (1998): 387–431.

Mettler, Suzanne. *The Submerged State: How Invisible Government Policies Undermine American Democracy*. Chicago: University of Chicago Press, 2011.

Murphy, Liam, and Thomas Nagel. *The Myth of Ownership: Taxes and Justice*. Oxford: Oxford University Press, 2002.

Pevnick, Ryan. "Democratizing the Nonprofit Sector." *Journal of Political Philosophy* 21 (2013): 260–282.

Pozen, David. "Remapping the Charitable Deduction." *Connecticut Law Review* 39 (2006): 531–601.

Putnam, Robert D. *Bowling Alone: The Collapse and Revival of American Community*. New York: Simon & Schuster, 2000.

Reich, Rob, Chiara Cordelli, and Lucy Bernholz, eds. *Philanthropy in Democratic Societies: History, Institutions, Values*. Chicago: University of Chicago Press, 2016.

Salamon, Lester M., and Stefan Toepler. *The International Guide to Nonprofit Law*. New York: John Wiley, 1997.

Saunders-Hastings, Emma. "Plutocratic Philanthropy." *Journal of Politics* 80, no. 1 (2018): 149–161.

Surrey, Stanley S., and Paul R. McDaniel. *Tax Expenditures*. Cambridge, MA: Harvard University Press, 1985.

Wuthnow, Robert. *Saving America? Faith-Based Services and the Future of Civil Society*. Princeton, NJ: Princeton University Press, 2004.

CHAPTER 13

Why Are Nonprofits Exempt From the Corporate Income Tax?

Michael Rushton

Rushton, Michael, "Why are Nonprofits Exempt from the Corporate Income Tax?" *Nonprofit and Voluntary Sector Quarterly 36* (2007): 662–675.

The basic structure of how nonprofits are treated under the corporate income tax (CIT) in the United States can be summarized as follows. Under the Internal Revenue Code Section 501(c)(3), an organization is exempt from the CIT if it is designed for a charitable purpose, which includes

religious, charitable, scientific, testing for public safety, literary, or educational purposes, or to foster national or international amateur sports competition (but only if no part of its activities involve the provision of athletic facilities or equipment), or for the prevention of cruelty to children or animals.

The organization must not distribute net earnings to any private shareholder or individual (the "nondistribution constraint," which Hansmann [1980] took as the defining feature of nonprofits) and is restricted in its ability to carry out political lobbying. For such organizations, the unrelated business income tax (UBIT), which is very similar to the CIT, applies to any net earnings from business regularly carried out by the organization but which is unrelated to the purpose under which the organization claimed tax exemption under Section 501(c)(3). Finally, exemption from the CIT under 501(c)(3) may be denied if the organization engages in too much unrelated business.

In this article, I want to ask whether the overarching structure of the corporate tax treatment of nonprofits is efficient.

Two terms that frequently arise in debates over tax reform are *efficiency* and *fairness*. It is worthwhile stating at the outset how these terms will be treated.

Efficiency means that the productive resources of the economy—labor, land, and investments in productive capital—are allocated across sectors of the economy, both in terms of what goods and services are produced and in what amounts and in terms of organizational form, between for-profit corporations, other types of for-profit business, and nonprofits, such that there is no possible reallocation of resources that could increase the total value of production. An efficient tax system is one that collects revenue while keeping the total value of production as high as possible.

DOI: 10.4324/9780367696559-17

Fairness, in terms of the tax system, means first that individuals who are in similar economic circumstances should pay similar amounts of tax, that is, there should not be arbitrary differences in tax burden across like individuals (horizontal equity), and, second, that those individuals with a higher ability to pay tax should pay more tax (vertical equity). Clearly, fairness will be more contested than efficiency. The value of output can be measured, and so inefficiencies in the tax system can be estimated, but fairness depends on subjective accounts of what it means to be in "similar economic circumstances," on what constitutes the best measure of "ability to pay," and on the rate at which taxes should rise with ability to pay (i.e., the optimal degree of progressiveness in the tax system).

With those definitions in mind, I suggest that the analysis of the treatment of nonprofits in the corporate tax system should focus on efficiency and, in practical terms, whether there are low administration and compliance costs. Nonprofits were exempt from the CIT from its introduction in 1913, and the only significant change since was the introduction of the UBIT in 1950, so it can hardly be the case that for-profit investors are earning low returns as a result of recent changes favoring nonprofits.

Because we have a political system that rewards lobbying by organized groups of producers for protection against competition, we have such lobbying. Although the statements by industry lobbyists will use the word *unfair* (almost as often as they use the phrase *in the public interest*), in reality the sole concern is for those who have investments in an industry to find new restrictions on their competition so that their own profits can rise, whether it is for-profit firms claiming that the tax treatment of nonprofits is unfair, firms claiming that competition by government is unfair, firms lobbying for regulatory rules that would restrict the entry of new firms (Stigler, 1971), firms lobbying for tariffs and quotas on foreign competition which

somehow has an unfair advantage (Bhagwati, 1989), and all the way back to manufacturers of candles seeking regulations to protect them from the unfair competition by the sun (Bastiat, 1845).

Impartial analysis of tax policy is sidetracked only when it ventures into discussions of the so-called unfairness of the nonprofit tax exemption. The true concern is efficiency: Is the tax treatment of nonprofits structured such that our economy uses its productive resources to produce the highest value of goods and services? In particular, does the tax system encourage goods and services to be produced by for-profit or nonprofit firms according to which organizational form provides a better mix of high quality and low costs? Many of the papers on the tax treatment of nonprofits raise the question of unfairness and, in their defense, it must be noted that even the Treasury Regulations regarding the UBIT state that

> the primary objective of adoption of the [UBIT] was to eliminate a source of unfair competition by placing the unrelated business activities of certain exempt organizations upon the same tax basis as the nonexempt business endeavors with which they compete.
> (Section 1.513-1(b))

But this article will not pursue that particular definition of unfairness.

Prior Theories of the Nonprofit CIT Exemption

Three classes of arguments have been put forth on why nonprofits are exempt from the CIT: that net income cannot be coherently defined for nonprofits, that nonprofits are deliberately being subsidized by government through the exemption, and that nonprofits have an historic legacy of being excluded from the tax base (for a survey of theories of the nonprofit CIT exemption, see, in addition to the references that follow in this section, Fishman & Schwarz, 2003).

The first argument is that public service (as opposed to mutual benefit) nonprofit organizations "do not realize 'income' in the ordinary sense of the word" (Bittker & Rahdert, 1976, p. 305). Bittker and Rahdert (1976) state that net income is well defined for for-profit organizations because they are in the business of maximizing it. For nonprofits, they claim, we cannot coherently define the tax base because there is no pursuit of profit. But it is not easy to see why the definition of net income is so difficult for nonprofits. The definition of profit as applied to for-profits for tax purposes does not hinge on their being effective at profit maximization. As for nonprofits, "one has the sneaking suspicion that Harvard could come up with a taxable income number if pressed to do so" (Colombo & Hall, 1995, p. 24).

There are multiple arguments for explaining the CIT exemption as a deliberate subsidy. One is that the CIT exemption represents a subsidy to the sector (in addition to the deductibility from the personal income tax of donations made to nonprofits and various other tax exemptions) to encourage its provision of services that are generally in the public interest. A possible way to define public interest is to use the evidence provided by the fact that individuals are willing to donate to the organization above and beyond payments for goods and services received. Hall and Colombo (1991) would restrict the tax exemption only to those organizations receiving a significant proportion of their income from donations (hence their proposal is known as a "donative" theory of the tax exemption; also see Colombo, 2002). In this model, commercial nonprofits would not receive a tax exemption. Atkinson (1990, 1997) sees room for a broader scope of the tax exemption, noting that even for commercial nonprofits, the founders who invested the initial capital have made a decision to forgo personal profit from that capital, and this represents a form of donation.

Does the subsidy argument for the nonprofit tax exemption need to be tied to the charitable nature of the organization? Not necessarily. Hansmann (1981) suggests that a good reason to subsidize the entire nonprofit sector is that the nondistribution constraint hampers the ability of nonprofits to raise equity capital, and so a CIT exemption is needed so that nonprofits can use all retained earnings for capital expansion if necessary. Crimm (1998) notes that because nonprofits are restricted in terms of which sectors are deemed eligible for the tax exemption, they cannot diversify risks in the way that shareholders of for-profits can, and so an exemption from the CIT is a justifiable subsidy.

Of course there are many sectors where nonprofits and for-profits share the market, which leads to questions of whether for-profits in such sectors should also receive a subsidy or conversely whether the tax exemption for a specific nonprofit organization should be contingent on its providing a service distinctly different from its for-profit competitors. But as it stands, there is generally a difference in tax treatment between for-profit and nonprofits, and this has allocation effects. Hansmann (1987) provides evidence, from U.S. states and those sectors where nonprofits and for-profits tend to compete, that the higher the state CIT rate, and thus the greater the difference in tax treatment between for-profit and nonprofit firms, the higher the proportion of businesses that are nonprofit. He suggests there might be a justification for the exemption if (a) there is a public policy reason to favor nonprofit providers (e.g., perhaps they better serve the poor) or (b) it corrects for another market failure, such as the difficulties nonprofits face in raising capital (Hansmann [1987] presents evidence on this front, showing that when demand for a service rapidly increases, it is generally for-profits that move to increase supply faster). Steinberg (1991) supports the general tax exemption, even where there are no clear external benefits, on the grounds that nonprofits often generate important innovations in the delivery of services and constitute an alternative and, in turn, useful competition to government. Beyond that, as Atkinson (1990, 1997) notes, a subsidy for nonprofits can be a way for the government to make a statement of sorts about the values it places on altruism and volunteerism by the public.

The third argument is that the tax exemption is in recognition of the historic exclusion from the tax base of the nonprofit sector, an acknowledgement by the state of the value of an independent sector with minimal duties to report to the state (and in turn with obligations to refrain from its involvement with political affairs, hence the restrictions on lobbying activity for 501(c)(3) organizations). This view is argued by Brody (1998, 1999). Recognition of the sovereignty of the nonprofit sector view explains why there are tax subsidies to nonprofits instead of direct grants (a way of avoiding state-nonprofit entanglement) and the existence of the UBIT (to limit the sphere of the nonprofits).

The Corporate Tax Exemption: A New Theory

All of the theories recounted above, for all their differences with one another, have something in common: They all seek to explain the nonprofit CIT exemption by asking, "What is it that makes nonprofits special?" They provide a variety of answers—nonprofits do not have a clearly definable measure for net income, they cannot easily raise equity capital or diversify risks, they provide goods and services in the public interest, they are the place where we can mobilize our altruistic and volunteer impulses, they have a long tradition of independence from the state—but they all begin with the same question. I would like to begin with a different question.

Return to the question of why for-profit corporations are taxed at the corporate level. It

is because the goal is to ensure that the income individuals earn on their investments does not escape taxation by flowing through a corporation. The goal of the CIT is not so much to tax corporations as it is to tax income. This is why a perfectly integrated personal tax capturing, and not distinguishing between, income earned through businesses and through labor earnings remains the desiderata of economists.

Nonprofits are exempt from the CIT because net income earned by nonprofits is not attributable to, and does not have the ultimate destination of, a private individual. This is not to say that individuals do not benefit from the existence of nonprofits; employees benefit from having a place to work, and clients benefit from the goods and services provided by nonprofits (even when they are paying a market price for a good provided by a nonprofit, most individuals will be placing a value on the good higher than the price paid—i.e., they will be receiving some consumer surplus). But the wages of nonprofit employees are taxed through the personal income tax, and we do not attempt in any circumstance to tax the consumer surplus received by individuals, which in any case is unobservable. What net income is left after paying for inputs (including wages) and delivering outputs must ultimately be reinvested by the organization. That is the essence of the nondistribution constraint. For-profit corporate income is taxed precisely because it can be distributed, and the CIT is a way, albeit imperfect, of ensuring it does not escape taxation at the personal level.

The tax exemption appears to be a "subsidy" only as the result of an inefficiently designed CIT that creates an effective tax rate even on marginal investments, when ideally they should face zero tax. If there were an effective means of attributing and taxing at the individual shareholder level all net profits earned through corporations, there would be no need for the CIT, and the apparent subsidy to nonprofits from the CIT exemption would disappear.

This would not be the result of changing views of the need to subsidize nonprofits, or of their sovereignty from government, or of the impossibility of defining their net income, but simply of repairing an inefficiently designed corporate tax.

In other words, there has been misplaced emphasis on the CIT exemption for nonprofits, where it has been treated as a departure from the norm of taxation. Instead, it is the tax levied on for-profit corporations that requires explanation, and which is explained as a practical measure not so much to tax businesses as it is to ensure that all income accruing to individuals is taxed. Notice that this new explanation for the tax exemption can also explain why the tax exemption is not treated as a "tax expenditure" in the federal budget, that it represents income outside the normal tax base (this question is raised by Brody & Cordes, 1999, p. 152).

But if we accept this rationale for the non-profit tax exemption—that there is no need to subject nonprofit net income to tax because it does not and will not end up in the hands of a private shareholder—then how do we explain the UBIT, which does tax part of the net earnings of nonprofits? Hansmann (1989) justifies the UBIT using the subsidy argument for the general tax exemption:

> The rationale for taxing unrelated business is basically the same as the rationale for granting the basic exemption, not to all nonprofit corporations, but only to those nonprofits that pursue activities deemed worthy of subsidy; there is no point in subsidizing nonprofit firms to provide services that can be performed just as efficiently by for-profit firms.
>
> (p. 625)

But because this article asserts that subsidy is not the rationale for the general tax exemption, where does that leave the UBIT?

The UBIT

Recent scholarship on the UBIT has looked both into how nonprofit organizations reduce tax liability by reporting as many costs as possible from all the organization's activities as being associated with the commercial "unrelated" business (Sansing, 1998; Yetman, 2003) and into whether a nonprofit's willingness to engage in commercial activities is related to its ability to shift costs (Cordes & Weisbrod, 1998). Evidence suggests that cost shifting is prevalent, and so the government revenues from the UBIT are strikingly low, although, as Hansmann (1987) points out, repeal of the UBIT might still be costly, as it would not only forfeit the (small) revenues collected from UBIT but would also likely greatly reduce CIT revenues, as for-profit firms would have increased incentives to convert to nonprofit status.

But the question remains as to whether an effective UBIT is efficient in the first place. If it makes sense, as argued above, to make nonprofits' net earnings from mission-related activities tax exempt, why not exempt all their earnings? Analysis of the UBIT cannot be separated from the nonprofit exemption from the CIT.

How does the nonprofit exemption from the CIT in their mission-related activities affect investment in the for-profit corporate sector? Begin with Rose-Ackerman's (1982) critique of the notion that the exemption harms for-profit business. She points out that if it is easy for investment capital to shift from one sector to another, then even if the nonprofit tax exemption causes a lower rate of return to investment in the related for-profit part of the sector, capital will simply move to where it can earn a higher return, so no investor will be at a loss. Investment in firms that compete with nonprofits only occurred at all because the returns that could be earned from such investment were at least as high as could be earned elsewhere.

However, suppose it was not so easy to shift investment capital and that the competition from nonprofits was not anticipated by investors. Rose-Ackerman (1982) goes on to say that the entry of nonprofits into the sector will only lower returns to for-profit investors if the nonprofits enter the sector to a larger degree than it was expected that other for-profits would. For example, suppose an investor in a for-profit long-term care facility expects that she or he will face competition from 12 other for-profit facilities and no nonprofits. If it turns out to be the case that the competition is from just 6 other for-profits and 6 nonprofits, there should be no effect on the return to investment. Only if there were "excessive" entry by nonprofits would the return to the for-profit investor fall. But why would nonprofits ever enter a sector, such as long-term care, in numbers that exceed what for-profits would have done? This would occur if "nonprofits have excess cash to invest and the return they can obtain by lending their money on the bond market is lower than the rate of return on active, entrepreneurial investments" (Rose-Ackerman, 1982, pp. 1027–1028). But she points out that for-profits can only be harmed by nonprofit entry if (a) nonprofits are so concentrated in certain sectors that their presence is able to lower the return to for-profit investment, (b) there are for-profits earning just-competitive returns to investment and no more, and (c) nonprofits have the excess cash available to make these investments.

But nonprofits do not represent a large proportion of the total investment capital in the country, and if it were spread evenly across all sectors, it would have no discernable impact on the returns to for-profit firms. Furthermore, those for-profit firms earning better than competitive returns will remain in business in any case. And finally, nonprofits might not have such cash available for investments. If nonprofits are managed less efficiently (in terms of profit maximization), they may have to pay higher interest rates to lenders worried about the nonprofit enterprise failing.

Rose-Ackerman's (1982) conclusion is that the UBIT is exactly the wrong policy to deal with the potential losses to for-profit investors from nonprofit competition: The UBIT, by design, concentrates nonprofit investments in a limited number of sectors, and it is only through this concentration that returns to for-profit investors are lowered.

Hansmann (1989), on the other hand, supports the UBIT and argues for a narrow reading of the tax exemption from the CIT. How does he come to the opposite conclusion from Rose-Ackerman? On one point they agree: If the UBIT were removed, so that nonprofits could invest in any sector and remain tax exempt, it is unlikely that they would cause a decrease in returns to for-profit firms. After all, presumably, nonprofits are only engaged in "unrelated" activities to earn profits to fund mission-related work, and it would not be profit maximizing to so heavily invest in a sector that prices would be pushed downward. Instead, Hansmann writes, "In the absence of UBIT, one would expect nonprofit firms to displace for-profit firms, not by driving them out of business through price competition but rather by purchasing them" (pp. 611–612). There would be significant incentives to purchase such firms, especially those subject to high rates of CIT.

The principal focus of Hansmann is how repeal of the UBIT would have unintended inefficiencies. First, nonprofits would find that because CIT would remain on for-profit firms in which the nonprofit might have invested in stock, but there would be no CIT on for-profit firms wholly owned by the nonprofit, there would be a tax incentive for nonprofits to shift to the riskier investment strategy of wholly owned businesses rather than a portfolio of common stock. After all, as Steinberg (1991) writes, as it stands, nonprofits have sound reasons to favor passive income in diversified investments, and there are not good reasons to change that situation.

Second, Hansmann worries that without the UBIT the return to investment in nonprofits is above that for the economy as a whole, and so nonprofits will tend to oversave and underspend on current mission-related activities. Given that it might well be the case that the endowments of large nonprofits are already too big (see Hansmann, 1990, on universities; Gentry, 2002, on hospitals; and Fisman & Hubbard, 2003, on the governance problems that arise from big endowments), the UBIT might put a brake on excessive savings.

Third, in sectors where nonprofits compete with for-profits, the advantage to nonprofits from the tax exemption would allow leeway for poor management practices. The UBIT ensures that nonprofits only enter a sector, other than those defined as having a public purpose, where they can perform at least as well as for-profits. This result is also established by Sansing (1998). In addition, it might well be the case that nonprofits only enter a commercial sector when its rate of return exceeds the return to passive investments by a nontrivial amount because donors might not be pleased by investments in running commercial activities and so would reduce their giving by some amount (Cordes & Weisbrod, 1998).

Following on this last point, we can begin to see a rationale for the UBIT even in the face of the earlier argument that nonprofits are generally tax exempt, not because they are deserving of subsidy or represent a sovereign sector in the economy that warrants a greater degree of noninterference by the state, but because their net earnings are not ultimately personal income for shareholders. The goal is to ensure that nonprofit investments in unrelated business activities are not treated differently than proprietary firms so as to avoid a distortion in the choice of organizational form. Without the UBIT, nonprofits would enter unrelated activities where they were less efficient than for-profit firms, again not so much because the nonprofit is "subsidized" as it is that the for-profit sector is "penalized" by the inefficient design of the CIT. Were the CIT to be redesigned such that the EMTR were zero, the UBIT would become unnecessary, as even without the UBIT a nonprofit would only open an unrelated business where through some advantage (say economies of scope) it could produce the service at lower cost than its for-profit competitors.

Conclusion

This article advanced the following two hypotheses. First, the exemption of nonprofits from the CIT is best explained by the fact that nonprofit income is not ultimately owned by any individuals, whereas the CIT is an (inefficiently designed) attempt to ensure that individual income does not escape taxation by being earned behind the corporate veil. This is a different argument than the traditionally advanced arguments that the tax exemption is either (a) a result of the lack of a coherent definition of nonprofit net income, (b) a deliberate subsidy to the nonprofit sector, or (c) a consequence of the state's historic exclusion from the tax base of the nonprofit sector. Second, the UBIT is made necessary by the effective marginal tax rate (EMTR) on for-profit corporations arising from the CIT's inefficient design and ensures that nonprofits are not given an artificial cost advantage in unrelated businesses.

References

Atkinson, R. (1990). Altruism in nonprofit organizations. *Boston College Law Review, 31*(3), 501–639.

Atkinson, R. (1997). Theories of the federal income tax exemption for charities: Thesis, antithesis, and synthesis. *Stetson Law Review, 27,* 395–431.

Bastiat, F. (1845). A petition from the manufacturers of candles, tapers, lanterns, sticks, street lamps, snuffers, and extinguishers, and from producers of tallow, oil, resin, alcohol, and generally of everything connected with lighting. In *Sophismes Économiques.*

Bhagwati, J. (1989). *Protectionism.* Cambridge, MA: MIT Press.

Bittker, B. I., & Rahdert, G. K. (1976). The exemption of nonprofit organizations from federal income taxation. *Yale Law Journal, 85*(3), 299–358.

Brody, E. (1998). Of sovereignty and subsidy: Conceptualizing the charity tax exemption. *Journal of Corporation Law, 23,* 585–629.

Brody, E. (1999). Charities in tax reform: Threats to subsidies overt and covert. *Tennessee Law Review, 66,* 687–763.

Brody, E., & Cordes, J. J. (1999). Tax treatment of nonprofit organizations: A two-edged sword? In E. T. Boris & C. E. Steuerle (Eds.), *Nonprofits and government: Collaboration and conflict* (pp. 141–175). Washington, DC: Urban Institute.

Colombo, J. D. (2002). Commercial activity and the charitable tax-exemption. *William and Mary Law Review, 44,* 487–567.

Colombo, J. D., & Hall, M. A. (1995). *The charitable tax exemption.* Boulder, CO: Westview.

Cordes, J. J., & Weisbrod, B. A. (1998). Differential taxation of nonprofits and the commercialization of nonprofit revenues. In B. A. Weisbrod (Ed.), *To profit or not to profit: The commercial transformation of the nonprofit sector* (pp. 83–104). New York: Cambridge University Press.

Crimm, N. J. (1998). An explanation of the federal income tax exemption for charitable organizations: A theory of risk compensation. *Florida Law Review, 50,* 419–462.

Fishman, J. J., & Schwarz, S. (2003). *Taxation of nonprofit organizations: Cases and materials.* New York: Foundation Press.

Fisman, R., & Hubbard, R. G. (2003). The role of nonprofit endowments. In E. L. Glaeser (Ed.), *The governance of not-for-profit organizations* (pp. 217–233). Chicago: University of Chicago Press.

Gentry, W. M. (2002). Debt, investment and endowment accumulation: The case of not-for-profit hospitals. *Journal of Health Economics, 21,* 845–872.

Hall, M. A., & Colombo, J. D. (1991). The charitable status of nonprofit hospitals: Towards a donative theory of tax exemption. *Washington Law Review, 66,* 307–411.

Hansmann, H. B. (1980). The role of nonprofit enterprise. *Yale Law Journal, 89*(5), 835–901.

Hansmann, H. B. (1981). The rationale for exempting nonprofit organizations from corporate income taxation. *Yale Law Journal, 91*(1), 54–100.

Hansmann, H. B. (1987). The effect of tax exemption and other factors on the market share of nonprofit versus for-profit firms. *National Tax Journal, 40,* 71–82.

Hansmann, H. B. (1989). Unfair competition and the unrelated business income tax. *Virginia Law Review, 75,* 605–635.

Hansmann, H. B. (1990). Why do universities have endowments? *Journal of Legal Studies, 19,* 3–42.

Rose-Ackerman, S. (1982). Unfair competition and corporate income taxation. *Stanford Law Review, 34,* 1017–1039.

Sansing, R. (1998). The unrelated business income tax, cost allocation, and productive efficiency. *National Tax Journal, 51,* 291–302.

Steinberg, R. (1991). "Unfair" competition by nonprofits and tax policy. *National Tax Journal, 44,* 351–364.

Stigler, G. J. (1971). The theory of economic regulation. *Bell Journal of Economics and Management Science, 2,* 3–21.

Yetman, R. J. (2003). Nonprofit taxable activities, production complementarities, and joint cost allocations. *National Tax Journal, 56,* 789–799.

PART V

Economic Theories of the Nonprofit Sector (*)

Most economic theories of the nonprofit sector try to answer questions about the roles of nonprofit sector organizations and the functions they serve in three-sector political-economic societies. Many rich, useful economic theories have withstood the test of time. Notably, some economic theories seek to explain why nonprofits exist—or exist in a particular form—in a society with a particular blend of political dynamics, entrepreneurial capitalism, and a government that organizes, provides, and regulates many services.

Economic theories of the sector may be loosely divided into two categories: *role theories*—theories that try to explain why the sector and its organizations exist in the economic, political, and/or political economy system; and *functional theories*—theories that attempt to explain what organizations in the nonprofit sector do, how they function, and why.

Numerous economic role theories have examined the "failures" of the market, of government, and of contracts as justifications for the existence and characteristics of the nonprofit sector.[1] Political scientists, economists, and sociologists alike have used *niche theories* to explain why some nonprofits cluster in certain functional and geographical areas.[2] At a different level, economic theorists and researchers have used *rational choice theories*, *principal-agent theories*, and *transaction cost theories*, among others, to help explain why government agencies prefer to contract for services instead of provide services directly, why government has preferred to contract for some types of services with organizations in the nonprofit sector instead of for-profit businesses, but why government does not appear to have a preference between nonprofits and for-profits when it comes to many other services. Answers to questions such as these are important for decision-making practitioners in all three sectors as well as for university teachers and researchers. As Kurt Lewin wisely reminded us decades ago, "There is nothing so practical as a good theory."[3]

Economists have been interested in the nonprofit sector clear back to the times of Adam Smith's *The Wealth of Nations*. Smith, who is widely acknowledged as being the father of modern economics, divided all labor into two categories: *productive labor* and *unproductive labor*. According to Smith, productive labor "adds to the value of the subject upon which it is bestowed."[4] Unproductive labor does not add value.

In one of the fundamental formative documents of economic theory, for example, Adam Smith classified many common activities, today called "voluntary," as "nonproductive" and set them entirely, and perhaps permanently, outside the bounds of economics. The theoretical basis of this perspective is itself a negation: Smith's concept of "unproductive labor." Subsequently, most economists tended to dismiss activities in the nonprofit sector as "unproductive labor" and the sector as

DOI: 10.4324/9780367696559-18

not value-producing well up into the 1980s. The sector had been viewed by many mainstream economists as being outside the realm of rational economics, because it was not profit-driven, and thus it was largely ignored.

Major Changes in Nonprofit Revenue Sources That Started During the 1970s and 1980s

The nonprofit sector entered a period of major changes in its revenue sources during the 1970s and 1980s. Many nonprofit organizations that had primarily relied on charitable donations began turning to contracted services and funding from government agencies. These basic changes in revenue sources became evident first in the fields of mental health and intellectual challenges but spread rapidly into other areas of the human services, health care, and to an extent in community development and housing.[5] The changes in revenue sources affected almost all aspects of nonprofit organizations' missions, structures, and operations. The changes also extended to less obvious dimensions of the sector such as the professionalism of management, the roles of boards of trustees, and the relationship between nonprofits and their communities.[6]

While many nonprofits were growing increasingly reliant on government contracts starting in the 1980s, many also turned aggressively to a second alternative revenue source. They became more "corporatized" and were surprisingly successful at learning to be competitive entrepreneurs in their business strategies. Many found they could compete directly with for-profit firms in a surprising number of lines of business.[7]

Overall, the resulting effects from these basic shifts in funding have affected the nonprofit sector for the past 50 plus years and have dramatically altered the identities, roles, activities, and arguably the character of many organizations in the nonprofit sector.[8] As more and more nonprofit sector organizations began to look and act like for-profit businesses or contracted "captives" of government agencies, they caught the attention of economists. Theorists in other social sciences (and a few economists)[9] also began asking whether government contracting and commercialization had irreparably damaged the long-term value, social contributions, and integrity of the sector.[10]

Nonprofits and Mainstream Economic Theory

Nonprofit organizations provide an interesting challenge for mainstream economic theory. For example, according to mainstream economic theory, the market establishes housing prices through interactions between the supply of houses and apartments on the market and consumers' (potential buyers' or renters') demand for housing. Because high housing prices make it difficult for low-income persons to enter the housing market, nonprofit organizations such as Habitat for Humanity co-build homes with the future occupants and sell them to the future occupants at far less than the prices they could command on the open market. Governments also affect the housing market in cities using any of the many regulatory policy tools available to them. From the perspective of mainstream economic theory, nonprofit and government actions such as these artificially influence the natural working of the market and thereby disturb its functioning and decrease its efficiency.

What economic theorists have found most compelling about nonprofit organizations—particularly the rapidly growing number of "professionalized" or "commercialized" nonprofit organizations that look and act like private businesses—is that they exist *at all*.[11] The central questions for mainstream economic theory thus lead back to Adam Smith's distinction between productive and unproductive labor: What can nonprofit organizations offer that profit-seeking firms cannot provide more efficiently? For decades, the economists' responses to this question relied mostly on several *failure theories*. Failure theories explain the existence or actions of one phenomenon by the failure of another phenomenon. In the earlier housing example, the presence and actions of nonprofit organizations in the market are explained by the failure of the market to satisfy the demand for housing and by the failure of government to alleviate the problem. Nonprofit organizations have a presence in the housing market and function as they do because the market and government have failed to satisfy needs in communities for low-cost housing. Therefore, Lester Salamon's "Market Failure" theory and Dennis Young's "Government Failure Theory" and "Contract Failure Theory" are reprinted in this part.

Economic Models

The argument that the sum of individual choices leads to the aggregate good is controversial, but the failure of markets to meet this idealistic view does not invalidate the usefulness of economic models for attempting to predict economic behavior. Models are built to simplify complex sets of relationships and to explain the interactions among the most meaningful elements. They are not intended to explain all minute details, and it would be unfair to hold them to a standard of precise accuracy. Although economic models obviously have limits, they are highly useful for testing theories and explaining or predicting the effects of government and business policies and the actions of individuals and organizations in the market. Sometimes, however, reality differs too much from the assumptions built into an economic model, the effects differ dramatically from predictions, and it becomes necessary to factor in conditions that cause the model to fail.

Market Failure Theory

According to the economists, markets usually fail for one of two reasons.[12] First, as noted in the housing example, markets fail when something interferes with them. Even in an ideal world where a market mirrors what is best for both individuals and society, when markets lose their competitive edge the suppliers of goods and services gain the ability to raise prices. For example, reduced competition allows firms to charge higher prices than they would in a more competitive market. If the suppliers of goods or services exercise this ability, the market fails to operate as it should, and society's well-being is reduced.

The second cause of market failure is the behavior of consumers. In a perfectly competitive market, individuals who value particular goods or services the most will pay more than anyone else. The resulting aggregate allocation of goods benefits society more than any other method of allocation. Quite obviously, this lofty set of assumptions can fall short of what happens in the real world. Factors that cause goods to be allocated in less than optimal ways—as defined by economic theory—cause the second type of market failure.

When the market fails, opportunities are created for nonprofit organizations to enter the market, and the effectiveness of for-profit businesses is diminished. Although market failures take many forms, the four market failures that are most useful for helping to explain the existence, roles, and functions of organizations in the nonprofit sector are *transaction costs, information asymmetries, externalities,* and *public goods.*

Transaction costs are the costs associated with market exchanges ("transactions"), including the costs of obtaining the information needed to participate wisely in a transaction, transporting the goods or services and the buyers to and from the place where the transaction will occur, pooling resources, and holding both parties to the terms of a contract (enforcing a contract). Economists assume that transaction costs do not exist in a "perfect market." In reality, some transaction costs almost always exist, but they are seldom high enough to disrupt or distort market transactions. When they are disruptive, government often is invited in to correct—to regulate—the market failure, or nonprofits are invited in to offset the effects of the failure.

Nonprofit organizations may reduce or help consumers or sellers overcome a variety of transaction costs. The cost of obtaining information is a good example. Sometimes information is important but isn't valued in the market, and nonprofits fill the void or niche. Many nonprofit organizations thus collect, analyze, and provide information to educate people about how to make decisions in the market. The incredible increase in the use of the internet and the proliferation of web-based consumer information over the past two decades has made it much easier for nonprofits to inform consumers. Examples include the Better Business Bureaus, consumer credit counseling services, Angie's List, TripAdvisor, Consumers Union,[13] and mutual benefit nonprofits that help communities of immigrants learn to survive in their new environment or that provide advice to aging citizens to help them avoid becoming victims of fraud.

Many nonprofits pool resources to acquire goods or to achieve shared purposes. Pooling resources allows multiple individuals to donate relatively small amounts of money or time to help create, preserve, or expand a community asset. Pooling resources, however, can be costly. Thus, some nonprofits absorb the costs of pooling the resources needed to create community centers, parks, Little League baseball fields, places of worship, and to protect nature. A few examples of the latter include the Nature Conservancy, the Wildlife Federation, Ducks Unlimited, many land trusts, and the Sierra Club.

Information asymmetry is a second variety of market failure that helps to explain the existence, roles, and functions of nonprofit organizations. Information asymmetry occurs when the producer or seller of a good or service has more knowledge about the good than the consumer. Asymmetries may be related to a good's cost, quality, or quantity. Three factors tend to cause information asymmetries: the complexity of goods, incompetence of those who receive goods, and goods that are consumed by people other than those who purchase them.[14] Information asymmetry leads to contract failure when consumers believe that they cannot judge a good or service and their discomfort prevents them from entering into a transaction that would have otherwise occurred.[15] In addition to reducing the costs of obtaining information, nonprofit organizations also help prevent or overcome contract failure by creating trust, for example through the existence of the *nondistribution constraint*.[16]

Complex goods is the second cause of information asymmetry. It is difficult to accurately judge the quality of many goods or services. Examples of information asymmetries where consumers have difficulty evaluating the quality of services include many types of healthcare, services to individuals with developmental disabilities, mental illness, and dementia. In the absence of accurate information about quality, consumers tend to place higher trust in organizations that do not have profit as their primary reason for existence. The third type of information asymmetry, goods that are consumed by people other than those who purchase them, include services paid for by third parties, including for example, long-term health care, international relief programs, and arrangements whereby individuals receive vouchers for food, housing, and education.

Externalities are the indirect effects of a transaction that are not reflected in the market price.[17] Sometimes persons who are not party to a transaction either suffer or benefit from the transaction, but the cost of their suffering or value of the benefit they receive is not included in the market price. Pollution created in a production process is a good example of a negative externality. People and towns downriver from a paper mill or downwind from a coal-powered power plant pay some of the costs of producing the paper and electricity. They pay to clean up the river water or in higher incidences of diseases and thus healthcare costs, and in lowered housing valuations and lost tourism because fish cannot live in the water or ugly air pollution drives tourists away.

In contrast, when a person paints the exterior of her house, clears trash out of the yard, or plants a flower garden, positive externalities are created. Neighbors benefit from the improved environment and the value of their houses increases. To repeat: *Externalities* are a category of market failure because the total costs and benefits of the transaction are not limited to—do not accrue to—the buyer and seller. The market doesn't work as it is supposed to.

Some nonprofit organizations exist to discourage negative externalities and others to encourage positive externalities.[18] Environmental advocacy nonprofit organizations that attempt to stop air and water pollution or the destruction of animal habitat are examples of nonprofits that discourage negative externalities. Examples of nonprofit activities that create positive externalities include adult education programs that raise the employability and literacy of unemployed citizens, and community center volunteer groups that provide recreation opportunities to help keep at-risk youth "off the street." In both types of cases, others benefit—the benefits are not limited to the direct recipients of the services.

A *public good* is a commodity or service that is not depleted by an additional user and for which it is almost impossible to exclude people, even those who refuse to pay.[19] Commonly cited examples of public goods include national defense, clean air, and scenery. Public goods cannot be divided, and people cannot be excluded from using them. If one citizen benefits, all others will also. In most cases, it is absurd to consider restricting or regulating the use of public goods. Even if some people could be charged for "consuming" a public good, for example, looking at the scenery out their windows, other free riders could not be excluded. Because public goods are difficult to monitor and are available to free riders as well as people who might be willing to pay for them, public goods tend to be undersupplied and abused in a free market.[20] Abuses of public goods cause negative externalities—a market failure. Thus, some nonprofit organizations exist to provide public goods that are undersupplied in the market or to discourage abuse of public goods that already are present.[21]

Government Failure Theories

When the market fails, economists tend to look to government to step in, but when government fails to respond satisfactorily to a market failure, demands are left unsatisfied. Some organizations in the nonprofit sector have been created to satisfy unmet needs caused by failures of the market and government.

Government failure theory holds that nonprofit organizations complement government in meeting demands for goods and services. The three most frequently cited rationales for government failure are: (1) individuals and minority groups demand goods or services beyond the norm or beyond the demands of the majority group (see Part VI, "Political Theories of the Nonprofit Sector"); (2) officeholders have shorter time horizons than the long-term public interest requires; and (3) government fails to have compelling information and/or not enough citizens come forward to inform the government and plead for services.[22] Although government failure theories are relatively new in their formal sense, they have been a part of the nonprofit literature for centuries.[23]

Criticisms of the Failure Theories

Economic theories have enlightened, but they also have created contention. The "failure theories" in particular have been criticized mostly for what they ignore—the values-based contributions that organizations in the nonprofit sector make to a society. Critics of the failure theories also argue that economists have remained narrowly focused on economic efficiency while ignoring the core values the nonprofit sector brings to communities, including trust, civil society, social capital, altruism, and compassion.

The nonprofit sector cannot be understood or appreciated when attention is limited to the failures of other institutions and markets, and when the values and contributions that are central to its existence and roles are ignored. This criticism was the cause for the title of Roger Lohmann's article, "And Lettuce is Nonanimal: Toward a Positive Economics of Voluntary Action." In it, Lohmann argues that economic failure theories distort reality in order to make the roles and behaviors of the nonprofit sector conform to economic theory. "Failure theories tell us more about what the nonprofit sector is not than they do about what it is."[24]

Readings Reprinted in Part V

As Henry Hansmann explains in "Ownership and Organizational Form: Nonprofit Firms," nonprofit organizations are firms without owners. In these nonprofit organizations or firms,

> control [of the organization] is separated from the claim to residual earnings by imposing a bar (the "nondistribution constraint") on the distribution of the firm's net earnings or assets to persons who control the firm. . . . By removing strong incentives for the firm's managers to earn profits, the incentive to exploit the firm's patrons is reduced.

The nondistribution constraint thereby creates trust and possibly reduces *transaction costs* especially in markets where information asymmetries make it difficult for consumers or third party payers to gauge the quantity or quality of services provided. "Nursing homes for the elderly—where, for example, sedating patients into inexpensive tractability is a tempting strategy for the producers—are evidently an example."

Sometimes nonprofit organizations are the best way to organize a new industry or type of service. Once efficient and effective monitoring and evaluation methods are available, for-profit firms can step in. Hansmann reminds, however, that once entrenched, nonprofit organizations may remain in the market for long periods of time, such as with nonprofit savings banks, mutual life insurance companies, and nonprofit hospitals.

In "Market Failure," Lester Salamon posits that the U.S. market system works well for many items people consume individually, but does not handle well "those things that can only be consumed collectively. . . . [T]hese so-called public goods" involve a "serious 'free rider' problem." To correct for the failure of the market and ensure that all who benefit pay, government may step in and, for example, impose a tax. An alternative correction mechanism is for nonprofit organizations to pool peoples' resources "to produce collective goods they mutually desire . . . but cannot convince a sufficient majority . . . to support [through government action]." *Information asymmetry* is a second form of market failure that was introduced earlier. When information asymmetries exist, such as with nursing homes that serve persons with dementia, nonprofit organizations may become preferred service providers because they do not exist primarily to earn profits, are more widely trusted, and *transaction costs* are lower.

In "Contract Failure Theory," Dennis Young emphasizes the centrality of contract failure for market failure theory. In readings reprinted here, Young uses James Douglas's "five sources of constraints on governmental action that create unsatisfied demands for public service to which private nonprofits may respond" to explain "government failure." The essence of *government failure theory* is that when government and markets do not satisfy the demands of individuals, people organize to do something about it. Thus, government failure theory provides insights about how nonprofit organizations operate in reality. The interfaces and interactions among nonprofits, government, and individuals represent components of the informal infrastructure that we refer to as community.

Maitreesch Ghatak's "Economic Theories of the Social Sector: From Nonprofits to Social Enterprise" introduces earlier economic theories of the nonprofit sector that mainly reflected contract failure theory and explains why these earlier theories cannot explain the emergence of hybrid organizations and social enterprise (see Part IX), newer organizational forms that tend to be more flexible. Ghatak proposes conditions when a hybrid social enterprise is likely to be preferable to a for-profit or nonprofit alternative. He also highlights the importance of hiring and retaining personnel who are motivated by the organization's mission.

Notes

* We are grateful to E. Brigham Daniels, now a professor at Brigham Young University's J. Reuben Clark Law School, for his wise advice, uniformly useful suggestions, and gentle but accurate criticisms, as well as for his drafts of portions of this introductory essay for the first edition of this volume.

1. See particularly "Contract Failure Theory" and "Government Failure Theory" by Dennis R. Young and "Market Failure" by Lester M. Salamon. All three are reprinted here. Also see Kirsten A. Grønbjerg, "Markets, Politics, and Charity: Nonprofits in the Political Economy," in *Private Action and the Public Good*, ed., Walter W. Powell and Elisabeth S. Clemens (New Haven: Yale University Press, 1998), 137–150; and, Roger Lohmann, "And Lettuce Is Nonanimal: Toward a Positive Economics of Voluntary Actions," *Nonprofit and Voluntary Sector Quarterly*, 18 (1989): 367–383.

2. Pamela Popielarz and Miller McPherson, "On the Edge or in Between: Niche Position, Niche Overlap, and the Duration of Voluntary Association Memberships," *American Journal of Sociology*, 101 (1995): 698–720.

3. Alfred J. Marrow, *The Practical Theorist: The Life and Works of Kurt Lewin* (New York: Basic Books, 1969).

4. Adam Smith, *Wealth of Nations* (1776; reprint, New York: Penguin, 1973).

5. The initial changes in revenue sources were closely associated with the "de-institutionalization movement" in mental health and intellectual challenges in the late 1960s and early 1970s and to distrust of local government among members of the Richard Nixon administration. See Kirsten Grønbjerg and Lester Salamon, "Devolution, Marketization, and the Changing Shape of Government-Nonprofit Relations," in *The State of Nonprofit America*, 2nd ed., ed. L. M. Salmon (Washington, DC: Brookings Institution Press, 2012), 549–586.

6. See Part VII for more about the relationship between nonprofits and communities, and the multiple roles nonprofits play in communities.

7. U.S. Small Business Administration, *Unfair Competition by Nonprofit Organizations with Small Business: An Issue for the 1980s*, 3rd ed. (Washington, DC: U.S. Government Printing Office, June 1984); James T. Bennett and Thomas J. DiLorenzo, *Unfair Competition: The Profits of Nonprofits* (Lanham, MD: Hamilton Press, 1989); Dan Pallotta, *Uncharitable: How Restraints on Nonprofits Undermine their Potential* (Medford, MA: Tufts University Press, 2008).

8. Steven Rathgeb Smith and Michael Lipsky, *Nonprofits for Hire* (Cambridge, MA: Harvard University Press, 1993); Ralph M. Kramer, "Voluntary Agencies and the Contract Culture: 'Dream or Nightmare'?" *Social Science Review*, 68 (1994): 33–60; James M. Ferris, "The Double-Edged Sword of Social Service Contracting," *Nonprofit Management and Leadership*, 3 (1993): 363–376; Melissa Middleton Stone, "Competing Contexts: The Evolution of a Nonprofit Organization's Governance System in Multiple Environments," *Administration and Society*, 28 (1996): 61–89.

9. Burton A. Weisbrod, ed., *To Profit or Not to Profit: The Commercial Transformation of the Nonprofit Sector* (Cambridge: Cambridge University Press, 1998).

10. Smith and Lipsky, *Nonprofits for Hire*.

11. Smith and Lipsky, *Nonprofits for Hire*; Weisbrod, *To Profit or Not to Profit*.

12. See for example, Paul Krugman and Robin Wells, *Microeconomics*, 5th ed. (New York: Worth Publishers, 2018); and, Robert S. Pindyck and Daniel L. Rubinfeld, *Microeconomics*, 8th ed. (Upper Saddle River, NJ: Prentice Hall, 2012).

13. The nonprofit consumer research organization that publishes *Consumer Reports* and provides product price and quality information by telephone and the internet.

14. Dennis R. Young, "Contract Failure," in *International Encyclopedia of Public Policy and Administration*, ed., Jay M. Shafritz (Boulder: Westview Press, 1998), 516–518. Reprinted in this part.

15. Henry B. Hansmann, "Economic Theories of Nonprofit Organization," in *The Nonprofit Sector: A Research Handbook*, ed., Walter W. Powell (New Haven: Yale University Press, 1987) 27–42; and, Henry B. Hansmann, "The Role of Nonprofit Enterprise," *Yale Law Journal*, 89 (1980): 835–902.

16. Elisabeth S. Clemens, "The Constitution of Citizens: Political Theories of Nonprofit Organizations," in *The Nonprofit Sector: A Research Handbook*, 2nd ed., eds., Walter W. Powell and Richard Steinberg (New Haven, CT: Yale University Press, 2006), 207–220, and reprinted in Part VI.

17. Krugman and Wells, *Microeconomics*.

18. Robert Scott Gassler, *Beyond Profit and Self-Interest: Economics with a Broader Scope*. (Northampton, MA: Edward Elgar, 2004).

19. Pindyck and Rubinfeld, *Microeconomics*; William J. Baumol and Alan S. Blinder, *Economics: Principles and Policy*, 9th ed. (London and New York: Pearson, 2018); and William J. Baumol, Alan S. Blinder, and John L. Solow, *Economics: Principles and Policy*, 14th ed. (Boston: Cengage, 2020).

20. Baumol, Blinder, and Solow, *Economics: Principles and Policy*; and, Pindyck and Rubinfeld, *Microeconomics*.

21. Weisbrod, *The Nonprofit Economy*.

22. James Douglas, *Why Charity?* (Beverly Hills, CA: Sage, 1983); Dennis Young, "Government Failure" reprinted in this part.

23. Recall Tocqueville's "theory" that nonprofit associations thrived in colonial United States due to the lack of established institutions, particularly government (Part II).

24. Roger A. Lohmann, "And Lettuce Is Nonanimal: Toward a Positive Economics of Voluntary Actions," *Nonprofit and Voluntary Sector Quarterly*, 18 (1989): 367–383.

Bibliography

Anheier, Helmut K., *Nonprofit Organizations: Theory, Management Policy* (2nd ed.) (Abingdon, UK: Routledge, 2014).

Bacchiega, Alberto, and Carlo Borzaga, "The Economics of the Third Sector: Toward a More Comprehensive Approach." In Helmut K. Anheier and Avner Ben-Ner (Eds.), *The Study of the Nonprofit Enterprise: Theories and Approaches* (pp. 27–48) (New York: Springer, 2003).

Baumol, William J., Alan S. Blinder, and John L. Solow, *Economics: Principles and Policy* (14th ed.) (Boston: Cengage, 2020).

Besley, Timothy, and Maitreesh Ghatak, "Pro-social Motivation and Incentives." *Annual Review of Economics*, 10 (2018).

Boris, Elizabeth T., "Nonprofit Organizations in a Democracy: Varied Roles and Responsibilities." In Elizabeth T. Boris and C. Eugene Steuerle (Eds.), *Nonprofits & Government: Collaboration & Conflict* (pp. 1–36) (Washington, DC: Urban Institute Press, 2006).

Clemens, Elisabeth S., "The Constitution of Citizens: Political Theories of Nonprofit Organizations." In Walter W. Powell and Richard Steinberg (Eds.), *The Nonprofit Sector: A Research Handbook* (2nd ed., pp. 207–220) (New Haven, CT: Yale University Press, 2006).

Coase, Ronald H., "The Problem of Social Cost." *Journal of Law and Economics*, 3 (1960): 1–44.

Gassler, Robert Scott, *Beyond Profit and Self-Interest: Economics with a Broader Scope.* (Northampton, MA: Edward Elgar, 2004).

Ghatak, Maitreesh, "Economic Theories of the Social Sector: From Nonprofits to Social Enterprise." In Walter W. Powell and Patricia Bromley (Eds.), *The Nonprofit Sector: A Research Handbook* (3rd ed., pp. 319–332) (Palo Alto, CA: Stanford University Press, 2020).

Gibbons, Robert, and John Roberts (Eds.), *The Handbook of Organizational Economics.* (Princeton, NJ: Princeton University Press, 2013).

Glaeser, Edward, and Andrei Shleifer, "Not-for-Profit Entrepreneurs." *Journal of Public Economics*, 81 (2001): 99–115.

Grønbjerg, Kirsten A., "Markets, Politics, and Charity: Nonprofits in the Political Economy." In Walter W. Powell and Elisabeth S. Clemens (Eds.), *Private Action and the Public Good* (pp. 137–150) (New Haven, CT: Yale University Press, 1998).

———, and Lester M. Salamon, "Devolution, Marketization, and the Changing Shape of Government-Nonprofit Relations." In Lester M. Salamon (Ed.), *The State of Nonprofit America* (2nd ed., pp. 549–586) (Washington, DC: Brookings Institution Press, 2012).

Hansmann, Henry B., "Economic Theories of Nonprofit Organizations." In Walter W. Powell (Eds.), *The Nonprofit Sector: A Research Handbook* (pp. 27–42) (New Haven, CT: Yale University Press, 1987).

———, "Ownership and Organizational Form: Nonprofit Firms." In Robert Gibbons and John Roberts (Eds.), *The Handbook of Organizational Economics* (pp. 907–909) (Princeton, NJ: Princeton University Press, 2013).

———, "The Role of Nonprofit Enterprise." *Yale Law Journal*, 89 (1980): 835–901.

Kramer, Ralph M., "Voluntary Agencies and the Contract Culture: 'Dream or Nightmare'?" *Social Science Review*, 68 (1994): 33–60.

Krugman, Paul, and Robin Wells, *Microeconomics* (5th ed.) (New York: Worth Publishers, 2018).

Lohmann, Roger A., "And Lettuce Is Nonanimal: Toward a Positive Economics of Voluntary Action." *Nonprofit and Voluntary Sector Quarterly*, 18 (1989): 367–383.

Marrow, Alfred J., *The Practical Theorist: The Life and Works of Kurt Lewin* (New York: Basic Books, 1969).

Pallotta, Dan, *Uncharitable: How Restraints on Nonprofits Undermine their Potential* (Medford, MA: Tufts University Press, 2008).

Pindyck, Robert S., and Daniel L. Rubinfeld, *Microeconomics* (9th ed.) (London and New York: Pearson, 2018).

Popielarz, Pamela, and Miller McPherson, "On the Edge or in Between: Niche Position, Niche Overlap, and the Duration of Voluntary Association Memberships." *American Journal of Sociology*, 101 (1995): 698–720.

Rushton, Michael, "Why are Nonprofits Exempt from the Corporate Income Tax?" *Nonprofit and Voluntary Sector Quarterly*, 36 (2007): 662–675.

Salamon, Lester M., "Market Failure." In Lester M. Salamon (Ed.), *America's Nonprofit Sector: A Primer* (2nd ed., pp. 12–19) (New York: Foundation Center, 1999).

———, *Partners in Public Service: Government-Nonprofit Relations in the Modern Welfare State* (Baltimore: Johns Hopkins University Press, 1995).

Smith, Adam, *Wealth of Nations* (1776; reprint, New York: Penguin, 1973).

Smith, Steven Rathgeb, and Michael Lipsky, *Nonprofits for Hire: The Welfare State in the Age of Contracting* (Cambridge, MA: Harvard University Press, 1993).

Steinberg, Richard, "Economic Theories of Nonprofit Organizations." In Helmut K. Anheier and Avner Ben-Ner (Eds.), *The Study of the Nonprofit Enterprise: Theories and Approaches* (pp. 277–309) (New York: Springer, 2003).

Vaceková, Gabriela, *The Nonprofit Sector in Economic Theory: Beyond Mainstream Explanations* (Brno, Check Republic: Masaryk University, 2016).

Weisbrod, Burton A., "The Future of the Nonprofit Sector: Its Entwining with Private Enterprise and Government." *Journal of Policy Analysis and Management*, 16 (1997): 541–555.

———, *The Nonprofit Economy* (Cambridge, MA: Harvard University Press, 1988).

—— (Ed.), *To Profit or Not to Profit: The Commercial Transformation of the Nonprofit Sector* (Cambridge, UK: Cambridge University Press, 1998).

Young, Dennis R., "Contract Failure." In Jay M. Shafritz (Ed.), *International Encyclopedia of Public Policy and Administration* (pp. 516–518) (Boulder, CO: Westview Press, 1998).

——, "Government Failure." In Jay M. Shafritz (Ed.), *International Encyclopedia of Public Policy and Administration* (pp. 1006–1008) (Boulder, CO: Westview Press, 1998).

——. (Ed.), *Wise Economic Decision-Making in Uncertain Times: Using Nonprofit Resources Effectively* (New York: Foundation Center, 2006).

CHAPTER 14

Ownership and Organizational Forms: Nonprofit Firms

Henry Hansmann

Originally published in Robert Gibbons and John Roberts, eds., *The Handbook of Organizational Economics*. Copyright © 2013 Princeton University Press. Reprinted by permission of Princeton University Press.

For some goods and services, the costs of contracting between firms and one or another class of their patrons is potentially extremely high, but at the same time the class of patrons in question cannot be organized to serve as effective owners at any feasible cost. In these cases, the efficient solution may be to create a nonprofit firm, that is, a firm without owners. In these firms, control is separated from the claim to residual earnings by imposing a bar (the "nondistribution constraint") on distributions of the firm's net earnings or assets to persons who control the firm. The consequence is that all the firm's revenues must be devoted to providing services. By removing strong incentives for the firm's managers to earn profits, the incentive to exploit the firm's patrons is reduced.

Asymmetric information between a firm and its customers is typically the source of the contracting costs involved. More particularly, the problem is often that the firm's customers cannot observe the quantity of product or service that the firm provides in return for the price they pay. Such a situation arises commonly when an individual, out of philanthropic motives, seeks to purchase services to be delivered to needy third parties in distant places. Payments to an organization like Oxfam to deliver food to famine victims in Africa are an example. The contributors are in no position to determine how their individual contributions are used. If such a firm were owned by someone other than its customers, the firm would have an incentive to provide few or no services in return for the payments it receives. Prospective customers, expecting this behavior, would refuse to patronize the firm. At the same time, however, the firm's customers (referred to as "donors") are too transient and dispersed to be organized, at any acceptable cost, as owners capable of monitoring effectively the firm's managers. Consequently, customer ownership is not a viable solution. A similar problem faces firms producing public goods, such as cancer research or commercial-free broadcasting: a contributor may be able to observe both the quantity and quality of services that the firm is producing but cannot determine whether, at the margin, her own contribution induced an increase in quantity or quality.

 DOI: 10.4324/9780367696559-19

Of course, once those who control the firm are deprived of the profit motive, one must ask what incentive they have to put any effort whatsoever into managing the firm, much less into producing a level of quantity and quality acceptable to customers. The best explanation is that, in the absence of competing "high-powered" profit incentives, the managers' actions are guided by "low-powered" nonpecuniary incentives, including pride, professionalism, and identification with the goals of the organization (Glaeser and Shleifer 2001).

The nonprofit form seems most commonly to be a response to the problems of contracting when quantity is (at the margin) unobservable. In particular, this problem generally occurs in organizations supported by donations, from the Salvation Army to the performing arts to universities. But there are also situations in which the nonprofit form is evidently a response to unobservable or unverifiable quality.[1] In such situations, one can find nonprofit firms that derive all their revenue from prices charged to their customers. Nursing homes for the elderly—where, for example, sedating patients into inexpensive tractability is a tempting strategy for the producers—are evidently an example.

However, the observed distribution of nonprofit firms across industries cannot be assumed to be a strong reflection of their comparative efficiency vis-à-vis other ownership types. In comparison with firms with owners, transactions in control (and particularly conversions out of the nonprofit form) may not occur when they would be efficient. In principle, a nonprofit corporation can sell its business as a going concern to a proprietary firm and either donate the proceeds to another nonprofit organization and liquidate, or invest the proceeds in another activity that the nonprofit can manage more efficiently. By virtue of the nondistribution constraint, however, the managers who control a nonprofit cannot gain financially from such a transaction; they may in fact suffer from it both in financial (salary) and in nonpecuniary (interest and status of employment) terms. In this regard, it is particularly

significant that the managers of a nonprofit firm do not bear the opportunity cost of the capital that the firm has accumulated. Moreover, a nonprofit firm can survive indefinitely, even if it earns only a zero net rate of return on its (self-owned) capital, and can in fact grow if it earns any positive rate of return, no matter how small. Consequently, survivorship cannot be taken as an indication of the efficiency of the nonprofit form as confidently as it can with proprietary forms of ownership.

This problem is compounded by the evolution of industries over time. The nonprofit form is sometimes the best or only way to organize production in the early stages of developing a new service, before effective mechanisms to monitor and pay for the service have been developed. When those mechanisms subsequently come into place, proprietary firms can take over production, and the nonprofit form becomes anachronistic. Yet, because market mechanisms are weak in inducing exit by nonprofit firms, they may long continue to account for a large share of the industry's production. A conspicuous example is offered by nonprofit savings banks, which arose in the United States (and elsewhere) in the early nineteenth century, because (as with life insurance), in the absence of public regulation, depositors could not trust that their savings would still be intact for withdrawal after many years in a proprietary bank's possession. Although regulation and deposit insurance long ago removed this reason for the nonprofit form, it continued to have a large presence in the industry until recent times (Rasmusen 1988; Hansmann 1996, 246–264). Similarly, there is evidence that nonprofit hospitals—originally institutions supported by donations that provided services to the poor—retain a large market share today, not because they are more efficient than proprietary hospitals but because of weak mechanisms to induce exit (Hansmann et al. 2003).

The distinction between formally nonprofit firms and firms that simply have extremely weak owners is vanishingly small at the margins. Mutual life insurance companies, for example, are in formal terms collectively owned by their policyholders (i.e., they are consumer cooperatives) and hence are in principle proprietary firms. Yet the firms' highly fragmented policyholders have little incentive or ability to exercise effective control over the firms' managers. As a consequence, most US life insurance companies, from the time of their initial formation, have effectively been nonprofit firms, controlled by self-perpetuating boards of directors and holding a growing pool of assets whose value the policyholders do not entirely appropriate. Similarly, there is today little meaningful difference in the United States between mutual savings and loan associations, which are formally depositors' cooperatives, and mutual savings banks, which (despite the term "mutual") are formally nonprofit entities.

Large business corporations with highly dispersed shareholdings that are largely free from the market for corporate control, as some US firms arguably have been over substantial periods, may likewise be little different from nonprofit entities with respect to the costs of ownership—which, for nonprofit firms, consist principally of managerial agency costs. There are, in fact, some industrial firms that are formally organized as nonprofit corporations or very close to it. The most conspicuous examples are the "industrial foundations" that are common in northern Europe (though effectively proscribed by tax law in the United States). These are business firms that are either organized as a nonprofit firm or are entirely controlled by one. The available empirical evidence fails to show that these industrial foundations are less efficient than their investor-owned counterparts (Thomsen and Rose 2004), lending some support to the judgment that, even at the extreme, the agency costs of delegated management are relatively modest in comparison with other costs of ownership and with the costs of market contracting.[2] Even with no owners at all—or, as we might say, even with a true "separation of ownership from control"—firms can be managed with fair efficiency.

Notes

1. Glaeser and Shleifer (2001) interpret their model, which is the best we have, in terms of unverifiable quality, though it can as easily be interpreted in terms of unobservable quantity.

2. Even if these results prove robust and are not idiosyncratic to the Danish environment, it is possible that the particular dual-level structure of these firms is an important factor. The industrial firms in the sample are themselves organized as business corporations, with a controlling majority of their shares held by a separate nonprofit foundation. Thus, in a sense, the industrial firms are proprietary firms with an owner—namely, the foundation. And though the foundation is nonprofit, its management may think of the operating company principally as a source of revenue for the foundation and hence seek to assure that the company is managed with substantial efficiency. In a sense, this structure is an extreme form of a company with a dual board system—an outside supervisory board that chooses an inside managerial board—which is itself a formal extension of the idea of having a single board with a majority of outside directors. For analogous results involving nonprofit hospitals in the United States, see Hansmann et al. (2003).

References

Glaeser, Edward, and Andrei Shleifer. 2001. "Not-for-Profit Entrepreneurs." *Journal of Public Economics* 81: 99–115.

Hansmann, Henry. 1996. *The Ownership of Enterprise.* Cambridge, MA: Harvard University Press.

Hansmann, Henry, Daniel Kessler, and Mark McClellan. 2003. "Ownership Form and Trapped Capital in the Hospital Industry." In Edward Glaeser, ed., *The Governance of Not-for-Profit Organizations,* 45–70. Chicago: University of Chicago Press.

Rasmusen, Eric. 1988. "Stock Banks and Mutual Banks." *Journal of Law and Economics* 31: 395–422.

Thomsen, Steen, and C. Rose. 2004. "Foundation Ownership and Financial Performance: Do Companies Need Owners?" *European Journal of Law and Economics* 18: 343–364.

▶ **CHAPTER 15**

Market Failure

Lester M. Salamon

In addition to modernization theories that attribute the development of nonprofit organizations to the growing complexity of social and economic life, a second set of theories points to the limitations that even modern social institutions exhibit to explain the emergence of a nonprofit sector. Especially noteworthy here are certain inherent limitations of the market, what classical economic theory refers to as *market failures*. According to this line of theory, the market system works quite well for supplying private goods, the things we consume individually, such as shoes, cars, clothing, and food. But it has difficulty responding to demands for public or collective goods, that is, those things that can only be consumed collectively, such as clean air, national defense, or safe neighborhoods. What sets these so-called public goods apart is the serious "free-rider" problem that attends their production because, once they are produced, everyone can benefit from them even if they have not shared in the cost. Therefore, each individual has an incentive to let his or her neighbors bear the cost of these public goods, knowing full well that he or she can nevertheless still share in the benefits. Since everybody has the same incentive, however, the inevitable result of relying solely on the market to produce such collective goods is that far less of them will be produced than people really want, creating an unsatisfied demand for collective goods.

In classical economic theory, it is this unsatisfied demand for collective goods that provides the ultimate economic rationale for government, since government can overcome the free-rider problem by compelling all citizens to share in the cost of desired collective goods. But students of the nonprofit sector have pointed out that government itself has inherent limitations in supplying collective goods, even in a democracy. According to one line of argument, this is particularly true in circumstances where religious, ethnic, or racial diversity makes it difficult for citizens to come to agreement on the range of collective goods they want, thus making it impossible to generate the majority support needed to trigger a governmental response in a democracy.[1] Ideological and economic disputes can also lead to government inaction.

To meet the unsatisfied demands for collective goods in such situations, another mechanism is needed, and nonprofit organizations provide such a mechanism. These organizations allow groups of individuals to pool their resources voluntarily to produce collective goods they mutually desire or find it important to provide but cannot convince a sufficient majority of their countrymen, or those in positions of power, to support. Indeed, support for reliance on such organizations has at times been used as a rationale to avoid extending governmental protections and the taxation and regulation it can bring with it.[2]

Notes

1. This line of argument has been applied to the nonprofit sector most explicitly in Burton Weisbrod, *The Voluntary Nonprofit Sector* (Lexington, MA: Lexington Books, 1978).

2. See, for example, Lester M. Salamon, "Of Market Failure, Voluntary Failure, and Third-Party Government: Toward a Theory of Government-Nonprofit Relations in the Modern Welfare State," *Journal of Voluntary Action Research* 16, nos. 1–2 (January–June 1987): 29–49.

► **CHAPTER 16**

Contract Failure Theory

Dennis R. Young

[Contract failure is an] economic theory that helps to explain the existence of nonprofit organizations in a market economy. It is a particular aspect of the more general economic theory of "market failure" that specifies conditions under which unfettered competition among profit-making firms fails to provide particular goods or services efficiently.

The condition of contract failure is said to occur where consumers feel unable to judge competently the quality or quantity of services they are receiving (Hansmann 1987). In this circumstance, consumers will be reluctant to purchase the goods and services they need, for fear of being cheated. Hence, markets composed solely of unregulated profit-making firms will fail to allocate economic resources to their most highly valued uses.

The basic source of contract failure is a condition called "information asymmetry" where producers have more accurate knowledge of the quantity, quality, and cost of services delivered than do consumers. There are three basic causes of information asymmetry. First, certain goods and services may be inherently complex or their quality may be difficult to judge. The technical and multifaceted natures of medical care or higher education illustrate this case. Second, the consumer himself or herself may simply not be competent to evaluate the services he or she is receiving. Preschool care or services to the mentally ill or the impaired elderly are examples of this type. Third, certain services may not be purchased by the same individual that consumes them. In this instance, the purchaser does not experience the service directly and may not be in a position to obtain good information from the consumer. Again, day care for young children purchased by parents, or nursing home care purchased by children of elderly parents, illustrates this condition. Another example is international relief services financed by donors in one country to help victims in another country distant from the first. (Note, for purposes of this discussion, donors can be considered one variety of consumer of nonprofit organization services.) One or more of these conditions may characterize a particular service, creating conditions of contract failure that inhibit the efficient functioning of normal markets because consumers may fear the possibility of exploitation.

DOI: 10.4324/9780367696559-21

The utilization of nonprofit organizations is just one possible remedy to conditions of contract failure. Other potential remedies include licensing and regulation of profit-making providers such as in the case of automobile repair; standards of practice and oversight by professional associations or accrediting bodies as in dentistry or teaching; or purchasing control by expert third parties, such as doctors who behave as consumer proxies for hospital care or insurance companies that oversee medical care purchases.

There is no clear-cut theory for determining which of the latter solutions best fits each circumstance of contract failure or when the participation of nonprofit organizations provides the best remedy. However, some sense of the latter can be discerned from the premises that underlie different theoretical approaches to the question of why participation of nonprofit organizations serves as a correction to contract failure. There are basically three streams of thought that purport to explain how nonprofit organizations help overcome the problems of contract failure and hence provide particular services more efficiently than profit-making firms. The most prominent explanation, developed by Hansmann (1980), is that the nondistribution constraint governing nonprofit organizations creates a disincentive for nonprofit organizations to exploit their customers or patrons. In essence, the nondistribution constraint prohibits those who control the organization (managers, trustees) from distributing financial surpluses (profits) for their personal benefit. If this constraint is effectively policed, for example by government authorities, then nonprofits will allocate all of their resources to the promulgation of their missions, and will have little incentive to cheat those who finance or consume its services. In this context, consumers and donors will find nonprofit organizations "trustworthy" and will exhibit less reluctance to utilize and pay for their services.

A second stream of theory, advanced by Young (1983) and Hansmann (1980), postulates that nonprofits become trustworthy by a different mechanism: the selection and screening of leaders. In this framework, executive leaders of organizations come to their positions with a variety of different motivations ranging from self-interested income and power seeking to the pursuit of personal beliefs and public ideals. The differences between profit-making and nonprofit organizations, including the presence of the nondistribution constraint for nonprofits, cause the pool of potential leaders to sort itself out among the sectors according to motivational differences, with the public service–oriented executives going into the nonprofit sector and the more wealth-seeking executives clustering in the profit sector. The result of this motivational sorting is to make the nonprofit sector more trustworthy by virtue of the kinds of people attracted to it, providing consumers and supporters with the confidence they require to overcome contract failure.

A third line of theory focuses less on the nondistribution constraint and more on other structural aspects of the nonprofit form that allow consumers and supporters to have greater control over service provision. Easley and O'Hara (1983) postulate that a nonprofit firm is distinguished from a for-profit firm by the fact that its managers accept a fixed amount of compensation and promise to devote all other resources to the costs of producing its services. In contrast, a for-profit firm contracts only on the basis of producing a given output for a given price. In this model, although the output of the nonprofit organization is difficult to measure, its expenditures on executive compensation and other inputs can be monitored and policed, helping to assure that the organization delivers what it has promised.

Ben-Ner (1986) takes still another view of nonprofits, arguing that they are distinguished by the fact that their donors and consumers play a more intensive role in governance of the nonprofit organization than they would in a for-profit organization. In this view, the nonprofit is a kind of consumer cooperative in which production and consumption of a service are integrated within the organization. This resulting close control by consumers overcomes information asymmetry by giving consumers an insider's view.

Each of these strands of theory suggest that under conditions of information asymmetry, the nonprofit form will serve consumers by promising that such organizations behave in more trustworthy fashion. Weisbrod (1988) elaborates on how more trustworthy behavior should manifest itself. In particular, he makes the distinction between "type 1" and "type 2" attributes of a good or service. A type 1 attribute, such as the physical appearance of a nursing home, is easily observable; a type 2 attribute, such as the caring nature of the relationship between attendants and elderly nursing home patients, is difficult for the outsider to observe. Weisbrod argues that if contract failure theory is correct, nonprofits should be superior to for-profits in the provision of type 2 attributes, but no different than for-profits in providing type 1 attributes. He points out, however, that verifying this hypothesis through research is intrinsically challenging: "Gathering data is difficult. If differences in type 2 dimensions of behavior persist across institutions, they must be difficult to discern—for analysts as well as consumers" (147).

Nonetheless, empirical research has been carried out with some success (Steinberg and Gray 1993). For example, surveys provide some evidence that people do distinguish between nonprofit and for-profit institutions and that they express more confidence in nonprofits. Studies of behavioral differences between nonprofits and for-profits within particular industries also provide some verification. For example, Weisbrod (1988) studied long-term care facilities for elderly, mentally handicapped, and psychiatric patients, finding that nonprofits were more likely than for-profits to provide family members with detailed information, less

likely to sedate their patients heavily, and more likely to achieve higher levels of expressed satisfaction by patients' families. He interprets these data cautiously to suggest that nonprofits, especially those that are religiously affiliated, offer a more trustworthy alternative to for-profits in industries where type 2 attributes prevail.

While providing a powerful framework for understanding why nonprofits exist in certain areas of the economy, the theory of contract failure is not a comprehensive theory and leaves some unanswered puzzles (Steinberg and Gray 1993). Most obvious is the fact that the theory does not fully distinguish between private, nonprofit organizations and government agencies, which are also technically nonprofit in a financial sense and which presumably should also engender greater trustworthiness than for-profit firms. Thus, a separate segment of theory has developed to explain why private nonprofits exist alongside government and are more efficient than government in some circumstances. However, an interesting sidelight to this question is the issue of governmental contracting with nonprofit organizations for the provision of public services.

Here the question also arises as to whether the government should utilize the services of for-profit firms or restrict its contracting to nonprofits (Smith and Lipsky 1993). If government as consumer/contractor also suffers the problem of information asymmetry, then the theory of contract failure can provide insight on its selection of nonprofit versus for-profit suppliers under various circumstances (Brodkin and Young 1989). For example, if a service such as garbage collection is primarily of a type 1 variety, there is less reason for the government to prefer nonprofit contractors. However, for services such as children in foster care, contract failure provides a stronger rationale for nonprofit contractors. Moreover, the governmental choice of contractors is presumably influenced by the mechanism through which government chooses to finance privately supplied public services. If that mechanism is direct contracting with a few suppliers, government officials may be more able to police contractor behavior, whether profitmaking or nonprofit. But if the mechanism is subsidy of consumers who must make the choice of suppliers and monitor the services they receive, but are limited in their abilities to do so, the theory of contract failure suggests a preference for utilizing nonprofits.

Another lacuna in the theory of contract failure is that it does not directly address the puzzle of why we observe "mixed industries," such as day care for children or nursing homes for the elderly, in which profit-making and nonprofit organizations coexist. If nonprofits are more efficient in certain industries characterized by information asymmetry, why do they not drive for-profits in those industries out of business? While this question is unresolved, contract failure theory contains within it one source of explanation: If consumers vary in their levels of understanding and information about service quality, they might choose to utilize a variety of types of institutions. Well-informed consumers, confident in their ability to discern whether or not they were receiving a good bargain, might choose a for-profit provider, especially if it were cheaper or provided a variety of service closer to their personal preferences. A less competent consumer, or one who didn't have the time to gather sufficient information, might prefer to rely on a nonprofit organization in which he or she could place greater trust.

A related puzzle, however, is that if nonprofits enjoy greater trust in certain situations, why wouldn't some for-profit businesses disguise themselves as nonprofit organizations in order to exploit consumers' fears and drain away resources for their own benefit through various indirect means such as inflated salaries and sweetheart contracts with suppliers? Clearly the answer to this question depends on the effectiveness with which the nondistribution constraint or other structural aspects of

the nonprofit form are assumed to police such behavior. If "for-profits in disguise" can successfully infiltrate the nonprofit sector, analysts have shown that this could seriously undermine confidence in nonprofits in general, destabilizing mixed industries and driving nonprofits out unless other means were implemented to ensure the survival of honest nonprofits (Steinberg 1993).

Contract failure is not just of interest to theorists, or to policymakers wishing to discern within what areas of the economy nonprofits should be encouraged to operate. This concept also highlights an important principle for managers and trustees of nonprofit organizations: the essential currency of nonprofit organizations is trust. When that is undermined, nonprofits lose an important reason for their existence and the confidence of those who support them or utilize their services.

References

Ben-Ner, Avner. 1986. "Non-Profit Organizations: Why Do They Exist in Market Economies?" In Susan Rose-Ackerman, ed., *The Economics of Nonprofit Institutions*, 94–113. New York: Oxford University Press.

Brodkin, Evelyn Z., and Dennis Young. 1989. "Making Sense of Privatization: What Can We Learn from Economic and Political Analysis?" In Sheila B. Kamerman and Alfred J. Kahn, eds., *Privatization and the Welfare State*, 121–154. Princeton, NJ: Princeton University Press.

Easley, David, and Maureen O'Hara. 1983. "The Economic Role of the Nonprofit Firm." *Bell Journal of Economics* 14: 531–538.

Hansmann, Henry. 1980. "The Role of Nonprofit Enterprise." *Yale Law Journal* 89: 835–901.

———. 1987. "Economic Theories of Nonprofit Organization." In Walter W. Powell, ed., *The Nonprofit Sector: A Research Handbook*, 27–42. New Haven, CT: Yale University Press.

Smith, Steven R., and Michael Lipsky. 1993. *Nonprofits for Hire*. Cambridge, MA: Harvard University Press.

Steinberg, Richard. 1993. "Public Policy and the Performance of Nonprofit Organizations: A General Framework." *Nonprofit and Voluntary Sector Quarterly* 22: 13–32.

Steinberg, Richard, and Bradford H. Gray. 1993. "The Role of Nonprofit Enterprise in 1993: Hansmann Revisited." *Nonprofit and Voluntary Sector Quarterly* 22: 297–316.

Weisbrod, Burton A. 1988. *The Nonprofit Economy.* Cambridge, MA: Harvard University Press.

Young, Dennis R. 1983. *If Not for Profit, for What?* Lexington, MA: D. C. Heath and Company.

Government Failure Theory

D ENNIS R. Y OUNG

G overnment failure is a] segment of economic theory that explains the conditions under which governmental provision of public goods and services is inefficient. Charles Wolf, Jr. (1979) described a variety of circumstances under which government intervention in the private economy to correct market failures may produce new inefficiencies and conditions under which government may over- or underproduce public services or provide them at too high of a cost.

Government failure is an important component in the theory of private nonprofit organizations. In particular, this body of theory has been used to explain why private nonprofit organizations arise to provide public goods and services on a voluntary basis, even in the presence of governmental provision. Government failure theory applied to nonprofit organizations focuses on the limitations of government and how private nonprofit organizations may fill in the niches left unserved by governmental action (Hansmann 1987).

James Douglas (1983, 1987) identified five sources of constraint on governmental action that create unsatisfied demands for public service to which private nonprofits may respond:

1. The "categorical constraint" results from the necessity of governments to provide goods and services on a uniform and universal basis. This constraint implies that the demands of individuals whose preferences for public services differ from the norm will go unsatisfied. This situation creates niches for nonprofit organizations to provide additional public services on a voluntary basis. Moreover, since government must provide its services universally to all its citizens, it is limited in its ability to experiment on a small scale with new programs, which creates another niche for private nonprofit organizations.

2. The "majoritarian constraint" of government reflects the fact that in a diverse population there may be multiple conceptions of the public good and what government should be doing. If government responds to the majority, it leaves niches for private nonprofit organizations to respond to minority issues and demands.

3. The "time horizon" constraint of government reflects the relatively short tenures of government officeholders and their consequent incentive to focus on short-term issues and results. This constraint leaves another area of

 DOI: 10.4324/9780367696559-22

action for private nonprofit organizations—the addressing of long-term societal issues and concerns.

4. The "knowledge constraint" connotes that government bureaucracies are organized in a relatively monolithic, hierarchical way and, hence, cannot be expected to generate all of the relevant information, ideas, and research needed for intelligent decisionmaking on public issues. This, too, creates a niche for private nonprofit advocacy groups, research centers, and other institutions.

5. The "size constraint" reflects the view that government bureaucracy is typically large and intimidating, thus, it is difficult for ordinary citizens to engage government. This situation creates a niche for nonprofit organizations to serve as "mediating institutions" between government and the citizenry (see Berger and Neuhaus 1977).

Burton Weisbrod's (1975) seminal economic theory of nonprofit organizations focuses essentially on James Douglas's categorical constraint. Weisbrod considers the implications of government as a provider of a particular public service to constituents with diverse preferences (demands) within a given political jurisdiction. The service is assumed to be a classical "pure public good," which is simultaneously consumed in the same quantity by all constituents once it is provided, and from which no one can be excluded. The government finances this good by imposing the same "tax-price" per unit of output on all citizens, no matter how much or little each values the good. Moreover, the government is assumed to use a voting mechanism to decide how much of the good to provide. For example, the use of majority voting would lead the government to provide an amount of the good that would correspond to the preferences of the "median voter," that is, the voter whose preferences fell in the middle of the distribution of voter preferences for this good.

The particular voting mechanism utilized is beside the point. The essential result is that one particular level of public goods provision will be selected and consumed by all voters, no matter what their individual preferences. Some voters may thus find the marginal value of the good less than the imposed tax-price and, hence, would prefer less of the good, and others may find the marginal value more than the tax-price and would prefer the government to provide more. Only those voters whose preferences resembled that of the median voter would be relatively satisfied. Thus, government is seen to be potentially inefficient in its provision of the good because it provides too much of it to some citizens and too little of it to others.

Weisbrod (1975) has considered various mechanisms available to correct such inefficiency. For example, he noted that people can move to different jurisdictions, where their preferences more closely match those of their neighbors (Tiebout 1956). He has also pointed out that private goods can be purchases as partial substitutes when citizens desire more than government provides. For example, people can buy watchdogs and install burglar alarms to make up for a lower-than-desired level of police services. Finally, Weisbrod pointed out that when mobility and private consumption fail to fill the gap, nonprofit organizations can arise to provide public goods on a private, voluntary basis. For example, neighborhood watch organizations may arise to supplement governmental police services.

One of the important predictions of the Weisbrod theory of government failure is that it suggests that the nonprofit sector will be most active where citizen populations are most diverse, and that nonprofit organizations are important for satisfying the service needs of political minorities. Thus, the theory gives us insights into the important role of nonprofit organizations in a democracy in accommodating the needs of diverse groups and averting conflicts over government service policy (Douglas 1987). It also helps to explain, at the international level, why some countries more than others rely on the nonprofit sector to provide public services. Estelle James (1987), for example, noted that the cultural diversity of such countries as Holland and Belgium helps to explain why these countries have more significant nonprofit sectors than more homogeneous countries such as Sweden.

Other evidence of the utility of government failure to understand the role of private nonprofit organizations derives from examination of the sources of funding of these organizations (Weisbrod 1988). In particular, Weisbrod presumes that if the function of the nonprofit sector is to provide public goods on a voluntary basis then a substantial fraction of their financing should derive from charitable contributions, gifts, or grants, rather than revenues from sales or membership fees. He thus created a "collectiveness index" from the ratio of contributions, gifts, and grants to that of the total revenues of nonprofit organizations in a variety of fields. The ratio was found to vary widely among industries in which nonprofit organizations participate, but substantial evidence was found to support the notion that nonprofit organizations classified as charitable (501[c][3]) by the Internal Revenue Service enjoyed relatively high collectiveness indices (typically in the range of 20% to 40%) and hence were indeed providing collective goods on a voluntary basis.

Bibliography

Berger, Peter L., and Richard J. Neuhaus, 1977. *To Empower People*. Washington, DC: American Enterprise Institute.

Douglas, James, 1983. *Why Charity?* Beverly Hills, CA: Sage.

———, 1987. "Political Theories of Nonprofit Organization," chap. 3, pp. 43–54. In Walter W. Powell, ed., *The Nonprofit Sector: A Research Handbook*. New Haven: Yale University Press.

Hansmann, Henry, 1987. "Economic Theories of Nonprofit Organization," chap. 2, in pp. 27–42. In Walter W. Powell, ed., *The Nonprofit Sector: A Research Handbook*. New Haven: Yale University Press.

James, Estelle, 1987. "The Nonprofit Sector in Comparative Perspective," chap. 22, pp. 397–415. In Walter W. Powell, ed., *The Nonprofit Sector: A Research Handbook*. New Haven: Yale University Press.

Tiebout, Charles, 1956. "A Pure Theory of Local Government Expenditure." *Journal of Political Economy* (October): 414–424.

Weisbrod, Burton A., 1975. "Toward a Theory of the Voluntary Non-Profit Sector in a Three-Sector Economy." In Edmund S. Phelps, ed., *Altruism, Morality, and Economic Theory*. New York: Russell Sage Foundation.

———, 1988. *The Nonprofit Economy*. Cambridge: Harvard University Press.

Wolf, Charles, Jr., 1979. "A Theory of Nonmarket Failure: Framework for Implementation Analysis." *Journal of Law and Economics* (April): 107–139.

CHAPTER 18

Economic Theories of the Social Sector: From Nonprofits to Social Enterprise

Maitreesh Ghatak

Ghatak, Maitreesh, "Economic Theories of the Social Sector: From Nonprofits to Social Enterprise." In Walter W. Powell and Patricia Bromley (Eds.), *The Nonprofit Sector: A Research Handbook* (3rd. ed.) 319–332 (Palo Alto, Calif.: Stanford University Press, 2020).

1. Introduction

Internationally, nongovernmental organizations (NGOs), a subset of organizations in the nonprofit sector that engage specifically in international development, have been supplementing and sometimes replacing government agencies in the provision of relief and welfare, social services, and various projects in developing countries. The number of international NGOs rose from less than 200 in 1909 to nearly 1,000 in 1956 to more than 20,000 in 2005 (Werker and Ahmed, 2008).

This substantial presence of nonprofits in the economy presents several conceptual challenges to economists.

First, if a private organization does not seek to maximize profits, it becomes a challenge to model its behavior. After all, financial incentives are an important engine of economic activity in a market economy. If the objective of a nonprofit is not profit, then what exactly is it, and how do we know that this supposed objective is not profit maximization by another name? If the objective is some form of social welfare, how can we be sure that the rational, utility-maximizing agent of economics textbooks (often referred to as *homo economicus*) will in fact pursue it? How can we be sure that such an agent will not pursue a selfish objective, such as capturing rents? How can an organization that does not maximize profits survive competition from for-profit organizations, particularly in markets where there are no entry barriers?

Second, the existence of nonprofits calls into question the neat division of economic activity into two spheres: the market sphere and the government sphere. It points to a gray zone in the neat, black-and-white picture of the economy that divides all economic activity into (a) a profit-driven private sector that produces private goods efficiently and (b) a public sector that corrects market failures, provides public goods, and carries out redistribution to serve equity objectives.

Even within the framework of mainstream economics, some scholars are questioning these traditional views related to the motivation of economic agents. They are also questioning the simplistic model that equates for-profit firms with the production of private goods and

DOI: 10.4324/9780367696559-23

government entities with the provision of public goods.

A large body of empirical work, especially within the field of experimental economics, has increasingly called into question the view of individuals as being driven by narrow self-interest.[1] Recent theoretical work in economics has, in light of this growing body of empirical evidence, moved beyond stylized models of motivation based on a narrow view of *homo economicus*—an archetypal figure who cares only about money and leisure—and has embraced a wider perspective on motivation. Broadly speaking, this work has focused on different approaches to prosocial motivation, such as commitment to a mission, commitment to an identity (being a "good" or "responsible" person, a good teacher or doctor or friend or parent), commitment to an "in-group" (e.g., family, community, tribe), intrinsic rewards, reputational concerns and social norms, status rewards, and pure altruism.[2]

At the same time, a large body of evidence has accumulated on varieties of government failure related to, for example, corruption, waste, absenteeism, and poor service quality. A related development involves the rising importance of private social-sector organizations, including not only nonprofits but also hybrid organizational forms such as social enterprises, public-private partnerships, and contracting-out of public service provision to private providers. The rising importance of this sector highlights the limitation of equating the provision of public goods and services with provision through government agencies.[3]

A central research objective of modern microeconomic theory has been to understand how the economic institutions that underlie the "invisible hand" of the market actually work. The starting point of modern organizational theory in economics is to understand the boundaries of the firm, i.e., the classic "make or buy" decision—how much to produce in-house and how much to procure from outside. The literature that has emerged has advanced our understanding of how the scope, size, and organizational form of a firm

and how it manages workers or raises capital depends on the nature of the production process, various contracting frictions, transactions costs, and informational asymmetries.[4]

A large literature on the economics of nonprofits has emerged since the early 1970s (see Hansmann, 1987, for a review), and this literature addresses alternative theories of nonprofits that I will review in the next section (Section 2). I argue that this literature does not provide a clear framework to explain the rise of hybrid organizational forms—social enterprises, in particular—that flexibly combine features of both nonprofit and for-profit organizations. In Section 3, I will discuss the rise of social enterprises and provide some examples. In Section 4, I will discuss a new agency problem that I call the "mission-integrity problem." In Section 5, I will discuss the self-selection of motivated managers into social enterprises. In Section 6, I will offer some concluding observations on the emerging research agenda in the economic theory of social sector organizations.

2. Existing Theories of Nonprofits

Many of the leading theories of nonprofits can be traced to the core insight of the multi-tasking literature (Holmström and Milgrom, 1991) in contract theory. The term "multi-tasking" refers to situations where a job involves multiple tasks and the performance in these are not all equally measurable. The general lesson from this literature is, if an organization has multiple outputs and its non-pecuniary outputs are difficult to measure, then a muting of financial incentives may be necessary. Moreover, if the social outputs of an organization are of great value to its owner or principal or stakeholders, then they may opt for the nonprofit form to decrease managers' incentive to pursue financial profits by sacrificing social objectives.

The existing literature on nonprofits, building on the work of Hansmann (1980) and Weisbrod (1988), with more recent contributions by Glaeser and Shleifer (2001), identifies the nonprofit sector as a residual sector that arises to overcome market and government failure in the provision of some goods and services. According to this work, a non-distribution constraint (henceforth, NDC) serves as a mechanism to overcome certain contractual problems, which Hansmann calls as "contract failure." The NDC (Hansmann, 1980) used by nonprofits stipulates that nonprofits can earn revenues or generate a financial surplus, so long as they are retained for future spending, distributed to beneficiaries in some form, or given to employees who lack control rights.

This literature shows that an NDC may be a constrained optimal choice in the presence of agency problems. Motivating an agent on a contractible task (effort in increasing output or reducing costs) might produce undesirable outcomes because it leads to neglect of a non-contractible task (effort in improving quality). Given this cost-quality trade-off, for-profit entities will tend to lower costs at the expense of product or service quality, whereas nonprofits have little incentive to compromise quality in that way (see Glaeser and Shleifer, 2001). The choice of organizational form thus depends on how much the principal of an organization values quality (or any other non-pecuniary aspects of production) as opposed to profits.

This is a cost-quality trade-off, which is an example of contract failure. A more general version of this trade-off occurs when a firm chooses an action that can be of two types, a pro-social one and a commercial one. The former type has a potential social benefit but is also costly, while the latter type has no social benefit but is low in cost. A nonprofit organization has no financial incentive to take a commercial action, while a for-profit firm has no incentive to take a social action.

A clarifying remark about using simple models to illustrate different economic theories may be helpful here. A simple model is meant to focus attention on one particular force (e.g., the cost-quality trade-off) whose variation will

determine whether a specific organizational form will emerge. However, there are several other variables that are being held constant (the *ceteris paribus* assumption). For example, a simple theory of the nonprofit form may posit that this form is merely a means to attract a motivated workforce that will work at lower wages (e.g., Preston, 1989; Weisbrod, 1988) or a means to get tax benefits. Alternatively, where a cost-quality trade-off exists, something other than a pure nonprofit or a pure for-profit firm may emerge. For example, a profit-sharing partnership may be optimal when it is hard to assess service quality (see Levin and Tadelis, 2005), and such partnerships are common in professional service industries—such as law, accounting, medicine, investment banking, architecture, advertising, and consulting—but not elsewhere. Unlike a general theory, a simple model indicates a likely association or a central tendency but allows for a range of possibilities that may deviate from that tendency and yet be consistent with it.

A variant of this argument suggests that charities should take a nonprofit form in order to assure donors that their money will indeed reach beneficiaries and not be pocketed by the managers of a donee organization. Contract failure arises in situations where the quality of a good or a service cannot be ascertained before (or sometimes even after) its consumption—a situation that leaves considerable scope for opportunism. Common examples of this situation include plumbing and car repair, health care, education, and child or elder care. An NDC is said to protect against opportunism: managers have a reduced incentive to compromise quality since they cannot pocket financial profits directly.[5]

It is not clear that having an NDC will eliminate opportunistic behavior. That profits cannot be directly distributed does constrain the way that surplus can be extracted from a nonprofit, but salaries and perks provide a mechanism through which nonprofit managers can extract surplus. Indeed, the starting point of the work of Glaeser and Shleifer (2001) is that nonprofit managers extract surplus in an indirect and possibly inefficient way: for every dollar they extract in the form of perks or benefits, they receive only a fraction of that value, and this effect mutes their incentive to compromise quality. After all, direct cash is preferable to perquisites in the form of goods and services. The same effect reduces their incentive to maximize revenues. The literature correctly notes the downside of nonprofits that is implied by this logic: if nonprofit managers have little incentive to pursue profits at the expense of non-contractible quality, they also have little incentive to cut costs in socially productive ways. In this respect, for-profit firms are preferable.[6]

Barring a few exceptions, the economics literature on nonprofits has placed relatively little focus on the motivation of those who manage or work in those organizations (Handy, 1995; Preston, 1989; and Weisbrod, 1988, are exceptions). It is often remarked that these individuals systematically differ in terms of their pro-social motivation from the rest of the population.[7] A key factor in the effectiveness of nonprofits may well be their ability to attract employees who are committed to a cause, as noted by Preston (1989), Weisbrod (1988), and Besley and Ghatak (2005).

3. Emergence of Social Enterprise

Because of the rise of social enterprises in the last few decades, the classification of all organizations as discrete nonprofit, for-profit, or government entities is no longer possible. Social enterprises belong [to] a set of organizations that are neither traditional profit-maximizing firms nor nonprofit organizations nor publicly owned and controlled government agencies. These hybrid forms of organization are often referred to as "social enterprises" even though, as Martin and Osberg (2007) acknowledge, many other types of firms operate under that banner.[8]

The defining goal of a social enterprise is to balance making profits with pursuing a social mission (Katz and Page, 2010). As Dees (1998) puts it, social enterprises combine "the passion of a social mission with an image of business-like discipline, innovation, and determination commonly associated with, for instance, the high-tech pioneers of Silicon Valley." They aim to bring entrepreneurial approaches to social problems, thereby providing an alternative to the perceived rigidity and inefficiency of existing institutions in the government and philanthropic sectors.

I should also clarify that many organizations—including for-profit firms—have multiple objectives, including social and commercial ones. What matters is which objective[s] have priority. We can think of for-profit firms as operating under strict market discipline, which requires them to prioritize profit maximization while respecting a minimum threshold for meeting certain social objectives (e.g., environmental standards). Likewise, we can view nonprofits as working to maximize a social objective, subject to a break-even constraint and an NDC. In contrast, social enterprises have a flexible approach: in some circumstances they maximize a social objective, subject to a break-even constraint; in other circumstances they maximize a financial objective, subject to the constraint that their actions do not fall short of a minimum threshold for meeting their social objective.

Indeed, in the management literature, social enterprises are viewed as aiming to balance making profits with advancing a social mission (see Katz and Page, 2010) and as avoiding the rigidity of either a nonprofit or a for-profit form. They are viewed as pursuing profit and social good in tandem, in part by making considered choices to pursue one over the other at any given time (Reiser, 2010). The underlying premise is that there is a trade-off between these objectives and that both nonprofit and for-profit entities face constraints that make resolving this trade-off difficult. Managers of a for-profit firm, meanwhile, have a legal obligation to maximize profits for the firm's owners. Also, market forces push them to give priority to profit maximization over social objectives; otherwise, they risk losing both market share and investor confidence.[9]

Like most nonprofits, social enterprises are allowed to earn revenue, but unlike nonprofits, they face no equivalent of an NDC that restricts the distribution of residual earnings—no constraint, that is, other than the requirement that its activities align with its social mission. However, as Dees (1998) points out, "For social entrepreneurs, the social mission is explicit and central. This obviously affects how social entrepreneurs perceive and assess opportunities. Mission-related impact becomes the central criterion, not wealth creation."

The role of social enterprises in the economy has attracted increasing attention in recent years, partly in response to the growing number of real-world examples of social enterprises in both the developed and developing worlds (see Porter and Kramer, 2011). The management literature presents many interesting case studies. Consider the following examples:

In Africa, where children frequently die of diarrhea from bad sanitation, Isaac Durojaiye runs a franchise system for public toilets. He supplies mobile toilets to slum areas, where previously unemployed young people operate the toilets and charge a small fee for their use. These operators keep 60% of the income and pass the rest to Durojaiye's company, Dignified Mobile Toilets, which uses the money to buy new toilets.

Nic Frances runs a group that aims to cut carbon emissions in 70% of Australian households over 10 years. His group, Easy Being Green, gives low-energy light bulbs and low-flow showerheads to households that agree to sign over the rights to the carbon-emission credits that use of the equipment will earn. The group then sells those credits to companies and use[s] the proceeds to finance its activities. Easy Being Green now aims to expand globally.[10]

A common theme in the literature on social enterprises is the tension between their commercial and social missions. In the commercial microfinance sector, for example, the social mission of relaxing borrowing constraints on the poor comes head-to-head with profit-seeking that may occur at the expense of the poor, raising the specter of "mission drift" (see Yunus, 2011). Ben & Jerry's, an ice-cream brand that was established to follow strong ethical norms (e.g., using hormone-free milk sourced from local farms) while pursuing commercial ends, was sold to Unilever at the behest of shareholders, raising questions about its future as a social enterprise (see Page and Katz, 2012).

4. The Mission-Integrity Problem

What nonprofits, social enterprises, and the kinds of hybrid organizations discussed in the previous section have in common is that they are all mission-driven organizations that operate in settings where principals or agents may have non-pecuniary motivations and where outputs cannot be measured well enough to make standard incentive contracts useful. But given that social enterprises claim to be flexible in balancing social and commercial objectives, they require a mechanism that can balance those objectives in a way that is consistent with a broad mission. Besley and Ghatak (2017a) call this challenge the "mission-integrity" problem.

Suppose it is possible to verify whether a manager has undertaken the pro-social action or the commercial action. Now suppose that there are two types of situations that can arise. In one, social considerations outweigh financial considerations, and so taking the pro-social action is the right thing to do. In the other, financial considerations outweigh social considerations, and so the commercial action is the appropriate one to undertake.

However, only the manager can observe the true facts of the situation, and therefore we cannot figure out whether the manager is doing the right thing merely by observing his or her actions. What matters is that the production or distribution of a good entails a potential conflict between social and commercial objectives, and yet the underlying reason for taking an action is not observable by outsiders, including the owners or principals of an enterprise.

There are several applications that would fit this scenario.

Think of situations in which the goal is to widen access to certain goods or services; education, health care, and legal services are important examples. Now the pro-social action can be interpreted as providing access to "deserving" beneficiaries at preferential terms (e.g., free treatment for the poor), while the commercial action involves offering no special access or concessions. The manager may observe an individual who is to be served (say, a patient or a student or a potential beneficiary of a targeted welfare program) and decide what action to choose.

The social objective may also be related to externalities associated with the good's production. For example, environmental externalities may arise requiring firms to balance cost efficiency against the social costs of pollution. Suppose the commercial action is to use a standard technology, while the pro-social action is to use a costlier but more environmentally sound technology. The manager's choice is to decide whether it is worth giving up profits by choosing the latter technology if the environmental benefits that are external to the firm are substantial enough.

One way to ensure mission integrity is to impose a rigid mission on an organization. Nonprofit organizations, for example, are designed to protect mission integrity by following a clear social mission. Many sectors of the economy—in particular, health, education, and poverty relief—rely heavily on such organizations. The downside of this arrangement is that from a social welfare point of view, there may be times when commercial considerations outweigh social considerations. In this scenario, nonprofits are inefficient.

In the existing framework, which I discussed in Section 2, the separation of for-profit and nonprofit entities might seem like an efficient division of labor between the provision of private goods and the provision of public goods. But the rigidity that characterizes both nonprofit and for-profit entities has a downside. From a social welfare point of view, there are times when engaging in profit-oriented activities is most desirable and times when pursuing other ends is most desirable. Thus, it makes sense to seek a more nuanced way to balance those two types of activity. That is indeed one of the claimed advantages of social enterprises: they eschew the rigidity of both nonprofit and for-profit forms. The question is, how do they guarantee mission integrity? To be effective, in other words, social enterprises have to solve the problem of achieving the right trade-off between profit and purpose.

In the absence of contractual solutions, the mission-integrity problem creates a role for what Katz and Page (2010) call "mission-sympathetic parties" who are appointed to achieve an optimal trade-off between commercial and social considerations. Selection on the basis of motivation can thus become a mechanism to achieve mission integrity. Besley and Ghatak (2017a) formalize this argument and show that one key mechanism through which social enterprises can achieve mission integrity while eschewing the rigid approach of nonprofit and for-profit forms is the selection of managers who are motivated by a social mission. In that case, managers can be given a financial stake in their organization, and this incentive structure will ensure that they will "do the right thing" depending on the situation—namely, maximizing profits when that is appropriate but deviating from that practice when social objectives are more important. However, external monitoring by stakeholders offers another option to make sure that the performance of social enterprises conforms to their social objectives.

Consider all three organizational forms: for-profit, nonprofit, and social enterprise. With a for-profit firm or a social enterprise, the manager is a full residual claimant on profits, whereas the manager of a nonprofit earns only a flat wage. For-profit and nonprofit entities curb the autonomy of managers by stipulating a rigid mission. In a social enterprise, the manager has discretion over the balance between profit and purpose.

If managers are sufficiently motivated (that is, if they put sufficiently high weight on a social payoff), nonprofits and social enterprise are equivalent, as managers of this type will always put more weight on social objectives than on profits. However, for moderately motivated managers, the flexibility of social enterprises mitigates the mission-profit trade-off, and giving them discretion over action is more efficient than the rigid approach followed by either non-profits or for-profit firms.

However, this effect has to be balanced against the fact that if the social payoff is very valuable to a principal or owner (or if the social state is much more frequent than the commercial one), then the nonprofit form should be chosen over both for-profit and social enterprise forms. Similarly, if the commercial payoff is more valuable to a principal or owner (or if the commercial state is much more frequent than the social one), then the for-profit form is the correct option.

This framework allows us to move beyond the for-profit versus nonprofit trade-off, which has been a primary focus of the existing literature on social enterprises. Another interesting implication of this framework is that when owners or principals do not like a social payoff (when, for example, they put a negative weight on it due to ideological considerations), they face a problem that resembles a standard agency problem, with the social payoff functioning like a private benefit to a firm's manager. Thus, for-profit firms that prohibit taking a pro-social action will be the preferred organizational form among owners or principals who object to a social payoff. This insight is in keeping with the well-known claim by Friedman (1970) that the only social responsibility of business is to make profits.

5. Selection of Socially Motivated Managers

The approach taken in the previous section challenges a central tenet of standard economic design, in which the assumption of *homo economicus* restricts attention to agents with narrowly self-interested goals. Even though, as I noted above, the potential role of nonprofits in attracting motivated managers is recognized (see, for example, Weisbrod, 1988), the formal theoretical literature on nonprofits has not explicitly considered the role of intrinsically motivated managers and how their presence and selection interacts with underlying agency problems. A key insight of the Besley and Ghatak (2017a) framework is to show that once the heterogeneity of manager motivation and self-selection is taken into account, social enterprises emerge as a natural alternative that allows the social sector to go beyond the standard for-profit versus nonprofit trade-off.

This insight provides an interesting contrast with certain assumptions that prevail in the existing literature on nonprofits. In that literature, it is assumed that managers have no non-pecuniary motivation and care only about money and their disutility of effort. As a result, nonprofit status are seen as necessary to manage the cost-quality trade-off. Once we allow for managers who have non-pecuniary motivation, nonprofit status ceases to be a necessary condition for aligning commercial and social objectives. Allowing for pro-social motivation therefore opens the door for more-flexible organizational forms, such as social enterprise.

However, a key question then emerges: How do social enterprises select for socially motivated managers? Motivation, like ability or conscientiousness, is not readily observable, and one must have mechanisms in place to ensure selection of the right kinds of individuals. An empirical implication of this argument is that social enterprises will spend much more time and effort on recruiting managers who are committed to a social mission than for-profit firms do.

There is ample empirical evidence that non-profit and public-sector organizations recruit individuals who have more "public-service motivation." There is also some evidence that social enterprises tend to hire workers who are highly motivated to achieve an organization's mission and who fit with the values espoused by the organization (Brolis, 2017).

Put differently, the selection of workers and managers for nonprofits and the choice of the nonprofit form are not independent, as it would appear from the existing literature, in which one strand of research (e.g., Weisbrod, 1988) focuses on the selection aspect while another strand (e.g., Hansmann, 1980) focuses on the role of the NDC in curbing incentives for managers to let commercial considerations override pro-social considerations. The main argument for nonprofits—namely, that it removes commercial considerations from decision-making—is reinforced if there are grounds to believe that not every decision-maker fully agrees with the mission of his or her organization. Likewise, if decision-makers are indeed committed to the mission, then contract failure is less likely and one can consider relaxing the rigidities of the NDC (e.g., if the NDC limits an organization's ability to access capital).

However, a key question remains: how do organizations solve the selection problem? If individuals are heterogenous in terms of their commitment to the mission of an organization and if information on their commitment level is not observable, how can the organization make sure that it selects the right managers? This is the classic problem of self-selection: if the quality of an applicant is subject to private information, is it possible to design a compensation package that will select for the "right" kind of applicant?

Suppose two types of organizations are in place, a nonprofit and a hybrid, and the former offers a flat wage w_N and the latter offers both a flat wage w_H and a share of profits λ as a bonus. Is it possible to set these values in a way that satisfies the mission-integrity constraints of both organizations *and* in a way that leads selfish agents to self-select for the nonprofit and motivated agents to self-select for the hybrid organization? A distinctive aspect of the problem, as it turns out, is that meeting those conditions is not possible. In standard problems that involve asymmetric information, we typically worry about the self-selection constraint on one type of agent but not both. Yet here, we have to worry about the self-selection constraints on both types of agents. To make the nonprofit attractive to selfish agents, the flat wage has to be high, but in that case motivated agents will also be attracted to the nonprofit: they get the social payoff by choosing the pro-social action in both states of the world. To make the hybrid attractive to motivated agents, the bonus has to be set high (as high as the mission-integrity constraint will permit) to offset the lower flat wage, but in that case the hybrid becomes attractive to selfish agents as well!

That means there are two possible options. First, one can set the wage in hybrid organizations so low that selfish agents will not join them, while motivated agents will opt to join nonprofits instead. Second, one can set the nonprofit wage at a level that is unattractive to motivated agents, but in that case selfish agents will be drawn to hybrid organizations. Both options have downsides: a selfish agent in a hybrid organization will pursue only financial objectives since they get a share of the profits as a bonus and do not value the social objectives by the assumption of being selfish, while a motivated agent in a nonprofit will pursue only social objectives since financial incentives are absent.

There are two factors that suggest that the former is likely to be the preferred "second-best" option. First, there is a paucity of motivated agents relative to selfish agents in the population. Screening out selfish agents, therefore, is a much bigger concern than screening in motivated agents. Second, within the social sector, the loss from pursuing a commercial objective when a social objective should receive priority is likely to be of greater concern than the loss from pursuing a social objective when a commercial objective should receive priority.

We do not have direct evidence to support the model outlined above. However, existing work on nonprofit wage differentials suggests that it should be possible to carry out similar work with respect to social enterprises. There is also evidence that those who work in the nonprofit sector believe they are underpaid but choose to continue to work in the sector for reasons that are value-based and because they find certain job characteristics appealing (Handy et al., 2007). There is also evidence that measures of pro-social motivation predict the decision to work in the nonprofit sector, and that workers in the sector accept a wage discount for that reason (Serra et al., 2011).

6. Concluding Remarks

An emerging research area seeks to understand the social sector from an economic point of view and to integrate the sector either into a standard economic framework that applies to for-profit firms producing private goods (e.g., economics of contracts and organizations, industrial organization, finance, labor) or into a standard framework that applies to government entities providing public goods (e.g., standard public economics).

Much of the economic reasoning that underpins the standard understanding of resource allocation in the private sector does not quite apply to the social sector. To start with, the quality of goods and services provided in the social sector—which include experience goods to credence goods—is typically non-contractible. Also, many of these goods and services have externalities: that is, their benefits or costs are partly external to the organization that provides them. According to Coase (1960) the inefficiencies that arise from externalities have to do with

the difficulty of creating property rights. In fact, "creating property rights" and "contractibility" are very similar concepts. If output is hard to measure and/or attribute to a given agent (e.g., in the moral hazard problem that applies to teams), then how do you pay people appropriately for their marginal product? If quality is non-contractible, then how do you charge buyers a price that reflects the value that they place on it? The core issue in the kinds of problems that I have discussed—the kinds of problems that have traditionally been the focus of public economics—is non-contractibility, namely, when the output is difficult to measure and price. If non-contractibility is not the issue and output is measurable, then non-rivalry (namely, one person's consumption not reducing another person's consumption as is the case with standard private goods like apples) simply changes the pricing formula (e.g., subscription or rental rates for cable TV) from that of standard private goods, without requiring any major change in the analytical framework.

There are several important potential areas of research in this emerging literature. Of particular interest is the financing of social enterprises. For example, one advantage of social enterprises over nonprofits is that the former can raise equity while the latter can only incur debt. More generally, there are several fascinating areas of future research related to the continuum of organizations that spans from for-profit firms to social enterprises of various kinds to nonprofits. With respect to social enterprises, topics for future research include the following: the organization design (e.g., delegation, ownership structure) and the implicit and explicit incentive mechanisms (e.g., reputation, career advancement, incentive pay) that these organizations use; the quality, performance, and impact assessment of the outputs of these organizations; how these organizations interact at an industry level and how they interact with other types of organizations; and government regulatory policy regarding these organizations.

Notes

1. See Besley and Ghatak (2018) for a review of this literature.

2. This work can be separated from behavioral economics, which studies departures from certain consistency axioms in a rational choice framework. One can have many objectives other than maximizing private wealth or consumption of private goods and yet be strictly rational. Even in standard public economics models, people care about public goods and services. In this literature, the premise is that there is some failure in government provision of public goods, regulations, and private voluntary actions by individuals (e.g., models of voluntary charitable contributions).

3. See Besley and Ghatak (2017b) for a discussion.

4. See Gibbons and Roberts (2013).

5. More generally, reputation can be an important incentive mechanism when the quality of a good is intangible, as in the case of experience goods.

6. This is a modified version of the multi-tasking argument of Holmström and Milgrom (1991).

7. See Ortmann (1996) for a discussion.

8. Terms like public benefit corporations (Shiller, 2012) or B Corporation (Reiser, 2010), social enterprise (Dees, 1998, Bornstein, 2004), social business (Yunus, 2007), and community interest company (Reiser, 2010) are part of an emerging lexicon, but all stand for somewhat different organizational forms.

9. See Reiser (2010) for a discussion from a law and economics perspective. The legal framework for hybrid organizations is evolving, and there are many unresolved questions. For example, as Culley and Horwitz (2015) note, a key question focuses on how to solve legal disputes that occur when profit making and social purpose conflict.

10. See Kristof (2007).

Bibliography

Besley, Timothy and Maitreesh Ghatak, [2005], "Competition and Incentives with Motivated Agents," *American Economic Review*, 95, 616–636.

Besley, Timothy and Maitreesh Ghatak, [2017a], "Profit with Purpose? A Theory of Social Enterprise," *American Economic Journal—Economic Policy*, 9(3), 19–58.

Besley, Timothy and Maitreesh Ghatak, [2017b], "Public-Private Partnership for the Provision of Public Goods: Theory and an Application to NGOs," *Research in Economics*, 71(2), 356–371.

Besley, Timothy and Maitreesh Ghatak, [2018], "Pro-social Motivation and Incentives," *Annual Reviews of Economics*, 10.

Bornstein, David, [2004], *How to Change the World: Social Entrepreneurs and the Power of New Ideas*, Oxford University Press.

Brolis, Olivier, [2017], "Do Social Enterprises Attract Workers Who Are More pro-Socially Motivated than Their Counterparts in for-Profit Organizations to Perform Low-Skilled Jobs?" *International Journal of Human Resource Management*, 1–19.

Coase, Ronald, [1960], "The Problem of Social Cost," *Journal of Law and Economics*, 3(1), 1–44.

Culley, Rachel and Jill R. Horwitz, [2015], "Profits v. Purpose: Hybrid Companies and the Charitable Dollar," in Edward A. Parson (ed.) *A Subtle Balance: Expertise, Evidence, and Democracy in Public Policy and Governance, 1970–2010*, McGill-Queens University Press.

Dees, J. Gregory, [1998], "The Meaning of Social Entrepreneurship," available at www.caseatduke.org/documents/dees_sedef.pdf

Friedman, Milton, [1970], "The Social Responsibility of Business is to Increase its Profits," *The New York Times Magazine*, September 13, 1970, available at www.colorado.edu/studentgroups/libertarians/issues/friedman-soc-resp-business.html

Gibbons, Robert and John Roberts, [2013], *Handbook of Organizational Economics*, Princeton University Press.

Glaeser, Edward and Andrei Shleifer, [2001], "Not-for-profit Entrepreneurs," *Journal of Public Economics*, 81, 99–115.

Handy, Femida [1995], "Reputation as Collateral: An Economic Analysis of the Role of Trustees of Nonprofits," *Nonprofit and Voluntary Sector Quarterly*, 24(4), 293–305.

Handy, Femida, Laurie Mook, Jorge Ginieniewicz, and Jack Quarter, [2007], "The Moral High Ground: Perceptions of Wage Differentials Among Executive Directors of Canadian Nonprofits," *The Philanthropist*, 20(2), 109–127.

Hansmann, Henry, [1980], "The Role of Nonprofit Enterprise," *Yale Law Journal*, 89, 835–901.

Hansmann, Henry, [1987], "Economic Theories of Nonprofit Organization," in W.W. Powell (ed.) *The Nonprofit Sector*, Yale University Press.

Holmström, Bengt and Paul Milgrom, [1991], "Multi-task Principal-Agent Analyses: Incentive Contracts, Asset Ownership, and Job Design," *Journal of Law, Economics and Organization*, 7, 24–52.

Katz, Robert A. and Antony Page, [2010], "The Role of Social Enterprise," *Vermont Law Review*, 35, 59–103.

Kristof, Nicholas, [2007], "Do-Gooders With Spreadsheets," *New York Times*, January 30.

Levin, Jonathan and Steven Tadelis, [2005], "Profit Sharing and the Role of Professional Partnerships," *The Quarterly Journal of Economics*, 120(1), 131–171.

Martin, Roger L. and Sally Osberg, [2007], "Social Entrepreneurship: The Case for Definition," *Stanford Social Innovation Review*, Spring, 29–39.

Ortmann, Andreas, [1996], "Modern Economic Theory and the Study of Nonprofit Organizations: Why the Twain Shall Meet," *Nonprofit and Voluntary Sector Quarterly*, 25(4), 470–484.

Page, Antony and Robert A. Katz, [2012], "The Truth About Ben and Jerry's," *Stanford Social Innovation Review*, 10, 1–10.

Porter, Michael E. and Mark R. Kramer, [2011], "Shared Value," *Harvard Business Review*, January/February 62–77.

Preston, A.E., [1989], "The Nonprofit Worker in a For-Profit World," *Journal of Labor Economics*, 7, 438–463.

Reiser, Dana Brakman, [2010], "Blended Enterprise and the Dual Mission Dilemma," *Vermont Law Review*, 35, 105–116.

Serra, Danila, Pieter Serneels, and Abigail Barr, [2011], "Intrinsic Motivations and the Non-Profit Health Sector: Evidence from Ethiopia." *Personality and Individual Differences,* 51(3), 309–314.

Shiller, Robert, [2012], *Finance and the Good Society*, Princeton University Press.

Weisbrod, B.A., [1988], *The Nonprofit Economy*, Harvard University Press.

Werker, Eric and Faisal Z. Ahmed, [2008], "What Do Nongovernmental Organizations Do?," *Journal of Economic Perspectives*, 22(2), 73–92.

Yunus, Muhammad, [2007], *Creating a World Without Poverty: Social Business and the Future of Capitalism*, New York: Public Affairs.

Yunus, Muhammad, [2011], "Sacrificing Microcredit for Megaprofits," *New York Times*, January 14, 2011.

PART VI

POLITICAL THEORIES OF THE NONPROFIT SECTOR

In comparison with the economists and sociologists, political scientists were relatively slow to develop an interest in the nonprofit sector, and it is difficult to find a serious attempt at a political theory of the nonprofit sector before the mid-1980s.[1] Most of the early political theories of the nonprofit sector focused on explanations and rationales for nonprofits influencing public policy and changes in public policy concerning economic dimensions of the sector such as tax exemption and tax deductible contributions (see Part IV), Unrelated Business Income Tax (UBIT), competition with businesses (see Part IX), restrictions on private foundations, and initiated referendums that have attempted to eliminate tax exemption for religious organizations.

James Douglas was the standout pioneer in articulating theories about the relationships among nonprofit organizations and democratic systems of government.[2] Douglas articulated a political theory of nonprofit organizations that used a market model of democracy. Governments would deliver the services desired by the majority leaving the less desired or more controversial services desired by the minority to nonprofit organizations. Nonprofits also provided the gathering places for collective political action for the mobilization of disadvantaged or disgruntled constituencies[3] and as an "expression of the diversity of commitments in a pluralist society."[4] Individuals learned long ago that they do not have the ability to influence changes in public policy. They need collective voices, staying power, and political skills. Nonprofit organizations are where most of this happens.

In the 2010s and 2020s, nonprofit organizations have been drawing the interest of more political scientists for a variety of important practical reasons that can benefit from scholarly inquiry, including for example:

- INGOs attempting to influence politics and governance in countries around the globe (Parts III and X).
- NGOs increasingly becoming involved in the governance processes of nations, through partnerships (Part IX) as well as through advocacy (Part X).
- Political Action Committees (PACs) that collect and distribute huge sums to candidates and issues are registering and filing as 501(c)(4) organizations (instead of as 527 organizations—Parts II and IV).
- The nonprofit sector's role in the development of future community political leaders and civil society more generally—trust, and strengthening of social networks in communities—emerging as community political issues that had been primarily a "community issue" and thus mostly

 DOI: 10.4324/9780367696559-24

the interest of sociologists[5] (Part VII) as they relate to civil society, trust, friendships, and the strengthening of social networks.

Therefore, political scientists internationally and domestically have become notably more interested in nonprofit organizations during the 2010s and early 2020s because of their expanding influence on politics and governance and because of governments' efforts to control their activities and influence.

Contributions to Collaborative Governance and to a Democratic Form of Government

It is important to consider the many ways organizations in the nonprofit sector help strengthen collaborative governance and a democratic system of government. Not all nonprofits make these types of contributions to a society, but many do. These contributions provide the foundation and the context for the political theories of the sector.[6]

Nonprofit organizations prepare citizens for participation in democratic institutions and processes or *collaborative governance*, especially nonprofit organizations that use volunteers.[7] It has long been assumed that citizenship skills are learned and tested by volunteering with nonprofit organizations, and credentials are built which are needed to be competitive for elected and appointed leadership positions in public organizations.[8] If this is a valid assumption, then nonprofit organizations are major contributors to developing citizenship and maintaining our democratic system of government.[9]

> 'Citizenship' is a broad umbrella term. . . . According to the most expansive definition it includes participation in various forms of democratic politics: voting, working in political campaigns, contacting public officials, serving on local government boards, attending demonstrations, and the like preferences for political involvement and feelings of attachment to community.[10]

These contributions to citizenship and politics by nonprofit organizations are of particular importance for individuals who have been excluded from educational and occupational opportunities to build citizenship/political skills, perhaps because of their gender or ethnic backgrounds.

Collaborative governance requires citizens who have *community leadership* skills that often are developed and sharpened through participation on a nonprofit organization's board of trustees or as a program volunteer. Nonprofit organizations are where "linking social capital" and "bonding social capital" are created, often spanning different ethnic and socioeconomic groups.[11] By volunteering and serving on boards of trustees, citizens engage with and become committed to others and to their communities.[12] For example as we state in the introduction to Part VII:

> as volunteers associate at regular meetings of a board of trustees to coordinate a neighborhood watch program or to help the local PTA offer children a safe Halloween experience . . . [both] are creating social capital. . . . The benefits of social capital come later to the participating individuals, to the networks to which they belong, and to the community—as a side effect of their associations.

In the United States and other democratic nations, governments at all levels represent the majority while also attempting to protect the rights of the minority. A number of nonprofits represent people and groups who may hold unpopular views that tend to be ignored or opposed by the majority and therefore may not receive government attention.[13] It often falls to nonprofit organizations to carry the fight for the protection of minority interests through legislative processes and government administrative systems. The ACLU, Doctors for Clean Air, Mothers Against Drunk Driving, the AIDS foundations, state alliances for the mentally ill, and the Nature Conservancy are good examples. In a pluralistic society, "there is not one will of the people but several, sometimes conflicting wills.[14] Nonprofit organizations often give voice to under-represented views.

Also, many nonprofit organizations assist with the integration and reintegration of groups into society. Immigrants, political refugees, recovering substance abusers, and prison parolees often receive myriad support services from nonprofit organizations that help them become functioning citizens.[15]

Developing Community Leaders

Community leadership differs in many ways from leadership at work. Community leadership depends on *collaborative leadership* and *horizontal leadership*[16]—leadership that crosses boundaries among organizations that are working together for a common, shared, public good goal. In community leadership, leadership is usually collaborative and shared because no one is completely in charge. At times, it may be necessary for participants in a community initiative to place the good of the community ahead of one's own organization.[17]

> Collaborative leadership focuses on power sharing among organizations (e.g., Crosby and Bryson 2010; Newell, Reeher, and Ronayne 2012). It deemphasizes the roles of both leaders and followers in order to emphasize the needs of the network, system, environment, or community, resulting in a collaborative style (Jackson and Stainsby 2000; Kettl 2006). Collaborative theory emphasizes the need to support the health of communities and the environment for the good of all.[18]

Thus, community leadership has emerged as a field of study and practice of high importance to the nonprofit sector. It draws on theories from many fields, including political science, organizational communication, and inter-organizational theory.[19] If nonprofit organizations do develop community leadership skills, then nonprofit organizations are indeed major contributors to the future of a democratic system of government. Although this list is far from complete, *community leadership* requires—

- *Passion*—for causes such as social justice.
- *Vision and creativity*—the ability to envision do-able solutions to community problems and ways to capitalize on opportunities.
- *Values*—to know deep down inside one's self what is worth fighting for (or against).
- *A well-developed personal ethics code*—to understand and act upon what is right for the community—and for sub-populations within the community.
- *Spirit*—to conceive of a "greater good" that goes beyond the self-interests of family, friends and associates.
- *Energy and enthusiasm*—because community leadership consumes time and requires energy, patience, fortitude, frustration tolerance, and diplomacy.
- *The ability to acquire and use power and influence through networks*—without resorting to authority.
- *Courage*—the willingness to take risks while leading that could bring harm to one's self, family, and friends. Community leadership is not for cowards.

> To lead is to live dangerously because when leadership counts, when you lead people through difficult change, you challenge what people hold dear—their daily habits, tools, loyalties, and ways of thinking—with nothing more to offer perhaps than a possibility. . . . People push back when you disturb the personal and institutional equilibrium they know.[20]

Perhaps the most important aspect of *community leadership* that differentiates it from intra-organizational leadership and makes it difficult to measure is that it requires an understanding of what someone truly stands for, what a person cares enough about to be willing to give up time with family and on the job, and what is important enough to one's personal being to stand up and take personal risks. Without this understanding, a person lacks authenticity, perseverance, and the courage to take risks. Others will sense and will not follow. Why should they when their participation is voluntary? But, when these understandings are in alignment and an individual makes the commitment to lead with passion and to be guided by shared, strong, clear values, others will follow. Obviously not everyone will follow, but those who share the passion and values and are convinced of the vision will. When people agree to follow another in building community, *community leadership* is happening. When community leadership is happening, *shared governance* is also.

Keep in mind that it is in nonprofit organizations where people are likely to gather who share hopes, worries, values, passions, and dreams. Nonprofits are where a passionate citizen is most likely to find others who are willing to commit time and energy to improve their community—to follow or to join in shared community leadership.

Politically Active Nonprofit Organizations

Although 501(c)(3) nonprofit organizations are limited in their ability to participate in political activity, other types of nonprofits are permitted to do so with considerable flexibility. The two types of politically active nonprofit organizations that have received considerable public and media attention in recent years are the 527 *political organizations* and 501(c)(4) *social welfare organizations*. These two types of organization are tax exempt but contributions to them are not deductible.

> Entities organized under section 527 of the tax code are considered "political organizations," defined generally as a party, committee or association that is organized and operated primarily for the purpose of influencing the selection, nomination or appointment of any individual to any federal, state or local public office, or office in a political organization.[21]

Most political parties, political committees, and "Super PACs" (Political Action Committees) at all levels of government used to be 527 organizations. Although 527s may not directly advocate for particular candidates and may not collaborate with a candidate's campaign organization, they can engage in issue advocacy that often is difficult to separate from candidates' advertisements. 527s do not have maximum contribution or spending limits. They must, however, disclose their donors, register with the IRS, and file reports of contributions and expenses.[22] The IRS established the 527 designation for the specific purpose of allowing political organizations to solicit funds for political purposes. Because 527s must disclose their donors, however, a number of Super PACs have elected to file instead as 501(c)(4) "social welfare organizations."

501(c)(4) organizations are "civic leagues or organizations not organized for profit but operate exclusively for the promotion of social welfare."[23] 501(c)(4) nonprofits are allowed to raise unlimited amounts of contributions and are not required to disclose their donors. 501(c)(4) organizations that engage in political activity without being required to disclose their donors are labeled *action organizations.*

> Seeking legislation germane to the organization's programs is a permissible means of attaining social welfare purposes. Thus, a section 501(c)(4) social welfare organization may further its exempt purposes through lobbying as its sole or primary activity without jeopardizing its exempt status.[24]

The United States Supreme Court's 2010 ruling in *Citizens United* has jettisoned 527s—and 501(c)(4)s—into the center of political life and the public's eye.

> In 2010, the Supreme Court's landmark "Citizens United" decision cleared the way for corporations and labor unions to raise and spend unlimited sums of money, and register for tax-exempt status under the section 501(c)(4) designation. Applications [for 501(c)(4) designations] more than doubled following the High Court's ruling.[25]
>
> Crossroads GPS, the conservative group co-founded by Karl Rove is one well-known example. On the other end of the political spectrum is Organizing for Action, which is what President [Barack] Obama's campaign operation turned into after the 2012 election. Often, organizations will have multiple arms, including a nonprofit and a super PAC. American Crossroads, for example, is a super PAC affiliated with Crossroads GPS.[26]

The *Citizens United* decision opened the door for an enormous influx of money into the election process, raising questions about donor disclosure and political activities by tax-exempt organizations. "It gave corporations and unions the green light to spend unlimited sums on ads and other political tools, calling for the election or defeat of individual candidates."[27] Why should huge sums of primarily corporation and union donations to support political activity benefit from tax protection? The Supreme Court ruled, in effect, that political spending is a form of protected speech under the First Amendment to the U.S. Constitution and cannot be limited.

The existence of 527 and 501(c)(4) organizations and the Court's "money is speech and thus restrictions on contributions would be a denial of free speech" decision in *Citizens United* have placed the nonprofit sector in the eye of an enormous controversy about the influence money can have in elections and the role of tax exempt nonprofit organizations as major political fund-raising organizations. Do 527s and 501(c)(4) organizations enhance our democratic system of government by facilitating a form of free speech as they raise and distribute funds, or are they undermining our representative democracy by enhancing the ability of large corporations and unions to gain disproportionate influence with elected and appointed public officials?

INGOs and NGOs as Political Actors

As we discussed in the introduction to Part III, the primary functions of most INGOs are to transfer resources from more developed countries to less developed countries for humanitarian assistance, development assistance, and/or recovery and rehabilitation purposes; or to advocate. A few well-known examples of assistance-type INGOs include Save the Children International, Oxfam International, Médecins San Frontières, and CARE International. Although the primary means by which INGOs attempt to influence governments is through advocacy, humanitarian assistance and development assistance also can be strategies for political influence and therefore are sometimes resisted by governments. When the extremely severe Cyclone Nargis struck Myanmar in May 2008, relief efforts were hampered by the military government initially refusing international assistance fearing political interference until India successfully persuaded officials to allow outside help.[28] It was not until the massive 2008 Sichuan earthquake that the government of China was willing to open its doors to disaster assistance from INGOs. Development assistance can be perceived as equally politically intrusive. See Abby Stoddard's reading, "International Assistance," in Part III for explanations and examples.

Advocacy is, however, the primary way that INGOs are active politically within nations. They attempt to create political and economic pressure on governments to change policies and practices, particularly practices involving human rights and protection of the environment. Although these may not sound particularly "political," they are. Public advocacy in these two areas give countries "black eyes" across the globe and are often in opposition to practices of industries that reduce costs and are important to local economies.

A few human rights examples include China reportedly holding thousands of Muslim Uighurs in re-education camps, and sex trafficking and slavery in most countries around the globe. Protecting the environment often comes into direct conflict with short-term economic development. Common economic development advocacy examples include the widely publicized protection of Canadian seals by limiting hunts, reducing industrial carbon emissions especially in developing countries, industrial safety in Bangladesh (also a human rights issue), and dumping of toxic waste in lakes, rivers, and oceans. Protecting the environment may hurt nations' economies in the short term and therefore are often vigorously opposed by industries, especially in lesser developed countries. Examples of INGOs that predominantly advocate include Amnesty International, Human Rights Watch, Free Tibet, Greenpeace, and World Wildlife Federation. Some INGOs engage in both assistance and advocacy.

Indigenous NGOs are active politically if the government permits. Many governments do, but many do not.[29] As in the U.S., attempts to influence public policy are a primary reason why NGOs exist: for example, the Council of German Women, DCI-France, Friends (in Sweden), CARE India, and the Zimbabwe Human Rights NGO Forum. We urge you to read Part X, especially Benjamin L. Reid and Robert Pekkanen's revised and updated reading, "Organizations That Straddle the State-Society Divide: Illuminating Blind Spots of Existing Paradigms."

Readings Reprinted in Part VI

Elisabeth S. Clemens's "The Constitution of Citizens: Political Theories of Nonprofit Organizations," which is reprinted here, wrestles with an array of intriguing political issues including, notably, the validity of Douglas's[30] theories about nonprofit organizations allowing for the provision of services to minorities that do not have the support of the majority, and how nonprofit associations open doors to political participation and influence for persons with different backgrounds. Clements's chapter is centered on a series of questions:

> Do voluntary associations and nonprofit organizations generate greater democratic participation? Are these organizational forms effective and legitimate vehicles for political engagement? Does reliance on or collaboration with nonprofits improve the efficiency of publicly funded services or generate innovative programs and new solutions to policy problems? In sum, are voluntary associations and nonprofit organizations a necessary or even desirable component of democratic politics?

In answering these questions, Clements considers nonprofit organizations as a crucial means for political socialization and social capital development; political engagement; advancing the politics of partnership, participatory governance and voluntarism; increasing autonomy from formal political institutions, broadening connections to social networks, and expanding orientations to the values of flexibility and diversity.

In "The Influence of Nonprofit Organizations on the Political Environment," Kelly LeRoux and Mary K. Feeney argue that nonprofit organizations are important fixtures in the political landscape. They describe and explain the many ways in which nonprofit organizations participate in politics and policy-making. These include, for example, legal limitations on public charities in the political arena, different types of nonprofit organizations that participate in the political arena and how they influence policy-making; activities and strategies nonprofits use in political mobilization, political representation role activities and strategies; and ways in which nonprofit organizations provide political education for citizens and elected and appointed officials.

The rules and roles are completely different for 501(c)3 public charities than for lobbying groups and interest groups. Therefore, it is common for nonprofits that see the need to be involved in politics and policy-making to create multiple nonprofit organizations under one corporate umbrella.

> One common arrangement is to have a 501(c)3, a related 501(c)4, a connected Political Action Committee, and a 527 organization. . . . Although organizations that choose a complex corporate structure such as this cannot actually combine or share day-to-day operations, they can have overlapping members on their boards of directors, share advocacy plans, collaborate on strategies of action, and manage their resources in ways that allow for maximizing their political goals.

Michal Almog-Bar, in "Insider Status and Outsider Tactics: Advocacy Tactics of Human Service Nonprofits in the Age of New Public Governance," presents findings from a study on the advocacy tactics of 47 nonprofit human service organizations (NPHSOs) in Israel, focusing on ways that partnership policies affect their activities. He concludes that this age of New Public Governance has increased governmental funding and contracting with nonprofits which in turn has increased opportunities for the NPHSOs to influence public policy. Interestingly, Almog-Bar also concludes that cooperative "insider" advocacy tactics tend to be more effective than more confrontational "external" tactics. They can effectively utilize more confrontational approaches only after establishing insider status.

Notes

1. James Douglas, *Why Charity?* (Beverly Hills, CA: Sage, 1983); and James Douglas, "Political Theories of Nonprofit Organization," in *The Nonprofit Sector: A Research Handbook*, ed., Walter W. Powell (New Haven: Yale University Press, 1987), 43–53.

2. Douglas, "Political Theories of Nonprofit Organizations." 43–53.

3. Elisabeth S. Clemens, "The Constitution of Citizens: Political Theories of Nonprofit Organizations," in *The Nonprofit Sector: A Research Handbook*, 2nd ed., ed., Walter W. Powell and Richard Steinberg (New Haven, CT: Yale University Press, 2006), 207–220, 208 (reprinted in this part); see also Kathleen D. McCarthy, *American Creed: Philanthropy and the Rise of Civil Society, 1700–1865* (Chicago, IL: University of Chicago Press, 2003).

4. Elisabeth S. Clemens, "The Constitution of Citizens: Political Theories of Nonprofit Organizations" (2006): 208. Reprinted in this part.

5. Meghan Elizabeth Kallman and Terry Nichols Clark, *The Third Sector: Community Organizations, NGOs, and Nonprofits* (Urbana, IL: University of Illinois Press, 2016).

6. Parts of this section are adapted from Christopher A. Simon, Melissa Yack, and J. Steven Ott, "MPA Program Partnerships with Nonprofit Organizations: Benefits to MPA Programs, MPA Students and Graduates, Nonprofit Organizations, and Communities," *Journal of Public Affairs Education*, 19 (2013), 355–374.

7. Kelly LeRoux, "Nonprofits as Civic Intermediaries: The Role of Community-based Organizations in Promoting Political Participation," *Urban Affairs Review*, 42 (2007), 410–422; Robert D. Putnam, *Bowling Alone: The Collapse and Revival of American Community* (New York: Simon & Schuster, 2000).

8. Michael Edwards, *Civil Society*, 2nd ed. (Cambridge, UK: Polity Press, 2009); Rosemarie Hunter, Sarah Munro, Linda Dunn, and K. Olson, "Bridging University and Community: The Power of Collaborative Partnerships for Social Change," in *Public Universities and Regional Development*, ed., Kathryn Mohrman, Jian Shi, Sharon E. Feinblatt, and King W. Chow (Chengdu, China: Sichuan University Press, 2009), 289–310.

9. Ronald A. Heifetz and Marty Linsky, *Leadership on the Line: Staying Alive Through the Dangers of Leading* (Boston, MA: Harvard Business School Press, 2002).

10. Marc A. Musick and John Wilson. 2008. "Citizenship and Prosocial Behavior," in Musick and Wilson, *Volunteers: A Social Profile*. Bloomington: Indiana University Press.

11. Jo Anne Schneider, "Organizational Social Capital and Nonprofits," *Nonprofit and Voluntary Sector Quarterly*, 38 (2009), 643–661.

12. Michael Edwards, *Civil Society*, 2nd ed.; Joanne Schneider, "Organizational Social Capital and Nonprofits," reprinted in Part VI of this volume.

13. Douglas, "Political Theories of Nonprofit Organizations." 43–53.

14. Douglas, "Political Theories of Nonprofit Organizations."

15. Alfreda P. Inglehart and Rosina M. Becerra, *Social Services and the Ethnic Community: History and Analysis*, 2nd ed. (Long Grove, IL: Waveland Press, 2011).

16. Also known as facilitative leadership, integral leadership and catalytic leadership. Montgomery Van Wart, "Lessons from Leadership Theory and the Contemporary Challenges of Leaders," *Public Administration Review*, 73 (2013), 553–565.

17. John Kania and Mark Kramer, "Collective Impact," *Stanford Social Innovation Review*, Winter 2011. https://ssir.org/articles/entry/collective_impact. And John Kramer and Mark Kramer, "Embracing Emergence: How Collective Impact Addresses Complexity," *Stanford Social Innovation Review*, January 2013. https://ssir. org/articles/entry/social_progress_through_collective_impact#. See also, William A. Clark and Daniel Gast (Eds.), *Collaborative Parish Leadership: Contexts, Models Theology* (New York: Lexington Books, 2018), and Gilbert Steil, *The Collaboration Response: Eight Axioms that Elicit Collaborative Action for a Whole Organization, a Whole Community, a Whole Society* (Scotts Valley, CA: CreateSpace Independent Publishing Platform, 2018).

18. Van Wart, "Lessons from Leadership Theory and the Contemporary Challenges of Leaders," p. 559.

19. See Chapter 8, "Theories of Organizations and Environments," and Chapter 9, "Theories of Organizations and Societies," in *Classics of Organization Theory*, 8th ed., ed. Jay M. Shafritz, J. Steven Ott, and Yong Suk Jang (Boston: Wadsworth/Cengage Books, 2015).

20. Ronald A. Heifetz and Marty Linsky, *Leadership on the Line: Staying Alive Through the Dangers of Leading*: 2.

21. Federal Election Commission, *Quick Answers to General Questions*. www.fec.gov/ans/answers_general.shtml#527 Also see the Internal Revenue Service, "Tax Information for Political Organizations," www.irs.gov/Charities-&-Non-Profits/Political-Organizations

22. Center for Public Integrity, *527 Frequently Asked Questions*. http://projects.publicintegrity.org/527/default.aspx?act=faq#5

23. U.S. Internal Revenue Service, "Types of Organizations Exempt under Section 501(c)(4)." www.irs.gov/Charities-&-Non-Profits/Other-Non-Profits/Types-of-Organizations-Exempt-under-Section-501%28c%29%284%29

Local associations of employers and in some cases homeowners associations and volunteer fire companies may be included under section 501(c)(4).

24. U.S. Internal Revenue Service, "Action Organizations." www.irs.gov/Charities-&-Non-Profits/Action-Organizations

25. Sean Sullivan, "What Is a 501(c)(4), Anyway?" *Washington Post*, May 13, 2013. www.washingtonpost.com/blogs/the-fix/wp/2013/05/13/what-is-a-501c4-anyway/

26. Sullivan, Sean, "What Is a 501(c)(4), Anyway?"

27. John Dunbar, "The 'Citizens United' Decision and Why It Matters: Nonprofits or Political Parties?" *The Center for Public Integrity*, October 18, 2012. www.publicintegrity.org/2012/10/18/11527/citizens-united-decision-and-why-it-matters?

28. *The Guardian*, Burmese regime blocked international aid to cyclone victims, report says. February 27, 2009. www.theguardian.com/world/2009/feb/27/regime-blocked-aid-to-burma-cyclone-victims

29. Francesco Cavatorta, Civil Society Activism under Authoritarian Constraints. In *Civil Society Activism under Authoritarian Rule*, ed. Francesco Cavatorta (Abington: Routledge, 2013), 1–12.

30. Douglas, "Political Theories of Nonprofit Organizations."

Bibliography

Almog-Bar, Michal. "Insider Status and Outsider Tactics: Advocacy Tactics of Human Service Nonprofits in the Age of New Public Governance." *Nonprofit Policy Forum*, 8(4) (2018), 411–428.

Anheier, Helmut K. *Nonprofit Organizations: Theory, Management, Policy*, 2nd ed. (Abingdon: Routledge, 2014).

Boris, Elizabeth T., and C. Eugene Steuerle, eds. *Nonprofits & Government: Collaboration & Conflict*, 3rd ed. (Washington, DC: Urban Institute Press, 2017).

Bryson, John M., Barbara C. Crosby, and Laura Bloomberg, eds. *Creating Public Value in Practice: Advancing the Common Good in a Multi-Sector, Shared-Power, No-One-Wholly-in Charge World* (London and New York: CRC Press, 2015).

Cavatorta, Francesco. "Civil Society Activism under Authoritarian Constraints." In Francesco Cavatorta, ed., *Civil Society Activism under Authoritarian Rule* (Abington: Routledge, 2013), 1–12.

Clark, William A., and Daniel Gast, eds. *Collaborative Parish Leadership: Contexts, Models Theology* (New York: Lexington Books, 2018).

Clemens, Elisabeth S. "The Constitution of Citizens: Political Theories of Nonprofit Organizations." In Walter W. Powell and Richard Steinberg, eds., *The Nonprofit Sector: A Research Handbook*, 2nd ed., 207–220 (New Haven, CT: Yale University Press, 2006).

———. "Nonprofits as Boundary Markers: The Politics of Choice, Mobilization, and Arbitrage." In Walter W. Powell and Patricia Bromley, eds., *The Nonprofit Sector: A Research Handbook*, 3rd ed., 192–207 (Stanford, CA: Stanford University Press, 2020).

Crosby, Barbara C., and John M. Bryson. *Leadership for the Common Good: Tackling Public Problems in a Shared-Power World* (San Francisco: Jossey-Bass/Wiley, 2005).

Dahl, Robert A. *Dilemmas of Pluralist Democracy* (New Haven, CT: Yale University Press, 1982).

Douglas, James. "Political Theories of Nonprofit Organization." In Walter W. Powell, ed., *The Nonprofit Sector: A Research Handbook*, 43–53 (New Haven, CT: Yale University Press, 1987).

Dunbar, John. "The 'Citizens United; Decision and Why It Matters: Nonprofits or Political Parties?" *The Center for Public Integrity*, October 18, 2012. www.publicintegrity.org/2012/10/18/11527/citizens-united-decision-and-why-it-matters

Edwards, Michael. *Civil Society*, 2nd ed. (Cambridge: Polity Press, 2009), 3rd ed., 2014.

Glasius, Marlies. "Dissident Writings as Political Theory on Civil Society and Democracy." In Francesco Cavatorta, ed., *Civil Society Activism under Authoritarian Rule: A Comparative Perspective*, 57–72 (Abington: Routledge, 2013).

Grønbjerg, Kirsten A., and Lester M. Salamon. "Devolution, Marketization, and the Changing Shape of Government-Nonprofit Relations." In Lester M. Salamon, ed., *The State of Nonprofit America*, 2nd ed., 549–586 (Washington, DC: Brookings Institution Press, 2012).

Heifetz, Ronald A., and Marty Linsky. *Leadership on the Line: Staying Alive Through the Dangers of Leading* (Boston, MA: Harvard Business School Press, 2002).

Inglehart, Alfreda P., and Rosina M. Becerra. *Social Services and the Ethnic Community: History and Analysis*, 2nd ed. (Long Grove, IL: Waveland Press, 2011).

Kallman, Meghan Elizabeth, and Terry Nichols Clark. *The Third Sector: Community Organizations, NGOs, and Nonprofits* (Urbana, IL: University of Illinois Press, 2016).

Kramer, John, and Mark Kramer. "Collective Impact." *Stanford Social Innovation Review*, Winter 2011. https://ssir.org/articles/entry/collective_impact

——. "Embracing Emergence: How Collective Impact Addresses Complexity." *Stanford Social Innovation Review*, January 2013. https://ssir.org/articles/entry/social_progress_through_collective_impact#

Lechterman, Ted, and Rob Reich. "Political Theory and the Nonprofit Sector." In Walter W. Powell and Patricia Bromley, eds., *The Nonprofit Sector: A Research Handbook*, 3rd ed., 171–191 (Stanford, CA: Stanford University Press, 2020).

LeRoux, Kelly. "Nonprofits as Civic Intermediaries: The Role of Community-based Organizations in Promoting Political Participation." *Urban Affairs Review*, 42 (2007), 410–422.

——, and Mary K. Feeney. "The Influence of Nonprofit Organizations on the Political Environment." In K. LeRoux and M. K. Feeney, eds., *Nonprofit Organizations and Civil Society in the United States* (New York: Routledge, 2015).

Levine, Peter. *The Future of Democracy: Developing the Next Generation of American Citizens* (Medford, MA: Tufts University Press, 2007).

Lundåsen, Susanne Wallman. "Democratic Values and Civic Engagement of Local Voluntary Associations." *Nonprofit Management & Leadership*, 24 (2014), 263–283.

Musick, Marc A., and John Wilson. *Volunteers: A Social Profile* (Bloomington, IN: Indiana University Press, 2008).

Newell, Terry, Grant Reeher, and Peter Ronayne. *The Trusted Leader: Building the Relationship that Makes Government Work*, 2nd ed. (Washington, DC: CQ Press, 2012).

Phillips, Susan D., and Steven Rathgeb Smith, eds. *Governance and Regulation in the Third Sector: International Perspectives* (New York: Routledge, 2011).

Powell, Walter W., and Patricia Bromley, eds. *The Nonprofit Sector: A Research Handbook*, 3rd ed. (Stanford, CA: Stanford University Press, 2020).

Putnam, Robert D. *Bowling Alone: Revised and Updated: The Collapse and Revival of American Community* (New York: Simon & Schuster, 2021).

Shafritz, Jay M., J. Steven Ott, and Yong Suk Jang, eds. *Classics of Organization Theory*, 8th ed. (Boston: Wadsworth/Cengage Books, 2015).

Simon, Christopher A., Melissa Yack, and J. Steven Ott. "MPA Program Partnerships with Nonprofit Organizations: Benefits to MPA Programs, MPA Students and Graduates, Nonprofit Organizations, and Communities." *Journal of Public Affairs Education*, 19 (2013): 355–374.

Skocpol, Theda. *Diminished Democracy: From Membership to Management in American Civic Life* (Norman, OK: University of Oklahoma Press, 2003).

Smith, Steven Rathgeb. "Nonprofits and Public Administration: Reconciling Performance Management and Citizen Engagement." *American Review of Public Administration*, 40(2) (2010), 129–152.

Steil, Gilbert. *The Collaboration Response: Eight Axioms that Elicit Collaborative Action for a Whole Organization, a Whole Community, a Whole Society* (Scotts Valley, CA: CreateSpace Independent Publishing Platform, 2018.)

Sullivan, Sean. "What Is a 501(c)(4), Anyway?" *Washington Post*, May 13, 2013. www.washingtonpost.com/blogs/the-fix/wp/2013/05/13/what-is-a-501c4-anyway/

U. S. Federal Election Commission. *Quick Answers to General Questions*. www.fec.gov/ans/answers_general.shtml#527

U.S. Internal Revenue Service. "Action Organizations." www.irs.gov/Charities-&-Non-Profits/Action-Organizations

———. "Tax Information for Political Organizations." www.irs.gov/Charities-&-Non-Profits/Political-Organizations

———. *Types of Organizations Exempt under Section 501(c)(4)*. www.irs.gov/Charities-&-Non-Profits/Other-Non-Profits/Types-of-Organizations-Exempt-under-Section-501%28c%29%284%29

Van Wart, Montgomery. "Lessons from Leadership Theory and the Contemporary Challenges of Leaders." *Public Administration Review*, 73 (2013), 553–565.

Walzer, Michael. *Spheres of Justice: A Defense of Pluralism and Equality* (New York: Basic Books, 1983).

Warren, Mark R. *Dry Bones Rattling: Community Building to Revitalize American Democracy* (Princeton, NJ: Princeton University Press, 2001).

Young, Dennis R. "Complementary, Supplementary, or Adversarial? Nonprofit-Government Relations." In *Nonprofits & Government: Collaboration & Conflict*, eds. Elizabeth T. Boris and C. Eugene Steuerle, 37–80 (Washington, DC: Urban Institute Press, 2006).

The Constitution of Citizens: Political Theories of Nonprofit Organizations

Elisabeth S. Clemens

From the perspective of political theory, associations and organizations are problematic as well as potent. Incorporated or not, associations are potential sites and resources for political activity outside of formal political institutions. Whether or not they are operated for profit, corporations are political creations (Novak 2001). These creations are endowed with rights—of legal existence and property holding—but are not strictly accountable to the sovereigns or legislatures that bestow these rights.[1] Such organizations are political constructions but are not part of the formal political system.

To date, one theory of politics has claimed pride of place as *the* political theory of nonprofit organizations: a market model of democracy (following Buchanan and Tullock 1962; Dahl 1982; Olson 1971). As articulated by James Douglas (1987), this theory built on an image of individual citizens holding distinctive preferences for public services as well as votes (or opinions in polls) with which to express those preferences. Public services or goods that gain support from a majority of constituents will be provided by public agencies; those that are more controversial or preferred by only a minority will be provided by nonprofits (albeit often subsidized by public funds; see Salamon and Abramson 1982; Smith and Lipsky 1993, 27). This approach has been developed to explain patterns of public-private partnership; its core logic is consistent with both economic models of nonprofit organization (e.g., Weisbrod 1988) and demographic or "entrepreneurial" models (e.g., James 1987). Deploying the imagery of choice that is central to much of contemporary economics and political science (March and Olsen 1989), these arguments use the traits and preferences of citizens to explain the development of nonprofit sectors and the distribution of activities across states, markets, households, and the variously defined "third sector."

Market models of democracy, however, do not exhaust the field of political theory. A range of political theories and theories of state development make important claims about the role of nonprofit organizations and associations,

DOI: 10.4324/9780367696559-25

although their terminology may diverge from the conventions of nonprofit research. Most notably, political theories of nonprofit organizations are increasingly entwined with broad debates over civil society, social capital, and the rights of association within a liberal polity. Rather than assuming citizens with preferences already well defined, these approaches problematize the constitution of citizens and constituencies as well as their capacities for political action.

Tocqueville's classic *Democracy in America* (1835–1840) is a touchstone for an alternative vision in which associational activities are constitutive of citizens as actors, of preferences and interests, and of the capacity to make effective demands on government (Frumkin 2002, ch. 2). From this vantage point, associations are understood to generate a capacity for collective or political action that may be exercised as an extension of elite power (Hall 1992), as a vehicle for the mobilization of disadvantaged or disgruntled constituencies (Clemens 1997; McCarthy 2003), or as an expression of the diversity of commitments in a pluralist society (Walzer 1984). Despite their many differences, these arguments concur in viewing the role of associations and formal politics as complementing one another in a democratic polity.

As this line of argument has gained prominence through the "civic engagement" debates of the 1990s (Putnam 2000; Skocpol and Fiorina 1999), critical voices and cautions have multiplied. Not all participatory organizations sustain values consistent with democracy, nor are all voluntary associations or nonprofit organizations participatory in the degree assumed by many celebrations of Tocqueville (Chambers and Kopstein 2001; Eliasoph 1998; Gutmann 1998; Kaufman 2002; Skocpol 2003). In combination, transformations of government that increase the influence of organized groups (Crenson and Ginsberg 2002) and lower levels of participation within these groups (due to professionalization and formalization) may actually reverse the presumed relationship of associational participation

and democratic values, leading to extremism and gridlock (Fiorina 1999).

For political science and sociology, much of the recent interest in voluntary associations and nonprofit organizations has been fueled by these concerns with the "input" side of democracy: citizenship, participation, and influence. For theorists concerned with governmental services, however, different questions have generated interest in the relations of privately governed associations and public institutions. As with civic participation, these concerns have a Tocquevillian lineage, echoing his claim that the capacity for local citizens to solve problems through associated action forestalls the extension of government responsibility (Tocqueville 1969, 515). Whereas this may lead to an understanding of charities and nonprofit organizations as substitutes for government action (Douglas 1983), other arguments highlight complementarities and collaborations (Smith and Grønbjerg 2006). State expansion may take the form of borrowing capacity from nonprofit organizations (Smith and Lipsky 1993; Ullman 1998), or states may actively sponsor the formation and growth of nonprofit entities that then implement policy (Salamon 1987), accommodating to and potentially transforming the local communities in which they operate (Evans 1997; Schorr 1997). This line of argument illuminates another role for nonprofit organizations on the "input" side, as sources of experimentation (Douglas 1987), innovation (Frumkin 2002), and policy models that may then feed back into deliberations over future public programs (Dorf and Sabel 1998; Sirianni and Friedland 2001). Here too, however, there is a "dark side" variant of the argument. The increasing delivery of publicly funded programs through nonprofit organizations may obscure relationships of accountability, distort citizens' understandings of how tax revenues are spent, and allow governments to displace the risks of downsizing and policy shifts onto nongovernmental entities (Pierson 1994).

Even within the context of the advanced industrialized democracies and within the United States in particular, there are diverse and conflicting claims about the implications of nonprofit organizations and voluntary associations for the quality of democracy as well as for the efficacy of government. Whereas Douglas's initial formulation drew on market models of democracy to ask "why are some services provided by governments and others by nonprofit organizations?" these broader theoretical debates ask about the consequences for democracy of participation in voluntary associations or production through nonprofit organizations. The divergent arguments about the place of nonprofits and voluntary associations in democratic polities are increasingly relevant as these organizational models are exported to developing nations and formerly socialist states.

Basic questions lie at the core of these debates. Do voluntary associations and nonprofit organizations generate greater democratic participation? Are these organizational forms effective and legitimate vehicles for political engagement? Does reliance on or collaboration with nonprofits improve the efficiency of publicly funded services or generate innovative programs and new solutions to policy problems? In sum, are voluntary associations and nonprofit organizations a necessary or even desirable component of democratic polities? While eluding definitive answers thus far, these questions have fueled renewed attention to the complex social terrain that is neither purely market nor purely state.

Political Socialization and Social Capital

Much of the interest of political theory in associations and nonprofit organizations stems from the presumption that associations are, or should be, embodiments of the constitutional forms, organizational skills, and political virtues required by a liberal democracy.[2] Eagerly appropriating the mantle of Tocqueville, such arguments contend that a wide range of formal and informal associations socialize citizens for democratic participation (Fleischacker 1998; Putnam, Leonardi, and Nanetti 1993; Wuthnow 1991, 1998) or that this capacity for democratic socialization should guide the legal regulation of associations (for a critical discussion, see Rosenblum 1998a). Empirical studies lend support to the connection between internal democracy and individual commitment to associations (Knoke and Wood 1981). Nonpolitical voluntary associations—along with workplaces and religious organizations—are settings in which citizens may practice skills such as letter writing, planning meetings, and making speeches (Verba, Schlozman, and Brady 1995, 310–320).

Through a commitment to internal democratic governance, such associations ideally sustain a sphere of relative equality decoupled from the structures of privilege that organize other social domains (Walzer 1983). For such arguments, associations are foundational to democracy insofar as they are sites for the cultivation of democratic values and skills. This contention is captured by the argument's theoretical imagery: associations are "schools of citizenship."

Where associations are permitted and even encouraged, their capacity to generate political socialization appropriate for a democratic polity depends on a series of organizational features. As the legal framework for association developed in the United States, organizational constitutions often required democratic practices such as the election of officers; as associations were increasingly incorporated and regulated by state governments, these political arrangements were required for all but religious associations (on the "corporation sole," see Dane 1998) and benevolent corporations governed by appointed or self-perpetuating trustees. Material conditions also often encouraged participatory governance; low budgets, low reserves, and little or no professional staff tended to forestall the logic of Michels's "iron law of oligarchy." Instead, membership served as a political apprenticeship, instilling mastery of skills such as public speaking and the intricacies of Robert's Rules of Order (Doyle 1977). The widespread cultivation of these skills sustained the circulation of citizens through large voluntary associations.

Fueled by recent claims about the contributions of social capital to democracy (Putnam, Leonardi, and Nanetti 1993; Putnam 2000; for a critical review, see Portes 1998), a new wave of research is addressing the role of associations in political socialization. Historical overviews trace the decline of the participatory organizations that were central to the Tocquevillian imagery of American democracy.

Against the background of this large-scale shift in American civic life, considerable heterogeneity remains in the organizations in which individuals may become politically socialized. Many groups continue to provide opportunities for individuals to acquire civic skills, including, most obviously, organizations that are explicitly committed to participatory governance (Polletta 2002). Among adolescents, participation in extracurricular activities is associated with increased political involvement during adulthood (Jennings 1981; Glanville 1999). But political skills are also cultivated in less obvious settings. Religious organizations may be incubators of political capacities or provide imageries for political action and may compensate for the obstacles to participation for the poor, minority groups, and women.

In important respects this literature extends a long-standing concern in comparative politics for the cultural foundations of democracy. Classic works such as Almond and Verba's *Civic Culture* (1963) addressed the importance of adult socialization in generating the values and practices that sustain democratic polities; associations, not surprisingly, are demonstrated to be important sites of socialization. In an analysis of comparative political stability, Eckstein (1966) argued that *congruence* between the

forms of authority that prevailed within families or associations and the system of formal political authority was critical. The closer the fit, the more stable the regime. More recently, Putnam, Leonardi, and Nanetti (1993) contributed to the revival of interest in the social foundations of democratic governance—and economic development—in their collaborative study of regional government in Italy.

The effects attributed to participatory associations cannot be assumed for nonprofit organizations in general. For nonprofit scholars the key question is whether the "associations" featured in these political analyses are equivalent—and in what way—to nonprofit organizations. As Skocpol has argued (2003, 234), the decline of large membership-based voluntary associations and the proliferation of more professionalized organizations has transformed the relations between civic associations and political participation. Thus, as nonprofit organizations become increasingly professionalized (Brint and Levy 1999; Hall 1999)—and thus both organizationally distinct from participatory voluntary associations and more likely to survive (Minkoff 1993)—we should not expect them to generate the same levels and socioeconomic distribution of democratic political socialization.

Evidence of these connections among organizational structure, resources, and participation can be found throughout the research literature on nonprofit organizations. As nonprofits become more dependent on external funding, they tend to become more bureaucratic and professionalized (Smith and Lipsky 1993, 100–108; Grønbjerg 1993, 169–198); recent calls for new models of outcomes-based assessment evince a hope that this connection can be broken (Frumkin 2000; Salamon 1987, 113–115; Schorr 1997, ch. 4). In a study of advocacy organizations in the peace movement,[3] Edwards (1994, 317) found that larger organizations were "more likely than small to be formally organized, have higher levels of procedural formality, prefer to elect their leaders, and have more centralized financial decision making." Smaller peace organizations were "more likely than large to have higher rates of member participation, to prefer to operate without formally designated leaders, and make decisions by consensus."

As a general rule, the larger and richer and more formalized the organization, the fewer the opportunities for participatory governance and democratic socialization of members (to the extent that they exist at all). Thus, the opportunities for participation and leadership may be greatest in those organizations with the fewest resources—in members or money—to harness to civic causes. Successful participatory movement organizations have discovered distinctive internal structures that combine some of the advantages of centralization with a commitment to continuous engagement with local activities and leaders (Ganz 2000; M. R. Warren 2001) or falter as organizational growth outstrips the capacities to practice direct democracy within a movement (Polletta 2002).

To the extent that nongovernmental associations can cultivate political capacities among relatively disadvantaged groups within developing nations or the global economy, this may have important consequences for the balance of power and processes of decision making. Brown (1998; Brown and Tandon 1993) argues that nongovernmental organizations have the potential to serve as "bridges" among parties with varying power and distinctive interests (see also Ostrom 1997). Local nongovernmental organizations may even give rise to transnationally effective coalitions, engaging in decision making with national governments and intergovernmental organizations (Brown et al. 2000, 276).

Despite the tremendous allure of democratic socialization, to the extent that nonprofit organizations are highly professionalized, have large budgets and staffs, or work within the constraints of government programs, they are far less likely to promote the kind of adult political socialization long attributed to participation in voluntary associations. These large and professionalized nonprofits may advance the interests of the disadvantaged or of the public good through their advocacy work (Boris and Krehely 2003), but advocacy for others raises a host of issues about legitimate representation (Dovi 2002) that are elided in the process of self-representation through participatory governance.

Incivility and Apathy: Critical Reflections on Associationalism

Increasingly, critics of the optimistic accounts of political socialization contend that even participatory organizations may fail to generate the skills necessary for democratic participation or that they may cultivate values that are actually hostile to liberal democracy. The more neutral variant of this critique asserts that the simple absence of formal organizational structure and professionalization does not guarantee that participation will nurture political socialization. In a comparative ethnography of local organizations, Eliasoph documents that organizations of volunteers, country-western dancers, and even environmental activists may be infused with "etiquettes" of participation that contribute to "political evaporation," the suppression of conversation around value commitments, public issues, and political challenges (1998, 6–7). Community volunteering, "the hegemonic image of good citizenship" (1998, 25), actually frustrated efforts to engage in the political conversations that are central to models of participatory democracy (Polletta 2002). Instead, individual volunteers often spent considerable time alone on preset activities that they themselves had not participated in planning. When conversation did occur, Eliasoph observed that the volunteers kept the conversation focused closely on what was local and practical:

> Volunteer work embodied, above all, an effort aimed at convincing themselves and others

that the world makes sense and that regular people really can make a difference. . . . Community-spirited citizens judged that by avoiding "big" problems, they could better buoy their optimism. But by excluding politics from their group concerns, they kept their enormous, overflowing reservoir of concern and empathy, compassion and altruism, out of circulation, limiting its contribution to the common good.

(1998, 63)

Other revisionist arguments go much further, arguing that voluntary associations may serve as vehicles for the cultivation of separatism, intergroup hostility, and even antidemocratic values. Revisiting the "golden age of fraternity" in late nineteenth-century America, Kaufman (2002) argues that the rich array of Masonic, Pythian, and other lodges cultivated identities grounded in racial, ethnic, and gender separateness. This culture of organization, he argues, undermined support for more universal public programs and fostered an atmosphere of group conflict. The Klan, the Nazi party, hate organizations—all have been held up as potent counter-organizations to the facile equation of participation with democratic values (Fiorina 1999; Rosenblum 1998b; Skocpol 1999, 69). Whereas nonprofit scholars have long been attuned to problems of "philanthropic particularism" and the large proportion of charitable donations that sustain cultural activities of interest to those with the income to donate (Salamon 1987, 111–112), these critical reflections go beyond the absence of genuine altruism to raise the possibility that voluntary and nonprofit organizations may nurture intolerance and damaging exclusion. As with arguments for democratic socialization, associations are understood to constitute political actors, but not necessarily democratic citizens.

Associations that practice internal self-governance may also be problematic insofar as they restrict some citizens from membership.

The tension between free association and detrimental restrictions on membership has also been central to judicial reflections on the place of voluntary associations in a democratic polity, turning on the "conflict between the values of free association and those of nondiscrimination" (Gutmann 1998, 6–11). Recent decisions concerning the Jaycees and the Boy Scouts of America delineate "intimate associations" from groups legitimately subject to requirements of open accommodation and nondiscrimination.

For liberal theorists the "dark side" of participation poses a particular problem, demanding a balancing of individual liberties to join associations with concerns for the preservation of core liberal commitments. In debates over the relation of multiculturalism and liberalism (Barry 2001; I. M. Young 1990), theorists contest the proper relation of deference to distinctive group values and adherence to core liberal principles. Similar questions are provoked by nonprofit status—particularly standing as a "public charity"—with its expectation that legal privileges recognize the provision of some public good or service to some social value. Whether challenged by the presence of "nonprofits in disguise" or by nonprofit organizations promoting controversial as well as illiberal values, the automatic equation of nonprofit status with civic virtues is undermined.

As with the positive claims for the role of voluntary associations in cultivating democratic values and practices, this critical view resonates beyond the advanced industrialized democracies. In the field of international development, international nongovernmental organizations may act to preserve authoritarian government or advance market penetration by firms in the donor country (B. H. Smith 1998). Whereas some projects may be designed to promote civic participation and cultivate democratic skills (Brown and Tandon 1993), other models of intervention may constitute an "anti-politics machine."

Here, the optimistic reading of Tocqueville is countered with insights from Foucault on the operation of power (and depoliticization) through seemingly neutral practices and expert discourses. The consequences of organizational auspice for democratic practices and values are shaped not only by internal organizational structure or values but also by the relation of organizations to broader structures of power. The "anti-politics machine" of technocratic implementation is one possibility; the "Velvet Revolution" of eastern Europe in 1989 another. Thus, voluntary associations and nonprofit organizations matter not only as potential sites of political socialization for individuals but also as vehicles for social regulation.

Political Engagement

Any assessment of the political consequences of voluntary associations and nonprofit organizations must directly address the forms of engagement between these private entities and formal political institutions.

This connection is shaped by the direct regulation of political participation. Many arguments for the contribution of associationalism to democracy presume that the skills and values cultivated in associations are easily transposed to formal politics by way of individual behavior, but the legal decoupling of "charitable" nonprofits from significant political engagement disrupts this presumed connection (Berry and Arons 2003, 47–65; Boris and Krehely 2003; Wolch 1990, 62–74).

Throughout history, rulers have been wary of "privately held public power." The long history of restrictions on association reminds us that voluntary organizations may be potent forces of change (whether or not current elites like the direction of that change) (McCarthy 2003). Given their potential as vehicles for political conflict, we should expect access to political arenas itself to be the object of contestation. If at least some voluntary associations or nonprofit organizations are sites for democratic

socialization and mobilization, such organizations are not necessarily equally available to all social groups or for all causes. In addressing these issues, research has become somewhat bifurcated between charities, foundations, and philanthropies that are generally recognized as core concerns for nonprofit research and more politically engaged voluntary associations such as labor unions that are more frequently treated in other research literatures.[4]

In a very fundamental sense, the lineage of the nonprofit immunization may be traced to efforts by elites to craft a means to extend their wishes in time (beyond the limits of their own mortal existence) and in scale (beyond the capacities of single individuals). As laid out in the Elizabethan Statute of 1601, the law of charities enabled durable and/or collective forms of activity beyond the bounds of the state, so long as that activity was dedicated to purposes approved by the state (Ware 1989). These efforts were initially viewed with suspicion; indeed, many states revoked English law in the wake of the Revolution, leaving such efforts without the foundation of the Elizabethan Statute of Charities (Zollman 1924). As Peter Dobkin Hall (1992, 2006) has documented in his studies of what would come to be recognized as "nonprofit organizations" in American history, through the nineteenth century this organizational form represented a controversial but effective vehicle for nationalizing projects of northeastern elites. Well into the twentieth century, the activities and resources of these publicly chartered yet privately governed entities raised political suspicion. State legislation repeatedly enacted tradeoffs of permission or subsidy of private activities for increases in government oversight (Clemens 2006; Novak 2001). The suspicion of resources controlled by private associations persisted in laws limiting the property that could be held.

In the United States this period of innovation and expansion on the part of elite philanthropy and foundations was accompanied by important changes in the organization of popular voluntary associations. As Tocqueville observed, early nineteenth-century American society was unusual in its extent of voluntary activity,[5] and by the second half of the century many of these organizations had large memberships and were national in scope (Skocpol 2003). Mobilizing farmers, workers, women, and other constituencies, these voluntary associations served as vehicles for large-scale political engagement that deeply changed American political institutions (Clemens 1997; Sanders 1999).

These early disagreements foreshadowed a history of legislative oversight in which excessive political activity by foundations or nonprofit organizations triggered threats to the exempt status and legal standing of these organizations (Jenkins 1998; Reid 1999, 310–321; Wolch 1990, 62–69; D. R. Young 1999, 5661). In the United States, as federal intervention in community and social issues expanded from the 1960s onward, existing community associations and social movement organizations were torn between the appeal of new resources and the perceived threat that engagement with public programs would in time curb their political activities (Andrews 2001; Castells 1983, ch. 13). Similar concerns were prompted by grants from foundations committed to social change (Jenkins 1998, 212–215). Tensions also rose between these politically engaged movement organizations and preexisting voluntary and service agencies that had expectations of greater control over new sources of public largesse (Castells 1983, 116). By the end of the decade both social service and environmental organizations had experienced hostile bouts of regulation in reaction to their advocacy activities (Wolch 1990, 63–67).

Through their tax-exempt status and receipt of public funds, both advocacy and service organizations remain vulnerable to political efforts to use the leverage of these economic advantages to channel or choke off political activity. In the early 1990s the US Congress repeatedly considered—and defeated—a proposal from Congressman Istook "to curtail advocacy by nonprofit groups receiving grants" (Reid 1999, 316; see also Berry and Arons 2003, 66–92). Although these proposals failed, they suggest the durable tension between contestation and collaboration as imageries of the relation of governments to nonprofit organizations and voluntary associations more generally. This decoupling of nonprofit associations and political activity has become still more problematic as nonprofits become ever more active in delivering publicly funded services.

The Politics of Partnership

If the role of nonprofits and associations in political mobilization has been carefully policed, the activity of these organizations in the provision of services has also been a topic of concern, perhaps the central topic in nonprofit scholarship. In Powell (1987), James Douglas turned to democratic theory to address the question of why some services are provided by nonprofit organizations rather than by government agencies. His answer emphasized the "demand structure" for services (e.g., majority versus minority in democratic polities) as well as the capacity of nonprofits to maintain diversity and to provide a corrective to bureaucratic inflexibility. The object of his influential essay (1987, 43) was to develop a political analogue to the economic theories of nonprofit organizations surveyed by Hansmann (1987) in the same volume (see also Weisbrod 1988). Drawing parallels with the economic concept of "market failure," Douglas asks, "why, given the extensive range of services provided by the public (or government) sector, we need to supplement them by private endeavors that are not accountable through the same political channels" (1987, 44; for critical discussions, see DiMaggio and Anheier 1990, 140–141; Ware 1989, ch. 1). Thus, voters with clear preferences are assumed by the argument, thereby eliding important questions about how the establishment of such partnerships in the delivery of services may transform processes of political socialization and the constitution of interests.

The explanatory logic emphasizes choice rather than the feedback of policies to recognized preferences (Pierson 1994). If a majority desires some form of social provision, those preferences will support government provision of services. In cases where a minority desires a service, nonprofit organizations represent an alternative vehicle for provision. Consequently, governments may facilitate the formation of nonprofit organizations in order to increase the level of satisfaction with the overall mix of services. Such a "combination of public provision and voluntary provision for public purposes makes it possible to accommodate the views and preferences of a greater range of the community than could public provision alone" (Douglas 1987, 45). The resulting argument offers both an explanation for existing distributions of activities across organizational forms and a guide to future decisions over when services should be provided by public agencies *or* nonprofit organizations. If the existing mix meets the preferences of citizens, it should be maintained; if not, policy should be altered to match those preferences.

This conceptualization of public and nonprofit provision as mutually exclusive alternatives—discrete choices—has been challenged by a growing body of empirical research on the role of nonprofit organizations in modern welfare states. Whereas Douglas's argument conceptualizes nonprofit activities as *alternatives* to government provision, Salamon documents that in the United States the nonprofit sector has grown as a *complement* to government programs. Further, rather than viewing nonprofit organizations as a consequence of the absence of majority support for public provision, Salamon contends that the expansion of government programs is better understood as a consequence of *voluntary failure* (2003, 33–49; for an overview see D. R. Young 1999).[6]

In contrast to studies of political socialization and participatory governance, research on the division of labor between nonprofits and government often rests on a decidedly thin sense of the distribution of preferences and the exercise of choice within democratic polities. Diverging from imageries of conflict and contestation, these arguments assume political actors as individuals with existing preferences for services rather than as already-organized communities and claimants. Consequently, this approach to the division of labor between government agencies and nonprofit organizations obscures the political process by which partnerships are constituted and politics are remade.

Under what conditions do states turn from predominantly public forms of social provision to more extensive collaboration with nonprofit organizations? And what are the implications of such delegation for democratic governance and the legitimacy of public programs? Douglas (1987) provided a clear answer to the first of these questions: Governments will collaborate with nonprofits—rather than providing services directly—insofar as those services are preferred by less than a majority of citizens or where the "categorical constraint" of uniformity and equity is not met. Recent scholarship, however, has tended to develop more dynamic or processual accounts of the turn of welfare states toward greater reliance on or collaboration with nonprofit organizations. This turn from relatively ahistorical economic models has highlighted how policy makes politics and thus how the expanding partnership between government and nonprofits has reconstructed the political roles of each. During the War on Poverty, for example, the US federal government adopted a "contracting regime" intended to promote innovation and participation as well as to allow a rapid expansion of organizational capacity (Smith and Lipsky 1993; Smith and Grønbjerg 2006). The resulting growth of government funding of nonprofit activities led, in turn, to a perception of those nonprofits as interest groups lobbying selfishly for increased funding (Berry and Arons 2003, 79–85) and calls—most notably in the oft-defeated Istook amendment—to forbid lobbying activity on the part of nonprofit organizations receiving public funds (although existing legislation already forbade the use of federal funds to support such political activities). Thus, the expansion of government-nonprofit partnerships has led to the increasing politicization of nonprofits as providers of public services even as they are increasingly wary of engaging as political actors.

Where the expansion of the welfare state took place primarily through public agencies, support for increased partnerships with nonprofits could be advanced as solutions to the "crisis" of the welfare state. In Europe well-developed welfare states have turned to expanded collaborations with nonprofits in the face of fiscal crises and "crises of technique" in which traditional bureaucratic methods prove ill suited to policy problems (Ullman 1998).

Insofar as governments turn to extensive collaboration with nonprofit entities, what are the implications for governance and legitimacy? As Milward and Provan (2000) argue, principal-agent theory helps to clarify what is at stake.

Insofar as nongovernmental entities are increasingly visible as the providers of social services, the legitimacy of public provision—increasingly restricted to funding rather than implementation—may be undermined. In the early 1980s surprise greeted studies by Lester Salamon and Alan Abramson (1982) that documented the extent to which nonprofit organizations were dependent on public funding. In an era when the case for delegation and decentralization is routinely joined to a stylized critique of public bureaucracies as necessarily ineffective (e.g., Chubb and Moe 1990, 38–39; Chubb and Peterson 1989, ch. 1; Schorr 1997, ch. 3), evidence of the efficacy of nonprofit organizations—and increasingly "faith-based" programs—is contrasted to the purported failure of public programs. Some commentators argue that such contrasts feed the stream of antistatism in American political culture (Block 1996; Weisberg 1996) at the same time that others see decentralization of policy provision as a path to the revitalization of democratic participation at the local level (Putnam 2000).

The questions raised by contracting out are rather different when viewed from the perspective of constituting citizens with distinct political interests and capacities for participation. To the extent that nongovernmental organizations deliver publicly funded services, it becomes more difficult for citizens to answer the question of "what are my tax dollars doing?" and easier to misrecognize public services as private benefits. This raises the possibility that as publicly funded services are increasingly mistaken for—or at least experienced as—private and charitable, this will undermine political support for continued public spending on these services. A second concern invokes the problems of patronage politics: Will increased government-nonprofit partnerships facilitate elected officials' cooptation of these "schools of citizenship"? With the transnational turn to privatization and devolution, the answers to these explicitly political questions are not yet clear, but the asking of them is obscured when we consider such partnerships only from the perspective of the quality of service delivery. If voluntary associations and nonprofit organizations are valued, in part, because of their capacity to constitute citizens, then the increasing ties of nonprofits to the states signal an important shift in the relations that constitute democratic polities.

Beyond Participation and Provision

The proliferation of claims for the political salience of voluntary associations or nonprofit organizations underscores how ambiguity about organizational forms pervades research and theorizing on nonprofit entities. For the majority of these claims, the "not-for-profit" status of organizations is less relevant than other traits assumed to be linked to this status: participatory governance and voluntarism, control by a delimited social group and some autonomy from formal political institutions, connections to broader social networks and orientation to particular values, and flexibility and diversity.

From the perspective of political theory, nonprofits matter not simply as providers of services but also as potential sites for the constitution of citizens and vehicles for expressing articulated interests and values. The capacity of nonprofit organizations to serve these functions depends on features of organizational structure: the degree of formal hierarchy and professionalism, the opportunities for practicing participation. But, as those wary of "bad civil society" have argued, even the most participatory organizational structure is not a guarantee that the values and practices the organization advances will be consistent with any given understanding of democracy. Consequently, the status of nonprofit organizations and voluntary associations will continue to be fundamentally contested as democratic polities strive to find balance between concerns for freedom of expression and limits on intolerance or exclusion.

Whereas the delineation of freedom of association in a democratic polity is a fundamental issue for liberal theory (Gutmann 1998), it is also an ongoing policy question as nonprofit organizations become ever more entwined in the governance and provision of public services. Just as the increase in the size and professionalism of nonprofits should prompt reconsideration of their role in political socialization, so the increasing ties between these nongovernmental—as well as not-for-profit—entities and the state raise important questions about the changing relations of the components of civic society to the formal institutions of representation and rule. In the place of a "political theory of nonprofits,"

the current moment requires close attention to the implication of nonprofit organizations in diverse projects of state building and political mobilization. If "policy makes politics," the increasingly complex web of relations among government agencies and nonprofit organizations will not lead to a simple—or singular—political outcome.

Notes

1. For a historical overview of nonprofit corporations in the United States, see Hall (2006). On sovereignty versus subsidiary concepts of nonprofit organizations, see Brody and Cordes (1999).

2. These arguments often combine a number of distinct claims: that participation in associations contributes to the development or maintenance of a sense of community, to the preservation of freedom, or to the capacity for self-governance (M. E. Warren 2001, 17).

3. For an extended discussion of local or grassroots associations, see Smith (2000).

4. The study of social movement philanthropy (Jenkins 1998, 2006; Ostrander 1995) represents an important exception to this generalization. For example, in the post-Reconstruction South, money from the Rosenwald Fund aided disenfranchised blacks in "leveraging the state" to expand public education for black children (Strong et al. 2000). Community associations and self-help organizations are also central to the nonprofit literature, another exception to this generalization.

5. Although recent research questions these estimates of the level of voluntary activity, the basic comparative insight into the differences with European societies of the time stands. A 1981 survey of associational membership in twelve industrialized democracies found the highest level in the United States (76 percent), followed by Northern Ireland (66 percent), with the lowest levels reported in Italy (26 percent) (reported in Verba, Schlozman, and Brady 1995, 80).

6. Other scholars retain Douglas's causal order—some limitation on government activities generates a turn to nonprofit or voluntary

provision—while invoking mechanisms other than majoritarian rule. In a comparative-historical study of Britain and the United States, Ware (1989) argues that the association of nonprofit organizations with particular domains of activity is best understood as an institutional legacy. Mutual and cooperative associations took root in what were once marginal economic areas, serving as savings banks and providing home loans. The characteristic organizational forms persisted even as the scale and importance of these economic activities grew. Thus, Ware argues, the distribution of economic activities across public, for-profit, and not-for-profit entities cannot be attributed to contemporary distributions of preferences within the electorate.

References

Almond, Gabriel A., and Sidney Verba. 1963. *The Civic Culture*. Princeton, NJ: Princeton University Press.

Andrews, Kenneth T. 2001. "Social Movements and Policy Implementation: The Mississippi Civil Rights Movement and the War on Poverty, 1965–1971." *American Sociological Review* 66: 71–95.

Barry, Brian. 2001. *Culture and Equality: An Egalitarian Critique of Multiculturalism*. Cambridge, MA: Harvard University Press.

Berry, Jeffrey M., with David F. Arons. 2003. *A Voice for Non-profits*. Washington, DC: Brookings Institution Press.

Block, Fred L. 1996. *The Vampire State: And Other Myths and Fallacies about the US Economy*. New York: The New Press.

Boris, Elizabeth T., and Jeff Krehely. 2003. "Civic Participation and Advocacy." In *The State of Non-profit America*, edited by Lester Salamon. Washington, DC: Brookings Institution Press.

Brint, Steven, and Charles S. Levy. 1999. "Professions and Civic Engagement: Trends in Rhetoric and Practice, 1875–1995." In *Civic Engagement in American Democracy*, edited by Theda Skocpol and Morris P. Fiorina. Washington, DC: Brookings Institution Press.

Brody, Evelyn, and Joseph J. Cordes. 1999. "Tax Treatment of Nonprofit Organizations: A Two-Edged Sword?" In *Nonprofits and Government*, edited by Elizabeth T. Boris and C. Eugene Steuerle. Washington, DC: Urban Institute Press.

Brown, L. David. 1998. "Creating Social Capital: Nongovernmental Development Organizations and Intersectoral Problem Solving." In *Private Action and the Public Good*, edited by Walter W. Powell and Elisabeth S. Clemens. New Haven, CT: Yale University Press.

Brown, L. David, Sanjeev Khagram, Mark H. Moore, and Peter Frumkin. 2000. "Globalization, NGOs, and Multisectoral Relations." In *Governance in a Globalizing World*, edited by Joseph S. Nye and John D. Donahue. Washington, DC: Brookings Institution Press.

Brown, L. David, and R. Tandon. 1993. *Multiparty Collaboration for Development in Asia*. New York: United Nations Development Programme.

Buchanan, James M., and Gordon Tullock. 1962. *The Calculus of Consent*. Ann Arbor: University of Michigan Press.

Castells, Manuel. 1983. *The City and the Grassroots: A Cross-Cultural Theory of Urban Social Movements*. Berkeley and Los Angeles: University of California Press.

Chambers, Simone, and Jeffrey Kopstein. 2001. "Bad Civil Society." *Political Theory* 29(6): 837–865.

Chubb, John E., and Terry M. Moe. 1990. *Politics, Markets, and America's Schools*. Washington, DC: The Brookings Institution.

Chubb, John E., and Paul E. Peterson, eds. 1989. *Can the Government Govern?* Washington, DC: The Brookings Institution.

Clemens, Elisabeth S. 1997. *The People's Lobby: Organizational Innovation and the Rise of Interest Group Politics in the United States, 1890–1925*. Chicago: University of Chicago Press.

———. 2006. "Lineages of the Rube Goldberg State: Public Finance and Private Governance, 1900–1940." In *Rethinking Political Institutions: The Art of the State*, edited by Ian Shapiro, Stephen Skowronek, and Daniel Galvin. New York: New York University Press.

Crenson, Matthew A., and Benjamin Ginsberg. 2002. *Downsizing Democracy: How America Sidelined Its Citizens and Privatized Its Public*. Baltimore: Johns Hopkins University Press.

Dahl, Robert A. 1982. *Dilemmas of Pluralist Democracy*. New Haven, CT: Yale University Press.

Dane, Perry. 1998. "The Corporation Sole and the Encounter of Law and Church." In *Sacred Companies*, edited by N. Jay Demerath et al. New York: Oxford University Press.

DiMaggio, Paul J., and Helmut K. Anheier. 1990. "The Sociology of Nonprofit Organizations and Sectors." *Annual Review of Sociology* 16: 137–159.

Dorf, Michael C., and Charles F. Sabel. 1998. "A Constitution of Democratic Experimentalism." *Columbia Law Review* 98: 267–473.

Douglas, James. 1983. *Why Charity?* Beverly Hills, CA: Sage.

———. 1987. "Political Theories of Nonprofit Organization." In *The Nonprofit Sector: A Research Handbook*, 1st ed., edited by Walter W. Powell. New Haven, CT: Yale University Press.

Dovi, Suzanne. 2002. "Preferable Descriptive Representatives: Will Just Any Woman, Black, or Latino Do?" *American Political Science Review* 96: 729–743.

Doyle, Don H. 1977. "The Social Functions of Voluntary Associations in a Nineteenth-Century American Town." *Social Science History* l(3): 333–355.

Eckstein, Harry. 1966. *Division and Cohesion in Democracy: A Study of Norway*. Princeton, NJ: Princeton University Press.

Edwards, Bob. 1994. "Semiformal Organizational Structure among Social Movement Organizations: An Analysis of the US Peace Movement." *Nonprofit and Voluntary Sector Quarterly* 23(4): 309–333.

Eliasoph, Nina. 1998. *Avoiding Politics: How Americans Produce Apathy in Everyday Life*. New York: Cambridge University Press.

Evans, Peter, ed. 1997. *State-Society Synergy: Government and Social Capital in Development*. International and Area Studies Research Series, 94. Berkeley: University of California Press.

Fiorina, Morris P. 1999. "Extreme Voices: A Dark Side of Civic Engagement." In *Civic Engagement in American Democracy*, edited by Theda Skocpol and Morris P. Fiorina. Washington, DC: Brookings Institution Press.

Fleischacker, Sam. 1998. "Insignificant Communities." In *Freedom of Association*, edited by Amy Gutmann. Princeton, NJ: Princeton University Press.

Frumkin, Peter. 2000. "After Partnership: Rethinking Public-Nonprofit Relations." In *Who Provides? Religion and the Future of Social Welfare in American Democracy*, edited by Mary Jo Bane, Brent Coffin, and Ronal Thiemann. Boulder, CO: Westview Press.

———. 2002. *On Being Nonprofit: A Conceptual and Policy Primer*. Cambridge, MA: Harvard University Press.

Ganz, Marshall. 2000. "Resources and Resourcefulness: Strategic Capacity in the Unionization of California Agriculture, 1959–1966." *American Journal of Sociology* 105(4): 1003–1062.

Glanville, Jennifer L. 1999. "Political Socialization or Selection? Adolescent Extracurricular Participation and Political Activity in Early Adulthood." *Social Science Quarterly* 80(2): 279–291.

Grønbjerg, Kirsten A. 1993. *Understanding Nonprofit Funding: Managing Revenues in Social Services and Community Development Organizations*. San Francisco: Jossey-Bass.

Gutmann, Amy, ed. 1998. *Freedom of Association*. Princeton, NJ: Princeton University Press.

Hall, Peter Dobkin. 1992. *Inventing the Nonprofit Sector and Other Essays on Philanthropy, Voluntarism, and Nonprofit Organizations*. Baltimore, MD: Johns Hopkins University Press.

———. 1999. "Vital Signs: Organizational Population Trends and Civic Engagement in New Haven, Connecticut, 1850–1998." In *Civic Engagement in American Democracy*, edited by Theda Skocpol and Morris P. Fiorina. Washington, DC: Brookings Institution Press.

———. 2006. "A Historical Overview of Philanthropy, Voluntary Associations, and Nonprofit Organizations in the United States." In *The Nonprofit Sector: A Research Handbook*, 2nd ed., edited by Walter W. Powell and Richard Steinberg, 32–65. New Haven, CT: Yale University Press.

Hansmann, Henry. 1987. "Economic Theories of Nonprofit Organization." In *The Nonprofit Sector: A Research Handbook*, 1st ed., edited by Walter W. Powell. New Haven, CT: Yale University Press.

James, Estelle. 1987. "The Nonprofit Sector in Comparative Perspective." In *The Nonprofit Sector: A Research Handbook*, 1st ed., edited by Walter W. Powell. New Haven, CT: Yale University Press.

Jenkins, J. Craig. 1998. "Channeling Social Protest: Foundation Patronage of Contemporary Social Movements." In *Private Action and the Public Good*, edited by Walter W. Powell and Elisabeth S. Clemens. New Haven, CT: Yale University Press.

————. 2006. "Nonprofit Organizations and Political Advocacy." In *The Nonprofit Sector: A Research Handbook*, 2nd ed., edited by Walter W. Powell and Richard Steinberg, 307–332. New Haven, CT: Yale University Press.

Jennings, M. Kent. 1981. *Generational Politics: A Panel Study of Young Adults and Their Parents.* Princeton, NJ: Princeton University Press.

Kaufman, Jason. 2002. *For the Common Good? American Civic Life and the Golden Age of Fraternity.* New York: Oxford University Press.

Knoke, David, and James R. Wood. 1981. *Organized for Action: Commitment in Voluntary Associations.* New Brunswick, NJ: Rutgers University Press.

March, James G., and Johan P. Olsen. 1989. *Rediscovering Institutions: The Organizational Basis of Politics.* New York: Free Press.

McCarthy, Kathleen D. 2003. *American Creed: Philanthropy and the Rise of Civil Society, 1700–1865.* Chicago: University of Chicago Press.

Milward, H. Brinton, and Keith G. Provan. 2000. "Governing the Hollow State." *Journal of Public Administration Research and Theory* 10(2): 359–380.

Minkoff, Debra C. 1993. "The Organization of Survival: Women's and Racial-Ethnic Voluntarist and Activist Organizations, 1955–85." *Social Forces* 71(4): 887–908.

Novak, William J. 2001. "The American Law of Association: The Legal-Political Construction of Civil Society." *Studies in American Political Development* 15: 163–188.

Olson, Mancur. 1971. *The Logic of Collective Action.* Cambridge, MA: Harvard University Press.

Ostrander, Susan A. 1995. *Money for Change: Social Movement Philanthropy at Haymarket People's Fund.* Philadelphia, PA: Temple University Press.

Ostrom, Elinor. 1997. "Crossing the Great Divide: Coproduction, Synergy, and Development." In *State-Society Synergy: Government and Social Capital in Development*, edited by Peter Evans. International and Area Studies Research Series, 94. Berkeley: University of California Press.

Pierson, Paul. 1994. *Dismantling the Welfare State? Reagan, Thatcher and the Politics of Retrenchment.* New York: Cambridge University Press.

Polletta, Francesca. 2002. *Freedom Is an Endless Meeting: Democracy in American Social Movements.* Chicago: University of Chicago Press.

Portes, Alejandro. 1998. "Social Capital: Its Origins and Applications in Modern Sociology." *Annual Review of Sociology* 24: 1–24.

Powell, Walter W., ed. 1987. *The Nonprofit Sector: A Research Handbook*, 1st ed. New Haven, CT: Yale University Press.

Putnam, Robert D. 2000. *Bowling Alone: The Collapse and Revival of American Community.* New York: Simon and Schuster.

Putnam, Robert D., with Roberto Leonardi and Raffaela Y. Nanetti. 1993. *Making Democracy Work: Civic Traditions in Modern Italy.* Princeton, NJ: Princeton University Press.

Reid, Elizabeth J. 1999. "Nonprofit Advocacy and Political Participation." In *Nonprofits and Government*, edited by Elizabeth T. Boris and C. Eugene Steuerle. Washington, DC: Urban Institute Press.

Rosenblum, Nancy L. 1998a. "Compelled Association: Public Standing, Self-Respect, and the Dynamic of Exclusion." In *Freedom of Association*, edited by Amy Gutmann. Princeton, NJ: Princeton University Press.

————. 1998b. *Membership and Morals: The Personal Uses of Pluralism in America.* Princeton, NJ: Princeton University Press.

Salamon, Lester M. 1987. "Partners in Public Service: The Scope and Theory of Government-Nonprofit Relations." In *The Nonprofit Sector: A Research Handbook*, 1st ed., edited by Walter W. Powell. New Haven, CT: Yale University Press.

————. 2003. "The Resilient Sector: The State of Nonprofit America." In *The State of Nonprofit America*, edited by Lester Salamon. Washington, DC: Brookings Institution Press.

Salamon, Lester M., and Alan J. Abramson. 1982. *The Federal Budget and the Nonprofit Sector.* Washington, DC: Urban Institute Press.

Sanders, Elizabeth. 1999. *Roots of Reform: Farmers, Workers, and the American State, 1877–1917.* Chicago: University of Chicago Press.

Schorr, Lisbeth. 1997. *Common Purpose: Strengthening Families and Neighborhoods to Rebuild America.* New York: Anchor Books.

Sirianni, Carmen, and Lewis Friedland. 2001. *Civic Innovation in America: Community Empowerment, Public Policy, and the Movement for Civic Renewal.* Berkeley and Los Angeles: University of California Press.

Skocpol, Theda. 1999. "How Americans Became Civic." In *Civic Engagement in American Democracy,* edited by Theda Skocpol and Morris P. Fiorina. Washington, DC: Brookings Institution Press.

———. 2003. *Diminished Democracy: From Membership to Management in American Civic Life.* Norman: University of Oklahoma Press.

Skocpol, Theda, and Morris P. Fiorina, eds. 1999. *Civic Engagement in American Democracy.* Washington, DC: Brookings Institution Press.

Smith, Brian H. 1998. "Nonprofit Organizations in International Development: Agents of Empowerment or Preservers of Stability?" In *Private Action and the Public Good,* edited by Walter W. Powell and Elisabeth S. Clemens. New Haven, CT: Yale University Press.

Smith, David Horton. 2000. *Grassroots Associations.* Thousand Oaks, CA: Sage.

Smith, Steven Rathgeb, and Kirsten A. Grønbjerg. 2006. "Scope and Theory of Government Nonprofit Relations." In *The Nonprofit Sector: A Research Handbook,* 2nd ed., edited by Walter W. Powell and Richard Steinberg, 221–242. New Haven, CT: Yale University Press.

Smith, Steven Rathgeb, and Michael Lipsky. 1993. *Nonprofits for Hire: The Welfare State in the Age of Contracting.* Cambridge, MA: Harvard University Press.

Strong, David, Pamela Barnhouse Walters, Brian Driscoll, and Scott Rosenberg. 2000. "Leveraging the State: Private Money and the Development of Public Education for Blacks." *American Sociological Review* 65: 658–681.

Tocqueville, Alexis de. 1969. *Democracy in America.* New York: Anchor Books.

Ullman, Claire F. 1998. *The Welfare State's Other Crisis: Explaining the New Partnership Between Nonprofit Organizations and the State in France.* Bloomington: Indiana University Press.

Verba, Sidney, Kay Lehman Schlozman, and Henry E. Brady. 1995. *Voice and Equality: Civic Voluntarism in American Politics.* Cambridge, MA: Harvard University Press.

Walzer, Michael. 1983. *Spheres of Justice: A Defense of Pluralism and Equality.* New York: Basic Books.

———. 1984. "Liberalism and the Art of Separation." *Political Theory* 12(3): 315–330.

Ware, Alan. 1989. *Between Profit and State: Intermediate Organizations in Britain and the United States.* Princeton, NJ: Princeton University Press.

Warren, Mark E. 2001. *Democracy and Association.* Princeton, NJ: Princeton University Press.

Warren, Mark R. 2001. *Dry Bones Rattling: Community Building to Revitalize American Democracy.* Princeton, NJ: Princeton University Press.

Weisberg, Jacob. 1996. *In Defense of Government: The Fall and Rise of Public Trust.* New York: Scribner.

Weisbrod, Burton A. 1988. *The Nonprofit Economy.* Cambridge, MA: Harvard University Press.

Wolch, Jennifer R. 1990. *The Shadow State: Government and Voluntary Sector in Transition.* New York: The Foundation Center.

Wuthnow, Robert. 1991. *Between States and Markets: The Voluntary Sector in Comparative Perspective.* Princeton, NJ: Princeton University Press.

———. 1998. *Loose Connections: Joining Together in America's Fragmented Communities.* Cambridge, MA: Harvard University Press.

Young, Dennis R. 1999. "Complementary, Supplementary, or Adversarial? A Theoretical and Historical Examination of Nonprofit-Government Relations in the United States." In *Nonprofits and Government,* edited by Elizabeth T. Boris and C. Eugene Steuerle. Washington, DC: Urban Institute Press.

Young, Iris Marion. 1990. *Justice and the Politics of Difference.* Princeton, NJ: Princeton University Press.

Zollman, Carl. 1924. *American Law of Charities.* Milwaukee, WI: Bruce.

CHAPTER 20

The Influence of Nonprofit Organizations on the Political Environment

KELLY LEROUX AND MARY K. FEENEY

LeRoux, Kelly, and Mary K. Feeney. *Nonprofit Organizations and Civil Society in the United States.* (New York. Routledge, 2015).

Introduction

Nonprofit and civil society organizations are influential actors in American policy-making and politics. These organizations shape policy-making and the electoral process at all levels of government in the form of lobbying groups, service organizations, political parties, and policy research institutes or "think tanks." In addition to these types of organizations that have a more direct role in the policy and politics arena, many other types of nonprofit organizations, including associations, human service organizations, and churches provide outlets for political dialogue, social networking, and volunteerism. Thus, these latter groups also contribute to American political life by serving as vehicles for promoting civic engagement, political discourse, and furthering democratic ideals.[1]

This chapter examines three critical roles that nonprofit organizations play in shaping public policy and politics in the US: political representation, political mobilization, and political education. These roles are inter-related. Some nonprofit organizations perform all three roles in their efforts to influence policy or election outcomes.

We will examine not only the types of nonprofit organizations that perform political roles, but also the many ways in which these organizations help to shape American democracy by promoting connections between ordinary citizens and their government. When the timing is right for dramatic political change, nonprofit organizations engaged in political representation, mobilization, and education can be catalysts in the process for creating broad-based social change.

Before moving into our discussion of nonprofits' political representation, mobilization, and education roles, there are some fundamental differences in the laws governing the political activities of public charities and other types of nonprofit organizations that are important to understand. The next section examines the key distinctions between public charities (501(c)3 organizations) and social welfare organizations, labor and business league organizations, and other lobbying organizations (501(c)4 and 501(c)6 organizations) that fall under other sections of the tax code. We then discuss how nonprofit organizations shape the political environment through political representation, mobilization, and education activities.

DOI: 10.4324/9780367696559-26

Critical Differences in Nonprofits' Political Activities

The vast majority of the nonprofit organizations registered with the Internal Revenue Service (IRS) are 501(c)3 organizations (otherwise known as public charities) including arts, education, science, healthcare and social service organizations. Despite their large proportion of the nonprofit universe, prevalence in society, and thus their collective impact on the political landscape, many people carry the misconception that public charities are not involved (or should not be involved) in the political arena.[2] Although public charities can engage in political activities, they are required by law to do so on a more limited scale, which includes strict prohibitions on supporting or endorsing political candidates.

Because the primary mission of public charities is to provide a particular service or public good, rather than influence policy, the federal government places strict legal limits on the political activities (and lobbying) of public charities. These legal limits often cause confusion and misconceptions about the ways in which nonprofit organizations are allowed to participate in public policy. Tax-exempt nonprofit organizations are allowed to lobby, but there are limitations on how that lobbying can work. First, in general, they cannot use federal funds or contract funds to lobby on legislative matters or for electioneering purposes. But, 501(c)(3) organizations can use general-purpose funds to lobby and community foundations can earmark grants for lobbying. Second, 501(c)(3) nonprofits cannot endorse candidates. But nonprofits can lobby within a set of limits.

Public charities cannot carry out political activities in an ideological, or **partisan**, fashion; they must be nonpartisan, meaning they cannot endorse candidates for office, make political contributions to candidates or parties, or advocate in favor of or against the platform of a particular candidate or party.[3]

Lobbying Groups and Interest Groups: 501(c)4, 501(c)5, and 501(c)6 Organizations

In comparison to public charities, there are classifications of nonprofit organizations that are allowed to lobby for and advance the political interests of a particular cause or group of individuals. "Social welfare" organizations 501(c)4, such as the Sierra Club and National Rifle Association, and 501(c)5 and (c)6 labor and business league organizations, such as the AFL-CIO and the Chambers of Commerce, are all allowed to engaged in political activities, endorse candidates, and partake in partisan activities. These organizations, often referred to as **lobbying groups** or **interest groups**, are created specifically for the purpose of representing a particular cause or the needs and interests of their members. They constitute a much smaller share of the US nonprofit sector, as compared to 501(c)3 public charities, but play a critical role in the American political process. These organizations can more or less engage in as much lobbying as their resources enable, and they are free to be partisan in their messages. In other words, they can publicly endorse candidates for office, encourage their followers or members to vote for particular candidates, create and fund advertisements designed to help bolster or undermine a candidate with regard to a particular issue. As we shall examine shortly, organizations that fall within these categories of the nonprofit sector are the "heavy hitters" of political influence in Washington D.C., and they can also be powerful forces in state-level policy-making and elections.

Some leaders of public charities (e.g. service-providing nonprofit organizations) would like to benefit from the political activism that is allowed for 501(c)4, 501(c)5, and 501(c)6 organizations. They want to more aggressively pursue political goals and advocate for policies that would benefit their organizations and their clientele. This has led some 501(c)3 organizations to create partner or sister organizations that have an alternative legal status (lobbying or interest group), enabling them to engage more directly in the political process. By creating linked 501(c)3 and 501(c)4 organizations, as well as associated Political Action Committees (PACs) and other organizational vehicles to pursue their political goals, many leaders of public charities have found a way to work within the confines of the law and enjoy the best of both worlds.

BOX 1 PUBLIC CHARITIES, "SISTER" ORGANIZATIONS, AND TRANSPARENCY

For nonprofit leaders that want to get involved in politics and policy, the choice of incorporating with 501(c)4 status is a double-edged sword. On the one hand, this status allows the organization to make a clear statement about which political candidates it supports and to freely encourage its members to vote for those candidates, and allows the organization to engage in unlimited lobbying. On the other hand, 501(c)4 status poses a clear disadvantage from the perspective of fundraising and sustaining a base of paying members since organizations with this status cannot offer donors or members a tax write-off in exchange for their membership dues or any additional donations made to the organization, a benefit which is reserved exclusively for 501(c)3 organizations, or public charities.

Many nonprofit leaders have found a way to "have their cake and eat it too." It has become increasingly common for strategic nonprofit leaders to create multiple nonprofit organizations of different types under one corporate umbrella. One common arrangement is to have a 501(c)3, a related 501(c)4, a connected Political Action Committee, and a 527 organization.[4] Consider The Sierra Club, for example. The Sierra Club is a 501(c)4 membership organization whose primary purpose is lobbying in the interest of environmental issues. The Sierra Club Foundation, which is a 501(c)3, is its related charitable and educational arm, while the Sierra Club PAC was set up to make political contributions, and the Sierra Club Voter Education Fund is its related 527 organization created to get-out-the-vote for environmentally friendly candidates.

Although organizations that choose a complex corporate structure such as this cannot actually combine or share day-to-day operations, they can have overlapping members on their boards of directors, share advocacy plans, collaborate on strategies of action, and manage their resources in ways that allow for maximizing their political goals.

According to one expert on this matter,[5] there are many potential concerns with these arrangements. The little bit of information that is required on the IRS reporting form may make it difficult to determine "who is really behind an organization" and how the various inter-connected nonprofit entities are related for political purposes. This lack of transparency also has implications for donors and members, who might be concerned about whether their contribution is being put toward its intended purpose. Finally, those in charge of overseeing these organizations within the government may not even be able to detect whether funds have been diverted to purposes that are inconsistent with an individual organization's tax status, or whether political activities have been financed with inappropriate donations.

Do most donors know the difference between the public charity and the lobbying organization? Should they? Are these inter-connected nonprofit organizational arrangements problematic? What evidence suggests that they are problematic? And if they are problematic, what should be done?

Shaping the Political Environment: Nonprofits and Political Representation

Representation is a key component of the political system in the United States. As a representative democracy, Americans are continually asked to elect representatives or entrust representatives to elect officials on their behalf. Just as politicians represent districts and citizens, organizations can represent our interests in the political system. Professional **lobbyists**, people whose business is to influence legislation on behalf of the group of individuals who hire them, work on behalf of private interests (e.g. oil companies), nonprofit interests (e.g. universities), and public interests (e.g. protection of public lands or better air quality).

The **political representation** role requires nonprofit organizations "to speak for, act for, look after the interests of respective groups."[6] Nonprofit organizations primarily carry out their representation role through lobbying and advocacy activities. Whether it is a critical-care physician paying membership dues to the American Medical Association to support lobbying for higher Medicare reimbursement rates, or a homeless family whose need for safe and affordable long-term housing is represented through the advocacy efforts of the National Coalition for the Homeless, lobbying and advocacy organizations act *on behalf of* those they represent, giving voice to the needs of their members and clients in the political system. In the discussion that follows, we will examine some of the strategies and tactics nonprofit lobbying and advocacy groups use in their efforts to provide political representation for their group members.

What Is Lobbying and Advocacy?

Lobbying can be defined as "attempts to influence legislation or government spending plans in order to achieve an outcome more favorable to a group's agenda or objectives."[7] These attempts to influence legislation or government spending are also frequently referred to as **advocacy**, especially when performed by certain kinds of nonprofits, such as public charities. While the terms lobbying and advocacy are often used synonymously, some have suggested there are differences, with advocacy encompassing a broader set of activities. In general discourse, the term lobbying is used when describing business, labor, or industry groups' attempts to influence policy or politicians while the term advocacy is more frequently used to describe attempts to influence policy by public charities or public interest lobbying groups, such as the American Association of Retired Persons (AARP).

In popular language, lobbying often implies promoting private corporate interests, while advocacy implies promoting social or public interests. Lobbying is concerned with influencing government and policy, while advocacy advances an agenda in both the political arena and society at large. Both lobbying and advocacy are mechanisms for representation in the political system, but advocacy also sometimes includes mobilization and education roles as well.

Lobbying and advocacy organizations employ a wide range of strategies and tactics to influence public policy, and these efforts can be targeted at local, state, or federal levels, or any combination thereof. The pressure for change exerted by groups may be directed toward elected political officials—lawmakers, administrative agencies, or both—depending on whether the organization is (a) taking a stand on a proposed or pending piece of legislation, (b) trying to influence administrative rules for a bill or ordinance that already exists, (c) trying to influence the budget process, or (d) simply trying to increase awareness of the organization's cause or needs of its members or service population. Common activities carried out by nonprofit lobbying and advocacy groups include: testifying before legislative bodies; advocating on behalf of, or against, proposed legislation; making a statement during the public comment portion of government meetings; submitting amicus briefs or statements in court; informally talking and meeting with policy-makers about their organizations and the needs of a group's membership or service population; and participating in government planning or advisory groups.[8]

Although advocacy involves a few more strategies and tactics than lobbying—those aimed at educating and mobilizing—the goals of these activities are ultimately the same. Lobbying and advocacy has four goals:[9] (1) influencing legislation or regulations; (2) improving governmental service programs; (3) securing government funds; and (4) obtaining special benefits for members or clients.

Why Do We Need Lobbying and Advocacy Groups?

Would our democracy work better if we eliminated lobbyists? Instead of lobbyists, citizens could just contact their elected officials individually to express their views. Instead of responding to lobbying groups with excessive resources to advance a special interest, political officials and representatives would need to respond to individual citizens. Pluralist theory and collective action theory help to provide some insight into the role of lobbyists in American representative democracy.

From the pluralist perspective, an abundance of interest groups representing all segments of society is good for democracy and ensures that no single group or interest can become all-powerful, nor can the public become victims of government tyranny. Pluralists argue that multiple, competing groups vying for political influence, public resources, and greater expression of their values in the public arena contribute to a more robust democracy and ensure a fairer and more just distribution of public resources. This system of competing interest groups, along with ever-changing political leadership in both the executive and legislative branches of government,

ensures that all groups get their way on some issues some of the time, but not on all issues all of the time.

Collective action theory argues that citizens organized and working together as a group around a common cause or issue are a more efficient and effective way to exert influence over policy and politicians than citizens working alone as individuals. Collective action theory views nonprofit groups—especially lobbying and advocacy groups—as emerging to accomplish what one person cannot do alone. Collective action theory portrays nonprofits as organizations arising to express group interests—members of a group share common values, beliefs, preferences, or goals. By uniting together around these shared values, beliefs, preferences, or goals, individuals can pool their resources, establish coordinated strategies and action plans, and be more effective at getting the attention of legislators. While elected officials might not be inclined to listen to the views of any one particular voter, most want to be re-elected and therefore cannot afford to ignore or alienate large groups of voters.

Does Lobbying and Advocacy Disproportionately Benefit the Existing Power Elite?

Not all lobbying and advocacy groups are the same. Some groups, such as Greenpeace and the AARP, are described as "public interest" lobbying groups because they advocate for policies that the group believes are of benefit to society as a whole—the environment and care for retired people respectively. These groups would argue that by achieving their goals they create benefits for all of society. By lobbying to protect the environment, Greenpeace's activities result in policies that create healthier oceans and air for all people. Similarly, by protecting the interests of retired people, AARP creates benefits for the families that might support retired individuals and all those who will someday retire themselves. The legislative victories of these public interest lobbying groups create benefits (or consequences, depending on your views) that cannot be limited only to those who pay dues or contribute to the organization. In essence, nonmembers and regular citizens become "free riders," benefitting from the activities of these organizations without being burdened with the cost of supporting those activities.

Of course, that which constitutes the "public interest," and benefits or costs, lies in the eye of the beholder. Consider the National Rifle Association (NRA), a well-known and influential public interest lobbying group. The NRA was founded in 1871 with the mission of promoting firearm competency, safety, and ownership. The NRA provides training and firearm proficiency courses for many police departments. The NRA has a century long history of lobbying for the protection of the Second Amendment right to keep and bear arms and against firearm legislation that might threaten or limit that right.

The NRA is one of the most powerful and politically influential public interest lobbying groups in the US,[10] with a budget of $231 million and a membership over 5 million in May 2013.[11] But some Americans do not believe that the NRA serves the public interest; they disagree with the NRA's mission and have organized their own groups, such as Moms Demand Action for Gun Sense and the Brady Campaign to Prevent Gun Violence. These organizations are also working in the public interest, but with an opposing mission to that of the NRA. One might argue that each of these groups serves the public interest, since they ensure that two sides of the issue are represented in our political system. But, at the same time, the outcomes of their activities might injure or threaten the interests of one or more opposing groups. Whose public interest is more important, that of NRA members or those on the side of Moms Demand Action?

Public interest lobbying groups exist to represent a wide variety of issues and populations

in the US including many organizations that advocate on behalf of underrepresented groups. There are lobbying groups that represent ethnic and racial minorities such as the National Association for the Advancement of Colored People (NAACP) and the Hispanic 100 Policy Committee, and organizations representing several vulnerable populations such as the Disabled American Veterans Foundation and Americans for Children's Health. These advocacy groups work on behalf of populations that have traditionally been marginalized in the political system. The Human Rights Campaign, for example, is a national nonpartisan organization with a mission to lobby lawmakers and educate the public to ensure the rights of lesbian, gay, bisexual, transgender, and queer (LGBTQ) individuals are protected. This organization "engages in direct lobbying, provides grassroots and organizing support, and educates the public to ensure that LGBTQ individuals can be open, honest, and safe at home, at work, and in the community."

Many public interest advocacy groups tend to rely upon grassroots mobilization strategies and national leadership to build a broad membership base by identifying committed members to create and lead state and local chapters to expand their influence around the country. Thus, the power of these advocacy groups is often found in their numbers. Large memberships enable the mobilization of resources to engage in direct phone call or mailing campaigns, marches, and demonstrations. Modern technologies, including the Internet and social media, have made it incredibly fast and simple for these organizations to mobilize members to contact their legislators via text, e-mail, and phone. A simple tweet or Facebook post can quickly mobilize hundreds of members, and potentially reach thousands of nonmembers who are connected to members through social media.

In addition to nonprofit organizations whose main purpose is lobbying and advocacy, public charities and human service organizations also engage in lobbying and advocacy (with some legal constraints). Since public charities (501(c)3 organizations) must carefully balance their service delivery roles with their political representation roles, rather than lobby directly they often work in conjunction with lobbying organizations.

Some human service organizations join coalitions or intermediary groups that function as advocacy "umbrellas," taking on the representation role for public charities. For example, public charities that provide child welfare services may choose to join another nonprofit, The Alliance for Children and Families, which is a national organization that provides advocacy on behalf of nearly 350 nonprofit child welfare service providers throughout the United States. Advocacy umbrellas enable human service organizations to ensure that they have a voice in the political process, without requiring them to directly engage in lobbying activities.

While it is true that the wealthy and powerful are not the only ones to benefit from lobbying groups, it is also true that they probably benefit disproportionately. There is a famous saying by E. E. Schattschneider that "the flaw in the pluralist heaven is that the heavenly chorus sings with a strong upper-class accent."[12] Translated into plain English, the most powerful and well-funded lobbying groups tend to be those representing corporate America—business and industry groups. In contrast to public interest lobbying groups, labor and industry lobbying groups exist to represent the interests of prestigious and wealthy professionals such as doctors, lawyers, and realtors, as well as businesses such as hospitals, restaurant owners, and beer distributors. While these types of lobbying groups may also have large numbers of members to mobilize, their real power is in their financial resources and their ability to persuade elected officials that the health of the American economy rests on the legislators' support of spending decisions (and sometimes laws or rules) that benefit the industry group.

In sum, nonprofit lobbying and advocacy groups play a critical role in the American political system representing the interests of American businesses, private citizens, underrepresented groups, marginalized populations, and the public interest. Lobbying groups, though they seek to advance the interests of their membership, often advance legislation and policies that have beneficial effects for others in society, creating public outcomes for nonmembers. And while some nonprofit organizations are established with the sole purpose of engaging in lobbying and advocacy, other types of nonprofits, specifically public charities, often find mechanisms for engaging in lobbying, either through umbrella organizations or through coalitions with advocacy groups. The complex political system in the United States gives ample opportunities for nonprofit organizations to engage in the political system and represent the interests of their membership or the public at large.

Shaping the Political Environment: Nonprofits and Political Mobilization

While the representation role involves nonprofit organizations speaking *on behalf of* the needs and interests of clientele groups, nonprofits' **political mobilization** role encourages citizens to *directly participate* in the political process. Mobilization activities include encouraging members or clients to attend public hearings or meetings to express their views; persuading or assisting members in writing, calling, e-mailing, or contacting via social media their legislators at local, state, or congressional levels; registering members to vote and encouraging their participation in elections; and, sometimes, encouraging participation in a demonstration, rally, boycott, or protest.

Nonprofits Mobilizing Public Voice

Many local chapters of advocacy organizations mobilize members and the general public to attend state or local public hearings or legislative sessions to express their support or opposition to a proposed ordinance or bill. For example, as the Illinois state legislature debated a bill in 2013 that would allow concealed carry of firearms in the state, the Illinois and Chicago chapters of the gun control group Moms Demand Action worked to turn out citizens at the state capitol speaking out in opposition to the bill, some of whom shared personal testimony about family members who had been victims of gun violence. The Chicago chapter of the organization also worked to mobilize residents of area municipalities considering local gun control ordinances to attend city meetings and speak out in support of these measures. As a result of the pressure put on city governments by members of this group, many suburban communities such as Evanston, Hazel Crest, and Homewood adopted their own gun control measures, including assault weapons bans, giving them local control over the issue before the state legislature passed the concealed carry law. Another frequent scenario involves human service organizations mobilizing clients to give personal testimony at budget hearings or debates, to express opposition to proposed cuts or to plead for expanded services. Many nonprofit mental health organizations, for example, have been successful in staving off or minimizing cuts to Medicaid services by turning out staff, clients, family members, and caregivers in large numbers to protest these cuts at the state budget hearings and county commission meetings.

Historically, those with the highest incomes and education have dominated political participation in the US. While the relationship still exists to some extent, nonprofit organizations have played a critical role in making democracy more inclusive and widening the scope of political participation. The Internet has also been instrumental in this regard, dramatically enhancing the mobilization function of nonprofits. Every major advocacy organization (and many public charities as well) now enables members, clients, and other interested parties to subscribe to "action alert" listservs in order to receive e-mails about specific bills and budget issues that encourage them to contact elected officials and express their views.

Moreover, the process of contacting legislators has been simplified as many nonprofits performing the mobilization role allow visitors to their websites to search for their representatives by zip code and to send e-mails with pre-filled messages just by clicking on a button. Based on the zip code entered, the site generates a listing of all federal and state representatives for the user with boxes alongside the legislators' names that the user can check off in order to compose one letter that can be sent to all selected representatives. Some of the largest and most well-funded advocacy organizations, such as The Christian Coalition, offer mobile apps that enable users to obtain and act on their legislative alerts more quickly through a smartphone. Advocacy organizations and other types of politically inclined nonprofits are also increasingly relying on social media such as Facebook and Twitter to advance mobilization efforts.

Community-organizing groups are a specific type of organization that embodies the political mobilization role of nonprofits. While community-organizing groups may also press for legislative change and social reform using some of the same approaches as advocacy organizations, community-organizing groups differ in that they seek to empower residents and promote the general well-being of entire communities rather than specific interest groups. These objectives are typically accomplished by identifying and training community leaders to become activists, facilitating coalitions, mobilizing community members to vote, pressuring local lawmakers and government administrators for reforms that will benefit the community, developing issue campaigns, and organizing protest activities if conventional strategies fail to bring about the desired social change.

Nonprofits Mobilizing Voters

The mobilization of voters in the United States is an important activity of both partisan and nonpartisan nonprofit organizations. Political parties are one of the most important partisan groups seeking to encourage voting in the US. The two major political parties in the US—the national Republican Party, the Democratic Party—and with other smaller political party organizations such as the Green Party and Tea Party are tax-exempt organizations. These organizations work around the clock during election seasons to register voters and **get-out-the-vote (GOTV)** for candidates who are members of their party, and also work in hopes of persuading undecided voters. Political parties generally do this work through door-to-door canvassing to register voters or asking them to sign pledge cards promising to vote for a particular candidate or slate of candidates. These same organizations also use phone canvassing to mobilize voters, especially for reminding people to get to the polls. Political parties have become very sophisticated in their methods for targeting their efforts at prospective voters, by partnering with private research firms to obtain data that allows them to focus canvassing efforts on neighborhoods where they are most likely to persuade voters in their favor. Many lobbying and advocacy organizations also engage in voter registration or get-out-the-vote work typically with a partisan agenda, going door-knocking or phone-calling, or holding community-based voter registration drives.

Along with political parties, many other types of nonprofits are playing an increasingly influential role in the American political landscape by mobilizing clients, members, and the general public to participate in elections. A wide range of nonprofit organizations participate in elections by holding voter registration drives and working to ensure that registered voters show up to the polls on election day through *nonpartisan* GOTV efforts. Many community-organizing groups, churches, voting rights groups, ethnic and immigrant service organizations, and human service agencies work to mobilize voters regardless of particular political issues or views.

While political parties, labor unions, and lobbying groups of all types have a long history of working to get-out-the-vote for their preferred candidates, the widespread involvement of nonpartisan groups in elections is a more recent phenomenon. Some nonpartisan groups, such as the League of Women Voters, have worked to encourage voter turnout for many decades. However, it was not until the passage of the National Voter Registration Act (NVRA)—also known as the "Motor Voter" law—in 1993 that nonpartisan voter registration and GOTV efforts spread to other types of nonprofit organizations. Signed into law by President Clinton, the goal of the NVRA was to reduce historic disparities in voter turnout rates that fall along lines of race, income, age, and disability.[13]

Many community-organizing groups organize events and assign staff and volunteers to go door-to-door with voter registration forms during election season, in an effort to register new voters, but not to persuade them to vote for any particular candidate. These groups often make phone calls or go door-knocking again in the final days before the election (and on Election Day) to remind people to get to the polls. Other organizations offer "agency-based" voter registration opportunities on-site at the service delivery agency, such as Health Access, or do some combination of agency-based voter registration and door-to-door registration in the community.

Through agency-based voter registration, nonprofit human service organizations play an important role in electoral mobilization. Even after voter registration opportunities were expanded through the 1993 National Voter Registration Act, registration rates remained disproportionately lower among low-income citizens and racial minorities. By performing nonpartisan voter registration and get-out-the-vote (GOTV) activities, human service organizations help to make democracy more inclusive by engaging low-income citizens and marginalized populations in the voting process. In addition to their frequent contact with low-income clients, nonprofits are often more highly trusted by clients than services provided by government voter registration offices. For example, one study shows that black and Hispanic citizens (and citizens from Spanish-speaking households) are more than twice as likely to register to vote via third-party nonprofit groups than white citizens and those from English-speaking households.[14]

Some organizations that offer voter registration go a step further in their voter mobilization efforts by providing information on voter registration deadlines, candidate policy positions and voting records, ballot measures, polling locations, and any other nonpartisan activity intended to increase the likelihood of voting and casting informed votes.[15] Some of these organizations even work to reduce physical barriers to voting, such as providing rides to the polls or helping people obtain absentee ballots, particularly organizations serving elderly persons, or persons with disabilities who may have difficulty getting around in the community. At least with regard to human service organizations, there is strong evidence that nonpartisan voter registration and voter mobilization efforts make a big difference in increasing voter turnout rates of low-income voters.[16]

Nonprofits Mobilizing Public Action

Finally, some nonprofit organizations mobilize their clients for direct participation in the political process through demonstrations, rallies, protests, or boycotts. While these activities constitute more "unconventional" political participation,[17] their potential to politically empower groups can be exceedingly effective, particularly when they are linked to broader social change efforts.

Some political scientists and organizers would argue that political action (through protest,

march, or demonstration) and defiance against government laws or authority and protests that lead to mass disruption are a true source of political power, particularly for the poor who have limited means to effect policy change in other ways. It has been argued that protest forms of political participation are the only actions that have ever produced large-scale dramatic policy reforms.[18] One need only to consider the organized actions of citizens and community-based organizations engaged in the Labor Movement or the Civil Rights Movement to see the merit in this argument. Consider the powerful effects of lunch counter sit-ins, bus boycotts, and marches during the segregation era.

Most organizations that pursue political action strategies to mobilize their members or clientele use them as a limited part of a more comprehensive approach to their advocacy, rather than the main tactic. For example, environmental groups devote most of their resources to direct lobbying, grassroots mobilization, and shaping public opinion through political education, but on occasion determine that a rally or protest is deemed the best strategy for influencing policy.

In order to avoid some of the stigma associated with the term "protesting," some nonprofit organizations have developed alternative terminology. The grassroots pro-life public charity Bound4LIFE organizes "Silent Sieges" through its local chapters across the country, indicating in bold print throughout its website and print materials: "It's not a protest. It's a prayer meeting!"[19] Chapter leaders are required to organize volunteers to participate in Silent Sieges at least monthly to stand outside Planned Parenthood and courthouses with red tape over their mouths bearing the word "life." Although for most organizations (particularly public charities) these types of activities would be rare and part of a broader social change strategy, in the case of Bound4LIFE these public demonstrations are the primary activity of the organization whose stated mission is: "Bound4LIFE exists to mobilize the nation to Fast and Pray for the ending of abortion."

Some nonprofit organizations are attempting to put a positive spin on political demonstrations by "reverse protesting" or assembling in groups in public to demonstrate their appreciation for legislators whose votes align with the group's mission. For example, the grassroots group Moms Demand Action organized a series of "stroller jams" outside the district offices of US Senators voting in favor of background checks for gun buyers in 2013.

It is clear that nonprofit organizations play a critical role in mobilizing groups and individuals to become more engaged in the political process, through direct contact with political officials, voting, and political action. Mobilization activities include encouraging members to contact political officials, enlisting people to register to vote, supporting efforts to get individuals to vote, and inspiring individuals to organize toward political action, be it a march, a bike ride, or a silent sit-in. Each of these activities enables nonprofit organizations to engage in the political system and mobilize their membership and others toward some political goal.

Shaping the Political Environment: Nonprofits and Political Education

The third way that nonprofit organizations engage in the political environment is through **political education**. One type of nonprofit organization that plays a critical role in advancing political education is the public policy research institute, also known as "**think tanks**." These organizations employ professionals, including economists and policy analysts, who conduct research on policy issues and produce reports that are informative for both policymakers and others inside the political decision-making world, but are also a useful source of information for the public. Think tanks seek

to influence policy by providing information to citizens, voters, activists, the media, and policy-makers. While many think tanks claim to be nonpartisan, most of them operate from an ideological perspective, which is often apparent in the policy issues they choose to focus upon, as well as the policy recommendations issued by these organizations. For example, a think tank that focuses on freedom from government interference, tax policy, and gun rights might be assumed to be conservative, while a think tank focused on urban education, poverty, and social justice might be considered liberal.

Some think tanks are more overt in their political leanings than others, and clearly aim to support policies aligned with a distinct ideology. For example, organizations such as the Cato Institute and Heritage Foundation make clear in their mission statements that they work to promote conservative policies, while, at the liberal end of the spectrum, the Center for American Progress and Demos engage in research that supports progressive policies. On the other hand, some nonprofit think tanks have a reputation for being more nonpartisan and generating information that is more objective and politically neutral. Examples of these organizations include Rand Corporation, Brookings Institution, and the Urban Institute.

Government **watchdogs** are another type of nonprofit that performs political education. These organizations play an important role in the political landscape by making more transparent for the public everything from lawmakers' voting decisions, to campaign financing, and government rule-making. These organizations not only provide helpful and unbiased information for citizens trying to better understand their government, but they keep legislators and government bureaucrats more accountable to the public. Some types of government watchdog groups such as the League of Women Voters have been around since the reform movement took hold in America in the early 20th century. However, the Internet has dramatically increased the impact of nonprofit watchdog organizations, making it simple for the average citizen to obtain information on his or her elected officials quickly and at no cost (other than the price of monthly home Internet). Organizations such as Project Vote Smart provide comprehensive information on the voting records of every US Senator and Representative in Congress, as well as the voting records of state lawmakers on key votes in each of the 50 states. The information produced by Project Vote Smart allows prospective voters to familiarize themselves with the positions and values of their legislators, so that the voter can become more informed and decide at election time whether or not they want to re-elect that person to represent them, or whether another candidate might do the job better.

Other government watchdog organizations serve to publicize financial contributions to political campaigns and officials. For example, Opensecrets.org educates the public on the source of campaign funds for federal lawmakers, including the President. Opensecrets.org has a search engine that allows users to find politicians by name and view how much funds were raised for each campaign, as well as the amounts contributed by individuals, Political Action Committees, and lobbying groups. Alternatively, users can also search Opensecrets.org to find contributions and financial activities of specific lobbying organizations.

Other types of nonprofit watchdog groups focus their efforts on educating the public about proposed rules that are developed by bureaucrats within federal agencies. For example, the Center for Effective Government is a watchdog group whose goal is to ensure "government reflects the needs and priorities of the American people, as defined by an informed, engaged citizenry"[20] and aims to make transparent the workings of government in a limited number of priority areas including Citizen Health and Safety, Revenue and Spending, and Openness and Accountability.

Finally, many types of public charities engage in political education activities. Human service organizations play a particularly important role in this regard because many of them provide services to lower-income citizens, who are, statistically speaking, the least likely to be politically engaged.[21] Low-income citizens are often disadvantaged by insufficient education and information needed to participate in the political process.

Nonprofits educate their clients about the rights granted to them under state and federal laws. This may include education related to entitlement programs, due process rights, rights within a particular service system, or basic citizenship rights. Human service organizations also educate their clients about proposed laws and regulations that have the potential to affect them. Many nonprofit women's health and family planning clinics educate their clients, who are often on low incomes, about proposed laws and judicial rulings that may threaten their reproductive freedoms. These types of organizations may also provide clients with education on the positions taken by candidates running for office, including judicial candidates who are prospective appointees to the state and federal bench.

Nonprofit human service organizations also provide political education for their clients by structuring opportunities for them to learn about democratic deliberation and effective political participation. Human service organizations help their clients develop democratic participation skills by providing opportunities for them to serve on client advisory boards and committees, participate in program planning, and serve on ad hoc agency work groups or policy development committees within the organization. By participating in the work of a service agency, clients can acquire the experience and skills required for participation in a democratic society.

Summary

Nonprofit organizations are an important fixture in the American political landscape, engaging in political representation, mobilization, and education roles. Nonprofit organizations fulfill the representation role by lobbying government officials, sometimes in the interests of corporate industries or narrowly defined groups, while other organizations engage in policy advocacy that is aimed at the broader public interest. Through their mobilization roles, nonprofit organizations encourage citizens to become active participants in the political process, by facilitating contact with elected officials or government agencies, registering voters, and encouraging voter participation. Many types of nonprofits provide political education, both partisan and nonpartisan, including think tanks, and policy research institutes, advocacy groups, and many types of public charities provide nonpartisan political education. Lobbying and advocacy groups play a particularly prominent role in the American political arena. While public charities engage in all of these three key roles of political representation, mobilization, and education, these activities cannot comprise a substantial part of their activities and they must be carried out in a strictly nonpartisan fashion.

Websites

Open Secrets: www.opensecrets.org

Project Vote Smart: http://votesmart.org/

Bolder Advocacy: Change the world with advocacy. Navigate the Rules http://bolderadvocacy.org/navigate-the-rules

Notes

1. Skocpol, Theda. 2003. *Diminished Democracy: From Membership to Management in American Civic Life.* Norman, OK: University of Oklahoma Press.

2. Berry, J. M., and D. F. Arons. 2003. *A Voice for Nonprofits.* Washington, DC: Brookings Institution Press.

3. They can, however, publicly adopt a position on a specific issue.

4. Reid, Elizabeth. 2001. Nonprofit Advocacy and Political Participation. In E. T. Boris and C. E. Steuerle (eds), *Nonprofits and Government: Collaboration and Conflict.* Washington, DC: Urban Institute Press, pp. 291–325.

5. Reid (2001).

6. Pitkin, H. F. 1967. *The Concept of Representation.* Berkeley, CA: University of California Press, p. 117.

7. The Business Dictionary. Accessed July 11, 2013 at www.businessdictionary.com/definition/lobby.html

8. LeRoux, Kelly, and Holly Goerdel. 2009. Political Advocacy by Nonprofit Organizations: A Strategic Management Explanation. *Public Performance and Management Review*, 32(4): 514–536; Berry, J. M., and D. F. Arons. 2003. *A Voice for Nonprofits.* Washington, DC: Brookings Institution Press; Ezell, M. 1991. Administrators as Advocates. *Administration in Social Work*, 15(4): 1–18.

9. Kramer, Ralph M. 1981. *Voluntary Agencies and the Welfare State.* Berkeley, CA: University of California Press.

10. Fortune Releases Annual Survey of Most Powerful Lobbying Organizations. *Timewarner.com*, November 15, 1999. Accessed February 12, 2014 at http://archive.is/vni2b

11. Korte, Gregory. 2013. Post-Newtown, NRA Membership Surges to 5 Million. *USA Today.* Accessed February 12, 2014 at www.usatoday.com/story/news/politics/2013/05/04/nra-meeting-lapierre-membership/2135063/

12. Schattschneider, E. E. 1960. *The Semi-Sovereign People.* New York: Holt, Rinehart and Winston.

13. Piven, Frances Fox and Richard A. Cloward. 1977. *Poor People's Movements: Why They Succeed, How They Fail.* New York, NY: Vintage/Knopf Doubleday.

14. Donovan, Megan K. 2011. *States Move to Restrict Voting: What Nonprofits Can Do to Defend the Right to Vote.* Webinar given by the Fair Elections Legal Network, October 27, 2011.

15. See IRS Revenue Rule 2007–41 for specific examples of non-permissible activities and cases illustrating their application. Accessed at www.irs.gov/pub/irs-drop/rr-07–41.pdf

16. LeRoux, Kelly, and Kelly Krawczyk. 2012. Can Nonprofit Organizations Increase Voter Turnout? Findings from an Agency-Based Voter Mobilization Experiment. *Nonprofit and Voluntary Sector Quarterly*, 43(2): 272–292.

17. Patterson, Thomas. 2004. *We the People. A Concise Introduction to American Politics*. New York, NY: McGraw-Hill; Reeser, L., and I. Epstein. 1990. *Professionalization and Activism in Social Work: The Sixties, the Eighties, and the Future*. New York: Columbia University Press.

18. Piven and Cloward (1977).

19. https://bound4life.com/the-silent-siege/. Accessed July 12, 2013.

20. Center for Effective Government. www.foreffectivegov.org/what-we-do. Accessed July 12, 2013.

21. Brady, H. E., S. Verba, and K. L. Schlozman. 1995. Beyond SES: A Resource Model of Political Participation. *American Political Science Review*, 89(2): 271–294.

CHAPTER 21

Insider Status and Outsider Tactics: Advocacy Tactics of Human Service Nonprofits in the Age of New Public Governance

Michal Almog-Bar

Almog-Bar, Michal. Insider Status and Outsider Tactics: Advocacy Tactics of Human Service Nonprofits in the Age of New Public Governance. *Nonprofit Policy Forum 8*(4)(2018). 411–428.

Introduction

Policy advocacy, defined as efforts to influence public policy and thus to effect changes in the nonprofits' operating environment (Boris and Mosher-Williams 1998, 488; Ljubownikow and Crotty 2016), is widely regarded as an eminent feature of the activities of nonprofit organizations (NPOs). This allows them to engage and represent their constituencies; give voice to diverse views and demands; promote economic and social justice; contribute to a more vital, active civil society, and strengthen democracy and equality of opportunity. While interest in nonprofit advocacy has grown in recent years, many studies have focused on those organizations whose main goal and core activity is advocacy (Child and Gronbjerg 2007; Gormley and Cymrot 2006; McCarthy and Castelli 2002). However, these amount to only a small percentage of the NPOs active in many countries. In human services, most nonprofit activity is undertaken by organizations that combine advocacy with the

provision of social services—usually their core activity (Bass, Abramson, and Dewey 2014). They represent disadvantaged, excluded, and vulnerable populations, mediating between these groups and government agencies, and providing a way to bring group concerns to broader public attention, and push for policy or broader social change (Berry 2001; Buffardi, Pekkanen, and Smith 2017; Kimberlin 2010; Pekkanen, Smith, and Tsujinaka 2014; Reid 1999; Salamon and Geller 2008). Policy advocacy by NPOS has been criticized for promoting "special interests" and exerting disproportionate powerful influence on political decision making through large expenditures of organizational funds for advocacy, as well as for promoting socially and politically conservative policy agendas (Reid 1999).

While interest has been growing in the role of nonprofit human service organizations (NPHSOs) in policy advocacy, there is still scant knowledge about the ways in which they carry-out their advocacy activities, and how changes related to governments' adoption of New Public Governance ideas are affecting them. This lack of

DOI: 10.4324/9780367696559-27

scholarly research is especially evident in settings outside the USA (Almog-Bar and Schmid 2014).

The present article aims to broaden understanding of advocacy tactics in the age of New Public Governance. It presents findings of an exploratory study of advocacy activities undertaken by 47 NPHSOs providing services to children, youth, and people with disabilities in Israel. The research utilized qualitative methods to address two main questions: a) how do NPHSOs perceive and analyze their tactical choices and their outcomes? and b) how do they interpret their tactics and relations with the government in the context of their organizational environment, characterized as it is by the contracting-out of social services and collaboration between the government and the NPHSOs.

As in many other countries, Israel has witnessed a tremendous growth of its nonprofit sector. This was especially evident during the 1990s. In economic terms, the Israeli non-profit sector is now one of the largest in the world, funded primarily from public sources (Salamon et al. 2013). In parallel with other places, the political and social environments in which NPHSOs operate in Israel have altered dramatically in the last decade. These changes relate mainly to the growing international perception of the relations between nonprofits and government as a partnership, and to the increasing dependency of government upon NPOs for the delivery of social services under contract. In recent years the partnership approach has become the prevalent model for nonprofit-government relations in developed countries, linking the two in a wide assortment of fields (Bode and Brandsen 2014; Salamon and Toepler 2015). Relying on theories of New Public Governance, describing the pluralistic nature of the contemporary state, in which multiple actors contribute to the policymaking system and the delivery of public services (Dickinson 2016; Osborne 2006), the partnership approach emphasizes the interdependence between the state and various other social actors—including nonprofit organizations—and sees the emergence

of widespread patterns of collaboration among them. New Public Governance emphasizes the significant strengths that nonprofit organizations can bring to the provision of publicly-financed services (Salamon and Toepler 2015). There have been claims that, due to their proximity to specific user groups, nonprofit organizations have a significant advantage over other providers of public services by contributing unique knowledge, innovative skills, flexibility, and an ability to mobilize resources such as volunteers and private charitable resources (Bode and Brandsen 2014).

NPHSOs are major providers of government-funded social services to children, youth, and people with disabilities in Israel. This large group of NPHSOs is highly dependent on the government not only for its funding, but also for the relevant work conditions, regulation, and supervision (Schmid 2003). However, these organizations have an additional role in enhancing human and social rights, in order to protect and advance the well-being of the clients they represent: advocacy, an essential component of their mission as civil society organizations. This study aims, therefore, to shed light on NPHSOs' perceptions of advocacy, and the tactics they employ in the current era of New Public Governance.

Advocacy Tactics and Modes of Operation of NPHSOs

The literature presents an extensive range of potential advocacy activities that NPHSOs may use in their efforts to influence public policy. They are usually grouped into clusters that include: legislative advocacy; administrative advocacy; grassroots advocacy; judicial (legal) advocacy; electoral advocacy; media advocacy; research and public education; coalition building; and direct actions (Casey 2011; Guo and Saxton 2010; Reid 1999; McCarthy and Castelli 2002).

Which advocacy tactics do NPHSOs use in their efforts to influence public policy? Several studies suggest taxonomy of different types of tactics and activities. Berry and Arons (2003) divide nine different advocacy tactics into two groups: The first comprises legislative, aggressive, and confrontational tactics, including those such as lobbying for a bill or policy; testifying in hearings; releasing research reports; and encouraging members to call or write to policy-makers. The second group comprises less aggressive administrative tactics. These include more cooperative forms of interaction such as meeting with government officials; working in a planning or advisory group; responding to requests for information; and socializing with government officials.

In their research Berry and Arons (2003) found a strong tendency among the NPOs they surveyed in the USA to rely on administrative advocacy and cooperative tactics. The authors suggest that the consistent strategic approach of most nonprofit leaders who work with government is to create relationships that enhance the position of their organization within the governmental process. The key for these leaders is to understand what government bureaucracies want from NPOs, build those capacities into the organization, and develop personal relationships with the policy-makers whose decisions affect the nonprofit. As trust is established, the nonprofit hopes it will increasingly be integrated in the governmental process, and will be able to work alongside policymakers. They conclude that "nonprofit leaders do not think so much of tactics of advocacy as they do of ways to insinuate themselves inside government" (Berry and Arons 2003, 104).

Similarly, Onyx et al. (2010) found that Australian nonprofits are much more likely to undertake institutional than radical advocacy action. Such actions—which the authors term "advocacy with gloves on"—are perceived as more professional, enabling organizations to establish constructive working partnerships with the government, and facilitating access to policy-making processes, while protecting them from punishment and governmental repression.

Other scholars have presented similar findings, revealing that activities vis-à-vis government agencies such as correspondence with, visiting, or calling government officials—which are perceived as "softer" and less demanding, and relying on the expert power of professionals—are the most prevalent tactics among NPHSOs in different countries. By contrast, more radical, confrontational tactics such as protest activities and grassroots lobbying are the least prevalent (Buffardi, Pekkanen, and Smith 2017; Donaldson 2007; Salamon and Geller 2008; Schmid, Bar, and Nirel 2008; Verschuere and De Corte 2015).

Some studies use a more common classification of activities, differentiating between insider and outsider strategies and tactics (Gais and Walker 1991; Gormley and Cymrot 2006; Onyx et al. 2010). Insider tactics are intended to change policy through direct work with policy-makers and other institutional elites that emphasize working 'inside the system'. Outsider tactics, sometimes termed 'indirect' (Mosley 2011), refer to extra-institutional tactics that emphasize working outside the system, such as public education; mass media; protests; boycotts, and demonstrations. These studies point to evidence that NPHSOs prefer insider tactics, and use them far more often than outsider tactics. One example of this is their participation in the development or revision of regulations. Such insider tactics are considered particularly important and effective in influencing policy (Bass et al. 2007; Buffardi, Pekkanen, and Smith 2017; Donaldson 2007; Gormley and Cymrot 2006; Hoefer 2001; Mosley 2011). According to Mosley (2011), organizations that are dependent on governmental funding may advocate for the protection of vital funding streams that can ensure funding stability. They also build relationships with decision-makers, creating advocacy opportunities that would not otherwise arise.

What can explain the greater use of insider, institutional, and less confrontational tactics by NPHSOs? The processes of privatization and the contracting-out of services have led to the growing mutual dependency of NPHSOs and government agencies. Government is increasingly dependent on local nonprofit organizations to provide services, feedback, and expertise in the implementation of programs in relation to social needs. On the other hand, nonprofit organizations are dependent on the government for funding. Such increased collaboration regarding program design, implementation, and evaluation may be making insider tactics part of the routine interactions between nonprofit organizations and government (Bass et al. 2007; Mosley 2011).

Collaborative work creates an opportunity to shape policies and programs, and exert influence. While fundamental decisions about funding and the broad outlines of social policy lie far beyond the reach of nonprofit executives, at the next level of decision-making—regarding the specifics of public policy and the allocation of funds within the sector—the directors of these organizations have a real opportunity to participate in and influence these processes. However, while institutional, insider tactics may ensure access to key players and deliver policy change, in the reality of nonprofit dependency on state resources, a close-knit, elite group of nonprofit organizations may be created that is, in effect, part of the state machinery. These are vulnerable to co-option, and risk the alienation of advocates from their respective memberships and constituencies (Onyx et al. 2010).

Method

The study presented in this article examined the perceptions of NPHSOs regarding the tactics they employ in order to influence public policy-making, in the context of New Public Governance.

Population and Data Collection
The research population included 650 NPHSOs that serve two different target groups: children and youth, and people with disabilities. We chose these organizations because they represent two major areas of social services in Israel, as reflected both in the number of organizations operating in each field, and the scope and variety of services they provide. From this list of organizations a sample of 47 organizations was chosen. All the organizations received some funding from the government—mostly through contracts for governmental services—ranging from 50–90 per cent of their total budget. 51% of the total income of the nonprofit sector in Israel is derived from government funding. However, the share of government funding to social service-providing nonprofits is higher (Almog-Bar 2016).

The main activity of the organizations in the sample was the provision of social services: They did not define themselves as advocacy organizations. Most of the organizations provided direct care, educational services, counseling, and support.

The sample of organizations was varied with respect to age, size, and geographic location.

Data were collected using 47 semi-structured, in-depth interviews with CEOs of the NPHSOs. 19 of the CEOs interviewed were women and 27 were men. The interview protocol consisted of open-ended questions about the policy advocacy activities of the respective organizations; their perception of advocacy, and the tactics they employed; the main spheres of political activity, and their objectives for change. The interviews were recorded, and then transcribed.

Data Analysis
We used a qualitative content analysis design to explore the social meaning attributed to advocacy strategies and tactics. This approach derived from the theoretical framework of social construction, which informed our analysis (Berger and Luckmann 1967). Against this background, we employed a qualitative, thematic analysis of the content to explore the strategies and tactics of NPHSOs, by identifying key issues and arguments as they were constructed in the interviews.

To ensure reliable results, two analysts analyzed the data.

Findings

Advocacy as Partnership

The majority of the CEOs interviewed defined their main strategy of advocacy as cooperation, as part of what they defined as their partnership with the government. One CEO explained: "We believe in cooperation and in the need to reach compromises which will allow all sides to achieve their policy goals." Another stated: "We would usually implement strategy of cooperation with an inside and quiet approach."

Others claimed that the dependency of these organizations on the government has led to strategies of cooperation. Cooperation includes working behind the scenes and quiet, ongoing dialogue with people in the government for reaching compromises and understandings. The main tactics that the CEOs reported were insider, cooperative administrative tactics, including meetings with government officials— mainly people in middle positions in the ministries of welfare and education; participation in government committees, e.g., participating in the development or revision of regulations; responding to requests for information; letter and e-mail correspondence; and deliberating with government officials.

A key component that the organizations perceive as important in their advocacy within the framework of cooperation is their professional expertise. Many of the organizations serve on professional committees and in governmental planning and advisory groups. They therefore try to position themselves as the main suppliers of information and research regarding the relevant issues. They present information about services and clients to the government, using this to highlight problems, move issues to a higher status on the agenda, and initiate policy solutions and services for the populations they serve.

Another insider tactic that many organizations use is forming and utilizing personal connections with people in government, including socializing with government officials. The CEO of a large organization serving people with hearing impairments explained that he devotes a lot of effort to maintaining personal relationships with government officials and ministers and members of parliament. When a government committee, dealing with large-scale reform in the Israeli educational system, ignored the special educational needs and services of people with hearing impairments, representatives of the organization used their personal ties to approach the Minister of Education at a social event, and requested her help. The next day, the organization received an invitation to a meeting with the head of the government committee.

Another CEO explained: "When needed, we send people that we know, who have connections in the right places." While forming good connections with people in positions of authority may support the organization in its efforts to change policies, it can also restrain the ability of NPHSOs to confront government. Thus, the cooperative form of advocacy is also a function of the dependency of NPHSOs on the government and the fear of sanctions.

What kinds of issues and aims are promoted when advocacy is framed as partnership? Analyzing the different examples of advocacy activities cited by the CEOs in the interviews, it is clear that most NPHSOs are greatly concerned with issues related to the specific populations they serve and their immediate problems. Far-reaching societal issues relating to more broadly-defined populations are not usually part of their advocacy work.

Most of the organizations promote issues related to governmental budget allocations. However, a distinction needs to be made between two different sets of issues: The first comprises issues dealing with securing or increasing budgets for an organization's maintenance and survival; of ensuring current governmental subsidies and financial support or increasing future governmental support; or matters related to the NPHSO's tax payments. The second set of issues concerns advocacy about the adequacy and appropriateness of governmental responses to social needs, including expressing concerns about changes in policy, entitlements, benefit levels, and social investment, as well as advocacy in support of new investment, new policy and innovative approaches to addressing social problems.

While the line between these two sets of issues is not always clear, it is important to note the difference between them. The first is characterized by the organization's self-interest, and focuses on its survival in the institutional environment (Mosley 2012). The second focuses more on the clients' needs and the services they receive. Most organizations interviewed in the study reported advocacy efforts and campaigns related to the second set of issues, focusing more on clients' needs and rights than on organizational survival and maintenance. This included new legislation that they proposed and promoted (more than 25 proposals of legislation), focusing on rights and services for their clients.

Insider Status and Outsider Tactics

Most of the organizations in the study emphasized their preference for cooperative strategies and their efforts to achieve insider status in policy-making processes through the use of tactics associated with institutional, administrative tactics, such as meetings, ongoing dialogues, and socializing with people in the government. Achieving insider status was perceived as important, as it facilitates accessibility to decision-making processes, and secures organizational legitimacy. However, together with the predominance of such insider tactics, many NPHSOs described the common utilization of tactics such as exerting pressure on government officials through the media and elected politicians.

Most organizations referred to the use of both insider and outsider tactics when they explained their advocacy modus operandi. As one CEO explained:

> Our advocacy strategy is cooperation and professional compromise that is constantly accompanied by the willingness to [apply] public pressure on government through the media. We will usually start with professional, quiet dialogue, [and] will try to reach professional compromises, but if it does not happen, we will turn to a louder mode of operation, [and] will try to create supportive public opinion and media pressure. We will present people with disabilities (who are our clients) in the media and will use our political connections.

However, many organizations contended that the employment of outsider tactics is possible only after establishing good connections with people in the government, establishing the organization as an expert in its field of service and the government as dependent on the organization's knowledge and provision of services.

Outsider tactics are usually employed as a reactive pattern to policy actions by the government, and are not usually the organization's first choice. In one case, an organization of parents to children with developmental disabilities on the autism spectrum heard rumors that the Ministry of Health was planning to violate the right of disabled children to receive public rehabilitation services and severely cut the budget of the treatment center that is the main public facility for such children in northern Israel—one of the largest facilities in the country. After unsuccessful meetings with ministry officials, they decided to publish an advertisement in a leading daily newspaper, accusing the ministry of abandoning these children, and calling it to protect them rather than harming them. One day after the publication of the advertisement, the Ministry of Health announced that it would not cut the center's budget. The CEO of the organization explained that the ministry is deeply dependent on the existence of this center, as the only such facility in the north of the country, serving hundreds of children and providing services that the ministry itself does not supply, including diagnostic services.

While the most common outsider tactics used were pressure through media and elected politicians, thirty (30) organizations reported that, in recent years, they had appealed to the Supreme Court against government ministries and institutions. Others were involved in strikes and in demonstrations in front of government ministries and parliament. In a few cases the organizations attacked government officials personally, delegitimizing them in the media. As mentioned above, many organizations were involved in lobbying activities as part of their attempt to promote new legislation in parliament, mostly through coalitions of NPHSOs. In most of these cases, the government opposed the legislation; e.g., the Subtitles Law, ensuring that television shows include subtitles for people with hearing impairments, or the implementation of the Rehabilitation Day-care Centers Law, which proclaims the right of children with disability to a day-care center with rehabilitation services.

Although lobbying is not restricted by law in Israel, it could carry some harsh consequences for the NPHSOs that have contracts with the government. The NPHSOs participating in the study mentioned a few risks and penalties that they associate with lobbying in particular and outsider tactics in general. One of the CEOs explained: "High officials in the ministries perceive our efforts to be involved in policy-making as an attempt to cause them personal and professional damage, and are looking for instances where they can punish us." The "punishments" consisted of delays, mainly in relation to the amount of time taken to deal with issues and obtain governmental approval.

Another penalty is the labeling of the organization as one that opposes the government, thereby de-legitimizing both its management and its services. This can sometimes lead to threats of cutting the organization's budget, and to its exclusion from meetings and consultations. However, when specifically asked about this, none of the organizations could cite an instance when the government carried out such threats. One CEO stated that: "The threats are always in the background of our activity, but I do not think that they will cut our budgets. They have never done so." Some CEOs contended that the use of more aggressive, outsider tactics leads the organization to a position of more power and respect in the eyes of the government.

Another CEO commented that "the professional power and prestige of the organization, as well as the fact that—while we rely heavily on government budgets—we have budget sources from donations, limiting the ability of government to harm us." Thus, while the organizations are aware of the risks associated with outsider activities, they do not perceive this as a realistic threat to their survival.

Discussion and Conclusions

This article presents findings on advocacy tactics employed by NPHSOs in Israel in their efforts to influence governmental policies. These NPHSOs frame their advocacy as partnership with the government; they widely use cooperative, administrative, institutional, and insider tactics; they try to achieve insider status in order to secure their participation in decision-making processes and attain a better position from which to promote policy issues (Berry and Arons 2003). The importance that they attribute to achieving insider status can be explained by their high dependency on the government for funding and legitimacy as part of the contracting-out culture: These organizations now supply more services for the government than they used to do in the past and, in order to survive in their new environments and secure these resources, they wish to retain this support (Schmid 2003).

These findings are consistent with other studies that suggest a preference among nonprofits for insider, softer, and less-confrontational tactics (Almog-Bar and Schmid 2014; Buffardi, Pekkanen, and Smith 2017). Verschuere and De Corte (2015) contend that the choice of softer-insider advocacy tactics is especially the case for nonprofit organizations that are active under third-party government, in which they have developed strong ties with the public sector for implementing social services. The findings of this study reveal that, in the Israeli case too, NPHSOs that have been accepted by policy-makers as legitimate players and part of the partnership with government, wish to reinforce their status by using insider, cooperative tactics.

However, the study reveals that the tendency towards the use of insider tactics is accompanied by a variety of aggressive, confrontational, outsider tactics. These include exerting pressure through the media and politicians; appealing to the courts; participation in coalitions with other nonprofit organizations; aggressive lobbying, mobilizing and educating the public; and participation in demonstrations.

Since the government under 'partnership' policies is highly dependent on NPHSOs for information and the delivery of certain services, provider organizations that have insider status can attain more power. This is often translated into the utilization of tactics that challenge the government. While organizations are aware of the risks associated with implementing outsider tactics, it does not seem to restrict their use of them.

While the findings of this study support the argument that contracting-out of governmental services to nonprofits, as part of the partnership between the two sectors, gives NPHSOs more opportunities to influence policy (Mosley 2011), it challenges the notion that this is mainly done by using insider, cooperative tactics (Berry and Arons 2003; Mosley 2012; Onyx et al. 2010). They also reveal how organizations can use their insider status to attain more power and legitimacy, and thus influence the government from the outside.

Partnership in the age of New Public Governance entails greater mutual dependence between government and nonprofits (Salamon and Toepler 2015): The NPHSOs need government funding, while government relies almost entirely on NPHSOs to supply its services. The government lacks the infrastructure, mechanisms, technologies, and knowledge for supplying social services, and therefore has become dependent on NPHSOs (Bode and Brandsen 2014). Thus, NPHSOs are firstly concerned with establishing their insider status, using cooperative tactics to ensure a steady flow of resources through contracts and governmental support. Later, after achieving this status, they feel confident to turn to more aggressive tactics, utilizing their relative power as major providers of social services, with professional knowledge and expertise, and close relations with clients. In line with the argument of Resource Dependence Theory, NPHSOs continue to make efforts to change the power-dependence relations with their environment, and increase their autonomy, engaging different strategies (Pfeffer and Salancik 2003). In this way, the organizations develop their distinctive competence and organizational capacity, in an attempt to increase the dependence of government on the services that they provide.

Salamon and Toepler (2015) contend that one of the major concerns about government-nonprofit collaboration relates to the ability of nonprofits to pursue their advocacy or lobbying responsibilities while working closely with government agencies. Overall, the findings of this study imply that the shift towards increased government funding to nonprofits, and the policy emphasis on creating partnership and dialogue between the two parties as part of New Public Governance, may increase NPHSOs' opportunities to influence government, using a wide variety of tactics. The findings suggest that these organizations can be important players in social policy-making, and should be understood as interest groups who mobilize resources in order to create policy change—and not only as service providers (Bass, Abramson, and Dewey 2014).

In the Israeli case, rather than strictly conforming to governmental policies, these organizations strive to represent their clients and protect their rights, and not only advance their organization's self-interest. While most of the advocacy efforts do not call for over-arching, fundamental changes in social policies (Buffardi, Pekkanen, and Smith 2017), they still focus on policies and services related to the needs of vulnerable populations within the large, diverse communities of people with disabilities and children. Moreover, while partnering with the government, the organizations are not afraid of criticizing and challenging governmental policies related to the populations they serve. This suggests that, while operating within a more complex environment than before, NPHSOs in the age of New Public Governance can still find ways of fulfilling their advocacy roles as civil society organizations representing and promoting the rights of their clients. It seems that policies of partnership between government and nonprofits are intensifying the growing polarization between large, often multi-service nonprofits mainly funded by government and small, community-based organizations that often lack adequate funding and staffing, as well as close connections with government (Smith 2012). Thus, it may be that partnerships policies reinforce the voice of strong nonprofits which become a part of a close-knit community of policy-makers, while distancing smaller, less professional civil society organizations from forums of policy-making.

The findings reveal that the desire for budget expansion is clearly one of the major motivations for policy advocacy by NPHSOs. However more in-depth research is needed in order to distinguish between the different aims related to budget expansion, and especially between budgets for service improvement for clients and those for organizational maintenance and survival.

Finally, it is important to note that the findings of this study should be understood in the specific national, structural, and cultural context in which these organizations operate. However, they may be helpful for understanding advocacy tactics in other locations where policies of partnership inspired by the New Public Governance approach exist.

References

Almog-Bar, M. 2016. "Policy Initiatives Towards the Nonprofit Sector: Insights from the Israeli Case." *Nonprofit Policy Forum* 7 (2):237–256.

Almog-Bar, M., and H. Schmid. 2014. "Advocacy Activities by Nonprofit Human Service Organizations: A Critical Review." *Nonprofit and Voluntary Sector Quarterly* 43 (1):11–35.

Bass, G. D., A. Abramson, and E. Dewey. 2014. "Effective Advocacy: Lessons for Nonprofit Leaders from Research and Practice." In *Nonprofits and Advocacy: Engaging Community and Government in an Era of Retrenchment*, edited by R. Pekkanen, S. R. Smith, and Y. Tsujinaka, 254–294. Baltimore: Johns Hopkins University Press.

Bass, G. D., D. F. Arons, K. Guinane, and M. Carter. 2007. *Seen But Not Heard: Strengthening Nonprofit Advocacy*. Washington, DC: Aspen Institute.

Berger, P. L., and T. Luckmann. 1967. *The Social Construction of Reality*. New York: Anchor Books.

Berry, J. 2001. "Effective Advocacy for Nonprofits." In *Exploring Organizations and Advocacy: Strategies and Finances*, edited by E. Reid and M. Montilla, Vol. 2 (1), 1–8. Washington, DC: Urban Institute Press, Nonprofit Advocacy and the Policy Process.

Berry, J., and D. F. Arons. 2003. *A Voice for Nonprofits*. Washington, DC: The Brookings Institution.

Bode, I., and T. Brandsen. 2014. "State-Third Sector Partnerships: A Short Overview of Key Issues in the Debate: Introduction to the Special Issue on State-Third Sector Partnerships." *Public Management Review* 16:1055–1066.

Boris, E., and R. Mosher-Williams. 1998. "Nonprofit Advocacy Organizations: Assessing the Definitions, Classifications, and Data." *Nonprofit and Voluntary Sector Quarterly* 27:488–506.

Buffardi, A. L., R. Pekkanen, and S. R. Smith. 2017. "Proactive or Protective? Dimensions of and Advocacy Activities Associated with Reported Policy Change by Nonprofit Organizations." *Voluntas* 28 (3):1226–1248.

Casey, J. 2011. *Understanding Advocacy: A Primer on the Policy-Making Role of Nonprofit Organizations*. New York: Baruch College, City University of New York, Center for Nonprofit Strategy.

Child, C. D., and K. A. Gronbjerg. 2007. "Nonprofit Advocacy Organizations: Their Characteristics and Activities." *Social Science Quarterly* 88:259–281.

Dickinson, H. 2016. "From New Public Management to New Public Governance: The Implications for a 'New Public Service'." In *The Three Sector Solution: Delivering Public Policy in Collaboration with Not-For-Profits and Business*, edited by J. Butcher and D. Gilchrist, 41–60. Canberra: ANU Press.

Donaldson, L. 2007. "Advocacy by Nonprofit Human Service Agencies: Organizational Factors as Correlates to Advocacy Behavior." *Journal of Community Practice* 15:139–158.

Gais, T., and J. Walker, Jr. 1991. "Pathways to Influence in American Politics." In *Mobilizing Interest Groups in America*, edited by J. Walker, Jr., 103–121. Ann Arbor: University of Michigan Press.

Gormley, W., and H. Cymrot. 2006. "The Strategic Choices of Child Advocacy Groups." *Nonprofit and Voluntary Sector Quarterly* 35:102–122.

Guo, C., and G. D. Saxton. 2010. "Voice-In, Voice-Out: Constituent Participation and Nonprofit Advocacy." *Nonprofit Policy Forum* 1:1–25.

Hoefer, R. 2001. "Highly Effective Human Services Interest Groups: Seven Key Practices." *Journal of Community Practice* 9 (3):1–13.

Kimberlin, S. E. 2010. "Advocacy by Nonprofits: Roles and Practices of Core Advocacy Organizations and Direct Service Agencies." *Journal of Policy Practice* 9:164–182.

Ljubownikow, S., and J. Crotty. 2016. "Nonprofit Influence on Public Policy: Exploring Nonprofit Advocacy in Russia." *Nonprofit and Voluntary Sector Quarterly* 45:314–332.

McCarthy, J. D., and J. Castelli. 2002. "The Necessity for Studying Organizational Advocacy Comparatively." In *Measuring the Impact of the Nonprofit Sector*, edited by P. Flynn and V. A. Hodgkinson, 103–121. New York: Plenum Press.

Mosley, J. E. 2011. "Institutionalization, Privatization and Political Opportunity: What Tactical Choices Reveal about the Policy Advocacy of Human Service Nonprofits." *Nonprofit and Voluntary Sector Quarterly* 40:435–457.

Mosley, J. E. 2012. "Keeping the Lights On: How Government Funding Concerns Drive the Advocacy Agendas of Nonprofit Homeless Service Providers." *Journal of Public Administration Research and Theory* 22 (4):841–866.

Onyx, J., L. Armitage, R. Dalton, R. Melville, J. Casey, and R. Banks. 2010. "Advocacy with Gloves: The 'Manners' of Strategy Used by Some Third Sector Organizations Undertaking Advocacy in NSW and Queensland." *Voluntas* 21:41–61.

Osborne, S. P. 2006. "The New Public Governance?" *Public Management Review* 8 (3):377–387.

Pekkanen, R., S. R. Smith, and Y. Tsujinaka. 2014. *Nonprofits and Advocacy: Engaging Community and Government in an Era of Retrenchment*. Baltimore: Johns Hopkins University Press.

Pfeffer, J., and G. Salancik. 2003. *The External Control of Organizations: A Resource Dependence Perspective*, 2nd ed. Stanford, CA: Stanford University Press.

Reid, E. J. 1999. "Nonprofit Advocacy and Political Participation." In *Nonprofit and Government*, edited by E. T. Boris and C. E. Steuerle, 291–308. Washington, DC: The Urban Institute Press.

Salamon, L. M., and S. L. Geller. 2008. *Nonprofit America: A Force for Democracy*. Baltimore: Center for Civil Society Studies, Institute for Public Policy, Johns Hopkins University, communiqué no. 9.

Salamon, L. M., M. W. Sokolowski, M. Haddock, and H. Tice. 2013. *The State of Global Civil Society and Volunteering*. Baltimore: Johns Hopkins Center for Civil Society Studies.

Salamon, L. M., and S. Toepler. 2015. "Government-Nonprofit Cooperation: Anomaly or Necessity?" *Voluntas* 26 (6):2155–2177.

Schmid, H. 2003. "Rethinking the Policy of Contracting Out Social Services to Non-Governmental

Organizations: Lessons and Dilemmas." *Public Management Review* 5 (3):307–323.

Schmid, H., M. Bar, and R. Nirel. 2008. "Advocacy Activities in Nonprofit Human Service Organizations: Implications for Policy." *Nonprofit and Voluntary Sector Quarterly* 37:581–602.

Smith, S. R. 2012. "Changing Government Policy and Its Implications for Nonprofit Management Education" *Nonprofit Management and Leadership* 23 (1):29–41.

Verschuere, B., and J. De Corte. 2015. "Nonprofit Advocacy under a Third-Party Government Regime: Cooperation or Conflict?" *Voluntas* 26:222–241.

PART VII

Community and Civil Society Theories of the Nonprofit Sector

Nonprofit organizations do not simply exist in communities; they are essential elements or components of communities and community life. Voluntary nonprofits (or, as they sometimes are called, "donative nonprofits") in particular draw volunteer time and effort, leadership, gifts of money and supplies, government contracts, credibility, and membership in networks from their communities.[1] They give back to their communities directly through the services and programs they provide and also indirectly by creating opportunities for citizens to associate, create networks, express their creativity, grow personally, and develop community leadership skills.[2]

Because communities, civics, politics, government, the economy, and nonprofit organizations are inexorably intertwined, scholars from many fields have contributed to our knowledge and understanding of nonprofits in communities, but community theories are primarily from sociology. Civil society theories draw heavily from sociology but also from political science, economics, and philosophy. Because civil society theories overlap with and share many perspectives and issues with sociologists, they are included in this part.

Sociological theories tend to be "rich theories" that examine questions that are usually quite different from those of economists and political scientists. For example, sociologists have developed theories and research that help to explain the "place" of nonprofits in communities and the niches they fill, the complexity of relationships among nonprofit organizations, and interaction patterns among their stakeholders and other community institutions. Sociological theories also identify and explain the roles of community networks of individuals, groups, and organizations and the importance of community elites and influential nonprofits.

Voluntary Association in Communities

Community theories in the United States have a long and useful history. In the colonial era in the United States, people and families could not rely on government for assistance. They had to do things for themselves. When the task at hand was more than one family could do, they turned to each other for assistance. They had no alternative. Families had to work together to survive and carve out lives in the hostile environment. In the process of accomplishing needed tasks, people

DOI: 10.4324/9780367696559-28

drew closer to others, learned who could be trusted, and developed obligations to each other. Communities were strengthened. As we mentioned in Part II, when Alexis de Tocqueville, the "founder of the sociology of politics,"[3] visited the United States in the 1830s, "it was the Americans' propensity for civic association that impressed him the most as the key to their unprecedented ability to make democracy work."[4] Tocqueville's fascination with the American tendency to associate voluntarily is evident:

> Americans of all ages, all stations in life, and all types of disposition are forever forming associations in the U.S. and in many other societies. There are not only commercial and industrial in which all take part, but others of a thousand different types—religious, moral, serious, futile, very general and very limited, immensely large and very minute. Americans combine to give fetes, found seminaries, build churches, distribute books, and send missionaries to the antipodes. Hospitals, prisons, and schools take shape in that way. Finally, if they want to proclaim a truth or propagate some feeling by the encouragement of a great example, they form an association. In every case, at the head of any new undertaking, where in France you would find the government or in England some territorial magnate, in the United States you are sure to find an association.[5]

The lessons of the colonial days were learned well. The tradition of mutual support has lasted through the centuries, and Americans have always turned to voluntary associations as the primary institutions through which "community" finds expression and is enacted. It can be argued that it is because participation has always been an integral part of U.S. history that voluntary nonprofit organizations are so pervasive in our society and accepted so unquestioningly as community institutions in the U.S. and in democracies around the world.

Strengthening Civic Life and Communities: Social Capital Formation

Tocqueville continued:

> I shall have occasion hereafter to show the effects of association in civil life; I confine myself for the present to the political world. . . . The second degree in the exercise of the right of association is the power of meeting. When an association is allowed to establish centers of action at certain important points in the country, its activity is increased and its influence extended. Men have the opportunity of seeing one another; means of execution are combined; *and opinions are maintained with a warmth and energy that written language can never attain* [emphasis added].[6]

Tocqueville observed what is known today as *social capital*: "the change in relations among persons that facilitate actions," a change that is formed through ongoing association.[7] Social capital is intangible—it exists in the relationships among people. It is the warmth and trust that Tocqueville described—the bonds of trust, goodwill, and reciprocity that are created among community members while they work together to accomplish purposes they care about individually and collectively. Social capital is *a by-product of their engagement in activities*. Social capital decreases transaction costs and thereby facilitates getting future tasks done efficiently, easily, comfortably, and with mutual trust.[8] With social capital, the need for formal contracts, written agreements, rigid rules, inflexible policies, or bureaucratic controls decreases. "A group within which there is extensive trustworthiness and extensive trust is able to accomplish much more than a comparable group without that trustworthiness and trust."[9]

For example, as volunteers associate at regular meetings of a board of trustees to coordinate a neighborhood watch program or to help the local PTA offer children a safe Halloween experience, they are creating social capital—without consciously thinking about this secondary benefit that flows unintended from their association. All they care about at the moment is the program they are working on or the problem they are solving. The benefits of social capital come later to the participating individuals, to the networks to which they belong, and to the community—as a side effect of their associations.

> In a housing project built during World War II in an eastern city of the United States, there were many physical problems caused by poor construction: faulty plumbing, crumbling sidewalks, and other defects. . . . Residents organized to confront the builders and to address these problems in other ways. Later, when the problems were solved, the organization remained as available social capital that improved the quality of life for residents. Residents had resources available that they had seen as unavailable where they had lived before. (For example, despite the fact that the number of teenagers in the community was smaller, residents were *more* likely to express satisfaction with the availability of teenage babysitters.) [emphasis in the original][10]

Obligations are important for the formation of social capital. When I ask you for a favor, an obligation is created. Your granted favor, however, does not benefit only me, and the existence of my obligation to you is not necessarily a negative state. You (the grantor of the favor) also benefit by

> adding to a drawing fund of social capital available in a time of [future] need. If the [asker] can satisfy his need through self-sufficiency, or through aid from some official source without incurring an obligation, he will do so—and thus fail to add to the social capital outstanding in the community.[11]

Information and trustworthiness are other agents of social capital. When we share important information, this creates an obligation and thus social capital. For example, when a nonprofit becomes known as a source of accurate and reliable information, it benefits other individuals and organizations that ask for and use the information. The obligation strengthens the broader community by creating a reciprocal obligation—and social capital.

Although social capital can be created in any type of organization, nonprofits are ideal settings—particularly voluntary nonprofits. We give up some of our leisure time to volunteer with nonprofits because we care enough about something to give of our time.[12] Typically, no one tells us that we must volunteer, and most of us do not choose to associate with a nonprofit or its cause in order to increase our income.[13] When we care about something, we join together (associate), put energy and emotion into a task, and make things happen. While we are getting things done, we also create social capital and strengthen our community. Future community problems will be easier to solve and future tasks will be easier to accomplish because social capital has been created and we are now members of networks with shared trust and obligations.

Networks

> Networking, one of my mother's old phrases, musty slang of yesteryear. Even in her sixties she still did something she called that, though as far as I could see all it meant was having lunch with some other woman.[14]

Networks are connections created through stable, recurrent, formal, or informal interactions among individuals.

> Network structures serve both as important opportunities and barriers to actors' performances and their realization of ends. The fundamental assumption of network analysis is that the social structures generated by networks of social ties have important consequences both for the individual actors and for the system within which they are embedded.[15]

NGOs often serve as intermediary community structures helping to create and maintain networks of organizations among the three sectors. Nonprofits initiate endeavors that bring together individuals from private businesses, government agencies, and other nonprofits (sometimes private foundations) to solve community problems and capitalize on opportunities—individuals and organizations that would not ordinarily otherwise know each other or work together. Well-developed networks may become *community partnerships*. Walter Powell describes *network nonprofit organizations* as organizations that have no hierarchy and consist of nothing other than horizontal links and relationships based on trust, reciprocity, and reputation.[16] Increasingly these "horizontal links" are becoming community *partnerships* among organizations in all three sectors that are essential for solving community problems. Some national government agencies and some intermediate funding sources are requiring communities to form partnerships in order to be eligible for grants and contracts. Well-developed networks makes the formation and operation of these partnerships easier and more effective. We expand on *network nonprofit organizations* and *community partnerships* in Part IX.

Civil Society[17]

Civil society theories introduce the concept of a *public sphere* to address three big questions: What is the good society? What does it mean to be a good citizen? And where do voluntary associations— or voluntary nonprofit organizations—fit into the good society? The readings on civil society selected for inclusion in this chapter express different arguments for why civil society exists and why it matters for the nonprofit sector.

Scholars and policymakers do not agree on an exact meaning of *civil society*, but the contours are evident and widely shared. The political scientist and sociologist Larry Diamond has provided one frequently cited definition:

> [Civil society is] the realm of organized social life that is voluntary, self-generating, (largely) self-supporting, and autonomous from the state, and bound by a legal order or set of shared rules. It is distinct from "society" in general in that it involves citizens *acting collectively in a public sphere* to express their interests, passions, and ideas, exchange information, achieve mutual goals, make demands on the state, and hold state officials accountable. Civil society is an intermediary entity, standing between the private sphere and the state.[18]

Diamond's definition makes the connection between civil society and the nonprofit sector absolutely clear. Civil society encompasses voluntarily organized and sustained associations, usually in the form of nonprofit organizations (or NGOs). Interestingly, in parts of the world these organizations are sometimes called *civil society organizations* and the nonprofit sector is referred to as *civil society*. In highlighting the role that citizens play, Diamond also points to the inherently political and sociological nature of civil society.

For most observers, civil society is the world of voluntary associations through which individuals become part of something larger than themselves and learn how to be good citizens.[19] Small, local, nonprofit organizations foster solidarity and trust among neighbors, and the accumulation of social capital strengthens communities. This is an idealized, communitarian view of civil society.

The bottom-up movements for democracy around the globe in the post-Cold War era of the 1990s prompted numerous INGOs and national governments to attempt to export civil society models developed in North America and Western Europe to lesser developed areas and sites of unrest. Whether these efforts had positive impacts on local communities and governments is highly debatable. Civil society is not something that can be exported easily.

> When one examines how democracy has actually been deepened, poverty reduced, peace restored or maintained, and power relations and market economies transformed . . . it is clear that civil society is only one of many forces at work, and that it has often been a progenitor of these problems as well as a contributor to their resolution.[20]

Citizens need a vibrant public sphere to ensure that their voices are expressed and allowed to shape and reshape their civil societies. Jürgen Habermas has argued the desirability of "a public sphere of communicative rationality rooted in civil society that separates deliberation from the entanglements of corporations and government bureaucracies."[21] Habermas developed his theory of the public sphere from an analysis of the historical changes that took place in the eighteenth century when civil rights guaranteeing the freedom to associate and to expression were established. People voluntarily gathered in public spaces, such as coffeehouses and literary salons, to debate the issues of the day and read opinions published by a free press. The formation of fraternities and voluntary associations of all kinds from these encounters would prompt historians and social scientists to refer to this period as the "age of associations." "According to Habermas, a normative notion of public opinion crystallized around the conception of the common good that was established in these fragile but sheltered arenas of public discourse."[22]

The ideal public sphere in civil society is a space where people, regardless of gender or economic status, can participate in rational public debate about the common good.[23] The space where this deliberation occurs is separate from the home, from businesses, and from government—usually in civil society or nonprofit organizations. The interconnections among civil society, NGOs, the public sphere, private enterprise, and the state are complex and constantly changing. Consider, for example, the long-term effects on civil society of social distance imposed by many governments in order to contain the spread of the Coronavirus. Although technology enables communication without physical contact, civil society will be negatively affected—and so will communities.

Niches and Community Integration

In the language of sociology, a *niche* is a "property space for people and/or organizations, defined partially by the characteristics and preferences of members but also by other stakeholders."[24] Nonprofit organizations seek niches in communities for reasons of comfort and survival. *Niche-width* defines an organization's identity—its distinctiveness—and the community niche that it may therefore call "its own."[25] The most important application of niche theory for organizations in the NGO sector is the ability to attract and retain diverse groups of volunteers. David Horton Smith thus posits that *social integration* is one of the most important social benefits that the voluntary sector provides in communities:

> [The voluntary sector links] together individuals, groups, institutions and even nations that otherwise would be in greater conflict, or at least competition, with each other. . . . At the community level, a variety of voluntary associations will each tend to have as members a set of two or

more individuals representing differing and often opposing political, religious, cultural, or social perspectives and backgrounds. The coparticipation of this set of individuals in the same voluntary association can have significant moderating effects on the relationships among these individuals.[26]

Some research based on niche theory does not support Smith's optimistic vision.[27] Nonetheless, there is widespread recognition that social integration is a potentially beneficial outcome of voluntary association.

Readings Reprinted in Part VII

The first selection reprinted in this chapter is from Robert Putnam's groundbreaking book *Bowling Alone: The Collapse and Revival of American Community*. It is rare when a scholarly work of political science finds itself on the *New York Times* list of best-selling nonfiction books and is sold out in airport bookstands, but Putnam's arguments have resonated with many and have influenced policymakers and the media. He tapped into a sense shared among many Americans that something was missing—something had been lost—in our communities. Putnam found that "ordinary Americans shared this sense of civic malaise" that indicated we were not "on the right track morally or culturally."[28] What was missing was social capital. Without social capital, Putnam observes, civil society becomes impoverished. Putnam's early publications made the case that civil society in the U.S. was in decline as evidenced by a downward trend in social capital. He pointed out the irony of holding up Western democracies and the United States as models of civil society for emerging democracies to emulate.[29]

Putnam also has argued that voluntary associations—the family, churches, and neighborhoods— needed to be strengthened while the role of the state needed to be diminished, a philosophy that has come to be known as neo-Tocquevillian. Putnam's focus on the importance of social capital for community and democracy has stemmed from years of research. He has concluded that success in overcoming dilemmas of collective action and the opportunism that they spawn depends on the broader social context within which any particular game is played. Voluntary cooperation is easier in a community that has a substantial stock of social capital, in the form of norms of reciprocity and networks of civic engagement.[30]

In communities where the norm is to help neighbors and to engage with them socially and culturally, trust is created and deepened, allowing for collective action to benefit the community as a whole. In *Bowling Alone*, Putnam breathes life into civil society theory. The vignette that concludes this reading captures his overall argument: bowling together and making and remaking human connections is better than bowling alone and could even change, if not save, a life.[31]

The view that voluntary associations should be fostered and state interventions minimized has dominated much of the civil society discussion recently. Where Putnam sees social capital as what is missing in a malaise-filled America, Sabine Lang, in "Civil Society as a Public Sphere," views international and government efforts to revitalize civil society solely through funding civil society organizations (NGOs) as lacking. Although NGOs unquestionably play important roles as mediators between the state and its citizens, many question their legitimacy.

> Some see the NGO explosion of recent decades as an indicator of revitalized democracies across the globe. For others, the increasing number and influence of NGOs undermine the very foundations of representative democracy. Glorifying portrayals of NGOs as the savior of citizen involvement in public affairs compete with dismissive accounts of self-proclaimed and nonrepresentative groups bolstered by an unelected activist elite. The question at the core of

these strikingly different perceptions is: What makes NGOs legitimate players in late modern public affairs?[32]

What makes NGOs legitimate is their ability to involve citizens in public affairs, fostering civic engagement and making sure that the public is heard. Lang bases these conclusions on her reading of history.

The prevailing view of civil society as being only about NGOs and social capital has drawn attention and resources away from the important and necessary role that voluntary associations play as public actors. In Lang's analysis, the public has been written out of civil society by government policies and by private and public funders' agendas. NGOs need to find their voice if they are to be recognized as legitimate public actors. Only if NGOs find their voice and activate citizens in public affairs will they become legitimate, accountable public actors.

As the title of "Civil Society as Associational Life" by Michael Edwards states, this reading examines ways that types of civil society organizations (NGOs) contribute to associational life in widely different countries. Edwards

focuses on civil society as a *part* of society that is distinct from states and markets . . . civil society in this sense contains all associations and networks between the family and the state in which membership and activities are "voluntary," including NGOs of different kinds, labor unions, political parties, churches and other religious groups, professional and business associations, community and self-help groups, social movements, and the independent media.

Edwards presents arguments for and against including or excluding types of organizations from the population of civil society organizations, including explicitly political organizations, NGOs that sell goods and/or services in the market, and "uncivil society organizations"—organizations that engage in activities or are grounded in ideology that most people would not include in their conception of organizations that serve "the public good," such as hate groups. Edwards focuses on the roles that civil society organizations play in associational life in the Middle East and in Africa, two areas where cultures vary dramatically from the West. In the Middle East, for example, religion and authoritarian forms of government influence daily life in ways not familiar to those in the West which causes civil society organizations to take different forms and play different roles.

Although Peter L. Berger and Richard John Neuhaus's book *To Empower People: The Role of Mediating Structures in Public Policy* is more than 40 years old, its argument that "mediating structures" are needed in communities remains salient today.[33] *To Empower People* was expected to provide the Ronald Reagan administration with the philosophical justification for massive diffusion of public service programs out into the nonprofit sector—a key component of Reagan's agenda to shrink government. But the expectation did not materialize. The Reagan administration never used the argument effectively.[34]

The essence of the Berger and Neuhaus argument is: In a complex society, individuals need buffers—mediating structures—to help them cope with large public and private bureaucracies when they are trying to get problems solved. Community needs can be met best when citizens utilize neighborhood, family, church, and voluntary associations as these mediating structures.

Without institutionally reliable processes of mediation, the political order becomes detached from the values and realities of individual life. . . . When that happens, the political order must be secured by coercion rather than by consent. And when that happens, democracy disappears. . . . Such mediation cannot be sporadic and occasional; it must be institutionalized in *structures*. The structures we have chosen to study . . . exist where people are, and that is where sound public policy should always begin. [emphasis in original]

Notes

1. On "voluntary nonprofits," see Steven Rathgeb Smith and Michael Lipsky, "Nonprofit Organizations and Community," in *Nonprofits for Hire: The Welfare State in the Age of Contracting*, edited by Steven Rathgeb Smith and Michael Lipsky (Cambridge, MA: Harvard University Press, 1993), 20–40. On "donative nonprofits," see Henry Hansmann, "The Two Nonprofit Sectors: Fee for Service Versus Donative Organizations," in *The Future of the Nonprofit Sector*, edited by Virginia A. Hodgkinson and R. W. Lyman (San Francisco: Jossey-Bass, 1989), 91–102.

2. Carl Milofsky, *Smallville: Institutionalizing Community in Twenty-First-Century America* (Medford, MA: Tufts University Press, 2008). See also Part V, "Economic Theories of the Nonprofit Sector," and Part VII, "Community and Civil Society Theories of the Nonprofit Sector."

3. Lester A. Salamon, "Tocqueville, 1959," *Social Research* 27 (1960): 449–470, cited in Whitney Pope, *Alexis de Tocqueville: His Social and Political Theory* (Beverly Hills, CA: Sage, 1986), 12.

4. Robert D. Putnam, "Bowling Alone: America's Declining Social Capital," *Journal of Democracy* 6 (1995): 65; and Robert D. Putnam, *Bowling Alone: The Collapse and Revival of American Community* (New York: Simon & Schuster, 2000). A chapter from *Bowling Alone* is reprinted in Part VII.

5. Alexis de Tocqueville, "On the Use Which the Americans Make of Associations in Civil Life," in *Democracy in America*, edited by Alexis de Tocqueville, vol. 2 (New York: Doubleday/Anchor, 1969), 513.

6. Alexis de Tocqueville, "Political Associations in the United States," in *Democracy in America*, edited by Alexis de Tocqueville, vol. 1 (New York: Vintage, 1945), 199.

7. James S. Coleman, "Social Capital in the Creation of Human Capital," *American Journal of Sociology* 94 (1988): S100.

8. See Part V, "Economic Theories of the Nonprofit Sector."

9. Coleman, "Social Capital," S101.

10. Ibid., S108.

11. Ibid., S117.

12. We use the term "leisure" broadly here to include "serious leisure." See, for example, Robert A. Stebbins, "Volunteering: A Serious Leisure Perspective," *Nonprofit and Voluntary Sector Quarterly* 25 (1996): 211–224.

13. This is not to deny that sometimes people are motivated to volunteer primarily for résumé building and business networking purposes. See, for example, Jone L. Pearce, *Volunteers: The Organizational Behavior of Unpaid Workers* (London: Routledge, 1993).

14. Margaret Atwood, *The Handmaid's Tale* (1985), quoted in David Knoke and Miguel Guilarte, "Networks in Organizational Structures and Strategies," in *Current Perspectives in Social Theory: Recent Developments in the Theory of Social Structure*, Supplement 1, edited by J. David Knottnerus and Christopher Prendergast (Greenwood, CT: JAI Press, 1994), 77.

15. Knoke and Guilarte, "Networks in Organizational Structures and Strategies," 77–78.

16. Walter W. Powell, "Hybrid Organizational Arrangements: New Form or Transitional Development?" *California Management Review* 30 (1987): 67–87.

17. This discussion of civil society theories is adapted from the 3rd edition of this book, "Introduction to Part VII, Civil Society Theories of the Nonprofit Sector," authored by Charlene D. Orchard. We thank her for her contributions to this discussion of civil society.

18. Larry Diamond, "Rethinking Civil Society: Toward Democratic Consolidation," *Journal of Democracy* 5, no. 3 (1994): 4–18 (emphasis in the original). Two other examples of definitions include:

> Civil society is the domain that can potentially mediate between the state and private sectors and offer women and men a space for activity that is simultaneously voluntary and public; a space that unites the virtue of the private sector—liberty—with the virtue of the public sector—concern for the general good.
> —Benjamin R. Barber, "The Search for Civil Society," *New Democrat* 7, no. 2 (1995)

Civil society refers to a third sector of private associations that are relatively autonomous from both state and economy. They are voluntary, in the sense that they are neither mandated nor run by state institutions, but spring from the everyday lives and activities of communities of interest. The associations of this third sector, moreover, operate not for profit. . . . Even those activities of the third sector that involve providing goods and services for fees, however, are not organized towards the objectives of making profit and enlarging market shares.

—Iris Marion Young, *Inclusion and Democracy* (Oxford: Oxford University Press, 2000), 158

19. The importance of Alexis de Tocqueville to theories about the voluntary sector is discussed in several parts of this book, particularly Part II.

20. Michael Edwards, "Civil Society and the Geometry of Human Relations," in *The Oxford Handbook of Civil Society*, edited by Michael Edwards, 3–14 (New York: Oxford University Press, 2011), 12.

21. Harry C. Boyte, "Civil Society and Public Work," in Michael Edwards, *The Oxford Handbook of Civil Society*, 324–336, 325.

22. James Gordon Finlayson, *Habermas: A Very Short Introduction* (Oxford: Oxford University Press, 2005), 10.

23. Ibid., 10. Finlayson points out that Habermas agreed with critics who noted that the early salons and coffeehouses catered to elite males.

24. Pamela A. Popielarz and J. Miller McPherson, "On the Edge or in Between: Niche Position, Niche Overlap, and the Duration of Voluntary Association Memberships," *American Journal of Sociology* 101 (1995): 698–720.

25. Michael T. Hannan and John Freeman, "The Population Ecology of Organizations," *American Journal of Sociology* 88 (1977): 1116–1145.

26. David Horton Smith, "The Impact of the Voluntary Sector on Society," in *Voluntary Action Research*, edited by David Horton Smith (Lexington, MA: Lexington Books, 1973) (reprinted in Part II).

27. See Popielarz and McPherson, "On the Edge or in Between"; and Elisabeth Clemens, "The Constitution of Citizens: Political Theories of Nonprofit Organizations," reprinted in Part VI of this book.

28. Robert D. Putnam, *Bowling Alone: The Collapse and Revival of American Community* (New York: Simon & Schuster, 2000), 25.

29. Robert D. Putnam, "Bowling Alone: America's Declining Social Capital," *Journal of Democracy* 6, no. 1 (1995): 65–78.

30. Robert D. Putnam, *Making Democracy Work: Civic Traditions in Modern Italy* (Princeton, NJ: Princeton University Press, 1993), 167.

31. Ibid., 28.

32. Sabine Lang, *NGOs, Civil Society, and the Public Sphere* (New York: Cambridge University Press, 2013), 1.

33. Peter L. Berger and Richard John Neuhaus, *To Empower People: The Role of Mediating Structures in Public Policy* (Washington, DC: American Enterprise Institute for Public Policy Research, 1977). The excerpt reprinted in this part has been edited substantially in order to highlight the roles of voluntary associations, including churches.

34. Lester M. Salamon, "Nonprofit Organizations: The Lost Opportunity," in *The Reagan Record*, edited by John L. Palmer and Isabel V. Sawhill (Cambridge, MA: Ballinger, 1984), 261–284.

Bibliography

Aldrich, Daniel P. *Building Resilience: Social Capital in Post-Disaster Recovery* (Chicago: University of Chicago Press, 2012).

Alexander, Jeffrey C., ed. *Real Civil Societies: Dilemmas of Institutionalization* (Thousand Oaks, CA: Sage, 1998).

——. *The Civil Sphere* (Oxford: Oxford University Press, 2006).

Anheier, Helmut K. "International Aspects and Globalization." In *Nonprofit Organizations: Theory, Management, Policy*, edited by Helmut K. Anheier, 2nd ed., 471 (Oxford and New York: Routledge, 2014).

Ashman, Darcy, and Carmen Luca Sugawara. "Civil Society Networks: Options for Network Design." *Nonprofit Management and Leadership* 23: 389–406 (2013).

Barber, Benjamin R. "The Search for Civil Society." *New Democrat* 7, no. 2. (1995).

——. *A Place for Us: How to Make Society Civil and Democracy Strong* (New York: Hill and Wang, 1998).

Berger, Peter L., and Richard John Neuhaus. *To Empower People: The Role of Mediating Structures in Public Policy* (Washington, DC: American Enterprise Institute for Public Policy Research, 1977).

Bernhard, Michael, and Ekrem Karako. "Civil Society and the Legacies of Dictatorship." *World Politics* 59: 539–567 (2007).

Boulding, Carew. *NGOs, Political Protest, and Civil Society* (Cambridge: Cambridge University Press, 2014).

Boyte, Harry C. "Civil Society and Public Work." In *The Oxford Handbook of Civil Society*, edited by Michael Edwards, 324–336 (New York: Oxford University Press, 2011).

Bromley, Patricia. "The Organizational Transformation of Civil Society." In *The Nonprofit Sector: A Research Handbook*, edited by Walter W. Powell and Patricia Bromley, 3rd ed., 123–143 (Stanford, CA: Stanford University Press, 2020).

Burbidge, John, ed. *Beyond Prince and Merchant: Citizen Participation and the Rise of Civil Society* (West Hartford, CT: Kumarian Press, 1998).

Chambers, Simone, and Will Kymlicka, eds. *Alternative Conceptions of Civil Society* (Princeton, NJ: Princeton University Press, 2002).

Chen, Katherine K., Howard Lune, and Edward L. Queen. "How Values Shape and Are Shaped by Nonprofit and Voluntary Organizations: The Current State of the Field." *Nonprofit and Voluntary Sector Quarterly* 47: 856–885 (2013).

Chiavacci, David, Simona Grano, and Julia Obinger, eds. *Civil Society and the State in East Asia: Between Entanglement and Contention in Post High Growth* (Amsterdam, The Netherlands: Amsterdam University Press, 2021).

Clements, Elisabeth. "The Constitution of Citizens: Political Theories of Nonprofit Organizations." *American Journal of Sociology* 101: 698–720 (1995).

Cohen, Jean L., and Andrew Arato. *Civil Society and Political Theory: Studies in Contemporary German Social Thought* (Cambridge, MA: MIT Press, 1992).

Coleman, James S. "Social Capital in the Creation of Human Capital." *American Journal of Sociology* 94: S95–S120 (1988).

Delue, Steven M., and Timothy M. Dale. *Political Thinking, Political Theory, and Civil Society* (New York and London: Routledge, 2017).

Diamond, Larry. "Rethinking Civil Society: Toward Democratic Consolidation." *Journal of Democracy* 5, no. 3: 4–18 (1994).

Dionne, E. J. "Why Civil Society? Why Now?" *Brookings Review* 15: 4–8 (1997).

Duelund, Peter. "Jürgen Habermas, The Structural Transformation of the Public Sphere: An Inquiry into a Category of Bourgeois Society." *International Journal of Cultural Policy* 16: 26–28 (2010).

Eberly, Don E. *America's Promise: Civil Society and the Renewal of American Culture* (Lanham, MD: Rowman & Littlefield, 1998).

——. "The Meaning, Origins, and Applications of Civil Society." In *The Essential Civil Society Reader: Classic Essays in the American Civil Society Debate*, edited by Don E. Eberly, 3–29 (Lanham, MD: Rowman & Littlefield, 2000).

——. *The Rise of Global Civil Society: Building Communities and Nations from the Bottom Up* (New York: Encounter Books, 2008).

Edwards, Bob, Michael W. Foley, and Mario Diani, eds. *Beyond Tocqueville: Civil Society and the Social Capital Debate in Comparative Perspective* (Hanover, NH: University Press of New England for Tufts University, 2001).

Edwards, Michael, ed. *The Oxford Handbook of Civil Society* (New York: Oxford University Press, 2011).
———. *Civil Society*, 4th ed. (Cambridge, MA: Polity Press, 2020).

Ehrenberg, John. *Civil Society: The Critical History of an Idea* (New York: New York University Press, 1999).

Field, John. *Social Capital*, 3rd ed. (New York: Routledge, 2017).

Finlayson, James Gordon. *Habermas: A Very Short Introduction* (Oxford: Oxford University Press, 2005).

Foley, Michael W., and Bob Edwards. "The Paradox of Civil Society." *Journal of Democracy* 7: 38 (1996).

Fowler, Alan. "The Civil Society Index." In *Third Sector Research*, edited by Rupert Taylor, 49–59 (New York: Springer, 2010).

Gramsci, Antonio. "Selections from The Prison Notebooks" [1930–1935]." In *The Civil Society Reader*, edited by Virginia A. Hodgkinson and Michael W. Foley, 190–202 (Hanover, NH: University Press of New England for Tufts University, 2003).

Gutmann, Amy. *Why Deliberative Democracy?* (Princeton, NJ: Princeton University Press, 2004).

Hall, John A., and Frank Trentmann, eds. *Civil Society: A Reader in History, Theory, and Global Politics* (New York: Palgrave Macmillan, 2005).

Hannan, Michael T., Glenn R. Carroll, and Laszio Pòlos. "The Organizational Niche." *Sociological Theory* 21: 309–340 (2003).

Hodgkinson, Virginia A., and Michael W. Foley, eds. *The Civil Society Reader* (Hanover, NH: University Press of New England for Tufts University, 2003).

Hunter, Albert, and Carl Milofsky. *Pragmatic Liberalism: Constructing a Civil Society* (New York: Palgrave Macmillan, 2007).

James, Estelle, ed. *The Nonprofit Sector in International Perspective: Studies in Comparative Culture and Policy* (New York: Oxford University Press, 1989).

Keane, John. *Civil Society: Old Images, New Visions* (Stanford, CA: Stanford University Press, 1998).
———. *Global Civil Society?* (Cambridge: Cambridge University Press, 2003).

Lang, Sabine. *NGOs, Civil Society, and the Public Sphere* (New York: Cambridge University Press, 2013).

Ma, Qiusha. "The Governance of NGOs in China Since 1978: How Much Autonomy?" *Nonprofit and Voluntary Sector Quarterly* 31: 306 (2002).

Mendel, Stuart C. "Are Private Government, the Nonprofit Sector, and Civil Society the Same Thing?" *Nonprofit and Voluntary Sector Quarterly* 39: 717–733 (2010).

Mercer, Claire. "NGOs, Civil Society, and Democratization: A Critical Review of the Literature." *Progress in Development Studies* 2: 5–22 (2002).

Milofsky, Carl. *Smallville: Institutionalizing Community in Twenty-First-Century America* (Medford, MA: Tufts University Press, 2008).

Moore, Barrington. *Social Origins of Dictatorship and Democracy: Lord and Peasant in the Making of the Modern World* (Boston: Beacon Press, 1966).

Muukkonen, Martti. "Framing the Field: Civil Society and Related Concepts." *Nonprofit and Voluntary Sector Quarterly* 38: 684–700 (2009).

Natil, Ibrahim, Vanessa Malila, and Youcef Sai, eds. *Barriers to Effective Civil Society Organizations: Political, Social and Financial Shifts* (New York: Routledge, 2021).

Nielsen, Klaus. *Social Capital, Trust, and Institutions* (Northampton, MA: Edward Elgar, 2014).

O'Connell, Brian. *Civil Society: The Underpinnings of American Democracy* (Hanover, NH: University Press of New England, 1999).

Paik, Anthony, and Layana Navarre-Jackson. "Social Networks, Recruitment, and Volunteering: Are Social Capital Effects Conditional on Recruitment?" *Nonprofit and Voluntary Sector Quarterly* 40: 476–496 (2011).

Popielarz, Pamela A., and J. Miller McPherson. "On the Edge or in Between: Niche Position, Niche Overlap, and the Duration of Voluntary Association Memberships." *American Journal of Sociology* 101: 698–720 (1995).

Powell, Frederick. *The Politics of Civil Society: Neoliberalism or Social Left?* (Bristol, UK: Policy Press, 2007).

Putnam, Robert D. *Making Democracy Work: Civic Traditions in Modern Italy* (Princeton, NJ: Princeton University Press, 1993).

———. "Bowling Alone: America's Declining Social Capital." *Journal of Democracy* 6, no. 1: 65–78 (1995).

———. *Bowling Alone: Revised and Updated. The Collapse and Revival of American Community* (New York: Simon & Schuster, 2021).

Salamon, Lester M. *The Global Associational Revolution* (London: Demos, 1994).

———, and Megan A. Haddock. *Explaining Civil Society Development: A Social Origins Approach* (Baltimore, MD: Johns Hopkins University Press, 2017).

———, and S. Wojciech Sokolowski. *Global Civil Society: Dimensions of the Nonprofit Sector*, Vol. 2 (Bloomfield, CT: Kumarian Press, 2004).

Schneider, Jo Anne. "Organizational Social Capital and Nonprofits." *Nonprofit and Voluntary Sector Quarterly* 38: 643–661 (2009).

Seligman, Adam B. *The Idea of Civil Society* (New York: Free Press, 1992).

———. "Civil Society as Idea and Ideal." In *Alternative Conceptions of Civil Society*, edited by Simone Chambers and Will Kymlicka, 13–33 (Princeton, NJ: Princeton University Press, 2002).

Shiffman, Ron, Rick Bell, Lance Jay Brown, and Lynne Elizabeth, eds. *Beyond Zuccotti Park: Freedom of Assembly and the Occupation of Public Space* (Oakland, CA: New Village Press, 2012).

Sievers, Bruce R. *Civil Society, Philanthropy, and the Fate of the Commons* (Medford, MA: Tufts University Press, 2010).

Smith, David Horton. "The Current State of Civil Society and Volunteering in the World, the USA, and China." *China Nonprofit Review* 6: 132–150 (2014).

Smith, Steven Rathgeb, and Michael Lipsky. *Nonprofits for Hire: The Welfare State in the Age of Contracting* (Cambridge, MA: Harvard University Press, 1993).

Smith, Steven Rathgeb, and Ce Shen. "The Roots of Civil Society: A Model of Voluntary Association Prevalence Applied to Data on Larger Contemporary Nations." *International Journal of Comparative Sociology* 43: 93–133 (2002).

Stadelmann-Steffen, Isabelle, and Markus Freitag. "Making Civil Society Work: Models of Democracy and Impact on Civic Engagement." *Nonprofit and Voluntary Sector Quarterly* 40: 526–551 (2011).

Stoddard, Abby. "International Assistance." In *The State of Nonprofit America*, 2nd ed., edited by Lester M. Salamon, 332 (Washington, DC: Brookings Institution Press, 2012).

Tocqueville, Alexis de. "Political Associations in the United States." In *Democracy in America*, edited by Alexis de Tocqueville, Vol. 1 (New York: Vintage, 1945).

———. "On the Use Which the Americans Make of Associations in Civil Life." In *Democracy in America*, edited by Alexis de Tocqueville, Vol. 2, 513–517 (New York: Doubleday/Anchor, 1969).

Van Til, Jon. *Growing Civil Society: From Nonprofit Sector to Third Space* (Bloomington and Indianapolis: Indiana University Press, 2000).

Verba, Sidney, Kay Lehman Schlozman, and Henry E. Brady. *Voice and Equality: Civic Voluntarism in American Politics* (Cambridge, MA: Harvard University Press, 1995).

Walzer, Michael. "The Idea of Civil Society: A Path to Social Reconstruction." *Dissent* 39: 293–304 (1991).

Warren, Mark E. *Democracy and Association* (Princeton, NJ: Princeton University Press, 2001).

———. "Civil Society and Democracy." In *The Oxford Handbook of Civil Society*, edited by Michael Edwards, 377–390 (New York: Oxford University Press, 2011).

Wollebaek, Dag, and Per Selle. "Does Participation in Voluntary Associations Contribute to Social Capital? The Impact of Intensity, Scope, and Type." *Nonprofit and Voluntary Sector Quarterly* 31: 32–61 (2002).

———. "Social Capital." In *Third Sector Research*, edited by Rupert Taylor, 219–233 (New York: Springer, 2011).

Woolcock, Michael. "Civil Society and Social Capital." In *The Oxford Handbook of Civil Society*, edited by Michael Edwards, 197–208 (New York: Oxford University Press, 2011).

CHAPTER 22

Bowling Alone: Thinking About Social Change in America

ROBERT D. PUTNAM

No one is left from the Glenn Valley, Pennsylvania, Bridge Club who can tell us precisely when or why the group broke up, even though its forty-odd members were still playing regularly as recently as 1990, just as they had done for more than half a century. The shock in the Little Rock, Arkansas, Sertoma club, however, is still painful: in the mid-1980s, nearly fifty people had attended the weekly luncheon to plan activities to help the hearing- and speech-impaired, but a decade later only seven regulars continued to show up.

The Roanoke, Virginia, chapter of the National Association for the Advancement of Colored People (NAACP) had been an active force for civil rights since 1918, but during the 1990s membership withered from about 2,500 to a few hundred. By November 1998 even a heated contest for president drew only fifty-seven voting members. Black city councillor Carroll Swain observed ruefully, "Some people today are a wee bit complacent until something jumps up and bites them." VFW Post 2378 in Berwyn, Illinois, a blue-collar suburb of Chicago, was long a bustling "home away from

home" for local veterans and a kind of working-class country club for the neighborhood, hosting wedding receptions and class reunions. By 1999, however, membership had so dwindled that it was a struggle just to pay taxes on the yellow brick post hall. Although numerous veterans of Vietnam and the post-Vietnam military lived in the area, Tom Kissell, national membership director for the VFW observed, "Kids today just aren't joiners."[1]

Meanwhile, as Tewksbury Memorial High School (TMHS), just north of Boston, opened in the fall of 1999, forty brand-new royal blue uniforms newly purchased for the marching band remained in storage, since only four students signed up to play. Roger Whittlesey, TMHS band director, recalled that twenty years earlier the band numbered more than eighty, but participation had waned ever since.[2] Somehow in the last several decades of the twentieth century all these community groups and tens of thousands like them across America began to fade.

It wasn't so much that old members dropped out—at least not any more rapidly than age and

DOI: 10.4324/9780367696559-29

the accidents of life had always meant. But community organizations were no longer continuously revitalized, as they had been in the past, by freshets of new members. Organizational leaders were flummoxed. For years they assumed that their problem must have local roots or at least that it was peculiar to their organization, so they commissioned dozens of studies to recommend reforms.[3] The slowdown was puzzling because for as long as anyone could remember, membership rolls and activity lists had lengthened steadily.

In the 1960s, in fact, community groups across America had seemed to stand on the threshold of a new era of expanded involvement. Except for the civic drought induced by the Great Depression, their activity had shot up year after year, cultivated by assiduous civic gardeners and watered by increasing affluence and education. Each annual report registered rising membership. Churches and synagogues were packed, as more Americans worshiped together than only a few decades earlier, perhaps more than ever in American history.

The civic-minded World War II generation was, as its own John F. Kennedy proclaimed at his inauguration, picking up the torch of leadership, not only in the nation's highest office, but in cities and towns across the land. Summarizing dozens of studies, political scientist Robert E. Lane wrote in 1959 that "the ratio of political activists to the general populations, and even the ratio of male activists to the male population, has generally increased over the past fifty years." As the 1960s ended, sociologists Daniel Bell and Virginia Held reported that "there is more participation than ever before in America . . . and more opportunity for the active interested person to express his personal and political concerns."[4] Even the simplest political act, voting, was becoming ever more common. From 1920, when women got the vote, through 1960, turnout in presidential elections had risen at the rate of 1.6 percent every four years, so on a simple straight-line projection it seemed reasonable,

as a leading political scientist later observed, to expect turnout to be nearly 70 percent and rising on the nation's two hundredth birthday in 1976.[5]

By 1965 disrespect for public life, so endemic in our history, seemed to be waning. Gallup pollsters discovered that the number of Americans who would like to see their children "go into politics as a life's work" had nearly doubled over little more than a decade. Although this gauge of esteem for politics stood at only 36 percent, it had never before been recorded so high, nor has it since. More strikingly, Americans felt increased confidence in their neighbors. The proportion that agreed that "most people can be trusted," for example, rose from an already high 66 percent during and after World War II to a peak of 77 percent in 1964.[6]

The fifties and sixties were hardly a "golden age," especially for those Americans who were marginalized because of their race or gender or social class or sexual orientation. Segregation, by race legally and by gender socially, was the norm, and intolerance, though declining, was still disturbingly high. Environmental degradation had only just been exposed by Rachel Carson, and Betty Friedan had not yet deconstructed the feminine mystique. Grinding rural poverty had yet to be discovered by the national media. Infant mortality, a standard measure of public health, stood at twenty-six per one thousand births—forty-four per one thousand for black infants—in 1960, nearly four times worse than those indexes would be by the end of the century. America in *Life* was white, straight, Christian, comfortable, and (in the public square, at least) male.[7] Social reformers had their work cut out for them. However, engagement in community affairs and the sense of shared identity and reciprocity had never been greater in modern America, so the prospects for broad-based civic mobilization to address our national failings seemed bright.

The signs of burgeoning civic vitality were also favorable among the younger generation, as the first of the baby boomers approached college. Dozens of studies confirmed that education was by far the best predictor of engagement in civic life, and universities were in the midst of the most far-reaching expansion in American history. Education seemed the key to both greater tolerance and greater social involvement. Simultaneously shamed and inspired by the quickening struggle for civil rights launched by young African Americans in the South, white colleges in the North began to awaken from the silence of the fifties.

The baby boom meant that America's population was unusually young, whereas civic involvement generally doesn't bloom until middle age. In the short run, therefore, our youthful demography actually tended to dampen the ebullience of civil society. But that very bulge at the bottom of the nation's demographic pyramid boded well for the future of community organizations, for they could look forward to swelling membership rolls in the 1980s, when the boomers would reach the peak "joining" years of the life cycle. And in the meantime, the bull session buzz about "participatory democracy" and "all power to the people" seemed to augur ever more widespread engagement in community affairs. One of America's most acute social observers prophesied in 1968, "Participatory democracy has all along been the political style (if not the slogan) of the American middle and upper class. It will become a more widespread style as more persons enter into those classes."[8] Never in our history had the future of civic life looked brighter.

What happened next to civic and social life in American communities is the subject of this chapter. In recent years social scientists have framed concerns about the changing character of American society in terms of the concept of "social capital." By analogy with notions of physical capital and human capital—tools and training that enhance individual productivity—the core idea of social capital theory is that social networks have value. Just as a screwdriver

(physical capital) or a college education (human capital) can increase productivity (both individual and collective), so too social contacts affect the productivity of individuals and groups.

Whereas physical capital refers to physical objects and human capital refers to properties of individuals, social capital refers to connections among individuals—social networks and the norms of reciprocity and trustworthiness that arise from them. In that sense social capital is closely related to what some have called "civic virtue." The difference is that "social capital" calls attention to the fact that civic virtue is most powerful when embedded in a dense network of reciprocal social relations. A society of many virtuous but isolated individuals is not necessarily rich in social capital.

The term *social capital* itself turns out to have been independently invented at least six times over the twentieth century, each time to call attention to the ways in which our lives are made more productive by social ties. The first known use of the concept was not by some cloistered theoretician, but by a practical reformer of the Progressive Era—L. J. Hanifan, state supervisor of rural schools in West Virginia. Writing in 1916 to urge the importance of community involvement for successful schools, Hanifan invoked the idea of "social capital" to explain why. For Hanifan, social capital referred to

> those tangible substances [that] count for most in the daily lives of people: namely good will, fellowship, sympathy, and social intercourse among the individuals and families who make up a social unit. . . . The individual is helpless socially, if left to himself. . . . If he comes into contact with his neighbor, and they with other neighbors, there will be an accumulation of social capital, which may immediately satisfy his social needs and which may bear a social potentiality sufficient to the substantial improvement of living conditions in the whole community. The community as a whole will benefit by

the cooperation of all its parts, while the individual will find in his associations the advantages of the help, the sympathy, and the fellowship of his neighbors.[9]

Hanifan's account of social capital anticipated virtually all the crucial elements in later interpretations, but his conceptual invention apparently attracted no notice from other social commentators and disappeared without a trace firmly and finally on the intellectual agenda in the late 1980s, using it (as Hanifan had originally done) to highlight the social context of education.[10]

Social capital has both an individual and a collective aspect—a private face and a public face. First, individuals form connections that benefit our own interests. One pervasive stratagem of ambitious job seekers is "networking," for most of us get our jobs because of whom we know, not what we know—that is, our social capital, not our human capital. Economic sociologist Ronald Burt has shown that executives with bounteous Rolodex files enjoy faster career advancement. Nor is the private return to social capital limited to economic rewards. As Claude S. Fischer, a sociologist of friendship, has noted, "Social networks are important in all our lives, often for finding jobs, more often for finding a helping hand, companionship, or a shoulder to cry on."[11]

If individual clout and companionship were all there were to social capital, we'd expect foresighted, self-interested individuals to invest the right amount of time and energy in creating or acquiring it. However, social capital also can have "externalities" that affect the wider community, so that not all the costs and benefits of social connections accrue to the person making the contact.[12] A well-connected individual in a poorly connected society is not as productive as a well-connected individual in a well-connected society. And even a poorly connected individual may derive some of the spillover benefits from living in a well-connected community. If the crime rate in my neighborhood is lowered by neighbors keeping an eye on one another's homes, I benefit even if I personally spend most of my time on the road and never even nod to another resident on the street.

Social capital can thus be simultaneously a "private good" and a "public good." Some of the benefit from an investment in social capital goes to bystanders, while some of the benefit redounds to the immediate interest of the person making the investment. For example, service clubs, like Rotary or Lions, mobilize local energies to raise scholarships or fight disease at the same time that they provide members with friendships and business connections that pay off personally.

Social connections are also important for the rules of conduct that they sustain. Networks involve (almost by definition) mutual obligations; they are not interesting as mere "contacts." Networks of community engagement foster sturdy norms of reciprocity: I'll do this for you now, in the expectation that you (or perhaps someone else) will return the favor.

Sometimes, as in these cases, reciprocity is *specific*: I'll do this for you if you do that for me. Even more valuable, however, is a norm of *generalized* reciprocity: I'll do this for you without expecting anything specific back from you, in the confident expectation that someone else will do something for me down the road. The Golden Rule is one formulation of generalized reciprocity. Equally instructive is the T-shirt slogan used by the Gold Beach, Oregon, Volunteer Fire Department to publicize their annual fund-raising effort: "Come to our breakfast, we'll come to your fire." "We act on a norm of specific reciprocity," the firefighters seem to be saying, but onlookers smile because they recognize the underlying norm of generalized reciprocity—the firefighters will come even if *you* don't.

A society characterized by generalized reciprocity is more efficient than a distrustful society, for the same reason that money is more efficient than barter. If we don't have to balance every exchange instantly, we can get a lot more accomplished. Trustworthiness lubricates social life. Frequent interaction among a diverse set of people tends to produce a norm of generalized reciprocity. Civic engagement and social capital entail mutual obligation and responsibility for action. As L. J. Hanifan and his successors recognized, social networks and norms of reciprocity can facilitate cooperation for mutual benefit. When economic and political dealing is embedded in dense networks of social interaction, incentives for opportunism and malfeasance are reduced. This is why the diamond trade, with its extreme possibilities for fraud, is concentrated within close-knit ethnic enclaves. Dense social ties facilitate gossip and other valuable ways of cultivating reputation—an essential foundation for trust in a complex society.

Social capital—that is, social networks and the associated norms of reciprocity—comes in many different shapes and sizes with many different uses. Your extended family represents a form of social capital, as does your Sunday school class, the regulars who play poker on your commuter train, your college roommates, the civic organizations to which you belong, the Internet chat group in which you participate, and the network of professional acquaintances recorded in your address book.

Sometimes "social capital," like its conceptual cousin "community," sounds warm and cuddly. Urban sociologist Xavier de Souza Briggs, however, properly warns us to beware of a treacly sweet, "kumbaya" interpretation of social capital.[13] Networks and the associated norms of reciprocity are generally good for those inside the network, but the external effects of social capital are by no means always positive. It was social capital, for example, that enabled Timothy McVeigh to bomb the Alfred P. Murrah Federal Building in Oklahoma City. McVeigh's network of friends, bound together by a norm of reciprocity, enabled him to do what he could not have done alone. Similarly, urban gangs,

NIMBY ("not in my backyard") movements, and power elites often exploit social capital to achieve ends that are antisocial from a wider perspective. Indeed, it is rhetorically useful for such groups to obscure the difference between the pro-social and antisocial consequences of community organizations. When Floridians objected to plans by the Ku Klux Klan to "adopt a highway," Jeff Coleman, grand wizard of the Royal Knights of the KKK, protested, "Really, we're just like the Lions or the Elks. We want to be involved in the community."[14]

Social capital, in short, can be directed toward malevolent, antisocial purposes, just like any other form of capital.[15] Therefore it is important to ask how the positive consequences of social capital—mutual support, cooperation, trust, institutional effectiveness—can be maximized and the negative manifestations—sectarianism, ethnocentrism, corruption—minimized. Toward this end, scholars have begun to distinguish many different forms of social capital.

Some forms involve repeated, intensive, multistranded networks—like a group of steelworkers who meet for drinks every Friday after work and see each other at mass on Sunday—and some are episodic, single-stranded, and anonymous, like the faintly familiar face you see several times a month in the supermarket checkout line. Some types of social capital, like a Parent-Teacher Association, are formally organized, with incorporation papers, regular meetings, a written constitution, and connection to a national federation, whereas others, like a pickup basketball game, are more informal. Some forms of social capital, like a volunteer ambulance squad, have explicit public-regarding purposes; some, like a bridge club, exist for the private enjoyment of the members; and some, like the Rotary club mentioned earlier, serve both public and private ends.

Of all the dimensions along which forms of social capital vary, perhaps the most important is the distinction between *bridging* (or inclusive) and *bonding* (or exclusive).[16] Some forms of social capital are, by choice or necessity, inward looking and tend to reinforce exclusive identities and homogeneous groups. Examples of bonding social capital include ethnic fraternal organizations, church-based women's reading groups, and fashionable country clubs. Other networks are outward looking and encompass people across diverse social cleavages. Examples of bridging social capital include the civil rights movement, many youth service groups, and ecumenical religious organizations.

Bonding social capital is good for undergirding specific reciprocity and mobilizing solidarity. Dense networks in ethnic enclaves, for example, provide crucial social and psychological support for less fortunate members of the community, while furnishing start-up financing, markets, and reliable labor for local entrepreneurs. Bridging networks, by contrast, are better for linkage to external assets and for information diffusion. Economic sociologist Mark Granovetter has pointed out that when seeking jobs—or political allies—the "weak" ties that link me to distant acquaintances who move in different circles from mine are actually more valuable than the "strong" ties that link me to relatives and intimate friends whose sociological niche is very like my own. Bonding social capital is, as Xavier de Souza Briggs puts it, good for "getting by," but bridging social capital is crucial for "getting ahead."[17]

Moreover, bridging social capital can generate broader identities and reciprocity, whereas bonding social capital bolsters our narrower selves.

Bonding social capital constitutes a kind of sociological superglue, whereas bridging social capital provides a sociological WD-40. Bonding social capital, by creating strong in-group loyalty, may also create strong out-group antagonism. Under many circumstances both bridging and bonding social capital can have powerfully positive social effects.

Many groups simultaneously bond along some social dimensions and bridge across others.

The black church, for example, brings together people of the same race and religion across class lines. The Knights of Columbus was created to bridge cleavages among different ethnic communities while bonding along religious and gender lines. Internet chat groups may bridge across geography, gender, age, and religion, while being tightly homogeneous in education and ideology. In short, bonding and bridging are not "either-or" categories into which social networks can be neatly divided, but "more or less" dimensions along which we can compare different forms of social capital.

It would obviously be valuable to have distinct measures of the evolution of these various forms of social capital over time. However, like researchers on global warming, we must make do with the imperfect evidence that we can find, not merely lament its deficiencies. Exhaustive descriptions of social networks in America—even at a single point in time—do not exist.

"Social capital" is to some extent merely new language for a very old debate in American intellectual circles. Community has warred incessantly with individualism for preeminence in our political hagiology. Liberation from ossified community bonds is a recurrent and honored theme in our culture, from the Pilgrims' storied escape from religious convention in the seventeenth century to the lyric nineteenth-century paeans to individualism by Emerson ("Self-Reliance"), Thoreau ("Civil Disobedience"), and Whitman ("Song of Myself") to Sherwood Anderson's twentieth-century celebration of the struggle against conformism by ordinary citizens in *Winesburg, Ohio* to the latest Clint Eastwood film. Even Alexis de Tocqueville, patron saint of American communitarians, acknowledged the uniquely democratic claim of individualism,

> a calm and considered feeling which disposes each citizen to isolate himself from the mass of his fellows and withdraw into the circle of family and friends; with this little society

formed to his taste, he gladly leaves the greater society to look after itself.[18]

Our national myths often exaggerate the role of individual heroes and understate the importance of collective effort. Historian David Hackett Fischer's gripping account of opening night in the American Revolution, for example, reminds us that Paul Revere's alarum was successful only because of networks of civic engagement in the Middlesex villages. Towns without well-organized local militia, no matter how patriotic their inhabitants, were AWOL from Lexington and Concord.[19] Nevertheless, the myth of rugged individualism continues to strike a powerful inner chord in the American psyche.

At the conclusion of the twentieth century, ordinary Americans shared this sense of civic malaise. We were reasonably content about our economic prospects, hardly a surprise after an expansion of unprecedented length, but we were not equally convinced that we were on the right track morally or culturally. Of baby boomers interviewed in 1987, 53 percent thought their parents' generation was better in terms of "being a concerned citizen, involved in helping others in the community," as compared with only 21 percent who thought their own generation was better. Fully 77 percent said the nation was worse off because of "less involvement in community activities." In 1992 three-quarters of the US workforce said that "the breakdown of community" and "selfishness" were "serious" or "extremely serious" problems in America. In 1996 only 8 percent of all Americans said that "the honesty and integrity of the average American" were improving, as compared with 50 percent of us who thought we were becoming less trustworthy. Those of us who said that people had become less civil over the preceding ten years outnumbered those who thought people had become more civil, 80 percent to 12 percent. In several surveys in 1999 two-thirds of Americans said that America's civic life had

weakened in recent years, that social and moral values were higher when they were growing up, and that our society was focused more on the individual than the community. More than 80 percent said there should be more emphasis on community, even if that put more demands on individuals.[20]

It is emphatically not my view that community bonds in America have weakened steadily throughout our history—or even throughout the last hundred years. On the contrary, American history carefully examined is a story of ups and downs in civic engagement, *not just downs*—a story of collapse *and* of renewal. Within living memory the bonds of community in America were becoming stronger, not weaker, and it is within our power to reverse the decline of the last several decades. Is life in communities as we enter the twenty-first century really so different after all from the reality of American communities in the 1950s and 1960s? One way of curbing nostalgia is to count things. Are club meetings really less crowded today than yesterday, or does it just seem so? Do we really know our neighbors less well than our parents did, or is our childhood recollection of neighborhood barbecues suffused with a golden glow of wishful reminiscence? Are friendly poker games less common now, or is it merely that we ourselves have outgrown poker? League bowling may be passé, but how about softball and soccer? Are strangers less trustworthy now? Are boomers and X'ers really less engaged in community life? After all, it was the preceding generation that was once scorned as "silent." Perhaps the younger generation today is no less engaged than their predecessors, but engaged in new ways.

American society, like the continent on which we live, is massive and polymorphous, and our civic engagement historically has come in many sizes and shapes. A few of us still share plowing chores with neighbors, while many more pitch in to wire classrooms to the Internet. Some of us run for Congress, and others join self-help groups. Some of us hang out at the local bar association and others at the local bar. Some of us attend mass once a day, while others struggle to remember to send holiday greetings once a year. The forms of our social capital—the ways in which we connect with friends and neighbors and strangers—are varied.

We shall encounter currents and crosscurrents and eddies, but in each we shall also discover common, powerful tidal movements that have swept across American society in the twentieth century. The dominant theme is simple: For the first two-thirds of the twentieth century a powerful tide bore Americans into ever deeper engagement in the life of their communities, but a few decades ago—silently, without warning—that tide reversed and we were overtaken by a treacherous rip current. Without at first noticing, we have been pulled apart from one another and from our communities over the last third of the century.

Social capital turns out to have forceful, even quantifiable effects on many different aspects of our lives. What is at stake is not merely warm, cuddly feelings or frissons of community pride. Our schools and neighborhoods don't work so well when community bonds slacken. Our economy, our democracy, and even our health and happiness depend on adequate stocks of social capital.

A century ago, it turns out, Americans faced social and political issues that were strikingly similar to those that we must now address. From our predecessors' responses, we have much to learn—not least that civic decay like that around us can be reversed.

Before October 29, 1997, John Lambert and Andy Boschma knew each other only through their local bowling league at the Ypsi-Arbor Lanes in Ypsilanti, Michigan. Lambert, a sixty-four-year-old retired employee of the University of Michigan hospital, had been on a kidney transplant waiting list for three years when Boschma, a thirty-three-year-old accountant, learned casually of Lambert's need and unexpectedly approached him to offer to donate one of his own kidneys.

"Andy saw something in me that others didn't," said Lambert. "When we were in the hospital Andy said to me, 'John, I really like you and have a lot of respect for you. I wouldn't hesitate to do this all over again.' I got choked up." Boschma returned the feeling: "I obviously feel a kinship [with Lambert]. I cared about him before, but now I'm really rooting for him." This moving story speaks for itself, but the photograph that accompanied this report in the *Ann Arbor News* reveals that in addition to their differences in profession and generation, Boschma is white and Lambert is African American. That they bowled together made all the difference.[21] In small ways like this—and in larger ways, too—we Americans need to reconnect with one another. That is the simple argument of this book.

Notes

1. David Scott and Geoffrey Godbey, "Recreation Specialization in the Social World of Contract Bridge," *Journal of Leisure Research* 26 (1994): 275–295; Suzi Parker, "Elks, Lions May Go Way of the Dodo," *Christian Science Monitor*, August 24, 1998; John D. Cramer, "Relevance of Local NAACP Is Up for Debate," *Roanoke Times*, January 24, 1999; Dirk Johnson, "As Old Soldiers Die, VFW Halls Fade Away," *New York Times*, September 6, 1999. I am grateful to Professor David Scott for information about the Glenn Valley Bridge Club; "Glenn Valley" is a pseudonym for a college town in central Pennsylvania.

2. Christine Wicker, "A Common Thread of Decency," *Dallas Morning News*, May 1, 1999; David Streitfeld, "The Last Chapter: After 50 Years, Vassar Ends Its Famed Book Sale," *Washington Post*, April 28, 1999, Cl; Caroline Louise Cole, "So Many New Uniforms, But So Few Musicians," *Boston Sunday Globe Northwest Weekly*, September 5, 1999, 1.

3. Jeffrey A. Charles, *Service Clubs in American Society: Rotary, Kiwanis, and Lions* (Urbana: University of Illinois Press, 1993), 157.

4. Robert E. Lane, *Political Life: Why People Get Involved in Politics* (Glencoe, IL: Free Press, 1959),

94; Daniel Bell and Virginia Held, "The Community Revolution," *The Public Interest* 16 (1969): 142.

5. In fact, turnout in 1976 was 53 percent and falling. See Richard A. Brody, "The Puzzle of Political Participation in America," in *The New American Political System*, edited by Anthony King (Washington, DC: American Enterprise Institute for Public Policy Research, 1978).

6. George H. Gallup, *The Gallup Poll: Public Opinion 1935–1971* (New York: Random House, 1972); Karlyn Bowman, "Do You Want to Be President?" *Public Perspective* 8 (February–March 1997): 40; Robert E. Lane, "The Politics of Consensus in an Age of Affluence," *American Political Science Review* 59 (December 1965): 879; and Richard G. Niemi, John Mueller, and Tom W. Smith, *Trends in Public Opinion* (New York: Greenwood Press, 1989), 303. The version of the "trust" question used in the 1940s, 1950s, and 1960s is not directly comparable to the one that has become standard in most recent years.

7. See Thomas R. Rochon, *Culture Moves: Ideas, Activism, and Changing Values* (Princeton, NJ: Princeton University Press, 1998), xiii–xiv.

8. James Q. Wilson, "Why Are We Having a Wave of Violence?" *The New York Times Magazine*, May 19, 1968, 120.

9. Lyda Judson Hanifan, "The Rural School Community Center," *Annals of the American Academy of Political and Social Science* 67 (1916): 130–138, 130.

10. John R. Seeley, Alexander R. Sim, and Elizabeth W. Loosley, *Crestwood Heights: A Study of the Culture of Suburban Life* (New York: Basic Books, 1956); Jane Jacobs, *The Death and Life of Great American Cities* (New York: Random House, 1961); Glenn Loury, "A Dynamic Theory of Racial Income Differences," in *Women, Minorities, and Employment Discrimination*, edited by P. A. Wallace and A. Le-Mund (Lexington, MA: Lexington Books, 1977), 153–188; Pierre Bourdieu, "Forms of Capital," in *Handbook of Theory and Research for the Sociology of Education*, edited by John G. Richardson (New York: Greenwood Press, 1983), 241–258; Ekkehart Schlicht, "Cognitive Dissonance in Economics," in *Normengeleitetes Verhalten in den Sozialwissenschaften* (Berlin: Duncker and Humblot, 1984), 61–81; James S. Coleman, "Social Capital in the Creation of Human Capital," *American Journal of Sociology* 94 (1988): S95–S120; and James S. Coleman, *Foundations of Social Theory* (Cambridge, MA:

Harvard University Press, 1990). See also George C. Homans, *Social Behavior: Its Elementary Forms* (New York: Harcourt, Brace & World, 1961), 378–398. Except for a brief acknowledgment by Coleman of Loury's work, I can find no evidence that any of these theorists were aware of any of the preceding usages.

11. Ronald S. Burt, *Structural Holes: The Social Structure of Competition* (Cambridge, MA: Harvard University Press, 1992); Ronald S. Burt, "The Contingent Value of Social Capital," *Administrative Science Quarterly* 42 (1997): 339–365; and Ronald S. Burt, "The Gender of Social Capital," *Rationality and Society* 10 (1998): 5–46; Claude S. Fischer, "Network Analysis and Urban Studies," in *Networks and Places: Social Relations in the Urban Setting*, edited by Claude S. Fischer (New York: Free Press, 1977), 19; James D. Montgomery, "Social Networks and Labor-Market Outcomes: Toward an Economic Analysis," *American Economic Review* 81 (1991): 1408–1418, especially table 22.1.

12. In earlier work I emphasized this public dimension of social capital almost to the exclusion of the private returns to social capital. See Robert D. Putnam, "The Prosperous Community: Social Capital and Public Affairs," *The American Prospect* 13 (1993): 35–42, on which the present text draws.

13. Xavier de Souza Briggs, "Social Capital and the Cities: Advice to Change Agents," *National Civic Review* 86 (Summer 1997): 111–117.

14. *US News & World Report*, August 4, 1997, 18. Fareed Zakaria, "Bigger Than the Family, Smaller Than the State," *New York Times Book Review*, August 13, 1995, 1, pointed out that McVeigh and his co-conspirators spent evenings together in a bowling alley and concluded that "we would all have been better off if Mr. McVeigh had gone bowling alone." Sometimes, as in certain cults or clans, even the *internal* effects of social capital can be negative, but these are less common than negative *external* effects.

15. In Robert D. Putnam, *Making Democracy Work: Civic Traditions in Modern Italy* (Princeton, NJ: Princeton University Press, 1993), he ignored the possibility that social capital might have antisocial effects, but he recognized this possibility explicitly in "The Prosperous Community," published that same year.

16. So far as I can tell, credit for coining these labels belongs to Ross Gittell and Avis Vidal, *Community Organizing: Building Social Capital as a*

Development Strategy (Thousand Oaks, CA: Sage, 1998), 8.

17. Mark S. Granovetter, "The Strength of Weak Ties," *American Journal of Sociology* 78 (1973): 1360–1380; Xavier de Souza Briggs, "Doing Democracy Up Close: Culture, Power, and Communication in Community Building," *Journal of Planning Education and Research* 18 (1998): 1–13.

18. Alexis de Tocqueville, *Democracy in America*, edited by J. P Mayer, translated by George Lawrence (Garden City, NY: Doubleday, 1969), 506. See also Wilson Carey McWilliams, *The Idea of Fraternity in America* (Berkeley: University of California Press, 1972), and Thomas Bender, *Community and Social Change in America* (Baltimore, MD: Johns Hopkins University Press, 1978).

19. David Hackett Fischer, *Paul Revere's Ride* (New York: Oxford University Press, 1994).

20. *The Public Perspective* 8 (December–January 1997): 64; Robert Wuthnow, "The United States: Bridging the Privileged and the Marginalized?" In *Democracies in Flux: The Evolution of Social Capital in Contemporary Society* (Oxford and New York: Oxford University Press, 2002), 59–102.

21. Emma Jackson, "Buddy Had Kidney to Spare," *Ann Arbor News*, January 5, 1998.

Civil Society as a Public Sphere

SABINE LANG

[The social scientist's] aim is to help build and to strengthen self-cultivating publics.

—C. WRIGHT MILLS (1959, 186)

Civil society may be to 21st century democracies what political parties were to an earlier era: a litmus test for organized citizen voice and participation (Cohen and Arato 1992; Keane 1988; Kaldor 2003). A vibrant civic sphere, we assume, fosters social and cultural integration and facilitates engagement with a polity. As a result, "strengthening civil society" has become a formula for democracy frequently cited in government commissions, by donor agencies, as well as in the democratic transition and development literature. Whereas some theories emphasize civil society's role as a buffer against autocratic regime intervention, global economic neoliberalism, and social injustice (Cohen and Arato 1992; Rosanvallon 2007), others identify it as a source of economic wealth and personal happiness, guaranteeing economically favorable exchange conditions and a meaningful life to members of its community (Bellah 1985; Wolfe 1989; Putnam 2001).

Even though civil society is generally assumed to be good for democracy, the specifics of how civil societies might contribute to various properties of the public sphere are much less developed. Frequently, broad assumptions are made without much attention to how civil society and strong democratic publics are inherently linked. Terms such as "the public sphere of civic engagement" (Paterson 2000, 51) or the claim that civic engagement will somehow automatically endow strong civil societies with vibrant publics speak to this neglect.[1] During the Obama administration's town hall meetings on the proposed health care reform, organized Tea Party critics hijacked the microphones and shut down debates (Media Matters for America 2009). In short, not all modes of publicity originating within civil society are positive, not all associations allow for plurality of public voice, and not all public forums encourage and enable debate.

Although some theories of civil society tend to neglect the public sphere,[2] much focus has been put on civil society's role in building associations and in generating common norms and values. Why does this bias toward community and norm generation matter? On the most basic level, it influences citizenship practices and informs what we teach children or students about how to be good citizens. Do we highlight the importance of community and norm generation? Or do we emphasize the value of constructive dissent, communicative action,

 DOI: 10.4324/9780367696559-30

and contributions to public discourse? To put it differently, do we encourage volunteerism for the sake of association and helping others? Or do we put just as much emphasis on speaking out and on the conditions that enable citizen voice?

The focus of this chapter is to bring the public sphere back into civil society debate and thus establish conditions that make NGOs not just civic but also public actors. I offer two routes by which we can re-import the public into concepts of civil society: a historical path and a theoretical path. Historical evidence suggests that early modern civil society did not grow exclusively out of pre-political associations, but that it has deep roots in the idea of voice, citizens' public engagement with politics, and modern state-making of the late 18th and early 19th centuries. I argue that public and political advocacy were historically an integral part of emerging modern civil societies. In contrast, the civil society debate in the aftermath of the revolutions of 1989 highlights how civil society and the public sphere have been separated in their most recent theoretical iterations. Specifically, the theoretical turn toward communitarianism and social capital has obscured the public sphere mode of civil society.

A Historical Approach

Notwithstanding recent waves of attention, civil society is not a new concept. Its oldest iteration goes back to Aristotle's notion of *societas civilis* (cited in Kaldor 2003, 23). In its modern and liberal version it is a term of the old Europe (Kocka 2006). Advancing in step with the establishment of 18th-century bourgeois society and enlightenment ideas, it provided a platform for the rights-based aspirations of bourgeois men who envisioned not just a society free of censorship and repression but also a state that would actively value participation by its citizens (Zaret 2000; Lang 2001; Barker and Burrows 2002). Historical investigation provides evidence for questioning civil society's persistent image as

a purely association-based, pre-political, apolitical, or even anti-political realm set apart or in opposition to the state. Early modern civil societies were built on claims to publicity and to political advocacy, and both these claims showed civil society and the emerging modern nation-state to be strongly interrelated. The struggle to establish civic associations in 18th- and 19th-century Europe was thus, at its core, a *public* struggle in which organizational claims to voice and advocacy played a prominent role.

Publicity

Across late 18th- and early 19th-century Europe, bourgeois citizens articulated their right to form associations not simply as a right to meet, but specifically as a civic right to publicity.[3] The associational revolution that swept through the continent during this period was not new. People had assembled before—in guilds, around the bread oven, in pubs, and at markets. What was new was the attempt to bring strangers together and encourage them to communicate and debate as a public. The right to assemble was articulated as an inherent civic right to partake in public affairs. "Publicity" became its rallying call and a synonym for freedom of speech and bourgeois liberties.

The articulation of this right to publicity took many different forms: Patriotic associations advertised with the slogan that publicly educating citizens on the constitution was crucial for a nation's well-being. Civic groups disseminated their messages by staging public events with speakers, food, drink, and entertainment. Newspapers printed series of treatises on the principle of publicity, and censored editors or journalists retaliated by publicly demanding their right to publicity (Lang 2001).

Thus, the democratic order that European bourgeois activists fought for was directly linked to the principle of publicity. Finding one's voice and expressing it were perceived to be key to a democratic civil society reigned by "critical publicity" (Habermas 1989 [1962]).

Publicity was not just the term of democratic trade across early 19th-century Europe. In Tocqueville's rendering of American civil society, publicity likewise turned out to be more than a marginal afterthought. What Tocqueville admired in the American landscape of associations was that "men had bound themselves *publicly*[4] to a cause" (Tocqueville 1945 [1835], 114); in other words, citizens expressed public commitment and used public communication arenas to articulate their allegiances and opinions. When Americans form associations, Tocqueville wrote, they become "a power seen from afar, whose actions serve for an example and whose language is listened to" (114). Community in civil society thus is not a self-serving ideal, but has two public dimensions: It consists of people signaling publicly that they identify with a cause, and it produces public power, exemplary action, and messages that travel in the wider public sphere.

Politics

A second noteworthy feature of early 19th- century civil society was that it was neither pre-, nor a-, nor anti-political. Instead, its expansive organizations engaged in ongoing negotiations among themselves and with government about what "politics" and "political" were in the first place and about how "civic" and "political" should relate to each other.

Emerging civil society, populated by an increasing number of associations and publications, performed intricate strategic dances with authorities. These dances were aimed at carving out space for a repertoire of actions that actors claimed were merely civic and not political in a state-defined manner, but in effect redefined the political itself.

Specifically, groups that promoted liberal or democratic ideas in countries with monarchic or absolutist regimes used the claim to nonpolitical activity to broaden their arenas of involvement in public affairs (Darnton and Roche 1989;

Lang 2001). When an editor sought approval from government authorities for publishing a newspaper or a pamphlet, the claim to engaging in "nonpolitical" activity was what initially prevented all too harsh censorship. When women's groups came together to bake for the poor or to sew clothes for the army in need, their aspiration to nonpolitical, purely social activity belied the fact that their activities spoke to the politics of needs, to questions about distributive justice, and to the fact that they devised the category of "deserving and needy" in their own view. As Mary Ryan puts it for 19th-century American women's societies, "If social life was divided between male and female, public and private, the history enacted on each side of that shifting border was deeply politicized" (Ryan 1992, 273). In other words, the cover of being nonpolitical served well to strengthen civil society while holding interference from government at bay.

Governments all over Europe tried to defend their institutional monopoly over politics, while civil society action corroded this monopoly and not just demanded but also actively organized participation in public affairs. In effect, what came to be known as the "age of associations"—the network of clubs and philanthropic, civic, professional, and cultural associations—was "the arena, the training ground, and eventually the power base of a stratum of bourgeois men who were coming to see themselves as a 'universal class' and preparing to assert their fitness to govern" (Fraser 1992, 114). Beyond the bourgeois class, worker groups began to explore voice through their civic associations; rural populations organized to protest price increases for bread, demanding dismissal of politically nonresponsive officials—in short, claiming the right to political voice was the conduit of early civil society and not its antidote.

State

The third noteworthy aspect of this short historical exploration is the involvement of the modernizing state in shaping and sustaining civil society. In fact, civil society and the state were never strictly separate spheres. While trying to rein in the association revolution and its critical voices, modernizing governments across Europe at the same time confronted the need not only to accept but also to some degree embrace their emerging civil societies (Lang 2001; Clark 2006). This was often not an altogether cozy embrace. In part, it was merely the result of realizing that censors, police, and laws could not fully repress emerging civic spheres. Yet to some degree, governments also started to rely on civil society in the tumultuous transitions from absolutist Ancien Regimes to modernized constitutional polities. To gain legitimacy, modernizing states needed intermediary structures that could help communicate policies and develop public opinion around government agendas. State actors envisioned aggregate audiences that would serve both as recruitment pools and as critical echo chambers for government policies and that would become accountable partners in promoting and executing policies. Agricultural associations, women's charity clubs, and reading societies served as interpreters and activators for state policies. Moreover, accommodating bourgeois interests in political participation during a period of rapid expansion of trade and industry provided a bulwark against more radical workers' interests (Scambler 2001, 3).

Governments had a functional interest in grooming emerging civil societies, and this grooming could be just as restrictive as it could be enabling. Although the notion of a "government-enabled" civil society at first sight has a more continental European than an Anglo-American ring to it, it developed on both sides of the Atlantic. Even though we tend to interpret Tocqueville's exploration of the state of civil society in America as a purely "bottom-up" take on the importance of associationalism to fostering and sustaining democracy, recent research has pointed to the fact that "government made all that 'volunteerism' possible" (Skocpol 1996,

2). According to Skocpol, the evidence as to when, how, and why civil society flourished in American history points straight to the emerging modern state. It was government-sponsored and -implemented infrastructure, like the network of postal offices, that allowed faster communication and networking among citizens and their associations. It was in the interest of members of Congress to facilitate news dissemination by legislating cheap newspaper postal rates and increasing the frequency of delivery to remote areas of the country. Likewise, the associations that Tocqueville visited functioned as mediators between state and civil society. Many were not just local, but developed around citizens who aimed for party offices and government posts. In effect, civil society, even in its American heyday from the 1820s to the 1840s, was marked by government facilitation.

We can draw three broad conclusions from this historical exploration: (1) claims to publicity and to participation in public debates are an integral part of civil society, (2) association building in particular needs to be complemented with attention to who gets to have voice and at whose expense, and (3) governance conditions matter.

Yet the civil society that today speaks out of foundation brochures, municipal volunteer day celebrations, and classroom textbooks rarely makes these connections. There, the emphasis of civil society development tends to be rarely on citizen voice and reciprocally enabling state-society relations, but most often on the personally fulfilling element of individualized civic engagement—that is, "volunteering feels good"[5]—or on the role of the civic sector as compensating for government failure.

The Revival of Civil Society

After its ascendancy in the late 1800s to mid-1900s to public discourse, the concept of civil society lay dormant for more than a century.

Not until the 1980s did the term "civil society" resurface in the transitional movements in Central and East European countries and in the mobilization against military dictatorships in Latin America.

Independent associations and networks of trust are therefore necessary, but not sufficient anchors for conceptualizing civil society. It is civil society in its mode as a public sphere that provides the stimulus for social change.

Writing the Public out of Civil Society

Communitarian and social capital theories of civil society, in particular, have shaped discourses on civil society with paradigms that tend to marginalize or "write out"[6] the politically engaged public. What makes these discourses important for our purpose is that they do not just stay within the confines of universities and conference rooms; they influence how governments and donor agencies perceive or "construct" civil society actors and, more specifically, shape interaction with the nongovernmental sector.

In communitarian terms, civil society is made up of communities and associations that are not political and that "foster competence and character in individuals, build social trust, and help children become good people and good citizens" (Elshtain 1999, 13). It is based on norms of trust and solidarity in a "space of uncoerced human association" (Walzer 1995, 7) that people enter "for the sake of sociability itself" (Wolfe 1989, 38) and face-to-face community, and Nathan Glazer refers to it as the "fine grain of society" (Glazer 1998, 103). Within these tightly woven social structures, citizens can learn solidarity-based behavior that in turn is supposed to strengthen the foundation for democracy.

Public voice and advocacy are rarely addressed in communitarian versions of civil society. If we encounter a public at all in communitarian

territory, it is an intimate and locally bound public that dispels any notion of it being a contested site of different voices. We encounter a civil society that ultimately could just as well thrive without larger and competing publics.

A second contribution to writing out the public sphere can be attributed to the past decades' "onward sweep" (Mayer 2003) of the social capital paradigm. In most general terms, theories of social capital assess civil society with a set of indicators aimed at measuring the strength of its community-building associations (i.e., Edwards, Foley, and Diani 2001; Putnam 2001). Social capital "is about capacities for cooperation that are embedded in associations" (de Haart and Dekker 2003, 155). Associations are credited with generating trust, norms, and networks, which in turn become predictors of democratic salience and economic prosperity (Putnam 2001). In Robert Putnam's shorthand, the more choral societies and community picnics, the higher are government responsiveness and economic well-being.

What makes recent social capital theories so appealing is that they indeed provide the first systematic empirical measurements for assessing the overall state of civil societies (i.e., Edwards et al. 2001; Minkoff 2001; Hooghe and Stolle 2003). It is of interest here how these concepts capture public voice and advocacy, which can be extrapolated most clearly from survey-response-focused social capital literature.

Writing out the public sphere in social capital theories is a direct consequence of the premise that generating civic trust and norms within a nation of strong associations fuels a vibrant civil society. Social capital theories tend to de-emphasize conditions that enable these networks of trust to aggregate citizen voice, carry it into larger civic arenas, and practice public advocacy. This is not just a theoretical problem that stays confined within academic conference circles. The dominant social capital discourse of recent years has had repercussions for how states, parties, foundations, and other philanthropic donors have conceived of and sponsored civil society in Berlin, Baltimore, and Baghdad. A major effect of operationalizing civil society assistance on the basis of the social capital paradigm has been "association overload"— the creation of civic landscapes that display layers of NGOs, alliances, and networks, all founded for the sake of investing in social capital production. This overload might lead to the appearance of a dense civil society, but tells us little about civic voice or the ability to strategically join forces to practice effective public advocacy (Petrikova 2007).

Civil Society and Political Society

Writing out the public sphere might occur as fallout from theoretical attempts to shield civil society from becoming overly politicized.[7] Liberal theories, in particular, remain acutely sensitive to state intervention and insist on strong barriers between civil society and the political system. In normative terms, a benign realm of voluntary association is posited against the harsher realities of a political society dominated by institutional actors who attempt to influence politics. Whereas the former is said to sharpen our sense of morality in independent associations, the latter is driven by instrumental rationality and provides the connections to representative government (Wolfe 1989, 180). Instead of constructing civil society and the state as different aggregates within a range of forms of social organization, liberalism tends to present an artificial dualism in which "civil society is believed to be the realm of popular freedom because it is declared autonomous from and prior to the state, spontaneous in its workings, self-activating and naturalistic" (Somers 1995, 232). Thus liberal theories construct a "great dichotomy between a vilified dangerous public realm of the state (always lurking behind the tamed government of the people) versus a noncoercive voluntary and pre-political (hence private) realm of (civil) society" (232).

Yet even if civil society is perceived not as private per se, but as a realm in between public and private spheres, it comes across merely as a "public-lite." John Rawls claims that "the reason of associations in civil society is public with respect to their members, but nonpublic with respect to political society and to citizens generally" (Rawls 1993, 220). In his view, associations provide "publicness"[8] to their members because by joining an association, they leave the intimate privacy of their home and family. Yet at the same time and in contrast to associations in which citizens exercise *political* citizenship, such as parties or parliaments, civic associations remain private assemblies, organizing the personal lives of their members. Theorizing civil society as a sphere in between public and private fortifies the limited publicness of civil society, offering private citizens temporary and occasional public status, but at the same time keeping civic associations out of political society. Citizens "go public" as individuals by leaving the intimate sphere of their family, but they do not form publicly recognized collectives in civil society. In Rawls's theory, "churches and universities, scientific societies and professional groups," for example, are nonpublic expressions of civil society and belong to what he calls the "background culture in contrast with the public political culture" (Rawls 1993, 220). This liberal reflex to shield areas of society from public and political intervention has consequences for theorizing and practicing citizenship. In practical terms, separating civil and political society leaves political agency squarely within the dominion of institutionalized political actors and government.

The perspective advanced in this chapter is that neither political society nor civil society is essentially public or private. Nonstrategic domains of solidarity and association can establish public voice, and strategic debate in political society might happen behind closed doors and in privatized settings. A neighborhood street party can ignite the spark for collective action, while simultaneously political negotiations on the same issue take place between parties and unions in City Hall in back rooms and never acquire publicness. The feminist theory debates of the last two decades have shed light on the forces that continually *construct* public and private and thus the power relations within the realm of civil society (Scott 1988; Fraser 1992; Landes 1998).

In sum, the expulsion of the political public from civil society needs to be framed within a broader context of depoliticizing citizenship. The liberal claim to privacy or semi-publicity of civil society brackets questions about the spaces and the conditions by which voice and advocacy are constituted, trained, and practiced in this sphere.

Without the concept of the public sphere, the analysis of NGOs misses a central dimension of how these organizations channel and condition public voice and advocacy. Yet the limited perspective of influential civil society theories on the public sphere is only one obstacle to understanding the role of the nongovernmental sector within a framework of civil society. Another obstacle is created by approaches that convey an overly narrow view of the public sphere itself.

Bringing the Public Sphere Back In

Civil society and public sphere theories tend to promote a tacit division of labor: Some respected theories within the civil society paradigm write out public voice and concentrate on associations; working within a public sphere paradigm, meanwhile, often results in a focus on the media at the expense of associations. Civil society's centers are nongovernmental, noneconomic, and voluntary associations that anchor the communication structures of the public sphere in civil society. What specifically should be noted here is that the function of associations

goes beyond establishing networks of trust and solidarity. Habermas conceives of associations as *public* actors that ideally aggregate and disseminate citizen voice and provide space for public engagement. Moreover, in its mode as a public sphere, civil society generates debate and carries issues from the margins to the centers of power that might otherwise never get to be on the radar screens of institutional politics: "Through resonant and autonomous public spheres [it] develops impulses with enough vitality to bring conflicts from the periphery into the center of the political system" (Habermas 1992, 330).[9]

Who or what creates these impulses? The most common answers point to the mass media, assuming that only what makes it into the mass media is "truly" public. From this assumption, it is just a stone's throw to the idea that the media *are* the public sphere or that "the public sphere is what the media make of it" (Risse 2010, 115).

Dominant forms of communication frequently silence other voices by setting standards of dispassionate, rational discourse attuned to a bourgeois habitus. Constructivism challenges these theories of the public sphere to rethink the artificially drawn boundaries of the public and private, as well as the fencing off of the political sphere against all those who are not part of the institutional political system. Marginalized groups, in particular, are seen as providing specific voices that institutions frequently refuse to hear and media do not report, and that therefore politics neglects to take into account.

NGOs and the Public Sphere

A constructivist model of the public sphere, I submit, might be best equipped to provide analytical tools for assessing the role of NGOs in late modern publics. Constructivism positions NGOs not just at the margins of an established and mass-media-dominated public sphere, but acknowledges that NGOs and their networks might form subpublics or issue publics that act to some degree independently of dominant media, and make strategic decisions as to when and how they engage with the debates in other publics.

Moreover, a constructivist model of the public sphere awards legitimacy to NGO advocacy on grounds not only of expertise but also of engagement with uncrystallized interests at the margins of society that might, or might not, adhere to conventional repertoires of public expression. By taking into account forms of advocacy that run counter to dispassionate rational discourse, constructivism provides recognition of multiple forms and venues of expression. It recognizes Greenpeace's acts of civil disobedience just as much as human rights NGOs negotiating at the United Nations. Hence, a constructivist theory of the public sphere enables analysis of the conditions under which NGOs do or do not operate as (1) central communicative actors within mostly non-mass-mediated subpublics that (2) provide an organizational context for citizen voice and thus organize the "publicness" of civic concerns by (3) directing advocacy at different levels of the political or economic system via (4) discursive and nondiscursive means of expression.

NGOs Avoiding the Public

Although I propose that we treat NGOs essentially as public actors, some caveats are in order. One, there are associations that do not even aspire to contribute to public deliberation and advocacy because they see their mission in arenas other than organizing voice and influencing policy, such as service provision, entertainment, or mere socializing. Such NGOs might attain "publicness," for example, if they engage their constituents in debate about their mission or if they are challenged from the outside, but for the most part they do not actively seek it. Two, there are associations that shun public voice because of fear of appearing "too political" or "too polarizing." In effect, they discourage what Nina

Eliasoph in her study of associational cultures has called "frontstage" public communication (Eliasoph 1998): communication that employs more generalized, political, and principled talk. Eliasoph cites the story of Charles, an African American member of the Parent League and local NAACP representative, who wants to activate fellow parents to deal with a teacher who used racially disparaging language. Yet instead of investigating the issue, his fellow Parent League members divert attention by stating in different iterations that the incident should go "through the proper channels" (Eliasoph 1996, 276). Members of the group are hesitant to connect the issue to a larger problem and to discuss its implications for the group and beyond. In fact, they attempt to turn it over to other "channels," clearly not conceiving of themselves as an adequate public body to address it. Moreover, throughout the discussion, Charles gets the impression that he is too political and does not use the proper meaning-making rhetoric in the group. In sum, this voluntary parent association suppresses public deliberation rather than nurturing it.

Thus, rejecting abstract, political, or principled talk was, paradoxically, volunteers' way of looking out for the common good. Volunteers assumed that if they want to show each other and their neighbors that regular citizens really can be effective, they should avoid issues that they considered "political." In their effort to be open and inclusive, to appeal to regular, unpretentious fellow citizens without discouraging them, they silenced public-spirited deliberation—which was just what someone like Charles thought the group needed to have in order to involve new members. This creation of "the public," this civic practice, itself dissipated the public spirit from public settings (Eliasoph 1996, 279; see also Eliasoph 1998, 63).

If the public spirit of associations is so fragile, then what are the conditions under which associations develop public voice and advocacy? Or, to rephrase Thomas Risse, how do we know an associational public when we see one (Risse 2010)? This, as pointed out earlier, is a different question than probing the policy influence or issue salience of NGO politics. It focuses less on outcome than on modes of communication and strategies that enable public debate. I end this discussion by proposing a conceptual framework for analyzing NGO publics that is anchored in their communication practices.

Communication Repertoires of NGOs

On the most general level, we can assume that a public exists if actors communicate about the same issue, at the same time, using similar frames (see Habermas 1998, 160; Bennett 2009). If Oxfam UK and SHRO, the Sudan Human Rights Organization, both publicly criticize the politics of the Sudanese government and employ a genocide frame, they would analytically qualify as a public. To gauge the actual strength of an associational public, a more fine-grained set of quantitative and qualitative data is needed that assesses (1) the actual *density* of communicative ties, that is, how often an issue is being communicated about at the same time using similar frames; (2) the *modes* of communication, that is, whether the debate takes place primarily within the organization, between organizations, or also between organizations and nonmember citizens, and (3) the *target* of communication, that is, who the public debate is directed at and specifically whether the task involves mobilizing and enabling citizens for action.

NGOs are continuously involved in scaled modes of communication. An NGO might primarily communicate with its members—I refer to this mode as the practice of *internal* or *reflexive communication*. It might communicate directly with institutions or organizations that it is trying to influence, for example by offering expertise or consultation or contesting information and thus engaging in what I refer to as *institutional communication*. Finally, it might use means of communication to engage

in *public communication* practices to gain support from a wider array of citizens and to engage with those who are not part of their subpublic.

These modes of communication are by no means exclusive; in fact, civic activists tend to utilize them simultaneously. Yet from a public sphere viewpoint, they are not all equally "loud" and visible and not all equally inclusive. Even within these communication modes, NGOs make choices as to the degree of publicness that a communication will gain. Communicating within one's subpublic might take place in rather closed communication circuits, such as in chapter meetings of member organizations. Or it might take place via blogs or Twitter streams that are, in principle, accessible to others and maybe even posted to encourage wider debate. The institutionalized communication circuits of expert publics with their targets tend, for the most part, to be closed to others and often strategically even avoid going public because of possible repercussions. Yet, at times, if an NGO takes the expert's seat in institutional hearings, its communication officer might invite other NGO representatives or the media into the audience. In contrast, public communication modes by default involve broader outreach into untapped segments of an NGO's constituency and beyond. Hence, they tend to put more emphasis on broad visibility of public messages. Public communication repertoires of NGOs can, but do not necessarily involve traditional mass media. New media, in particular, have to some degree displaced traditional mass media as the prime public communication means. Moreover, NGO publics with such dense communicative links do not rely on incorporating a wide array of voices within *one single* public sphere. Strong NGO publics can be small, removed from dominant discourses, and formed solely to "invent and circulate counterdiscourses to formulate oppositional interpretations of their identities, interests, and needs" (Fraser 1992, 123). Ultimately, it is the combined strength of these three modes of communication that accounts for strong NGO publics. If NGOs use exclusively reflexive and institutional communication repertoires, their legitimacy is in jeopardy.

Conclusion

For civil society to be more than an empty euphemism for a gentler, better world, it needs to be held accountable, not just to what norms it fosters and what kinds of association it promotes but also to what kinds of publics it generates. In contrast, not strengthening civil society in its public sphere mode creates "a democratic time bomb" (Smismans 2006, 6) that breeds disappointment for those interested in meaningful associations, in citizen voice, and in seeing accountability and representativeness as outcomes of discursive interaction. Therefore, enhancing individualized social capital, which is the main civic engagement paradigm that currently informs community development policies across the world, is not an adequate response to strengthening anemic civil societies. At the same time, calls for the revival of associationalism miss the mark if they merely employ civil society as an arena in which declining state functions can be compensated for by activating citizens. The proliferation of voluntary associations "could easily advance parochial interests instead of serving democracy" (Tilly 2007, 86). It is only in the context of the debates within a public sphere that NGOs become accountable actors, able to engage citizens in public affairs.

Hence, assessing the role of the nongovernmental sector in the public sphere is not equivalent to measuring policy influence and outcome, and it is also not adequately captured by assessing their media presence. NGO publics have proliferated at the margins of, or sometimes even outside of, elite mass-media-driven public spheres. They use new means of communication that have the ability to connect members, supporters, and issues with greater frequency and depth, and possibly with a greater potential for activism than provided by traditional media. Density, modes, and targets of NGO communication have been identified as measurements that gauge how much an association contributes to civil society in its mode as a public sphere.

At the same time, not all NGOs are equally committed and strong enablers of publics. In the democratic transformation literature, in particular, NGOs have recently acquired a reputation for turning into technocratic operatives and for actually contributing to the decline of public engagement.[10] In this view, NGOs have become neoliberal stand-ins for empire-building interests, shortchanging those who are invested in building strong civil societies. How then did the NGO sector come to be perceived as the equivalent of civil society, and what are the implications for its role in the public sphere?

Notes

1. Michael Edwards, the former director of the Ford Foundation's Governance and Civil Society Program, noted this lack of focus on the public sphere as part of a somewhat "lazy thinking" in civil society theorizing (Edwards 2004, 10).

2. A number of civil society theories *do* put emphasis on the public sphere dimension (e.g., Fraser 1992; Cohen 1999; Chambers 2003; Edwards 2004; Alexander 2006).

3. For an analysis of early associations in Germany, see Dann (1984); for Belgium and the Netherlands, Ertman (2003); for England and Germany, Hellmuth (1990); for Great Britain, Clark (2000); and for an overview of civil society in Europe during the 19th century, see Bermeo and Nord (2003).

4. Emphasis added.

5. The combination of both "volunteering" and "feels good" brings up more than 2.1 million results in a Google search. The combination of "volunteering" and "public voice" has merely 900,000 hits (accessed February 1, 2012).

6. I owe this term to Jane Jenson (2008). She investigates the processes by which women are written out of EU policy imperatives; I focus on the arguments by which the public is written out of civil society narratives.

7. Margret Somers calls this the "metanarrative of Anglo-American citizenship theory" (Somers 1995, 2320). Its reach today extends far beyond its origin.

8. I use the term "publicness" here in conjunction with the more established term "public sphere." Whereas the German term "Öffentlichkeit" combines aspects of a *sphere* as well as a specific, namely public, *property* or characteristic of a setting, we need two terms to demarcate the difference in English, namely *public sphere* and *publicness*.

9. Whereas Habermas argues for the power of democratic discourse to deliver these impulses, Jeffrey Alexander (2006) rejects the notion that purely rational discursive practices devoid of emotional and cultural attachments can create a democratic civil sphere. For Alexander, "publicness is a social and cultural condition, not an ethical principle; it points to symbolic action, to performance, to projections of authenticity" (2006, 16).

10. See the debates in the Uganda NGO Forum at http://ngoforum.or.ug (accessed February 1, 2012).

References

Alexander, Jeffrey. 2006. *The Civil Sphere*. Oxford: Oxford University Press.

Barker, Hannah, and Simon Burrows, eds. 2002. *Press, Politics, and the Public Sphere in Europe and North America, 1760–1820*. Cambridge: Cambridge University Press.

Bellah, Robert. 1985. *Habits of the Heart*. Berkeley: University of California Press.

Bennett, Lance W. 2009. "Grounding the European Public Sphere: Looking Beyond the Mass Media." *KFG Working Paper*. Free University Berlin.

Bermeo, Nancy, and Phillip Nord, eds. 2003. *Civil Society Before Democracy: Lessons from Nineteenth-Century Europe*. Lanham, MD: Rowman & Littlefield.

Chambers, Simone. 2003. "A Critical Theory of Civil Society." In Will Kymlicka and Simone Chambers, eds., *Alternative Conceptions of Civil Society*, 90–110. Princeton, NJ: Princeton University Press.

Clark, Christopher. 2006. *Iron Kingdom: The Rise and Downfall of Prussia 1600–1947*. Cambridge, MA: Harvard University Press.

Clark, Peter. 2000. *British Clubs and Societies 1500–1800: The Origins of an Associational World*. New York: Oxford University Press.

Cohen, Jean. 1999. "American Civil Society Talk." In Robert K. Fullenwider, ed., *Civil Society, Democracy, and Civic Renewal*, 55–88. Lanham: Rowman & Littlefield.

Cohen, Jean, and Andrew Arato. 1992. *Civil Society and Political Theory*. Cambridge, MA: MIT Press.

Dann, Otto, ed. 1984. *Vereinswesen und bürgerliche Gesellschaft*. Munich: Oldenbourg.

Darnton, Robert, and Daniel Roche, eds. 1989. *Revolution in Print: The Press in France 1775–1800*. Berkeley: University of California Press.

De Haart, Joep, and Paul Dekker. 2003. "A Tale of Two Cities: Local Patterns of Social Capital." In Marc Hooghe and Dietlind Stolle, eds., *Generating Social Capital: Civil Society and Institutions in Comparative Perspective*, 153–169. New York: Palgrave Macmillan.

Edwards, Bob, Michael W. Foley, and Mario Diani, eds. 2001. *Beyond Tocqueville: Civil Society and the Social Capital Debate in Comparative Perspective*. Boston: University Press of New England.

Edwards, Michael. 2004. *Civil Society*. London: Polity Press.

Eliasoph, Nina. 1996. "Making a Fragile Public: A Talk-Centered Study of Citizenship and Power." *Sociological Theory* 14, no. 3, 262–289.

———. 1998. *Avoiding Politics: How Americans Produce Apathy in Everyday Life*. Cambridge: Cambridge University Press.

Elshtain, Jean Bethke. 1999. "A Call to Civil Society." *Society* 36, no. 5, 11–19.

Ertman, Thomas. 2003. "Liberalization, Democratization, and the Origins of a 'Pillarized' Civil Society in Nineteenth-Century Belgium and the Netherlands." In Nancy Bermeo and Phillip Nord, eds., *Civil Society Before Democracy: Lessons from Nineteenth-Century Europe*, 155–180. Lanham, MD: Rowman & Littlefield.

Fraser, Nancy. 1992. "Rethinking the Public Sphere: A Contribution to the Critique of Actually Existing Democracy." In Craig Calhoun, ed., *Habermas and the Public Sphere*, 109–142. Cambridge: Cambridge University Press.

Glazer, Nathan. 1998. *The Limits of Social Policy*. Cambridge, MA: Harvard University Press.

Habermas, Jürgen. 1989 [1962]. *Structural Transformation of the Public Sphere*. Cambridge, MA: MIT Press.

———. 1992. "Further Reflections on the Public Sphere." In Craig Calhoun, ed., *Habermas and the Public Sphere*, 421–461. Cambridge, MA: MIT Press.

———. 1998. "Does Europe Need a Constitution? A Response to Dieter Grimm." In Jürgen Habermas, ed., *The Inclusion of the Other*, 155–161. Cambridge: Polity Press.

Hellmuth, Eckhart. 1990. *The Transformation of Political Culture: England and Germany in the Late 18th Century*. London: Oxford University Press.

Hooghe, Marc, and Dietlind Stolle. 2003. *Generating Social Capital: Civil Society and Institutions in Comparative Perspective*. New York: Palgrave Macmillan.

Jenson, Jane. 2008. "Writing Women Out, Folding Gender In: The European Union 'Modernises' Social Policy." *Social Politics* 15, no. 2, 131–153.

Kaldor, Mary. 2003. *Global Civil Society: An Answer to War*. London: Polity Press.

Keane, John. 1988. *Democracy and Civil Society*. London: Verso.

Kocka, Jürgen. 2006. "Civil Society in Historical Perspective." In John Keane, ed., *Civil Society: Berlin Perspectives*. New York: Berghahn Publishers.

Landes, Joan B. 1998. "The Public and the Private Sphere: A Feminist Reconsideration." In Joan B. Landes, ed., *Feminism, the Public and the Private*, 135–163. New York: Oxford University Press.

Lang, Sabine. 2001. *Politische Öffentlichkeit im modernen Staat*. Baden-Baden: Nomos.

Mayer, Margit. 2003. "The Onward Sweep of Social Capital: Causes and Consequences for Understanding Cities, Communities, and Urban Movements." *International Journal of Urban and Regional Research* 27, no. 1, 110–132.

Media Matters for America. 2009. "CBS, Fox Reports on Town Hall Disruptions Ignore Conservative Strategy." August 5. Available at: http://media matters.org/research/200908050017 (accessed November 9, 2011).

Mills, C. Wright. 1959. *The Sociological Imagination*. New York: Oxford University Press.

Minkoff, Deborah. 2001. "Producing Social Capital: National Social Movements and Civil Society." In Bob Edwards, Michael W. Foley, and Mario Diani, eds., *Beyond Tocqueville: Civil Society and the Social Capital Debate in Comparative Perspective*, 183–193. Boston: University Press of New England.

Paterson, Lindsay. 2000. "Civil Society and Democratic Renewal." In Stephen Baron, John Field, and Tom Schuller, eds., *Social Capital: Critical Perspectives*, 39–55. Oxford: Oxford University Press.

Petrikova, Ivica. 2007. "Too Many Bad Cooks Spoiling the Broth? Effectiveness of NGOs in Addressing Child Labor in El Salvador." Digital Commons@Colby (Colby College). Available at: http://digitalcommons.colby.edu/honorstheses/281 (accessed March 11, 2010).

———. 2001. *Bowling Alone: The Collapse and Revival of American Community*. New York: Simon and Schuster.

Rawls, John. 1993. *Political Liberalism*. New York: Columbia University Press.

Risse, Thomas. 2010. *A Community of Europeans? Transnational Identities and Public Spheres*. Ithaca, NY: Cornell University Press.

Rosanvallon, Pierre. 2007. *The Demands of Liberty: Civil Society in France Since the Revolution*. Cambridge, MA: Harvard University Press.

Ryan, Mary. 1992. "Gender and Public Access: Women's Politics in Nineteenth-Century America." In Craig Calhoun, ed., *Habermas and the Public Sphere*, 259–288. Cambridge, MA: MIT Press.

Scambler, Graham, ed. 2001. *Habermas, Critical Theory, and Health*. London: Routledge.

Scott, Joan W. 1988. *Gender and the Politics of History*. New York: Columbia University Press.

Skocpol, Theda. 1996. "What Tocqueville Missed: Government Made All That 'Volunteerism' Possible." *Slate Magazine Online*, November 15. Available at: www.slate.com/id/2081 (accessed October 24, 2008).

Smismans, Stijn. 2006. "Civil Society and European Governance: From Concepts to Research *Agenda*."

In Stijn Smismans, ed., *Civil Society and Legitimate European Governance*, 3–23. Cheltenham, UK: Edward Elgar.

Somers, Margret. 1995. "Narrating and Naturalizing Civil Society and Citizenship Theory: The Place of Political Culture and the Public Sphere." *Sociological Theory* 13, no. 3, 229–274.

Tilly, Charles. 2007. *Democracy*. Cambridge: Cambridge University Press.

Tocqueville, Alexis de. 1945 [1835]. *Democracy in America*. New York: Vintage Books.

Walzer, Michael. 1995. "The Concept of Civil Society." In Michael Walzer, ed., *Toward a Global Civil Society*, 7–28. Providence: Berghahn Publishers.

Wolfe, Alan. 1989. *Whose Keeper? Social Science and Moral Obligation*. Berkeley: University of California Press.

Zaret, David. 2000. *Origins of Democratic Culture: Printing, Petitions, and the Public Sphere in Early-Modern England*. Princeton, NJ: Princeton University Press.

CHAPTER 24

Civil Society as Associational Life

Michael Edwards

Edwards, Michael, *Civil Society* (2nd ed.) (Cambridge, UK: Polity Press, 2009). 3rd ed., 2014.

In the late thirteenth century, Marco Polo was struck by the vibrancy of associational life in the Chinese city of Hangzhou, "noted for its charitable institutions as for its pleasures."[1] Public hospitals, market associations, free cemeteries, cultural groups, and homes for the elderly abounded. No doubt, earlier explorers would have seen similar things on their travels since associations like these have existed from at least the days of the pharaohs. Human beings are social creatures, and joining groups that help us to resolve the problems of collective action, advance the causes we believe in, find more meaning and fulfillment in life, or simply have some fun is a universal part of human experience. A life lived without such opportunities would be severely—perhaps unremittingly—diminished. For some, voluntary association is the natural state of humankind, invested with almost spiritual significance. "Human beings," writes J. Ronald Engel, "are made for the life of free association, and that divine reality, the Holy Spirit, is manifest in all associations committed to the democratic pursuit of justice in the common life."[2] It was Alexis de Tocqueville that started this romance on his travels to the United States in the 1830s. "Americans of all ages, conditions and dispositions," he declared in a now famous passage from his book *Democracy in America*, "have a constant tendency to form associations."[3] Today, more than 70 percent of all firefighters in the country are volunteers. Tocqueville would be proud of them, though he would also be worried that those volunteers are increasingly difficult to come by.[4]

This love affair has stirred passions on all sides of the political spectrum. Conservatives see associations as vehicles for rebuilding traditional moral values; liberals see them as counterweights to the power of government and business; and progressives see them as platforms for advancing new visions of society. Yet does this mean that voluntary action is always the best way to run a fire service or achieve social change? As long ago as 1911, Max Weber warned against romanticizing the effects of associations in his address to a congress of sociologists in Frankfurt: "the man of today is without doubt an association man in an awful and never dreamed of degree," he said, citing the negative effects on political engagement of the singing societies that were proliferating across Germany at the time—a fascinating anticipation of contemporary critiques of those such as Robert Putnam who praise the positive civic and political effects of choirs.[5] Associations matter hugely and they should be encouraged, but there is equal danger in expecting too much from associational life, as if it were a "magic bullet" for resolving intractable problems. Increasingly, it seems, voluntary associations are expected to organize social services, govern local communities, solve the unemployment problem, save the environment, and still have time to rebuild the moral life of nations. "Don't ask us to carry more than our capacity and then blame failure on us," as the Peruvian NGO leader Mario Padron once said. "We can't carry the load."

This [reading] focuses on civil society as a *part* of society that is distinct from states and markets, the most common of the understandings in use today and the direct descendant of de Tocqueville's ideas about nineteenth-century America. Commonly referred to as the "third" or "nonprofit" sector, civil society in this sense contains all associations and networks between the family and the state in which membership and activities are "voluntary," including NGOs of different kinds, labor unions, political parties, churches and other religious groups, professional and business associations, community and self-help groups, social movements, and the independent media. This is the "space of uncoerced human association," in Michael Walzer's famous phrase, "and also the set of relational networks—formed for the sake of family, faith, interest and ideology—that fill this space."[6]

Is There an "Associational Revolution" at Work in the World Today?

Voluntary associations have existed in most parts of the world for hundreds of years. The rural peasants' cooperatives that sprang into action after the French Revolution, for example; the Young Men's Lyceum in Springfield, Illinois, where Abraham Lincoln first practiced his oratory in 1838; the nineteenth-century reform movements such as Araya Samaj that pre-dated mass political action in India; and—despite the risks involved—the many dissident groups that

remained active in Eastern Europe throughout communist rule. Since the late 1980s, however, the expansion of some forms of associational life has been so rapid and so global that commentators have begun to talk of an "associational revolution" or a "power shift" of potentially momentous significance. Except in a small number of cases where authoritarian governments still block the development of NGOs and other voluntary associations, the numbers of registered nonprofits have increased at rates not seen before in history, though these data should always be treated with caution given differences in definitions and inaccuracies in measurement.

For example, India counted more than 3.3 million NGOs in 2015, up from approximately 1 million twenty years earlier, while both Brazil and Egypt had double the number in 2017 that they had in 2007 (at 400,000 and 46,000 respectively).[7] In Ghana, Zimbabwe, and Kenya, the sector provides 40 percent or more of all healthcare and education services, and even in China, where government policy remains suspicious, the number of foreign NGOs had increased from 2,000 in 2001 to 7,000 by 2016.[8] Paralleling this increase in numbers has been the growth of individual NGOs to cover the provision of services to large sections of the population, especially in South Asia—over 110 million people in 2017, for example, in the case of the Bangladesh Rural Advancement Committee.[9] In Western Europe and the United States, the trend is toward stability rather than rapid growth, but the numbers of voluntary associations are still impressive. There are approximately 1.5 million registered charities in the United States for example, and at least 200,000 in the United Kingdom, plus another 200,000 "informal" groups.[10]

However, these figures disguise important shifts in the composition of associational life. In both the United Kingdom and the United States, religious organizations, advocacy groups, service providers and formally registered "intermediary" NGOs have grown since the late 1980s, while non-religious membership groups and labor unions have declined, though there has recently been a resurgence in grassroots action among low-income and immigrant communities.[11] This decline has been especially acute in the labor movement—with unions in the United States representing only one-third of the workers they represented in the early 1950s[12]—and among what Theda Skocpol calls "locally rooted but nationally active" cross-class membership associations such as the American Legion. Skocpol concludes that as a consequence, US civil society has moved "from membership to management."[13] In other words, the traditional Tocquevillian core of associational life has been eroded.

At the international level, a new layer of nonprofits has emerged since the early 1990s, with more than 56,000 international NGOs and 25,000 transnational NGO networks active on the world stage, 90 percent of which have been formed since 1970. They include famous names such as Oxfam and Save the Children, campaigns such as those on land mines and arms control, global movements such as the Hemispheric Social Alliance (which already claims to have 49 million members), federations of community groups, such as Shack Dwellers International that links hundreds of thousands of people across three continents, and international associations of mayors, local authorities, business representatives, professionals, universities, and writers. Because the data for most of the world cover only registered organizations, trends in other areas of associational life are difficult to identify, especially those below the radar of academic research such as community groups and grassroots movements: only 5 percent of the 700,000 "voluntarily formed organizations" in Australia, for example, are run by professional staff.[14] We do not know whether past developments are a reliable guide to the future, though we do know that governments in China, Russia, Kenya, and many other countries are placing more restrictions on NGOs, and this is bound to feed through into their future size and numbers.

Who Is "In" and Who Is "Out"?

Civil society and the state have always been interdependent, with states providing the legal and regulatory framework civil society needs to function, and civil society exerting the pressure for accountability that keeps governments on track.

Sitting between associations and the state, however, is a gray area called "political society," which consists of parties and other explicitly political organizations and which has divided civil society scholars into two rival camps. The first camp sees political society as a crucial component of civil society, not because civic groups seek state power or because they aggregate the interests of individuals into political settlements but because they generate influence on politics through the life of democratic associations and unconstrained discussion in the public sphere. "In the long run, democratic political societies depend for their health on the depth of their roots in independent pre-political associations and publics."[15] Solidarity in Poland was both a labor union and a political party in waiting, and social movements usually have implicit political agendas. In Rajasthan, for example, the Mazdoor Kisan Shakti Sangathan, a "non-party political formation" that works with workers' and peasants' groups, has already fielded candidates in local elections,[16] while across Latin America "activists have not been contained by conventional civic or political categories, but rather have overflowed their boundaries, opening new democratic spaces or extending new ones in the process."[17] South Africa's Treatment Action Campaign began as an alliance of NGOs determined to change government policy on retroviral drugs for HIV/AIDS patients but then developed some of the characteristics of an opposition against the background of rule by the African National Congress. And leaders in countries such as Chile, the Philippines, and Brazil move regularly from NGOs to government and back.[18] After all, politics is where many people involve themselves in voluntary, collective action most intensively through channels that invariably bleed into the civil sphere, so to insist on a firewall between the two is unrealistic.

The second camp shudders at the corrupting influence of politics on associations since associations are assumed to be independent of any partisan political interests. If they weren't independent, they wouldn't be able to play the role that is claimed for them in cementing *generalized* trust and tolerance across different political communities or in promoting a genuine sense of the common interest. Any association that claims to promote the public interest is in dangerous water when it allies itself with a private political agenda because it forfeits its claim to represent the broader agenda of citizens in tasks that necessarily cross party lines—like preserving the freedom of the press or the integrity of the electoral system as a whole. This is exactly the problem that faces the United States today, where too many voluntary associations mirror the partisan divide. Perhaps that's why public reactions were so strong when President Donald Trump appeared to politicize the Boy Scouts of America in a speech he delivered to them in 2017.[19]

As sociologist Nina Eliasoph as shown,[20] many volunteers shy away from political involvement and debates because they add discomfort and division to the group. Perhaps this explains why there are few cases where civil society networks or social movements have made a successful and sustained transition into electoral politics.[21] In 2006, for example, the Nobel Peace Prize winner Muhammad Yunus tried to start a new political party in Bangladesh called Citizens' Power, but he found that even the deep networks of the Grameen Bank and other successful NGOs could not make inroads into the political establishment.[22] In the United States, it's true that religious conservatives have mobilized their political muscle through networks like the Moral Majority and the Christian Coalition of America which have strong links with insurgent elements in the Republican Party but, as the

2018 mid-term elections showed, this may not be enough to secure a hold over Congress.

So while the state is definitely "out" of civil society and non-partisan political activity is definitely "in," everything between these two extremes remains an object of dispute. The only acceptable compromise seems to be that political parties are *in* civil society when they are out of office and *out* of civil society when they are in.

In case the situation is not sufficiently muddy, the boundary between civil society and the market is even less clear. Here again, there is disagreement between those who fear for the purity of the civic spirit when contaminated by contact with business, and those such as Ernest Gellner[23] who argue that business is inescapably a part of civil society, or at least the private-property relations and market institutions that business needs to flourish. Going back at least to the writings of John Locke, this strand of theory has always seen private economic activity as a crucial mainstay of civil society because, at least in theory, it diffuses power away from states and helps to protect the freedom of individuals. This tradition is echoed today in the increasing use of nonprofit agencies in the provision of social and economic services and the rise of "philanthrocapitalism"—the increasing adoption of business thinking and market mechanisms by charities and foundations.[24]

At the opposite end of the spectrum, critics such as Michael Walzer and Christopher Lasch insist that civil society is a market-free zone—a sphere of life in which "money is devalued." In practice, however, it is difficult to draw these distinctions in such a watertight manner. It was the market women of Sierra Leone, for example, who (acting collectively) thronged the streets of Freetown in 1996 and 1997 to ensure that democratic elections went ahead. Likewise, Ashutosh Varshney's research has shown that business associations that tie together the economic interests of Hindus and Muslims in Indian cities have been crucial in reducing the incidence of intercommunal violence. And in

Cuba, it has often been small-scale, informal enterprises that have provided some space for independent organization whilst other forms of association were controlled by the state.[25]

In developing societies, most economic activity takes place in the informal sector, where social relations and market relations are inextricably interwoven. One also needs to distinguish between profit-seeking activities by individual enterprises and the civic or political role of business associations—such as the Transatlantic Business Dialogue or a national chamber of commerce. Logically, the former would be excluded from civil society but the latter would not. Such associations could have an important role to play in encouraging attitudes of cooperation and trust, as well as representing the interests of their members.

The most difficult and contested question about "who is in and who is out" revolves around the definition of "civil" and "uncivil" society. Models of associational life find it difficult to exclude any non-state or non-market institution so long as they meet the criteria [of] consensual membership and voluntaristic mechanisms of decision making. Of course, some writers do exclude associations of which they disapprove ideologically, but not on any grounds that can be defended without considerable intellectual gymnastics and the imposition of a particular—and therefore partial—definition of the good, the bad, and the ugly. There have always been liberal, conservative and progressive elements in civil society, as well as groups with no explicit political leanings at all.[26] In my view, structural models hold water only if all such voluntary associations are included, though a case can be made to exclude hate groups and other associations that seek to obliterate the rights and participation of others on the grounds of identity or ideology—and which therefore violate the basic rules of the civil society game. According to the Southern Poverty Law [Center],[27] there were 953 such hate groups in the United States in 2018, compared to 1.5 million registered voluntary associations as a whole. It seems reasonable to place these groups outside of civil society in any meaningful sense of the phrase, but elsewhere the boundaries between voluntary associations, states and markets are increasingly fluid.

Organizations and Ecosystems

Like a complex and fragile ecosystem, civil society gains strength when grassroots groups, nonprofit intermediaries and membership associations are linked together in ways that promote collective goals, cross-society coalitions, mutual accountability, and shared action-learning. This is one generalization that does hold up across many different contexts: "the landscape of the third sector is untidy but wonderfully exuberant . . . what counts is not the confusion but the profusion." Associations promote pluralism by enabling multiple interests to be represented, different functions to be performed, and a wide range of capacities to be developed.

Drawing from social capital theory, this means a balance between "bonding" (connections within groups), "bridging" (connections across them), and "linking" (connections between associations, government, and the market). Bonding may accentuate inequalities because associations will be used to promote the interests only of the groups concerned, and this can lead to gridlock in the system. Bridging should reduce this problem over time as people dissolve their differences in a sense of the wider common interest, and linking should help all groups to prosper by making the right connections with institutions that can offer them support, resources, opportunities, and influence.[28] However, without the security provided by strong in-group ties, bridging may expose those on the margins to environments in which they cannot operate on equal terms or benefit the few that can prosper at the expense of the many who are left behind.

Strongly bonded associations (such as community organizations) are more effective when they link together vertically and horizontally to form crosscutting networks and federations that can take the struggle to the next level of action, and alliances across the lines of difference that build from a strong grassroots base. "Just as life assembles itself into chains, nonprofits aggregate either by linking up interests, people or communities, or by linking to related organizations," concludes Paul Hawken in his study of the worldwide environmental movement.[29]

When civil society actors join forces on a scale and over a time span significant enough to force through more fundamental changes, they can be classified as social movements. Successful social movements (think civil rights in the United States, the movement of the landless in Brazil, and the environmental and women's movements worldwide) tend to have three things in common: a powerful idea, ideal, or policy agenda; effective communications strategies to get these ideas into politics, government, and the media; and a strong constituency or social base that provides the muscle required to make those targets listen and ensure that constituency views are accurately represented.[30] When these three things come together, success is possible even when the odds are stacked against them, though true social movements are relatively infrequent, in part because they are so emotionally intense and demand significant sacrifices of time, energy, and sometimes even life itself. Such movements often arise in response to a flashpoint, grievance, or obvious injustice which fires up a large-scale counterreaction, but others—like the struggle to promote action against climate change—are slow-burning. History shows that they are most effective in the long term when they are anchored in a broader repertoire of contentious politics that connects them to their targets and their allies over time.[31]

Contention is a central feature of social movements, which is why they tend to form and thicken when the temperature rises around elections, referenda, or "wedge issues" like abortion. Something of this nature happened in

the United States after the 2016 presidential election when a re-energized set of conservative movements locked horns with a host of new formations among liberals and progressives. They included the #MeToo movement, which revealed the true extent of sexual violence in society and led to a spate of high-profile arrests and convictions; the struggle against the Dakota Access Pipeline which united Native American and environmental activists; Black Lives Matter, which was born in the context of police violence against (mostly young) African-American men; and the rebirth of the movement for gun control in the aftermath of mass shootings at the Marjory Stoneman Douglas High School in Parkland, Florida and elsewhere. The same period saw large-scale women's marches, teachers' strikes, immigrant organizing, anti-austerity protests, and a renewed Poor People's Campaign modeled on the original that was launched by Dr Martin Luther King Jr just before his assassination in 1968.[32]

Interestingly, these new movements have some features that distinguish them from older efforts. For example, they make much more use of social media while retaining a core of face-to-face engagement, which allows them to organize horizontally and with less bureaucracy or central direction; they pay more attention to burnout and the need for healing among activists, which may help them to avoid descending into factionalism and fracturing in the future; and they have had significantly more success in attracting participation and leadership from the millennial generation, which may have already fed through into higher voting rates among young people in the 2016 mid-term elections.[33] But, like older movements, they remain solidly rooted in a constituency to whom they are accountable and from whom their leadership and vision emerges. This is what makes them especially important in driving deep-rooted and democratically directed social change. Of course, conservative movements like the Tea Party and the anti-tax movement have been influential too,[34] though they are often overlooked by liberals. Unfortunately, there is no mass movement to bridge the divide between these two camps, which is why other, non-social movement elements of the ecosystem are vital in tackling polarization and division.

These other elements—let's call them "apolitical" associations even though politics are never completely absent—play a much less high-profile but equally important role in engaging large numbers of people in community and civic action, from music and service societies to sports clubs to Weightwatchers. Most people will spend more of their time and energy in associations like these than in social movements, so if we are interested in the development of particular norms and relationships or the emergence of a new sense of the common interest, then they are likely to provide more of the channels and meeting grounds in which these things take shape. Informal associations at the grassroots are often ignored or neglected, but they were vital to the struggle, for example, against apartheid in South Africa or for democracy in China today—organizations such as yard and street resident committees, burial and temple societies, farmers' associations, and youth clubs. Revolutions may start in the streets but they can't stop there, so while movements like #MeToo occupy the headlines, it is the health of the associational ecosystem as a whole that matters most.

As in a real ecosystem, all parts need to be present and connected if the system is to operate effectively. There has been a worldwide professionalization of the nonprofit sector in a technocratic sense and a gradual distancing of associations from their social base—a process variously described as "NGO-ization," "corporatization" and the rise of the "NonProfit Industrial Complex."[35] This process is advanced among conservative groups as well as among liberals and progressives.[36] Funding has gone overwhelmingly to larger NGOs, well-known think tanks, and advocacy groups in capital cities, while northern NGOs have dominated the emergence of transnational networks.

Associational Life in Cross-Cultural Perspective

For the most part, civil society theory has been developed in Europe and the United States, and it makes a series of assumptions about the characteristics of voluntary associations that may not travel well across different countries. They may not even be accurate for different communities within the same country—African-American associational life in America, for example, or Islamic associations in England, or groups led by women rather than by men. Norms of participation are different among whites and African-Americans in the United States, with the latter more likely to take part in protest and campaigning activities as part of an oppositional culture that characterizes many of their associations.[37] Confucian cultures think differently about belonging, solidarity, and citizenship, in part because of a stress on the collective rather than the individual. Social memberships—at least historically—were non-optional and priority was given to the needs of the social whole, so it is no surprise that associations in countries like China have always found it difficult to exist outside of government control. This does not, however, mean that they are powerless.[38] Similarly, Islam's communal character necessitates that the autonomy of individuals must sometimes give way to the needs of the broader community, though also that all such ethical questions must be constantly and collectively reevaluated.[39] The reality of associational life in non-western cultures is always one of "mix and match" because they have been subject to so many external influences in both the colonial and postcolonial eras. To enlarge on this point, it may be useful to look at the combination of associational cultures in more detail in two regions that are of particular interest to civil society watchers: the Middle East and Africa.

Associational Life in the Middle East

Most famously for Ernest Gellner, civil society cannot exist in non-western societies since it is the product of a specific period in the evolution of the West. Gellner refused to believe that regions like the Middle East with strong Islamic traditions could ever develop a meaningful civic life because Islam as an institution cannot be left and entered freely. As recent events have shown, however, such judgments are far too crude to provide an accurate guide to the diverse realities of associational life in Middle Eastern societies, where many different kinds of Islamic organization coexist, cooperate, and compete with secular NGOs, think tanks, women's groups, protest movements, labor unions, media outlets, and bloggers. The resulting mix changes markedly from one country to another, so associational life in Oman or Libya is very different to that in Jordan, Egypt, or Kuwait. The focus of attention is on actualizing forms of civic and democratic behavior that are feasible under different political and religious regimes.

When a college-educated Tunisian street vendor named Mohamed Bouazizi set fire to himself in a protest over political and economic conditions in 2011, he set in motion a train of events that challenged Gellner's hypothesis afresh. Variously described as the "Arab Spring," the "Arab Awakening," and the "Arab Intifada," the large-scale popular protests that spread rapidly across the region after this event seemed to signify a watershed for civil society in the region. As of 2018, and in common with previous experiences of civil society uprisings in Eastern Europe and Latin America, this sense of euphoria has been harshly tempered, but it has not disappeared.[40] The path to democracy rarely leads directly from the streets to the offices of the state. Yet the condition of associational life in the Middle East will surely never be the same.

The Arab Spring did not spring from nowhere. Nor was it launched spontaneously by social media, though the occupation of Cairo's Tahrir Square and other iconic public spaces did unfold without much warning or formal preparation.[41] Its origins lie much further back in the history of associational life in the region, through a wide variety of groups whose activities in neighborhoods, factories, mosques, and universities helped to underpin the eventual emergence of large-scale protest.[42] Recent scholarship has shown that elements of voluntarism existed even in traditional Islamic associations such as guilds (or *asnaf*), trusts, and foundations funded by endowments (called *waqfs*), charities funded through tithes (or *zakat*), and *ayan*, or groups of "urban notables." These groups coexisted with tribal institutions, merchants' groups, labor unions, secular organizations of intellectuals, and professional associations before the repression of civic activity by post-independence governments in the Arab world who sought to consolidate their newfound power in the face of what some saw as threats to national unity.[43] Beginning in the 1980s, these patterns began to open up in response to economic liberalization (which created space for service-providing NGOs), limited political reforms, and the spread of Islamist movements.

In Turkey, for example, independent associations of urban working women with freely chosen memberships coexist with Islamic associations that are closed to other faiths, while in Jordan and Morocco, students' organizations, youth and women's groups and proto-social movements are beginning to influence mainstream Muslim discourse. At the opposite end of the political spectrum (in countries such as Saudi Arabia, Qatar, and the United Arab Emirates) independent citizens' organizations are prohibited and state-run "NGOs" are the norm, along with semi-official Islamic charities (called *diwaniyyas*) and quasi-official research institutes and think tanks.

In these authoritarian contexts, there is little prospect that associational life is about to flourish. The question that then presents itself is clear: how will different kinds of civil society associations take advantage of the spaces that emerge? Despite the diversity of associational life in the region, it is Islamist movements that tend to dominate debates about the answers to this question, especially those that have achieved (albeit fleeting) electoral success, such as Hamas, Hezbollah, and the Muslim Brotherhood. Such movements are themselves diverse, of course. Some elements combine the need to engage in democratic politics in order to gain political power with the continuation of anti-democratic sentiments once they have achieved it, while others—like Hamas in the Gaza Strip—are active in promoting community development and civic restoration, a surprising conclusion, perhaps, to those who identify this movement solely with political violence.[44] Relationships between these groups and other voluntary associations in the Middle East are obviously tense because they involve contests over control, but given the strong ties that Islamists enjoy with large grassroots constituencies and the elite-based nature of many NGOs and advocacy groups (often dependent on funding from outside their own societies), such movements offer a natural vehicle for politics and the development of the social mores governing political and economic life. Islamists enjoy the popular support and legitimacy required to challenge the moral and political authority of incumbent regimes, while NGOs (even if externally funded and restricted in their roles) have a presence at both grassroots and international levels that can pull in resources and develop skills that may eventually translate into change higher up the system. Through that process, there might yet be a democratic resolution of the ongoing "internal struggle over who gets to define the Islamic reformation that is already underway in most of the Muslim world."[45]

That struggle includes liberal NGO activists, feminist leaders, moderate Islamists, "repentant Jihadists" (former Islamic militants who have won release from prison by renouncing violence), and scholars such as Adullahi An-Na'im, who are developing new visions of civil and political life rooted firmly in the Islamic tradition *and* explicitly committed to equal citizenship and respect for human rights, under a democratic, secular state.[46] There are certainly problems with associational life in the Middle East—as shown by the continued intransigence of governments in the face of the Arab Spring—but this is not because civil society is "un-Islamic." "The compatibility or incompatibility of Islam and democracy is not a matter of philosophical speculation but of political struggle," concludes Asef Bayat, which is why the evolution of locally rooted visions of associational life holds one of the keys to the future of the Muslim world.[47]

Associational Life in Africa

Early work on civil society in Africa tended to deny the applicability of the concept completely or look for patterns of associational life that replicated those familiar from the West. Neither approach proved convincing, and today there is renewed interest in creating civil society theories and practices with distinctly African flavors.[48] The starting point in this effort is to recognize the impact of colonialism on the ways in which different forms of associational life were categorized and dealt with by the colonial authorities. As Mahmood Mamdani has shown, using examples from South Africa and Uganda, the bifurcation of British rule into indirect authority exercised through customary law in rural areas, and direct authority exercised through civil law in urban centers, had important consequences for civil society and governance that still reverberate today. One of these consequences has been an ongoing debate between "liberal modernists and Africanist communitarians" about the relative importance of "modern" (urban) and "traditional" (rural) associations that reflects this historical divide.

It is important to note that the bifurcation of civil and customary authority was a deliberate strategy to consolidate colonial rule, but it also overemphasized the differences between traditional and modern forms of association. Social structures based on tribe and clan are characteristic of African societies, and they have given rise to strong ascriptive associations based on ethnicity in which membership is inherited, as opposed to voluntary in the sense implied by western civil society theory. But excluding them from civil society makes no sense when they occupy such an important position in the fabric of associational life by organizing forms of collective action from mutual aid to informal debate and decision making. In Uganda, Ghana, and Nigeria, for example, ethnicity has provided a focus for popular mobilization in contexts where existing power arrangements have closed down other routes to participation. Of course, it has also been used to mobilize violence and dispossession in recent electoral competitions in Kenya and elsewhere, but often what appear as ethnic conflicts are more straightforward struggles over access to power and resources that are manipulated along clan or tribal lines.[49]

Even in colonial Africa, a wide variety of different associations coexisted. Nationalist movements emerged alongside independent churches, women's and self-help groups, professional and neighborhood associations, credit and burial societies, labor unions, farmers' organizations and politico-cultural networks. These associations were spurred on by urbanization and rural–urban migration, increasing access to education, and the development of the market economy (which both required and created an increasing range of intermediaries, mutual-support and interest-based associations); by the struggle for independence, in which civil society activists often played key roles (especially in Southern Africa); and by the trend toward decentralization and democracy in the post-independence era, when development and human rights NGOs began to emerge across the continent.[50]

The debate alluded to by Mamdani has been brought into sharper focus by recent criticisms of NGOs in Africa which are largely urban based but have little connection to a domestic constituency or supporter base, raising questions about their legitimacy, sustainability, and ability to lever changes in politics and economics. On the other hand, strongly rooted associations that are often organized around ethnicity may face difficulties in building relationships across different groups, which tend to be important in consolidating a democratic political culture. This is one reason why broad-based civic action in Africa is quite rare, often emerging only at times of crisis and difficult to sustain beyond the first or second wave of democratic elections—even in South Africa, where NGOs and community-based organizations were so influential prior to and after the end of apartheid.[51]

What is intriguing in this picture is not whether "modern" NGOs or "traditional" community associations are most important but how these different elements intertwine so that the "whole is more than the sum of its parts," as this is the only way in which the civil society ecosystem will be able to influence larger questions. Clearly, factors other than the structure of associational life are important in this respect, principally the nature of political regimes. In most African countries, these regimes continue to restrict the ability of anyone in civil society to influence public affairs, regardless of the kind of associations to which they belong, with infiltration or direct control of associations by the state widespread in countries such as Cameroon, Benin, Ethiopia, and Sudan.

The reality is that people draw on a wide range of cultural resources and identities, whether modern, traditional, or somewhere in between. The debate highlighted by Mamdani may never be settled, but moving "beyond the backlash" against both African NGOs and customary associations will help us to understand and encourage the different ways in which the ecosystems of associational life are evolving across the continent.[52] Far from being a problem, the diverse development of these ecosystems across Africa, the Middle East, and other regions is a cause for celebration because it means that what emerges in the future—hybrid, fluid, and maybe surprising to commentators in the West—might be able to avoid some of the problems encountered by civil society in the United States and Europe. This may help to answer the charge that NGOs and other associations in these regions are simply pawns of foreign powers. Associational life in every country is a process of constant evolution, with lots of different elements recombining over time. The consequences of this process are always uncertain, particularly in contexts where radically different cultures of identity and belonging coexist. This is why there are no simple relationships between the forms, norms, and achievements of voluntary associations.

Notes

1. Goody (2002: 157).
2. From Engels's foreword to Adams (1986: viii).
3. De Tocqueville (1945: vol. 2, 114).
4. Bodin (2017). On the general decline in volunteering in the United States, see Grimm and Dietz (2018).
5. Cited by Adams (1986: 160).
6. Walzer (1998: 124).
7. Data from Non-Profit Action (2015), Anacleto (2015), and Najjar (2017).
8. Wu (2017).
9. BRAC at a glance: www.brac.net
10. Edwards (2016), Bureau of Democracy, Human Rights and Labor (2017).
11. Gottesdiener (2012).
12. Lichtenstein (2002).

13. Skocpol (1999, 2003), Verba et al. (2012).
14. Hughes (2018).
15. Cohen and Arato (1992: x).
16. *The Economist*, January 13, 2001: 42.
17. Alvarez et al. (2017), Ice and Yovanovich (2018).
18. Lewis (2008).
19. Cillizza (2017).
20. Eliasoph (1998, 2011, 2013).
21. For a useful comparative review of cases, see Pinckney (2018).
22. Ramesh (2007).
23. Gellner (1994).
24. Edwards (2010).
25. Edwards (1999: 94), Varshney (2002), Peters and Scarpacci (1998).
26. See Davies (2014) and Martin (2015) for useful historical surveys; and Youngs (2018) for an account of conservative associations and networks worldwide.
27. www.splcenter.org/hate-map
28. Woolcock (1998), Edwards (2000).
29. Hawken (2007).
30. Tarrow (2012).
31. See Tilly and Tarrow (2007), Tarrow (1998), Hawken (2007).
32. Freeman-Woolpert (2018).
33. See Harris (2017).
34. See Martin (2015).
35. INCITE (2007), Choudry and Kapoor (2013), Dauvergne and LeBaron (2013).
36. See Youngs (2018).
37. Dawson (2001).
38. Howell and Pearce (2001), Unger (2008), Teets (2016).
39. See Aslan (2005a), Khilnani and Kaviraj (2002).
40. See Yerkes and Ben Yahmed (2018).
41. Hassan (2012).
42. Kienle (2012).
43. Kandil (1995), Salam (2002), Hawthorne (2004), Paya (2004), Bamyeh (2005).
44. Roy (2013).
45. Aslan (2005b).
46. Tamman (2008), An-Na'im (2008).
47. Bayat (2007), Kelsay (2002).
48. Obadare (2014), Mathews (2017).
49. Orvis (2001).

50. Bayart (1986), Mamdani (1996), Comaroff and Comaroff (1999), Lewis (2004).

51. Lehman (2008), Obadare (2014).

52. Obadare (2014).

References

Adams, J. L. (1986) *Voluntary Associations*. Chicago: Exploration Press.

Alvarez, S., Rubin, J., Thayer, M., Baiocchi, G., and Laó-Montes, A. (eds) (2017) *Beyond Civil Society: Activism, Participation, and Protest in Latin America*. Durham, NC: Duke University Press.

Anacleto, M. (2015) "NGOs in Brazil." https://prezi.com/kyasgfxjrzwr/non-governmental-organizations-in-brazil/

An-Na'im, A. (2008) *Islam and the Secular State: Negotiating the Future of Shari'a*. Cambridge, MA: Harvard University Press.

Aslan, R. (2005a) *No God But God: The Origins, Evolution and Future of Islam*. New York: Random House.

Aslan, R. (2005b) "From Islam, Pluralist Democracies Will Surely Grow." *Chronicle of Higher Education*, March 11.

Bamyeh, M. (2005) "Civil Society and the Islamic Experience." *ISIM Review* (Spring): 40–41.

Bayart, J.-F. (1986) "Civil Society in Africa," in P. Chabal (ed.), *Political Domination in Africa*. Cambridge: Cambridge University Press.

Bayat, A. (2007) *Making Islam Democratic: Social Movements and the Post-Islamist Turn*. Stanford, CA: Stanford University Press.

Bodin, M. (2017) "Volunteer Fire Departments Are Struggling to Retain Firefighters, While 911 Calls Are Surging." www.govtech.com/em/disaster/EM-Summer-2017-Dwindling-Force.html

Bureau of Democracy, Human Rights and Labor, US State Department. (2017) "NGOs in the United States." www.state.gov/j/drl/rls/fs/2017/266904.htm

Choudry, A. and Kapoor, D. (2013) *NGOization: Complicity, Contradictions and Prospects*. London: Zed Books.

Cillizza, C. (2017) "The 29 Most Cringe-worthy Lines from Donald Trump's Hyper-political Speech to the Boy Scouts." www.cnn.com/2017/07/25/politics/donald-trump-boy-scouts-speech/index.html

Cohen, J. and Arato, A. (1992) *Civil Society and Political Theory*. Cambridge, MA: MIT Press.

Comaroff, J. and Comaroff, J. (eds) (1999) *Civil Society and the Political Imagination in Africa*. Chicago, IL: University of Chicago Press.

Dauvergne, P. and LeBaron, G. (2013) *The Corporatization of Activism*. Cambridge: Polity.

Davies, T. (2014) *NGOs: A New History of Transnational Civil Society*. New York: Oxford University Press.

Dawson, M. (2001) *Black Visions: The Roots of Contemporary African-American Mass Political Ideologies*. Chicago: University of Chicago Press.

De Tocqueville, A. (1945) *Democracy in America*, 2 vols. New York: Knopf.

Edwards, M. (1999) *Future Positive: International Cooperation in the 21st Century*. London: Earthscan.

Edwards, M. (2000) "Enthusiasts, Tacticians and Skeptics: Civil Society and Social Capital." *Kettering Review* 18(1): 39–51.

Edwards, M. (2010) *Small Change: Why Business Won't Save the World*. San Francisco, CA: Berrett-Koehler.

Edwards, M. (2016) "Back to the Future?" *IDS Bulletin* 47(2): 169–178.

Eliasoph, N. (1998) *Avoiding Politics: How Americans Produce Apathy in Everyday Life*. Cambridge: Cambridge University Press.

Eliasoph, N. (2011) *Making Volunteers: Civic Life after Welfare's End*. Princeton, NJ: Princeton University Press.

Eliasoph, N. (2013) *The Politics of Volunteering*. Cambridge: Polity.

Freeman-Woolpert, S. (2018) "A Renewed Poor People's Campaign Revives King's Dream of Challenging Divides." www.opendemocracy.net/transformation/sarah-freeman-woolpert/renewed-poor-people-s-campaign-revives-king-s-dream-of-challen

Gellner, E. (1994) *Conditions of Liberty: Civil Society and Its Rivals*. London: Hamish Hamilton.

Goody, J. (2002) "Civil Society in an Extra-European Perspective," in S. Khilnani and S. Kaviraj (eds.), *Civil Society: History and Possibilities*. Cambridge: Cambridge University Press.

Gottesdiener, L. (2012) "A New Face of the New Labor Movement." www.WagingNonViolence.org

Grimm, R. and Dietz, N. (2018) *Where Are America's Volunteers*. College Park, MD: Do Good Institute, University of Maryland.

Harris, M. (2017) *Kids These Days: The Making of Millennials*. New York: Back Bay Books.

Hassan, K. (2012) "Making Sense of the Arab Spring: Listening to the Voices of Middle Eastern Activists." *Development* 55(2): 232–238.

Hawken, P. (2007) *Blessed Unrest: How the Largest Movement in the World Came into Being and Why No One Saw It Coming*. New York: Penguin.

Hawthorne, A. (2004) *Middle Eastern Democracy: Is Civil Society the Answer?* Democracy and Rule of Law Project, Paper No. 44. Washington, DC: Carnegie Endowment for International Peace.

Howell, J. and Pearce, J. (2001) *Civil Society and Development: A Critical Exploration*. Boulder, CO: Lynne Rienner.

Hughes, V. (2018) "Whatever Happened to Civil Society?" www.opendemocracy.net/transformation/vern-hughes/whatever-happened-to-civil-society

Ice, R. and Yovanovich, G. (eds) (2018) *Re-Imagining Community and Civil Society in Latin America and the Caribbean*. London: Routledge.

INCITE (2007) *The Revolution Will Not Be Funded: Beyond the Non-Profit Industrial Complex*. Cambridge, MA: South End Press.

Kandil, A. (1995) *Civil Society in the Arab World*. Washington, DC: CIVICUS.

Kelsay, J. (2002) "Civil Society and Government in Islam," in R. Post and N. Rosenblum (eds.), *Civil Society and Government*. Princeton, NJ: Princeton University Press.

Khilnani, S. and Kaviraj, S. (eds) (2002) *Civil Society: History and Possibilities*. Cambridge: Cambridge University Press.

Kienle, E. (2012) "Egypt without Mubarak, Tunisia after Bin Ali: Theory, History and the Arab Spring." *Economy and Society* 41(4): 532–557.

Lehman, H. (2008) "The Emergence of Civil Society Organizations in South Africa." *Journal of Public Affairs* 8: 115–127.

Lewis, D. (2004) "Old and New Civil Societies in Bangladesh," in M. Glasius, D. Lewis and H.

Seckinelgin (eds.), *Exploring Civil Society: Political and Cultural Contexts*. Abingdon: Routledge.

Lewis, D. (2008) "Crossing the Boundaries between Third Sector and State: Life-work Histories from the Philippines, Bangladesh and the UK." *Third World Quarterly* 29(1): 125–141.

Lichtenstein, N. (2002) *State of the Union: A Century of American Labor*. Princeton, NJ: Princeton University Press.

Mamdani, M. (1996) *Citizen and Subject: Contemporary Africa and the Legacy of Late Colonialism*. Princeton, NJ: Princeton University Press.

Martin, I. W. (2015) *Rich People's Movements: Grassroots Campaigns to Untax the One Percent*. New York: Oxford University Press.

Mathews, S. (2017) *NGOs and Social Justice in South Africa and Beyond*. Durban: University of Kwa-Zulu-Natal Press.

Najjar, F. (2017) "Why Is Egypt's New NGO Law Controversial?" www.aljazeera.com/indepth/features/2017/05/egypt-ngo-law-controversial-170530142008179.html

Non-Profit Action (2015) "Facts and Stats about NGOs Worldwide." http://nonprofitaction.org/2015/09/facts-and-stats-about-ngos-worldwide/

Obadare, E. (ed) (2014) *The Handbook of Civil Society in Africa*. New York: Springer.

Orvis, S. (2001) "Civil Society in Africa or African Civil Society?" *Journal of Asian and African Studies* 36(1): 17–38.

Paya, A. (2004) "Civil Society in Iran: Past, Present and Future," in M. Glasius, D. Lewis, and H. Seckinelgin (eds.), *Exploring Civil Society: Political and Cultural Contexts*. Abingdon: Routledge.

Peters, P. and Scarpacci, J. (1998) *Cuba's New Entrepreneurs: Five Years of Small-Scale Capitalism*. Arlington, VA: Alexis de Tocqueville Institution.

Pinckney, J. (2018) *When Civil Resistance Succeeds: Building Democracy after Popular Nonviolent Uprisings*. Washington, DC: International Centre on Nonviolent Conflict.

Ramesh, R. (2007) "Nobel Winner Starts Anti-graft Party." *Guardian Weekly*, March 2–8.

Roy, S. (2013) *Hamas and Civil Society in Gaza: Engaging the Islamist Social Sector*. Princeton, NJ: Princeton University Press.

Salam, N. (2002) *Civil Society in the Arab World: The Historical and Political Dimensions*. Occasional

Paper 3, Islamic Legal Studies Program, Harvard Law School.

Skocpol, T. (1999) "Advocates Without Members: The Recent Transformation of American Civic Life," in T. Skocpol and M. Fiorina (eds.), *Civic Engagement in American Democracy*. Washington, DC: Brookings Institution Press.

Skocpol, T. (2003) *Diminished Democracy: From Membership to Management in American Civic Life*. Oklahoma City: University of Oklahoma Press.

Tamman, H. (2008) "Repentant Jihadists and the Changing Face of Islam." *Arab Reform Bulletin*, September. http://carnegieendowment.org/2008/09/09/repentant-jihadists-and-changing-face-of-islamism-in-egypt/eiaa

Tarrow, S. (1998) *Power in Movement: Social Movements and Contentious Politics*. Cambridge: Cambridge University Press.

Tarrow, S. (2012) *Strangers at the Gates: Movements and States in Contentious Politics*. Cambridge: Cambridge University Press.

Teets, J. (2016) *Civil Society under Authoritarianism: The China Model*. Cambridge: Cambridge University Press.

Tilly, C. and Tarrow, S. (2007) *Contentious Politics*. London: Paradigm.

Unger, J. (ed) (2008) *Associations and the Chinese State: Contested Spaces*. London: M. E. Sharpe.

Varshney, A. (2002) *Ethnic Conflict and Civic Life: Hindus and Muslims in India*. New Haven, CT: Yale University Press.

Verba, S, Schlozman, K., and Brady, H. (2012) *The Un-Heavenly Chorus: Unequal Political Voice and the Broken Promise of American Democracy*. Princeton, NJ: Princeton University Press.

Walzer, M. (1998) "The Idea of Civil Society: A Path to Social Reconstruction," in E. J. Dionne (ed.), *Community Works: The Revival of Civil Society in America*. Washington, DC: Brookings Institution Press.

Woolcock, M. (1998) "Social Capital and Economic Development: Toward a Theoretical Synthesis and Policy Framework." *Theory and Society* 27(2): 151–208.

Wu, D. D. (2017) "More than 7,000 Foreign NGOs in China: Only 91 Registered So Far." https://thediplomat.com/2017/06/more-than-7000-foreign-ngos-in-china-only-72-registered-so-far/

Yerkes, S. and Ben Yahmed, Z. (2018) *Tunisians' Revolutionary Goals Remain Unfulfilled*. Washington, DC: Carnegie Endowment for International Peace.

Youngs, R. (ed) (2018) *The Mobilization of Conservative Civil Society*. Washington, DC: Carnegie Endowment for International Peace.

CHAPTER 25

To Empower People: The Role of Mediating Structures in Public Policy

PETER L. BERGER AND RICHARD JOHN NEUHAUS

Originally published as *To Empower People: The Role of Mediating Structures in Public Policy*. Washington, DC: American Enterprise Institute for Public Policy Research, 1977. Reprinted with permission of the American Enterprise Institute.

Mediating Structures and the Dilemmas of the Welfare State

Two seemingly contradictory tendencies are evident in current thinking about public policy in America. First, there is a continuing desire for the services provided by the modern welfare state. Partisan rhetoric aside, few people seriously envisage dismantling the welfare state. The serious debate is over how and to what extent it should be expanded. The second tendency is one of strong animus against government, bureaucracy, and bigness as such. This animus is directed not only toward Washington but toward government at all levels. Although this essay is addressed to the American situation, it should be noted that a similar ambiguity about the modern welfare state exists in other democratic societies, notably in Western Europe.

Perhaps this is just another case of people wanting to eat their cake and have it too. It would hardly be the first time in history that the people wanted benefits without paying the requisite costs. Nor are politicians above exploiting ambiguities by promising increased services while reducing expenditures. The extravagant rhetoric of the modern state and the surrealistic vastness of its taxation system encourage magical expectations that make contradictory measures seem possible. As long as some of the people can be fooled some of the time, some politicians will continue to ride into office on such magic.

But this is not the whole story. The contradiction between wanting more government services and less government may be only apparent. More precisely, we suggest that the modern welfare state is here to stay, indeed that it ought to expand the benefits it provides—but that *alternative mechanisms are possible to provide welfare state services*.

The current anti-government, anti-bigness mood is not irrational. Complaints about impersonality, unresponsiveness, and excessive interference, as well as the perception of rising costs and deteriorating service—these are based upon empirical and widespread experience. What first appears as contradiction, then, is the sum of equally justified aspirations. The public policy goal is to address human needs without exacerbating the reasons for animus against the welfare state.

Of course there are no panaceas. The alternatives proposed here, we believe, can solve *some* problems.

The basic concept is that of what we are calling mediating structures. The concept in various forms has been around for a long time. What is new is the systematic effort to translate it into specific public policies. For purposes of this study, mediating structures are defined as *those institutions standing between the individual in his private life and the large institutions of public life.*

Modernization brings about an historically unprecedented dichotomy between public and private life. The most important large institution in the ordering of modern society is the modern state itself. In addition, there are the large economic conglomerates of capitalist enterprise, big labor, and the growing bureaucracies that administer wide sectors of the society, such as in education and the organized professions. All these institutions we call the *megastructures.*

Then there is that modern phenomenon called private life. It is a curious kind of preserve left over by the large institutions and in which individuals carry on a bewildering variety of activities with only fragile institutional support.

For the individual in modern society, life is an ongoing migration between these two spheres, public and private. The megastructures are typically alienating, that is, they are not helpful in providing meaning and identity for individual existence. Meaning, fulfillment, and personal identity are to be realized in the private sphere. While the two spheres interact in many ways, in private life the individual is left very much to his own devices, and thus is uncertain and anxious. Where modern society is "hard," as in the megastructures, it is personally unsatisfactory; where it is "soft," as in private life, it cannot be relied upon. Compare, for example, the social realities of employment with those of marriage.

The dichotomy poses a double crisis. It is a crisis for the individual who must carry on a balancing act between the demands of the two spheres. It is a political crisis because the megastructures (notably the state) come to be devoid of personal meaning and are therefore viewed as unreal or even malignant. Not everyone experiences this crisis in the same way. Many who handle it more successfully than most have access to institutions that *mediate* between the two spheres. Such institutions have a private face, giving private life a measure of stability, and they have a public face, transferring meaning and value to the megastructures. Thus, mediating structures alleviate each facet of the double crisis of modern society. Their strategic position derives from their reducing both the anomic precariousness of individual existence in isolation from society and the threat of alienation to the public order.

Our focus is on four such mediating structures—neighborhood, family, church, and voluntary association. This is by no means an exhaustive list, but these institutions were selected for two reasons: first, they figure prominently in the lives of most Americans and, second, they are most relevant to the problems of the welfare state with which we are concerned. The proposal is that, if these institutions could be more imaginatively recognized in public policy, individuals would be more "at home" in society, and the political order would be more "meaningful."

Without institutionally reliable processes of mediation, the political order becomes detached from the values and realities of individual life. Deprived of its moral foundation, the political order is "delegitimated." When that happens, the political order must be secured by coercion rather than by consent. And when that happens, democracy disappears.

Democracy is "handicapped" by being vulnerable to the erosion of meaning in its institutions. Cynicism threatens it; wholesale cynicism can destroy it. That is why mediation is so crucial to democracy. Such mediation cannot be sporadic and occasional; it must be institutionalized in *structures*. The structures we have chosen to study have demonstrated a great capacity for adapting and innovating under changing conditions. Most important, they exist where people are, and that is where sound public policy should always begin.

This understanding of mediating structures is sympathetic to Edmund Burke's well-known claim: "To be attached to the subdivision, to love the little platoon we belong to in society, is the first principle (the germ as it were) of public affections." And it is sympathetic to Alexis de Tocqueville's conclusion drawn from his observation of Americans: "In democratic countries the science of association is the mother of science; the progress of all the rest depends upon the progress it has made." Marx too was concerned about the destruction of community, and the glimpse he gives us of post-revolutionary society is strongly reminiscent of Burke's "little platoons." The emphasis is even sharper in the anarcho-syndicalist tradition of social thought.

In his classic study of suicide, Emile Durkheim describes the "tempest" of modernization sweeping away the "little aggregations" in which people formerly found community, leaving only the state on the one hand and a mass of individuals, "like so many liquid molecules," on the other. Although using different terminologies, others in the sociological tradition—Ferdinand Toennies, Max Weber, Georg Simmel, Charles Cooley, Thorstein Veblen—have analyzed aspects of the same dilemma. Today Robert Nisbet has most persuasively argued that the loss of community threatens the future of American democracy.

Also, on the practical political level, it might seem that mediating structures have universal endorsement. There is, for example, little political mileage in being anti-family or anti-church. But the reality is not so simple. Liberalism—which constitutes the broad center of American politics, whether or not it calls itself by that name—has tended to be blind to the political (as distinct from private) functions of mediating

structures. The main feature of liberalism, as we intend the term, is a commitment to government action toward greater social justice within the existing system.

American liberalism has been vigorous in the defense of the private rights of individuals, and has tended to dismiss the argument that private behavior can have public consequences. Private rights are frequently defended *against* mediating structures—children's rights against the family, the rights of sexual deviants against neighborhood or small-town sentiment, and so forth. Similarly, American liberals are virtually faultless in their commitment to the religious liberty of individuals. But the liberty to be defended is always that of privatized religion. Supported by a very narrow understanding of the separation of church and state, liberals are typically hostile to the claim that institutional religion might have public rights and public functions. As a consequence of this "geometrical" outlook, liberalism has a hard time coming to terms with the alienating effects of the abstract structures it has multiplied since the New Deal. This may be the Achilles heel of the liberal state today.

The left, understood as some version of the socialist vision, has been less blind to the problem of mediation. Indeed the term alienation derives from Marxism. The weakness of the left, however, is its exclusive or nearly exclusive focus on the capitalist economy as the source of this evil, when in fact the alienations of the socialist states, insofar as there are socialist states, are much more severe than those of the capitalist states.

On the right of the political broad center, we also find little that is helpful. To be sure, classical European conservatism had high regard for mediating structures, but, from the eighteenth century on, this tradition has been marred by a romantic urge to revoke modernity—a prospect that is, we think, neither likely nor desirable. On the other hand, what is now called conservatism in America is in fact old-style liberalism. It is the laissez-faire ideology of the period before the New Deal, which is roughly the time when liberalism shifted its faith from the market to government. *Both* the old faith in the market *and* the new faith in government share the abstract thought patterns of the Enlightenment. In addition, today's conservatism typically exhibits the weakness of the left in reverse: it is highly sensitive to the alienations of big government, but blind to the analogous effects of big business. Such one-sidedness, whether left or right, is not helpful.

As is now being widely recognized, we need new approaches free of the ideological baggage of the past. The mediating structures paradigm cuts across current ideological and political divides.

The argument of this essay—and the focus of the research project it is designed to introduce—can be subsumed under three propositions. The first proposition is analytical: *Mediating structures are essential for a vital democratic society.* The other two are broad programmatic recommendations: *Public policy should protect and foster mediating structures,* and *Wherever possible, public policy should utilize mediating structures for the realization of social purposes.*

The analytical proposition assumes that mediating structures are the value-generating and value-maintaining agencies in society. Without them, values become another function of the megastructures, notably of the state, and this is a hallmark of totalitarianism. In the totalitarian case, the individual becomes the object rather than the subject of the value-propagating processes of society.

The two programmatic propositions are, respectively, minimalist and maximalist. Minimally, public policy should cease and desist from damaging mediating structures.

The maximalist proposition ("utilize mediating structures") is much riskier. There is the real danger that such structures might be "co-opted" by the government in a too eager embrace that would destroy the very distinctiveness of their

function. The prospect of government control of the family, for example, is clearly the exact opposite of our intention. The goal in utilizing mediating structures is to expand government services without producing government oppressiveness.

Our point is not to attack the megastructures but to find better ways in which they can relate to the "little platoons" in our common life.

The theme is *empowerment*. One of the most debilitating results of modernization is a feeling of powerlessness in the face of institutions controlled by those whom we do not know and whose values we often do not share. Lest there be any doubt, our belief is that human beings, whoever they are, understand their own needs better than anyone else—in, say, 99 percent of all cases. The mediating structures under discussion here are the principal expressions of the real values and the real needs of people in our society. They are, for the most part, the people-sized institutions. Public policy should recognize, respect, and, where possible, empower these institutions.

Neighborhood

At first blush, it seems the defense of neighborhood is a motherhood issue. The neighborhood is the place of relatively intact and secure existence, protecting us against the disjointed and threatening big world "out there." Around the idea of neighborhood gravitate warm feelings of nostalgia and the hope for community.

While no doubt influenced by such sentiments, the new interest in neighborhoods today goes far beyond sentimentality. The neighborhood should be seen as a key mediating structure in the reordering of our national life. As is evident in fears and confusions surrounding such phrases as ethnic purity or neighborhood integrity, the focus on neighborhood touches some of the most urgent and sensitive issues of social policy.

To put it simply, real community development must begin where people are.

For public policy purposes, there is no useful definition of what makes a good neighborhood, though we can agree on what constitutes a bad neighborhood. With respect to so-called bad neighborhoods, we have essentially three public policy choices: we can ignore them, we can attempt to dismantle them and spread their problems around more equitably, or we can try to transform the bad into the better on the way to becoming good. The first option, although common, should be intolerable. The second is massively threatening to the nonpoor, and therefore not feasible short of revolution. The third holds most promise for a public policy that can gain the support of the American people.

One pays the price for the neighborhood of one's choice. Making that choice possible is the function of the *idea* of neighborhood as it is embodied in many actual neighborhoods. It is not possible to create the benefits of each kind of neighborhood in every neighborhood. One cannot devise a compromise between the cohesion of a New England small town and the anonymity of the East Village without destroying both options.

The mediating structures paradigm requires that we take seriously the structures, values, and habits by which people order their lives in neighborhoods, wherever those neighborhoods may be, and no matter whether they are cohesive or individualistic, elective or hereditary.

The empowerment of people in neighborhoods is hardly the answer to all our social problems. Neighborhoods empowered to impose their values upon individual behavior and expression can be both coercive and cruel. Government that transcends neighborhoods must intervene to protect elementary human rights. Here again, however, the distinction between public and private spheres is critically important. In recent years an unbalanced emphasis upon individual rights has seriously eroded the community's power to sustain its democratically determined values in the public sphere. It is ironic, for example, to find people who support landmark commissions that exercise aesthetic censorship—for example, by forbidding owners of landmark properties to change so much as a step or a bay window without legal permission—and who, at the same time, oppose public control of pornography, prostitution, gambling, and other "victimless crimes" that violate neighborhood values more basic than mere aesthetics.

Many different streams flow into the current enthusiasms for neighborhood government. Sometimes the neighborhood government movement is dubbed "the new Jeffersonianism." After two centuries of massive immigration and urbanization, we cannot share Jefferson's bucolic vision of rural and small-town America, just as we do not indulge the re-medievalizing fantasies associated in some quarters with the acclaim for smallness. Our argument is not against modernity but in favor of exploring the ways in which modernity can be made more humane.

If neighborhoods are to be key to public policy, governmental action is necessary to fund neighborhood improvement. Without a direct assault upon the free enterprise system, the possibilities of evasion and subterfuge in order to invest money where it is safest or most profitable are almost infinite. To strengthen the mediating role of neighborhoods we need to look to new versions of the Federal Housing Administration assistance programs that played such a large part in the burgeoning suburbs after World War II. Such programs can, we believe, be developed to sustain and rehabilitate old communities, as they have been used to build new ones. The idea of urban homesteading, for example, although afflicted with corruption and confusion in recent years, is a move in the right direction. At a very elementary level, property tax regulations should be changed to encourage rather than discourage home improvement.

Neighborhoods will also be strengthened as people in the neighborhood assume more and more responsibility for law enforcement, especially in the effort to stem the tide of criminal terrorism.

We should examine the informal "law enforcement agents" that exist in every community—the woman who runs the local candy store, the people who walk their dogs, or the old people who sit on park benches or observe the streets from their windows.

All of which is to say that the goal of making and keeping life human, of sustaining a people-sized society, depends upon our learning again that parochialism is not a nasty word. Like the word parish, it comes from the Greek, *para* plus *oikos*, the place next door. Because we all want some choice and all have a great stake in the place where we live, it is in the common interest to empower our own places and the places next door.

Family

For most Americans, neighborhood and community are closely linked to the family as an institution.

Of course, modernization has already had a major impact on the family. It has largely stripped the family of earlier functions in the areas of education and economics, for example. But in other ways, modernization has made the family more important than ever before. It is the major institution within the private sphere, and thus for many people the most valuable thing in their lives. Here they make their moral commitments, invest their emotions, plan for the future, and perhaps even hope for immortality.

We can take positive measures to protect and foster the family institution, so that it is not defenseless before the forces of modernity.

This means public recognition of the family *as an institution*. It is not enough to be concerned for individuals more or less incidentally related to the family as institution. Public recognition of the family as an institution is imperative because every society has an inescapable interest in how children are raised, how values are transmitted to the next generation.

The sovereignty of the family over children has limits—as does any sovereignty in the modern world—and these limits are already defined in laws regarding abuse, criminal neglect, and so on. The onus of proof, however, must be placed on policies or laws that foster state interference rather than on those that protect family autonomy. In saying this we affirm what has been the major legal tradition in this country.

Conversely, we oppose policies that expose the child directly to state intervention, without the mediation of the family. We are skeptical about much current discussion of children's rights—especially when such rights are asserted *against* the family. Children do have rights, among which is the right to a functionally strong family.

The implications of our policy concept may be clarified by looking briefly at three currently discussed issues—education vouchers, day care, and the care of the handicapped. The idea of education vouchers has been around for a while and has had its ups and downs, but it remains one of the most intriguing possibilities for radical reform in the area of education. In this proposal, public funding of education shifts from disbursement to schools to disbursement to individuals. Parents (or, at a certain age, their children) choose the schools where they will cash in their vouchers, the schools then being reimbursed by the state. Essentially the proposal applies the paradigm of the GI Bill to younger students at earlier periods of education. This proposal would break the coercive monopoly of the present education system and empower individuals in relating to the megastructures of bureaucracy and professionalism, with special benefits going to lower-income people. In addition, it would enhance the diversity of American life by fostering particularist communities of value—whether of life style, ideology, religion, or ethnicity.

Turning to our second example, we note that day care has become a public issue, as more and more mothers of small children have entered the labor force and as many people, spurred by the feminist movement, have begun to claim that working mothers have a right to public services designed to meet their special needs.

Three positions on national day care policy can be discerned at present. One is that the government should, quite simply, stay out of this area. Another position endorses a federally funded, comprehensive child-care system attached to the public schools. A third position is much like the second, except that the national program would be less closely linked to the public school system.

It should come as no surprise that we favor the third position. We do so because there is a real need and because the need should be met in a way that is as inexpensive and as unintrusive as possible. The mediating structures concept is ideally suited to the latter purpose and may also advance the former. Vouchers would facilitate day-care centers that are small, not professionalized, under the control of parents, and therefore highly diversified.

The third issue mentioned is care of the handicapped. An important case in this area is the so-called special child—special children being those who, for a broad range of nonphysical reasons, are handicapped in their educational development.

Innovative thinking today moves toward using the family as a therapeutic context *as much as possible*. This means viewing the professional as *ancillary* to, rather than as a substitute for, the resources of the family. It may mean paying families to care for a handicapped child, enabling a parent to work less or not at all, or to employ others.

The principal public policy interest in the family concerns children, not adults. This interest is common to all societies, but in democratic society there is an additional and urgent interest in fostering socialization patterns and values that allow individual autonomy. That interest implies enhanced protection of the family in relation to the state, and it implies trusting people to be responsible for their own children in a world of their own making.

Church

Religious institutions form by far the largest network of voluntary associations in American society. Yet, for reasons both ideological and historical, their role is frequently belittled or totally overlooked in discussions of social policy. Whatever may be one's attitude to organized religion, this blind spot must be reckoned a serious weakness in much thinking about public policy. The churches and synagogues of America can no more be omitted from responsible social analysis than can big labor, business corporations, or the communications media. Not only are religious institutions significant "players" in the public realm, but they are singularly important to the way people order their lives and values at the most local and concrete levels of their existence. Thus they are crucial to understanding family, neighborhood, and other mediating structures of empowerment.

From the beginning, we have emphasized the importance of mediating structures in generating and maintaining values. Within the family, and between the family and the larger society, the church is a primary agent for bearing and transmitting the operative values of our society. This is true not only in the sense that most Americans identify their most important values as being religious in character, but also in the sense that the values that inform our public discourse are inseparably related to specific religious traditions. In the absence of the church and other mediating structures that articulate these values, the result is not that the society is left without operative values; the result is that the state has an unchallenged monopoly on the generation and maintenance of values. Needless to say, we would find this a very unhappy condition indeed.

Our proposal is that the institutions of religion should be unfettered to make their maximum contribution to the public interest. In some areas of social service and education, this means these institutions should be free to continue doing what they have historically done.

Again, and in accord with our maximalist proposition, we expect increased public funding for the meeting of human needs in a wide range of policy areas; our particular contention is that mediating institutions, including religious institutions, be utilized as much as possible as the implementing agencies of policy goals. Contrary to some public policy and legal thinking today, such increased funding need not require an increase in governmental control and a consequent war on pluralism.

Voluntary Association

There is a history of debate over what is meant by a voluntary association. For our present purposes, a voluntary association is a body of people who have voluntarily organized themselves in pursuit of particular goals. (Following common usage, we exclude business corporations and other primarily economic associations.) Important to the present discussion is the subject of volunteer service. Many voluntary associations have both paid and volunteer staffing. For our purposes, the crucial point is the free association of people for some collective purpose, the fact that they may pay some individuals for doing work to this end not being decisive.

At least since de Tocqueville the importance of voluntary associations in American democracy has been widely recognized. Voluntarism has flourished in America more than in any other Western society and it is reasonable to believe this may have something to do with American political institutions. Associations create statutes, elect officers, debate, vote courses of action, and otherwise serve as schools for democracy. However trivial, wrongheaded, or bizarre we

may think the purpose of some associations to be, they nonetheless perform this vital function.

Apart from this political role, voluntary associations are enormously important for what they have actually done. Before the advent of the modern welfare state, almost everything in the realm of social services was under the aegis of voluntary associations, usually religious in character. We are interested in one type within the vast array of voluntary associations—namely, associations that render social services relevant to recognized public responsibilities.

Assaults on voluntary associations come from several directions, from both the right and left of the political spectrum. Some condemn them as inefficient, corrupt, divisive, and even subversive. Many subscribe to the axiom that public services should not be under private control. From the far left comes the challenge that such associations supply mere palliatives, perpetuate the notion of charity, and otherwise manipulate people into acceptance of the status quo.

The problem confronting us arises when the vested interests in question use coercive state power to repress individual freedom, initiative, and social diversity. We are not impressed by the argument that this is necessary because voluntary associations often overlap with the functions of government agencies. Overlap may in fact provide creative competition, incentives for performance, and increased choice. But our more basic contention is against the notion that anything public must *ipso facto* be governmental. That notion is profoundly contrary to the American political tradition and is, in its consequences, antidemocratic.

Our present problem is also closely linked with the trend toward professionalization. Whether in government or nongovernment agencies, professionals attack allegedly substandard services, and substandard generally means nonprofessional. Through organizations and lobbies, professionals increasingly persuade the state to legislate standards and certifications that hit voluntary associations hard, especially those given to employing volunteers. The end result is that the trend toward government monopoly operates in tandem with the trend toward professional monopoly over social services. The connection between such monopoly control and the actual quality of services delivered is doubtful indeed.

Professional standards are of course important in some areas. But they must be viewed with robust skepticism when expertise claims jurisdiction, as it were, over the way people run their own lives. Again, ordinary people are the best experts on themselves.

So long as voluntary work is genuinely voluntary—is undertaken by free choice—it should be cherished and not maligned. It is of enormous value in terms of both the useful activity offered to volunteers and the actual services rendered. In addition, because of their relative freedom from bureaucratic controls, voluntary associations are important laboratories of innovation in social services; and, of course, they sustain the expression of the rich pluralism of American life.

The policy implications of our approach touch also on the role of nonprofit foundations in our society. Technically, there are different kinds of foundations—strictly private, publicly supported, operating, and so on—but the current assault applies to all of them. The argument is summed up in the words of the late Wright Patman whose crusade against foundations led to Title I of the Tax Reform Act of 1969:

> Today I shall introduce a bill to end a gross inequity which this country and its citizens can no longer afford: the tax-exempt status of the so-called privately controlled charitable foundations, and their propensity for domination of business and accumulation of wealth. . . . Put most bluntly, philanthropy—one of mankind's more noble instincts—has been perverted into a vehicle

for institutionalized deliberate evasion of fiscal and moral responsibility to the nation. (*Congressional Record*, August 6, 1969)

Of course, foundations have engaged in abuses that need to be curbed, but the resentment and hostility manifested by the curbers also needs to be curbed if we are not to harm the society very severely. The curbers of foundations make up an odd coalition. Right-wing forces are hostile to foundations because of their social experimentation (such as the Ford Foundation's programs among inner-city blacks), while others are hostile because of the role of big business ("the establishment") in funding foundations.

While large foundations would seem to be remote from the mediating structures under discussion, in fact they are often important to such structures at the most local level, especially in the areas of education and health. Were all these institutions taken over by the government, there might be a more uniform imposition of standards and greater financial accountability than now exists (although the monumental corruption in various government social services does not make one sanguine about the latter), but the price would be high. Massive bureaucratization, the proliferation of legal procedures that generate both public resentment and business for lawyers, the atrophying of the humane impulse, the increase of alienation—these would be some of the costs. Minimally, it should be public policy to encourage the voluntarism that, in our society, has at least slowed down these costs of modernity.

As always, the maximalist side of our approach—that is, using voluntary associations as agents of public policies—is more problematic than the minimalist. One thinks, for example, of the use of foster homes and half-way houses in the treatment and prevention of drug addiction, juvenile delinquency, and mental illness. There is reason to believe such approaches are both less costly and more effective than using bureaucratized megastructures (and their local outlets). Or one thinks of the successful resettlement of more than 100,000 Vietnam refugees in 1975, accomplished not by setting up a government agency but by working through voluntary agencies (mainly religious). This instance of using voluntary associations for public policy purposes deserves careful study. Yet another instance is the growth of the women's health movement, which in some areas is effectively challenging the monopolistic practices of the medical establishment. The ideas of people such as Ivan Illich and Victor Fuchs should be examined for their potential to empower people to reassume responsibility for their own health care. Existing experiments in decentralizing medical delivery systems should also be encouraged, with a view toward moving from decentralization to genuine empowerment.

Empowerment Through Pluralism

The theme of pluralism has recurred many times in this essay. This final section aims simply to tie up a few loose ends, to anticipate some objections to a public policy designed to sustain pluralism through mediating structures, and to underscore some facts of *American* society that suggest both the potentials and limitations of the approach advanced here.

It should be obvious that by pluralism we mean much more than regional accents, St. Patrick's Day, and Black Pride Days, as important as all these are. Beyond providing the variety of color, costume, and custom, pluralism makes possible a tension within worlds and between worlds of meaning. Worlds of meaning put reality together in a distinctive way. Whether the participants in these worlds see themselves as mainline or subcultural, as establishment or revolutionary, they are each but part of the cultural whole. Yet the paradox is that wholeness is experienced through affirmation of the

part in which one participates. This relates to the aforementioned insight of Burke regarding "the little platoon." In more contemporary psychological jargon it relates to the "identity crisis" which results from "identity diffusion" in mass society. Within one's group—whether it be racial, national, political, religious, or all of these—one discovers an answer to the elementary question, "Who am I?" and is supported in living out that answer. Psychologically and sociologically, we would propose the axiom that any identity is better than none. Politically, we would argue that it is not the business of public policy to make value judgments regarding the merits or demerits of various identity solutions, so long as all groups abide by the minimal rules that make a pluralistic society possible. It is the business of public policy not to undercut, and indeed to enhance, the identity choices available to the American people (our minimalist and maximalist propositions throughout).

This approach assumes that the process symbolized by "E Pluribus Unum" is not a zero-sum game. That is, the *unum* is not to be achieved at the expense of the *plures*. To put it positively, the national purpose indicated by the *unum* is precisely to sustain the *plures*. Of course there are tensions, and accommodations are necessary if the structures necessary to national existence are to be maintained. But in the art of pluralistic politics, such tensions are not to be eliminated but are to be welcomed as the catalysts of more imaginative accommodations. Public policy in the areas discussed in this essay has in recent decades, we believe, been too negative in its approach to the tensions of diversity and therefore too ready to impose uniform solutions on what are perceived as national social problems. In this approach, pluralism is viewed as an enemy of social policy planning rather than as a source of more diversified solutions to problems that are, after all, diversely caused and diversely defined.

Throughout this paper, we have emphasized that our proposal contains no animus toward those charged with designing and implementing social policy nor any indictment of their good intentions. The reasons for present pluralism-eroding policies are to be discovered in part in the very processes implicit in the metaphors of modernization, rationalization, and bureaucratization. The management mindset of the megastructure—whether of HEW Sears Roebuck, or the AFL-CIO—is biased toward the unitary solution. The neat and comprehensive answer is impatient of "irrational" particularities and can only be forced to yield to greater nuance when it encounters resistance, whether from the economic market of consumer wants or from the political market of organized special interest groups. The challenge of public policy is to anticipate such resistance and, beyond that, to cast aside its adversary posture toward particularism and embrace as its goal the advancement of the multitude of particular interests that in fact constitute the common weal. Thus, far from denigrating social planning, our proposal challenges the policy maker with a much more complicated and exciting task than today's approach.

Throughout this essay we have frequently referred to democratic values and warned against their authoritarian and totalitarian alternatives. We are keenly aware of the limitations in any notion of "the people" actually exercising the *kratein*, the effective authority, in public policy. And we are keenly aware of how far the American polity is from demonstrating what is possible in the democratic idea. The result of political manipulation, media distortion, and the sheer weight of indifference is that the great majority of Americans have little or no political will, in the sense that term is used in democratic theory, on the great questions of domestic and international policy. Within the formal framework of democratic polity, these questions will perforce be answered by a more politicized elite. But it is precisely with respect to mediating structures that most people do have, in the most exact sense, a political will. On matters of

family, church, neighborhood, hobbies, working place, and recreation, most people have a very clear idea of what is in their interest. If we are truly committed to the democratic process, it is *their* political will that public policy should be designed to empower. It may be lamentable that most Americans have no political will with respect to US relations with Brazil, but that is hardly reason to undercut their very clear political will about how their children should be educated.

The subculture that envisages its values as universal and its style as cosmopolitan is no less a subculture for all that. The tribal patterns evident at an Upper West Side cocktail party are no less tribal than those evident at a Polish dance in Greenpoint, Brooklyn. That the former is produced by the interaction of people trying to transcend many particularisms simply results in a new, and not necessarily more interesting, particularism. People at the cocktail party may think of themselves as liberated, and indeed they may have elected to leave behind certain particularisms into which they were born. They have, in effect, elected a new particularism. *Liberation is not escape from particularity but discovery of the particularity that fits.* The goal of public policy in a pluralistic society is to sustain as many particularities as possible, in the hope that most people will accept, discover, or devise one that fits.

While our proposal is, we hope, relevant to modern industrialized society in general, whether socialist or capitalist, its possibilities are peculiarly attuned to the United States. (We might say, to North America, including Canada, but some aspects of particularism in Canada—for example, binationalism between French- and English-speaking Canadians—are beyond the scope of this essay.) There are at least five characteristics of American society that make it the most likely laboratory for public policy designed to enhance mediating structures and the pluralism that mediating structures make possible. First is the immigrant nature of American society. The implications of that fact for pluralism need no elaboration. Second, ours is a relatively affluent society. We have the resources to experiment toward a more humane order—for example, to place a floor of economic decency under every American. Third, this is a relatively stable society. Confronted by the prospects of neither revolution nor certain and rapid decline, we do not face the crises that call for total or definitive answers to social problems. Fourth, American society is effectively pervaded by the democratic idea and by the sense of tolerance and fair play that make the democratic process possible. This makes our society ideologically hospitable to pluralism. And fifth, however weakened they may be, we still have relatively strong institutions— political, economic, religious, and cultural— that supply countervailing forces in the shaping of social policy. Aspirations toward monopoly can, at least in theory, be challenged. And our history demonstrates that the theory has, more often than not, been acted out in practice.

Of *this* we are convinced: America has a singular opportunity to contest the predictions of the inevitability of mass society with its anomic individuals, alienated and impotent, excluded from the ordering of a polity that is no longer theirs. And we are convinced that mediating structures might be the agencies for a new empowerment of people in America's renewed experiment in democratic pluralism.

PART VIII

THEORIES OF GIVING AND PHILANTHROPY

Giving is one of the most distinctive features of the nonprofit sector, and theories of giving and philanthropy help explain this central element of the sector. How traditions and norms of giving have evolved requires looking back essentially to the beginning of modern civilization.[1]

Why do people give of their money, time, and effort? Why do some people give more than others? Why do people give to certain organizations and purposes but not to others? To what extent is giving influenced by altruism, sympathy, empathy, guilt, a sense of justice, outrage at an injustice, or by rational calculation of personal utility? Is altruism an inherited personality trait or a "drive," or is it learned from others around us developmentally? How and why do people's giving patterns change at different life stages? How is philanthropy similar and different among people with different ethnic heritages?[2] Does the motivation for giving even matter? These types of questions are the focus of theories of giving and philanthropy. They provide a glimpse about the complexity of giving, and no single theory or group of theories can adequately explain it.

It should not be surprising that an understanding of giving is as important for the trustees and executives of NGOs who rely on philanthropy as it is for academicians. Giving theories provide important clues about what causes who to give how generously to which particular charitable causes and organizations and when—knowledge that is vital for the survival and growth of nonprofit organizations. Yet, giving theories also provide clues to academicians about the nature of the human condition and human motivations.

Different types of theories of giving present contrasting views, for example, about the degree to which giving is shaped by internalized motivations and/or social influences.[3] Theories also differ in their assumptions about the nature of human beings. Do people rationally calculate utilities before deciding to give, or do events and circumstances merely trigger gifts to specific organizations that have already been selected consciously or unconsciously? These diverse assumptions reflect differences among the four academic disciplines that have produced most of the theories of giving: psychology, philosophy, sociology/anthropology, and economics. *Psychological theories* of giving focus mostly on individual motivations for giving and cognitive processes leading to giving; *philosophical theories* mostly seek to answer questions about the nature of human beings; *sociological/ anthropological theories* emphasize cultural influences, including socialization processes, social norms and pressures, and the role of institutionalized religion; *economic theories* mostly start from rational public choices—decision processes that lead people to donate instead of allocating their resources for other utilitarian uses.

The next sections of this essay introduce and define concepts that are central to theories of giving, review a few implications of giving theories, and present intriguing ideas about giving as espoused

 DOI: 10.4324/9780367696559-33

by Maimonides (1135–1204), a Jewish philosopher and astronomer, and Benjamin Franklin (1706–1790), a founding father of the United States. Both represent philosophies of giving that are as useful in the twenty-first century as they were when written.

Definitions

Giving theory is an umbrella term that incorporates four interrelated concepts and four separate bodies of literature: *philanthropy, altruism, charity,* and *voluntarism.*[4] There is disagreement about definitions of these concepts among practitioners and theorists, but the disagreements serve a useful purpose: they highlight the main differences among the alternative theories. For example, Ilchman defines *philanthropy* as:

> Voluntary giving, voluntary serving, and voluntary association to achieve some vision of the public good; includes charity, patronage, and civil society. . . . The usual inclusive contemporary definition of philanthropy is "values, organizations, and practices that entail voluntary action to achieve some vision or the public good" or the "private" production of "public goods."[5]

Private Foundations are the primary secular institutions for philanthropy in many Northern countries including the U.S. Foundations are—

> nonprofit, nongovernmental organizations that promote charitable giving and other public purposes usually by giving grants of money to nonprofit organizations, qualified individuals, and other entities. . . . Foundations are formed by individuals, families, and business corporations, which usually donate money, property, or other financial assets.[6]

Foundations serve as intermediaries between donors and recipients of philanthropy, a role that in Maimonides's era was reserved for churches alone. In the U.S., foundations developed out of long traditions of secular and religious giving. Donors create foundations for reasons that vary widely, and these motivations reflect different theories of giving. Despite widespread public belief to the contrary, relatively few foundations are formed simply to avoid paying taxes, although tax incentives may influence the amount of money given to a foundation.[7] Several giving theories are introduced in this chapter, and many more are referenced in the Bibliography at the end of this introduction.

Some donors create and give their fortunes to foundations because of a deeply imbedded religious background or a tradition of family social responsibility and concern for the poor, while others have political or ideological beliefs they wish to advance. Some give to foundations because they want to try to improve the human condition around the world. Others feel a commitment to give back to a community or a cause. Some seek to create a memorial to themselves or their families or because of pressure from their peers to be philanthropic.

The concepts of *charity* and *philanthropy* overlap but differ in emphasis.[8] They overlap on donations and gifts of money, property, and time or effort to needy and/or socially desirable purposes, but *philanthropy* is a broader term than *charity*. Whereas *charity* traditionally has been used to mean the alleviation of individual *cases* of, for example, chronic illness, poverty, or homelessness, *philanthropy* tends to refer more to efforts to eliminate the *causes* of the problems that charity seeks to alleviate. Alan Wolfe's explanation of categories of theories of *altruism* demonstrates that theoretical perspectives shape definitions of why people give, or otherwise act or appear to act charitably.

Giving Theories of Benjamin Franklin and Maimonides

Although theories of giving may sound dry and ethereal, they can be fascinating. For example, theories that provide links between historical thinking and actions in today's circumstances are not far removed. To demonstrate, we introduce you to Benjamin Franklin's and Maimonides's theories.

Benjamin Franklin

Benjamin Franklin advised about responding to requests for help in approaching others to ask for gifts.

[The Speaker of the House of Representatives] is hereby required to sign an Order on the Provincial Treasurer for the Payment of Two Thousand Pounds in two yearly Payments, to the treasurer of the said Hospital, to be applied to the Founding, Building and Finishing of the same. This Condition carried the Bill through. . . . And then in soliciting Subscriptions among the People we urg'd the conditional Promise of the Law as an additional Motive to give, since every Man's Donation would be doubled. Thus the Clause work'd both ways. The Subscriptions accordingly soon exceeded the requisite sum, and we claim'd and receiv'd the Public Gift which enabled us to carry the Design into Execution. A convenient and handsome Building was soon erected, the Institution has by constant Experience been found useful, and flourishes to this Day. And I do not remember any of my political Manoeuvres, the Success of which gave me at the time more Pleasure. . . .

It was about this time that another Projector, the Revd. Gilbert Tennent, came to me, with a Request that I would assist him in procuring a Subscription for erecting a new Meeting-house. . . . Unwilling to make myself disagreeable to my fellow Citizens, by too frequently soliciting their Contributions, I absolutely refus'd. He then desir'd I would furnish him with a List of the Names of Persons I knew by Experience to be generous and public-spirited. I thought it would be unbecoming in me, after their kind Compliance with my Solicitations, to mark them out to be worried by other Beggars, and therefore refus'd also to give such a List. He then desir'd I would at least give him my Advice. That I will readily do, said I; and, in the first Place, I advise you to apply to all those whom you know will give something; next to those whom you are uncertain whether they will give any thing or not; and show them the List of those who have given; and lastly, do not neglect those who you are sure will give nothing; for in some of them you may be mistaken. He laugh'd, thank'd me, and said he would take my Advice. He did so, for he ask'd of *every body*; and he obtain'd a much larger Sum than he expected, with which he erected the capacious and very elegant Meeting-house that stands in Arch Street. (NOTE: The Second Presbyterian Church, organized in 1743, opened its new building at Arch (Mulberry) and Third Streets in 1752.)

[emphasis in original][9]

Maimonides

Maimonides, a Jewish scholastic philosopher and rabbi, is believed to have lived in Spain from 1135 to 1204. Maimonides's "code" was one of the earliest recorded attempts to identify degrees of goodness in giving or, if you will, to articulate a theory of giving.[10] The values that differentiate Maimonides's levels of giving are reflected in many of the theories reprinted in this volume. For example, Maimonides's highest level of "almsgiving" is a gift or loan made to another to "strengthen his hand"—a gift that allows the recipient to become employed or open a business, become self-sufficient, and not need to beg again. Centuries later, Andrew Carnegie echoed this theme in his admonitions:

In bestowing charity, the main consideration should be to help those who will help themselves; to provide part of the means by which those who desire to improve may do so; to give those who desire the aids by which they may rise. . . . Neither the individual nor the race is improved by alms-giving.

(Carnegie's "The Gospel of Wealth" is reprinted in Part II.) And like the philosophy of Carnegie's contemporary, John D. Rockefeller, Maimonides saw the primary purpose for giving as ensuring one's place in the afterlife: "Whosoever serves food and drink to poor men and orphans at his table, will, when he calls to God, receive an answer and find delight in it."

> There are eight degrees of almsgiving, each one superior to the other. The highest degree, than which there is none higher, is one who upholds the hand of an Israelite reduced to poverty by handing him a gift or a loan, or entering into a partnership with him, or finding work for him, in order to strengthen his hand, so that he would have no need to beg from other people. Concerning such a one Scripture says, *Thou shalt uphold him; as a stranger and a settler shall he live with thee* (Lev. 25:35), meaning uphold him, so that he would not lapse into want.
>
> Below this is he who gives alms to the poor in such a way that he does not know to whom he has given, nor does the poor man know from whom he has received. This constitutes the fulfilling of a religious duty for its own sake, and for such there was a Chamber of Secrets in the Temple, whereunto the righteous would contribute secretly, and wherefrom the poor of good families would draw the sustenance in equal secrecy. Close to such a person is he who contributes directly to the alms fund. . . .
>
> Below this is he who knows to whom he is giving, while the poor man does not know from whom he is receiving. He is thus like the great among the Sages who were wont to set out secretly and throw the money down at the doors of the poor. . . .
>
> Below this is the case where the poor man knows from whom he is receiving, but himself remains unknown to the giver. He is thus like the great among the Sages who used to place the money in the fold of a linen sheet which they would throw over their shoulder, whereupon the poor would come behind them and take the money without being exposed to humiliation.
>
> Below this is he who hands the alms to the poor man before being asked for them.
>
> Below this is he who hands the alms to the poor man after the latter has asked for them.
>
> Below this is he who gives the poor man less than what is proper, but with a friendly countenance.
>
> Below this is he who gives alms with a frowning countenance. . . .
>
> He who provides maintenance for his grown sons and daughters—whom he is not obligated to maintain . . ., and likewise he who provides maintenance for his father and mother, is accounted as performing an act of charity. Indeed it is an outstanding act of charity, since one's relative has precedence over other people.[11]

The values that separate Maimonides's degrees of almsgiving are anonymity of the donor, anonymity of the recipient, giving before being asked, and giving cheerfully. The first two presage current theories and debates about, for example, the relative worth of giving "out of true altruism" versus giving to receive public recognition and acclaim, or giving because of sympathy or empathy for the plight of recipients versus giving to advance a principle or a cause.

Readings Reprinted in Part VIII

Amy A. Kass's "Giving Well, Doing Good," is an exploration into the enterprise of philanthropy that seeks to illuminate fundamental questions about the idea and practice of philanthropy. Kass begins with a brief historical overview of the development of philanthropy and positively assesses philanthropy's current and near-term future health. She then introduces a number of concerns and challenges facing philanthropy and philanthropic institutions. Kass closes with six "difficult, complex and unlikely to be settled once and for all" questions facing philanthropic leaders—and public policy leaders—including (1) longer-term goals and intentions for philanthropy; (2) rights and responsibilities involving gifts, donors, recipients and grants, grantors, and grantees; (3) strengthening bequests and legacies; (4) the effectiveness of philanthropy; (5) accountability to whom and for what, and (6) the future of philanthropic leadership.

Alan Wolfe introduces the essence and intensity of the competing approaches to giving theories in the opening sentences of his article, "What Is Altruism?"

> A debate over the relative importance of altruism and egoism is the latest chapter in the long-running story of how social scientists think about human behavior. That story . . . has pitted an economic conception of human beings against a sociological one. The economic conception views the individual as a utilitarian calculator of self-interest, the sociological as an other-regarding member of some larger group or society.[12]

"What Is Altruism?" identifies three concepts of altruism—behavioral, motivational, and environmental—identifies their assumptions and disciplinary bases; and assesses the advantages and risks of adopting the three approaches. The *behavioral approach to altruism* examines "what an organism does, irrespective of the state of mind." It views altruism as a predetermined reality, not as behavior that can be developed and learned. The behavioral approach ignores the possibility of an altruistic personality. "Altruism is not a state waiting to be activated but rather something that requires aspects of mind . . . before it can be said to exist." Altruism is not predetermined as the behaviorists assume. "We do not, when we act altruistically, respond to hard-wired programs for sacrificial behavior that have been written into our genes through millennia of evolutionary response."

Wolfe's *motivational approach to altruism* emphasizes "the missing ingredient in behavioral accounts . . . is *intent*; to be altruistic, an act must be directed specifically toward an altruistic end." A distinction is needed between "purity of motives" and "purity of behavior." Motivational theories are usually presented by psychologists, are individualistic, and often overlook the importance of social influences on individual motivations. "The incompleteness of many of the psychological accounts of altruism indicates that the larger social environment may well be an important factor in encouraging or discouraging altruism." The *environmental approach to altruism* incorporates the roles of culture and institutions in influencing altruism. Wolfe argues that to fully understand altruism, all three approaches are needed—behavioral, motivational, and environmental. "Altruism requires that an individual make choices in the context of particular situations," and thus no single approach is adequate. "Such choices must be a reflection of the way individuals think and develop as they confront contexts within which they must make decisions."

During the past two decades, there has been a dramatic increase in research on charitable activities. Most of the studies that have included the demographic variables "black," Hispanic," and "non-white" have reported significantly lower levels of giving and volunteering by people in these groupings in the U.S.[13] Bradford Smith, Sylvia Shue, Jennifer Lisa Vest, and Joseph Villarreal's reading, "Philanthropy in Communities of Color," examines the differences in giving patterns and approaches among eight ethnic groups in the San Francisco Bay Area: Chinese, Japanese, Filipino, Mexican, Guatemalan, Salvadoran, Korean, and African American. They found that commonly used survey research questions and categorizations fail to reveal the true extent of giving within ethnic groups. They conclude that giving is much more prevalent among ethnic groups than is usually reported, and:

- Ethnic philanthropy is inextricably linked with family and kinship.
- Religion plays a very important role in ethnic philanthropy.

- Little ethnic philanthropy is directed toward mainstream charitable organizations other than churches. Most ethnic philanthropy is informal.
- There is a similarity of giving-related customs (and even terms) across the [ethnic] groups studied.

Michael Mascarenhas examines the current state of global humanitarianism from a critical perspective, in "New Humanitarianism and the Crisis of Charity: Good Intentions on the Road to Help." He asks, for example, to what extent are global acts of charity truly motivated by humanitarianism? Are businesses and INGOs using international aid funds to benefit populations in need? And, are Northern countries sending aid internationally while ignoring needs locally? "Walmart, for example, reported a $2 million donation to the Red Cross for tsunami relief, yet many of their employees rely on food stamps to subsidize their low wages in the United States." The overall question that Mascarenhas attempts to address is

as the shared interests that make humanitarianism possible have grown and the networks among them have strengthened, how is this assemblage of global actors transforming the politics (decisions over who gets aid, when, and under what conditions) and power-knowledge dynamics (notions of expertise, data, and measurement) of humanitarian policy and practice?

Notes

1. Kevin C. Robbins, "The Nonprofit Sector in Historical Perspective: Traditions of Philanthropy in the West," in *The Nonprofit Sector: A Research Handbook*, 2nd ed., eds., Walter W. Powell and Richard Steinberg (New Haven, CT: Yale University Press, 2006): 13–31. For the U.S. history, see Peter Dobkin Hall, "A Historical Overview of Philanthropy, Voluntary Associations, and Nonprofit Organizations in the United States, 1600–2000," also in *The Nonprofit Sector: A Research Handbook*, 2nd ed. (New Haven, CT: Yale University Press, 2006): 32–65; or Oliver Zunz, *Philanthropy in America: A History* (Princeton, NJ: Princeton University Press, 2012).

2. Daniel M. Oppenheimer and Christopher Y. Olivola, eds., *The Science of Giving: Experimental Approaches to the Study of Charity* (New York: Psychology Press, 2011).

3. Angela M. Eikenberry, *Giving Circles: Philanthropy, Voluntary Association, and Democracy* (Bloomington and Indianapolis, IN: Indiana University Press, 2009).

4. Most students of the nonprofit sector use *philanthropy* as an overarching term that *includes both charity and voluntarism*. They are listed separately here as a reminder that these three concepts are included in our usage of the term *giving theory*. These two terms are used almost interchangeably in this part.

5. Warren F. Ilchman, "Philanthropy," in *International Encyclopedia of Public Policy and Administration*, ed., J. M. Shafritz (Boulder: Westview Press, 1998): 1654.

6. Elizabeth T. Boris, "Foundations," in *International Encyclopedia of Public Policy and Administration*, ed., Jay M. Shafritz (Boulder: Westview Press, 1998): 928.

7. Boris, "Foundations," pp. 931, 932, reporting on John Edie's study in "Congress and Foundations: Historical Summary," in *America's Wealthy and the Future of Foundations*, ed., Teresa Odendahl (New York: Foundation Center, 1987).

8. Judith Lichtenberg, "What Is Charity?" *Philosophy & Public Policy Quarterly* 29 (2009): 16–20; also, J. Steven Ott and Jay M. Shafritz, *The Facts on File Dictionary of Nonprofit Organization Management* (New York: Facts on File, 1986): 284.

9. Benjamin Franklin, *The Autobiography of Benjamin Franklin*, ed., Ralph L. Ketcham, Helen C. Boatfield, and Helene H. Fineman (New Haven: Yale University Press, 1964): 201, 202.

10. Lichtenberg, "What is Charity?"

11. Maimonides, *The Code of Maimonides, Book Seven, The Book of Agriculture*, trans. from the Hebrew by Isaac Klein (New Haven: Yale University Press, 1979): 91, 92.

12. Alan Wolfe, "What Is Altruism?" in *Private Action and the Public Good*, ed., Walter W. Powell and Elisabeth S. Clemens (New Haven, CT: Yale University Press, 1998): 36.

13. Bradford Smith, Sylvia Shue, Jennifer Lisa Vest, and Joseph Villarreal, "Philanthropy in Communities of Color" (Bloomington and Indianapolis, IN: Indiana University Press, 1999): 2. Reprinted in this Chapter.

Bibliography

Acs, Zoltan J. *Why Philanthropy Matters: How the Wealthy Give, and What It Means for Our Economic Well-being* (Princeton, NJ: Princeton University Press, 2013).

Anheier, Helmut K. *A Dictionary of Civil Society, Philanthropy and the Third Sector* (London: Routledge, 2005).

———. *Nonprofit Organizations: Theory, Management, Policy* (2nd ed.) (New York: Routledge, 2014).

Barclay, Pat. *Reputation and the Evolution of Generous Behavior* (New York: Nova Science Publishers, 2010).

Barman, Emily. "The Social Bases of Philanthropy." *Annual Review of Sociology 41* (2017): 22-1-22.20. https://doi.org/10.1146/annurev-soc-060116-053524

Batson, C. Daniel. *Altruism in Humans* (New York: Oxford University Press, 2015).

———. *A Scientific Search for Altruism: Do We Care Only About Ourselves?* (New York: Oxford University Press, 2019).

Bedford, Kristen Corning. *A Generous Heart: Changing the World Through Feminist Philanthropy* (Independently Published, 2020).

Bhati, Abbishek, and Angela M. Eikenberry. "A Critical Fundraising Perspective: Understanding the Beneficiary Experience." In Angela M. Eikenberry, Roseanne M. Mirabella, and Billie Sandberg (Eds.), *Reframing Nonprofit Organizations: Democracy, Inclusion, and Social Change* (Irvine, CA: Melvin & Leigh, 2019): 154–167.

Boris, Elizabeth T. "Congress and Foundations: Historical Summary." In Teresa Odendahl (Ed.), *America's Wealthy and the Future of Foundations* (New York: Foundation Center, 1987).

———. "Foundations." In Jay M. Shafritz (Ed.), *International Encyclopedia of Public Policy and Administration* (Boulder, CO: Westview Press, 1998): 928–935.

Burlingame, Dwight F. (Ed.). *Philanthropy in America: A Comprehensive Historical Encyclopedia* (Santa Barbara, CA: ABC-CLIO, 2004).

Clift, Elayne. *Women, Philanthropy, and Social Change: Visions for a Just Society*, 2nd ed. (Medford, MA: Tufts University Press, 2008).

Clotfelter, Charles T., and Thomas Ehrlich (Eds.). *Philanthropy and the Nonprofit Sector in a Changing America* (Bloomington and Indianapolis, IN: Indiana University Press, 2001).

Coles, Robert. *The Call of Service: A Witness to Idealism* (Boston: Houghton Mifflin, 1993).

Damon, William V. B. (Ed.). *Taking Philanthropy Seriously: Beyond Noble Intentions to Responsible Giving* (Bloomington and Indianapolis, IN: Indiana University Press, 2007).

Eikenberry, Angela M. *Giving Circles: Philanthropy, Voluntary Association, and Democracy* (Bloomington and Indianapolis, IN: Indiana University Press, 2009).

Faulk, Lewis, and Jasmine McGinnis Johnson. "Philanthropy: Shaping and Being Shaped by Public Policy." In Elizabeth T. Boris and C. Eugene Steuerle (Eds.), *Nonprofits and Government: Collaboration and Conflict* (Lanham, MD: Rowman & Littlefield, 2017): 237–262.

Franklin, Benjamin. *The Autobiography of Benjamin Franklin*. Eds. Leonard W. Labaree, Ralph L. Ketcham, Helen C. Boatfield, and Helene H. Fineman (New Haven: Yale University Press, 1964).

Friedman, Lawrence J., and Mark D. McGarvie (Eds.). *Charity, Philanthropy, and Civility in American History* (Cambridge: Cambridge University Press, 2004).

Frumkin, Peter. *Strategic Giving: The Art and Science of Philanthropy* (Chicago: University of Chicago Press, 2007).

Gates, Melinda. *The Moment of Life: How Empowering Women Changes the World* (New York: Flatiron Books/Macmillan, 2019).

Goldin, Milton. "The Founding Fathers of Modern Philanthropy." *Fund Raising Management 99* (1988): 48–50.

Hall, Peter Dobkin. "A Historical Overview of Philanthropy, Voluntary Associations, and Nonprofit Organizations in the United States, 1600–2000." In Walter W. Powell and Richard Steinberg (Eds.), *The Nonprofit Sector: A Research Handbook*, 2nd ed. (New Haven, CT: Yale University Press, 2006): 32–65.

Hammack, David C., and Steven Heydemann. *Globalization, Philanthropy, and Civil Society: Projecting Institutional Logics Abroad* (Bloomington and Indianapolis, IN: Indiana University Press, 2009).

Havens, John J., Mary A. O'Herlihy, and Paul G. Schervish. "Charitable Giving: How Much, by Whom, to What, and How?" In Walter W. Powell and Richard Steinberg (Eds.), *The Nonprofit Sector: A Research Handbook*, 2nd ed. (New Haven, CT: Yale University Press, 2006): 542–567.

Ilchman, Warren F. "Philanthropy." In Jay M. Shafritz (Ed.), *International Encyclopedia of Public Policy and Administration* (Boulder, CO: Westview Press, 1998): 1654–1661.

Jackson, William J. *The Wisdom of Generosity: A Reader in American Philanthropy* (Waco, TX: Baylor University Press, 2009).

Kass, Amy A. *Giving Well, Doing Good* (Bloomington and Indianapolis, IN: Indiana University Press, 2008).

Lichtenberg, Judith. "What Is Charity?" *Philosophy & Public Policy Quarterly 29* (2009): 16–20.

Maimonides. *The Code of Maimonides, Book Seven, The Book of Agriculture*. Trans. and ed. Isaac Klein (New Haven: Yale University Press, 1979).

McCully, George. *Philanthropy Reconsidered: Private Initiatives—Public Good—Quality of Life* (Bloomington, IN: AuthorHouse, 2008).

Moody, Michael. "We Need New Theories About Philanthropy." *Council on Foundations*, February 26, 2013. www.cof.org/blogs/re-philanthropy/2013-02-26/we-need-new-theories-about-philanthropy

Moon, Seong-gin, and Sang Ok Choi. "Ethnic Giving versus Mainstream Giving by Foreign-born Korean Immigrants in California." *Nonprofit and Voluntary Sector Quarterly 42* (2013): 781–802.

Odendahl, Teresa. *Charity Begins at Home* (New York: Basic Books, 1990).

Oppenheimer, Daniel M., and Christopher Y. Olivola (Eds.). *The Science of Giving: Experimental Approaches to the Study of Charity* (New York: Psychology Press, 2011).

Patton, Michael Quinn, Nathaniel Foote, and James Radner. "A Foundation's Theory of Philanthropy: What It Is, What It Provides, How to Do It." *The Foundation Review 7*(4) (2015): 7–20.

Payton, Robert L. *Philanthropy: Voluntary Action for the Public Good* (New York: American Council on Education/Macmillan, 1988).

——, and Michael P. Moody. *Understanding Philanthropy: Its Meaning and Mission* (Bloomington and Indianapolis, IN: Indiana University Press, 2008).

Reich, Rob. *Just Giving: Why Philanthropy Is Failing Democracy and How It Can Do Better* (Princeton, NJ: Princeton University Press, 2018).

Robbins, Kevin C. "The Nonprofit Sector in Historical Perspective: Traditions of Philanthropy in the West." In Walter W. Powell and Richard Steinberg (Eds.), *The Nonprofit Sector: A Research Handbook*, 2nd ed. (New Haven, CT: Yale University Press, 2006): 13–31.

Salamon, Lester M. *Leverage for Good: An Introduction to the New Frontiers of Philanthropy and Social Investment* (New York: Oxford University Press, 2014).

——. *New Frontiers of Philanthropy: A Guide to the New Tools and New Actors that Are Reshaping Global Philanthropy* (New York: Oxford University Press, 2014).

Sapolsky, Robert M. *Behave: The Biology of Humans at Our Best and Worst* (New York: Penguin Books, 2017).

Sievers, Bruce R. *Civil Society, Philanthropy, and the Fate of the Commons* (Medford, MA: Tufts University Press, 2010).

Smith, Bradford, Sylvia Shue, Jennifer Lisa Vest, and Joseph Villarreal. *Philanthropy in Communities of Color* (Bloomington and Indianapolis, IN: Indiana University Press, 1999).

Smith, David H. *Good Intentions: Moral Obstacles and Opportunities* (Bloomington and Indianapolis, IN: Indiana University Press, 2005).

Soskis, Benjamin. "George Soros and the Demonization of Philanthropy." *The Atlantic*, December 5, 2017. www.theatlantic.com/business/archive/2017/12/soros-philanthropy/547247/

Thümier, Ekkehard, Nicole Bögelein, Annelie Beller, and Helmut K. Anheier. *Philanthropy and Education: Strategies for Impact* (New York: Palgrave Macmillan, 2014).

Vakoch, Douglas A. (Ed.). *Altruism in Cross-Cultural Perspective* (New York: Springer, 2013).

Wilson, David Sloan. *Does Altruism Exist? Culture, Genes, and the Welfare of Others* (New Haven, CT: Yale University Press, 2015).

Wolfe, Alan. "What Is Altruism?" In Walter W. Powell and Elisabeth S. Clemens (Eds.), *Private Action and the Public Good* (New Haven, CT: Yale University Press, 1998): 36–46.

Zunz, Oliver. *Philanthropy in America: A History* (Princeton, NJ: Princeton University Press, 2012).

Giving Well, Doing Good

AMY A. KASS

Philanthropy and American Society

Philanthropy in the United States is flourishing. Every year millions of Americans donate large amounts of money, time, and energy in organized efforts to promote numerous civic goods. The scale of giving is unprecedented, as are the range of activities that receive philanthropic support. At the same time, however, American philanthropy also faces unprecedented challenges, in part the result of its ever-growing importance and the changes that have accompanied its success. Both the promise and the perils of philanthropy's present and future may be better appreciated if we sketch first an outline of philanthropy's past, showing the emergence of some of its key features and potential tensions: religious versus secular, local versus national (or even global), charitable relief versus social reform, volunteer or amateur versus professional, private versus governmental.

America's philanthropic beginnings, traceable back to colonial times, were religiously inspired. In his 1710 pamphlet *Bonifacius* ("Doing Good"), Cotton Mather, the leading clergyman in the Massachusetts Bay Colony,

summoned fellow citizens to create voluntary associations in the service of social betterment: "Neighbors, you stand Related unto One another; And you should be full of Devices, That all the Neighbors may have cause to be glad of your being in the Neighborhood." The spirit of philanthropy derived from the Christian obligation of charity ("love of neighbor"), and its early practice revolved around local churches.

But the practice of philanthropy soon spread to other venues as voluntarism acquired more secular engines, fueled especially by the rationalist optimism of the Enlightenment. The quintessential new philanthropist was, of course, Benjamin Franklin, whose early "Dogood Papers"—clearly a response to *Bonifacius*—sought to re-found the philanthropic spirit on purely secular ground. Later, as a young tradesman in Philadelphia, Franklin started the "Junto," a club of civic-spirited young artisans, whose deliberations launched a vast array of public philanthropic projects, including, among others, the paving, cleaning, and lighting of public streets; the creation of a lighthouse, a volunteer fire department, a fire insurance association, a hospital, and a circulating library; and the

 DOI: 10.4324/9780367696559-34

founding of the American Philosophical Society for Useful Knowledge as well as an Academy for the Education of Youth (forerunner of the University of Pennsylvania). By the early nineteenth century, American philanthropic activity and voluntary associations were in full flower. They captured the attention of Alexis de Tocqueville, whose magisterial *Democracy in America* praises as quintessentially American (in contrast to European) the impulse to set up churches, hospitals, schools, universities, orphanages, and countless other such organizations throughout the land. In towns and cities, large and small, these associations, now comprising the "nonprofit sector," became—and have remained—the pillars of rich civic life.

The early decades of the twentieth century witnessed the emergence of philanthropy on a national scale, with the rise of the first large foundations—among them, the Russell Sage Foundation (1907), the Carnegie Corporation of New York (1911), the Rockefeller Foundation (1913), and, later, the Ford Foundation (1936). These large foundations differed from earlier philanthropic enterprises not only in their abundant resources but also in their purpose. Rather than fund responses to local needs or sponsor "palliatives," they hoped to use their wealth to attack the "root causes" of social ills.

The next innovations involved new roles for government and for (paid) philanthropic professionals. It is hard in the age of the welfare state to imagine it, but until the 1960s philanthropic activity in America ran largely on private money and depended mainly on unpaid volunteers; voluntary associations were still the center of beneficent works and deeds. To be sure, hospitals, schools, museums, symphonies, and other service-providing nonprofit institutions were—and still are—supported also by contributions from state and local governments, as well as by income earned from those who use their services (making these institutions subject to pressures from the market). But the federal government stayed out of philanthropic ventures. Indeed,

the emerging large foundations explicitly saw themselves as providing what the federal government would not: the vision and the wherewithal to manage the social, educational, and scientific needs of an advanced industrial nation. The federal government cooperated in the growth of private philanthropy only indirectly, encouraging the proliferation of foundations through the federal tax code, which excluded charitable contributions from income subject to federal taxation.

After World War II, the federal government's role began to change. Security considerations and international competition in science and technology (especially with the Soviets, and after Sputnik) brought the federal government into supporting higher education and scientific research. The civil rights and anti-poverty movements led to a raft of federal legislation and activity, culminating in the Great Society programs of the 1960s. With federal funding flowing freely, government support of nonprofit activities soon equaled and, eventually, surpassed private donations. The explicit goal of this massive federal initiative was to effect social change, especially for victims of poverty and discrimination; under the protection of federal legislation, many minority groups established nonprofit organizations to advance their own causes. But the influx of federal funding had unanticipated and unintended consequences for the ways and means of philanthropic organizations. Programs were reformatted to meet federal goals and guidelines; nonprofit boards lost some of their independence, as their organizations became subject to public review and national legislation; many nonprofit organizations shifted from volunteer to paid professional staff; and the interests and influence of individual donors were curtailed by new restrictions and competition.

Notwithstanding these changes, private philanthropy still occupies a central place in American civic life, generating civic energy and promoting civic renewal. As in the past, the extraordinary generosity of American philanthropy—institutional and independent, communal and personal—sustains schools and hospitals, research laboratories and churches, museums and operas, magazines and radio stations, and myriad activities to feed, clothe, house, train, and succor the needy and the dispossessed. Of perhaps equal significance, philanthropic activity continues to mobilize the energy and dedication of hundreds of thousands of our fellow citizens as active participants in promoting robust and responsible civic life. In these respects, the current state of philanthropy could hardly be more encouraging.

Philanthropic Activity, Present and Projected

American philanthropy is, in fact, booming. In 2004, nearly 1.4 million nonprofits registered with the Internal Revenue Service.[1] Nearly half of American adults volunteer their time.[2] In addition, the nonprofit sector employs almost 10 percent of our total workforce—double that of 25 years before.[3] Perhaps most significant, the number of active grant-making foundations—especially small, medium-sized, and community foundations—continues to rise dramatically. According to the Foundation Center, they numbered nearly 68,000 in 2004, more than double their number in 1991 and triple that of 1981. Their total assets are also rising, as is the amount of foundation money directed toward charities. Foundations gave away an estimated $33.6 billion in 2005, and foundation giving has nearly tripled since 1995.[4]

Active grantmaking by foundations is, however, but a small part of America's philanthropic largesse, estimated as only 11.5 percent of total giving in 2005. Individual Americans, meanwhile, gave 76.5 percent (or $199.07 billion) of all charitable funds.[5] And in times of crisis, the generosity of Americans has, in recent years, outdone itself. The personal and communal outpouring following 9/11 was extraordinary.

So too were the responses to the natural disasters of 2005—the Asian tsunami, the Pakistan earthquake, and the Gulf Coast disasters caused by hurricanes Katrina and Rita. Yet even these manifestly heroic contributions to disaster relief in emergencies are dwarfed by the steady, mundane, and largely unheralded generosity of the American people in support of ordinary charitable causes. Indeed, individual giving for the three disasters of 2005—currently estimated at $5.83 billion—represents less than 3 percent of what Americans typically donate to charities and churches every year.[6]

Projections for the coming decades suggest that philanthropic giving will rise, very likely massively. According to a highly respected wealth simulation model, developed by Paul Schervish and John Havens, the next 50 years will see ever-increasing and unprecedented philanthropic activity, owing to record intergenerational transfers of many newly made fortunes. By a conservative estimate, $41 trillion is expected to change hands through inheritance,[7] and much of this money will find its way into new philanthropic activity, dwarfing that of today and likely transforming how philanthropy is practiced.

Other changes are also making their influence felt. Billionaire Warren Buffett has recently announced the transfer of 85 percent of his wealth to philanthropic causes, strong evidence for researchers' claim that, despite reductions in estate taxes, our wealthiest Americans are not trying to maximize the transfer of wealth to their personal heirs but looking for larger and deeper purposes for their material means.[8] We are also witnessing the rise of a new breed of philanthropists, "venture philanthropists"—young, successful entrepreneurs who bring expectations gleaned from business to bear on their philanthropic ventures—as well as "philanthropreneurs"—those whose philanthropic and business ventures merge as they seek to harness the marketplace for charitable purposes (and sometimes profit). In recent years, there have also been large increases in "values-driven" philanthropy, especially among members of evangelical churches. In addition, new technologies that drive down costs of starting and maintaining foundations make it likely that small, as well as mega, foundations will continue to proliferate. Finally, the rise of the Internet has massively expanded the networks in which people enmesh themselves, creating a new "gift economy" of exchange of services and enabling many more philanthropists, and on a global scale, to leverage funds and collaborators for their pet projects. For all these reasons, philanthropy's future role in American life seems likely only to increase.

Growing Concerns and Suggested Remedies

Yet despite—and perhaps because of—these new and promising developments, all is not well with philanthropy, especially in the world of foundations. Critics—including some insiders—express growing concerns about unmet needs, unresponsive donors, doubtful effectiveness, irresponsible practices, and inadequate accountability. The foundation boom has gone hand-in-hand with increasing professionalization—the reliance on specialized experts to develop, implement, evaluate, and promote projects—with the consequence of ever-increasing administrative expenses. Thanks to the professionalization and bureaucratization of foundations, access to funds has become more complicated, threatening philanthropy's hitherto much praised ability to be more nimbly and immediately responsive than big government. Success in securing grants often goes not to the best proposals or the most needy organizations but to the most skilled competitors, who, knowing the secrets of grantsmanship, deftly tweak their programs to appear to comply with foundation priorities. Nationwide, more than 90

percent of grant proposals to foundations are turned down; many small nonprofit associations, including faith-based and minority institutions, go underfunded, understaffed, and, according to some, systematically unrecognized, working hard just to make ends meet and often handicapped by inexperience with new information technologies. Finally, the growing reliance on Internet networking, for all its efficiency, raises new concerns about the impact of such "virtual relationships" on genuine civic engagement and face-to-face philanthropic activities.

Philanthropy's problems have become substantive as well as procedural. The philanthropic sector has been drawn into controversies about the state of our culture and about philanthropy's role in fostering controversial educational and cultural change. Battles over "the culture wars" or "political correctness," as well as serious disagreements about whether certain philanthropic activities are in fact achieving their desired goals, have put foundations on the defensive and increasingly at the center of public attention and controversy. Today more than before, one hears about donors discontented with the uses made of their benefactions, and some large gifts to prestigious universities have been withdrawn for such reasons. In addition, heightened concern for our national security has had some worrisome repercussions for philanthropy, with increased private anxiety and public scrutiny over where money is being spent. The relative invisibility of foundations is a thing of the past; today they are objects of intense public, even governmental, attention.

Especially significant has been the public outcry over, and Congress' direct response to, several well-publicized egregious examples of irresponsible managerial practices in the foundation world, including self-dealing, nepotism, and cronyism. Today, although no new regulatory legislation has yet been enacted, the very fact of public scrutiny has ushered in a period of intense and critical self-examination, as the philanthropic sector is again making efforts to improve accountability and insure probity.

Not everyone in the world of philanthropy believes that major change is needed. Many organizations—including the Association of Small Foundations, Independent Sector, and the Alliance for Charitable Reform (spearheaded by the Philanthropy Roundtable)—have been lobbying against any new legislative strictures. Others, however, have seen in the recent scandals an opportunity for much needed reform. Suggestions include more vigorous self-regulation, updated and strengthened statutory and regulatory standards, and increased resources devoted to oversight by the IRS, state attorneys general, and the philanthropic sector itself.[9] Proponents of reform argue that better regulations regarding accountability and stricter standards of enforcement—whether self-imposed or directed by Congress—will inspire more public trust. They also suggest that new and improved codes of ethics can articulate ideals toward which philanthropic practice should strive and offer rough guidelines to govern more specific conduct.

But if one takes a large view of the field, it is clear that new codes, rules, and regulations will not be enough, not even to accomplish their purpose of improving professional integrity. Such strictures abstract from the rich context of moral choice, ignore the motives and passions that lead people to give, and fail to reach the moral sensibilities and habits of the heart of particular agents. They also pay little if any attention to the big practical question: how to get people to practice what is preached. Most important, by focusing only on the prevention of misconduct, they ignore a much more fundamental need, namely, assessing how philanthropy, once freed of misconduct, should be conducted: what does it mean *to give well* and *to do good* in the twenty-first century? New codes and regulations cannot address the growing interest in larger questions about the future of American philanthropy—questions about goals and purposes, relations between donors and recipients (grantors and grantees), wisdom in legacies and bequests, assessment of success, public accountability, and philanthropic leadership.

The new opportunities and new challenges for philanthropy invite a self-conscious return to these questions. Indeed, with philanthropy on the threshold of an exciting new era, it is especially fitting that present and future philanthropists reflect more deeply on the whys and wherefores of their activities.

Themes and Questions

1. *Goals and Intentions:* American philanthropy has long been devoted to a variety of ends, including direct alleviation of suffering, promoting social change, advancing social justice, developing and sustaining civic life, enhancing education and culture, and correcting social ills through research into their "root causes" and efforts to counter them with public policy. Although philanthropists commonly appeal to serving "the public good" or promoting "the general welfare," they often differ widely on the meaning of these ideals and how best to promote them. There is indeed little agreement even about the most basic question, "What *is* philanthropy?" and how it is related to "charity." And despite a general historic shift in institutional giving, from more specific goals (for example, ending yellow fever) to broader social goals (for example, promoting civic society), the social goods that are being served have become less clear.

What are the goals of philanthropy as practiced today? How are they related to the goals of governmental programs and public policy, or to the activities of voluntary associations, including religious institutions? What is the relation between philanthropy and charity? Above all: *What should today's philanthropy aim to do? Should its energies be directed mainly toward securing the floor—removing obstacles such as poverty and disease, somatic and psychic—or toward lifting the ceiling—promoting excellences such as learning and the fine arts? Should the major targets today be equality and social justice? Freedom and self-governance? Moral and spiritual renewal? Something else?*

2. *Gifts, Donors, Recipients; Grants, Grantors, Grantees:* Champions of democratic participation have long been in favor of giving potential recipients and beneficiaries a greater role in the grant-making process. But whether it is reasonable to try to do so depends in no small part on what exactly one understands a grant to be. Grantor-grantee relations will be affected, often profoundly, by the operative understanding of "grantor" and "grantee" and by the fundamental meaning of "a grant."

For example, when the federal government first began sponsoring research, it realized that, in order to get what it wanted, it would also have to support the kind of research that universities wanted to do. This gave rise to a dual system of relationships, one based on contracts, the other on grants. Over time, however, the distinction seems to have become blurred. Is a grant really a contract? Or is it more like a gift?

If philanthropic practice is to become more democratic, as well as more effective and more accountable, the crucial elements of philanthropic exchange require clarification. *What is the meaning of a grant? How is it similar to or different from a gift? From a contract? What sorts of relationships and obligations does a grant imply for givers and receivers? How should grant- or gift-making decisions be rendered?*

3. *Bequests and Legacies:* The ability of established foundations to make grants depends in large part on the bequests of founders and major donors. Family foundations, increasingly important actors in American philanthropy, are born largely from bequests made and legacies left by parents and other ancestors. In recent years, much public attention has been directed to measures needed to encourage more such gifts (for example, the debates about the pros

and cons of eliminating the estate tax). Less attention has been paid to what is arguably even more important: what is required to give and receive such gifts wisely and well.

Although bequests and legacies that are explicitly directed beyond the family may avoid the pitfalls of intergenerational strife, an equally vexing issue may arise here as well, connected to the deference owed to—and claimed for—the intent governing the donor's bequest. Hence, every kind of bequest and legacy may well require not only greater clarity about expectations but also prior preparation if the expectations are to be realized. *What is the relationship between a bequest and legacy? What should guide people who make a bequest? What should guide heirs and trustees? How should we prepare the next generation?*

4. *Effectiveness:* There has long been much interest in getting better and more reliable—more measurable—information about the effectiveness of grants or gifts, be they from private charity, foundations, or government. And for good reasons: No one wants to do harm in the name of doing good; no one thinks that good intentions are an acceptable excuse for bad results; everyone realizes that ignorance in the name of doing good can undermine doing real good, and no one condones the arrogance of such ignorance. But although everyone wants good results, people differ on the *meaning* of a good result, or even on whether results can accurately be measured or assessed in a timely or useful way. No wonder there are today more than one hundred conflicting approaches to measurement and evaluation.

But the difficulty of assessment is more than methodological. For it is one thing to gauge whether grant recipients are performing the particular activities that they said they would; or whether they are proceeding according to their proposed plan; or whether the available resources are being effectively managed; or even whether recipients have delivered the promised concrete results. It is quite another, and more difficult, thing to discern what sort of an impact a grant really has, whether it has really made a difference for good, and if so, how, where, when, and to whom. *What is effective philanthropy? How should we judge its success? What attitudes, dispositions, or measures are conducive to effective philanthropy?*

5. *Accountability:* Everyone today seems to agree that philanthropy should be more accountable and responsive to some overseeing authority. As one observer puts it, "it is time to put the response back into responsibility." But there is little agreement regarding the authority to which philanthropy should respond. *Who should be the arbiter of what is—and what is not—in the "public good"?* Likewise, everyone seems to agree that grantors as well as grantees ought to explain what they are doing and why. But, again, it is unclear what sort of account is warranted, as well as to whom it should be addressed.

These matters become especially urgent (and far more complicated) once we look beyond the ethics of managerial conduct to consider also the purposes and contents of grants, or more generally, to the interests and goals of philanthropists. Are there limits on what responsible philanthropy should be free to promote—especially in a post-9/11 world? The federal government grants special privileges to the nonprofit sector, notably in matters of taxation. Do these privileges carry special responsibilities, not merely for administrative integrity but also for the character of organizations and activities that philanthropy supports? Transparency is surely a good thing, but one must still wonder whether the activities of philanthropy can be made transparent without jeopardizing the very freedom that foundations treasure. Account-giving is also a good thing, but one may wonder what sort of account-giving might justify the civic privileges that philanthropy enjoys. *For what should philanthropy be responsible? To whom should philanthropy be accountable? How should we educate for responsibility?*

6. *Philanthropic Leadership:* Many foundation leaders agree that one can learn quickly much of what one needs to know to keep a foundation out of trouble. There is far less agreement, however, about what it takes or means positively to lead well. Some believe that no professional training is necessary. Indeed, they claim that a cadre of professionally trained leaders would not only be a positive disadvantage to the field in general, but also a strong disincentive for anyone who might otherwise be interested in entering it. Yet "philanthropy training," especially in the form of nonprofit management programs, as well as "leadership training" are growing industries.

Is philanthropy a profession? Is there a body of knowledge that its leaders should master? Are there specific skills, attitudes, or virtues required for excellent leadership in philanthropy, and do they differ from those required for other forms of leadership (for example, statesmanship or religious leadership)? Is effective leadership in philanthropy dependent upon (or separable from) one's ideological beliefs and commitments? Are nonprofit management or leadership programs helping or hindering the development of excellent leaders? *What should we expect of philanthropic leaders?*

The questions raised above are difficult, complex, and unlikely to be settled once and for all. Different people will approach and answer them differently. As there are many mansions in the house of philanthropy, there is no need to divide the house. For all who live under its roof—be they donors, grantors or professionals in philanthropy, or leaders of nonprofits—share (or *should* share) certain common attributes: a benevolent disposition, thoughtfully expressed, in concrete deeds, freely chosen, for some public (as opposed to merely personal) ends. Philanthropists of every stripe can benefit from reflecting more deeply on what it means—for their own preferred form of giving—to give well and to do good.

Notes

1. According to the Urban Institute's National Center for Charitable Statistics.

2. See the Independent Sector's *Giving and Volunteering in the United States* (2001).

3. See the Independent Sector's *Nonprofit Almanac* (2002).

4. See *Foundation Yearbook* (2006).

5. See *Giving USA* (2006).

6. See *Giving USA* (2006).

7. In 2002 dollars. John J. Havens and Paul G. Schervish, "Why the $41 Trillion Wealth Transfer Is Still Valid: A Review of Challenges and Questions," *The Journal of Gift Planning* (2003).

8. See Paul G. Schervish, John Havens, and Albert Keith Whitaker, "Leaving a Legacy of Care," *Philanthropy* (Jan/Feb 2006).

9. See Rick Cohen, "Hearings and Roundtables: NCRP Brings Philanthropic Accountability Standards to Capitol Hill," *Politics of Philanthropy* (2004).

What Is Altruism?

ALAN WOLFE

A debate over the relative importance of altruism and egoism is the latest chapter in the long-running story of how social scientists think about human behavior. That story, since at least the nineteenth century, has pitted an economic conception of human beings against a sociological one. The economic conception views the individual as a utilitarian calculator of self-interest, the sociological as an other-regarding member of some larger group or society. This battle has never stopped (Schwartz 1986), and it is not likely to do so in the future. The economistic version has, in recent years, won numerous adherents, often in fields far removed from economics, including sociology (Coleman 1990). But the more popular rational choice theory becomes, the more contested it is; many see rational choice theory as increasingly limited, which raises the possibility of the emergence of a new paradigm that once again pays attention to altruism (Piliavin and Charg 1990; Batson 1990, 1991; Simmons 1991).

It is no longer possible to argue, as it was just a decade or two ago, that assumptions of self-regarding behavior are more realistic or predictive than assumptions of other-regarding behavior. To be open to the world around them, social scientists need to go beyond monocausal explanations of human behavior that achieve a certain formal elegance, but do so at the price of prematurely closing off the complexities of human behavior.

If the need for a theoretical appreciation of altruistic behavior is increasingly accepted by social scientists, problems of conceptualization remain formidable. Altruism is a far more tricky concept philosophically than self-interest, for it involves not only defining the motives of an individual actor, but also dealing with the consequences of those actions for a multitude of other actors.

These difficulties suggest the need for some stock-taking with respect to the way social scientists have tried to theorize about and understand altruistic behavior. Such a task could be carried out in two ways. One would be to examine the theoretical and conceptual difficulties facing any attempt to operationalize what altruistic behavior might be. The other is to put such conceptual issues on hold, at least for a while, in an attempt to examine presumptively altruistic behavior in real world or approximate real world conditions. My aim in this chapter is to start with real world or

 DOI: 10.4324/9780367696559-35

approximate real world efforts to understand altruism, and from them to generalize back to theoretical and conceptual problems rather than the other way around.

Daniel Bar-Tal (1985/86) has distinguished between behavioral and motivational conceptions of altruism. To these I would add a third: environmental. Each approach to altruism carries both advantages and risks.

Behavioral Altruism

Behavioral approaches examine what an organism does, irrespective of the state of mind of the organism that does it. (Indeed, some organisms can act altruistically without having any state of mind at all, if by *state of mind* we mean the complex cognition associated with humans and perhaps some other primates.) "Altruism," J. Phillipe Rushton writes, "is defined as social behavior carried out to achieve positive outcomes for another rather than for the self" (1980, 8). Behavioral definitions of altruism thus have a seemingly great contribution to make; they seem to prove that, despite Hobbesian pessimism, there are solutions to prisoners' dilemma situations that are based on something more solid than temporary agreements or contingent contracts.

It is a short step from a behavioral definition of altruism to the conclusion that human beings are by nature cooperative, social, or even, in some accounts, moral (Wilson 1993). Considering the fact that nineteenth-century intellectual traditions left us with a legacy of claims that self-interest is biologically based, it is refreshing to believe that the opposite may be the case. Refreshing though such a case may be, it is not, however, persuasive. Do human beings act altruistically without having altruistic motives? This is an impossible question to answer definitively, given the notorious problems of establishing what motives are, but there are sufficient hints in what we know about

altruistic behavior to suggest that the behavioral model has serious empirical flaws.

First, the behavioral approach imagines altruism as a state that is activated by a genetic switch. There are two reasons to question such an approach. One is that altruism possesses clear *developmental* features. One can quibble with Jean Piaget's or Lawrence Kohlberg's account of the stages of moral development, but there is little doubt that as human beings mature, they become more capable of taking the position of an abstract other (Zahn-Waxler 1991). Similarly, we know that altruistic behavior varies from one society to another. The question is not so much whether, in any given organism (or society), altruism exists or not, but rather, how much of a disposition to altruism (or, for that matter, egoism) exists?

In addition, it is by no means clear that a precise conceptualization of altruism, one which imagines such behavior as being turned on automatically, corresponds with the way in which individuals pursue activities that have public-regarding intentions or consequences. Such a point of view imagines altruistic behavior as an emerging reality, whereas behavioral approaches to altruism imagine it as a determined reality.

A second problem with behavioral approaches to altruism is that they ignore the existence of an altruistic personality. Altruism is not a state waiting to be activated but rather something that requires aspects of mind—cognition, self-perception, identity formation, empathy—before it can be said to exist. What differentiated rescuers of Jews from nonrescuers in the study by Samuel and Pearl Oliner was their state of mind: altruistic people tend to believe in the existence of a just world, are more inward looking, and tend to be the children of parents who emphasized similar values. These findings have been replicated in laboratory and everyday life situations by social psychologists (Carlo et al. 1991; Bierhoff et al. 1991). Mental activity is a dynamic component of altruistic behavior:

altruism happens because people use their minds to interpret the world around them and, basing themselves on that information, decide to act in one way rather than another.

Third, although altruism is learned, it does not take heroic amounts of education or training to instill it. To be sure, there will always be saints whose altruism stands as an unattainable ideal for ordinary people, but most real world altruism is learned through others in the course of everyday life. Altruism, for one thing, usually involves a substantial amount of conformist behavior. For example, people are more likely to give money to the Salvation Army if they see others do it (Hurley and Allen 1974; Krebs 1970). A variety of laboratory studies indicate that when some people act altruistically, others do as well (Reykowski 1980). Even heroic acts of altruism can have a conformist dimension. Rescuers of Jews in Nazi Europe, for example, were more likely to appear in parts of Europe where the moral climate credited their activities. And although rescue was by its very nature secret—and therefore not likely to be conformist—there is evidence that rescuers' neighbors knew of many rescue activities and silently acknowledged them, an indirect form of social approval (Oliner and Oliner 1988, 125).

Altruism, like selfishness, is facilitated by rewards; the reward of selfishness may be increased material benefit, while that of altruism is attachment to group norms. Group solidarity can be as important as individual conscience in contributing to prosocial behavior (Dawes et al. 1988). Moreover, just as altruism has a conformist dimension, interestingly, so does nonaltruism: the famous bystander effect—that is, people will be more likely not to act altruistically when they know that others are present—demonstrates the importance of conformity in nonaltruistic responses (Latané and Darley 1970). Learning from others—watching what they do and then deciding to do something similar—is a constitutive feature of altruistic behavior.

Taken together, all these factors are indirect evidence that, at least in human beings, altruism is not a product of preconscious or unconscious drives. We do not, when we act altruistically, respond to hard-wired programs for sacrificial behavior that have been written into our genes through millennia of evolutionary response. What is most important about altruism is precisely what behaviorism leaves out, namely, the activating factors that transform an instinct into something worth knowing about. When altruism exists, something happens. Behavioral definitions willfully choose to ignore what that something might be.

Whatever the empirical problems facing a naturalistic explanation of altruism, there are normative problems as well. Because hard-wired explanations of human behavior are usually associated with such notions as those of a "selfish gene" (Dawkins 1976), we usually think of biological theories as insufficiently altruistic because they allow little room for imagining people as making complex moral choices. Ironically, such theories are also problematic because they are, in a sense, too altruistic. Altruism in and of itself is not a good. The fact that animals sacrifice themselves for the sake of their offspring does not mean that a human being who did so would be acting in an altruistically appropriate way. Society would face as much trouble reproducing itself if everyone were other-regarding all the time as it would if everyone were self-regarding all the time.

This is not the place for asserting my own normative commitments and judging any particular approach to altruism a failure because it fails to appreciate them. But I do think it appropriate to argue that a minimum normative standard can be developed from empirical grounds. If altruism means an effort to do good for others, then the minimal normative principle that a definition of altruism should meet is respect for pluralism, given that conceptions of the good will be contested (Mansbridge 1998). A pluralistic perspective on human behavior would be suspicious of any kind of moral perfection or imperfection. People are by nature neither saints nor sinners. Behavioral approaches to altruism are insufficiently appreciative of those problems. A society that was perfectly altruistic but that, as a result, lacked a human capacity to err would not necessarily be a good society. We might well prefer a society in which there was some cruelty to others—crime, for example—to one in which such cruelty was completely abolished if the former contained the freedom that makes such things as crime possible.

Assumptions of psychological pluralism, then, raise questions about behavioral approaches to altruism on both empirical and normative grounds. At a time when psychologists themselves have moved well beyond behaviorism, it makes little sense for other social scientists to adopt their discarded models in seeking to understand a phenomenon as complex as human altruism.

Motivational Altruism

Some experimental social psychologists trying to understand prosocial behavior have turned to an examination of the motives people have for taking others into account. The missing ingredient in behavioral accounts, they argue, is *intent*; to be altruistic, an act must be directed specifically toward an altruistic end. The most parsimonious definition of motivational altruism comes from Daniel Batson and Laura Shaw: "Altruism is a motivational state with the ultimate goal of increasing another's welfare" (Batson and Shaw 1991, 108).

Batson makes a distinction between purity of motives and purity of behavior. Batson and his colleagues have tried to show that altruistic goals will be more likely to be chosen when an individual identifies empathically with other people (Batson et al. 1991; Batson et al. 1989; Batson et al. 1989; Batson et al. 1988; Dovidio et al. 1990). Such empathy is not the by-product of benefits to the self, such as the relief brought about by minimizing another's distress. There is such a thing as pure motivational altruism, Batson claims. We really are capable of caring for others (Batson 1990).

Batson's work has not been universally accepted by social psychologists. Some are critical of his work because the concept of a motive does not seem to account either for behavior that is without motives or behavior that is guided by motives that cannot be fully articulated.

Nancy Eisenberg (Eisenberg et al. 1989; Eisenberg 1991, 29) makes an important distinction in this context between empathy, which in her view involves feeling what the other feels, and sympathy, which involves wanting the other person to feel better. To the degree that altruism involves empathy, it involves sentiments which are not quite the same as conscious motivations; generally speaking, we feel what another person feels not after considering the matter and being motivated to do so, but out of a spontaneous emotional reaction. From this point of view, Batson's motivational account of altruism is too demanding; to meet its standard, human beings must not only react empathically to another, but do so by meeting a standard of rationality that is rarely found in real world situations.

Yet from another point of view, Batson's definition does not set a high enough standard of rational conduct. One of the most fully elaborated theoretical accounts of how morality develops is that of Kohlberg, who argues that the most moral acts are those which rise beyond convention and situation to principled reasoning in line with the essentially impersonal Kantian criterion of judgment (Kohlberg 1981). Whatever one thinks of such an account, altruism, in the higher stages of moral development, would not be produced by motives that grow out of empathic identification with the other. It would instead be a reflective response to norms of justice that have been internalized by a particular individual (Eisenberg 1991, 128–129). As every Kantian knows, there are occasions in which the upholding of a norm of justice requires cruelty in specific circumstances; that is, to achieve a higher form of altruism, one must *resist* the desire to act out of empathy in a particular situation. Batson's definition, which tends to exclude emotional identification with a specific other, also tends to exclude rationalized identification with a general principle.

One way of combining these critiques of purely motivational theories of altruism is to point out that motives, like altruism in general, are rarely in one state or another. When we act altruistically, we can be responding at a number of levels and attempting to meet a variety of mixed goals (Mansbridge 1998). Our inclination to act altruistically could originate in an emotion, as when, confronted with another's pain, we want to do something for that person. At the same time, such a response to another's pain can reflect a principled, cognitive commitment, namely, that it is right that we respond to the pain of another. Not surprisingly, emotions usually accompany altruistic acts: we think of the sacrifices people make for their children, which generally grow out of love, as the most altruistic of acts. Surprising as it may seem, however, altruistic acts are also often motivated by a commitment to principle.

Emotional appeals without any appeal to principle, for one thing, can backfire, exhibiting what has been called psychological reactance (Brehm 1966). When door-to-door solicitors for a charity showed potential contributors pictures of handicapped children, they did find such an effect (Isen and Noonberg 1979). In most cases, showing pictures did not bring about additional contributions; the best that could be said in support of emotional appeals to altruism was that they did not hurt contributions (Thorton et al. 1991). In addition, much real world altruistic behavior is motivated by commitments to abstract norms of justice. Psychologists have demonstrated that altruistic behavior *is* associated with an orientation toward norms; those who help others usually possess a strong sense that they *ought* to act in ways to help others (Schwartz 1977; Schwartz and Howard 1982). These internalized norms have important real world consequences. We know, for example, that those who have a strong sense of moral obligation are more likely to be blood donors (Zuckerman and Reiss 1978) and that repeat blood donors are more likely to act on the basis of principle than first-time blood donors (Charg et al. 1988). Similarly, individuals are more likely to ignore opportunities to act as free riders when they have a strong sense of moral obligation. For example, individuals are more likely to participate in a recycling program when they believe it is the right thing to do (Hopper and Nielsen 1991).

Because the motives that lie behind altruistic acts are complex, combining, as they do, both emotion and principle, motivational theories of altruism can be faulted, not because they all pay attention to motives, but because they reduce all motives to one thing. Batson is surely correct to stress the importance of motivation; behavior that has altruistic consequences without any altruistic motive is less altruistic than behavior which is intended to help others but which actually harms them. We would be more likely to view the action of someone who tries to save a drowning man but fails as altruistic than the actions of someone whose passing boat acts as a life raft to bring a drowning person to shore. Moreover, there are clear normative advantages to a motivational account; one generally wants to believe that individuals are responsible for their acts and that when they act well it is because they were motivated to achieve the goal of acting well. But Batson runs into problems when he identifies motives with the pursuit of one goal only, for such an account does not give full appreciation to real world, as opposed to laboratory, conditions.

Motivational theories ought to be viewed as establishing necessary but not sufficient conditions for an understanding of altruism. Perhaps because they are usually advocated by psychologists, motivational theories tend to be individualistic, stressing how motives are internally arrived at as people examine the world around them. In this way, motivational theories accept a distinction between a private realm in which motives matter and a public realm in which people act on the basis of their motives. But this distinction, as Calhoun argues, is problematic (Calhoun 1998). His point applies as much to theories of motivation as it does to other efforts to draw a sharp line between private and public activity. Motives come from somewhere. To the degree that the place from which they come lies outside individuals and their particular cognitive or emotional makeup, to that extent is a motivational account of altruism unsatisfactory.

Some evidence exists that the normative principles associated with altruistic acts *do* come from outside individuals themselves. In her study of blood donations in specific communities, Jane Piliavin found that personal norms did not account fully for variations in altruistic behavior. Any particular individuals' motives for giving blood were reenforced in those communities which were perceived as valuing such acts. In other words, personal norms were connected to social norms and could not be fully understood without an appreciation of the connection (Piliavin and Libby 1985/86). One need not take a Durkheimian position that society stands outside the individual and acts as a conscience for individuals; it is sufficient to recognize that individual motives toward altruism are influenced by the degree to which the society in which the individual lives values altruism. Obviously, as the examples of the rescue of European Jews illustrate, societies that denigrate altruism can still manifest it. Still, real world conditions underscore the point that motivations come from somewhere. We are more likely to see altruism occurring in societies that give social approval to altruism, just as we are more likely to see extreme egoism in cultures that, because they lack the rudiments

of self-sufficiency, cannot make care of others a primary goal (Turnbull 1972).

Environmental Altruism

The incompleteness of many of the psychological accounts of altruism indicates that the larger social environment may well be an important factor in encouraging or discouraging altruism. (In using the term *environment* in this context, I am not referring to the natural or ecological environment.)

One way to illustrate the role that environmental factors play in encouraging or discouraging altruistic behavior is to consider the question of religion because religious beliefs and institutions, since Durkheim, have been understood to be part of the larger social structure—what I am calling the environment—that influences individual conduct. We would generally expect that the more religious people are, the more altruistic their behavior.

Somewhat to their surprise, the Oliners discovered that rescuers could not be distinguished from nonrescuers on the basis of religious belief (1988, 156). Similarly, the sociologist Robert Wuthnow wrote, "Participation in religious organizations, it appears, has a genuine, but limited, effect on charitable behavior" (1991, 126). If this were the end of the story, Chaves's argument that religion is a public good which contributes directly and indirectly to philanthropic activity would be hard to explain (Chaves 1998). But in fact, religion is an important factor in encouraging altruism, even if the relation is indirect.

This indirect relation can be best understood if we think of religious beliefs and institutions as frameworks that enable people to understand the meaning and consequences of altruism. In order to grasp what altruistic behaviors are, Wuthnow argues, we need to look beyond those behaviors themselves to "the languages we use to make sense of such behaviors, the cultural understandings that transform them from physical motions into human action" (1991, 45). Chaves argues against the notion that religious organizations engage in charitable behavior in order to hold on to or gain members. But he does not go completely in the opposite direction of arguing that religious organizations are directly altruistic. Rather, he suggests, religious organizations generally have "unclear goals, unclear technologies, and fluid participants." The role of religion in encouraging altruism is indirect because organizations, like individuals, have multiple objectives and pursue the good in a variety of ways.

One must be careful about relying too much on environmental explanations of altruistic variation. We have already seen that religious belief does not correlate strongly with altruism; neither, in the Oliners' study, did political affiliation or social class (1988, 156–159). Other environmental factors, however, do seem to correlate with altruistic behavior. For all their methodological difficulties, many studies demonstrate that women tend to be more altruistic than men (Russell and Mentzel 1990; Mills et al. 1989). There are stages in the life cycle which suggest that people's level of altruism is correlated with age (Midlarsky and Hannah 1989). Cross-cultural variations in the degree of altruism have frequently been observed (Johnson et al. 1989). Altruism is more frequent in rural areas than in urban ones (Kamal et al. 1987). Gender may account for the fact that lesbians tend to be much more altruistic than male homosexuals (Weller and Benozio 1987)—and, for that matter, nurses usually more than doctors (Chambliss 1996)—but questions of lifestyle and cultural choice are also involved. Because some things seem to explain altruism better than others, we ought to remind ourselves that environmental explanations of altruism do not offer a foolproof guide to empirical observations; they play a major role, but they always have to be interpreted with some caution.

Environmental approaches to altruism stress the role to be played, not only by culture, but also by social institutions. Bureaucratic organization can make it possible for altruism to exist in the absence of altruists. Sweden is often viewed as a very altruistic society composed of people who do not want to take any *personal* responsibility for the fate of their neighbors. When altruism is embodied in institutions, as Merton and Gieryn have pointed out, "the institutional arrangements of the professions tend to make it a matter of self-interest for individual practitioners to act altruistically" (1982, 119). From an institutional perspective, motives are the raw materials that are transformed by the institutions into something else, including behavior quite at variance with the original motive. As Selznick has argued, organizations can produce immoral outcomes from the intentions of moral people, but they can also do the opposite, create moral responsibility out of indifferent or even ill-intentioned persons (1992, 265–280). Just as markets can channel a disposition to act for the sake of others into a tendency to act out of self-interest, social institutions can transform selfish intentions into a collectively altruistic result.

There seems little question, then, that a good deal of real world altruistic behavior is related to the strength of social factors like culture and institutions. No empirical account of altruism can be complete without moving from the psychological level to the social. It would, I believe, be a mistake to move from extreme psychological accounts of altruism that emphasize what individuals do and ignore social and environmental factors to extreme environmental explanations in which individuals' motives are downplayed. Although environmental explanations are polar opposites of genetic ones, both have a tendency to downplay individual acts in favor of determinations at another level: either below the individual in the genes or above the individual in a Durkheimian reification of society. Moreover, it is a hotly contested question—one that cannot be resolved here—whether it would be preferable to live in a nonaltruistic society filled with altruists or in an altruistic society filled with indifference. On both empirical and normative grounds, there is much to say for environmental accounts of altruism, but such accounts should be used judiciously.

Conclusion

People will always act in a variety of ways: any theory which reduces their behavior to one way of acting is therefore problematic on scientific grounds. But even more, people should act in multiple ways. The best way to avoid the twin extremes of pure value relativism and preaching is to recognize the complexity of human objectives.

Respect for pluralism can be illustrated in two ways from the literature on altruism. In the first place, any theory of human behavior should not posit that egoism always rules over altruism or vice versa. What emerges from the literature in many forms is a sense that altruism and egoism do not constitute mutually exclusive categories. In experimental social psychology, it is recognized that human beings do respond out of empathy for the plight of others, as Batson has shown (for an overview of his work, see Batson and Shaw 1991), but at the same time that empathy often satisfies the relatively selfish function of stress reduction, as Batson's main critic, Cialdini (1991), has argued. (For a compromise position, see Stiff et al. 1988.) Likewise, the sociological study of real world altruism, such as blood or kidney donation, indicates that, in the words of Roberta Simmons, "it is very difficult to untangle altruistic and egoistic motives" (1991, 5).

Much the same mixture of motives seems to underlie altruistic professions and institutions. Altruistic professions are caught between many imperatives, not all of them altruistic. On the one hand, those usually helped by such professions increasingly reject altruism as a model

that gives meaning to the help provided them; among the deaf, for example, there has been a clear rejection of the notion of giving, replaced by an assertion of rights (Lane 1992). On the other hand, those who entered altruistic professions in order to give end up organizing themselves into unions, engaging in efforts to prevent their exploitation in the name of altruism, and feeling burned out by the demands placed upon them (Chambliss 1996).

Even the most extraordinary altruistic behavior—such as the acts of those who rescued the European Jews—supports the idea that altruism and its opposite exist in a kind of uneasy simultaneity. In their study of rescuers, the Oliners point out that

they were and are "ordinary" people. They were farmers and teachers, entrepreneurs and factory workers, rich and poor, parents and single people, Protestants and Catholics. Most had done nothing extraordinary before the war nor have they done much that is extraordinary since. Most were marked neither by exceptional leadership qualities nor by unconventional behavior. They were not heroes cast in larger-than-life molds. What most distinguished them were their connections with others in relationships of commitment and care.

(259)

So "normal" were the people who rescued Jews, often at great risk to themselves, that, when interviewed many years later, a number of them appeared to be completely conventional, some even vaguely anti-Semitic.

If the models we develop to represent reality are to be as complex as the reality we want to represent, such models should be pluralistic in nature. A pluralistic model would make the following assumptions about human behavior: both egoism and altruism exist; most real world examples of human behavior contain elements of both simultaneously; efforts to attribute to one or the other the determining role in explaining human behavior are inevitably contrived; and as a result, social scientists should use a wide variety of techniques, methods, and approaches to gain insights to how human beings actually act.

Just as we ought to assume a pluralistic position when it comes to identifying egoism and altruism, so we ought to be pluralistic with respect to the approaches to altruism discussed in this chapter. It may be that a combination of these approaches best fulfills a commitment to pluralism. Although there are valuable aspects associated with behavioral approaches, they tend to be difficult to incorporate into a pluralistic theory because they tend to reduce all behavior to one thing. We ought, therefore, to think of altruism as containing primarily motivational and environmental components compared to behavioral ones. Most altruistic acts occur in an environment friendly to altruism but require the normative motivation that only individuals can provide.

I think of altruism—or, for that matter, of selfishness—as a template, a preframed response that guides but does not determine individual behavior. When we are called upon to make a decision, these bundles of responses called altruism are out there, available to us, helping us frame the complex reality we confront. In most situations, we are fully aware of which reactions are selfish and which are altruistic, and this makes it possible for us to reflect on how we make our decisions as we are in the process of making them.

But it is not culture that determines whether any particular choice we make will be selfish or altruistic. Only our individual attributes—the way we think, the lessons we have internalized, the reactions to past experience—shape how we will respond to the preexisting templates available to us. Only on the rarest possible occasions will we choose either template in its entirety. Most of the time, what we do involves an uneasy combination of motives and intentions, some of them selfish, others altruistic. Indeed,

it is precisely because there is nearly always a gap between how we act and the ways that our culture tells us we should act that we have such a thing as a conscience.

Altruism, then, represents that bundle of cultural practices which insist that the decisions we make be made in the light of their consequences for others. In this sense, altruism is primarily an environmental phenomenon; it exists in the stories, traditions, beliefs, and institutional memories of a society, handed down from generation to generation. The giving of accounts will be influenced by the norms of the society, norms which themselves are derived from the cultural practices that establish standards of altruism. But every individual will have a different relation to those social norms. There will never be clear markers of who is likely to be more altruistic and who is likely to be less. It is theoretically possible for a particular individual to lack any degree of altruism at all. But for society as a whole, there will always be both altruistic codes and altruistic behavior or else there will be no society.

This is a relatively weak definition of altruism, one that seems to downplay the heroically altruistic—the rescuers of the European Jews, for example. But I think it worth emphasizing that with both self-interest and altruism, we generally find as much as our definitions allow. If social scientists define self-interest broadly and altruism narrowly, they will certainly find more self-interest than altruism.

There are, I believe, two major threats to a pluralistic understanding of altruism contained in recent social science and social theory. On the one hand, strongly individualistic theories are based on the notion that people already know their preferences, making it unnecessary for them to have strong social institutions and structures that help shape preferences. Individuals under such a construct are singular; we generally know what they want because their preferences are either constant or transitive. On the other hand, certain communitarian tendencies, presumably the opposite of individualistic ones, can, as Calhoun argues (1998) emphasize national values in ways that reduce all people to singularity as well; we know what they want because we know the country to which they belong.

Both points of view overtheorize. Both approach individuals as people whose behavior and choices are already shaped. But altruistic acts, as one of the most important things that people do, may not be shaped at all. Altruism requires that an individual make choices in the context of particular situations. Such choices must be a reflection of the way individuals think and develop as they confront contexts within which they must make decisions. Weak definitions of altruism are important because they tend to produce stronger conceptions of individual choice. If we know what altruism is, we need to know little about individuals who act altruistically. If we leave the definition of altruism relatively open, both our understanding of people and our appreciation for their multiple objectives are likely to be enhanced.

References

Bar-Tal, Daniel. 1985/86. "Altruistic Motivation to Help: Definition, Utility, and Operationalization." *Humboldt Journal of Social Relations* 13:3–14.

Batson, C. Daniel. 1990. "How Social an Animal? The Human Capacity for Caring." *American Psychologist* 45:336–346.

———. 1991. *The Altruism Question: Towards a Social-Psychological Answer*. Hillsdale, NJ: Erlbaum Associates.

Batson, C. Daniel, Judy G. Batson, Cari A. Griffitt, Sergio Barrientos, et al. 1989. "Negative-state Relief and the Empathy-Altruism Hypothesis." *Journal of Personality and Social Psychology* 56:922–933.

Batson, C. Daniel, Judy G. Batson, Jacqueline K. Slingsby, Kevin Harrell, et al. 1991. "Empathic Joy and the Empathy-Altruism Hypothesis." *Journal of Personality and Social Psychology* 61:413–426.

Batson, C. Daniel, Janine L. Dyck, Randall J. Brandt, Judy G. Batson, et al. 1988. "Five Studies Testing Two New Egoistic Alternatives to the Empathy-Altruism Hypothesis." *Journal of Personality and Social Psychology* 55:52–77.

Batson, C. Daniel, Kathryn C. Oleson, Joy L. Weeks, Sean P. Healy, et al. 1989. "Religious Prosocial Motivation: Is It Altruistic or Egoistic?" *Journal of Personality and Social Psychology* 57:873–884.

Batson, C. Daniel, and Laura L. Shaw. 1991. "Evidence for Altruism: Toward a Pluralism of Prosocial Motives." *Psychological Inquiry* 2:107–122.

Bierhoff, Hans W., Renate Klein, and Peter Kramp. 1991. "Evidence for the Altruistic Personality from Data on Accident Research." *Journal of Personality* 59:263–280.

Brehm, J. W. 1966. *A Theory of Psychological Reactance*. New York: Academic Press.

Calhoun, Craig. 1998. "The Public Good as a Social and Cultural Project." In Walter W. Powell and Elisabeth S. Clemens, eds., *Private Action and the Public Good*, 20–35. New Haven, CT: Yale University Press.

Carlo, Gustavo, Nancy Eisenberg, Debra Troyer, and Galen Switzer. 1991. "The Altruistic Personality: In What Contexts Is It Apparent?" *Journal of Personality and Social Psychology* 61:450–458.

Chambliss, Dan. 1996. *Beyond Caring: Hospitals, Nurses, and the Social Organization of Ethics*. Chicago: University of Chicago Press.

Charg, H. V., J. A. Piliavin, and P. L. Callero. 1988. "Role Identity and Reasoned Action in the Prediction of Repeated Behavior." *Social Psychology Quarterly* 51:303–317.

Chaves, Mark. 1998. "The Religious Ethic and the Spirit of Nonprofit Entrepreneurship." In Walter W. Powell and Elisabeth S. Clemens, eds., *Private Action and the Public Good*, 47–65. New Haven, CT: Yale University Press.

Cialdini, Robert B. 1991. "Altruism or Egoism? That Is (Still) the Question." *Psychological Inquiry* 2:124–126.

Coleman, James S. 1990. *Foundations of Social Theory*. Cambridge, MA: Harvard University Press.

Dawes, Robyn M., Alphons J. C. van de Kragt, and John M. Orbell. 1988. "Not Me or Thee But We:

The Importance of Group Identity in Eliciting Cooperation in Dilemma Situations: Experimental Manipulations." *Acta Psychologica* 68:83–97.

Dawkins, Richard. 1976. *The Selfish Gene.* New York: Oxford University Press.

Dovidio, John F., Judith L. Allen, and David A. Schroeder. 1990. "Specificity of Empathy-Induced Helping: Evidence for Altruistic Motivation." *Journal of Personality and Social Psychology* 59:249–260.

Eisenberg, Nancy. 1991. "Values, Sympathy, and Individual Differences: Toward a Pluralism of Factors Influencing Altruism and Empathy." *Psychological Inquiry* 2:128–131.

Eisenberg, Nancy, Paul A. Miller, Mark Schaller, Richard Fabes, et al. 1989. "The Role of Sympathy and Altruistic Personality Traits in Helping: A Reexamination." *Journal of Personality* 57:41–67.

Hopper, Joseph R., and Joyce M. Nielsen. 1991. "Recycling as Altruistic Behavior: Normative and Behavioral Strategies to Expand Participation in a Community Recycling Program." *Environment and Behavior* 23:195–220.

Hurley, Dennis, and Bern Allen. 1974. "The Effect of the Number of People Present in Nonemergency Situations." *Journal of Social Psychology* 92:27–29.

Isen, A. M., and A. Noonberg. 1979. "The Effect of Photographs of the Handicapped on Donations to Charity: When a Thousand Words May Be Too Much." *Journal of Applied Social Psychology* 9:426–431.

Johnson, Ronald C., George P. Danko, Thomas J. Darvill, Stephen Bochner, et al. 1989. "Cross-Cultural Assessment of Altruism and Its Correlates." *Personality and Individual Differences* 10:855–868.

Kamal, Preet, Manju Mehta, and Uday Jain. 1987. "Altruism in Urban and Rural Environment." *Indian Psychological Review* 32:35–42.

Kohlberg, Lawrence. 1981. *The Philosophy of Moral Development.* New York: Harper and Row.

Krebs, Dennis L. 1970. "Altruism—An Examination of the Concept and a Review of the Literature." *Psychological Bulletin* 73:258–302.

Lane, Harlan. 1992. *The Mask of Benevolence: Disabling the Deaf Community.* New York: Knopf.

Latané, Bibb, and John Darley. 1970. *The Unresponsive Bystander: Why Doesn't He Help?* Englewood Cliffs: Prentice-Hall.

Mansbridge, Jane. 1998. "On the Contested Nature of the Public Good." In Walter W. Powell and Elisabeth S. Clemens, eds., *Private Action and the Public Good,* 3–19. New Haven, CT: Yale University Press.

Merton, Robert K., and Thomas F. Gieryn. 1982. "Institutional Altruism: The Case of the Professions." In Robert K. Merton, ed., *Social Research and the Practicing Professions,* with an introduction by Aaron Rosenblatt and Thomas F. Gieryn, 109–134. Cambridge, MA: Apt Books.

Midlarsky, Elizabeth, and Mary E. Hannah. 1989. "The Generous Elderly: Naturalistic Studies of Donations across the Life Span." *Psychology and Aging* 4:346–351.

Mills, Rosemary S., Jan Pedersen, and Joan E. Grusec. 1989. "Sex Differences in Reasoning and Emotion about Altruism." *Sex Roles* 20:603–621.

Oliner, Samuel P., and Pearl M. Oliner. 1988. *The Altruistic Personality: Rescuers of Jews in Nazi Europe.* New York: Free Press.

Piliavin, Jane Allyn, and Hong-Wen Charg. 1990. "Altruism: A Review of Recent Theory and Research." *Annual Review of Sociology* 16:27–65.

Piliavin, Jane Allyn, and Donald Libby. 1985/86. "Personal Norms, Perceived Social Norms, and Blood Donation." *Humboldt Journal of Social Relations* 13:159–194.

Reykowski, Janusz. 1980. "Origin of Prosocial Motivation: Heterogeneity of Personality Development." *Studia Psychologia* 22:91–106.

Rushton, J. Phillipe. 1980. *Altruism, Socialization, and Society.* Englewood Cliffs: Prentice-Hall.

Russell, Gordon W., and Robert K. Mentzel. 1990. "Sympathy and Altruism in Response to Disasters." *Journal of Social Psychology* 1990:309–316.

Schwartz, Barry. 1986. *The Battle for Human Nature.* New York: Norton.

Schwartz, S. H. 1977. "Normative Influences on Altruism." In L. Berkowitz, ed., *Advances in Experimental Social Psychology,* 221–279. New York: Academic Press.

Schwartz, S. H., and J. A. Howard. 1982. "Helping and Cooperation: A Self-Based Motivational Model." In J. Derlega and J. Grzelak, eds.,

Cooperation and Helping Behavior: Theories and Research, 327–353. New York: Academic Press.

Selznick, Philip. 1992. *The Moral Commonwealth: Social Theory and the Promise of Community*. Berkeley: University of California Press.

Simmons, Roberta G. 1991. "Altruism and Sociology." *The Sociological Quarterly* 32:1–22.

Stiff, J. B., J. P. Dillard, L. Somera, H. Kim, and C. Sleight. 1988. "Empathy, Communication, and Prosocial Behavior." *Communication Monographs* 55:198–213.

Thorton, Bill, Gayle Kirchner, and Jacqueline Jacobs. 1991. "Influence of a Photograph on a Charitable Appeal: A Picture May Be Worth a Thousand Words When It Has to Speak for Itself." *Journal of Applied Social Psychology* 21:433–445.

Turnbull, Colin M. 1972. *The Mountain People*. New York: Simon and Schuster.

Weller, Leonard, and Motti Benozio. 1987. "Homosexuals' and Lesbians' Philosophies of Human Nature." *Social Behavior and Personality* 15:221–224.

Wilson, James Q. 1993. *The Moral Sense*. New York: Free Press.

Wuthnow, Robert. 1991. *Acts of Compassion: Caring for Others and Helping Ourselves*. Princeton: Princeton University Press.

Zahn-Waxler, Carolyn. 1991. "The Case for Empathy: A Developmental Perspective." *Psychological Inquiry* 2:155–158.

Zuckerman, M., and H. Y. Reiss. 1978. "Comparison of Three Models for Predicting Altruistic Behavior." *Journal of Personality and Social Psychology* 36:468–510.

CHAPTER 28

Philanthropy in Communities of Color

Bradford Smith, Sylvia Shue, Jennifer Lisa Vest,
and Joseph Villarreal

Excerpted from *Philanthropy in Communities of Color*: 1–8, 146–170. Copyright © 1999 by The University of San Francisco and reprinted by Indiana University Press. Reprinted with permission.

"Philanthropy" often refers to the altruism of the wealthy: John D. Rockefeller and Andrew Carnegie a century ago, Bill Gates and George Soros now. Yet as John Gardner once remarked, philanthropy in America is largely a "Mississippi River of small gifts." Of the $150 billion donated in 1996, the largest portion came not from billionaires and mega-foundations but from individuals giving the proverbial widow's mite to their churches, scout troops, and local soup kitchens.

After countless studies of elite philanthropy, scholars have recently begun to give some attention to the altruistic behavior of laborers, farmers, immigrants, women, people of color, and the poor. The social history of American immigration has revealed an astonishing array of mutual assistance groups, ethnic/religious organizations, and other mechanisms by which immigrants helped each other as well as needy people in their homelands and, as time went on, society at large. Feminist studies have thrown much light on the philanthropy of middle-class and poor women as well as that of wealthy women. Very little attention, however, has been given to charitable behavior within communities of color. Minority people are often portrayed as takers rather than givers, significantly less generous than white Americans, but there has been little research to evaluate this characterization.

Ethnic philanthropy is the phenomenon of sharing and helping within communities of color. This chapter reports an ethnographic study that examined in close detail the altruistic behavior, attitudes, and values of 260 individuals from eight communities of color in the San Francisco Bay Area. The Mexican, Guatemalan, Salvadoran, Filipino, Chinese, Japanese, Korean, and African American participants were interviewed by members of their own ethnic groups in two phases of the study, in 1991 and 1993.

Conceptual Framework

Culture

Not only has research on ethnic philanthropy failed to keep pace with the rapidly increasing size and importance of America's minority

393 DOI: 10.4324/9780367696559-36

groups, but the cultural dimensions of philanthropic behavior within these ethnic communities remain virtually unexplored. All cultures construct reality differently; within each unique cultural community, beliefs and behavior have meanings that are often not shared or understood by the outside world. Some cultural meanings are manifest and easily recognized; others are latent and subtle, requiring systematic observation in order to produce accurate analysis. Thus, the cultural dimensions of gift giving, financial assistance, sharing, and the distribution of income and wealth all have a variety of meanings from culture to culture.

In most cultures characterized by traditional patrilineal systems of kinship, authority, and inheritance, the extended family is the main source of support, assistance, caretaking, and self-help for individuals. In the Chinese tradition, for example, principles of filial piety dictate that elderly family members receive respect, care, and support from the younger generations (Chang 1983). Particularly in rural Chinese communities, this eliminated the need for community-based care for the elderly. Chinese people entering American urban settings are likely to perceive non-kin-based support services as unnecessary and even shameful. Similar tenets of family- and community-based self-help permeate the Hispanic and African American cultural traditions as well. Understanding patterns of cultural and family tradition is essential to understanding giving and volunteering within a particular cultural group.

The uses of wealth, prestige, and power are also important to the cross-cultural analysis of charitable behavior. In some cultures, for example, gift giving and charity involve formalized systems of wealth redistribution that annually reaffirm the power base of local leaders. In other cultures gift giving may signal a wish for reconciliation or improved relationships between families or clans (Gibbs 1973; Gulliver 1977). Subtle gift-giving rituals can signal appropriate degrees of honor and shame, reaffirm cultural

precepts, and allow positive channels for "face-saving" behavior. In such cultural contexts giving a gift or being asked to give (particularly to a stranger) can easily create suspicion on the part of the potential donor or create a situation in which the gift giver perceives that he or she has been placed in a subservient position (Van Loo 1990).

Acculturation and assimilation into American society, however, tend to weaken traditional practices. Each generation's experience with family caretaking and the use of external community services creates a different set of attitudes about the value and appropriateness of community programs and charitable support for such efforts.

Philanthropy

No one suggests that goods and services given to nuclear family members should be counted as philanthropy. Nor does anyone count as philanthropy goods and services directly exchanged for money or some other economic value. What interests students of philanthropy is *the giving of goods and services outside the nuclear family without any apparent expectation of economic return.* In accounting terms, a gift or grant results in the net asset of the grantor being reduced by an amount equal to an increase in net assets of the grantee (Boulding 1981). This definition leaves open the question of the role of noneconomic values such as status, recognition, control, acceptance, face, spiritual insurance, and feelings of self-worth. A giver may receive social rather than economic goods in return for a gift. This study will focus on giving as defined above, in relation to eight ethnic communities, and will explore ethnic giving in the context of its roots in the nuclear and extended family as well as in the larger context of social and economic exchange.

The fundamental question in any study of philanthropy is, Why do individuals give money, goods, and services to others? Altruistic or apparently altruistic behavior among humans and animals has long intrigued philosophers, psychologists, economists, anthropologists, biologists, and historians, not to mention fundraisers. This chapter investigates indigenous conceptualizations and patterns of giving within the eight ethnic communities studied. The differences are unsurprising given the sharply different historical experiences of the eight groups. The similarities, however, may help us understand philanthropic behavior generally.

This study focused on enumerating and describing the specific practices and customs of giving money, goods, and services within each of the eight communities. One of the common patterns identified in this study is that the giving of money, goods, and services originates in the nuclear family and moves outward through a series of roughly concentric circles of beneficiaries. These beneficiary groups are defined as follows:

- Nuclear family: mother and/or father and unmarried children. (Members of the nuclear family are not considered as beneficiaries of philanthropy in this study.)
- Extended family: people related by marriage, common ancestry, or fictive kinship not necessarily living together.
- Nuclear community: people known by the individual who is giving money, goods, or services.
- Extended community: organizations with whom an individual feels a cultural identification.
- United States: organizations within the United States.
- The world: organizations throughout the world.
- Other: ancestors, nature, and deities.

This study examines the ever-changing boundaries that exist between nuclear family support, economic exchange, social exchange, mutual assistance, and gifts. Such boundaries are inevitably arbitrary, as are the boundaries between the beneficiary groups.

Observations made within one cultural setting began to inform observations made in other settings.

Ethnicity

The principal focus of this study is ethnicity—specifically, the relationship of ethnicity to charitable behavior. Do people of color give and volunteer, and if so, in what ways, to whom, for what reasons, to what degree? Do minority Americans give more or less than, or about the same as, white Americans? As suggested above, the evidence on this last question is somewhat contradictory.

The research reported in this chapter found that in all eight minority groups, respondents were much more likely to speak of giving to or helping needy individuals, families, and informal groups rather than organizations. Much of the giving occurs outside of organizations. However, it still serves the same function as giving to organizations: Instead of providing aid to many people, most of whom are unknown to the donors, the groups studied here focused their giving on fewer people, but people they knew and could count on to return the favor if needed.

Further, the terminology of questions asked in ethnic philanthropy research may significantly impact the conclusions. The survey research studies use words such as "charity," "contributions," "volunteering," and the like. The present study found that such terms did not work at all for the participants, who were much more likely to describe their experiences as "sharing" and "helping." The word "charity" carried negative connotations for some groups.

The present study suggests that the *amount* (relative to personal resources) of minority giving may be roughly consistent with that of white America but that the *forms and beneficiaries* of minority giving may be quite different.

It is worth noting that the customs and practices of giving described here strongly resemble the "sharing and helping" traditions of earlier Americans, who often shared goods and services prior to the development of more formal government and philanthropic aid organizations (Boorstin 1969, ch. 3; Hawke 1988; Schlesinger 1944–45). Historically, American life was filled with interdependent networks. Quilting bees, barn raisings, and harvest-time cooperation are just a few of the more familiar examples of groups coming together to help individuals. These cooperative arrangements continued into the industrial age. As time went on, various forms of mutual assistance were replaced by more formal and organized government and philanthropic aid. However, familial and communal networks still play an important role in the giving habits of many Americans, perhaps especially in communities of color due to recent immigration, discrimination, and cultural factors.

A note on terminology: Following the general usage of the 260 participants, this reading uses "African American" and "black" interchangeably and, for the other seven ethnic groups, generally uses single-word descriptions such as "Chinese community" and "Filipinos" rather than "Chinese American community," "Filipino Americans," and so forth.

Research Approach and Methodology

This cross-cultural ethnography focused on giving and volunteering in eight communities of color. The eight ethnic groups were selected primarily because of their prevalence and importance in the San Francisco Bay Area. Focused interviews, typically an hour and a half in length, with 260 individuals were conducted by members of the same ethnic groups. While an attempt was made to select respondents representatively across age, generation, and gender, the interviewee group was not intended to be and was not a true random sample. The interviews were conducted at the participants' homes or places of work from January to September of 1991 and from April to September of 1993. The first phase included five groups: Chinese, Japanese, Filipino, Mexican, and Guatemalan Americans. The second phase added Salvadoran, Korean, and African Americans.

These interviews provided the principal data from which the conclusions of the study were drawn. Additional insights came from participation in informal group sessions in each ethnic community. Some participants were interviewed more than once, particularly community leaders and individuals conversant with social science concepts and methods.

Conclusion

Philanthropy is often associated with wealthy people giving large amounts of money to a charitable organization and indirectly to people they do not personally know: for example, Andrew Carnegie's and Bill Gates's commendable support of libraries. Ethnic philanthropy is almost totally different: It consists primarily of people sharing modest or meager wealth with other people, most of whom the givers know well.

This chapter reports an ethnographic cross-cultural study of giving and volunteering in eight communities of color in the San Francisco Bay Area and is based on focused interviews with 260 individuals from those communities. Several major findings emerged from the study:

Ethnic philanthropy is inextricably linked with family and kinship. Ethnic charity, like other charity, truly begins at home. While transactions involving money, goods, and services within the nuclear family cannot be considered "philanthropy" or "charity," they powerfully prepare family members for charitable activities that go beyond the nuclear family. In the eight communities studied, there is typically a seamless transition between intra- and extrafamilial sharing and helping. Parents' care for their children, children care for their parents, and sharing and helping among siblings move almost imperceptibly outward to grandparents and grandchildren, aunts and uncles, nieces and nephews, cousins, friends, neighbors, fellow church members, coworkers, classmates, other members of the ethnic community, relatives and friends living in the homeland, and, finally, people and organizations in the larger society both in the United States and abroad. Many stories told by participants revealed a steady addition of beneficiaries in ever-widening circles of sharing and helping.

The dominant culture's definition of (nuclear) family as parents and children and the distinction between family and extended family (including also some relatives and fictive kin) are largely ignored by the ethnic communities studied. As one participant put it, family means "people you truly love who love you back." Blood relationships begin but do not end the concept of family in the communities studied. Several respondents went out of their way to criticize the dominant culture's notion of family as narrow and lacking appropriate scope of love and responsibility.

Family broadly defined is not only the prime teacher and model of ethnic philanthropy but also its prime recipient. The great bulk of philanthropy (giving money, goods, and services outside the nuclear family with no expectation of economic return) in the eight communities studied comes from and goes to the family broadly defined and the ethnic community, including churches and other organizations primarily serving the ethnic community. While this study made no effort to quantify ethnic giving and volunteering, a reasonable estimate based on the interviews is that 80 to 90 percent of time spent helping and money and goods shared were directed toward the "family" and the ethnic community.

Respondents volunteered many reasons for this: One's primary obligation is to one's own—"family" members and fellow members of the ethnic community. To paraphrase many responses:

These are the people you know best and love most. These are the people who have given or will give you most in return. These are the people whose needs are most evident and immediate; they need help right here, right now. These are the people who count on you for help, and on whom you may count some day.

There was also, in all eight communities, a strong sense of the special needs of the community, resulting from poverty, discrimination, language differences, or all of the above. Obligation to family came first, obligation to the community a close second. To many respondents, it simply did not make sense to support mainstream charitable agencies while there were such pressing needs in one's "family" and community. Charity was not a matter of the best use of discretionary income; it was a matter of the survival of loved ones.

Families and kinship groups practice reciprocity as well as charity. People care for their elderly parents at least partly so that they will be cared for when they are old. Families give elaborate and expensive wedding gifts to cousins and neighbors partly so that their own children will receive similar help as they start families. The family is the first teacher of reciprocity as well as charity: As you give, so will you get.

Fictive kinship was important in all the communities studied. In the African American community, for example, much emphasis is placed on helping one's "brothers" and "sisters," who might be relatives, former classmates, friends, members of the same church, or simply other members of the black community. In Latin American cultures "uncle" might mean your father's brother or simply his good friend. These fictive kin are also "family" who help and are helped in times of need.

In most of the communities studied, there were overlapping kinship groups such as family-surname associations and homeland-district associations. Many such kinship groups and ethnic mutual benefit associations were created in America for support and solidarity in response to discrimination and other hardships. In such groups, as in the nuclear and extended family, charity and reciprocity are almost inextricably mixed.

Research on charitable behavior as well as common notions of philanthropy in the United States rightly excludes gifts of money, goods, and time within the nuclear family. However, ethnic philanthropy cannot be understood without careful reference to family and kinship interactions. The social context of philanthropy for most Americans is quite different. As a result of urbanization, industrialization, and other socioeconomic changes, the roles of family and kinship group in caring for the aged, providing relief for the poor, and other such activities have increasingly been assumed by government, nonprofit, and some for-profit institutions, including soup kitchens, homes for the elderly, schools, and insurance companies (Mintz and Kellogg 1988; Espiritu and Hunt 1964; Dalton 1971). But nearly two-thirds of the world's population still lives in villages in close association with large numbers of their kin (Shoumatoff 1985, 204). This is relevant to understanding not only the local but also the international dimensions of American ethnic philanthropy. Many respondents described how they support relatives and friends who remain in the homeland.

Religion plays a very important role in ethnic philanthropy. In all eight communities studied religion plays an important role in shaping the philanthropic behavior of community members. In four of the groups (Mexican, Guatemalan, Salvadoran, and Filipino) Catholicism is the dominant religious influence. In two groups (Korean, African American) Protestantism is dominant. In the Chinese and Japanese communities Confucianism and Buddhism play an important but different, less direct role, and many community members also belong to Protestant churches.

Catholicism provides a sacramental context, model, teacher, and recipient of ethnic philanthropy. Sacramental events tied to major life changes—baptisms, confirmations, marriages, funerals—are the occasion for many forms of giving and volunteering, as are religious/cultural practices such as *compadrazgo* (copaternity, godparenthood) and *quinceañera* (a girl's fifteenth birthday and coming-out celebration). But the church's role in ethnic philanthropy goes far beyond such events and practices. The weekly collection at mass, parish food drives, Catholic schools and religious education programs, religious festivals, church societies to help the poor, church efforts to assist immigrants and refugees, and many other activities are occasions for ethnic giving and volunteering. Through its charitable activities, the church practices, teaches about, and receives philanthropy. Ethnic philanthropy in the Catholic tradition, like family and kin interactions, also mixes charity and reciprocity: Gifts to the *santos* (saints) bring benefits in return.

Catholicism has had a profound effect on the cultures of Mexico, Guatemala, El Salvador, and the Philippines in recent centuries. Though recently losing ground somewhat to secularism and evangelical Protestantism, Catholicism continues to exert considerable influence in shaping the values of people living within these countries, values that are then brought to the United States when people immigrate here. In addition to their devotional aspects, religious ceremonies and festivals in the home countries promote communal solidarity. This emphasis on community, and attendant customs such as *compadrazgo*, reflect and reinforce similar values of the communal and kin-based societies of Latin America and the Philippines.

For many respondents religious giving was primarily devotional. This was especially true among the Guatemalans interviewed and some of the more recent immigrants from Mexico and the Philippines.

Protestantism is the religious choice of 70 percent of Koreans, with Buddhism attracting most of the rest. The church is a very important part of Korean philanthropy and is active in the educational, social, economic, and political lives of Koreans. Korean churches helped raise money to support the independence movement in the homeland.

Protestantism is also the overwhelming choice of African Americans, although in recent decades Islam has attracted a sizable number of blacks. The church is by far the most important philanthropic organization in the African American community. Charitable church programs include food and clothing drives, services to the sick and elderly, college scholarship funds, day care and after-school centers, tutoring, counseling, recreation, and many others. In addition to formal church charities, much of the personal and family-based philanthropy within the black community is inspired and organized by the church. As one respondent said, "You know, it'd be 'Sister Jones is sick and shut in, so therefore we'd like to have you take her a meal.'"

The black church also plays an important role in directing charitable resources to other organizations, both within and outside the African American community. Such is the influence of the black church that Carson (1989) believes the future of African American charitable organizations will depend on the support and endorsement of black religious leaders.

Confucianism and Buddhism teach and support philanthropic values but do not play the same activist philanthropic role that Catholicism and Protestantism do in the communities studied. Both Buddhism and Confucianism provide centuries-old ethical precepts relating to charity. In particular, these wisdom traditions convey the central importance of community, oneness, and connection with others.

In all the groups studied, it was clear that the philanthropic aspects of religion could not be seen as separate and distinct from family, kinship, and ethnic group. Local religious congregations were largely composed of members of the same ethnic groups, and the congregations included many families related to each other by kinship or fictive kinship ties. In other

words, it is difficult and probably impossible to isolate the specific effect of religion on ethnic philanthropy, since for religiously active people of color, religious influence continually and extensively interacts with the effects of the ethnic group, family, and kinship. Religion both shapes and expresses culture (Geertz 1973). There is no way to separate fully religion and culture.

Little ethnic philanthropy is directed toward mainstream charitable organizations other than churches. Most ethnic philanthropy is informal and probably goes unrecorded in tax returns and Gallup surveys because it is given directly by one person to another. Respondents mentioned giving to or volunteering for a number of nonchurch charitable organizations, both ethnic agencies (National Association for the Advancement of Colored People, Mexican American Legal Defense and Educational Fund, Japanese American Citizens League, Chinese for Affirmative Action) and mainstream nonprofit organizations (YMCA and YWCA, Boy and Girl Scouts, Red Cross, March of Dimes, Easter Seals, Salvation Army, Goodwill Industries, United Way) as well as organizations in their countries of origin. However, giving and volunteering to secular charitable organizations constitute a relatively small portion of ethnic philanthropy, most of which goes to the extended family, including fictive kin, and the church. Several respondents expressed distrust of mainstream charitable organizations, seeing them as large, impersonal institutions operated by strangers and benefiting strangers. A young second-generation Guatemalan woman said bluntly, "Latins do not follow the American model of charity; we do not give to strangers."

The present study found that philanthropy in the eight minority communities studied had very little to do with giving to organizations other than churches and temples. Nearly all giving and volunteering—or sharing and helping—within these communities of color was person to person, family to family, neighbor to neighbor, church member to church member. Much of this ethnic philanthropy consisted of bringing food, visiting, taking in someone who didn't have a place to stay—all activities that are difficult to place a monetary value on, difficult to measure. It is easy to record the value of a donation sent to Amnesty International or clothes given to Goodwill Industries, but it is difficult to record the value of bringing shoes to a neighbor's nephew in Guatemala. Defining charity or philanthropy as giving to and volunteering for incorporated nonprofit charitable organizations simply excludes most of the reality of ethnic philanthropy. Survey research based on such a definition becomes a Procrustean bed, to accommodate which major parts of philanthropic behavior are cut away. The present study suggests that this approach does great disservice to the understanding of at least minority philanthropy and probably other philanthropy as well. If, hypothetically, the dominant philanthropic pattern of white Americans is to give to charitable organizations and *not* to relatives, friends, and members of their ethnic/national origin group, while people of color give primarily within their extended family (including fictive kin) and ethnic group, research focused largely or exclusively on giving to organizations will always "prove" that whites give much more than people of color.

There is a similarity of giving-related customs (and even terms) across the groups studied. The eight groups studied have very different histories, both in their lands of origin and in the United States. The differences go back centuries and are expressed in social, political, and economic structures; art, music, and literature; philosophy, religion, and culture. Some of the countries of origin have warred with each other, and in the United States some of the groups have had tense relationships with one another. In spite of all these differences, there are strong similarities in the groups' customs, practices, and even terminology related to sharing and helping.

In most of the groups studied much giving and volunteering takes place in connection with major life events such as birth, coming of age, marriage, moves, and death. The obvious explanation is that people need extra money, goods, help, and emotional support at such times; a communal response helps ease the burden. For example, the birth of a baby occasioned giving in different forms: the Filipino *pakimkim* (money and gifts to the godchild at baptism), the Chinese *Mún yuht laib sih* (money given to the newborn by all married individuals in attendance at the Red Egg and Ginger birthday party), the Japanese *oiwai* (money and gifts of congratulation), the Mexican *bolo* (money thrown to children at the baptism), *batea* (tray full of gifts given to the parents and child), *aguacero* (shower for the newborn; gifts and money for the mother), and so forth.

Respect for parents and the elderly in general was a common philanthropic theme in the groups studied. Such values and practices clearly go back to times and countries where the extended family is the sole means of support for the elderly, but the values have remained strong even in the United States of the 1990s, where different values and support systems are in place.

Customs and terms such as *compadrazgo*, *padrino/a*, and *quinceañera* appear in the four groups with a Catholic Hispanic background and clearly reflect the language and culture of that background. They are, however, similar to godparenthood and coming-of-age practices in the other four communities studied as well as other religious and cultural groups.

A detailed comparative list of customs and terms for five of the eight groups (Chinese, Japanese, Filipino, Mexican, Guatemalan) may be found in Smith, Shue, and Villarreal (1992, 227–249).

Significant amounts of money and goods are sent to family, kin, and communities outside the United States. With the exception of the African American community, all of the groups studied directed a significant part of their philanthropy to their countries of origin. This pattern of giving is strongly reminiscent of the practices of European immigrant groups (Irish, Italian, Polish, Jewish, and so forth) during the nineteenth century. If the first rule of philanthropy is "charity begins at home," the second is "people help their own," both here and in the homelands. Sending money abroad is clearly related to recency of immigration: Americans of English, Irish, German, French, and African descent send little money to their countries of origin, whereas Americans of Mexican, Filipino, Guatemalan, Korean, and other ancestries do because of the recency of direct family and kinship ties.

In the groups studied there was a continual flow of visitors and migrants back and forth between the United States and the countries of origin. These people were carriers and often recipients of ethnic philanthropy. Money and goods sent abroad mostly went to relatives and friends, but some went to more general causes. For example, people who had done well economically in the United States might build a new school or clinic in the town they came from. Sometimes there are sending-off parties and welcome-back parties. These events both help pay the expenses of the trip and provide the travelers with gifts to people in the homeland. Visiting the homeland can be expensive. One Filipino respondent said that the required gift giving there usually costs more than the plane tickets.

Any attempt to quantify American ethnic philanthropy must take into account this large-scale transfer of money and goods out of the United States. Some respondents estimated that these transfers account for a significant percentage of revenue flowing into some of the countries of origin. If the practices reported by the 240 respondents from seven groups here (not counting the African American group) are any indication of general practices within these communities, the total annual value of these philanthropic transfers would be in the hundreds of millions of dollars, and possibly higher.

Members of ethnic communities often report caretaking activities that in the mainstream society are more likely to be performed by government and nonprofit organizations. This study did not systematically compare ethnic philanthropy practices with those of the dominant culture, but some apparent differences were revealed in participants' statements with regard to care for the elderly, children and youth from troubled homes, and the needy. In some cases these differences were rooted in strong cultural values, such as respect for the elderly. Generally the ethnic caretaking practices were brought over from the homeland. In many cases there was a noticeable element of reciprocity: People care for elderly parents partly in the hope that their children will care for them in later years.

Many respondents expressed surprise and even shock at the way mainstream Americans dealt with the elderly and other vulnerable populations. To some respondents, it was unthinkable that one's parents or grandparents would have to finish their years in a nursing home.

Higher income respondents consistently spoke of their obligation to help others in their community achieve success in the same way they themselves were helped by members of their family and community. While people of color are disproportionately represented in lower-income groups, some groups and some members of all groups have achieved significant economic success. Do these people help the less fortunate in their own ethnic groups? The self-reports in this study suggest that this is generally the case. Many participants expressed strong feelings of obligation toward those in "the community" who had not fared so well. The assistance comes in many ways. Frequently people spoke of professionals who could have made more money by leaving the ethnic community but who took lower pay to serve in the community. Some of the successful made financial donations, such as to college scholarship funds. Volunteering was a common form of "payback": tutoring, coaching, or providing other services to young people. Jobs are an important form of payback. People in jobs that hire others try to hire some members of the ethnic community. Shop owners sometimes hire extra workers even when they don't need to.

Knowledge of people's ethnicity does not help to predict the proportion of their total yearly household expenditures or total number of hours a year they give outside their nuclear family, but knowledge of people's ethnicity does help to predict the forms and beneficiaries of giving and volunteering outside the nuclear family. One of the major conclusions of the study is that the apparent disparity between white and minority giving may be largely spurious, a result of the way questions are worded in national surveys. The national surveys report that whites give twice as much as blacks and Hispanics: Whites give about two percent of their income to charity while blacks and Hispanics give one percent or less. The present study showed that members of eight communities of color, including blacks and Hispanics, are extensively involved in sharing and helping. In these communities these activities are usually personal, direct, informal, and of their very nature not likely to be recorded and reported in tax returns and Gallup polls. The key question may turn out to be a definitional one: What do "charity," "philanthropy," "giving," and "volunteering" include? If the definition is restricted largely or exclusively to activities directed toward organizations, people of color will fall short. But if all giving of money, goods, and services outside the nuclear family is counted, people of color may turn out to be as generous as whites, if not more so. It must be stressed again that the present study did not test but rather generated this hypothesis.

It seems appropriate to end this report with a brief discussion of the concept of social exchange. It is clear to most who study charitable activity that there is some form of exchange in any act of sharing or giving (see, for example, Mixer 1993). Capitalist economies

are based largely on the idea and practice of economic exchange, but the interviews reported here clearly verify that other types of exchange are common. For example, contributions of money and time often result in social approval. Within the Asian communities in particular there is an explicit discussion of "face," or the dignity, prestige, and respect a person maintains in the community. Giving can bring prestige to the giver; conversely, giving must be done in a way that preserves the dignity and self-respect of the recipient. This process of maintaining "face" in the community is observed in all social groups, though perhaps with less self-awareness and discussion than found in the Asian groups studied here.

A related issue is the value of social cohesion, which can bring many benefits to the individual: identity, security, a feeling of belonging, protection from threats from outside, and the like. People want acceptance and recognition, want to feel part of a group. Helping and sharing create social cohesion and generate for individual givers the resulting benefits. Many of the giving customs identified in this study are used to establish and maintain social ties.

Finally, there is often an implicit social contract in giving and volunteering. Gifts of money and time are often made with the understanding that an obligation is being created that will be repaid at some time in the future or that an obligation is being discharged that was established at some time in the past. The notion of "payback" was present more or less subtly in all the groups studied.

References

Boorstin, Daniel J. 1969. *The Decline of Radicalism: Reflections on America Today.* New York: Random House.

Boulding, Kenneth E. 1981. *A Preface to Grants Economics: The Economy of Love and Fear.* New York: Praeger.

Carson, Emmett D. 1989. "Church Support of Individuals and Organizations: Patterns of Black and White Giving." 1989 Spring Research Forum Working Papers. Washington, DC: Independent Sector.

Chang, Betty L. 1983. "Care and Support of Elderly Family Members: Views of Ethnic Chinese Young People." In *Culture, Ethnicity, and Identity: Current Issues in Research*, edited by William C. McCready. New York: Academic Press.

Dalton, George. 1971. *Economic Anthropology and Development*. New York: Basic Books.

Espiritu, Socorro C., and Chester L. Hunt, eds. 1964. *Social Foundations of Community Development: Readings on the Philippines*. Manila, Philippines: R. M. Garcia Publishing House.

Geertz, Clifford. 1973. *The Interpretation of Cultures*. New York: Basic Books.

Gibbs, Jr. James. 1973. "Two Forms of Dispute Settlement among the Kpelle of West Africa." In *The Social Organization of Law*, edited by Donald Black and Maureen Mileski. New York: Seminar Press.

Gulliver, P. H. 1977. "On Mediators." In *Social Anthropology and Law*, edited by I. Mamnet. New York: Academic Press.

Hawke, David F. 1988. *Everyday Life in Early America*. New York: Harper and Row.

Mintz, Steven, and Susan Kellogg. 1988. *Domestic Revolutions: A Social History of American Family Life*. New York: The Free Press.

Mixer, Joseph R. 1993. *Principles of Professional Fundraising: Useful Foundations for Successful Practice*. San Francisco: Jossey-Bass.

Schlesinger, Arthur M. 1944–45. "Biography of a Nation of Joiners." *American Historical Review* 50: 1–25.

Shoumatoff, Alex. 1985. *The Mountain of Names: A History of the Human Family*. New York: Vintage Books.

Smith, Bradford, Sylvia Shue, and Joseph Villarreal. 1992. *Asian and Hispanic Philanthropy: Sharing and Giving Money, Goods, and Services in the Chinese, Japanese, Filipino, Mexican, and Guatemalan Communities in the San Francisco Bay Area*. San Francisco: Institute for Nonprofit Organization Management, University of San Francisco.

Van Loo, M. Frances. 1990. "Gift Exchange: A Brief Survey with Applications for Nonprofit Practitioners." 1990 Spring Research Forum Working Papers. Washington, DC: Independent Sector.

CHAPTER 29

New Humanitarianism and the Crisis of Charity: Good Intentions on the Road to Help

Michael Mascarenhas

On December 26, 2004, in the Northern Hemisphere we watched and witnessed the human devastation from a massive 9.0 magnitude earthquake centered off the western shores of Indonesia. The earthquake triggered a series of devastating tsunamis that inundated the coasts of fourteen countries along the rim of the Indian Ocean, killing nearly 230,000 people, injuring tens of thousands more, and displacing more than 10 million men, women, and children. The scale of the harm to life and damage to the local economy, infrastructure, and government was unprecedented. In the days that followed, the South Asian tsunami became a truly global affair. Bombarded with media reporting and seduced by YouTube videos, we watched live as millions of helpless people lost their homes, livelihoods, and, in many cases, their lives. These horrific images, combined with the seemingly arbitrariness of their fate, provoked an outpouring of empathy and generosity of global proportions. Governments, corporations, and individuals[1] from around the world scrambled to offer aid, medicine, other vital supplies, and technical support to the helpless victims of this tragedy.

Airlines provided free travel for relief workers. The Coca-Cola Company and PepsiCo donated thousands of cases of bottled water. Drug makers and medical companies sent shipments of medical supplies and cash donations. Pfizer announced plans to donate $10 million to local and international relief organizations, including Save the Children and the International Rescue Committee, as well as about $25 million of its health-care products to the relief efforts. Bristol-Myers Squibb sent antibiotics and other supplies, in addition to a $100,000 donation through the American Red Cross. Abbott Laboratories' charitable fund donated supplies, including nutritional supplements, valued at $2 million, as well as an additional $2 million in cash. Merck made a cash donation of $250,000. Johnson & Johnson contributed $2 million in cash and matched employee donations to the Red Cross. General Electric pledged $1 million to the Red Cross's International Response Fund and $100,000 to the United Nations Children's Fund (UNICEF) (*Wall Street Journal* News Roundup 2004). Similar donations poured in from other corporate sectors and governments from around the world, and, within six months, official aid and private donations raised over $13 billion for the victims of this natural[2] disaster!

The emotional imagery of debris-laden coastlines, destroyed school buildings and decimated roads, tent camps and temporary shelters, and mass graves ensured that this story would not leave the public spotlight for some time. In the weeks that followed, the media turned its attention from relief efforts to restoration and recovery. It was at this point that large international nongovernmental organizations (INGOs) began to take center stage, for their participation as first responders was deemed a vital component of relief efforts to restore normal life in the region. Humanitarian agencies seized the media opportunity and pasted their logos on every available surface and raised their flags on every restored structure. And, for a while, we all felt rewarded for our efforts and hopeful about the future.

However, over the succeeding weeks, a different story came to the fore: the transparency and accountability of these large INGOs involved in the rebuilding of tsunami-ravaged areas. "I was exhausted and I was completely disillusioned with the entire [humanitarian] system," reflects Adrian Roberts, about his four-month volunteer experience with the Thai Red Cross. "I started seeing all of these organizations like World Vision and faith-based organizations," he recalled, "rebuilding people's homes and farming operations in the name of Christianity. . . . But there was no transparency. . . . Someone would get 'a five-star hotel' for [their] chickens," while other families "weren't being helped out. . . . Money was being spent," Roberts remembered, "Lots of money was being spent," but "many families who I helped weren't getting the help they desperately needed."

As the media pressed the issue of where the aid was going, we found out that diverting donations to other projects is a generally accepted practice of humanitarian organizations. In some cases, much of the aid pledged (about half, in some cases) never ends up reaching the poorest people affected by these disasters.[3] Much of the money raised is used to purchase urgently needed goods and materials, such as food and medicine; ambulances and mobile medical clinics, portable water, sanitation, and housing;

clothing, blankets, and other personal belongings. "Right after the tsunami hit, I volunteered for a local humanitarian organization involved in the delivery of emergency health services," recalled Naomi Cohen.

> On my first day I was able to acquire a large quantity of hospital coats. They needed that immediately. We had a whole bunch of doctors and nurses going over to Aceh, and they needed those gowns donated. I spent all day on the phone and was able to get a huge amount donated from hospital supply companies.

Gowns, in addition to [a] long list of necessary relief items, are donated from the private sector or purchased from government contractors or other suppliers—all located in donor countries. In other cases, international pledges, in some cases up to millions of dollars, take the form of redevelopment contracts that are given to domestic companies. These multinational for-profit companies then offer their technical assistance and engineering capacity, as well as other forms of expertise, necessary for extensive redevelopment projects in the devastated regions or countries. For example, as part of its pledge to the Sri Lanka Tsunami Reconstruction Program, the United States Agency for International Development (USAID) awarded CH2M Hill a $33 million contract to lead infrastructure redevelopment efforts in parts of Sri Lanka damaged by the tsunami.[4] Some of the redevelopment aid, however, was used to fund large-scale construction for tourism and other economic activities, which further displaces fishing and farming villages along attractive coastlines (Klein 2007). A humanitarian response of this scale, after all, could not help attracting some controversy about how funds were spent, and it is important that these types of funding issues are raised. The real question I want to explore, however, is: as the shared interests that make humanitarianism possible have grown and the networks among them have strengthened, how is this assemblage of global actors transforming the politics (decisions over who gets aid, when, and under what conditions) and power-knowledge dynamics (notions of expertise, data, and measurement) of humanitarian policy and practice? How are we to make sense of the complex formal and informal partnerships that seem to be forming among states, businesses, and civil society organizations as they join efforts—and change roles—in a concerted effort to alleviate the crisis conditions of the world's poor and dispossessed? How can this new humanitarian network be analyzed and understood? And how has the production of crises and understanding of need served to organize this particular humanitarian conjuncture?

In an effort to find empirical answers to these theoretical questions, I examine the unprecedented rise in nongovernmental organizations (NGOs) and their interconnected response with donor (Northern) governments and the business sector. What does it mean if private Northern NGOs and for-profit corporations channel large sums of government and private funds, resources, and people (employees and volunteers) to the Global South as a result of their involvement in new humanitarian efforts? A great deal of debate and scrutiny has arisen in response to the transfer or channeling of funds around the globe by government and nongovernment agencies interested in global security, terrorism, and migration. Governments have blocked bank accounts and confiscated assets when they determined that funds circulating around the world were tied to various forms of corruption or terrorism. One way to identify corrupt activities, criminals, and terrorists, governments argue, is to "follow the money." By comparison, the same sense of scrutiny or concern has not seemed to follow funds that circle the globe in the name of this new humanitarianism, in spite of their growth and magnitude. Total government funds transferred by and through Northern NGOs (i.e., from industrialized counties) from 1970 to 1990 alone increased

at twice the rate of international aid as a whole. In addition, government funding of Northern NGOs has grown at a faster rate than support for the general public during this period (United Nations Development Programme 1991). Why are Northern businesses so engaged in humanitarian efforts in the Global South? Walmart, for example, reported a $2 million donation to the Red Cross for tsunami relief, yet many of their employees rely on food stamps to subsidize their low wages in the United States. How can we understand this seemingly humanitarian contradiction? Wouldn't it make more sense to pay their employees higher wages and better benefits rather than advocate charitable measures to aid strangers around the globe? What is it about the current humanitarian complex that enables corporations to be good Samaritans, on the one hand, and callous employers, on the other? And to what extent are those charitable funds a direct result of exploitative labor practices and, in some cases, criminal behavior? As corporations like Walmart and JPMorgan Chase continue to funnel some of their profits to humanitarian causes, it becomes increasingly important to recognize the way in which these rising profits are generated in the name of good corporate citizenship and to question to what extent this charity is, in fact, a gift.

New Humanitarianism

The crisis conditions of the post–Cold War era, epitomized by virulent conflicts, inhuman genocides, and rising rates of inequality, have led to intense debates over the role and responsibility—and if we were truly honest with ourselves, the apathy and culpability—of the international community in the prevention of human suffering and intervention in genocidal events (Power 2013). Moreover, the changing nature of violence, as exemplified in the genocides in Kosovo and Rwanda—to name only two in "the age of genocide"—have called into question the principles of classic humanitarianism and the monopoly power of sovereignty, pertaining in particular to the violence of citizens. Critics have argued that traditional humanitarian aid, based on the principles of humanity, impartiality, neutrality, and independence, is not only unable to protect the most vulnerable but, in some cases, may have been complicit in their dispossession. "What got under my skin," writes Roméo Dallaire, the force commander for the United Nations Assistance Mission for Rwanda (UNAMIR), in his memoir *Shake Hands with the Devil: The Failure of Humanity in Rwanda* (2003, 493),

> was the way the aid community so unthinkingly rallied behind its first principle: no matter what, they had to protect their neutrality. It was my opinion that, in this new reality we had all inherited, they were defining their independence so narrowly it often impeded their stated aims.

This neutrality that NGOs clung to, Dallaire (2003, 493) insists, "needs to be seriously rethought."

But it is not only humanitarian organizations that have clung to the principle of neutrality when marshalling their efforts to aid the dispossessed. In their countless opportunities to mitigate and prevent slaughter, Samantha Power (2013) writes, US policy makers and presidents clung to their neutrality and insisted that genocidal affairs in other sovereign states were not their business. However, Dallaire observes that when NGOs were given military escort by the Rwandan Patriotic Front (RPF), which, in effect, granted them sovereign protection, they "moved in to feed and aid these supposedly displaced," while also "providing aid and comfort to a belligerent" (2003, 299). From Dallaire's vantage point, the relief work of some NGOs and the inaction of the international community "aided and abetted genocide in Rwanda" (2003, 323). Recalling the failure of the United

Nations Security Council and the international humanitarian community to act in a decisive manner in Rwanda and the former Yugoslavia, then–Secretary-General Kofi Annan asked, "if humanitarian intervention is, indeed, an unacceptable assault on sovereignty, how should we respond to a Rwanda, to a Srebrenica, to gross and systematic violation of human rights that offend every precept of our common humanity?" (United Nations 2014).

The debate at the heart of Annan's inquiry and Dallaire's concern was whether states have unconditional sovereignty over their affairs or whether the international community has a responsibility to intervene in a country for humanitarian purposes, and at what point does the right to intervene supersede state legitimacy? In 2004, the High-Level Panel on Threats, Challenges, and Change, set up by Annan, declared that the international community had a responsibility to protect people, by force if necessary, "in the event of genocide and other large-scale killing, ethnic cleansing and serious violations of humanitarian law which sovereign governments have proved powerless or unwilling to prevent" (High-Level Panel on Threats 2004, 57). In effect, this "new humanitarianism" gave the international community the right to intervene in sovereign affairs when it deemed necessary. In September 2005, at the United Nations World Summit, all member states formally accepted this R2P[5] principle ushering in a new global era in humanitarian governance.

Fiona Fox (2001, 275) argues that this "new humanitarianism" is "principled, human rights based, politically sensitive, and geared towards strengthening those forces that bring peace and stability to the developing world." Whereas actors engaged in classic humanitarianism—most notably, Médecins Sans Frontières (MSF; Doctors Without Borders) and the International Committee of the Red Cross (ICRC)—have generally defended their practice on ethical terms and resisted attempts to instrumentalize it, the new humanitarianism is directly

TABLE 29.1 Classic Humanitarianism and New Humanitarianism

Classic Humanitarianism	New Humanitarianism
Humanity	Directed
Impartiality	Limited
Neutrality	Principled
Independence	Political
Universal	**Instrumental**

instrumental, guiding purposive action for specific outcomes—such as overthrowing oppressive groups or regimes, maintaining peace, and introducing democracy (see Table 29.1).

In addition to introducing new actors, new humanitarianism has also blurred the boundaries of what constitutes humanitarian intervention and relief, extending them to include the training of armed forces, the support of international human rights reform, and the strengthening of the domestic justice system through regulatory reform or regime change (Labbe 2012). In effect, this ends the distinction between development and humanitarian relief by linking aid and charity to broader political and economic decision-making structures (Fox 2001; Labbe 2012; Neuman 2012). In making this observation, I am not suggesting the classic humanitarian intervention somehow lacked political and economic motivations. However, what distinguishes new from classic humanitarianism is the way in which human rights issues and political and economic reform are now joined with humanitarian intervention. In the future, Fox (2001, 280) writes, "responding to human needs will be conditional on achieving human rights and wider political objectives."

However, although it may relegitimize the role and responsibilities of the international community in the face of extreme poverty, human conflicts, and even genocide, new humanitarianism also signals the rejection of a universal right to relief in times of crisis. In effect, this technique of humanitarian governmentality

permits the creation of "deserving and undeserving victims" (Fox 2001). Who becomes deserving and not deserving in this new goal-oriented system of relief is unclear. However, one thing is certain: decisions about who is deserving and who is not will be made based on more than need alone, leading to decisions in which aid might be withheld or suspended because of broader political and or economic objectives, or in which racial, ethnic, gender, or religious identities might influence or even take precedence over human suffering. It begs the question as to whether the international humanitarian community should be making life and death decisions—decisions previously associated with state sovereignty—in the Global South. And, if so, on what grounds will these highly political decisions be made, given the complicated and uneven power-knowledge dynamics within the global humanitarian complex?

The "State of Exception"

If the South Asian tsunami has taught us anything, it is that one enduring feature of the postcolonial condition has, and continues to be, humanitarian emergencies. Consider the genocides in East Timor, Rwanda, Congo, Liberia, Sierra Leone, and the former Yugoslavia; the ongoing ethnic conflict between Israel and Palestine; the enduring conflicts in Iraq, Afghanistan, Yemen, and, now, Syria; the current humanitarian crises in Darfur and South Sudan; and the most recent earthquakes in Haiti, China, Japan, and Italy. Walter Benjamin's (1942, 392) well-known formula that "the 'state of exception' . . . has become the rule" increasingly appears to be not only a technique of government but also a subjective fact of life shared among those in the North as well as the South (Agamben 2005). Nowhere is this relationship more pronounced than in the humanitarian spectacle that engulfed the tiny Caribbean country of Haiti, dubbed by some the "NGO Republic of Haiti," after its devastating earthquake in 2010. The worst natural disaster in the history of the Western Hemisphere also swiftly became a lightning rod for the stark contradictions and lopsided relationships embedded in today's humanitarian complex.

These enduring, and by some measures worsening, conditions of global poverty and insecurity have prompted a humanitarian response by civil society organizations of epic proportions. Data assembled by the Union of International Associations (UIA) show that three-quarters of the estimated 27,472 INGOs active in 2005 were formed after 1975 (Union of International Associations 2008). Employment at nonprofit organizations in the United States grew every year between 2000 and 2010 despite two recessions. According to a recent Urban Institute report, the number of nonprofit organizations in the United States increased 25 percent, meaning that their growth rate exceeded that of both industry and government over that decade (Salamon, Sokolowski, and Geller 2012). The annual Giving USA report on philanthropy reported that charitable giving rose 3.5 percent in 2012, to $316.23 billion, an all-time record that surpassed the high-water mark of $311 billion before the financial crisis began in 2007 (Center on Philanthropy 2013). In 2010, public charities in the United States alone, the largest component of the nonprofit sector in the country, reported $1.51 trillion in revenue, $1.45 trillion in expenses, and $2.71 trillion in assets. The 21st Century NGO report

stated that the not-for-profit sector "could now rank as the world's eighth-largest economy" (Beloe et al. 2003). This now-thriving sector employs more than 19 million people and is rapidly becoming the career of choice for many college graduates in fields from engineering and the social sciences to law and those with a master's degree in business administration. Moreover, charity workers' salaries have started to rise rapidly in recent years, with those in executive positions often earning incomes of more than six figures, making humanitarianism an attractive career choice (Canadian Broadcasting Corporation 2011). According to the 2012 Urban Institute report, in addition to rising donations and employment opportunities, more than one-quarter (27 percent) of adults in the United States volunteered with an organization (Blackwood, Roeger, and Pettijohn 2010).[6]

New humanitarian government and governmentality,[7] as expressed in the Haiti earthquake and the South Asian tsunami relief efforts, have created a way to penetrate the Global South and ignore existing laws, conventions, or constraints (Duffield 2007). Moreover, Mark Duffield (2007) suggests that this newly acquired authority to describe and define the crisis conditions among the world's poor has ensured that so-called civil society actors now wield significant international political and economic power. Some scholars have argued that their endless decision-making authority concerning how particular humanitarian conditions are defined, who will be helped, how to go about helping them, and, consequently, who can be left behind amounts to a new form of sovereignty or even empire (Barnett 2011; Foucault 1997, 2008; Hardt and Negri 2001). This type of political and economic power does not reign over citizens, per se, but, rather, populations of people that are described and organized with particular conditions, such as water insecurity, ill health, or poverty (Barnett 2011; Chatterjee 2004). The strength of this nonstate or petty sovereign power, as I illustrate, comes not only from its ability to form boundaries around particular territories, peoples, and ideas but also from its ability to transgress geographic boundaries, translate meanings, and transform value, all in the name of humanitarianism. Making these thick[8] and obscure sites of humanitarian production visible offers us a glimpse of the political and economy systems, knowledge-making practices, and institutional networks associated with a global humanitarian assemblage, which seeks to do massive social good in the face of mounting humanitarian crises.

As a result of their involvement in humanitarian efforts, multinational corporations, such as CH2M Hill, are not simply rebuilding productive infrastructure that had been damaged or destroyed by a tsunami, earthquake, or war. Rather, these actors are now productive agents in a humanitarian aid/development complex that seeks to reassert and extend its humanitarian mission through its interactions with multiple and interconnected sites of production from the boardroom of CH2M Hill to the shores of Sri Lanka. It therefore becomes important to assess the degree to which CH2M Hill's humanitarian effort in Sri Lanka is as much about bridge engineering as it is also about social engineering. Similarly, we need to ask to what extent Water for People's baseline assessment in Rwanda is as much about counting existing water and sanitation facilities as it is also about producing certain types of knowledge and expertise. These new thick transnational assemblages, most often associated with military and security functions and global development policy, are increasingly comingling the ethos of humanitarianism with the apparatuses of the global political economy. Indeed, it is becoming increasingly difficult to distinguish military from humanitarian intervention, as they have often become one [and] the same.

Although humanitarian crises in the Global South have benefited civil society actors and multinational corporations in the Global North, allowing them to ignore existing laws, conventions, and constraints and secure a foothold in otherwise prohibitive markets, such crises have also provided an economic boost to distressed countries. For example, the Asian Development Bank reported that the 2004 tsunami—paradoxically—brought a measure of stability to the Sri Lankan economy, which had been straining under growing macroeconomic imbalances (Weerakoon, Jayasuriya, Arunatilake, and Steele 2007). In Sri Lanka's case, the devastation from the tsunami provided an unanticipated source of foreign capital inflows for the relief and reconstruction effort and enabled the country to avoid a slide into a currency crisis. In effect, the tsunami prevented Sri Lanka from descending into a currency crisis and falling into a recession.

However, although the ongoing crisis conditions among much of humanity has provided the impetus for rethinking the modern humanitarian system and its moral sentiments, very little attention has been given to the way in which this transnational complex continues to expand throughout the globe, growing new productive tentacles, overlapping with and reinforcing other sectors of society, including academia, finance capital, agriculture, and information and communication technology, to name some of the most salient, and concomitantly interweaving new threads of power, politics, and indeed cultural change, into humanitarian theory, practice, and policy. The rapid growth of institutions involved in new humanitarianism has not only aided in its expansion as an ideology, a profession, and a new social movement but also influenced the means and methods by which we attempt to do massive social good in the face of global crisis conditions. It is crucial for us to understand how diverse institutions that spread throughout the world are being pieced together as part of a global agenda that is supposed to do massive social good, in an effort to locate and understand the types of logics, functions, and subjectivities that are embedded in this new global social project. Such knowledge and understanding are vital for thinking through the paradox of modern capitalism—a system that, on the one hand, has allowed unprecedented advances in the material conditions for some, and, on the other hand, has produced its opposite for others—"massive underdevelopment and impoverishment, untold exploitation and oppression" (Escobar 1995, 4).

The Present Humanitarian Conjuncture

Many development scholars and practitioners recognize the importance of President Harry S Truman's 1949 Inaugural Address as a watershed moment in constituting a global project of poverty alleviation and development of those countries and peoples who had suffered under colonialism. Truman ([1949] 1964) proclaimed that:

> More than half the people of the world are living in conditions approaching misery. Their food is inadequate. They are victims of disease. Their economic life is primitive and stagnant. Their poverty is a handicap and a threat to them and to more prosperous areas. . . . I believe that we should make available to peace-loving peoples the benefits of our store of technical knowledge in order to help them realize their aspirations for a better life.

This postwar development period pioneered an institutional reform of global proportions—one that would create complex interdependencies between so-called developed and underdeveloped countries. Since its inception more than sixty years ago, the notion of development has formed a remarkably stable problem-space within which contemporary questions about the growing polarity of postcolonial life and its relationship to state, market, and global civil society can be understood.

However, what began as a post–World War II era of state-led development to assist countries and people in the Global South recover from the ravages of war and colonialism, what Gillian Hart calls "development with a big D," has shifted to one in which nonstate actors have introduced an overtly interventionist approach to improving the human condition, "development with a small d" (Hart 2001, 2004, 2009).

Linking this form of intervention to the notion of humanitarianism—that a deep-[seated] human ethos or moral obligation exists to help improve and promote the welfare and flourishing of those in need—has made it difficult to foster a critical perspective on this form of aid/development policy and practice. How could one possibly be against this now universal principle of humankind? Moreover, the urgency associated with humanitarian crises in which [governments] and NGOs are scrambling with the immediate consequences of saving lives makes it acutely inconvenient to reflect on the causes of particular crises and how they may be prevented, or best mitigated, in the future. Given the particular urgency—lack of access to housing, medical services, food, or water—there is little tolerance for second guessing. "We just have to do our best" was the reprimand I received by another volunteer on a baseline assessment project in Rwanda to questions that others and I had raised about the method that continued to plague our analysis. "Facts," it seems, are a distant second in the race to do massive social good. Similarly, the steadily growing humanitarian caseload has led many practitioners dedicated to relief work and the protection of human rights to turn a blind eye to ethical matters of those who support their efforts. "Does it matter how funds are raised," some ask, "as long as it is contributing to social good?" In short, humanitarian government and governmentality has become a cultural commodity, and the pressures to get involved have resulted in the fact that "everyone's doing it" (Salamon 1994, 110).

Additionally, those on the frontline of redefining the cultural boundaries of the humanitarian system have asked, "What does it matter if executives of major humanitarian organizations are making six-figure salaries, if that is the cost of expertise in this and other sectors of society?" Moreover, the notion that free trade, self-regulating markets, good investments, and entrepreneurial ingenuity combined in the "right way" can ameliorate the crisis conditions of the world's poor is a provocative one. In many ways, this coming together of profit and welfare represents a new social contract for the twenty-first century—not a contract between citizen and state but, rather, a contract between rich and poor.[9]

NGOs continue to be a growing force in facilitating this new social contract. In addition to opening up to a number of nontraditional development actors, such as business and the military, NGOs have also cultivated partnerships with multilateral organizations such as the United Nations, the World Bank, the World Trade Organization, and the World Economic Forum in Davos. Over 1,550 INGOs have been granted consultative status by the Economic and Social Council (ECOSOC), and in 1997 an NGO Working Group was established as part of the United Nations Security Council (Opoku-Mensah 2001). At the same time, NGOs have started to take on more traditional roles of government in the name of humanitarianism, such as training of armed forces or volunteer groups on international norms and standards, advocating for the enactment of international law in domestic legislation, and strengthening of the domestic justice system regarding international human rights and refugee law (Labbe 2012). Not surprisingly, as NGOs' influence on global decision-making structures has increased, they have requested that the boundaries of humanitarianism be further expanded to include the areas of disaster risk reduction, long-term development programs, education, peacekeeping, conflict resolution, and human rights advocacy.

This new humanitarianism seeks to address not only the symptoms but also the systemic causes of humanitarian crises worldwide through the use of pre-emptive humanitarian intervention toward achieving human rights and political goals (Fox 2001; Macrae 2002). The question, then, is no longer whether NGOs are too close for comfort, as development scholars Michael Edwards and David Hulme (1996) asked a decade ago, but, rather, in what ways are they assembled and whose interests are best represented in this current formulation of modern humanitarianism.

Part of what makes this current humanitarian conjuncture so extraordinary is the way in which the convergence of finance capital, corporate philanthropy, social entrepreneurialism, and business management principles have converged and been reconfigured to solve the most pressing problem of modern society. Today, private aid has dwarfed official government aid several times over. This recent transformation means that future humanitarian support will largely hinge on the generosity of corporate philanthropy, not to mention the fluctuations of markets. This rapidly growing network connects investment bankers in New York, engineers in London, water technicians in Montreal, celebrities in Los Angeles, and volunteers from around the globe in an uncertain and ephemeral humanitarian assemblage.

The everyday discursive practices of new humanitarianism have proved to be powerful allies in reformulating the role of NGOs, which have increasingly become the conduit for forging all sorts of political and economic relationships, not only among countries within the North-South world system but also between rich people and poor people, or more specifically between the rich white minority in the North and the poor brown majority in the South. The persuasive power of new humanitarianism has helped NGOs receive funds from overseas governments, work as private subcontractors for local governments, and benefit from rising rates of corporate philanthropy. Therefore, the degree to which NGOs work in the service of imperialism, as James Petras (1999) has pointed out, receives little attention or is seen as a necessary evil in the larger global effort to do massive social good. The immediate consequence is that today new humanitarianism is still largely interpreted as an act of charity from Northern countries and business (Goldman 2005). Moreover, impediments to those acts of kindness are most often attributed to the innate corruption and irrationality of leaders or cultures of the Global South. "Corruption," World Bank president Kim warned, "is the biggest obstacle in the fight against poverty . . . it is simply stealing from the poor." In an effort to hold corrupt Bangladeshi officials accountable, Kim cancelled a $1.2 billion loan from the bank in support of the Padma Multipurpose Bridge project (World Bank 2012). However, corruption emanating from major donors in the North—Walmart, JPMorgan Chase, SAC Capital, and Johnson & Johnson, to name a few—is reduced to a few bad apples on the otherwise healthy humanitarian tree. This double standard, Michael Goldman (2005) argues, has deep colonial roots that profoundly influence our capacity to analyze the practice and outcomes of humanitarianism within its larger political and economic complex.

Changing the Way the World Tackles Poverty

The important question of how poverty can be eradicated is one that continues to disturb and agitate modern society. Despite years of intense Western involvement and trillions of dollars in charity and aid to so-called developing countries and humanitarian campaigns aimed at alleviating poverty and social insecurity, the welfare of the world's needy is not only still a problem but, as the United Nations (UN-Habitat 2003) and now the World Bank (Lakner and Milanovic

2013) have recently acknowledged, a problem that is actually worsening.

Debates rage over why poverty continues to increase. Within the expansive development literature, two opposing views have framed the way in which this postcolonial project has been both understood and implemented. Neither of these views does justice to the complex assemblages that constitute today's modern humanitarian practice and policy. However, both perspectives suggest that NGOS have an important role to play in the long-term fight against global poverty. One theoretical approach in the sociology of development literature has been to focus on development as a historically produced discourse or system of representation, language, and practice. This extensive body of critical scholarship extends colonial and feminist studies to reveal the many ways in which the technical discourse and strategy of development have produced its opposite—"massive underdevelopment and impoverishment, untold exploitation and oppression"—all the while obscuring the political effects (Appadurai 1990; Escobar 1995, 4; Rist 2008). Authors such as Homi Bhavva (1990), Chandra Mohanty (1991a, 1991b), Gilbert Rist (1997, 2008), and Edward Said (1979) have introduced new ways of thinking about representations of "third world" practices and peoples. Others in the development as discourse framework have chosen to examine the multitude and fragmented ways in which global domination or Empire is resisted, avoided, and negotiated (Burawoy 2001; Burawoy et al. 2000; Hardt and Negri 2004; Scott 1998). Within this perspective, NGOs are often theorized as enablers of uneven global development (Harvey 2006, 2010; O'Connor 1998; Smith 1998). Some scholars argue that they actually direct uneven development, thereby functioning as the "Trojan horses for global neoliberalism" (Wallace 2003). This perspective, however, tends to ignore the degree to which the convergence of finance capital, corporate philanthropy, social entrepreneurialism, and business management principles are shaping the way in which humanitarianism is both conceptualized and addressed by NGOs.

From an instrumentalist perspective NGOs are often seen as an important and necessary actor in influencing humanitarian policy and practice. In his book *Dams and Development. Transnational Struggles for Water and Power*, Sanjeev Khagram (2004) argues that the growing struggles and campaigns over human rights, as well as indigenous peoples and the environment, can be explained, in part, by the rapid rise of transnational NGOs. The rapid rise of transnational NGOs has become a common feature of world politics, Khagram argues. As "transnational nongovernmental organizations, coalitions, and networks interact over time," they influence "the degree to which norms and principles in issue areas, such as the environment, human rights, and indigenous peoples . . . spread globally and become institutionalized in the procedures and structures of states, multilateral agencies, and multinational corporations" (Khagram 2004, 18). However, for all the persistent optimism about the power of policy design to solve the problem of poverty, the instrumentalist perspective continues to ignore the politics of science and technology *in* humanitarianism. In so doing, critics argue, the instrumentalist perspective not only ignores long-standing traditions of domination but also contributes to permanent biopolitical restructuring—in defining the state of exception and necessity—of the world's poor (Agamben 2005; Escobar 1995; Hardt and Negri 2001).

The new visibility of NGOs as international government actors is a subject of growing interest among international relations and development scholars. Part of that attention has come from the rapid expansion of this newly (re)forming sector of civil society. In fact, NGOs have greatly proliferated in the past two decades, and some of the more established ones, such as Oxfam, Save the Children Fund, CARE, or World Vision, have expanded not only in size but also in the scope of their activities. These changes in both the magnitude and the scope of NGOs, together with growing concerns about their legitimacy, have repeatedly called for an urgent need to review and, in some cases, further transform the NGO sector (Beloe et al. 2003).

For instance, Weiss and Gordenker (1996) define NGOs as "a special set of organizations that are private in their form but public in their purpose," thus distinguishing them from either intergovernmental organizations (IGOs) or transnational corporations (TNCs). However, this characterization fails to acknowledge how both the form and practices of NGOs have become aligned with private and government interests alike. NGOs have become crucial to the United Nations' future and a salient phenomenon in international policy making and execution (Weiss and Gordenker 1996), and, at the same time, they have also been at the forefront of reforming humanitarian consultancy, education, entrepreneurialism, and financial services (Bebbington 1997).

The challenge to understanding the role of NGOs comes in part from conventional ways of thinking about globalization, development, and humanitarianism. Most metanarratives condense all cultural developments into a single program or trajectory: the emergence of the global era. For example, modernization theory, argues that, over time, "underdeveloped areas" of the globe will emerge from traditional societies to modern. The causes of many problems associated with underdevelopment—lack of access to drinking water, poverty, and military conflict, for example—are assumed to be mostly internal to a given country, and the solutions to these social problems to lie in more ties to the West. This conventional approach to theorizing globalization and development often pits NGOs and other civil society groups against the incapacities of sovereign state power.

Moreover, even in making the observation that unregulated global markets have caused and continue to cause enormous harm to rich and poor societies alike, those at the so-called cutting edge of poverty reduction strategies continue to insist that maximizing economic integration is the best strategy in the war on poverty.

One goal of this [reading] is to challenge the deeply held belief that to achieve poverty reduction "there is no alternative" to integrating the poor into the global economy. This belief is rooted in the assumption that the crisis conditions of the world's poor and dispossessed are largely a result of their social exclusion from modern life and economy, and the only way to end this condition is to include and integrate them into the world economy. What makes this particular approach noteworthy is the manner in which investment strategies, business principles, and entrepreneurialism have converged in an effort to alleviate the rising rates of inequality and conspicuous poverty that has been the hallmark of the past forty years of neoliberalism. In addition to supporting an enhanced role for free trade and economic integration, this approach has also shifted the burden of poverty reduction strategies away from national and international aid to programs supported by private donations. In the past, aid from rich countries to African and Asian governments has tended to be in the form of large concessional loans or grants (Moyo 2010). The problem for debtor countries is that these loans often come with obligations, such as selling off commonly held resources, privatizing national industries, and removing protective trade barriers, in addition to repayment of principle and interest. This form of indebtedness amounts to a new and deepening system of dependency in which debtor countries are forced to relinquish the very government assets that are needed for urgent economic recovery and long-term repayment. Moreover, critics have observed that food aid can actually undermine local agricultural production by saturating local food markets, thereby adding to the burden of farmers who

were already struggling to sell their agricultural products on a heavily subsidized global commodities market. This shift from government aid to private investment, venture philanthropists argue, will reduce poverty by extending opportunities for economic integration in the developing countries and transition them away from the debt dependence that has epitomized national and international aid programs of the past forty years. In the absence of another political economic alternative, those involved in poverty reduction campaigns are encouraged to harness the power of markets in the war on poverty.

For their part, the non-profit sector have experienced unprecedented growth in recent years. In some instances, they have replaced failing government agencies or helped to staff particular bureaucracies with paid employees or volunteers. In other instances, they have become strategic business partners or investment vehicles that are traded on global markets. In still other instances, they have advanced information and communications technology (ICT) and platforms that support and enhance their transnational networks, and, in other cases, they are actively involved in research design and data collection associated with specific humanitarian projects or emergency relief efforts. Proponents of this rapidly growing humanitarian complex argue that it merges the power of finance, the generosity of corporate charity, the spirit of entrepreneurialism, and the acumen of business to "change the way the world tackles poverty" (Zaidman 2013). Yet in spite of what amounts to sovereign decision-making authority to give life and take it away, we know very little about how humanitarian needs and efforts are determined, how money is raised, spent, or invested, how markets are "enhanced," how technology is used, how expertise is established, and how poverty reduction programs are supposed to work, and why they usually fail. Moreover, we know very little about the manner in which these new transnational networks of humanitarianism are assembled, expand, or are maintained. More generally, however, it remains unclear to what extent this new humanitarian complex can cope with the conflicting ambitions of human welfare and profit maximization. When people set out to change the crisis conditions in most of the world, the devil is truly in the details.

Notes

1. At the time I was a graduate student at Michigan State University and, like so many others, felt compelled to donate as much as I could afford.

2. Questions continue to surface regarding the manner in which natural barriers, particularly coral reefs, mangroves, and sand dunes, have been removed to make way for shrimp farms, tourism, and other economic activities. Many countries across Asia, including Indonesia, Sri Lanka, and Bangladesh, have encouraged expansion of their aquaculture industries by destroying the coral reefs surrounding their beaches. Moreover, many reefs areas around the Indian Ocean have been exploded with dynamite because they impede shipping, an important part of the South Asian economy. This ecological damage, environmentalists argue, have left coastal communities around the world more vulnerable to natural calamities (Browne 2004).

3. Max Lawson of the charity Oxfam told CBC Radio. Lawson said when Hurricane Mitch ravaged Central America in 1998, only a third of the money promised got to the people of Nicaragua and Honduras (Canadian Broadcasting Corporation 2006).

4. AECCafe.com (www10.aeccafe.com/nbc/articles/view_article.php?articleid=292462&interstitial_displayed=Yes/). For more information on the redevelopment projects, see www.careers.ch2m.com/worldwide/en/engineering-projects/sri-lanka-tsunami.asp.

5. R2P states that sovereignty no longer exclusively protects states from foreign interference; it is a charge of responsibility that holds states accountable for the welfare of their people.

6. Volunteers contributed 15.2 billion hours, worth an estimated $296.2 billion.

7. Through this reading, I use the terminology of humanitarian government and governmentality.

Humanitarian government entails any attempt to shape with some degree of deliberation aspects of our humanitarian behavior. This conduct is conveyed according to particular sets of norms and interests that frame and constrain ways of thinking about questions of "doing good." Governmentality refers to the way in which humanitarian actors (state, business, and non-profits), exercise this control over, or govern, the way in which we think and act upon our humanitarian aspirations, practices, and policies.

8. Here I am referring to the strategy of anthropologist Clifford Geertz towards an interpretative theory of culture where thick description ethnography is used "in the hope of rendering mere occurrences scientifically eloquent" (Geertz, C. 1973, 28).

9. For all its consequence, this social contract is rarely subjected to empirical analysis at the macro level. Of course, there is much at stake in problematizing this now-dominant approach to poverty alleviation. My fear in conducting such an analysis is that it will alienate the very audience with whom I want to have a conversation. Moreover, it strikes me that "those in the thick" of this humanitarian complex will have little tolerance or time to be self-reflective about the politics of such an approach.

Bibliography

Agamben, Giorgio. 2005. *State of Exception*. Chicago: University of Chicago Press.

Appadurai, Arjun. 1990. "Disjuncture and Difference in the Global Cultural Economy." In *Global Culture: Nationalism, Globalization and Modernity*, ed. Michael Featherstone, 295–310. London: Sage.

Barnett, Michael. 2011. *Empire of Humanity: A History of Humanitarianism*. Ithaca: Cornell University Press.

Bebbington, Anthony. 1997. "New States, New NGOs? Crises and Transitions among Rural Development NGOs in the Andean Region." *World Development* 25:1155–1765.

Beloe, Seb, John Elkington, Katie Fry Hester, and Sue Newell. 2003. *The 21st Century NGO in the Market for Change*. London, UK: Sustainability. http://www.sustainability.com/library/the-21st-century-ngo/.

Benjamin, Walter. 1942. "On the Concept of History:" In *Walter Benjamin: Selected Writings: Vol. 43 1938–1940*, ed. Howard Elland and Michael W. Jennings, Cambridge, MA: Harvard University Press, 2003.

Bhavva, Homi. 1990. "The Other Question: Difference, Discrimination, and the Discourse of Colonialism." In *Out There: Marginalization and Contemporary Culture*, ed. Russell Ferguson, Martha Gever, Trinh T. Minh-ha, and Cornell West, 71–89. Cambridge, MA: MIT Press.

Blackwood, Amy S., Katie L. Roeger, and Sarah L. Pettijohn. 2010. "The Non-Profit Sector in Brief: Public Charities, Giving, and Volunteering, 2012." The Urban Institute, Washington, DC.

Browne, Andrew. 2004. "Tsunami's Aftermath on Asia's Coasts: Progress Destroys Natural Defenses." *Wall Street Journal*, December 31. http://onlinewsj.com/news/articles/SBI0443750029213098.

Burawoy, Michael. 2001. "Manufacturing the Global." *Ethnography* 2:147–159.

Burawoy, Michael, Joseph A. Blum, Sheba George, Zsuzsa Gille, Teresa Gowan, Lynne Haney, Maren Klawiter, Steve H. Lopez, Sean O'Riain, and Millie Thayer. 2000. *Global Ethnography: Forces, Connections, and Imaginations in a Postmodern World*. Berkeley: University of California Press.

Canadian Broadcasting Corporation. 2006. "How Charities Spend." *CBC News*. www.cbc.ca/news/background/asia_earthquake/how-charities-spend.html.

———. 2011. "Thousands of Charity Workers Earn Big Salaries: Report." *CBC News*, July 10. www.cbc.ca/news/canada/thousands-of-charity-workers-earn-big-salaries-report-1.1022805.

Center on Philanthropy. 2013. "Giving USA 2013. The Annual Report on Philanthropy for the Year 2013. 58th Annual Issue." Center on Philanthropy at Indiana University, Bloomington, IN.

Chatterjee, Partha. 2004. *The Politics of the Governed. Reflections on Popular Politics in Most of the World*. New York: Columbia University Press.

Dallaire, Roméo. 2003. *Shake Hands with the Devil: The Failure of Humanity in Rwanda*. Cambridge, MA: Da Capo Press.

Duffield, Mark. 2007. *Development, Security and Unending War. Governing the World of Peoples*. Cambridge: Polity Press.

Edwards, Michael, and David Hulme. 1996. "Too Close for Comfort? The Impact of Official Aid on Nongovernmental Organizations." *World Development* 24:961–973.

Escobar, Arturo. 1995. *Encountering Development. The Making and the Unmaking of the Third World*. Princeton: Princeton University Press.

Foucault, Michel. 1997. *Michel Foucault: "Society Must Be Defended." Lectures at the College de France, 1975–1976*, ed. M. Bertani and A. Fontana; gen. ed. Francois Ewald and Alessandro Fontana; trans. David Macey. New York: Picador.

———. 2008. *The Birth of Biopolitics: Lectures at the College de France, 1978–1979*. New York: Palgrave Macmillan.

Fox, Fiona. 2001. "New Humanitarianism: Does It Provide a Moral Banner for the 21st Century?" *Disasters* 25:275–289.

Geertz, Clifford. 1973. *The Interpretation of Cultures: Selected Essays*. New York: Basic Books.

Goldman, Michael. 2005. *Imperial Nature: The World Bank and Struggles for Social Justice in the Age of Globalization*. New Haven: Yale University Press.

Hardt, Michael, and Antonio Negri. 2001. *Empire*. Cambridge, MA: Harvard University Press.

———. 2004. *Multitude: War and Democracy in the Age of Empire*. New York: Penguin Press.

Hart, Gillian. 2001. "Development Critiques in the 1990s: Culs de Sac and Promising Paths." *Progress in Human Geography* 25:649–658.

———. 2004. "Geography and Development: Critical Ethnographies of D/development in the Era of Globalization." *Progress in Human Geography* 28:91–100.

———. 2009. "D/developments after the Meltdown." *Antipode* 41:117–141.

Harvey, David. 2006. *Spaces of Global Capitalism. Towards a Theory of Uneven Geographical Development*. London: Verso.

———. 2010. *The Enigma of Capital and the Crises of Capitalism*. New York: Profile Books.

High-Level Panel on Threats, Challenges and Change. 2004. "A More Secure World: Our Shared Responsibility." United Nations, New York.

Khagram, Sanjeev. 2004. *Dams and Development: Transnational Struggles for Water and Power*. Ithaca: Cornell University Press.

Klein, Naomi. 2007. *The Shock Doctrine: The Rise of Disaster Capitalism*. New York: Metropolitan Books.

Labbe, Jeremie. 2012. "Rethinking Humanitarianism: Adapting to 21st Century Challenges." International Peace Institute, New York.

Ladika, Susan. 2012. "Transforming Lives." *International Educator* 21:15–24.

Lakner, Christoph, and Branko Milanovic. 2013. "Global Income Distribution. From the Fall of the Berlin Wall to the Great Recession." World Bank Development Research Group Poverty and Inequality Team, New York.

Macrae, Joanna. 2002. "The New Humanitarianisms: A Review of Trends in Global Humanitarian Action." Overseas Development Institute, London, UK.

Mohanty, Chandra. 1991a. "Cartographies of Struggle: Third World Women and the Politics of Feminism." In *Third World Women and the Politics of Feminism*, ed. C. Mohanty, A. Russo, and L. Torres, 1–47. Bloomington: Indiana University Press.

———. 1991b. "Under Western Eyes: Feminist Scholarship and Colonial Discourses." In *Third World Women and the Politics of Feminism*, ed. Chandra T. Mohanty, Ann Russo, and Lourdes Torres, 51–80. Bloomington: Indiana University Press.

Moyo, Dambisa. 2010. *Dead Aid. Why Aid Is Not Working and How There Is Another Way for Africa*. London: Penguin Books.

Neuman, Michael. 2012. "The Shared Interests Which Make Humanitarianism Possible." *Humanitarian Aid on the Move Newsletter*. ED. 9 (March):2–4. http://reliefweb.int/sites/reliefweb.int/files/resources.Full%20Report_653.pdf.

O'Connor, James. 1998. *Natural Causes: Essays in Ecological Marxism*. New York: Guilford Press.

Opoku-Mensah, Paul. 2001. "The Rise and Rise of NGOs: Implications for Research." Institutt for Sosiologi og Statsvitenskap. www.svt.ntnu.no/iss/issa/0101/010109.shtml.

Petras, James. 1999. "NGOs: In the Service of Imperialism." *Journal of Contemporary Asia* 29:429–440.

Power, Samantha. 2013. *A Problem from Hell. America and the Age of Genocide*. New York: Basic Books.

Rist, Gilbert. 1997. *The History of Development from Western Origins to Global Faith*. London: Zed Books.

———. 2008. *The History of Development: From Western Origins to Global Faith*. 3rd ed. New York: Zed Books.

Said, Edward. 1979. *Orientalism*. New York: Vintage Books.

Salamon, Lester M. 1994. "The Rise of the Nonprofit Sector." *Foreign Affairs* 73:109–122.

Salamon, Lester M., S. Wojciech Sokolowski, and Stephanie L. Geller. 2012. "Holding the Fort: Nonprofit Employment During a Decade of Turmoil." Johns Hopkins Center for Civil Society Studies, Baltimore, MD.

Scott, James C. 1998. *Seeing Like a State: How Certain Schemes to Improve the Human Condition Have Failed*. New Haven: Yale University Press.

Smith, Neil. 1998. "Nature at the Millennium: Production and Re-enchantment." In *Remaking Reality: Nature at the Millennium*, ed. Bruce Braun and Noel Castree, 271–285. New York: Routledge.

Truman, Harry. [1949] 1964. *Public Papers of the Presidents of the United States: Harry Truman*. Washington, DC: U.S. Government Printing Office.

UN-Habitat. 2003. *The Challenge of the Slums: Global Report on Human Settlements 2003*. London: United Nations Human Settlements Programme.

Union of International Associations. 2008. *Yearbook of International Organizations 2007/2008: Volume 5: Statistics, Visualizations, and Patterns*. Brussels: Brill.

United Nations. 2014. "The Responsibility to Protect." Department of Public Information, United Nations, New York. www.un.org/en/preventgenocide/rwanda/pdf/Backgrounder%20R2P%202014.pdf.

Wallace, Tina. 2003. "NGO's Dilemmas: Trojan Horses for Global Neoliberalism." *Socialist Register* 40:202–219.

Wall Street Journal News Roundup. 2004. "Tsunami's Aftermath: Donations Pile in From Companies, Individuals." *Wall Street Journal*, December 30. http://online.wsj.com/news/articles/SB110424799797311011.

Weerakoon, Dushni, Sisira Jayasuriya, Nisha Aruna-tilake, and Paul Steele. 2007. "Economic Challenges of Post-Tsunami Reconstruction in Sri Lanka." Asian Development Bank Institute, Tokyo, Japan.

Weiss, Thomas, and Leon Gordenker. 1996. *NGOs, the UN, and Global Governance*. Boulder: Lynn Rienner.

World Bank. 2012. "World Bank Statement on Padma Bridge." World Bank, Washington, DC.

Zaidman, Yasmina. 2013. "An Approach to Building Diverse Global Networks and Unlikely New Alliances in an Interconnected World." Paper presented at "Framing the Global" Conference. September 26–28. Indiana University, Bloomington, IN.

PART IX

Theories of Relations and Collaboration Within and Between Sectors

Relationships among the public, business, and NGO sectors have undergone enormous changes repeatedly in many countries especially since the decade of the 1980s.[1] As a prime example in the United States, prior to Medicare and Medicaid (1966) and the early years of deinstitutionalization of persons with mental illness and intellectual challenges starting in the 1970s, few nonprofit organizations in any field depended on government funding.[2] Private donations were the primary source of revenue for most nonprofit organizations. Since then, however, government reliance on nonprofits in the U.S. for the provision of public goods and services has grown enormously especially in healthcare and for persons with mental illness, disabilities, youths and gangs, families, victims of abuse; to support and coordinate the arts; and to provide financial and political support, for example, for national parks, seashores, and rivers. Government funds reach nonprofit organizations through many paths. National government funds are distributed to provinces or states as grants, and these funds often flow to nonprofit organizations or to local governments that contract with NGOs for services. Some funds flow directly from government agencies to nonprofit organizations, such as research grants to research centers and universities.

Many cities, provinces or states, and counties no longer provide essentially any direct human services. They have contracted-out virtually all such services to organizations mostly in the NGO sector and have no service delivery capability left themselves.[3] Since the 1970s, the percentage of the NGO sector's income from sales of services and products directly to the general public, government agencies, and for-profit firms has increased markedly.[4] Many nonprofits have become aggressively commercial in their organizational strategies, often competing for business directly with businesses.

The nonprofit sector has always been positioned rather delicately between the business sector's market orientation and the government sector's drive to meet social needs. Despite the existence of rather clear boundaries between nonprofit organizations and organizations in the public and business sectors prior to the 1970s, the existence, roles, and functions of NGOs have always been affected by changes in the other two sectors. The impacts of the government changes resulting from the global Great Recession, the Arab Spring, and the U.S. Tax Reform Act of 2018 are vivid examples. Dramatic changes in the two other sectors that have continued into the new millennium continue to have impacts on organizations in the nonprofit sector.[5] Although the long-term trend toward the "blurring and blending of the sectors" has been widely acknowledged for many years,

 DOI: 10.4324/9780367696559-38

the nature, substance, and magnitude of the blending and blurring continue to change and also the resulting implications.

In the 1980s and 1990s, the phrase "blending and blurring of the sectors" usually meant contractual arrangements for the delivery of government services by nonprofits accompanied by heavy dependence of these nonprofits on the government for revenue, and entrepreneurial ventures by nonprofits that compete with for-profit firms (often called "social entrepreneurship"). Since the 2000s, "blending and blurring of the sectors" now also includes myriad partnerships, networks, hybrid organizations, and collaborative arrangements. Indeed, it can be argued that the most significant change in the practice of public administration over the past decade has been the emergence of partnerships and networks as the preferred means for accomplishing governments' domestic aims, and many of these partnerships are with NGOs.

Government funding for domestic services in many countries has been in a long-term decline, including in the U.S.[6] Liberals and conservatives alike in nations' capitals and statehouses continue to clamor for governments to be *downsized*, for the *devolution* of government services and fiscal responsibility to the lowest levels of government possible, and for the *diffusion* of government services and responsibility out into the NGO and for-profit sectors.[7] At the same time, nonprofits have been told they must be more businesslike if they hope to survive and grow. In particular, they must be more entrepreneurial in pursuing alternative sources of revenue, and they must manage their resources and programs more efficiently. And now, NGOs must also be integral members of partnerships with other NGO providers, government agencies, and businesses in order to be included in community networks that receive funding to solve or ameliorate societal problems. *Blending and blurring* is shorthand for the obvious: The more NGOs enter into long-term relationships with other organizations in all three sectors, and as they continue to be more and more dependent on each other, the more they share basic assumptions and the more they think and act similarly. Hybrid organizations—organizations that are partially in more than one sector—are even more dramatic examples of the blurring.[8]

These partnerships require deeper and more subtle forms of relationships, adding new complexities to the governance and management of NGOs and their relationships with other organizations.[9] A representative example has emerged as more and more government agencies and intermediate funding agencies such as the United Ways and private foundations are requiring community-wide collaborations among key organizations from all sectors as a condition for receiving grant funding.[10] Also, *network organizations* that are partly government and partly nonprofit have emerged as funding agencies, policy makers, and service providers have come to realize that no single organization or group of organizations in any one sector can have effective impacts on our most intractable social problems.[11]

Network approaches or *network theories of organization* represent a body of literature that starts from the assumption that all organizations depend for success—indeed for their survival—on their environments, and their environments consist of complex relationships and interactions among a variety of actors including "key suppliers, resource and product consumers, regulatory agencies, and other organizations that produce similar services and products."[12] While most organization theories see the environment as a *place* of transaction, a *source* of resources and legitimacy, and/or a *space* of competition, the network approaches view the organizational environment as a complex *web* of actual interactions and relationships among organizational actors. The networks constrain actors and in turn are shaped by them.[13]

"Collaboration" within partnerships and networks does not occur automatically. Collaboration across organizational and sectoral boundaries requires different leadership skills and attitudes about "owning" solutions to problems. (See the discussion about *community leadership* in Part VI.) Collaboration requires serious effort.[14] Somewhat surprisingly, nonprofits have been quite successful at meeting these challenges. Their successes, however, have created in turn numerous new challenges.[15,16]

Partnerships Among Organizations in the Public and Nonprofit Sectors

As the nonprofit sector emerged as the preferred deliverer of public services in the U.S. in the 1970s and 1980s, government became the primary source of revenue for nonprofits in several large subsectors.[17] The percent of total income that nonprofits receive from government varies by organizational purpose and program function, from a high in social and legal services to a low in education, advocacy, and the arts. Smith and Lipsky have been among the most articulate in describing the deep and lasting effects that dependence on government funding have on the governance, leadership, management, and character of organizations in the nonprofit sector. As dependence has grown, the lines that separate the sectors may have become more blurred than is good for government, the nonprofit sector, or for a society.[18]

Since the "Great Society" era of the 1970s, the U.S. government has imposed numerous administrative requirements on states and municipalities as conditions for receiving grants, including personnel systems and practices, budgeting procedures, and financial reporting standards.[19] For decades, the U.S. government attempted to strengthen the administration of state and local government agencies, and these agencies used similar approaches and tactics with contracted nonprofit service providers. Eligibility for contracts and contract awards often have been conditioned on nonprofits adopting government-like systems, policies, procedures, and practices. The substance of the requirements varies, but most are intended and thereby protect records of employees, clients, unserved individuals, records, and fiscal resources.

Some have argued that these government requirements with increased resource dependence have diminished the independence of nonprofits.[20] Others counter-argue that reliance on government funding does not necessarily decrease the ability of contracted nonprofits to remain true to their missions or to their community roots.[21] Whereas some argue that government's influence on the administration of a contracted nonprofit far exceeds the percent of income received from government,[22] others caution that "the source of resources determines the type of and standards for success and failure, the character of decision making, accountability, and the external relations of an organization."[23] Probably all of these arguments are at least partially correct. The standards and requirements that government agencies impose on contracted nonprofits can be stifling, but the resources provided by government contracts can support expanded services and innovations.[24]

Some effects of resource dependence appear to be predictable: The longer a nonprofit relies extensively on government contracts, the more it will tend to look, think, feel, and act like a small (or not so small) government agency.[25] Therefore, "one of the necessary shifts in intersectoral theory . . . is the abandonment of the notion of the third sector as independent."[26]

Other factors and trends have contributed to the blurring of the lines between the government and nonprofit sectors. As direct service provision shifts from government to nongovernmental providers, "where the action is" for employees moves also.[27] Nonprofit managers accept positions with municipal and state agencies, and government employees move out into nonprofit organizations. The managers in government funding agencies today may be the nonprofit service deliverers of tomorrow, and vice versa. Assuming that this movement continues, the historic differences in perspectives between employees in the two sectors eventually will diminish if not vanish.[28]

In another important trend, contracting relationships—the interorganizational means by which contracts are administered and monitored—have been steadily evolving away from traditional arms-length, legalistic contract relationships toward long-term partnership-like relationships.[29] Especially in human services systems, contract relationships have developed into problem-solving partnerships, network organizations, and hybrid organizations often with multiple players from more than one sector. Sooner or later, close working partnerships lead to increasingly shared perceptions, values, expectations, standards, and interdependence among organizations in the sectors. The dependence of nonprofits on government funding is not single-directional. Governments become dependent on NGOs and businesses. These inter-dependencies are potentially both "good news" and "bad news" for nonprofits, government agencies, clients, and the future of democratic civil society.[30]

Political scientists and public administration scholars have documented the enormous changes that outsourcing has had on governments worldwide.[31] The effects of the changes are felt most directly by civil service employees and lower- to middle-level public administrators, but they extend much further.

> [P]rogress may bring with it a weakening of neutral competence, merit, professionalism, and related values. . . .
>
> If we assume the worst, then reinventing government ["Reinventing government" includes but is not limited to contracting with nonprofits] as political ideology suggests the disempowerment of public employees and the career civil service. Privatization, debureaucratization, and decentralization reduce the size and scope of government; managerialism makes public servants more like corporate workers . . . and reinstate the politics/administration dichotomy. When central government is downsized and load shedding shifts government activities to the private or nonprofit sectors, public employees and organizations that represent them lose numbers, standing, influence and power. . . . Reinventing government tends to strengthen the hand of private sector forces, and to cause reallocations of power from legislative to executive branches.[32]

Obviously, globalization has had huge positive impacts on the economies of many countries, developed and lesser developed. The literature on globalization, however, has also contributed to the understanding of the effects of globalization's increased involvement of local and outside-of-the country businesses on sovereignty and governments' functioning, including public policy formulation.[33]

The negative effects of blurring between the public and NGO sectors should not be underestimated. Milward, Milward, and Provan[34] warn about the "hollow state" and the "gutting" of government's historic roles and functions that have occurred as nongovernmental organizations have taken over service delivery especially in the human services. "The issue of privatizing welfare raises the question and challenges long-standing notions of what constitutes the public arena and what responsibilities lie there."[35] Alexander, Stivers, and Nank take the argument a step further when they ask whether the blurring may threaten the future of civil society.[36]

While many nonprofits have increased their reliance on government contracts, the total amount of government money flowing into the human services, the arts, and environmental protection has declined in many countries in recent years including the U.S.[37] States or provinces, counties, and cities often have hesitated to replace these declining federal funds because reduced taxes tend to have strong public support. Although we are still early in the Coronavirus pandemic, it appears quite certain that the financial impacts on NGOs will be enormous.

Blurring Between the Business and Nonprofit Sectors

Because of the downward trends in the nonprofit sector's traditional revenue sources noted in the preceding section, nonprofits have needed to become more businesslike, entrepreneurial, and innovative. They have been challenged to find and develop new sources of income, increase their efficiency, and create venture partnerships with businesses—to *be more like businesses* in all respects. Board members, managers, and employees have had to sharpen their skills and increase their professionalism. Many nonprofits have done surprisingly well at meeting this challenge in recent decades, but many others have not and have closed their doors. The movement of NGOs into entrepreneurial business-like ventures is known as *social entrepreneurship*. Businesses also engage in social entrepreneurship. But whereas NGOs pursue entrepreneurial revenue generating ventures largely to support their mission, businesses engage in entrepreneurial ventures because:

> The social entrepreneur aims for value in the form of large-scale, transformational benefit that accrues either to a significant segment of society or to society at large. . . . The social entrepreneur's value proposition targets an underserved, neglected, or highly disadvantaged population that lacks the financial means or political clout to achieve the transformative benefit on its own. This does not mean that social entrepreneurs as a hard-and-fast rule shun profitmaking value propositions. Ventures created by social entrepreneurs can certainly generate income. . . . What distinguishes social entrepreneurship is the primacy of social benefit.[38]

Being socially entrepreneurial can yield large benefits for for-profit firms. For example, high tech firms include statements about being socially entrepreneurial in ads for products and services, and especially for recruitment of highly skilled new employees.[39]

Nonprofit organizations have been venturing entrepreneurially into a variety of commercial markets for years, seeking new sources of revenue to support their mission-related activities. For example, nonprofits in the health care subsector have competed directly with for-profit businesses for decades.[40] Most nonprofit hospitals and clinics own for-profit subsidiaries that provide corporate wellness programs, own condominium physicians' offices, and manage private health clubs. Mental health agencies and other nonprofits that serve mostly low-income populations regularly buy and manage companies that operate apartment houses, provide janitorial and lawn care service, pet stores, laundries, and many other historically low-wage service businesses. Many of these commercial ventures by nonprofits have proven to be enormously successful, profitable, and have served their clients well.

NGOs' commercial ventures provide multiple benefits for clients who receive services and for the nonprofit organization as an entity. These ventures often create employment opportunities while also making more services available. Nonprofits have learned the importance of paying careful attention to legal requirements and tax codes in order to limit Unrelated Business Income Taxes (UBIT) and to preserve their tax-exempt status with the IRS and state taxing authorities. It is easy to understand why nonprofit organizations' commercial ventures have incited vociferous cries of "unfair competition" from small businesses and legislators.[41]

Several other factors have contributed to the blurring of the line between the business and nonprofit sectors. First, for-profit businesses have "invaded turf" that historically had been served essentially exclusively by government agencies and nonprofit organizations. For example, for-profit chains have replaced nonprofits as the primary providers of hospital care in the United States. Private emergency medical services (EMS) companies have all but driven nonprofit ambulances out of urban and suburban markets and have made inroads in many rural areas. For-profits also have made aggressive entries in the fields of youth and adult corrections, mental health, intellectual challenges, substance abuse, and wellness.

Second, the professionalism of the managers of nonprofit organizations has increased dramatically. This has been necessary. Therefore, the number of professional master's degree programs and students has expanded nearly exponentially since 1980.[42] Nonprofit executives are often recruited from businesses, and in some subsectors they are paid *Fortune 500* wages.[43] "Passion for the cause" remains vitally important for NGO managers, and now also business management skills.

Third, a larger percentage of nonprofit organization directors—persons with policymaking responsibility—come from businesses while fewer are from government agencies and other non-profit organizations.

Finally, *social entrepreneurial* partnerships between businesses and nonprofits have become commonplace. Planned giving programs, social entrepreneurial ventures—including cause-related marketing—and businesses using nonprofit higher education research capabilities rather than investing in their own are only a few examples of intertwined relationships.[44]

In sum, nonprofit organizations have become more like businesses because:

- They are more businesslike in their revenue-generating activities—as they compete directly with profit-making businesses.
- They have been learning more about business ways of doing things and business perspectives from directors and executives recruited from businesses.
- They are gaining in their management sophistication as their personnel earn MPAs (masters of public administration), MNMs (masters of nonprofit management), MFAAs (masters of fine arts administration), MBAs (masters of business administration), and professional certificates.
- They are working collaboratively with businesses in partnerships and networks.

Lester Salamon warned that nonprofit organizations are in danger of losing public support and favored treatment from government *because they have been too successful in becoming like businesses.*[45] Burton Weisbrod asks:

> As the nonprofit sector grows in size and commercial activities, is it becoming indistinguishable from the private sector? . . . At its roots, this question asks whether nonprofit organizations deserve priority consideration for contracts and the favorable tax treatment they receive from national, state, and local governments.[46]

Conclusion

In this part on relationships within and among the sectors, we have attempted to pull important themes together that were introduced in most of the earlier chapters. Understanding the advantages, concerns about, and complexities of intra- and inter-sectoral relations, partnerships, social entrepreneurship, and collaborations requires knowledge about underlying factors and forces, including the sector's history and cultural roots, its distinctive values and contributions to society (Parts I, II, and III); the justification for tax exemption and tax deduction (Part IV); and the range of theories and research about the sector's existence, roles, and functions (Parts V through VIII).

Readings Reprinted in Part IX

"The Point of Partnering" by Stuart Mendel and Jeffrey Brudney addresses a key question for academicians and practitioners: Are partnerships worth the time and effort required to create and maintain them? This reading "examines and illustrates the conditions under which partnership is more or less beneficial to nonprofit organizations." The authors report on how nonprofit partnerships with other nonprofits, government agencies, and business enterprises change expectations, approaches, methods, and outcomes. Mendel and Brudney examine the clusters of benefits that may be hoped for when establishing partnerships among organizations in the different sectors. In other words, expected benefits to the participants are different for a nonprofit–for-profit partnership than for a government–nonprofit partnership or a nonprofit–nonprofit partnership.

Lester Salamon and Stefan Toepler challenge widely shared skepticism about the possibility for extensive cooperation among nonprofit organizations and government agencies, in "Government-Nonprofit Cooperation: Anomaly or Necessity?" They point to the shortcomings in market failure theory and government failure theory (see Part V) that have obscured key features of the nonprofit sector that tend to make cooperation between nonprofits and government effective. They also identify limitations of the public sector that make partnerships with nonprofits a natural and useful path toward effectiveness of government services. The reading concludes with a set of conditions that must be met in order for government–nonprofit partnerships to achieve their potential.

> As it turns out, the strengths of the nonprofit sector as a provider of public goods nicely complement the limitations of government both in originating and delivering such goods, while the strengths of government as a generator of revenue and of rights to benefits nicely complement the limitations of the nonprofit sector in these same areas.

"Public-Private Partnership in Turbulent Times" by Graeme Hodge and Carsten Greve investigates the nature of public-private partnerships (PPPs) where government enters into partnerships with for-profit firms as well as nonprofit organizations drawing heavily from experience with PPPs in the U.K. and Australia. The reading has three parts: Part I examines the various forms of PPPs and the different levels of government where they tend to exist and serve different purposes; Part II focuses on the criteria for "success" of PPPs using recent literature on "policy success" as a guide; and Part III attempts to identify expected long-term impacts of the global financial crisis (GFC)—"the Great Recession"—of 2008 on PPPs and their success—including both optimistic and pessimistic views.

> [T]here is a movement underway . . . looking . . . towards what we will here term 'emerging partnerships', because they are emerging . . . [a]cross organizational borders as well as countries, and can be expected to be found at the local level, the national level, the international level or some combination of these.

Whereas the first three readings reprinted in this chapter focus on partnerships, "Comparing New Hybrid Governance Arrangements: Better and Smarter?" by Joop Koppenjan, Katrien Termeer, and Philip Marcel Karré assesses hybrid organizations and arrangements—formal and informal organizations that are partly public and partly private. According to the authors, "smart hybrids" usually are created to cope with "wicked problems" that cross the boundaries of sectors and jurisdictions. This reading aims to determine how much hybrid governance arrangements tend to be truly smart and hence whether they have indeed met the challenge of being "smart hybrids." The authors propose four groups of values for assessing the "smartness" of hybrid organizations: (1) effectiveness and efficiency; (2) innovative uses of information technologies; (3) other public values are adhered to, including particularly equality, rules of law, representation, and participation; and (4) sustainability and reliance are realized through periods of uncertainty and volatility, and the erosion of trust in societal institutions.

Notes

1. For experiences in other countries, see Lester M. Salamon and S. Wojciech Sokolowski, eds., *Global Civil Society: Dimensions of the Nonprofit Sector*, vol. 2. (Bloomfield, CT: Kumarian Press, 2004); Benjamin L. Read

with Robert Pekkanen, eds., *Local Organizations and Urban Governance in East and Southeast Asia* (London and New York: Routledge, 2009); and Shawn Shier, "Beyond Corporatism and Civil Society: Three Modes of State-NGO Interaction in China," in *State and Society Responses to Social Welfare Needs in China: Serving the People*, eds. Jonathan Schwartz and Shawn Shieh (London and New York: Routledge, 2009): 22–42.

2. Chris Koyanagi, *Learning from History: Deinstitutionalization of People with Mental Illness as Precursor to Long-Term Care Reform* (Washington, DC: Kaiser Commission on Medicaid and the Uninsured, 2007); National Council on Disability, *Deinstitutionalization: Unfinished Business* (Washington, DC: National Council on Disability, 2012). www.ncd.gov/publications/2012/Sept192012/

3. Smith, Steven R. and Michael Lipsky. *Nonprofits for Hire: The Welfare State in the Age of Contracting* (Cambridge, MA: Harvard University Press, 1993).

4. National Center for Charitable Statistics, *NCCS Quick Facts* (Washington, DC: Urban Institute, May 2006). http://nccsdataweb.urban.org/NCCS/Public/index.php. This trend has been challenged by Curtis Child in "Whither the Turn? The Ambiguous Nature of Nonprofits' Commercial Revenue," *Social Forces*, 89 (2010): 1–17.

5. Joseph J. Cordes and C. Eugene Steuerle, "The Changing Economy and the Scope of Nonprofit-Like Activities," in *Nonprofits and Business*, eds. Joseph J. Cordes and C. Eugene Steuerle (Washington, DC: Urban Institute Press, 2008), 47–82.

6. U.S. Government Accountability Office (GAO). *Nonprofit Sector: Increasing Numbers and Key Role in Delivering Federal Services* (GAO-07-1084T Washington, DC: U.S. Government Printing Office, 2007); J. Steven Ott and Lisa A. Dicke, "Evolving Relationships: Managing under Government Contracts, through Networks and in Collaborations," Part VII in *Understanding Nonprofit Organizations*, 2nd ed., eds. Ott and Dicke (Boulder, CO: Westview Press/Perseus Books, 2011).

7. J. Steven Ott and Lisa A. Dicke, "HRM in an Era of Downsizing, Devolution, Diffusion, and Empowerment . . . and Accountability?" in *Strategic Public Personnel Administration/HRM: Building Human Capital for the 21st Century*, Vol. 1, ed. Ali Farazmand (Westport, CT: Praeger, 2007): 67–84.

8. See, Joop Koppenjan, Philip Marcel Karré, and Katrien Termeer, "New Governance Arrangements: Towards Hybrid and Smarter Government?" in *Smart Hybridity: Potentials and Challenges of New Governance Arrangements*, eds. Koppenjan, Karré, and Termeer (The Hague, Netherlands: Eleven International Publishing, 2019): 11–28; and David Billis, ed., *Hybrid Organizations and the Third Sector: Challenges for Practice, Theory and Policy* (Houndmills, Basingstoke, and Hampshire, UK: Palgrave Macmillan, 2010).

9. Patricia Bromley and John W. Meyer, "'They Are All Organizations': The Cultural Roots of Blurring between the Nonprofit, Business, and Government Sectors," *Administration & Society*, First published September 4, 2014 at https://doi.org/10.1177/0095399714548268.

10. John Kania and Mark Kramer, "Collective Impact," *Stanford Social Innovation Review*, 9(1) (Winter 2011). www.ssireview.org/blog/entry/channeling_change_making_collective_impact_work?cpgn=WP DL—Channeling Change.

11. See Henrich Greve, Tim Rowley, and Andrew Shipilov, *Network Advantage: How to Unlock Value from Your Alliances and Partnerships* (San Francisco: Jossey-Bass/Wiley, 2014); and Daniel J. Brass, Joseph Galaskiewicz, Henrich R. Greve, and Wipin Tsai, "Taking Stock of Networks and Organizations: A Multilevel Perspective," *Academy of Management Journal*, 47 (2004): 795–817.

12. Paul J. DiMaggio and Walter W. Powell, "The Iron Cage Revisited: Institutional Isomorphism and Collective Rationality in Organizational Fields," *American Sociological Review*, 48 (1983): 148.

13. Hee Soun Jang, Jesus N. Valero, and Kyujin Jung, *Effective Leadership in Network Collaboration: Lessons Learned from Continuum of Care Homeless Programs* (Washington, DC: IBM Center for the Business of Government, 2016).

14. See for example, John C. Morris and Katrina Miller-Stevens, eds., *Advancing Collaboration Theory: Models, Typologies, and Evidence* (New York: Routledge, 2016); Dennis Young and John Casey, "Supplementary, Complementary, or Adversarial? Nonprofit-Government Relations," in *Nonprofits & Government: Collaboration*

Lanham, MD, Rowman and Littlefield, 2017); and Hee Soun Jang, Jesus N. Valero, and Kyujin Jung, *Effective Leadership in Network Collaboration* (IBM Center for the Business of Government, 2016).

15. Lester M. Salamon, "The Current Crisis," in *Holding the Center*, ed. L. M. Salamon (New York: Nathan Cummings Foundation, 1997).

16. Thomas Diefenbach and Rune Todnem, eds. *Reinventing Hierarchy and Bureaucracy: From the Bureau to Network Organizations* (Bingley: Emerald Group, 2012).

17. Steven R. Smith, "Transforming Public Services: Contracting for Social and Health Services in the U.S.," *Public Administration*, 74 (1996): 113–127; and U.S. Government Accountability Office (GAO), *Nonprofit Sector: Increasing Numbers and Key Role in Delivering Federal Services* (GAO-07-1084T Washington, DC: U.S. Government Printing Office, 2007).

18. Steven R. Smith and Michael Lipsky, *Nonprofits for Hire* (Cambridge, MA: Harvard University Press, 1993).

19. Chapters 2, 3, and 4 in Jay M. Shafritz, E. William Russell, Christopher P. Borick, and Albert C. Hyde, *Introducing Public Administration*, 9th ed. (New York: Routledge, 2017); and chapter 1 in B. Guy Peters, *The Politics of Bureaucracy: An Introduction to Comparative Public Administration*, 7th ed. (New York: Routledge, 2018).

20. Judith R. Saidel, "Resource Interdependence: The Relationship between State Agencies and Nonprofit Organizations," *Public Administration Review*, 51 (1991): 543–553.

21. James M. Ferris, "The Double-Edged Sword of Social Service Contracting: Public Accountability versus Nonprofit Autonomy," *Nonprofit Management and Leadership*, 3 (1993): 363–376.

22. Smith and Lipksy, *Nonprofits for Hire.*

23. Ralph M. Kramer, "Voluntary Agencies and the Contract Culture," *Social Service Review*, 68 (1994): 33–60.

24. See Seok-Eun Kim, "Balancing Competing Accountability Requirements: Challenges in Performance Improvement of the Nonprofit Human Services Agency," *Public Performance & Management Review*, 29 (2005): 145–163; J. Steven Ott and Lisa A. Dicke, "Important but Largely Unanswered Questions about Accountability and Contracted Public Human Services," *International Journal of Organization Theory & Behavior*, 3 (2000): 283–317.

25. Smith and Lipsky, *Nonprofits for Hire.*

26. Judith R. Saidel, "Dimensions of Interdependence: The State and Voluntary-Sector Relationship," *Nonprofit and Voluntary Sector Quarterly*, 18 (1989): 336.

27. J. Steven Ott and Lisa A. Dicke, "Accountability Challenges Facing Public Sector HRM in an Era of Downsizing, Devolution, Diffusion, and Empowerment," in *Strategic Public Personnel Administration: Building and Managing Human Capital for the 21st Century*, Vol. 2, ed. Ali Farazmand (Westport, CT: Praeger, 2007): 67–84.

28. Smith and Lipsky, *Nonprofits for Hire.*

29. Ruth H. DeHoog, "Competition, Negotiation, or Cooperation: Three Models for Service Contracting," *Administration and Society*, 22 (1990): 317–340; Thomas Diefenbach and Rune Todnem, eds. *Reinventing Hierarchy and Bureaucracy: From the Bureau to Network Organizations* (Bingley: Emerald Group, 2012); D. J. Brass, J. Galaskiewicz, H. R. Greve, and W. Tsai, "Taking Stock of Networks and Organizations: A Multilevel Perspective," *Academy of Management Journal*, 47 (2004): 795–817; Henrich Greve, Tim Rowley, and Andrew Shipilov, *Network Advantage: How to Unlock Value from Your Alliances and Partnerships* (San Francisco: Jossey-Bass/Wiley, 2014).

30. Judith R. Saidel, "Devolution and the Politics of Interdependence: Management and Policy Trade-Offs in Government-Nonprofit Contracting," paper presented at *The American Society for Public Administration*, Seattle, WA, May 9–12, 1998.

31. For example, H. Brinton Milward and Keith Provan, "Managing the Hollow State: Collaboration and Contracting," *Public Management Review*, 5(1) (2010), 1–18.

32. Richard C. Kearney and Steven W. Hays, "Reinventing Government, the New Public Management and Civil Service Systems in International Perspective," *Review of Public Personnel Administration*, 18 (1998): 39, 46.

33. For example, Stella Z. Theodoulou and Ravi K. Roy, *Public Administration: A Very Short Introduction* (Oxford: Oxford University Press, 2016), and Ali Farazmand, "Globalization, The State and Public Administration: A Theoretical Analysis with Policy Implications for Developmental States," *Public Organization Review*, 1(4) (1999): 437–463.

34. See H. Brinton Milward and Keith G. Provan, "Governing the Hollow State," *Journal of Public Administration Research and Theory*, 10 (2000): 359–380; and H. Brinton Milward, "The Increasingly Hollow State: Challenges and Dilemmas for Public Administration," *Asia Pacific Journal of Public Administration*, 36(1) (2014): 70–79.

35. Meghan Cope, "Responsibility, Regulation, and Retrenchment: The End of Welfare?" in *State Devolution in America: Implications for a Diverse Society*, eds. Lynn A. Staeheli, Janet E. Kodras, and Colin Flint (Thousand Oaks, CA: Sage, 1997): 181–205.

36. Jennifer Alexander, Camilla Stivers, and Renee Nank, "Implications of Welfare Reform: Do Nonprofit Survival Strategies Threaten Civil Society?" *Nonprofit and Voluntary Sector Quarterly*, 28 (1999): 452–475.

37. Amy Blackwood, Brice McKeever, and Thomas H. Pollak, "Which Nonprofit Sectors Were the Biggest Winners and Losers in 2014?" *Nonprofit Quarterly*, 2016; and Amy Blackwood, Kennard T. Wing, and Thomas H. Pollak, *The Nonprofit Sector in Brief: Facts and Figures on the Nonprofit Almanac 2008: Public Charities, Giving, and Volunteering* (Washington, DC: The Urban Institute, 2008).

38. Roger L. Martin and Sally Osberg, "Social Entrepreneurship: The Case for Definition," *Stanford Social Innovation Review*, 5(2): 2007.

39. See for example, Teresa Chahine, *Introduction to Social Entrepreneurship* (Boca Raton, FL: Taylor & Francis, 2016); MeiMei Fox, "5 Reasons Why Social Entrepreneurship Is the New Business Model," *Forbes* (August 2016); and G. Gregory Dees, "Taking Social Entrepreneurship Seriously: Uncertainty, Innovation, and Social Problem Solving," *Society*, 44(3) (2007): 24–31.

40. Since about 1995, however, nonprofit hospitals have been losing the competition.

41. U.S. Small Business Administration, *Unfair Competition by Nonprofit Organizations with Small Business: An Issue for the 1980s*, 3rd ed. (Washington, DC: U.S. Government Printing Office, June 1984). And nonprofit credit unions have been a huge "thorn in the side" of commercial banks for decades.

42. Roseanne M. Mirabella, "University-Based Educational Programs in Nonprofit Management and Philanthropic Studies: A 10-Year Review and Projections of Future Trends," *Nonprofit and Voluntary Sector Quarterly*, 36 (2007): 11S–27S; Naomi Wish and Roseanne Mirabella, "Educational Impact on Graduate Nonprofit Degree Programs: Perspectives of Multiple Stakeholders," *Nonprofit Management and Leadership*, 9 (1999): 329–340.

43. The *U.S. News and World Report's* October 2, 1995, cover story exclaimed: "Tax Exempt! Many Nonprofits Look and Act Like Normal Companies—Running Businesses, Making Money. So Why Aren't They Paying Uncle Sam?"

44. See for example, Georgia Levenson Keohane, *Social Entrepreneurship for the 21st Century: Innovation across the Nonprofit, Private, and Public Sectors* (New York: McGraw-Hill Education, 2013); Chao Guo and Wolfgang Bielefeld, *Social Entrepreneurship: An Evidence-Based Approach to Creating Social Value* (San Francisco: Jossey-Bass/Wiley, 2014); Paul C. Light, *The Search for Social Entrepreneurship* (Washington, DC: Brookings Institution Press, 2008); and Johanna Mair, Jeffrey Robinson, and Kai Hockerts, eds. *Social Entrepreneurship* (New York: Palgrave Macmillan, 2006).

45. Lester M. Salamon, "The Current Crisis," in *Holding the Center: America's Nonprofit Sector at a Crossroads*, ed. Lester M. Salamon (New York: Nathan Cummings Foundation, 1997).

46. Burton A. Weisbrod, "The Nonprofit Mission and Its Financing: Growing Links Between Nonprofits and the Rest of the Economy," in *To Profit or Not to Profit: The Commercial Transformation of the Nonprofit Sector*, ed. Burton A. Weisbrod (Cambridge: Cambridge University Press, 1998): 4.

Bibliography

Abramson, Alan, Lester Salamon, and C. Eugene Steuerle. "Federal Spending and Tax Policies: Their Implications for the Nonprofit Sector," in E. Boris and C. E. Steuerle (eds.), *Nonprofits and Government* (2nd ed.) (Washington, DC: Urban Institute Press, 2006): 118.

Afflerbach, Thomas. *Hybrid Virtual Teams in Shared Services Organizations: Practices to Overcome the Cooperation Problem* (London and New York: Springer, 2020).

Alexander, Jennifer, Camilla Stivers, and Renee Nank. "Implications of Welfare Reform: Do Nonprofit Survival Strategies Threaten Civil Society?" *Nonprofit and Voluntary Sector Quarterly*, 28 (1999): 452–475.

Alexius, Susanna, and Staffan Furusten, eds. *Managing Hybrid Organizations: Governance, Professionalism and Regulation* (London and New York: Palgrave Macmillan, 2019).

Battilana, Julie, Matthew Lee, John Walker, and Cheryl Dorsey. "In Search of the Hybrid Ideal," *Stanford Social Innovation Review* (Summer 2012): 51–55.

Berry, Frances Stokes, and Ralph S. Brower. "Intergovernmental and Intersectoral Management: Weaving Networking, Contracting Out, and Management Roles into Third Party Government," *Public Performance & Management Review*, 29 (2005): 7–17.

Billis, David, ed. *Hybrid Organizations and the Third Sector: Challenges for Practice, Theory and Policy* (New York: Palgrave Macmillan, 2010).

Boccardelli, Paolo, Maria Carmela Annosi, Federica Brunetta, and Mats Magnusson, eds. *Learning and Innovation in Hybrid Organizations: Strategic and Organizational Insights* (London and New York: Palgrave Macmillan, 2018).

Boris, Elizabeth T., and C. Eugene Steuerle, eds. *Nonprofits & Government: Collaboration & Conflict*, 3rd ed. (Washington, DC: Urban Institute Press, 2017).

Bornstein, David, and Susan Davis. *Social Entrepreneurship: What Everyone Needs to Know* (New York: Oxford University Press, 2010).

Bowman, Woods, and Marion R. Fremont-Smith. "Nonprofits and State and Local Governments," in E. Boris and C. E. Steuerle (eds.), *Nonprofits and Government* (2nd ed.) (Washington, DC: Urban Institute Press, 2006): 191–194.

Bromley, Patricia, and John W. Meyer. "'They Are All Organizations': The Cultural Roots of Blurring between the Nonprofit, Business, and Government Sectors," *Administration & Society*, 49(7) (2017): 939–966.

Brothers, John. *Rebalancing Public Partnerships: Innovative Practice Between Government and Nonprofits from Around the World* (New York: Routledge, 2015).

Brown, Trevor L., and Matthew Potoski. "Transaction Costs and Contracting: The Practitioner Perspective," *Public Performance & Management Review*, 29 (2005): 326–351.

Carey, Gemma, Kathy Landvogt, and Jo Barraket, eds. *Creating and Implementing Public Policy: Cross-Sectoral Debates* (New York: Routledge, 2016).

Chandler, Susan Meyers. *Making Collaboratives Work: How Complex Organizational Partnerships Succeed* (New York: Routledge, 2019).

Cordes, Joseph J., and C. Eugene Steuerle, eds. *Nonprofits and Business* (Washington, DC: Urban Institute Press, 2008).

Elson, Peter R. *High Ideals and Noble Intentions: Voluntary Sector-Government Relations in Canada* (Toronto, Canada: University of Toronto Press, 2013).

Ferris, James M. "The Double-Edged Sword of Social Service Contracting: Public Accountability versus Nonprofit Autonomy," *Nonprofit Management and Leadership*, 3 (1993): 363–376.

Forrer, John J., James Edwin Kee, and Eric Boyer. *Governing Cross-Sector Collaboration* (San Francisco: Jossey-Bass/Wiley, 2014).

Gazley, Beth. "Why *Not* Partner with Local Government? Nonprofit Managerial Perceptions of Collaborative Disadvantage," *Nonprofit and Voluntary Sector Quarterly*, 39 (2010): 51–76.

Gazley, Beth, and Jeffrey L. Brudney. "The Purpose (and Perils) of Government-Nonprofit Partnership," *Nonprofit and Voluntary Sector Quarterly*, 36 (2007): 389–415.

Greve, Carsten, and Graeme Hodge, eds. *Rethinking Public-Private Partnerships: Strategies for Turbulent Times* (London: Routledge, 2013).

Grønbjerg, Kirsten A., and Lester M. Salamon. "Devolution, Marketization, and the Changing Shape of Government-Nonprofit Relations," in *The State of Nonprofit America* (2nd ed.), ed., Lester M. Salamon (Washington, DC: Brookings Institution Press, 2012): 549–586.

Jang, Hee Soun, Jesus N. Valero, and Kyujin Jung. *Effective Leadership in Network Collaboration: Lessons Learned from Continuum of Care Homeless Programs* (Washington, DC: IBM Center for the Business of Government, 2016).

Kim, Seok-Eun. "Balancing Competing Accountability Requirements: Challenges in Performance Improvement of the Nonprofit Human Services Agency," *Public Performance & Management Review*, 29 (2005): 145–163.

Kramer, Ralph M. "Voluntary Agencies and the Contract Culture: 'Dream or Nightmare?'," *Social Service Review*, 68 (1994): 33–60.

Light, Paul C. *The Search for Social Entrepreneurship* (Washington, DC: Brookings Institution Press, 2008).

Mair, Johanna, Jeffrey Robinson, and Kai Hockerts, eds. *Social Entrepreneurship* (New York: Palgrave Macmillan, 2006).

Marwell, Nicole P., and Maoz Brown. "Towards a Governance Framework for Government-Nonprofit Relations," in Walter W. Powell and Patricia Bromley (eds.), *The Nonprofit Sector: A Research Handbook* (3rd ed.) (Stanford, CA: Stanford University Press, 2020): 231–250.

Mendel, Stuart C. "Are Private Government, the Nonprofit Sector, and Civil Society the Same Thing?" *Nonprofit and Voluntary Sector Quarterly*, 29 (2010): 717–733.

Milward, H. Brinton, and Keith G. Provan. "Governing the Hollow State," *Journal of Public Administration Research and Theory*, 10 (2000): 359–380.

National Council on Disability. *Deinstitutionalization: Unfinished Business* (Washington, DC: National Council on Disability, 2012). www.ncd.gov/publications/2012/Sept192012/

Nicholls, Alex, ed. *Social Entrepreneurship: New Models of Sustainable Social Change* (Oxford: Oxford University Press, 2006).

Nohria, Nitin, and Robert Eccles, eds. *Networks and Organizations: Structure, Form, and Action* (Boston, MA: Harvard Business School Press, 1992).

Norris-Tirrell, Dorothy, and Joy A. Clay, eds. *Strategic Collaboration in Public and Nonprofit Administration: A Practice-Based Approach to Solving Shared Problems* (Boca Raton, FL: CRC Press, 2010).

Osborne, David, and Ted Gaebler. *Reinventing Government* (Reading, MA: Addison-Wesley, 1992).

Ott, J. Steven, and Lisa A. Dicke. "Accountability Challenges Facing Public Sector HRM in an Era of Downsizing, Devolution, Diffusion, and Empowerment," in Ali Farazmand (ed.), *Strategic Public Personnel Administration: Building and Managing Human Capital for the 21st Century*, vol. 2 (Westport, CT: Praeger, 2007): 67–84.

——. "Important But Largely Unanswered Questions about Accountability in Contracted Public Human Services," *International Journal of Organization Theory and Behavior*, 3 (2000): 283–317.

——. *Understanding Nonprofit Organizations: Governance, Leadership, and Management* (3rd ed.) (Boulder, CO: Westview Press/Perseus Books, 2015).

——, eds. *Understanding Nonprofit Organizations: Governance, Leadership, and Management* (4th ed.) (New York: Routledge, 2021).

Saidel, Judith R. "Dimensions of Interdependence: The State and Voluntary-Sector Relationship," *Nonprofit and Voluntary Sector Quarterly*, 18 (1989): 336.

——. "Resource Interdependence: The Relationship between State Agencies and Nonprofit Organizations," *Public Administration Review*, 51 (1991): 543–553.

Salamon, Lester M. "Resource Interdependence: The Relationship between State Agencies and Nonprofit Organizations," *Public Administration Review, 51* (1991): 543–553.

———, and S. Wojciech Sokolowski, eds. *Global Civil Society: Dimensions of the Nonprofit Sector*, vol. 2 (Bloomfield, CT: Kumarian Press, 2004).

Seitanidi, Maria May. *The Politics of Partnerships: A Critical Examination of Nonprofit-Business Partnerships* (London and New York: Springer, 2010).

Shafritz, Jay M., J. Steven Ott, and Yong Suk Jang, eds. *Classics of Organization Theory* (8th ed.) (Boston: Cengage, 2015).

Smith, Steven R. "Government Financing of Nonprofit Activity," in *Nonprofits & Government: Collaboration & Conflict* (2nd ed.), eds. Elizabeth T. Boris and C. Eugene Steuerle (Washington, DC: Urban Institute Press, 2006): 219–256.

———, and Kirsten Grønbjerg. "Scope and Theory of Government-Nonprofit Relations," in *The Nonprofit Sector: A Research Handbook* (2nd ed.), eds. Walter W. Powell and Richard Steinberg (New Haven, CT: Yale University Press, 2006): 221–242.

———, and Michael Lipsky. *Nonprofits for Hire: The Welfare State in the Age of Contracting* (Cambridge, MA: Harvard University Press, 1993).

U.S. GAO (United States Government Accountability Office). *Nonprofit Sector: Increasing Numbers and Key Role in Delivering Federal Services*. Testimony before the Subcommittee on Oversight, Committee on Ways and Means, House of Representatives (Washington, DC: U.S. GAO-07-1084T, July 24, 2007).

Weisbrod, Burton A. "The Future of the Nonprofit Sector: Its Entwining with Private Enterprise and Government." *Journal of Policy Analysis and Management, 16* (1997): 541–555.

———, ed. *To Profit or Not to Profit: The Commercial Transformation of the Nonprofit Sector* (Cambridge: Cambridge University Press, 1998).

Young, Dennis. "Third Party Government," in Jay M. Shafritz (ed.), *International Encyclopedia of Public Policy and Administration* (Boulder, CO: Westview Press, 1998): 2252–2254.

Zimmer, Annette. "Third Sector-Government Partnerships," in Rupert Taylor (ed.), *Third Sector Research* (New York: Springer, 2010): 201–217.

ZumBrunnen, Mary. *Transcendent Partnership: Aligning Agendas for Collective Impact* (McLean, VA: Difference Press, 2018).

CHAPTER 30

The Point of Partnering

STUART C. MENDEL AND JEFFREY L. BRUDNEY

Mendel, Stuart C. and Jeffrey L. Brudney, *Partnerships the Nonprofit Way: What Matters, What Doesn't.* (Indiana University Press, 2018).

Introduction

Three important insights offer a useful frame for understanding nonprofit-first partnership. The first insight is that partnership is recognized as a critical practice for nonprofit organizations. The second is that partnership engagement differs across different sectors, and that nonprofit executives have distinct expectations for achieving the benefits of partnership.[1] The third insight is that the nuances and subtle distinctions in the terminology of partnership are more than diplomacy or hairsplitting: instead, such language signifies important clarifications that have significant implications for the partner participants.[2]

The comments of a pair of nonprofit executives encapsulate these insights. The first, the director of a social services agency devoted to job skills development and placements for youth residing in the city of Cleveland, noted,

This partnership is one of as many as 16 partnership arrangements with which we engage . . . all of which have different features and benefits. . . . An organizational value is to actively seek collaboration and to engage in partnerships with other organizations . . . while

protecting our core work focus and competencies from incrementally moving away from our mission. We consider collaboration and partnership as a part of our overall sustainability strategy toward achieving our mission. . . . We are confident our partner would not describe . . . collaboration the same way.

The second nonprofit executive, who leads a social justice organization that brings leaders of all faiths together to encourage understanding and community-building, stated,

Yes, there is a difference between partnering with different industries. . . . Partnership between two nonprofits has undertones of competition. Many times, we did not want to acquiesce to do things to accommodate our partner . . . and the agreements in advance were really important for the purpose of establishing limits for the partners. . . . There are other huge problems with nonprofit partners as well. Barriers to enduring relationships include . . . [uncertainty] that both will take the same interest in the partner and their success. . . . When the relationship is between a nonprofit and a business or government, we did not sense competition as a factor whatsoever. In both types,

DOI: 10.4324/9780367696559-39

we felt unrestricted in our efforts to seek end results without interference with the program delivery. Businesses and governments are easier because of the power struggle and the visibility.

Ample comments from our sample of nonprofit executives among the cases they supplied express viewpoints supporting these observations. The executive of a growing social services agency seeking partnership opportunities with other nonprofits as a way to build organizational capacity to serve existing clients and to reach more stated,

> The intention of the partnership is that it will project an image of our organization as innovative, risk-taking, and entrepreneurial in our use of technology to enhance service delivery. The act of partnership with another organization also forces us to evolve by changing our practices and plans to account for joint endeavors. The changes in service delivery improve the quality of life for our clients and add employment training opportunities to our partner's clients and their families.

This chapter examines and illustrates the conditions under which partnership is more or less beneficial to nonprofit organizations. We show that partnership benefits accrue through the transactional actions of the two participating organizations as well as the creation of transformational outcomes to society at large. Our analysis of the cases provides examples of the ways in which the transactional and transformational benefits of partnership lead to the creation of public value and social value. We show differences across partnerships based on sector pairings: nonprofit-nonprofit, nonprofit-government, and nonprofit-business.

Validation Through Participation in Partnership

Many nonprofit executives look to partnership arrangements as a way to sustain their

organizations financially, but the decision whether or not to enter into a partnership also includes nonfinancial considerations. Nonprofit executives expressed two important nonfinancial benefits.

The first is the potential that a nonprofit organization and its partner will be validated or granted a measure of recognition by third parties or the larger community as trusted institutional actors by virtue of participation in an important partnership. Such an imprimatur reinforces in turn the significance of the partnership endeavor. Several executives described the rewards for engaging in partnership as a return on their investment of time and effort through the endorsement of credible third parties. According to one nonprofit executive, endorsement implied that the partner organizations were trustworthy, capable, deserving of attention in the community, and worthy of policy makers' interest.

The leader of a nonprofit research and community-coordinating institution promoting public sector support for the arts suggested that partnerships provided the opportunity to work with service providers in promoting the role and value of the arts in a thriving community. The partnership allowed his organization to tie the work of the arts community to more well-recognized economic development priorities. In this arrangement, the partnering organization served as an advocate and used its considerable strategic and operations expertise to improve business practices, conduct research, and collaborate on arts projects. This executive maintained that the partnership gave him new connections through which to advance his organization's credibility and influence among public policy makers.

The second nonfinancial benefit of partnership is a strong desire for continuous improvement in the delivery of partnership goals. When asked for their advice to other nonprofit organizations engaging in partnership, executives shared lessons learned as important to themselves personally and to building the capacity of their organization to succeed in future partnership endeavors. For example, the executive of a private grant-making institution entering into a partnership stated,

> In the beginning, there were a lot of problems with our partner, and this required adjustments to the project. . . . We hung in, though, because we had invested too much in terms of opportunity costs to simply cut and run. . . . Despite many stops and starts, the work eventually started to move forward because of our learning curve . . . and because of our adjustments . . . overall this is a good program that will be offered again.

The ways in which such experiential learning eventually overcame the challenges of partnership indicates, first, that nonprofit executives enter into partnerships with the expectation that partnerships can evolve from the lessons learned by the actors. Second, it indicates that learning from the partnership experience is perceived as a benefit by the partners. Many nonprofit executives attested that the experiences of performing a partnership strengthened their organization and further justified their investment in the endeavor.

The Most Common Nonfinancial Benefits of Partnership

The nonprofit executives rated their satisfaction with their partnerships on a 10-point scale where a score of 1 indicated a partnership that did not meet any of its goals and a score of 10 indicated a partnership that had met all of its goals. In 80 percent of the partnership cases, the nonprofit executives explained that at least one reason that their partnership failed to meet their performance expectations was because of vague, difficult-to-resolve challenges in the partnership design or arrangements. Process improvement and executives' own professional development are thus a desirable and overt benefit of partnership. In addition, in more than 87 percent of the cases, the nonprofit executives described

learning from the partnership experience as a valuable benefit. Learning included a broad range of practices and skills. At one extreme, simple exchanges of information contributed to better ways of understanding the nature of the work to be performed, and at the other, learning influenced the perspective, and in some cases the actions and performance, of the partner. As a nonprofit executive director of a grant-making institution noted,

> One of the factors for why the partnership was able to meet its goals is that our partner had a building rehabilitation operation already in place, and they also had the ability to conduct sales of homes that were rehabbed. They taught us how to price complex projects. Our experience and abilities were in putting financing packages together needed to secure the funding for rehabbing of the homes for this project. . . . They also used our model on other project work they performed outside the partnership.

In the most successful instances of experiential learning emanating from partnership, one or both partners gain a better grasp of collaboration itself.

In some cases, nonprofit executives described another type of beneficial experience often gained through partnerships. In one instance, executives' time investments were repaid by improved partnership program operations and outcomes. The executive rated as 7.5 on a 10-point scale a partnership of more than five years of community organizations dedicated to mutual fundraising because both participants needed to improve their understanding of the programs' effects on other stakeholder groups. A second nonprofit executive rated his partnership as 7 because it met a high number of its goals, but the organizers did not pay sufficient attention to project outcomes that should have signaled to them the need to make mid-course corrections. As a result, a primary goal that this partnership failed to meet was to continue the program.

Challenges to Partnerships

Despite the many nonfinancial benefits of partnership, executives also named significant challenges. One of the most daunting included a broad range of new burdens specific to the ongoing act of partnership, such as the challenges of hiring, training, and supervising new staff dedicated to the partnership endeavor; aligning two fiscal operating systems to comply with the accounting standards of a third-party funding source; and establishing clear lines of communication and responsibility across two organizational cultures, integrating a new program into an existing culture of work.

In most partnership cases described by the nonprofit executives, the effort put into overcoming the burdens of partnership also became a means of strengthening the nonprofit partner's capacity to set and reach goals. In some instances, the challenges were quite modest. The executive of a large social services organization in partnership with another sizeable organization devoted to complementary purposes noted, "Some of the burdens were as simple as finding time to communicate with our partners." More complex issues, though, involved responsibilities for measuring the performance and the impact of the partnership.

Other challenges dealt with basic understanding of the partner's limitations. One executive, for instance, shared that an important takeaway of his experience was to understand the partner organization's strengths and limits, and to take them into account in future partnerships. He further explained that some government agencies engaged in partnerships may change the agenda and commitment to an endeavor depending on the outcome of an election. He also gave the example of a partnership that began with one set of senior staff that was abruptly replaced by another without the benefit of a transition plan. As a consequence of this change, his organization was left responsible for ensuring that the partnership continued to function. The burden of having to assume the full stewardship of the partnership, which began as a public sector initiative, compelled the nonprofit partner to create an exit strategy and eventually to leave the partnership.

In a second example of the benefits of learning from experience, one executive shared that the primary factor working against meeting his partnership's goals was the nature of government funding. For example, the project work of the partnership required task completion and verification, submitting of detailed invoices, and then a thirty-day payment turnaround for all approved invoices. Typically, this process did not occur as a seamless set of transactions. The executive reported that the primary lesson that informed his learning was that public sector funds were released only after the completion of government procurement and contracting processes. In the meantime, the nonprofit partner organization had loaned its own discretionary dollars to the endeavor due to its government partner's lengthy reimbursement timelines.

TABLE 30.1 **Reasons for Cross-Sector Partnerships**

Nonprofit-Nonprofit (56%)	Nonprofit-Government (34%)	Nonprofit-Business (10%)
1. Mission Purpose	1. Leveraging Tax Dollars	1. Business Development
2. Simpatico Mission	2. Principal Agent Theory	2. Market Share
3. Shared Information	3. Greater Good and Public Value	

Nonprofit-Nonprofit Sector Partnership Benefits

Among the eighty-two examples of important partnership cases collected in our research, 56 percent occur between two nonprofit participants; nearly one-third, or approximately 34 percent, occur between a nonprofit and government actor; and the approximately 10 percent remaining occur between a nonprofit and a business. Table 30.1 documents these proportions and the affiliated reasons for cross-sector partnerships nonprofit executives gave and that we describe in the following paragraphs as distinctive of their partnership pairings.

Respondents presented three primary reasons for the nonprofit-nonprofit partnership pairings. First, executives shared that nonprofit organizations with similar or complementary missions are usually aware of one another, see each other as both peers and competitors, and can frame the benefits of partnership as a rationale to achieve their respective organizational missions. Despite the pressure of competing for limited funding opportunities, organizations with mutual missions and interests already have this common baseline understanding and drive to form partnership arrangements with each other.

A second reason nonprofit organizations often form partnerships is as a strategy toward fulfilling their own missions. In seeking a nonprofit peer, two nonprofit executives are more likely to coordinate by merit of familiar concepts, sources of income, ability to attract philanthropic giving, and technical language.

A third reason nonprofits benefit from partnerships with one another is that these arrangements have a better chance of success than partnerships proposed or prompted by a third party outside the partnership. According to nonprofit executives, the process of mutual partnership formation typically takes place between complementary organizations that come together through some combination of similar resource needs, aligned mission or vision, or shared perspectives on public problems needing attention. "We felt . . . the partnership itself as being important, and our major funder for the partnership (the State of Ohio) really liked the partnership and the partnership's ability to leverage their funding into other/new dollars."

Two examples illustrate these points about mutual interests as a catalyst to the formation of nonprofit-nonprofit partnerships that would not have occurred with public or business partners.

First, the executive of a statewide political advocacy organization prompted a partnership with advocates of the opposing political affiliation because the participants shared mutual interests related to the declining civility in public discourse as well as among public policy makers and political parties. Because each partner identified with a different part of the political spectrum, and those differences typically inhibited their collaboration, the partnership was conceived to utilize their combined staff and convening power to draw attention to policy issues and processes that they hope will contribute to the public good.

A second partnership was initiated by an interfaith social justice organization in the aftermath of the September 2001 terrorist attacks. According to the nonprofit executive, the partnership gave a voice to faith communities that previously had few institutional voices or advocates to raise awareness and understanding.

> The partnership was originally set up to create an educational forum to improve understanding of beliefs that were not one's own. The partnership exists because our organization had existing relationships with the Sikh, Hindu, Muslim, Jewish, and Christian communities, who were each members of the partnership. This initiative brought everyone together to create a single event which we

considered an important partnership. Our desire is that the event will stimulate dialog and pathways for future dialogue between the communities [and] better understanding and opportunities for advocacy by the groups with one another and with other players beyond our community.

Another frequently mentioned benefit realized by two nonprofit actors in a partnership was that both organizations shared their exclusive data and the expertise of program staff in ways that were more reciprocal than competitive. According to one nonprofit executive, providing access to propriety information was no small matter, but doing so as a practice of sharing helped meet the partners' highest aspirations: using their organizational data enabled the partnership to create a more efficient and well-targeted program.

Nonprofit-Government Sector Partnership Benefits

Scholars of public administration and management credit the nonprofit sector with mission fulfillment as supportive of the general good and also as a supplement and complement of government.[3] The nonprofit executives in our sample, however, related that public sector mission fulfillment differs in important ways from nonprofit sector mission fulfillment.[4] According to scholars, public sector organizations seek engagements that offer efficient use of tax dollars to produce value beyond a dollar of investment for a dollar of service. Nonprofit missions as defined by scholars of nonprofit management theory, by contrast, are realized through engagements where a societal condition requires institutional action by intermediary actors to fulfill a need or induce remedy or change.[5]

As a result, the challenge in tracing partnership benefits between the two sectors is that public sector actors consider contract-for-hire relationships with nonprofits "partnerships."[6] Although the nonprofit executives in this study maintain that a partner-as-funder can rise to the level of partnership when a steady dialogue and interchange occur between the participants regarding the outcomes and processes of the endeavor, they also note that very few of their contracted government relationships exhibit either the characteristics or the benefits of partnership in the sense that nonprofits intend or as they understand them. Instead, the nonprofit executives maintained that government drove arrangements whose primary features were contracted performances that prized accountability, compliance, and transaction outcomes.

Although these types of arrangements between public and private actors are frequently cast by government as a partnership, nonprofits asserted that partnership with the public sector was achieved through other means. They did offer some examples of collaboration with government that rose to the level of partnership. For example, one executive of a nonprofit social and human services agency explained that his view of nonprofit-government partnership required starting with the understanding that public agencies have different constituencies than nonprofits. Because they ultimately have to be responsible to the public, they are frequently limited in their ability to respond to their nonprofit partners. Still, in his experience, variations exist across government agencies: some exhibit flexibility and are designed to be responsive and adaptive to their nongovernmental partners; others are part of a larger public agency bureaucracy and are slower to meet obligations to their partners. Like many of our nonprofit respondents, his overall conceptualization of nonprofit-government partnership was that the relationship is top-down and prescribed by government. In the nonprofit view, these arrangements are not partnerships because government rules and procedures control the relationship, subordinating the nonprofit to simply meeting the public sector requirements.

The interviewees also suggested that the goals of public sector actors for partnership often differ from those of nonprofit actors. Public sector funding is typically a mechanism of nonprofit-government partnership that reflects the power, credibility, and authority of government leaders' mission to achieve a greater purpose and good.[7] For example, one nonprofit executive described a partnership with government that funded community-wide arts and cultural organizations. Prior to the partnership, his organization had no access to public funds; with the partnership, a new revenue stream was created through an approved "sin tax" on cigarettes and alcohol consumption in the county. The nonprofit executive explained that maintaining the custodial or stewardship role of the partnership endeavor, which he asserted meant that internal performance deadlines were kept and meetings to communicate and overcome problems were held, rested with his organization. This role also meant, as he explained below, that his organization accepted the responsibility for the partnership to communicate to the public the value of tax dollars committed to supporting arts and cultural institutions in the city.

Nonprofit-Business Sector Partnership Benefits

Even though the number of cases of nonprofit-business partnerships in our sample is small (n = 8 cases), the benefits and outcomes identified seem to differ from those of nonprofit-nonprofit and nonprofit-government partnership cases.[8] Engagement and community service are elements of these partnerships; however, the nonprofit executives described their nonprofit-business partnerships as based primarily on market share and business development. Typically, the partnership outcomes were facilitations

of transactions such as providing basic business services.

Desirable Conditions Leading to Partnership Benefits by Sector Pairings

Based on the nonprofit executives' case narratives demonstrating important and desirable conditions that support the creation of benefits for partnership, we identify and depict in table 30.2 the causes underlying nonprofit-first partnerships that are specific to the different partnership dyads.

Nonprofit-Nonprofit

The first major benefits cluster of answers provided by nonprofit executive respondents reflects benefits that are derived from the direct involvement of the nonprofit leader in the partnership. Each nonprofit executive sharing this insight asserted that the involvement of organizational leadership signaled to the partners and other stakeholders involved that the partnership constituted an organizational priority. The result of the partnership was active involvement of the senior leadership of the participating organizations in the rapid problem-solving and the addition of resources through an expedited path that cut through the bureaucracy of the partnering organizations.

The nonprofit interviewees also explained that the opportunity cost of the involvement of the executive, whose time and resources are the most limited in the organization, is a "wager" or risk undertaken by the organization that the partnership will produce a return on investment that justifies it as an organizational priority (and the use of the executive's scarce time). One executive noted that the return on investment for his organization due to the partnership was that it raised the stature of the organization among third parties, instilled confidence among

TABLE 30.2 Benefit Causes Underlying the Three Dyadic Sector Partnership Pairs

Nonprofit-Nonprofit	Nonprofit-Government	Nonprofit-Business
1. Active Involvement of Executive Director, Demonstrating Priority of Partnership	1. Shared Staff and Data	1. Funding Scholarships
2. Leverage Knowledge and Expertise	2. Increase in Awareness of Target Population	2. Alliance with Business Community Sponsorships
3. Strengthen Shared Values	3. Active Involvement of Government and Nonprofit Leaders	
	4. Mutual Engagement of Partners	
	5. Opportunities for Mutual Advocates	
	6. Convenes Constituents	

the staff in the quality of their work, and lent credibility to their partner organizations. He maintained that his commitment to the partnership could be seen as the time he dedicated to its shared mission and to communicating with the partner organization. The executive further explained the value of reciprocity:

> Factors that worked towards meeting goals were . . . openness, honesty, trust, tolerance, flexibility, and humor between the leaders of both organizations. . . . We made a commitment . . . to deliver on our promises as a value, because to not do so would have been to deliver upon our partner, harm.

A second major benefits cluster that nonprofit organization partners accrue in partnership with other nonprofits is new or leveraged knowledge and expertise gained when program staff are shared. This sharing between the two organizations allows the partners to influence each other. Although sharing information, program methodology, and responsibility between

the partners was unexpected at the outset, the nonprofit executives viewed sharing as added value.

In a third major benefits cluster, partnering nonprofits can often strengthen both shared and individual values and practices. For example, one nonprofit executive explained that his large social services agency maintained a partnership with a smaller peer organization. The executive observed that cross-training and career development practices in the smaller social services agency were effective in keeping staff motivated and working with greater intensity, while also creating avenues for staff succession and continuity in program delivery. The nonprofit executive maintained that these concepts and practices became a shared value influencing hiring practices in both organizations, which in turn strengthened the bond of partnership between organizations. "Exposing our organization to the values of our partner influenced our operating values, specifically in our hiring practices to include our own residents who are partner-trained to work in our office."

Nonprofit-Government

The major benefits clusters in these partnership dyadic pairs reflect benefits derived from the nonprofits' partnerships with government. The nonprofit executives elaborated that nonprofit-government partnerships were most effectual when the arrangement involved the leadership of the nonprofit organization and senior leadership from the public sector, which might include the legislative, executive, or administrative offices of government.

An important and distinctive benefit occasionally described by the nonprofit executives was the opportunity for advocacy by the nonprofit partner with elected legislators and other policy makers. The following case examples illustrate this point.

First, a small community social services organization looked to the separate offices of the mayor and the city council in order to receive funding and access to city departments for the coordination of service delivery to local residents, community education, and in-kind services such as additional space, dissemination of information, and opportunities for fundraising. The factors that led to meeting the goals of this partnership were that important, high-level members of city government both in the mayor's office and the city council became aware of the partnership and responded to the nonprofit directly. As the executive told us,

> There is a demonstrated acceptance of our mission by government as something worthy of their support and interest. . . . We have expertise and capacity that the City lacks to fulfill its commitment to the residents . . . and are a knowledge resource for the city.

In a second case example, a social services agency focused on youth and teen fathers partnered with the county Department of Human Services to drive referrals and the entrance of new clients into public sector human services counseling. The nonprofit executive explained that from his point of view, the partnership with the county educational services center was mutually beneficial; he identified repeated project renewals by the County as one measure of government commitment. Both partners demonstrated willingness to compromise in solving problems and overcoming barriers. He also observed that both organizations had strong individuals driving the endeavor, solid second-tier program leadership, and sufficient support staff committed to the program. As he related,

> The relationship is 9 on a scale of 10 . . . due to . . . the intent of the County to address the needs of the target population. . . . I consider the County a true partner . . . and the positive relationship with the County is because . . . of a regular evaluation that is neither punitive nor inhibited and helped by open and easy communication with County administrators. . . . The multi-year nature of the contract awarded through an RFP tell us that they appreciate us.

Other highly rated benefits of nonprofit-government partnership mentioned by over 70 percent of the fifty-two nonprofit executives included: perceived endorsement of one partner for the partner agency as a result of the partnership project; sharing staff across the partnership project who contributed labor and proprietary data (but not necessarily expertise); increase in the public consciousness of the target population by virtue of their receiving the services provided by the partnership endeavor; and the ability to convene public and private constituents. Mentioned less frequently were partnership benefits of in-kind resources; such as equipment and office space; funding contributed by the nonprofit from its discretionary funds; volunteer involvement; and increased target market share.

Nonprofit-Business

Within this major benefit cluster lie four categories, each defined by a distinctive perspective on the underlying motivations for nonprofit-business partnerships. The first sub-cluster includes nonprofits seeking sponsorship dollars from businesses. The second sub-cluster comprises nonprofits seeking to benefit from businesses that fulfill community service, public-values generation, or corporate social responsibility. The third sub-cluster involves the nonprofits lending their credibility to businesses for program expertise or to boost operational profitability and efficiency. The fourth sub-cluster consists of nonprofits lending their credibility to businesses that are trying to enhance market share: in this model, the clients or patrons of the nonprofit begin to associate the business with the "doing good" glow of the nonprofit.

Nonprofits Seeking Sponsorship Dollars From Businesses

One nonprofit executive shared a partnership case in which his organization, a statewide affiliate of a national health organization performing research and education to eradicate a particular disease, worked with the regional manager of a global corporation. The health organization was able to demonstrate its appeal as a partner to local and regional corporate sponsors, and the partnership was formed to raise money to support the research and operations of the national office of the nonprofit organization. Businesses were offered membership in the "team," which signaled to the local community that the business was a responsible corporate citizen, thus raising public perceptions of its corporate image.

Nonprofits Seeking to Benefit From Business Corporations Fulfilling Community Service, Public-Values Generation, or Corporate Social Responsibility

Another nonprofit executive described the origin of a nonprofit-business partnership as initiated by the business to make the community more inviting to commercial enterprise and residential neighborhood stability. The partnership began

as a funding relationship between his nonprofit and a community bank that had its headquarters in an urban neighborhood and eventually grew into an important partnership centered on services to youth. Although his nonprofit organization entered into the partnership seeking unrestricted operating support for its work in the community, the nonprofit understood the bank's motivation to find ways to help stabilize the neighborhood as a desirable place for the business to maintain its headquarters. The nonprofit executive also noted that the bank was a business anchor and gathering place for the local community, which lacked such amenities. In pursuit of these mutual benefits, the two organizations created a project to address the educational future of the neighborhood's youth and their families.

Nonprofits Lending Credibility to Businesses for Program Expertise

A third example consists of a partnership whose output includes arranging business placements for clients to whom the nonprofit organization provides training, social services, and hopefully relief from some social pathologies. One nonprofit executive explained that she valued the partnership with the business because a successful partnership of this type engenders respect among her peers.

> The partnership with a business is an ongoing relationship that began in 2008 because we find and train youth in low-income communities in Cleveland and East Cleveland, from which our partner, a national chain of retailer outlets selling clothes, housewares, and accessories at a discount, draws upon for qualified applicants for employment in its stores. . . . We entered into this partnership with [the] business by making the case to the business as relating to their profit goals and not based on philanthropy and donations. . . . The success of the relationship is a point of pride and accomplishment for our

organization and positions us as an expert among our peers.

The partnership assists the nonprofit by providing jobs to at-risk youth, and the business receives employees. The business also offered feedback to the nonprofit partner on the quality of its youth participants as workers.

Nonprofits Lending Credibility to Businesses Desiring Enhanced Market Share

Nonprofit organizations can also lend their credibility to a business seeking to enhance its market share, as illustrated in the following case example:

> The partnership was originally set up to expand the capacity of the microenterprise lending in Northeast Ohio. This was to help small businesses who would not be creditworthy otherwise. The partnership was initiated by the regional district office of a large commercial bank after the demise of a small nonprofit intermediary organization that served as a microlender to small businesses. The nonprofit partner was a small community foundation dedicated to strengthening entrepreneurial business start-ups. The goals of the partnership were to leverage more access to capital for aspiring entrepreneurs, but also to affiliate the bank as a friendly face to small business enterprise. The partnership had an impact on the target population, which was an increase in access to technical assistance and capital in the form of banking products.

Partnership Benefits and Public Value

We have described the benefits of partnership drawn from the viewpoint of nonprofit executives engaged in these endeavors. The benefits we ascertain from the executives are linked to the beliefs that their organizations would receive a

reasonable return on investment to the relationship, and that the partnership endeavor rose to the level of "important." One executive shared that his partnership had an impact on his organization through an increased operational budget, a larger staff, and an increase in clients served. He also pointed to stronger client retention.

Beyond the immediate and tangible transactional benefits of partnership for the partners, the nonprofit executives point to benefits that they believe contribute to a greater societal good. In many of the case narratives, the executives stated that the processes and activities of the partnership realize benefits for both partner participants as well as the greater society. Executives named forming and strengthening social networks, sustaining social capital, building community, and nurturing the bonds of trust that comprise civil society as transformational outcomes arising from partnership processes. The outcomes of such transformations can potentially resonate well beyond the work of the partnership and extend into benefits for the larger community, examples of which were suggested by nonprofit executives contributing cases as reduction in overall rates of crime rate, poverty, and illiteracy. In other cases, the benefits of partnership were credited as enhancing the standing of a partner as a community institution.

Transformational benefits are reflected in outcomes such as positive participant impressions, improvements in the conditions of society, and public dollars redirected through advocacy. The executive of the social services organization mentioned above explained that transformational benefits arising from his partnership were less directly observable or measurable. For example, he claimed that the benefits rose to the level of community impact because the increased number of clients served translated into a reduction of "distress" in the larger community.

Other examples of transformational benefits arising from partnerships are outcomes that strengthen the network of service providers, promote social change, improve public policy, or create public value. The nonprofit executive of an organization devoted to strengthening arts organizations receiving tax dollars explained that transformational impacts worked in two directions. From one perspective, the arts and cultural sector gained access to public sector funds that did not exist before the partnership. The creation of a public sector contribution to the arts enabled a new source of sustainability for private organizations that had not been available previously. From another perspective, arts and cultural organizations receiving public sector funding had greater responsibility to communicate the value of the arts to the public and to cast the dollars as an investment by the public, who could then contemplate the arts community as drivers of economic development and improved social and educational services to the region.

A third nonprofit executive stated that the partnership was established in order to build a community improvement district. The institutions that formed the partnership sought urban revitalization through property and institutional development, and the nonprofit members wanted to create plans for the strategic growth of all member institutions. The partnership provided transactional benefits to its members, who gained from collaboration and shared resources, and to the larger community, which then created the conditions for positive change in an urban neighborhood threatened by economic disinvestment and decline.

Conclusion

A central element in our inquiry into nonprofit-first partnerships has been the lens of sector pairings that form these arrangements. We show that nonprofit-nonprofit, nonprofit-government, and nonprofit-business partnerships produce differences in expectations, approaches, and methods, as well as outcomes meriting our attention. Among nonprofit-nonprofit partnerships, we note eight distinct and frequently mentioned outcomes listed in table 30.3.

First is an emphasis that both partners share the benefits and outcomes of the partnership while still pursuing their own missions. Second is a demonstrable commitment reflected by the hands-on involvement of the leaders in both organizations to the partnership and its outcomes. Third is mutuality in authority and responsibility between the partners. Fourth is that the risks and rewards are shared between participants. Fifth is a perceived reciprocity of financial and nonfinancial contributions by both partners toward carrying out the work of the partnership. Sixth is the willingness and interest of the parties to continue or renew the relationship beyond the partnership. Seventh is the perception that the process of partnership is itself a valued outcome of the endeavor. Eighth is the idea that the partnership contributes to the greater good and the creation of public value.

In nonprofit-government partnerships, by contrast, we note three main clusters of benefits. These outcomes are related to, but different than, the benefits noted for nonprofit-nonprofit partnerships. First is an emphasis on clarity in the roles and expectations of each member. Second is the requirement for a formalized agreement on the partnership, usually in the form of a contract for services between the two partners. Third is the understanding that relationships are focused on transactional work products and accountability for performance as specified in the contract agreement.

Although the nonprofit-business partnership dyads were the fewest in number as related by our nonprofit respondents, four benefits distinguish these ventures from the other two types of sector pairings. First is the for-profit businesses' concern with market share, reduced costs, and profit creation as motivations to engage with nonprofit organizations. Second is the understanding that many of the nonprofit partners enter into partnerships with business with the aspiration that the business will be flexible and adaptive to the circumstances of the partnership. Third is the realization that businesses enter into partnerships with nonprofits

TABLE 30.3 **Distinct and Frequently Mentioned Nonprofit-First Outcomes Associated With Cross-Sector Types**

#	*Nonprofit-Nonprofit*	*Nonprofit-Government*	*Nonprofit-Business*
1	Both partners share benefits and outcomes while pursuing their own missions	A priority is the emphasis on the roles and expectations of both partners	Desire to improve market share, reduce costs of doing business, and create profits
2	Both partners demonstrate commitment reflected by hands-on involvement of the organizations' leaders	The presence of a formal written agreement or contract between actors	Expectation by both partners that they will be flexible and adaptable to achieve their mission
3	Both partners perceive a mutuality of authority and responsibility	Agreement by both partners that the work of the partnership is focused on transactional outcomes and performance accountability	Businesses may support the nonprofit in its mission fulfillment, but that is secondary to profit achievement goals
4	Both partners share risks and rewards		Nonprofits may support business profitability goals if the business aids them in reaching their goals
5	Both partners perceive reciprocity of financial and nonfinancial contributions		
6	Both partners perceive the willingness to continue the partnership beyond its expiration		
7	Perception that the partnership itself is a worthy outcome beyond the work of the partnership		
8	Perception that the partnership contributes to the greater good of society		

for motivations other than the desire to engage in social enterprise or social innovation. Fourth is the insight that nonprofit partners were motivated to form partnerships with businesses based on the part the business would play in program completion, resources development, and a perceived legitimacy arising from the association.

The three insights that framed our growing understanding of nonprofit-first partnerships in this chapter have led us to identify both transactional and transformational benefits for the nonprofit participants. Nonprofits are validated by partnership and may gain both financial and nonfinancial benefits; the specifics of such gains, however, differ by nonprofit-nonprofit,

nonprofit-government, and nonprofit-business pairings. In this chapter, we developed clusters of benefits based on these three major pairings in order to better understand the benefits and values that each type can offer the nonprofit actor and the larger community thus served.

Notes

1. Forrer, John, James Jed Kee, and Eric Boyer. *Governing Cross-Sector Collaboration* (Hoboken, NJ: John Wiley & Sons, 2014); Bryson, John M., Barbara C. Crosby, and Melissa Middleton Stone. "The Design and Implementation of Cross-Sector Collaborations: Propositions from the Literature." *Public Administration Review* 66, no. s1 (2006): 44–55, https://doi.org/10.1111/j.1540-6210.2006.00665.x; Austin, James E. *The Collaboration Challenge: How Nonprofits and Businesses Succeed Through Strategic Alliances* (Hoboken, NJ: John Wiley & Sons, 2010), 109.

2. Teisman, Geert R., and Erik Hans Klijn. "Partnership Arrangements: Governmental Rhetoric or Governance Scheme?" *Public Administration Review* 62, no. 2 (2002): 197–205, https://doi.org/10.1111/0033-3352.00170; Linder, Stephen H. "Coming to Terms with the Public-Private Partnership: A Grammar of Multiple Meanings." *American Behavioral Scientist* 43, no. 1 (1999): 35–51, https://doi.org/10.1177/00027649921955146.

3. Powell, W. W., and R. Steinberg. *The Nonprofit Sector: A Research Handbook* (New Haven: Yale University Press, 2006); Bryson, John M., Barbara C. Crosby, and Melissa Middleton Stone. "The Design and Implementation of Cross-Sector Collaborations: Propositions from the Literature." *Public Administration Review* 66 no. s1 (2006): 44–55, https://doi.org/10.1111/j.1540-6210.2006.00665.x.

4. Benington, J., and M. Getters. "10 Partnerships as Networked Governance?" In *Local Partnership and Social Exclusion in the European Union: New Forms of Local Social Governance?* (Abingdon, UK: Routledge, 2013), 198; Young, Dennis R. "Complementary, Supplementary, or Adversarial? Nonprofit-Government Relations," edited by Elizabeth Boris and C. Eugene Steuerle entitled *Nonprofits & Government: Collaboration & Conflict.*

Urban Institute Press (2006): 37–80, https://doi.org/10.1515/npf-2015-0040.

5. Young, D. R. "Alternative Models of Government-Nonprofit Sector Relations: Theoretical and International Perspectives." *Nonprofit and Voluntary Sector Quarterly* 29, no. 1 (2000): 149–172; McDonald, Mary B. "Understanding Social Capital, Civic Engagement, and Community Building." In *Leadership in Nonprofit Organizations: A Reference Book*, ed. Kathryn Agard (Thousand Oaks, CA: Sage Publications, 2011), 46–55.

6. Gazley, Beth, and Jeffrey L. Brudney. "The Purpose (and Perils) of Government-Nonprofit Partnership." *Nonprofit and Voluntary Sector Quarterly* 36, no. 3 (2007): 389–415, https://doi.org/10.1177/0899764006295997; Young, Dennis R. "Alternative Models of Government-Nonprofit Sector Relations: Theoretical and International Perspectives." *Nonprofit and Voluntary Sector Quarterly* 29, no. 1 (2000): 149–172, https://doi.org/10.1177/0899764000291009; Salamon, Lester M. "The Nonprofit Sector and Government: The American Experience in Theory and Practice." In *The Third Sector: Comparative Studies of Nonprofit Organization* (Berlin and New York: Walter de Gruyter, 1990), 210–240, https://doi.org/10.1515/9783110868401.219.

7. Rainey, Hal G., and Barry Bozeman. "Comparing Public and Private Organizations: Empirical Research and the Power of the *A Priori*." *Journal of Public Administration Research and Theory* 10, no. 2 (2000): 447–470, <http://jpart.oxfordjournals.org/content/10/2/447. abstract>; Moore, Mark H. *Creating Public Value: Strategic Management in Government* (Cambridge, MA: Harvard University Press, 1995); Oliver, Christine. "Determinants of Interorganizational Relationships: Integration and Future Directions." *Academy of Management Review* 15, no. 2 (1990): 241–265, https://doi.org/10.5465/AMR.1990.4308156.

8. Eikenberry, Angela M., and Jodie Drapal Kluver. "The Marketization of the Nonprofit Sector: Civil Society at Risk?" *Public Administration Review* 64, no. 2 (2004): 132–140, https://doi.org/10.1111/j.1540-6210.2004.00355.x; Sagawa, Shirley, and Eli Segal. *Common Interest, Common Good: Creating Value through Business and Social Sector Partnerships* (Cambridge, MA: Harvard Business Press, 1999).

CHAPTER 31

Government-Nonprofit Cooperation: Anomaly or Necessity?

Lester M. Salamon and Stefan Toepler

Salamon, L. M., & Toepler, S. (2015). Government–Nonprofit Cooperation: Anomaly or Necessity? *Voluntas*, *26*(6), 2155–2177.

Introduction

Few facets of the nonprofit sector have been as thoroughly overlooked or as commonly misunderstood as the relationships between nonprofit organizations and the state. According to widespread beliefs, government and the nonprofit sector operate in separate spheres, pursue different objectives, and are, at best, indifferent to each other, and at worst, in active competition or antagonism. Europe, we had been told, developed a "welfare state" that rendered nonprofit organizations largely superfluous while America chose to rely instead on a robust nonprofit sector financed mostly by charitable gifts.

In fact, however, recent research has revealed that much of Europe actually developed a widespread "welfare partnership" linking government to nonprofit organizations in a wide assortment of fields (Salamon and Anheier 1994; Salamon et al. 2004; Gidron et al. 1992). And government support has been a central feature of America's nonprofit landscape since the founding of America's very first nonprofit organization (Harvard College) and had grown by the late 1980s to a point where it outdistanced private charitable support to nonprofits by a factor of 4:1 (Whitehead 1973, pp. 3–16; Salamon and Abramson 1981; Salamon 1987, 1995; Smith and Lipsky 1993).[1]

How can we explain this curious blind spot in comprehending the close relationship between nonprofit organizations and government in widely disparate countries around the world? While many factors have doubtless been at work, a central one has been the inadequacy of the conceptual lenses through which we have been examining both the nonprofit sector and the contemporary welfare state. Far from calling attention to this interdependent relationship and explaining why it makes sense, existing theories divert our attention from it and provide powerful reasons to doubt it could, or should, exist (Salamon 1987).

So far as the theory of the "welfare state" is concerned, scholars and politicians alike have focused on the dramatic expansion of government social welfare expenditures that began in late 19th century Europe, and considerably later in the United States, to jump understandably to the conclusion that what has been under way has been a gigantic enlargement of the bureaucratic apparatus of the modern state and

DOI: 10.4324/9780367696559-40

the displacement of other social institutions, among them private nonprofit groups. Both those on the left and those on the right have had reason to embrace such a "paradigm of conflict," moreover. For those on the left, denigration of the capabilities of charitable institutions has long been a crucial weapon in the battle to win political support for an expanded governmental role in social problem-solving. The left therefore had reason to exaggerate the capabilities of the state and dismiss the capabilities of the third sector in coping with the enormous challenges of urban, industrial societies. Those on the right have had an even stronger incentive to exaggerate the power of the modern welfare state and neglect to acknowledge the growing cooperation between the state and nonprofit groups. This is so because such acknowledgement would have contradicted the conservative narrative of an inherent conflict between the state and voluntary groups and the resulting inevitable displacement of voluntary groups as the state expands its reach (Nisbet 1962).[2]

But prevailing theories of the nonprofit sector have also done little to prepare us for a robust pattern of government–nonprofit cooperation. To the contrary, they have at least implicitly made such cooperation [appear] to be an aberration. In the process, they have shielded us from some inconvenient truths about the nonprofit sector as well as about the changing character of modern states. And they have complicated the task that governments around the world have faced in coming to terms with the challenges confronting them in coping with important public problems for which collaboration between states and nonprofit organizations has become essential.

To assist with this task, this article reviews some of the core tenets of recent nonprofit and public administration theorizing in an effort to establish a firmer understanding of the conceptual bases for government–nonprofit relationships, and a clearer comprehension of the prerequisites that such relationships require in order to function most effectively. We examine

some of the challenges such third-party relationships create and indicate some ways in which such challenges can be minimized. Foremost among these is the need for nonprofit involvement not just in the delivery of government-funded human services, but also in the design of the programs being delivered with government assistance. In the process, the article provides a framework against which the different national experiences detailed in the subsequent articles of this special issue can be assessed.

Part I. Prevailing Economic Theories of the Nonprofit Sector

The early economic theories of the nonprofit sector were not originally designed to explain patterns of government–nonprofit relations. The primary focus was to explain the very existence of nonprofits within the neo-classical two-sector conception of the economy. However, conceptually they provided an initial barrier to a fuller understanding of the relations between nonprofits and the state by implying the lack of a basis for such relations. Two strands of such theorizing can be discerned: one of them focusing on the demand side of the equation, that is, why clients, donors, or purchasers might prefer nonprofits in seeking to fulfill demand for some goods and services, and the other focusing on the supply side, explaining why entrepreneurs come forward to found nonprofit organizations rather than for-profit businesses.

Demand-Side Theories

Burton Weisbrod's (1975) seminal market failure/government failure, or heterogeneity, theory was among the earliest efforts to conceptualize a role for nonprofit organizations within the framework of neo-classical economics. Weisbrod's theory starts with the classical assumption of market failure—the inherent inability of the market to supply certain goods or services. This failure arises from the fact that the market only produces goods or services for customers willing and able to pay for them. But, as shown by Mancur Olson's (1965) analysis of collective action, public or collective goods, goods that can only be produced through collective action (e.g., clean air or national defense), once produced, are available to everyone independent of their willingness to pay, creating a "free-rider problem," since it is not economically rational to pay for goods or services available for free. Market mechanisms alone will therefore not lead to the production of the quantities of such goods that citizens actually desire, causing an undersupply of such public goods.

Government intervention—the assumption of public responsibility for the supply of such goods—is the standard prescription of classical economic theory for these kinds of market failures. As Weisbrod argued, in democratic societies, government only produces collective goods that are desired by a majority of citizens. In order to win elections, politicians accordingly tailor collective good provision to the preferences of the "median voter," which would ensure majority support. In societies in which population diversity yields highly heterogeneous collective goods demands, however, government cannot easily supply all of the collective goods demands that citizens have. This leaves considerable unsatisfied demand for such goods. It is to meet such demand, Weisbrod suggests that even classical economics must acknowledge a need for nonprofit organizations, for it is to fulfill such demand that nonprofit organizations exist. Such organizations are financed by the voluntary contributions of the dissatisfied voters interested in increasing the output of particular collective goods. Nonprofit organizations are therefore gap-fillers that emerge in response to private demands for collective goods not offered by government and not available from market providers because of their free-rider character.

Weisbrod's theory applies not only to the basic, but also to the more elaborate, forms of public goods (e.g., opera, recreational activity, religious worship, and many more), and its prediction that the number of nonprofit organizations will grow with the degree of diversity of a population appears to apply whether the diversity is defined not just in terms of the traditional indicators of ethnicity, language, age, or religion, but also in terms of wealth, income levels, occupations and professions, and many more.

What is most important about the market failure/government failure theory for our purposes here, however, is what it implies about government–nonprofit relations—and what it implies is that such relationships are unlikely to exist. This is so because the market failure/government failure theory predicts that nonprofit organizations arise precisely in fields where government does not operate and where government support is unavailable due to the lack of sufficient public demand. Indeed, Weisbrod is quite explicit about expecting nonprofits to be supported fundamentally by donative sources. Donations are expressions of preferences for collective goods not provided by either market or government. In the process, however, the Weisbrod theory delegitimizes government support for the voluntary sector and feeds a powerful social myth about the role that private philanthropy plays in the modern nonprofit sector.

The other major demand-side theory of the nonprofit sector emphasizes the element of *trust* as the key to the existence of the nonprofit sector, but it does not do much better at anticipating a robust pattern of government–nonprofit cooperation. As articulated by Hansmann (1987), this theory traces the existence of the nonprofit sector to situations in which information asymmetry impedes the operation of the market because the purchaser of goods or services is not the consumer of the goods or services. In such situations, the purchaser cannot easily know whether the good or service was worth the cost, breaking a link between consumer and producer that is crucial to market operations. Under these circumstances, an element of trust is required.

Because of the so-called "non-distribution constraint"—the widespread prohibition on the distribution of profits by nonprofits to their investors, directors, or others—nonprofit organizations are considered to be less likely to cut corners or cheat consumers even in the absence of the market's control mechanism of consumer sovereignty based on direct consumer experience with the purchased product (Hansmann 1987, p. 29).

Supply-Side Theories

In contrast to these theories emphasizing the demand for services, a second set of economic theories focuses on the supply side of the nonprofit market and seek[s] to explain why nonprofits come into existence, i.e., why entrepreneurs might come forward to form nonprofit, as opposed to for-profit, entities. To appreciate such supply-side approaches, one has to consider that they take a very different starting point from the demand-side theories. Instead of positing rational economic actors seeking collective benefits or a substitute for the absence of market-based economic signals, supply-side arguments posit a range of non-economic, non-monetary incentives for the creation and existence of nonprofit organizations. Thus, James (1987), for example, suggests that monetary goals may not be foremost in the minds of those who found nonprofit organizations, and even service provision to needy groups may not be as fundamental as other objectives—such as increasing the numbers of members, believers, or other types of adherents to one's religious community. She thus posits that nonprofits will be more numerous in areas where religious competition is most pronounced. To the extent that government enters a field, it reduces the gap that such religious or ideological zealots can exploit for their recruitment efforts. This would hardly incline them to favor such government efforts.

In short, like prevailing conceptions of the welfare state, prevailing economic theories of the nonprofit sector—whether on the demand side or the supply side, and whether positing unsatisfied demand for collective goods or a search for an alternative to market cues for the quality or cost of various services—leave us largely adrift in explaining one of the dominant social realities of modern society: the appearance of widespread cooperation between the state and nonprofit institutions in coping with modern social and economic problems. How, then, are we to account for this widespread phenomenon?

Part II. Voluntary Failure and New Governance Theory

Fortunately, an alternative body of theory that usefully fills this conceptual gap has recently become available. Known variously as "voluntary failure," "third-party government," "new governance," or "interdependence" theory, this body of thought emphasizes the interdependence between the state and various other social actors, among them private nonprofit organizations, and sees the emergence of widespread patterns of collaboration among them as a natural consequence as opposed to an unfortunate aberration (Salamon 1981, 1995, 2002). In the process, it fits the reality of extensive government–nonprofit partnerships into a more comprehensive framework of theorizing about both the nonprofit sector and the modern state. At the same time, it identifies the conditions under which such partnerships need to operate in order to capture the advantages of which they are capable.

Voluntary Failure Theory

Two strands of theorizing form the core of this voluntary failure line of thought. One of them—the "voluntary failure" component—relates most specifically to nonprofit organizations and seeks to explain why such organizations, whatever their origins, might turn to the state for assistance, and why both supply-side entrepreneurs and private consumers might find such an outcome desirable. The other—the "third-party government" or "new governance" component—seeks to explain why governments, consumers, (and voters) might favor such an approach.

So far as the first component is concerned, the voluntary failure theory acknowledges the problems of addressing public problems through both the market and the state, but it takes issue with the notion embodied in these other theories that the nonprofit sector is essentially derivative and secondary, filling in where these other systems fall short and operating in spheres in which the others are either incapable or unwilling to operate. Rather, it turns these other theories on their head, rejecting the view that government is always, or even usually, the first line of defense in cases of market failure, and seeing voluntary organizations as the primary response mechanism instead—even where extensive state systems of service provision are available, but where new problems arise to which state systems are slow to respond or where higher quality of performance is demanded than state-centered systems are able to supply.

The "transaction costs" involved in mobilizing governmental responses to shortages of collective goods tend to be much higher than the costs of mobilizing voluntary action. For governments, whether democratic or undemocratic, to act in response to some public problem, information must be assembled, substantial segments of the public must be aroused, public officials must be informed and persuaded, proposed solutions must be developed, laws must be formulated and passed, and programs must be put into operation. All of this takes time and resources. By contrast, to generate a voluntary-sector response, a handful of individuals, whether motivated by religious impulse, ideological fervor, professional conviction, or personal experience can take the initiative on

their own to address a problem. This highlights a unique characteristic of nonprofit organizations: alone among societal institutions, they are capable of mobilizing *individual initiative* for the *public good*. This differentiates them from market institutions, which mobilize individual initiative but for *individual gain*, and from governmental institutions, which pursue the public good but do so through *collective* action (Salamon 2012). It is therefore reasonable to expect that the private, nonprofit sector, not government or business, will frequently provide the first line of response to perceived "market failures."

But why would government–nonprofit cooperation result from such a situation instead of the splendid isolation posited by the economic theories? The answer to this question lies in the reality that, for all their advantages, nonprofit organizations have their own significant limitations that constrain their ability to respond to public problems. In addition to "market failure" and "government failure," in other words, there is "voluntary failure"—i.e., inherent limitations of the voluntary sector as a mechanism for meeting public needs (Salamon 1987, 1995). These include

- First, *philanthropic insufficiency:* the inability of voluntary organizations to generate the scale of resources adequate and reliable enough to cope with the human service problems of an advanced industrial society. What is more, philanthropic resources are often available where they are needed least and least available where they are needed most. Coupled with the inability of nonprofit organizations to generate equity capital due to the legal barriers on their distribution of profits, the result is too often an inability of nonprofit organizations to "scale up" their operations;
- Second, *philanthropic particularism:* the tendency of nonprofits and donors to focus on particular groups of clients or particular geographic areas to the exclusion of others. This

creates enormous disparities in the provision of needed assistance;

- Third, *philanthropic paternalism:* the difficulty these organizations have in establishing *rights* to benefits, as opposed to *privileges,* and hence the difficulty they have in fostering a true sense of empowerment self-worth; and
- Fourth, *philanthropic amateurism:* the lack of professionalism in volunteer-driven organizations and the consequent difficulty in bringing truly professional approaches to bear on complex human problems.

Significantly, these inherent limitations of the private nonprofit sector are mirror images of inherent strengths of government. Thus, for example, government's coercive powers, including the power to tax, can overcome the free ridership of voluntary contributions and mitigate the philanthropic insufficiency of the voluntary sector. Government's concern for equity and entitlements is a useful antidote to the particularism of the nonprofit sector. Through legitimate, democratic decision-making procedures, it can establish access to certain benefits as a "right" of citizens as opposed to a "gift" from wealthy donors. As such, it can counter the paternalism often characteristic of the charitable giving. So, too, through its ability to set quality standards and professional certification requirements, as well as its ability to provide resources sufficient to retain professional talent, it can overcome the amateurism that often limits even the most dedicated volunteer staff.

Third-Party Government and New Governance Theory

But why would government turn to nonprofit organizations to assist in supplying such public goods, and why might consumers and taxpayers support this? To answer this question, we must turn to the second component of the interdependence line of theories, which is known variously as "third-party government" or "new governance" theory (Salamon 2002).

Large government bureaucracies, it turns out, can become highly inefficient and overly cumbersome and unresponsive. Worse yet, according to some theorists, their personnel are too often driven by cravings for power and resources rather than by the selfless pursuit of the public interest (Tullock 1965). Other limitations of state action have also recently become evident. While suitable for delivering common-issue services, they lack the flexibility needed for many crucial human services, which must be delivered at a human scale by institutions capable of considerable flexibility. What is more, given the growing complexity of the problems government is being called on to address, governments often lack the resources and talents needed to respond effectively (Agranoff 2007; Goldsmith and Kettl 2009). It has become clear, for example, that going after complex non-point sources of pollution requires the mobilization not only of governmental capacities, but also broader citizen capacities through watershed alliances, "stream teams," and other forms of citizen mobilization (Siriani and Friedland 2001; Wurzel et al. 2013, pp. 77–132; Ringling 2002).

These various criticisms have given rise to a "public choice" theory of government and to the "new public management" (NPM) school of thought (e.g., Osborne 2006; Plumptre 1993; Lane 2000; Tullock 1965). The central argument of the NPM theory and its American counterpart, known as "reinventing government," was that these shortcomings in government operations could be overcome by introducing business-style management techniques such as strategic planning, management by objectives, evidence-based decision-making, and incentive-based reward systems into the administration of the public sector. The central premise was that government agencies need to be radically streamlined, their internal operations subjected to market-type incentives, and many, if not most, of their functions outsourced to private organizations through contracts and so-called "quasi-market" arrangements (LeGrand and Bartlett 1993a, b; Le Grand 2011).

New Governance Theory acknowledges many of the problems that have inspired the NPM, but parts company with the NPM approach on three crucial grounds. In the first place, New Governance Theory calls attention to the fact that the central premise of NPM—that major problems of public sector performance arise from the fact that government agencies are tightly structured hierarchies insulated from market forces and from effective citizen pressure, and therefore free to serve the personal and institutional interests of bureaucrats instead—does not characterize government operations in most of the countries at which the theory was aimed, and has not for decades. In a sense, NPM provided the right answer but to the wrong question in public administration reform (Salamon 2005). That question was: "How can hierarchical government bureaucracies be reshaped and re-invented to improve their performance?"

Largely overlooked in the NPM analysis, however, is the extent to which the operation of modern government in many of the countries around the world already embodied many of the features that the NPM reformers were proposing. Indeed, a veritable revolution had taken place in the operation of the public sector during the 50 years or more before this theory emerged, at least in much of the developed world. The heart of this revolution has been a fundamental transformation not just in the scope and scale of government action, but also in its basic *forms*— in the *tools* of public action, the instruments or means used to address public problems.

Certainly this has been a central feature of the American approach to public problems for decades and has involved collaboration not only with nonprofit human service, education, health, and related organizations, but also with a wide assortment of for-profit banks, industrial firms, construction organizations, and many more (Salamon 1995, 2002). Behind the potent myth of voluntarism through which 19th century America is often viewed, for example, lies a solid reality of extensive collaboration between local governments and private nonprofit groups. Indeed, by the end of the 19th century, many cities and states heavily supported private voluntary institutions to take care of the poor as well as prisoners, and this arrangement expanded massively when the national government entered the human service field in the mid-1960s.[3]

But this pattern of third-party government has hardly been restricted to the American scene. To the contrary, it is widely evident in countries throughout the world. Indeed, research carried out by teams of scholars working under the auspices of the Johns Hopkins Comparative Nonprofit Sector Project discovered that the much-vaunted European "welfare state" turns out on closer inspection to be a widespread "welfare partnership" involving extensive collaboration between government and the nonprofit sector. Clearly, a theory advancing as a solution to inadequate public sector performance a strategy that was already widely in place in a significant number of countries could hardly be relied on as a sufficient guide to the improvements that were needed—something else must be involved in the unsatisfactory performance of government than this.

This brings us, therefore, to a second departure of the New Governance Theory from the prevailing NPM approach. One of the comforting assumptions of NPM is that outsourcing governmental functions to third parties, and reliance on quasi-market mechanisms such as vouchers and tax expenditures simplifies governmental operations. According to this theory, such mechanisms capture the inherent efficiencies and automaticity of the market instead of having to rely on the cumbersome and inefficient mechanisms of public administration to achieve their results.

The New Governance Theory, by contrast, acknowledges the enormous challenges that attend the operation of indirect, third-party government. It does so by calling attention to a new "unit of analysis" in public management work. Where both traditional public administration and the NPM focus on the internal operations of *public agencies* as the central unit of analysis, the New Governance Theory shifts the focus instead to the distinctive *tools* or *instruments*—such as loans, grants, loan guarantees, contracting, regulation, insurance, tax expenditures, vouchers, and many more— through which public action is increasingly carried out. Each of these tools has its own operating procedures, its own skill requirements, its own delivery mechanism—indeed its own "political economy." Each therefore imparts its own "twist" to the operation of the programs that embody it. Loan guarantees, for example, rely on commercial banks to extend assisted credit to qualified borrowers. In the process, commercial lending officers become the implementing agents of government lending programs. Since private bankers have their own worldview, their own decision rules, and their own priorities, left to their own devices, they will likely produce programs that differ markedly from those that would result from direct government lending, not to mention outright government grants.

What is more, like loan guarantees, many of the most increasingly prevalent tools turn out to share a common feature: they are highly *indirect*. They rely on a wide assortment of "third parties"—commercial banks, private hospitals, social service agencies, industrial corporations, universities, daycare centers, other levels of government, financiers, construction firms, and many more—to deliver publicly financed services and pursue publicly authorized purposes.

What is involved here, moreover, is not simply the delegation of clearly defined ministerial duties to closely regulated agents of the state. That is a long-standing feature of government operations stretching back for generations.

What is distinctive about many of the newer tools of public action is that they involve the sharing with third-party actors of a far more basic governmental function: *the exercise of discretion over the use of public authority and the spending of public funds*. And thanks to the information asymmetries between principals and agents highlighted by the "principal-agent theory" of modern organizational theory, a major share—in many cases *the* major share— of the discretion over the operation of public programs routinely comes to rest not with the responsible governmental agencies but with the third-party actors that actually carry them out (on "principal-agent theory," see: Moe 1984; Pratt and Zeckhauser 1985; Kettl 1993).

Under these circumstances, the operation of indirect government actually turns out to be far more complicated and demanding than the operation of direct government. Where the latter "internalizes transactions" (Leman 2002), the former requires the anticipation of a wide range of potential contingencies to be structured in advance into formally binding contracts. Where the latter permits close supervision of governmental personnel, the latter requires complex negotiations with independent agencies over which government agencies have at best imperfect control. The result is not to eliminate or significantly scale back the need for public management, but to necessitate its expanded involvement, but in a new mode—as the balance wheel protecting important public interests in complex collaborative relationships involving multiple actors pursuing varied combinations of objectives within the structure of government-funded or -authorized programs. For this task, a new type of public manager is needed, one skilled in the techniques of network management and armed, not with the trappings of command and control, but with the more subtle techniques of negotiation and persuasion (Salamon 2002, pp. 16–18; Salamon 2005; see also Donahue and Zeckhauser 2011; Goldsmith and Eggers 2004).

Finally, unlike the NPM, which tends to emphasize reliance on the market and on market enterprises to take on functions formerly performed by governments, the New Governance Theory emphasizes as well the significant strengths that nonprofit organizations can bring to the provision of publicly financed services. This is so because nonprofit organizations offer significant advantages in delivering the services that governments are increasingly called on to provide. Among these, at least potentially, are the following:

- A significant degree of flexibility resulting from the relative ease with which agencies can form and disband and the closeness of governing boards to the field of action;
- Existing institutional structures in a number of program areas resulting from the fact that voluntary agencies frequently begin work in particular areas prior to the development of government programs in these areas;
- A generally smaller scale of operation, providing greater opportunity for tailoring services to client needs;
- A degree of diversity both in the content of services and in the institutional framework within which they are provided;
- A greater capacity to avoid fragmented approaches often created by government funding "silos," and to concentrate on the full range of needs that families or individuals face—to treat the person or the family instead of the isolated problem;
- Greater access to private charitable resources and volunteer labor, which can enhance the quality of service provided and "leverage" public dollars; and
- Mechanisms for promoting other important social values, such as group and individual freedom, diversity, a sense of community, and civic activism.

Because of these features, nonprofits can deliver human services at a human scale, and,

unlike for-profits, are less driven by the need to maximize profits and can thus endure dips in revenue that too often drive for-profit providers from a field. They thus have staying power—which is exceptionally important in fields where vulnerable clients rely on providers for assistance.

For all of these reasons, the New Governance Theory concludes that "the voluntary sector's weaknesses correspond well with government's strengths, and vice versa." Thus, extensive collaboration between government and the nonprofit sector emerges not as an unexplained aberration but as "a logical and theoretically sensible compromise" both for government and the third sector (Salamon 1995, pp. 48–49; Salamon 1987). Indeed, this feature has made the New Governance Theory especially attractive to European analysts, who faulted the NPM orthodoxy for failing to appreciate the challenges and subtleties of Europe's collaborative "welfare mix" and thereby threatening to create a dysfunctional and excessively commercial system of private provision (Ascoli and Ranci 2002; Evers 2005; Bode 2006). This in turn led to a growing disillusionment with market-based privatization and the business mechanism focus of the NPM movement. Since the beginning of the 2000s, NPM has therefore largely been overtaken by New Governance Theories that de-emphasize the need for market incentives and focus instead on service networks and the role of government in orchestrating a wide range of third parties. As Bode and Brandsen (2014, p. 1056) point out, for European observers of the modern state, "collaboration with the third sector is superior to mere public sector provision, given that the sector exhibits a particular potential of identifying the needs of citizens and may contribute to a more cost-efficient delivery through the use of volunteers." Despite its American origins, in other words, the tools of government approach have therefore immediate and growing applicability in both the Western European as well as Central European and Russian contexts, and likely more generally as well.

Overall, the voluntary failure theory and its broader New Governance conception thus emerge as two components of a particularly useful conceptual framework for both assessing and explaining patterns of government–nonprofit relationships.

Part III. Coping With the Challenges of Third-Party Government and Government–Nonprofit Cooperation

To say that third-party government and its specific manifestation in government–nonprofit cooperation holds enormous promise as a way to finance and deliver public services is not to say that this pattern is without its challenges. To the contrary, any relationship as complex as this one is likely to encounter immense strains and difficulties, especially given the somewhat different perspectives of the two sides. Government officials, for example, worry about the problems of exercising management supervision, ensuring a degree of accountability, and encouraging coordination when decision-making authority is widely dispersed and vested in institutions with their own independent sources of authority and support. Within the philanthropic community, the issues raised by the prevailing pattern of government support of nonprofit organizations are of a far different sort. Of central concern here are at least four potential dangers: (a) the potential *loss of autonomy* or independence that some fear can result from heavy dependence on government support; (b) "*vendorism*," or the distortion of agency missions in pursuit of available government funding; (c) *bureaucratization*, or over-professionalization resulting from government program and accounting requirements; and (d) the stunting of *advocacy activity* in order not to endanger public funding streams (Salamon 1995; Toepler 2010).

Writing in 1995, Salamon (p. 104) pointed out that "The message that emerges from the limited analysis to date is that many of the concerns about the partnership [in the American context] have not materialized to anywhere near the extent feared."

Nevertheless, the concerns are real and deserve attention, especially as the experience with government–nonprofit relations moves from countries with generally open political systems and multiple points of entry through which to fend off undue governmental influence to those in which resistance to such influence is harder to maintain. Certainly, the risks are real where financial dependency is high, and governments enjoy total, or near-total, control over available resources, as resource dependency theorists suggest (Pfeffer and Salancik 1978). Consequences can include the loss of an agency's ability to determine its own mission and goals or to set programmatic preferences and priorities freely (Anheier et al. 1997; Jung and Moon 2007). One way to minimize these risks is to nurture alternative sources of revenue—from charitable contributions, contributions of time, or fee-based income. Another is to diversify the sources of governmental support by approaching multiple offices or levels of government. More generally, nonprofit providers can take advantage of the information asymmetries identified in principal-agent theory as a major barrier to the type of detailed control that government funding is often feared to [have] created.

"Vendorism," or the perennial pursuit of government contracts without much regard to the particular objective or any involvement in setting the policy being pursued (Kramer 1981, p. 153), is a particular concern with the government contracting tool and has attracted a large literature both in the American context and elsewhere (see, for example: Smith and Lipsky 1993; Smith 2010; Ascoli and Ranci 2002; Buckingham 2012). Aside from the loss of mission focus, concerns arise over a number of more concrete specific managerial challenges that contracts pose for nonprofits, including payment delays, cash-flow management, off-putting contract boilerplate, limited coverage of true costs, disputed payments, limited contractual time-horizons, contract close-out disputes, and contract renewal problems. As public service contracting becomes more prevalent elsewhere, as in the U.K., for example, similar challenges and tensions for different types of local contractors also become more evident. Being typically undercapitalized and lacking financial slack makes it difficult for nonprofits to absorb the sudden cash-flow changes which result from delayed contract payments, underestimations of the actual costs involved in the contract, or other unanticipated expenditures. The resulting financial insecurity seems almost endemic to contracting arrangements. Worse yet are the pressures that contracts frequently create to displace organizational commitments to traditional community constituencies in order to comply with public sector equity and other norms (Smith and Lipsky 1993). In religiously affiliated organizations, for example, this can lead to a secularization of service delivery.

Perhaps a more pervasive, if subtle, consequence of government–nonprofit cooperation is the impact it can have on nonprofit organizations *qua* organizations. In a word, government–nonprofit cooperation can lead to the bureaucratization of nonprofit organizations. This results less from having to adapt to public sector values than from having to conform to the administrative procedures involved in applying for and managing government funds. Contracting rules for human services frequently build on the procedures used for other government procurement, which frequently call for a level of specificity and evidence of financial and administrative record-keeping that small nonprofits may find it difficult to provide. What is more, government program requirements, often advanced by nonprofits themselves in order to keep for-profit competitors at bay, frequently require certifications of staff capabilities and specified levels of service provision that smaller nonprofits may find it challenging to provide. Complicated reimbursement systems of the sort required for voucher-type programs only add to the difficulty and the resulting need for more professional, and more costly, staff.

A final major concern about government–nonprofit collaboration concerns the ability of nonprofits to pursue their advocacy or lobbying responsibilities while working closely with government agencies. To be sure, the evidence here is uneven. In the American context, it is uncertainties about the legal status of advocacy and lobbying, rather than politically inspired hostility to it, that seems to impede greater advocacy involvement (Bass et al. 2007). Salamon and Geller (2008) report that, far from declining, nonprofit involvement in advocacy activity actually increases with increases in government support, suggesting that nonprofits with a stake in public policy are more likely to engage in efforts to shape it.

Whatever the specific problems might be that arise in government–nonprofit cooperation, the underlying concern is that involvement in government programs will erode the distinctive roles and contributions that attract governments to partner with nonprofits in the first place. This means that a balance must be struck between the government's need for economy, efficiency, equity, and accountability and the nonprofit sector's need for a degree of self-determination and independence from governmental control. Based on the existing literature, it is possible to identify at least three clues about how this can best be done.

Accommodation by Government of the Organizational Needs of Nonprofit Organizations

In the first place, as noted above, care must be taken not to structure the government–nonprofit partnership in ways that undermine the distinctive characteristics of the nonprofit sector. This can occur if administrative arrangements are too cumbersome or confining; if performance requirements are too burdensome; or if special attributes of nonprofits, such as their community roots or their ability to give voice to new needs, are somehow curtailed.

Of special concern here is the advocacy function of nonprofits—the ability to give voice to the voiceless and call important matters of policy to the attention of governmental authorities. Indeed, these organizations may be in a unique position to serve as a link between individuals and communities, on the one hand, and the broader political process on the other. Indeed, there is a growing consensus among experts that committing to both service and advocacy is a key to high performance by nonprofits (Bass et al. 2014). "High-impact organizations . . . eventually realize that they cannot achieve large-scale social change through service delivery alone. . . . Ultimately, all high-impact organizations bridge the divide between service and advocacy" (Grant and Crutchfield 2007, p. 35).

Special Attention to the Management of the Partnership

As we have seen, although outsourcing services to nonprofits or other third-party actors is often assumed to reduce the management challenges of government, it more likely increases them (Salamon 2002, p. 38; Kettl 2002, pp. 490–510; van Slyke 2003). Indirect tools require advanced planning of far more operational details than is the case with more direct tools. In addition, incentives must be carefully structured to achieve the desired result from entities over which government has only imperfect control. And all of this must be done while avoiding damage to the underlying characteristics of the third-party partners.

Two sets of considerations have been identified in the literature as contributing to effective management of such partnerships:

first, *operational features* that take account of the capabilities and needs of the government's partner; and second, *access* for the partners to the design of the programs that form the heart of the partnership.

Regarding the *operational features*, governments often try to bring to the management of their partnerships the same procedures that govern the internal management of their own organizations. This is often a prescription for problems. Instead, attention needs to be devoted to operational features conducive to the needs of the partners as well, such as:

- Payment schedules on grants and contracts that avoid costly cash-flow problems for non-profit organizations;
- Avoidance of undue interference with the non-service functions of the organizations;
- The use of challenge grants or other funding devices that reward agencies for the use of volunteers or the generation of private-sector funds to supplement public resources; and
- Continued encouragement of private giving, which is crucial for the preservation of an element of independence and flexibility for non-profit agencies.

Beyond this, mechanisms for engaging partners in the design of programs can improve partnership operations. Nonprofit organizations often have knowledge of programmatic needs that can improve the effectiveness of programs; without access to the design phase of programs, and without continuing channels through which to offer suggestions for mid-course corrections, however, they can lose the opportunity to bring this knowledge to bear and be frustrated as a result.

Many European countries have established formal consultative relationships between the nonprofit sector and government to avoid this problem. In some cases, this takes the form of formal channels of consultation and joint policy development. A good example of this is the

German system, which is based on the principle of subsidiarity in welfare provision. The doctrine of subsidiarity essentially holds that the responsibility for caring for individuals' needs should always be vested in the units of social life closest to the individual—the family, the parish, the community, the voluntary association—and that larger, or higher level, units should be entrusted only when a problem clearly exceeds the capabilities of these primary units. What is more, the doctrine holds that the higher units have an obligation not only to avoid usurping the position of the lower units, but to help the lower units perform their role.

In Germany, the subsidiary principle was fully established in the Social Assistance Act of 1961, which obliges the "public bodies responsible for social assistance" to "collaborate with the public law churches and religious communities, and with the free welfare associations" and to do so in a way that acknowledges "their independence in the targeting and execution of their functions." In a sense, therefore, nonprofit organizations are not only guaranteed a share of public resources, but also a share of the authority for making public policy (Salamon and Anheier 1998).

While Germany's arrangements are longstanding and firmly enshrined in law, a slightly different arrangement with the same general objective has taken shape in the UK and has been copied by a number of other countries.

The vehicle here was the Voluntary Sector Compact. Worked out in collaboration between the UK government and the voluntary sector in the mid-1990s, the Compact commits the government to funding, to streamlined funding procedures, and to the involvement of voluntary-sector organizations in the design of public policy in the areas in which they operate (Plowden 2003). While the implementation of these arrangements has not been without issues, the idea of formal compacts has spread to a number of different countries over the last ten to fifteen years (Reuter et al. 2014).

Attention to the Tools of Action Through Which Partnerships Are Effectuated and a Level Playing Field for Nonprofits

A third clue to the effective operation of partnerships is paying serious attention to the particular tools through which partnerships are effectuated. This attention to the tools of action is a central feature of the New Governance Theory (Salamon 2002). Tools structure partnerships. In the process, they determine the operating procedures of programs, the partners on which programs will depend, and the degree of discretion left to these partners. Inevitably, some tools are more advantageous to nonprofits than others. Generally speaking, producer-side subsidies such as grants or contracts are much preferred to consumer side subsidies such as vouchers and tax expenditures, because the former deliver their benefits directly to the organizations whereas the latter put the resources in the hands of consumers, who can "shop" among providers. This puts nonprofit organizations at a disadvantage because they generally lack marketing skills and access to capital due to the constraint on their distribution of profits to potential shareholders. Lacking access to investment capital, they find it difficult to expand to meet the new demands often triggered by new government voucher programs. A key to the success of nonprofit providers in such circumstances is therefore to level the playing field for access to capital on their part, which can be done by offering various subsidies to investors in nonprofit organizations in these fields. The alternative is to trigger a significant loss of nonprofit market share as for-profits raise capital through stock issues and rapidly expand the supply of facilities to absorb the government-induced expanded demand for services—a process that has been very much under way in the United States (Salamon 2012, pp. 29–31, 2015, pp. 40–43). What is more, nonprofits typically prefer grants over contracts because grants typically offer more leeway for the beneficiary organizations, whereas contracts involve higher levels of specificity and mechanisms of accountability (van Slyke 2006). Tool knowledge, and knowledge of the particular design features of the tool embodied in a particular program, can thus determine the actual impact that involvement in a program can have for nonprofits. Attention to this facet of government policy would thus pay enormous dividends for both governments and nonprofit partners.

Conclusion

Despite prevailing, mostly economic, theories of the nonprofit sector, which treat government–nonprofit cooperation as, at best, an unexpected outcome and, at worst, a serious and unfortunate aberration, such cooperation has grown massively around the world and appears poised to continue to do so into the foreseeable future. As this article makes clear, however, prevailing theories of both the nonprofit sector and the state contain serious blind spots that have made it difficult for them to imagine how such cooperation could make both theoretical and practical sense. Partly as a consequence of this, opportunities to visualize and build upon such partnerships have not been fully enough taken or carefully enough structured.

Armed with the twin theoretical insights of "voluntary failure" and the New Governance, however, this option for pursuing public sector objectives comes fully into view not only as a theoretically legitimate, but also as a substantively necessary, means through which to improve the way societies address growing social, economic, and environmental challenges. As it turns out, the strengths of the nonprofit sector as a provider of public goods nicely complement the limitations of government both in originating and delivering such goods, while the strengths of government as a generator of revenue and of rights to benefits nicely complement the limitations of the nonprofit sector in these same areas. Hence, far from an aberration, government–nonprofit cooperation emerges through the lens of these

theories as a logical outcome of mutual interdependence and a highly effective way to organize a wide assortment of publicly financed services.

What is more, government–nonprofit cooperation—and the broader patterns of third-party government of which they are a part—provide a more compelling and encompassing conceptual map to a desirable future of public problem-solving than either the more limited and narrow NPM prescription or continued reliance on direct government alone.

For such a future to come within reach, however, greater attention will need to be paid to the dynamics built into the different tools, or instruments, through which programs are carried out. Among other things, this will require a new, collaborative style of public management and the engagement of government's partners not only in the execution of government programs, but also in their development and design. And it will require clearer understanding of how these tools operate and what consequences they have for those who benefit from them, for those who pay the bills, and for those who actually deliver the benefits. It is to the task of building that understanding that attention now needs to turn.

Acknowledgment

This article was prepared within the framework of a subsidy granted to the National Research University Higher School of Economics, Russian Federation by the Government of the Russian Federation for the implementation of the Global Competitiveness Program. None of the organizations with which the authors are affiliated or that have supported their work bear any responsibility for any errors or views expressed here. That is the authors' own responsibility.

Notes

1. Harvard College, America's oldest nonprofit institution, was created in the early part of the 17th

century by an act of the Massachusetts Commonwealth legislature and sustained through much of its early life by a dedicated tax on corn—the so-called "college corn." As of 1898, 60% of the funds that the City of New York was spending on the care of paupers and prisoners went to private benevolent institutions, and similar practices were evident in all but four American states (Fetter 1901/02, pp. 376, 360). Similarly, the very first national social service program in the United States took the form of a grant-in-aid to a nonprofit social service organization, and a sectarian one at that—the Little Sisters of the Poor in Washington, D.C. This program was enacted in 1874 (Warner 1894).

2. As conservative theorist Robert Nisbet (1962, p. 109) put it: "The real conflict in modern political history has not been, as is so often stated, between state and individual, but between state and social group."

3. By the start of the 21st century, direct provision of goods or services by government bureaucrats accounted for only 5% of the activity of the U.S. federal government. Even with income transfers, direct loans, and interest payments counted as "direct government," the direct activities of the federal government amounted to only 28% of federal activities. Far larger in scale, and accounting for over 70% of the federal government's financial activities, were the more indirect instruments of public action—contracting, grants-in-aid, vouchers, tax expenditures, loan guarantees, insurance, and regulation, to name just a few (Salamon 2002). While it is true that more direct activities are carried out at the state and local level in the United States, third-party government is a familiar and growing practice at these other levels as well (Goldsmith and Eggers 2004; Agranoff and McGuire 2003).

References

Agranoff, R. (2007). *Managing within networks: Adding value to public organizations*. Washington, DC: Georgetown University Press.

Agranoff, R., & McGuire, M. (2003). *Collaborative public management: New strategies for local governments*. Washington, DC: Georgetown University Press.

Anheier, H., Toepler, S., & Sokolowski, S. W. (1997). The implications of government funding for nonprofit organizations: Three propositions. *International Journal of Public Sector Management, 10*, 190–213.

Ascoli, U., & Ranci, C. (2002). *Dilemmas of the welfare mix: The new structure of welfare in an era of privatization*. New York: Springer.

Bass, G., Abramson, A., & Dewey, E. (2014). Effective advocacy: Lessons for nonprofit leaders from research and practice. In R. Pekkanen, S. R. Smith, & Y. Tsujinaka (Eds.), *Nonprofits and advocacy: Engaging community and government in an era of retrenchment*. Baltimore: Johns Hopkins University Press.

Bass, G., Arons, D., Guinane, K., & Carter, M. (2007). *Seen, but not heard: Strengthening nonprofit advocacy*. Washington, DC: Aspen Institute Press.

Bode, I. (2006). Disorganized welfare mixes: Voluntary agencies and new governance regimes in Western Europe. *Journal of European Social Policy, 4*, 346–359.

Bode, I., & Brandsen, T. (2014). State-third sector partnerships: A short overview of key issues in the debate, introduction to the special issue on state-third sector partnerships. *Public Management Review, 16*, 1055–1066.

Buckingham, H. (2012). Capturing diversity: A typology of third sector organizations' responses to contracting based on empirical evidence from homelessness services. *Journal of Social Policy, 41*, 569–589.

Donahue, J., & Zeckhauser, R. (2011). *Collaborative governance: Private roles for public goals in turbulent times*. Princeton: Princeton University Press.

Evers, A. (2005). Mixed welfare systems and hybrid organizations: Changes in the governance and provision of social services. *International Journal of Public Administration, 28*, 737–748.

Fetter, F. (1901/02). The subsidizing of private charities. *American Journal of Sociology, 7*, 359–385.

Gidron, B., Kramer, R., & Salamon, L. M. (1992). *Government and the third sector in comparative perspective: Experience in modern welfare states*. San Francisco: Jossey-Bass.

Goldsmith, S., & Eggers, W. D. (2004). *Governing by network: The new shape of the public sector*. Washington, DC: Brookings Institution Press.

Goldsmith, S., & Kettl, D. (2009). *Unlocking the power of networks: Keys to high-performance government*. Washington, DC: Brookings Institution Press.

Grant, H. M., & Crutchfield, L. R. (2007). Creating high-impact nonprofits. *Stanford Social Innovation Review, 5*, 32–41.

Hansmann, H. (1987). Economic theories of nonprofit organizations. In W. W. Powell (Ed.), *The nonprofit sector: A research handbook*. New Haven: Yale University Press.

James, E. (1987). The nonprofit sector in comparative perspective. In W. W. Powell (Ed.), *The nonprofit sector: A research handbook*. New Haven: Yale University Press.

Jung, K., & Moon, M. (2007). The double-edged sword of public-resource dependence: The impact of public resources on autonomy and legitimacy in Korean cultural nonprofit organizations. *The Policy Studies Journal, 35*, 205–226.

Kettl, D. (1993). *Sharing power: Public governance and private markets*. Washington, DC: Brookings Institution Press.

Kettl, D. (2002). *The transformation of governance: Public administration for the 21st century*. Baltimore: Johns Hopkins University Press.

Kramer, R. (1981). *Voluntary agencies in the welfare state*. Berkeley: University of California Press.

Lane, J. (2000). *New public management*. London: Routledge.

Le Grand, J. (2011). Quasi-market versus state provision of public services: Some ethical considerations. *Public Reason, 3*(2), 80–89.

Le Grand, J., & Bartlett, W. (Eds.). (1993a). *Quasi-markets and social policy*. London: Palgrave.

Leman, N. (2002). Direct government. In L. M. Salamon (Ed.), *The tools of government: A guide to the new governance*. New York: Oxford University Press.

Moe, Terry M. (1984). The new economics of organization. *American Journal of Political Science, 28*(November), 739–777.

Nisbet, R. (1962). *Community and power*. New York: Oxford University Press.

Olson, M. (1965). *The logic of collective action*. Cambridge, MA: Harvard University Press.

Osborne, S. P. (2006). The new public governance? *Public Management Review, 8*, 377–387.

Pfeffer, J., & Salancik, G. (1978). *The external control of organizations: A resource dependence perspective*. New York: Harper & Row.

Plowden, W. (2003). The compact attempts to regulate relationships between government and the voluntary sector in England. *Nonprofit and Voluntary Sector Quarterly, 32*, 415–432.

Plumptre, T. (1993). Public sector reform: An international perspective. In C. McQuillan (Ed.), *Proceedings of the Canada South-East Asia colloquium: Transforming the public sector*. Ottawa: Institute on Governance.

Pratt, John W., & Zeckhauser, R. J. (1985). Principals and agents: An overview. In J. W. Pratt & R. J. Zeckhauser (Eds.), *Principals and agents: The structure of business*. Cambridge: Harvard Business School Press.

Reuter, M., Wijkstrom, F., & von Essen, J. (2014). Policy tools or mirrors of politics: Government-voluntary sector compacts in the post-welfare state age. *Nonprofit Policy Forum, 3*(2).

Ringling, A. (2002). European experience with tools of government. In L. M. Salamon (Ed.), *The tools of government: A guide to the new governance*. New York: Oxford University Press.

Salamon, L. M. (1981). Rethinking public management: Third-Party government and the tools of government action. *Public Policy, 29*, 255–275.

Salamon, L. M. (1987). Of market failure, voluntary failure and third party government: The theory of government–nonprofit relations in the modern welfare state. *Journal of Voluntary Action Research, 16*, 29–49.

Salamon, L. M. (1995). *Partners in public service: Government–nonprofit relations in the modern welfare state*. Baltimore: Johns Hopkins University Press.

Salamon, L. M. (Ed.). (2002). *The tools of government: A guide to the new governance*. New York: Oxford University Press.

Salamon, L. M. (2005). Training professional citizens: Getting beyond the right answer to the wrong question in public affairs education. *Journal of Public Affairs Education, 11*(1), 7–19.

Salamon, L. M. (Ed.). (2012). *The state of nonprofit America* (2nd ed.). Washington, DC: Brookings Institution Press.

Salamon, L. M. (2015). *The resilient sector revisited: The new challenge to nonprofit America*. Washington, DC: Brookings Institution Press.

Salamon, L. M., & Abramson, A. (1981). *The federal government and the nonprofit sector: Implications of the Reagan budget proposals.* Washington, DC: The Urban Institute.

Salamon, L. M., & Anheier, H. (1994). *The emerging sector.* Baltimore: Johns Hopkins Institute for Policy Studies.

Salamon, L. M., & Anheier, H. (1998). The third route: Government–nonprofit collaboration in Germany and the United States. In W. Powell & E. Clemens (Eds.), *Private action and the public good.* New Haven: Yale University Press.

Salamon, L. M., & Geller, S. L. (2008). Nonprofit America: A force for democracy? *Listening Post Communiqué No. 9.* Baltimore: Johns Hopkins Center for Civil Society Studies. http://ccss.jhu.edu/publications-findings/?did=260.

Salamon, L. M., Sokolowski, S. W., & Associates. (2004). *Global civil society: Dimensions of the nonprofit sector* (Vol. Two). Greenwood: Kumarian Press.

Siriani, C., & Friedland, L. (2001). *Civic innovation in America.* Berkeley: University of California Press.

Smith, S. R. (2010). Managing the challenges of government contracts. In D. Renz, et al. (Eds.), *The Jossey-Bass handbook of nonprofit leadership and management.* San Francisco: Jossey-Bass.

Smith, S. R., & Lipsky, M. (1993). *Nonprofits for hire.* Cambridge, MA: Harvard University Press.

Toepler, S. (2010). Government funding policies. In B. Seaman & D. Young (Eds.), *Handbook of research on nonprofit economics and management.* Cheltenham: Edward Elgar.

Tullock, G. (1965). *The politics of bureaucracy.* Washington, DC: Public Affairs Press.

van Slyke, D. (2003). The mythology of privatization in contracting for social services. *Public Administration Review, 63,* 277–296.

van Slyke, D. (2006). Agents of stewards: Using theory to understand the government–nonprofit social service contracting relationship. *Journal of Public Administration Research and Theory, 17,* 157–187.

Warner, A. (1894). *American charities.* New York: Thomas Y. Crowell Publishers.

Weisbrod, B. A. (1975). Toward a theory of the voluntary nonprofit sector in a three-sector economy. In E. Phelps (Ed.), *Altruism, morality, and economic theory.* New York: Russell Sage.

Whitehead, J. (1973). *The separation of college and state: Columbia, Dartmouth, Harvard and Yale, 1776–1876.* New Haven: Yale University Press.

Wurzel, R. K. W., Zito, A. R., & Jordan, A. J. (2013). *Environmental governance in Europe: A comparative analysis of new environmental policy instruments.* Cheltenham: Edward Elgar.

CHAPTER 32

Public–Private Partnership in Turbulent Times

Graeme Hodge and Carsten Greve

Greve, Carsten, and Graeme Hodge. (Eds.), *Rethinking Public-Private Partnerships: Strategies for Turbulent Times* (London: Routledge, 2013).

Introduction

One of the paradoxes of the last few decades has been the continuity and even growth of infrastructure public–private partnerships (PPPs) despite the loud voices of critics and harsh judgements of some academics. Indeed, there is little doubt about the success of PPPs on the basis of global interest, the frequency of use in countries such as the UK and Australia or by the spectacular delivery of timely new infrastructure. There has been substantial work undertaken to date on the multiple meanings of PPP more generally, the multidisciplinary languages spoken by commentators, and on the evaluation challenges faced by those interested in assessing PPPs as projects or activities. Whilst acknowledging the considerable advocacy and assertions of those pushing such reforms, there has been less work undertaken on the theory of PPPs. There is a real need to articulate the potential causal factors behind why PPPs may be capable of producing superior performance compared to traditional arrangements. This chapter focuses in particular on meanings given to how PPP might be judged as successful by implementing governments. The specific aim of the chapter is to explore the notion of success—what constitutes success for PPP? The criteria appear to be both varied and multifaceted, while also mirroring the very goals of government in society. A recent contextual factor has been the global financial crisis (GFC) that hit the world in 2008, catapulting PPP into 'turbulent times'. So how might the aftermath of the GFC affect PPP success?

The chapter is divided into three parts. Part one examines the variety of forms and levels of PPP. Part two details the theoretically-based criteria for 'success', taking inspiration from some of the recent literature on 'policy success'. Part three explores what the GFC and the turbulent times that have followed it may mean for PPPs.

Public–Private Partnerships: A Variety of Forms and Levels

PPP has been defined as 'cooperation between public–private actors in which they jointly develop products and services and share risks, costs and resources which are connected with these products and services' (Van Ham and Koppenjan 2001: 598, quoted in Hodge and Greve 2005). Moreover, authors such as Weihe (2005) and Hodge and Greve (2007) have defined partnerships as encompassing several different families of activities; and the desire to articulate public–private partnership continues.

In the United Nations, PPPs are defined as 'voluntary and collaborative relationships between various parties, both state and nonstate, in which all participants agree to work together to achieve a common purpose or undertake a specific task, and to share risks and responsibilities, resources and benefits' (UN General Assembly 2005: 4; cited in Bull 2010: 480). Such partnerships can include those oriented towards resource mobilization, advocacy and policy goals, as well as long-term operations.

There are several crucial concepts here. One concept is 'risk'. In almost all definitions, sharing of risks in an explicit way is mentioned as one of the key aspects of PPP. This differs from earlier ideas on risk sharing through contracting out/outsourcing arrangements where this was more implicit.[1] Another key concept is 'innovation': the public sector and the private sector have to come up with new solutions and 'work together or achieve a common purpose'. More is expected of PPPs than just 'ordinary' collaboration. There is usually a sense of hope that the relationship is a long-term one—and desirably longer than the temporary relationship achievable through traditional 'contracting out' of services. Additionally, many partnerships entertain the notion of a certain degree of power sharing whilst working together jointly.

As witnessed in the last few decades, PPPs come in many shapes and sizes. Perhaps the most visible form of recent partnership has been the long-term infrastructure contract (LTIC) partnership. Another is the widespread co-operation between governments and non-profit organizations. This has been a tradition in some countries, especially in the USA where non-profit sector organizations run many public

services (Amirkhanyan 2010; Kettl 2009). In the UK, there has been a debate on the 'big society' since Prime Minister David Cameron took office. Recently, the 'big society' has also been suggested as a guide for research efforts, though universities express misgivings about that (*The Guardian*, 27 March 2011). There are also other newer forms of partnering where the public sector and the private sector team up in new innovative formats to solve common challenges. 'Gate21' is a current example of a partnership on environmental issues. What began as a sustainable future forum by local government quickly spread as relationships were forged with other local governments, private sector companies and non-profit organizations as well as universities and housing associations (www.gate21.dk).

PPPs are, moreover, found at various levels of government, from regional partnerships between local governments and local private sector companies or associations, to national governments that team up with national companies or associations, to international organizations that team up with multinational companies (Skanska) or associations (the Red Cross).

PPPs are also, clearly, more than projects (the building of a hospital or bridge). PPPs are now also associated with policies on how the government should interact with the private sector in order to improve public services or create innovation (the recent Danish government's 'Strategy for public–private partnerships and markets' is an example of this). At the UN level, there is a PPP policy (Bull 2010). At an even broader level, PPP could be a metaphor or a brand for how governments want their interaction with business and society viewed, or, alternatively, how they want the role of government in the economy viewed. And at a broader level still, the UN's Millennium Declaration (and the subsequent establishment of the Millennium Development Goals, MDGs) saw partnership being used in the context of developed countries having a role in aiding developing countries; Goal 8 here was to achieve a 'global partnership for development' through various means.[2]

Perhaps it makes sense to view PPP as being understood at many different levels. Hodge (2010b) formulated it in this way:

> PPPs can be understood as (1) a specific project or activity, (2) a management tool or organizational form, (3) a policy, or statement as to the role of the government in the economy, (4) a governance tool or symbol, or (5) an historical context and a cultural set of assumptions.

A Conceptual Model of the PPP Phenomenon

So PPP may indeed mean different things to different people. If this is the case, how might we build on this idea and develop a conceptual model in order to contribute to multiple jurisdictions and PPP debates around the globe?

At the narrowest level, PPP is viewed as a single project. At level B, PPP is viewed as a specific type of infrastructure delivery mechanism involving the use of contracted private finance to initially fund all works.

The next conceptual level takes this project tool one step further and sets the private finance delivery of PPP infrastructure as a policy preference for a jurisdiction. It may also operate at a wider policy level and recognizes explicitly that there is, in reality, not one single PPP type but a wide variety of alternative project delivery options available to governments, all of which use differing arrangements of public and private sector skills. The OECD list of acronyms is a manifestation of this: the breadth available here[3] is therefore essentially a policy statement that the private sector has a valid—and indeed major—role to play in today's mixed economy, whichever technical delivery option is chosen.

The use of huge private contracts with a consortium for the delivery of high-profile government projects is a strong regulatory tool in

governing.[4] Large economic incentives can be employed to ensure that the promise of early achievement of government objectives is met—even for complex projects and in controversial circumstances. PPPs can also function as a broader governance tool and mark a particular style of governance. For instance, the Labour government in the UK throughout the 1990s struggled to develop its relationship with the City of London. But as Hellowell (2010: 310) points out, PPP provided the incoming Tony Blair and his 'New Labour' government with advantages. Indeed, the use of private finance had the 'crucial [political] advantage that borrowing undertaken through it did not score against the main calculations of national debt', and borrowing was thus essentially 'invisible' to public sector borrowing and investment measurements. Blair's rebranding of the Private Finance Initiative (PFI) scheme as a public–private partnership policy was a further masterful political move under the 'third way' banner. Importantly, this PPP policy not only assisted New Labour in establishing a stronger relationship with the City of London, but also international promotion of PPP ideas then enabled this relationship to be cemented (Hellowell 2010). Both of these political characteristics of PPP suggest that it continues to have an inherently political, and thus governance, context in addition to any functional engineering or economic meaning.

In this model, each of the inner perspectives of PPP exist within the context of others. The notion that a PPP is simply a project delivery tool, for instance, carries with it many assumptions: the role of the private sector in the economy, how governance might occur in a country, as well as broader historical and cultural assumptions of that country. These dimensions are, to a strong degree, inherently bound together.

It is important to recognize that the PPP phenomenon exists within any one single cultural/historical tradition at each of the four levels. In Victoria, Australia, for example, the Bracks/Brumby governments (2000–10) branded a specific set of infrastructure delivery arrangements using private financing as PPP.[5] A broader and less partisan view of partnership would acknowledge that the latest PPP policy is simply the most recent step in a long developmental process in which the delivery of large infrastructure projects through the private sector has been progressively changing over the past three decades. The governments also branded their PPP policy as different to the PFI policy of the UK. This Australian PPP branding might be contrasted against the modern use of PPP terminology by a country such as the People's Republic of China. The huge Beijing Line 4 construction project has been labelled as a PPP, but the reality is that it most likely has public ownership of just above 92 per cent and would, by western analysts, be regarded essentially as a public–public partnership.[6] Notwithstanding, this arrangement clearly signals new directions in terms of institutional, contractual, professional and project delivery dimensions for China. In this sense, PPP in China represents an important symbolic move to innovate, to commercialize and to professionalize. PPP represents change.

In our conceptual model, therefore, each of the four levels of PPP meaning exist within a broader historical and cultural context. The above examples suggest that this is an important additional part of understanding the legitimate use of the PPP label as well as other dimensions covering the more technical-, institutional- or governance-related aspects.

Theoretical Criteria for PPP Success

In concept, success can be judged at each of the four levels of PPP. In this section we contemplate success from the narrowest of these perspectives (project level), to a broader (organizational) level, through to the perspective of government and the broadest levels of societal change and benefit.

At the narrowest end, the literature is full of claims of success based at the project level. We all enjoy brand-new facilities, whether they are hospitals, schools, courts, tunnels or roads; and given that the very specifications of PPP contracts indicate the need to deliver a project according to particular engineering, timing and financial standards, viewing success in this manner is hardly surprising. When a major infrastructure project is delivered according to the contracted standards, this is success. It may also have come in on time and on budget. A major attraction of declaring success at this level is its certainty, its visibility and its appeal to a common-sense judgment.

However the reasons for governments adopting PPP ideas are more sophisticated than simply delivering a project—they have been doing that for centuries. If we trace back over the explicit (and implicit) reasons for adoption, they are manifold.[7] The initial rationale under John Major's UK government was to get around restrictions on formal public sector debt levels. Private financing promised a way to provide infrastructure without increasing the Public Sector Borrowing Requirement (PSBR). This was followed by the promise that PPPs would 'reduce pressure on public-sector budgets'.[8] The third promise of PPPs was that this delivery mechanism provides better value for money (VfM) for taxpayers. This is a policy promise most worthy of examination and one that has also formed the primary PPP rationale in countries such as the UK and Australia. In addition to these three initial promises have been many more—some explicit such as: reduced risk to government from projects, better accountability, better on-time and on-budget delivery, and greater innovation; and some implicit such as: encouraging a more innovative public sector, improved business confidence, improved palatability for user funding for infrastructure, provision for long-term infrastructure life-cycle costs, and boosted sales of professional PPP services abroad. To these 13 PPP objectives we might

TABLE 32.1 Examples of forms of partnership (public–private) and dimensions of the PPP phenomenon

	Government–Private Company	Government–Non-profit	Government–Private Company–Non-profit
Project/activity	Hospital project, school project	Public sector employees 'opt out' to form own non-profit project	Gate21 in DK, a partnership on climate change issues
Organizational form	PFI organizational form	Red Cross running refugee camps on behalf of government	Networked partnership across multiple organizations
Policy/symbol	UK Treasury PFI policy	'Big society' agenda in UK	World Bank policy in private sector involvement
	Canadian PPP policy		
	Victoria, Australia PPP policy		
	European Commission PPP policy across directorates from 2010		
Governance tool or style	EU on the role of government in the European economy	Role of non-profits in delivery of specific services in the US because of pressing policy issues	Millennium goals in the UN
Historical context of public–private relations	Can market economy continue the same way after the financial crisis?	Associations' integral use in the building of the administrative state	UN global compact between developed and developing world

nowadays also add two more objectives following the recent credit market failures and stock market downturns. It may well be that two new implicit objectives for PPPs will be: the desire for governments to broadly support businesses and preferentially adopt the PPP mechanism in difficult market circumstances (the objective of business assistance), or the broader societal objective of economic development. Additional objectives, too, are also possible, but the point here is clear. There have been many separate objectives set for PPPs, ranging from narrow financial objectives such as project value for money and delivery goals, such as timeliness, to much broader efforts to change culture or implement policy, as well as better governing and the pursuit of economic development. These are shown in Table 32.2 below. Furthermore, these

TABLE 32.2 Objectives—both explicit and implied to date

Objective	Number	Objective/Promise Made by Government
Financial	1	Provide better VfM for taxpayers
	2	Reduce pressure on public sector budgets
Project delivery	3	Provide better on-time delivery
	4	Allow better on-budget delivery
Cultural change	5	Allow greater infrastructure (project) innovation
	6	Encourage a more innovative public sector
Policy	7	Enable provision of infrastructure without appearing to increase public sector borrowing
	8	Support businesses in difficult global market conditions (business assistance/subsidy)
	9	Improve political feasibility to impose user fees
	10	Reduce risks to government from infrastructure projects
Governance	11	Be a symbol of new (third way) government
	12	Help put infrastructure issues onto the public policy agenda
	13	Improve business confidence
	14	Improve government budget credentials
	15	Improve accountability
Economic	16	Provide a crucial tool to underpin the broad societal objective of economic development
	17	Boost sales of professional PPP services abroad
	18	Enable the full life-cycle costs of infrastructure to be provided

Source: Adapted from Hodge (2010a)

objectives have also altered over time, and today still remain slippery in the rough-and-tumble of government policy speak.

How might we determine, for example, if PPP has been successful in delivering projects more 'on time' (as promised as a delivery mechanism), encouraging a more innovative public sector (promised at the policy level), or improving business confidence and underpinning economic development (as implied at the governance level)?

A major contribution here has been the work of Jeffares *et al.* and Skelcher and Sullivan (2008), which builds on earlier work by Skelcher and Sullivan. Jeffares *et al.* have been concerned with how it is possible to measure the performance of partnership. Instead of taking the usual private sector route, and only asking if a partnership contributes to economic success, Jeffares *et al.* and Skelcher and Sullivan pointed to the need for a theory-based evaluation of partnership performance. In their work, Jeffares *et al.* talk about 'performance domains' that are linked explicitly to acknowledged bodies of theory. These performance domains (and the associated theoretical arenas) include: *democracy* (democratic theory); *policy* goal achievement (network theory); *transformation* to produce new public sector behaviours (institutional theory); *connectivity* to stimulate innovation (innovation theory, network theory); *co-ordination* to achieve synergies (resource dependency); and *coalition* to achieve sustainable partnerships (discourse theory). Each of these alternative dimensions is valuable and each brings different PPP values into the spotlight.

Crucially, Jeffares *et al.* acknowledge the need for a 'theoretically informed' evaluation framework and for any PPP assessment to consider 'performance' in a range of ways. However, they also are clear about 'the politically-loaded nature of PPPs as public policy instruments'. As they quite rightly state: 'PPPs are as much political as they are managerial entities'. Importantly, Jeffares *et al.* also articulate both a 'narrow' and a 'broad' definition of partnership performance.

Narrow Definition

> Partnership performance could be narrowly conceived as concerned with the achievement of particular service or outcome targets as set out in the partnership agreement (strategy, contract, business plan) and assessed in relation to other factors such as the cost of the partnership's operations.
>
> (JEFFARES *ET AL.* 2012)

In this narrow definition, partnership is therefore concerned with 'goal-based evaluation'; that is to evaluate success through criteria officially set out. This could be through Parliament and legislation, but often it is through the specific goals and objectives that were formulated by government or by the partners themselves prior to setting the partnership forth. It should then be relatively easy to be able to determine if a partnership was successful or not by going back to the 'original documents' and seeing what the objectives were.

Wider Definition

> Alternatively, partnership performance may be more broadly conceived and include consideration of the longer-term relationship that might exist beyond the delivery of a particular project or programme, the wider benefits to particular individuals or partner organizations or indeed to citizens and service users.
>
> (JEFFARES *ET AL.* 2012)

In the wider definition, there is clearly more work for those doing the evaluation to assess the degree to which 'success' has been achieved.

A further finding of the Jeffares *et al.* research was the articulation of a preliminary list of elements in an 'ideal partnership'. These elements were developed from eight partnership 'toolkits' made by various organizations (consultants and public organizations). Jeffares *et al.* identified the 12 composite partnership principles, the implication of which was twofold: first, that partnerships could be assessed across all dozen domains; and second, that an ideal PPP would presumably score well on all counts.

Added to this work has been that of Huxman and Hubbert (2009), along with other colleagues. Huxman and Hubbert picked out five types of success. They saw success as: (1) achieving outcomes, (2) getting the process to work, (3) reaching emergent milestones, (4) gaining recognition from others, and (5) acknowledging personal pride in championing a partnership. Of these types of success, perhaps the most well known from other parts of the literature are the first two. 'Achieving outcomes' is often considered to be the final decision on whether a project or a policy is judged a success or not—'mission accomplished' could be another expression for this. The second criteria is 'getting the process to work'. Many network analysts argue that it is not the output or outcome that is important to a reform and change effort, but more what the process brings with it. New and innovative elements can be discovered in a partnering process. If the process itself runs smoothly and helps create new ideas and satisfaction among participants, then the process could be a success criterion. The third point, 'reaching emerging outcomes', is about the content of that innovation that a smooth process can bring about. New goals and objectives may have risen because of a well-structured process, and a success factor could be that an invention is being discovered. The two remaining factors mentioned by Huxman and Hubbert relate to personal investment and the point of view of the actor making the change. If a partnership ensures 'recognition from others' and 'acknowledgment of personal pride' then that, in Huxman and Hubbert's view, also counts as a success factor.

Skelcher (2010) writes about PPP success from another angle—that of the governance of PPP. Acknowledging the existence of a wide range of PPP families, he writes about four different types of governance: legal, regulatory, democratic and corporate. In his view, the corporate governance aspect has been the least examined aspect of PPPs, with few studies having focused on the relationship between the board and the director, and the governance structures surrounding them. There has been some focus on legal governance and also regulatory governance, for example the regulatory framework of entering partnerships in the European Union (EU) (Tvarnø 2010).

At the broadest level, too, there are different kinds of criteria for 'success', which are associated with more disciplinary perspectives. Economists tend to look at economic factors concerning PPPs, political scientists and public policy scholars are likely to see if the political mandate is being fulfilled, while sociologists want to know the difference PPPs make at a broader societal level, including being clear about who the winners were as well as the losers. And in the world of auditing, there is now talk of the 'five Es' as opposed to the 'three Es' in the New Public Management (NPM) era. The five Es are economy, efficiency, effectiveness, equity, and environmental. While economists typically care about economy, efficiency and effectiveness, and political scientists and public policy people care about both effectiveness and equity, sociologists and other groups are increasingly beginning to focus more on environment (see, for example, the world famous sociologist Anthony Giddens' recent book on climate change).

So, at this broadest level of societal existence, how should PPP 'success' be seen? And knowing that PPP is as political a task as it is a technical or policy goal-oriented one, how can we think about judging the success of PPP at the highest level? Put another way, what precisely do governments mean when they view PPP as successful or not successful?

Like talk of 'good' governance and 'better' regulation, 'success' in government policy is an attractive linguistic. It is, as McConnell (2010) says, comforting and pleasing to everyone. We all desire success. It is clear that success is not an issue of 'all or nothing', and that governments, for example, may achieve success to a degree across many fronts. McConnell suggests that one major distinction in thinking about success from a theoretical perspective has been between the foundationalist and anti-foundationalist positions. In the first instance, success is seen as a matter of fact, because success can be assessed against identifiable standards. The opposite position is that of the anti-foundationalists. To them, success is purely a matter of interpretation. In this case, there are no identifiable standards for success because objectives and outcomes are supported and opposed by different actors. A road through a local community who does not want it can be seen as a failure, whilst the government perceives it as a success—but this is simply their view.

McConnell's 'realistic' definition of success acknowledges a midway position between these two extremes. To the realists, a policy can indeed be judged a success 'insofar as it achieves the goals that proponents set out to achieve'. He adds, however, that 'only those supportive of the original goals are liable to perceive, with satisfaction, an outcome of policy success. Opponents are likely to perceive failure, regardless of outcomes, because they did not support the original goals.' In other words, their definition of success accommodates the important, but thus far unstated, question—'Success for whom?'. It also begins to delve into the dual worlds of success viewed from the utilitarian goals and objectives perspective, on the one hand, and the more fluid world of politics on the other, where the words are the fundamental currency for framing meaning in the polity. The title of Edelman's 1977 book said it all: *Political Language: Words that Succeed and Policies that Fail*.

Importantly, McConnell (2010: 29) [acknowledges] that policy has to date been about process, about programmes and about the political dimension. As a consequence, he suggests that these three main dimensions provide a foundation for interpreting success, as shown in Table 32.3.

McConnell (2010: 54) put it well when he noted that governments *do process* (defining issues as problems, examining options, consulting, and so on), they *do programmes* (using a wide variety and combinations of policy instruments), and they *do politics* (engaging in activities that can influence electoral prospects, maintaining capacity to govern and steering policy direction).[9] Clearly, 'success can reside in each of these three spheres'.[10] These insights are, in our minds, crucial in our discussions of PPP success. And McConnell's framework neatly ties together some of our thoughts in this paper.

Other commentators such as Bebbington and McCourt (2007) have also observed the achievement of 'success' at the highest levels of societal change, and in the context of developing countries. Their work adopted the normative definition of success as 'the enhancement of human capabilities, in particular for the people who have the greatest

TABLE 32.3 The three main dimensions of policy success

Dimension	Elements
Process	• Preserving policy goals and instruments
	• Conferring legitimacy
	• Building a sustainable coalition
	• Symbolizing innovation and influence
Programmes	• Meeting objectives
	• Producing desired outcomes
	• Creating benefit for target groups
	• Meeting policy domain criteria
Politics	• Enhancing electoral prospects/reputation of governments and leaders
	• Controlling the policy agenda and easing the business of governing
	• Sustaining the broad values and direction of government

Source: McConnell (2010: 46)

capability deficits'. And whilst their work ana-lysing development success was clearly a more complex undertaking, their analysis of eight (southern) case studies had something to offer theories of 'success' in the north. They sug-gested that success was achieved through seven stages:[11] 'an initial upsurge in social energy' (to lay popular roots); 'generates a policy idea . . . or highlights an existing idea'; 'around which a coalition assembles'; this then 'throws up a leader who gets the idea on the policy agenda'; 'and overcomes opposition from supporters of the old dispensation'. The coalition is then 'institutionalized, empowering beneficiaries and deflecting patrons and rent-seekers'; and 'the policy is consolidated through feedback to adapt it to changing circumstances'. The importance of their contribution relates to the 'sociology of knowledge and the politics of ideas in policy processes' along with the 'multifarious membership of policy coalitions' (Bebbington and McCourt 2007: 241). And as they put it, understanding success is crucial not only for the practice of development but also in order to examine the role that governments can play. Perhaps PPP success in the north has owed much of its success to the power of the fundamental partnership ideal as well as to the more obvious policy coalitions hard at work?

Importantly, we have now mapped the terrain covered by two slippery concepts—the PPP phenomenon, and the idea of 'success'. Clearly, both of these domains remain complex; and whilst they do not fit into any single, neat meta-framework for evaluating PPP success, we at least now have some broad dimensions that would seem central to any analysis of PPP, its current success and its future. Indeed, irrespec-tive of how one looks at the issue of PPP (from its narrowest conception as an activity or a proj-ect through to the broadest conception of part-nership as symbolism and part of governance), the three broad success dimensions (process, programmes and politics) would seem to apply. And for all types of PPP, this success framework

suggests that issues of legitimacy, sustainability and innovation matter; utilitarian notions of meeting policy objectives, achieving outcomes and delivering benefits to target groups matter; and issues of enhancing one's own electoral prospects and sustaining the broad values of government also matter. In other words, PPP success would seem from these arguments to be as much about politics and the business of gov-erning strongly and legitimately as it is about policy objectives and technical issues such as VfM.

Public–Private Partnerships in Turbulent Times

PPPs have been affected by the financial crisis that hit the world in late 2008. Like other areas, however, it is not certain how serious and severe the consequences will be for PPPs. PPPs, at a minimum, are living through 'turbulent times' and there is no easy answer as to what will hap-pen to PPPs in the long run. What is certain is that, as Flinders (2010) remarked, the whole politics of the PPP debate has

> to a great degree been recast, or has at the very least taken on new emphasis, as a result of the global financial crisis from 2008 onwards. Assumptions regarding the dominance and superiority of the market that had become almost uncontested towards the end of the twentieth century are now receiving renewed attention, and this may have important rami-fications for the future utilization of PPPs.

This could also have influence on the topic of 'success' discussed in this chapter.

Judging from an impression of the literature and commentary so far, we might contemplate two different scenarios or interpretations as to the future: (1) a sceptical, technical and pes-simistic interpretation, and (2) an optimistic, holistic and political interpretation.

A Sceptical and Technical Interpretation

In a sceptical interpretation, PPPs have been affected hard by the financial crisis. According to the OECD in 2010, the financial crisis had an 'immediate negative impact on the volume of PPP projects in member countries'.

The events in the UK have also been examined by Connoly and Wall—the British banks' and the British government's responses to the financial crisis, and the practice of setting up a temporary bank within the Treasury. The result of this, for the time being, has therefore been a 'public–public partnership', as the Treasury as a public organization is financing the building of public sector organizations such as schools or hospitals.

An Optimistic and Political Perspective

The partnership ideal in which we aim to get the best of the government (in defining common interests) and the best of the private sector (to generate wealth) will not go away. There will be even more demand for PPPs in various forms in the future. The policy challenges are, increasingly, becoming too great for any one organization to cope with alone (Kettl 2009), which is also reflected in the broader 'collaborative governance' movement (O'Flynn and Wanna 2009). In the EU, the Commission is shifting its attention towards PPPs in a broader policy perspective. The Commission wants PPP to be a defining feature that will cut across many of the other policy areas. Instead of just being a policy that is relevant to the transport or infrastructure sector, a PPP policy is more about the role of European governments in the economy (European Commission 2011). The EU is therefore turning up the volume on what a PPP can be, and in our terminology here the EU is shifting focus from project and organizational form levels to a policy level. Of course, the future reality in any country will depend on local circumstances,

but it is also most likely to be somewhere along the continuum between these two extremes.

The future of the post-GFC PPP terrain is also likely to be influenced by several other trends and dynamics in the way that PPP success is being discussed currently. These include:

- *A change from projects and organizational forms to policy.* There appears to be a move away from only focusing on individual projects. In the beginning of the PPP literature, there was much focus on individual projects in the UK or North America. The evaluations were about the initial rounds of project experiences, and they were examined by individual researchers or by leading auditing institutions such as the National Audit Office in the UK. There has since been a move towards focusing more on broader policies that governments or international organizations form. Both Australia and the UK, for example, have been spearheading the formulation of PPP policies. PPP policy has, in some ways, therefore come of age and become part of broader discussions about a mixed economy.

- *A change from economic success criteria and political criteria to broader social criteria:* There appears to be a move away from only assessing 'success' as economic or financial for individual projects. This was very much the case in studies of specific projects in the UK and Canada. Now the focus is on broader success criteria, and moving towards broader 'programme' success criteria. 'Process' success criteria, such as user involvement or innovative practices, and the 'politics' success criteria of establishing ways of dealing with often competing values of government and private sector actors are also being considered.

- *A change from a sceptical to an optimistic view on partnerships in the long run, towards 'emerging' partnerships:* The GFC certainly put a damper on the economics-based families of the PPP phenomenon for a time. The 'partnership idea' is hard to suppress, however, and attention has shifted towards other types of partnerships, notably to partnerships with the non-profit sector (as currently witnessed by the advent of the 'big society' idea in the UK, although many observers think it is bogus). New ways to partner with private sector organizations are also being explored. This buzz can be found in new or rising policy areas, such as environment and climate issues, and in more enduring policy challenges such as urban development or town planning. The current interest in collaborative governance or 'nodal governance' can be aligned with the partnership discussion in the wider definition of the term. Emerging partnerships are likely to emphasize multiple partners rather than two, and new policy areas are also appearing through collaborations in the information and communication technology (ICT) arena.

In short, there is a movement underway from looking at 'established' PPPs such as long-term infrastructure contracts, which are often dependent on private finance, towards what we will here term 'emerging partnerships', because they are emerging around new and evolving public policy issues. These emerging partnerships cross organizational borders as well as countries, and can be expected to be found at the local level, the national level, the international level or some combination of these.

Studies of 'success' should therefore look to theories that can capture the advent of the emerging partnerships, and be sure to capture a broader view of their 'success'. In all likelihood this cannot be captured in only economic terms, but also requires a combination of process, programme and politics dimensions to understand partnership 'success' from a theoretical and empirical perspective.

Notes

1. See Montiero (2010) who sees risk explicitly at the centre of the OECD definition of PPP performance. In the OECD's words, 'the effectiveness of the alignment depends on a sufficient transfer of risk to the private partner'.

2. Whilst the UN's use of 'partnership' in the context of the MDGs, strictly speaking, calls on developed countries to assist developing countries, it is essentially a call for the wealth (both private and public) of developed countries to play a role in solving the common problem of poverty across developing countries.

3. The recent National Audit Office (NAO) (2009) review for the UK Parliament formally confirmed the breadth of the PPP idea, stating that 'we have mainly concentrated on the widely used PPP model called the Private Finance Initiative (PFI) . . . which has been adopted in the UK for more than £28 billion worth of projects.' They then noted that 'there are also hundreds of other types of PPPs, ranging from small joint ventures to the London Underground PPPs, which have a capital value of £18 billion'.

4. Braithwaite *et al.* (2007) suggested that the 'regulatory work' of government was increasing. They argued that work of governments broadly included three functions: providing, distributing and regulating. They observed that whilst the government's role in directly providing services is currently decreasing (through, for example, outsourcing and privatization), and their role in distributing (or redistributing) wealth will continue unabated through time, the government's role in regulating is increasing through a myriad of ways. The modern sense of regulation adopted here is broad and is construed as 'involving a sustained and focused attempt to alter the behaviour of others according to defined standards or purposes with the intention of producing a broadly identified outcome or outcomes' (Black 2002). Central to notions of how governments regulate, too, is the work of Freiberg (2010) who lists six different modes of regulating: through economic tools; through contracts (or grants); through authorization; through information; through structural means; and through law.

5. Thus the Bracks/Brumby Labor governments established their PPP policy platform in 2000 and through this action, implied that PPPs had essentially not existed prior to the year 2000. Whilst this is technically nonsense, given that the private funding of infrastructure had occurred at various points over the previous two decades, the political power of this PPP symbolism was also indisputable.

6. Of course, labels rarely tell the full story. 'Medibank Private' is an Australian government private health insurer. Established in 1976, it is Australia's largest health insurance provider. It was established through the Health Insurance Commission (now known as Medicare Australia) and currently operates commercially as a Government Business Enterprise. It is, despite its name, 100 per cent government owned (Source: http://en.wikipedia.org/wiki/Medibank_Private).

7. At the outset, of course, different stakeholders clearly have differing objectives for the delivery of a PPP. We focus simply on the objectives of government in this paper.

8. We might reflect that the private financing of a long-term infrastructure does not strictly reduce the call on the budget. A mechanism through which governments may turn a large, one-off capital expenditure into a series of smaller, annualized expenditures has simply been provided. Here, such an arrangement does reduce pressure on public sector budgets, because government has essentially purchased the infrastructure through the promise of funds from future (private) road users rather than using its own resources.

9. While most commentators are aware of both government 'programmes' (with a utilitarian emphasis) and government 'politics' (emphasizing electoral prospects), the additional thread of 'process' is useful. The case cited for the dimension of 'politics' was an episode in Australia's treatment of its Aborigines and Torres Strait Islanders. A shocking part of Australia's history was the forced removal, over the period 1910 to 1970, of between one tenth and one third of these children from their families. A two-year high-profile report on the scandal in 1997 suggested that a national apology should be undertaken as a first step, but the Howard government at the time refused, saying it could not say 'sorry' for something that was the responsibility of previous governments. The election in 2007 of a Labor government saw Prime Minister Kevin Rudd give a historic 'sorry' speech at Parliament House for all the pain and suffering caused. This official statement was a huge political success. It saw the government's opinion poll ratings soar, it diffused a sensitive political issue, and it symbolized a new governing direction that was more tolerant, inclusive and respectful of social diversity. The case cited for the third dimension of policy success, that of 'process', involved the electoral system

of British Columbia (BC) in Canada. The late 1990s saw the Liberal opposition committing itself to electoral reform after receiving 42 per cent of the vote, whilst the New Democrats party gained the majority of the seats in the legislature after receiving only 39 per cent. When the Liberals were elected in 2001, they established a diverse Citizens Assembly of 160 people, undertook 50 public hearings and extensive e-consultation, and produced a report recommending that the existing system be replaced with a more proportional one. This went to referendum in 2004, but received support from only 58 per cent of voters, just short of the required 60 per cent. This was a case of 'process success' where the government's goal was not closed (but was electoral reform subject to referendum endorsement), where the processes adopted suggested it was legitimate to proceed no further, where the Citizens Assembly initiative was seen an innovative way of tackling a difficult issue, and where these processes symbolized forward thinking and legitimate governance.

10. McConnell also suggests that for each of these dimensions we can assess policy success as being durable, conflicted, precarious or a failure (McConnell 2010: 67). These terms provide a sense of a continuum between clear success and failure, as well as a sense of the durability of relative success over time.

11. See Bebbington and McCourt (2007: 240).

References

Amirkhanyan, A. (2010) Monitoring Across Sectors: Examining the Effect of Non-Profit and For-Profit Contractor Ownership on Performance Monitoring in State and Local Contracts. *Public Administration Review* 70(5): 742–755.

Bebbington, A. and McCourt, W. (eds) (2007) Explaining (and Obtaining) Development Success. In *Development Success: Statecraft in the South*, edited by A. Bebbington and W. McCourt. New York: Springer, pp. 211–245.

Black, J. (2002) Critical Reflections on Regulation. *Australian Journal of Legal Philosophy* 27: 1–35.

Braithwaite, J., Coglianese, C. and Levi-Faur, D. (2007) Can Regulation and Governance Make a Difference? *Regulation and Governance* 1(1): 1–7.

Bull, B. (2010) Public–Private Partnerships: The United Nations Experience. In *International Handbook on Public–Private Partnerships*, edited by G. Hodge, C. Greve, and A. Boardman. Chel-tenham: Edward Elgar, pp. 479–495.

European Commission (2011) *Public–Private Part-nerships: The Implementation of the Commission's Communication.* Presentation by Elias Messaoudi for the Audit of Public–Private Partnership semi-nar arranged by the Bundesrechnungshof in Bonn, Germany, 9–11 February 2011 (http://bundesrechnungshof.de/the-audit-ofppp-key-speeches).

Flinders, M. (2010) Splintered Logic and Political Debate. In *International Handbook on Public–Private Partnerships*, edited by G. Hodge, C. Greve, and A. Boardman. Cheltenham: Edward Elgar, pp. 115–131.

Freiberg, A. (2010) *The Tools of Regulation.* Sydney: The Federation Press.

Guardian/Observer (27 March 2011) Academic Fury Over Order to Study the Big Society.

Hellowell, M. (2010) The UK's Private Finance Ini-tiative: History, Evaluation, Prospects. In *Inter-national Handbook on Public–Private Partnerships*, edited by G. Hodge, C. Greve, and A. Board-man. Cheltenham: Edward Elgar.

Hodge, G. (2010a) Reviewing Public–Private Part-nerships: Some Thoughts on Evaluation. In *Inter-national Handbook on Public–Private Partnerships*, edited by G. Hodge, C. Greve and A. Boardman. Cheltenham: Edward Elgar, pp. 81–112.

Hodge, G. (2010b) *On Evaluating PPP Success: Thoughts for Our Future.* Key note address to the Finnish Association of Administrative Sciences, Helsinki, November 2010.

Hodge, G. and Greve, C. (eds) (2005) *The Challenge of Public–Private Partnerships: Learning from International Experience.* Cheltenham: Edward Elgar.

Hodge, G. and Greve, C. (2007) Public–Private Part-nerships: An International Review. *Public Administration Review* 67(3): 545–558.

Huxman, C. and Hubbert, P. (2009) Hit or Myth? Stories of Collaborative Success. In *Collaborative Governance*, edited by J. O'Flynn and J. Wanna. Canberra: ANU Press.

Jeffares, S., Sullivan, H. and Bovaird, T. (2012) Beyond the Contract: The Challenge of Evaluat-ing the Performance(s) of Public-Private Partner-ships. In *Rethinking Public-Private Partnerships: Strategies for Turbulent Times,* edited by C. Greve and G. Hodge. London and New York: Rout-ledge, 166–187.

Kettl, D. F. (2009) *The Next Government of the United States: How Our Institutions Fail Us and How to Fix Them.* New York: W.W. Norton.

McConnell, A. (2010) *Understanding Policy Success: Rethinking Public Policy.* Basingstoke: Palgrave Macmillan.

Montiero, R. S. (2010) Risk Management. In *Inter-national Handbook on Public-Private Partnerships*, edited by G. Hodge, C. Greve and A. Boardman. Cheltenham: Edward Elgar, pp. 262–291.

National Audit Office (2009) *Private Finance Proj-ects.* A Report to the House of Lords Economic Affairs Committee.

O'Flynn, J. and Wanna, J. (eds) (2009) *Collaborative Governance.* Canberra: ANU Press.

Skelcher, C. (2010) Governance of Public–Private Part-nerships. In *International Handbook on Public–Pri-vate Partnerships*, edited by G. Hodge, C. Greve and A. Boardman. Cheltenham: Edward Elgar.

Skelcher, C. and Sullivan, H. (2008) Theory Driven Approaches to Analyzing Collaborative Perfor-mance. *Public Management Review* 10(6): 751–777.

Tvarnø, C. D. (2010) Law and Regulatory Aspects of Public–Private Partnerships: Contract Law and Public Procurement Law. In *International Hand-book on Public–Private Partnerships*, edited by G. Hodge, C. Greve and A. Boardman. Chelten-ham: Edward Elgar, pp. 216–236.

Van Ham, H. and Koppenjan, J. (2001) Building Public–Private Partnerships: Assessing and Man-aging Risks in Port Development. *Public Man-agement Review* 4(1): 593–616.

Weihe, G. (2005) *Public–Private Partnerships, Addressing a Nebulous Concept.* Working Paper No. 16. International Center for Business and Politics, Copenhagen Business School.

CHAPTER 33

Comparing New Hybrid Governance Arrangements: Better and Smarter?

Joop Koppenjan, Katrien Termeer, and Philip Marcel Karré

Hybrid governance arrangements may take many forms, and the nature and direction of the development towards smarter hybridity is not yet clear, nor well understood. Hybrid governance arrangements are not necessarily new, but the context, nature and scale of the use of hybridity have evolved over time. The theories and concepts at our disposal to analyse, understand and manage hybrid governance arrangements are still poorly developed. Moreover, our empirical knowledge about the phenomenon is limited. We examine the extent to which these arrangements meet the promises of tackling wicked problems in a better and smarter way. We do not address the question of whether hybridity in governance arrangements is a good idea by itself (as we see hybridity as an ongoing development that will not stop) but rather how these arrangements can be characterized, what mechanisms drive them, how they are managed, and what their effects are. Overall, we aim to determine whether these hybrid governance arrangements are really smart and hence whether they have indeed mastered the challenge of smart hybridity. In dealing with criticism, we propose four categories of values to assess the smartness of hybrid governance arrangements. First, smart hybridity refers to arrangements and strategies

that are both effective and efficient. They are smart in the sense that they avoid the high costs of large-scale reforms, by being incremental and tailor-made, and by using resources and opportunities that are already available. Second, information and information technologies play a prominent role in governance in the digital age. Innovative ways of using social media, digital platforms, or information disclosure systems are an important asset of smart governance arrangements. Overall, this should result in innovative, informed and evidence-based solutions. Third, besides being effective and efficient, other public values must also be adhered to the concept of smartness, such as (democratic) legitimacy, equality, rule of law, representation, participation, empowerment and ownership. Fourth, in light of uncertainties and volatility that characterize wicked problems and the erosion of trust in societal institutions, sustainability and resilience are important values to be realized as well.

Despite their variety and diversity, these new governance arrangements share a number of characteristics. They are utilized to tackle complex, wicked problems that involve a lack of consensus about their nature, causes and suitable solutions. Wicked problems also transcend organizational boundaries and administrative

DOI: 10.4324/9780367696559-42

levels, that is, they cannot be resolved by any one administrative actor (Head & Alford, 2015; Klijn & Koppenjan, 2016). Since they also cut across the borders of societal domains, they require collaboration with other social partners (*e.g.* citizens, societal organizations and businesses). Wicked problems are increasingly common in our rapidly changing society, in which society places heavy demands on government and its capacity to deliver, while at the same there is strong polarization and a loss of trust in existing institutions. The new governance arrangements strive to deal with these challenges in a context of uncertainty, ambiguity, volatility and limited resources. Instead of large-scale reforms, they involve mostly incremental changes that take place alongside existing forms of governance. Even in the case of the large-scale social care reform in the Netherlands, the hybridity of arrangement emerged on the shop floor, as a result of local actors trying to cope with the implications of the reform. The new, hybrid and smart governance arrangements complement, react to and compensate for the downsides of existing governance modes or other (large-scale) interventions, and in doing so bring about substantial and transformative changes with limited effort.

In this chapter, we compare the findings pertaining to the various practices of new, hybrid and smart governance arrangements.

1. What is the nature of these new hybrid governance arrangements used to address complex societal challenges, and what characteristics do they share?
2. What assumptions and mechanisms form the foundation of these new hybrid governance methods, and how have they manifested themselves in practice?
3. In what way do the new hybrid governance arrangements contribute to solving complex challenges, and to what extent are they actually smart, in terms of effectiveness, innovative

use of information systems and enhancing and safeguarding public values like legitimacy and resilience?

We build on the reflections of internationally renowned governance scholars from various countries in different parts of the world that put the empirical studies perspective to use and enrich our reasoning regarding smart hybridity.

1 What Characterizes the New Hybrid Governance Arrangements?

Sørensen and Torfing define what we understand to be smart hybridity as "a governance arrangement that combines elements of well-known and often lone-standing governance tools such as hierarchies, markets, self-governed communities, and cross-boundary networks and allows the various elements to coexist and merge in a relatively coherent way". They all deal with innovations in governance that are designed to tackle the wicked problems that transcend existing organizational boundaries and administrative levels. The governance arrangements described here are focused on coordinating the behaviour of parties from various sectors, domains and administrative layers. They are all a response to the inadequacy of traditional forms of government (hierarchy, market, networks, self-governance)—sometimes because these are simply ineffective or too expensive, sometimes because the scale of governance does not match the scale of the issues at hand and sometimes because government is underperforming or even absent, as at the start of a crisis situation. The use of client networks in the social care domain is a response to overly expensive and inefficient traditional provision of social care. Public private partnerships in delivering and managing public infrastructure is inspired by the belief that the government cannot do a good job on its own.

The governance arrangements described here strive to provide better and more suitable solutions for complex societal issues by mobilizing other social and private resources, since it is apparent that governance models based solely on hierarchy, market, networks or societal self-governance fall short. The new governance arrangements combine the potential of these models in order to deal with the complexity and dynamic nature of today's governance challenges. In the case of urban regional governance, network governance leads to a democratic shortage, whereas societal or hierarchical governance could have beneficial effects. Finally, [self]-governance in the social care domain and during crisis management show that professionals often play a prominent role in informal care and that citizens' social media platforms become more effective when professional emergency services and governments use them as well.

Therefore, the one characteristic that all forms of smart governance have in common is their hybrid nature (Brandsen & Karré, 2011; Johanson & Vakkuri, 2018; Karré, 2011; Skelcher & Smith, 2015): they combine the institutional logics of government, market and third sector. Although old governance modes make way for new ones, there is never an entirely clean break with the past. Today, we continue to expect the government to use its available resources well and set up its services in an efficient and effective manner, in addition to being responsive to our wishes as a society.

At the same time, it can be observed that hybrid arrangements differ from each other. They combine different logics in different ways, with different intentions and probably different implications too. What the effects are of hybridity and whether its strengths or weaknesses are dominant depends on the specific characteristics of the hybrid in question. The search for new and smart governance arrangements is not merely a Dutch affair, of course. Family group conferences were first introduced

in New Zealand. Design, build, finance, maintain and operate (DBFM(O)) contracts for public-private partnerships are based on the UK's example, which has since been adopted by countless other countries. Information platforms established by citizens appear all over the world during times of crisis. Similarly, the struggles with the question of regional governance and the certification of trade chains are international concerns as well.

2 What Are the Mechanisms Behind the New Hybrid Governance Arrangements?

What mechanisms characterize the new governance arrangements? How do these relate to, for example, scientific theories and society's dominant views on governance? Two of the governance arrangements that were studied have been strongly influenced by new institutional economics and thinking in terms of market instruments, as they were propagated in the 1990s under the label of New Public Management (NPM). For both the governance of global value chains and the development and maintenance of public infrastructure contracts, market stimuli and a focus on performance play major roles. Perhaps this is because these governance methods became popular during the heyday of neoliberalism and the New Public Management philosophy.

The new governance arrangements also appear to be influenced by ideas from more sociologically oriented governance and network theories, which are often grouped together under the term of New Public Governance (NPG) these days (Bryson, Crosby, & Bloomberg, 2014; Koppenjan, 2012; O'Flynn, 2007; Osborne, 2010; Torfing & Triantafillou, 2013). Forms of contractual governance are supplemented with relational contracting, discussion, round tables, and so on with the intention of committing parties to shared goals and collaboration. This type of governance is therefore less about realizing predefined agreements and targets and more about facilitating learning processes, discovering and realizing shared interests and dealing with shared challenges. Whereas traditional governance makes use of predefined targets and performances, this new way of working allows for a greater degree of flexibility.

The governance practices pertaining to family group conferences in the social care domain and Internet platforms used in crisis management focus on the mobilization of citizens and their resources and competences. This suits our modern times with its increased focus on self-governance and citizen initiatives as a result of the failure of the government and the market. These ideas on self-governance have a long history, but they became especially *en vogue* during the financial crisis. Many problems and challenges are too much for the government, market mechanisms and networks to handle, and hence they will have to be resolved by citizens and social organizations. With the help of proper training and the emergence of new information systems and technological innovations, they are increasingly up to the task (Bolívar & Meijer, 2016). This also offers a solution for governments, which lack the financial resources to face today's societal issues on their own.

Governance mechanisms reflect various theoretical notions about governance. The aforementioned consideration shows a shift from coercion and control to a more enabling approach. There is also more focus on a relational, sociological and political form of governance, moving away from the rational 'homo economicus'. There is a focus on public values and trust but also on power relations and irrationality (Lowndes & Roberts, 2013; O'Flynn, 2007; Peters, 2019). At the same time, self-governance and self-organization appear to be an important common ingredient: it is shared by family group conferences, regional governance, crisis management, trade chains and private-public partnerships. In all cases, the governance arrangements strive to create room for other, non-government parties to make an optimal contribution to the co-production of solutions and services based on self-organization (Brandsen & Pestoff, 2006; Koliba, Meek, Zia, & Mills 2018; Nederhand, Bekkers, & Voorberg, 2016).

3 Are the New Hybrid Governance Arrangements Smart?

Now we turn to the question whether hybrid arrangements are really smart. To what extent do they meet expectations, and what exactly are those expectations? Has there been an increase in effectiveness? Do they provide a solution for the erosion of the legitimacy of institutions and contribute to a more resilient society? Is innovation with information technologies realized? The contributions in this collection provide answers to these questions.

3.1 Effectiveness: Are New Governance Arrangements Smart Enough?

An important expectation attached to these new government arrangements is that they are more effective than traditional approaches. The effectiveness of urban regional governance strongly depends on what the parties involved choose to consider the important aims of their collaboration. What the various cases have in common is that a high degree of output legitimacy is reported. Apparently, hybrid urban regional governance can indeed be quite effective. The local citizen initiatives for crisis management are also valued for their contributions to the provision of emergency aid in situations where governments and NGOs fail to provide all that is needed. Nevertheless, the question remains as to whether the upscaling of these platforms practices can be successful and whether these practices will result in successful collaboration with governments.

If we make a distinction between the successful introduction of new governance arrangements and their ultimate performance in order to determine their effectiveness, we can say that regional governance, trade chains and public-private partnerships have had a successful and therefore effective implementation. This applies to a limited extent to family conferences and citizen platforms during crises, since their level of institutionalization is still low. It is possible that new smart governance arrangements have to go through a learning curve. After a difficult—or successful—start, the question remains as to the extent to which the parties involved can manage to consolidate or scale up the new practice. If they succeed, an increase in effectiveness is to be expected. It is quite possible that the effectiveness and smartness of governance arrangements are limited by time, that is, that they are smart only for a certain period.

3.2 Innovation and the Application of Information Systems: More Innovative Products and Services?

Most of the discussed governance arrangements show high knowledge intensity and new ways of using information. In the case of the information platforms used during crises and the certification of international value chains, information systems and the exchange of data are core elements of the new governance arrangement. The challenge is therefore to realize safeguards during the design and use of these systems that also guarantee parties' trust in the systems. Typical patterns can develop in principal-agent relationships under the influence of information asymmetry. Information systems, standard contracts and standardized assessment tools are attempts to streamline the information and minimize differences in interpretation and transaction costs.

The new governance arrangements can all be seen as examples of social innovation (Brandsen, Evers, Cattacin, & Zimmer, 2016; Cels, Jong, & Nauta, 2012; Mulgan, 2007, 2015; Tollefson, Zito, & Gale, 2012) because actors interact with each other in new ways. However, do these new practices also result in new and innovative products and services? IT platforms, the self-governance of trade chains and family group conferences can be cited as positive examples, although innovations in public-private partnerships disappoint and innovations in trade chains result in the perpetuation of existing interests.

3.3 Legitimacy: For Whom Are the New Smart Governance Mechanisms Actually Smart?

A leading thought behind the introduction of new smart governance arrangements was that its increased effectiveness would also result in more legitimacy for governments and institutions. The question of legitimacy as such is hardly being asked in the process of creating regional governance arrangements, and citizens and local politicians are only marginally involved. This may eventually put regional collaboration at risk.

There is yet another reason why effectiveness does not necessarily enhance legitimacy. The definition of 'effective' may vary depending on the position of the parties involved. New governance arrangements are not necessarily beneficial for everyone. Users, citizens and politicians are generally at a distance whenever governments and corporations collaborate on the development of infrastructure. Citizens and social organizations have to struggle to get involved in regional partnerships. Vulnerable clients have difficulty organizing their own care. Attempts to safeguard their position often put professionals in a central role, at the expense of clients and citizens.

So hybrid arrangements may result in an unequal allocation of values. The use of hybrids in cases 'of extreme misery and misfortune' may reinforce depersonalization, dehumanization and commodification, and give rise to pressing moral dilemmas.

Legitimacy and trust are based on commitment, involvement, participation opportunities and the feeling of being a co-owner of a solution, service or governance practice. In that sense, tension exists between striving towards efficiency and effectiveness, on the one hand, and participation and legitimacy, on the other. It is not easy to solve these tensions. It is not possible to optimize goals such as effectiveness, innovation, legitimacy and resilience all at once. Given these contradictory requirements, the legitimacy of these new governance arrangements depends on the extent to which they succeed in striking a balance between these various requirements and prioritizing certain values over others depending on the situation at hand (Jørgensen & Bozeman, 2007; Veeneman, Dicke, & de Bruijne, 2009). This involves issues of democratic legitimacy, accountability and morality: who decides, and on what grounds, how these values should be balanced, and how and to whom account is given about this?

3.4 Resilience: The Sustainability of Smart Hybridity

New governance arrangements based on the notion of smart hybridity are also expected to lead to more resilience. The contributions suggest that hybridity and the call for self-governance reinforce the robustness of solutions and services, as well as the resilience of the government and of society. The combination of governance methods and the involvement of corporations, social organizations and citizens means that more parties and resources are mobilized and deployed in order to deal with the complex challenges that our society faces. This leads to redundancy and synergy. It allows for the formation of various defensive lines and attack formations, which may reinforce each other. At

the same time, practices also show that these expectations are not always justified; vulnerable groups are left in the cold by these governance arrangements. The arrangements often support and reinforce each other where they are already strong or in such a way that parties with a lot of resources and capabilities benefit, while weak parties and public values tend to be neglected or underserved. The governance challenge is therefore to deploy these arrangements in such a way that institutional voids are filled, weak areas are reinforced and public values and the interests of vulnerable groups are safeguarded. Smart hybridity in this sense is not about finding shortcuts that result in low-cost, short-term gains but about the development of legitimate, sustainable practices that allow for long-term and widely accepted solutions that contribute to trustful relationships. In this respect, an important follow-up question to this research is, to what extent do hybrid arrangements remain successful over a longer period? Smart hybridity is not just about governing *by* hybridity, but also about the governing *of* hybridity. Hybridity can result in 'magical' marriages as well as 'monstrous' combinations (Jacobs, 1992; Howlett & Rayner, 2006). It has to be understood as a heads *and* tails issue, in the sense that benefits and risks most often are different sides of the same coin (Karré, 2011). That means the hybridity must be consciously recognized and managed.

4 Next-Step Challenges: Complications and Dilemmas

New hybrid governance arrangements do not necessarily lead to better results. In practice, those who implement them encounter complications and dilemmas. For example, major corporations are able to control the negotiations concerning certification systems, since the system will not function properly without their collaboration. Governments that try to act as smart clients can be [outsmarted] by private parties that offer smart counter-steering in public-private partnerships. Citizen initiatives for crisis management can get in the way of professional emergency aid providers, while the latter often fail to fully utilize the potential of these citizen platforms. In hybrid urban regional governance arrangements, those involved face the choice of increasing their effectiveness by moving tasks to the regional level at the expense of the influence of local representative bodies and democratic legitimacy. During attempts to put clients and their networks at the centre of the provision of care, at the risk of asking too much from vulnerable clients and their families, the question remains as to who is ultimately in charge: the client, professionals or government officials.

Smart hybridity, therefore, does not necessarily or automatically result in better or smarter governance practices. Hybrids, instead of providing solutions for wicked problems, could become the problem themselves, because they mask the 'toxic dynamics' when markets and hierarchies meet. Forms of self-organization may also result in chaos or the perpetuation of 'fake news'. Hybrids confront the parties involved with new, unexpected and complicated dilemmas. The extent to which these parties succeed in meeting the expectations associated with these new governance practices depends on their capabilities and competences. Therefore, the effective operation of hybrid governance requires actors and organizations involved to possess the capacity to manage them.

5 Beyond Government Arrangements: On the Importance of Learning and Responsiveness to a Plurality of Values and Ethics

An expectation underlying the new, smart and hybrid governance arrangements is that they have the potential to deal with the complexity, fragmentation and volatility of today's wicked problems. These expectations are met to a certain extent. This, however, is not always or necessarily the case. Therefore, the smartness of new hybrid governance arrangements should not be overrated. The studies of these arrangements show that although they are supposed to be smart, new governance arrangements are not necessarily smart for everyone and always come with new dilemmas and unintended side effects. After some initial or partial success, all of these new smart governance practices faced next-step challenges. This implies that these new governance practices require continuous reflection on the part of those who apply them, in order to monitor their impacts and adjust their functioning accordingly and in order to keep them on track and mitigate and correct their unintended by-effects.

What is also consistently notable is the fact that these new governance arrangements do not develop in isolation from existing and more traditional forms of governance and that new and older forms of governance have to find a way to relate to each other. Bringing in volunteers affects the role of professionals. Citizen initiatives during disasters must be coordinated with official emergency services and government activities. Public-private projects result in a call to focus less on the smartness of the contract and drastically change client-contractor relationships. Hybrid regional governance cannot simply break free from existing institutions of public law. Private certification systems must be reinforced by and complemented with government regulation.

The new, smart and hybrid governance arrangements do not automatically solve the complicated issues the parties are confronted with in dealing with wicked problems and complex societal challenges. The reason is that these governance practices are not neutral instruments, but in applying them values are allocated. These instruments are often biased in the way they allocate these values. In the processes in which these governance arrangements are put into practice, actors are, to varying degrees, able to protect and pursue their interests. Strong parties, in particular, have more opportunities to operate in a smart manner and are often better able to learn quickly. New, smart governance practices, therefore, are not about simply applying an instrument or arrangement but rather about new ways of governing that impose high demands on those in charge and must be accompanied by certain safeguards. Just like any other proposedly smart solution in any other context (*e.g.* smartphones, smart cities or smart grids) that promises to improve the quality of life, we have to remain cautious concerning possible drawbacks.

Dilemmas and competing values that are involved in new governance practices, as well as the diverse and dynamic contexts in which they are applied, mean that there are no standard prescriptions on what makes up the success of these arrangements and how they should be applied in order to mitigate those shortcomings and manage their hybridity. The variety of combinations of governance modes and of their contexts precludes generalizations. No macro, general theory on hybridity exists, that might be helpful, given the particular, unique potentials, dilemmas and risks the specifics of hybrid combinations bring along.

These arrangements tend to emerge as much as they are the result of intentional design. Even when designed, they end up being serendipitous recombinations of governance arrangements in response to the complexity of the circumstances and the context in which they are implemented (*see, e.g.* Christensen & Lægreid, 2010). Deliberate design is also constrained by context: historical-institutional traditions, polity features and environmental factors. Hybrid governance arrangements tend to be a result based on adaptive learning, with an important role of processes of trial and error and chance discoveries. Therefore, it is also likely that they cannot be prescriptively determined from the outset. As far as design is concerned, Sørensen and Torfing

(2016) suggest that smart hybrids be treated as design experiments. These experimental designs should include options for monitoring and evaluation, followed by either termination or adjustment or gradual upscaling and mainstreaming. This conforms to recommendations made by for instance Termeer, Dewulf, and Van Lieshout (2010), Termeer, Dewulf, Karlsson-Vinkhuyzen, Vink, and van Vliet (2016), and Pahl-Wostl (2009) on reflexivity and adaptive learning as generic conditions for the success of new governance arrangements.

This imposes high demands on the capacities and skills of actors involved. In addition to the willingness to collaborate and break free from the shadow of one's own organization, it also requires the ability to deal with changes and to keep learning. We would argue that given the complexity and the moral dimensions of the next-step challenges hybridity brings along, transparency, openness and accountability impose demands on the capabilities and ethics of those involved in hybrid governance. Smart hybridity should not be about bypassing administrative checks and balances, avoiding fair competition and participation in order to realize quick fixes, but should contribute to the realization of long-term and public values in a legitimate and sustainable way, enhancing trust and contributing to the resilience of the system.

The application of these new governance practices is also an organizational issue: How can public organizations be rearranged and managed internally in a way that facilitates new forms of hybrid governance and deals with them in an adaptive manner (Brandsen & Karré, 2011; Jessop, 2003; Johanson & Vakkuri, 2018; Karré, 2011)?

6 Conclusions: Towards Smart Hybridity

Not all hybrid governance arrangements are smart, and not all smart arrangements are hybrid.

We conclude with a summary of the features of governance arrangements characterized by smart hybridity, as described in the preceding chapters.

First, smart hybrids emerge as a more or less deliberate attempt to better deal with wicked problems that cross the boundaries of organizations, policy sectors, public-private domains and jurisdictions. These hybrids combine not only modes of governance and instruments but also various governance theories, contexts and cultures and institutionalized practices. Hybrid governance thus inherently involves processes of transformative change including barriers and resistance of existing governance regimes and related power systems.

Second, the evaluation of the level of smartness of new hybrid governance arrangements inherently requires a variety of criteria and values: Does the arrangement in question work (effectiveness)? Does it use new information (systems) and does it realize innovations (innovativeness)? Is it legitimate and for whom (legitimacy and accountability), and does it result in sustainable practices that help in realizing solutions and public services that hold in the long term (resilience)? Hybrids that focus merely on effectiveness and efficiency thus do not qualify as smart, since they neglect the variety of values society expects governments to take into account in dealing with complex challenges and providing public services.

Third, smart hybridity is hard to grasp. Owing to inherent connections across scales and domains in complex societal systems, an arrangement that qualifies as smart today may evolve into tomorrow's problem. Therefore, a crucial characteristic of smart hybridity is the capacity to learn, to adapt and to respond to foreseen and unforeseen circumstances and trade-offs. Thereby, special attention needs to be directed to the risk that hybrids may mask negative drawbacks. Smart hybrids require smart organizations and smart governance actors. By smart actors we mean actors who are reflective, who can bridge organizational boundaries and

logics and who have a strong moral compass that guides them in dealing with competing public values and moral dilemmas. Such actors are committed to working in open publicly accountable settings, in contrast to the smart people who 'created the mortgage derivatives market that led to the Great Recession of the late 2000s'.

Given bad experiences with opaque governance structures and failed hybridity, one can hold the position that hybridity is inherently problematic and that pure governance modes should be the norm. We believe that given the increasing complexity of both societal problems and governance systems, the question whether we want hybridity or not is a passed station. We now have to deal with the question of how hybridity can best be governed and how smartness can be realized. For example, we see hybridity as a pragmatic governance style, going beyond ideological gridlocks that stand in the way of new solutions and innovative services. We also agree with them that hybridity will not be a guarantee of success but that a pragmatic and experimental approach is needed. Since upfront knowledge about how to design smart hybridity perfectly does not exist, we should be prepared to learn, adapt and improve.

Seen in this way, the concept of smart hybridity provides practitioners within the public sector with a new perspective on how to deal with complex challenges and demanding assignments. It may help them to understand the tensions and dilemmas that need to be addressed in order to fruitfully manage the hybridity of the instruments and arrangements at their disposal and to fully use their potentials.

We suggest the following topics for future research into smart hybridity:

1. The possible and impossible combinations of various governance arrangements and the (toxic or magic) dynamics and added value these combinations bring about given the underlying mechanism and logics.

2. The specific next-step challenges and (moral) dilemmas that result from particular forms of hybrid governance and the strategies and coping mechanisms actors use to deal with them.

3. The further development of assessment models to evaluate the smartness of hybrid governance arrangements, more specially with attention to the use of information and (big) data, the plurality of public values involved, representation, participation, legitimacy, trust-building and accountability.

4. A life cycle analysis of hybrid governance arrangements, including their long-term effectiveness and sustainability and (conditions of) their termination, continuation, adjustment, upscaling, and mainstreaming.

5. The possibilities and limitations of deliberately designing hybrid government arrangements, especially the potentials of designing hybrids as experiments and the implications thereof.

6. The resources, capacities and skills of actors to successfully manage smart hybrid arrangements and deal with the (moral) dilemmas they encounter. This research might also address issues of supportive leadership, adaptive and learning capability and requirements for education and training.

7. The institutional conditions for the governance of smart hybrids, including the way public organizations are internally organized and managed to deal with hybrid arrangement. This research may also be aimed at making sectoral, regional and international comparisons to clarify how different contexts may impact on the evolvement and smartness of hybrid arrangements.

References

Bolívar, M. P. R., & Meijer, A. J. (2016). Smart governance: Using a literature review and empirical analysis to build a research model. *Social Science Computer Review*, 34(6), 673–692.

Brandsen, T., Evers, A., Cattacin, S., & Zimmer, A. (2016). Social innovation: A sympathetic and critical interpretation. In T. Brandsen, S. Cattacin, A. Evers, & A. Zimmer (Eds.), *Social innovations in the urban context* (pp. 3–18). Heidelberg, Germany: Springer Verlag. https://doi.org/10.1007/978-3-319-21551-8_1

Brandsen, T., & Karré, P. M. (2011). Hybrid organizations: No cause for concern? *International Journal of Public Administration*, 34(13), 827–836. https://doi.org/10.1080/01900692.2011.605090

Brandsen, T., & Pestoff, V. (2006). Co-production, the third sector and the delivery of public services: An introduction. *Public Management Review*, 8(4), 493–501.

Bryson, J. M., Crosby, B. C., & Bloomberg, L. (2014). Public value governance: Moving beyond traditional public administration and the new public management. *Public Administration Review*, 74(4), 445–456.

Cels, S., de Jong, J., & Nauta, F. (2012). *Agents of change: Strategy and tactics for social innovation.* Washington, DC: Brookings Institution Press.

Christensen, T., & Lægreid, P. (2010). Complexity and hybrid public administration: Theoretical and empirical challenges. *Public Organization Review*, 11, 407–423. https://doi.org/10.1007/s11115-010-0141-4

Head, B. W., & Alford, J. (2015). Wicked problems: Implications for public policy and management. *Administration & Society*, 47(6), 711–739. https://doi.org/10.1177/0095399713481601

Howlett, M., & Rayner, J. (2006). Convergence and divergence in 'new governance' arrangements: Evidence for European integrated natural resource strategies. *Journal of Public Policy*, 26(2), 167–189.

Jacobs, J. (1992). *Systems of survival: A dialogue on moral foundations of commerce and politics.* New York, NJ: Random House.

Jessop, B. (2003). Governance and meta-governance: On reflexivity, requisite variety and requisite irony. *Governance as Social and Political Communication*, 101–116.

Johanson, J.-E., & Vakkuri, J. (2018). *Governing hybrid organisations. Exploring diversity of institutional life.* London: Routledge.

Jørgensen, T. B., & Bozeman, B. (2007). Public values: An inventory. *Administration & Society*, 39(3), 354–381.

Karré, P. M. (2011). *Heads and tails: Both sides of the coin: An analysis of hybrid organizations in the Dutch waste management sector*. The Hague, The Netherlands: Eleven International Publishing.

Klijn, E. H., & Koppenjan, J. (2016). *Governance networks in the public sector*. London: Routledge.

Koliba, C., Meek, J., Zia, A., & Mills, R. (2018). *Governance networks in public administration and public policy* (2nd ed.). Oxfordshire: Routledge.

Koppenjan, J. F. M. (2012). *The new public governance in public service delivery*. The Hague, The Netherlands: Eleven International Publishing.

Lowndes, V., & Roberts, M. (2013). *Why institutions matter: The new institutionalism in political science*. New York, NY: Macmillan International Higher Education.

Mulgan, G. (2007). *Social innovation. What it is, why it matters and how it can be accelerated*. London: The Young Foundation.

Mulgan, G. (2015). Foreword: The study of social innovation—Theory, practice and progress. In A. Nicholls, J. Simon, & M. Gabriel (Eds.), *New frontiers in social innovation research*. Basingstoke: Palgrave Macmillan.

Nederhand, J., Bekkers, V., & Voorberg, W. (2016). Self-organization and the role of government: How and why does self-organization evolve in the shadow of hierarchy? *Public Management Review*, *18*(7), 1063–1084.

O'Flynn, J. (2007). From new public management to public value: Paradigmatic change and managerial implications. *Australian Journal of Public Administration*, *66*(3), 353–366.

Osborne, S. P. (2010). Introduction, the (New) Public Governance: A suitable case for treatment? In S. P. Osborne (Ed.), *The new public governance? Emerging perspectives on the theory and practice of public governance* (pp. 1–16). London and New York: Routledge.

Pahl-Wostl, C. (2009). A conceptual framework for analysing adaptive capacity and multi-level learning processes in resource governance regimes. *Global Environmental Change*, *19*(3), 354–365.

Peters, B. G. (2019). *Institutional theory in political science: The new institutionalism*. Cheltenham, UK and Northampton, MA: Edward Elgar Publishing.

Skelcher, C., & Smith, S. R. (2015). Theorizing hybridity: Institutional logics, complex organizations, and actor identities: The case of nonprofits. *Public Administration*, *93*(2), 433–448.

Sørensen, E., & Torfing, J. (Eds.). (2016). *Theories of democratic network governance*. Basingstoke, UK and New York: Palgrave Macmillan.

Termeer, C. J. A. M., Dewulf, A., Karlsson-Vinkhuyzen, S. I., Vink, M., & van Vliet, M. (2016). Coping with the wicked problem of climate adaptation across scales: The Five R governance capabilities. *Landscape and Urban Planning*, *154*, 11–19. https://doi.org/10.1016/j.landurbplan.2016.01.007

Termeer, C. J. A. M., Dewulf, A., & Van Lieshout, M. (2010). Disentangling scale approaches in governance research: Comparing monocentric, multilevel, and adaptive governance. *Ecology and Society*, *15*(4), 29.

Tollefson, C., Zito, A. R., & Gale, F. (2012). Symposium overview: Conceptualizing new governance arrangements. *Public Administration*, *90*(1), 3–18.

Torfing, J., & Triantafillou, P. (2013). What's in a name? Grasping new public governance as a political-administrative system. *International Review of Public Administration*, *18*(2), 9–25.

Veeneman, W., Dicke, W., & de Bruijne, M. (2009). From clouds to hailstorms: A policy and administrative science perspective on safeguarding public values in networked infrastructures. *International Journal of Public Policy*, *4*(5), 414–434.

PART X

THE NONGOVERNMENTAL (NGO) SECTOR IN OTHER COUNTRIES

Part I introduced the nonprofit or NGO sector without respect to geographical location. Part II provided an overview of the nonprofit sector in the United States. Part III then gave a "30,000 feet up" view of NGOs globally with emphasis on INGOs. Now in Part X, we explore domestic nongovernmental organizations—or simply NGOs—within countries outside of the United States. Obviously, we cannot include chapters about NGOs in all countries or even in all continents. There are far too many. Instead, this chapter focuses on the reasons why there are enormous differences in the status, role, strength, and functions of NGOs within countries. The readings present comparative analyses and examples from many countries with special emphasis on Mexico, Southeast Asia, and China.

As defined originally by United Nations ECOSOC resolution 288[X], Article 71, 1950, a nongovernmental organization or NGO is: "Any international organization which is not established by intergovernmental agreement shall be considered as a nongovernmental organization."[1] A more useful definition is offered by Archer:

> A group brought together by common aims and with a basic organizational structure; it does not rely upon governments for its formation or for most of the resources of its continued existence, and it is not profit-making in its aim.[2]

The size, resources, aspirations, and influence of the nonprofit sectors in most countries around the globe have expanded so rapidly and comprehensively that observers have referred to "an associational revolution."[3] Many NGOs now reach actively outside of their national boundaries to find new sources of funding with partners including humanitarian relief and private-development assistance organizations (INGOs), and interest associations (see Part III).[4,5]

NGOs have become important social, economic, and in some instances political actors in many less developed emerging nations but also in some more developed nations.[6]

> NGOs today are vitally important in providing additional checks on the legislative and executive branches of government. . . . I have seen the civil society groups at home and abroad . . . come to enjoy an impressive amount of influence over government policy-making and to play an important role in building civil society.[7]

   DOI: 10.4324/9780367696559-43

This "global associational revolution is a

> massive upsurge of organized private, voluntary activity in virtually every corner of the globe. . . . Known variously as the "nonprofit," the "civil society," . . . the "NGO," or the "charitable sector," this set of institutions includes within it a sometimes bewildering array of entities.[8]

In 2004, Salamon and Sokolowski ranked the strength of the NGO sectors in the 34 countries for which they had relatively complete data. These rankings were "based on each of the three major dimensions of our [Global Civil Society Index], and then the Composite Score (or 'Overall Score')."[9] The three major dimensions were capacity, sustainability, and impact. For the sake of comparison, the five strongest NGO sectors at that time were:

	Overall	Capacity	Sustainability	Impact
Netherlands	74	79	54	89
Norway	65	55	82	59
United States	61	76	54	54
Sweden	60	58	56	67
United Kingdom	58	366	60	50

Obviously, all of the strongest sectors are in northwestern Europe except the United States. Also notice that although the United States is ranked highly, it does not have the strongest sector. In contrast, the least strong sectors (lowest first) were in:

	Overall	Capacity	Sustainability	Impact
Pakistan	19	26	19	12
Romania	22	27	26	14
Mexico	24	23	29	19
Slovakia	24	32	28	13
Poland	25	30	38	7

A few other selected Composite Index scores of interest were Israel 54 (ranked 7th), Uganda 37 (tied for 18th), Japan 36 (19th), South Korea 35 (20th), and India 26 (29th). We stated earlier that the importance of the roles NGOs play in their country is highly influenced by the government's degree of democratization vs authoritarianism and the relative amount of funding that flows into the sector. Therefore, the Republic of Uganda, a lesser developed country with a modern history of turmoil and government instability having an Overall Index score of 37 next to highly developed stable countries such as Japan at 36 and South Korea at 35, is surprising. In this chapter, we attempt to explain some of the more important factors and forces that affect the strength of NGO sectors.

In Part III, we stated:

> As the Cold War continued, the U.S. government and a host of private citizens shared an interest in keeping newly emerging nations from opting for alliances with the Soviet Union. Accordingly,

the creation of private institutions to alleviate poverty and stimulate popular participation in the civic life of these societies became a major objective of U.S. foreign policy.[10]

And rapidly increasing globalization has continued to expand the resources and activities of INGOs and indigenous NGOs. *Globalization* is the interconnectedness of the world-wide economy, the interweaving of international and domestic organizations, governance systems, and communication capabilities that ignore boundaries of time and space. As globalization continues to expand as a reality, many political, legal, financial, and cultural barriers to INGOs and NGOs have been weakened or have fallen in countries around the globe.

Even in countries such as China that have feared and tightly controlled nonprofit organizations:

In May 2007, the European Union (EU) and the United Nations Development Programme (UNDP) signed an agreement with the Chinese government to support a large-scale initiative to strengthen the rule of law and civil society participation in China. . . . About half of the program's US$10.5 million budget will be devoted to strengthening the legal framework for civil society organizations (CSOs) and improving communication and coordination between CSOs, the government, and other social actors.[11]

The government of China

has been downsizing, transferring many economic and social responsibilities to a variety of social groups. . . . The first and essential step in this strategy was for the government to legalize and to promote nongovernmental organizations. Once they became legal and gained government support, dormant SOs [social organizations, shehui tuanti] were revitalized and new ones launched.[12]

The Roles and Functions of Nonprofits in Countries With Different Forms of Government

The role that NGOs play in nations around the world today depends largely on a particular government's views of the state and international relations.

A view of the state based on, for example, the U.S. Constitution might see it as a servant of the people and their needs. Insofar as these needs can be achieved by other means—by use of the market or by voluntary associations—then the state has less to do and private enterprise and civil society [and NGOs] are to the fore. . . . [In contrast,] a government that believes it has the monopoly of wisdom—as well as power—has little time for nongovernmental organizations.[13]

For example, almost all charitable establishments in Europe were formerly in the hands of private persons or of guilds. Today, they continue to be dependent on the state, and in many countries the state almost exclusively delivers the services directly and undertakes to supply bread to the hungry, assistance and shelter to the sick, work for the idle, and act as the sole reliever of all kinds of misery. Or the state controls the management and operations of the nonprofits that deliver the services. Alexis de Tocqueville's *secondary power* is what we refer to today as activities that service the public good, and Tocqueville's observations about concepts such as the *public good*, *common goods*, and *private goods*[14] continue today. Similar discussions also continue about the concept of *social capital*—networks of mutual trust, goodwill, and obligations that are created as by-products of people working together to achieve an end and that can be called upon in the future to achieve other ends.[15]

In non-democratic societies, governments may attempt "to control not only political and economic activities but also in the social, religious, and family spheres. Such governments have thus been opposed to the existence of independent nongovernmental organizations."[16] A government may suppress nonprofit organizations coercively or more subtly. For example, government decides the services it will contract out into the nonprofit sector and the regulations it will use to encourage or discourage the health—and often the existence—of organizations in the nonprofit sector.

> In the extreme, the state can proscribe NPOs, nationalize them, or prohibit consumers from using their services. . . . Thus, while the nonprofit sector flourishes at the will of the government, its existence also limits the power of the state, in democratic societies.[17]

Readings Reprinted in Part X

Nuno Themudo's "A Cross-National Philanthropic Puzzle" directly addresses the key issue for this chapter: why countries differ in the size, strength, and resilience of their NGO sectors. What theories and/or empirical data explain why, for example, Mexico has one of the weakest nonprofit sectors in the world despite having "intermediate levels of economic development and welfare spending, significant protection of civil liberties and political rights, and a favorable legal framework for non-profit organizations"? Themudo also examines economic and political ramifications of Mexico's anemic NGO sector, including low social trust, widespread corruption, less than vigorous economic development, and possibly social instability.

"A Cross-National Philanthropic Puzzle" attempts to find explanatory factors for the differences among nations (including Mexico). It tests—and largely rejects—the applicability of many different types of nonprofit theories and hypotheses before settling on Kuznets' U-shaped curve, a model that focuses on economic instability and overall risk. Because this reading includes widely ranging theories about the nonprofit sector drawn from many disciplines, it could also fit comfortably in Part I, III, or V, but we believe it contributes best here.

The second reading in this chapter, "Global Perspectives on the Legal Framework for Civil Society and Relational Governance" by Douglas Rutzen, examines "the extent to which legislation enables—or disables—civil society participation in relational governance." Rutzen's analysis of legal frameworks provides important insights into why civil societies differ widely and often unexpectedly. For example, are relational and authoritarian forms of governance diametrically opposed in how they enable or restrict the NGO sector?

> The legal framework for civil society 1) reflects governance theories and 2) serves as an agent of change. In other words, the legal framework reflects views on the roles of the state, the role of civil society, forms of engagement, and other societal norms.

The legal system also affects the extent to which NGOs can influence societal norms. The final reading in this chapter by Peifeng Liu adds specifics to Rutzen's analysis by examining the legal structure and its implications for NGOs in China.

Benjamin Read and Robert Pekkanen's "Organizations that Straddle the State-Society Divide: Illuminating Blind Spots of Existing Paradigms" has been revised from a chapter in their 2009 book, *Local Organizations and Urban Governance in East and Southeast Asia*. This reading addresses a series of questions about the "sprawling presence" of straddle groups—grassroots associations (NGOs) that span the divide between government and society—in many parts of Southeast Asia. Because none of the four conceptual frameworks the authors use is able to successfully explain the status of NGO sectors on its own, they utilize a combination of the four.

Read and Pekkanen answer three key questions about grassroots organizations that receive at least some state support and encouragement and often provide important services and communication channels "through which ordinary people can articulate demands, address local issues, and sometimes vote for representatives." (1) How do straddle associations interact with their members? (2) In what ways do they influence the broader political system? And (3), Do straddle groups help facilitate good governance, and if so, how? The authors conclude that straddlers are often "kinds of corporatist arrangements in that states use them in efforts to direct particular participation toward sanctioned channels." Yes in some contexts, straddlers serve as synergistic bridges between states and communities such that "each can possess valuable assets that the other requires: resources, reach, expertise, and authority on the hand and micro-level networks, interpersonal trust, and credibility on the other,"

In this chapter's final reading, Peifeng Liu[18] analyzes "nonprofit legislation in China as part of a broader examination of the development of civil rights in the country." As the reading by Douglas Rutzen makes clear, laws both reflect prevailing culture and also shape how NGOs are permitted to participate in civil society and governance. "Nonprofit Legislation in China" provides a fascinating example of the effects of legislation on the sector by tracing the changes in government stances that have resulted in "government legislation [that] has at times actively regulated and at other times passively reacted to [NGOs]." Importantly for understanding the NGO sector in China,

> Most nonprofits in China are corporatist (i.e., government-led) organizations. In the short term, Chinese nonprofits will not necessarily undermine government power but will more likely either contribute to or limit government power. . . . Only through this emerging civil society, can China establish a modern, integrated state and protect its people's civil rights.

Notes

1. United Nations, *ECOSOC Resolution 288[X]*, Article 71, 1950.

2. Clive Archer, "Nongovernmental Organization," in *International Encyclopedia of Public Policy and Administration*, ed. Jay M. Shafritz (Boulder, CO: Westview, 1998): 1504.

3. Michael Edwards, "Civil Society as Associational Life," in *Civil Society*, ed. M. Edwards (4th ed., Cambridge, MA: Polity Press, 2020); Lester M. Salamon and S. Wojciech Sokolowski, eds., *Global Civil Society: Dimensions of the Nonprofit Sector* (Vol. 2, Bloomfield, CT: Kumarian, 2004).

4. William E. DeMars, *NGOs and Transnational Networks: Wild Cards in World Politics* (London: Pluto Press, 2005).

5. Helmut K. Anheier, "International Aspects and Globalization," in *Nonprofit Organizations: Theory, Management, Policy*, ed. H. K. Anheier (2nd ed., London and New York: Routledge, 2014).

6. For examples, see: Jie Chen, *Transnational Civil Society in China: Intrusion and Impact* (Cheltenham: Edward Elgar, 2013); Julie Hearn, "African NGOs: The New Compradors?" *Development and Change* 38 (2007): 1095–1110; Mary Kay Gugerty, "The Emergence of Nonprofit Self-Regulation in Africa." *Nonprofit and Voluntary Sector Quarterly* 39 (2010): 1087–1112; Qiusha Ma, "The Governance of NGOs in China since 1978: How Much Autonomy?" *Nonprofit and Voluntary Sector Quarterly* 31 (2002): 305–328; Roseanne M. Mirabella, Giuliana Gemelli, Margy-Jean Malcolm, and Gabriel Berger, "Nonprofit and Philanthropic Studies:

International Overview of the Field in Africa, Canada, Latin America, Asia, the Pacific, and Europe," *Nonprofit and Voluntary Sector Quarterly* 36 (2007): 110S–135S.

7. Stuart E. Eizenstat, "Nongovernmental Organizations as the Fifth Estate," *Seton Hall Journal of Diplomacy and International Relations* 5 (2004): 15.

8. Lester M. Salamon, S. Wojciech Sokolowski, and Regina List, "Global Civil Society: An Overview," in *Global Civil Society*, eds. Lester M. Salamon and S. Wojciech Sokolowski (Vol. 2, Bloomfield, CT: Kumarian Press, 2004): 3.

9. Lester M. Salamon, and S. Wojciech Sikowski, "Measuring Civil Society; The Johns Hopkins Global Civil Society Index," in *Global Civil Society: Dimensions of the Nonprofit Sector*, eds. L. M. Salamon, S. W. Sokolowski, and Associates (Vol. II, Bloomfield, CT: Kumarian Press, 2004).

10. Brian H. Smith, "Nonprofit Organizations in International Development: Agents of Empowerment or Preservers of Stability?" in *Private Action and the Public Good*, eds. Walter W. Powell and Elisabeth S. Clemens (New Haven, CT: Yale University Press, 1998): 218.

11. Jonathan Schwartz, and Shawn Shieh, eds. *State and Society Responses to Social Welfare Needs in China: Serving the People* (London and New York: Routledge, 2009).

12. Qiusha Ma, "The Governance of NGOs in China Since 1978: How Much Autonomy?" *Nonprofit and Voluntary Sector Quarterly* 31 (2002): 306.

13. Archer, 1998, p. 1505.

14. Adapted from Alexis de Tocqueville, *Democracy in America* (Vol. 2, New York: Knopf, 1840). See also Part V, "Economic Theories of the Nonprofit Sector."

15. See also Part VI, "Political Theories of the Nonprofit Sector" and Part VII, "Community and Civil Society Theories of the Nonprofit Sector."

16. Archer, 1998, p. 1505.

17. Estelle James, "Introduction," in *The Nonprofit Sector in International Perspective: Studies in Comparative Culture and Policy*, ed. Estelle James (New York: Oxford University Press, 1989): 9.

18. Translated by Juliann H. Viksc, Research Fellow, Huamin Research Center, School of Social Work, Rutgers University.

Bibliography

Anheier, Helmut K. *Nonprofit Organizations: Theory, Management, Policy* (2nd ed., London and New York: Routledge, 2014).

Archer, Clive. "Nongovernmental Organization." In *International Encyclopedia of Public Policy and Administration*, ed. Jay M. Shafritz (Boulder, CO: Westview, 1998): 1504.

Bies, Angela, and Scott Kennedy. "The State and the State of the Art on Philanthropy in China." *Voluntas* 30(4) (2019): 619–633.

Brown, Rajeswary Ampalavanar, and Justin Pierce (Eds.). *Charities in the Non-Western World: The Development and Regulation of Indigenous and Islamic Charities* (New York: Routledge, 2013).

Caballero-Anthony, Mely, and Toshihiro Menju (Eds.). *Asia on the Move: Regional Migration and the Role of Civil Society* (New York: Japan Center for International Exchange, 2015).

Cavatorta, Francesco (Ed.). *Civil Society Activism Under Authoritarian Rule: A Comparative Perspective* (Abington: Routledge, 2013).

Clark, Janine A. "Relations Between Professional Associations and the State in Jordan." In *Civil Society Activism Under Authoritarian Rule: A Comparative Perspective*, ed. Francesco Cavatorta (Abington: Routledge, 2013): 158–180.

Cortina, Regina, and Constanza Lafuenta. *Civil Society Organizations in Latin American Education: Case Studies and Perspectives on Advocacy* (New York: Routledge, 2020).

Durac, Vincent. "Entrenching Authoritarianism or Promoting Reform? Civil Society in Contemporary Yemen." In *Civil Society Activism Under Authoritarian Rule: A Comparative Perspective*, ed. Francesco Cavatorta (Abington: Routledge, 2013): 135–157.

Edwards, Michael. *Civil Society* (4th ed., Cambridge, MA: Polity Press, 2020).

Elson, Peter R. *High Ideals and Noble Intentions: Voluntary Sector-Government Relations in Canada* (Toronto, Canada: University of Toronto Press, 2013).

Farmer, Jane, Carol Hill, and Sarah-Anne Munoz (Eds.). *Community Co-Production: Social Enterprise in Remote and Rural Communities* (Cheltenham: Edward Elgar, 2013).

Ferguson, Gretchen. "The Social Economy in Bolivia: Indigeneity, Solidarity, and Alternatives to Capitalism." *Voluntas* 29(6) (2018): 1233–1243.

Gugerty, Mary Kay. "The Emergence of Nonprofit Self-Regulation in Africa." *Nonprofit and Voluntary Sector Quarterly* 39 (2010): 1087–1112.

Ha, Seong-Kyu. "The Role of NGOs for Low-income Groups in Korean Society." *Environment and Urbanization* 14 (2002): 219–229.

Hansson, Lisa, and Asa Weinholt. "New Frontline Actors Emerging from Cross-Sector Collaboration: Examples from the Fire and Rescue Service Sector." *Public Organization Review* 19(4) (2019): 519–539.

Hearn, Julie. "African NGOs: The New Compradors?" *Development and Change* 38 (2007): 1095–1110.

Huang, Chien-Chung, Guosheng Deng, Zhenyoo Wang, and Richard L. Edwards (Eds.). *China's Nonprofit Sector: Progress and Challenges* (New York: Routledge, 2014).

Hustinx, Lesley, Dries Van den Bosch, and Chloë Delcour. "Money Makes the World Go Round: Voluntary Associations, Financial Support, and Social Capital in Belgium." *Nonprofit and Voluntary Sector Quarterly* 42 (2013): 1176–1196.

Ismail, Ayman, and Brendon Johnson. "Managing Organizational Paradoxes in Social Enterprises: Case Studies from the MENA Region." *Voluntas* 30(3) (2019): 516–534.

James, Estelle (Ed.). *The Nonprofit Sector in International Perspective: Studies in Comparative Culture and Policy* (New York: Oxford University Press, 1989).

Kravchenko, Zhanna, and Anastasiya Moskvina. "Entrepreneurial NPOs in Russia: Rationalizing the Mission." *Voluntas* 29(5) (2018): 962–975.

Lang, Sabine. *NGOs, Civil Society, and the Public Sphere* (New York: Cambridge University Press, 2013).

Liu, Peifeng, Nonprofit Legislation in China (2014). In, Huang, Chien-Chung, Guosheng Deng, Zhenyao Wang, and Richard L. Edwards (eds.), *China's Nonprofit Sector: Progress and Challenges* (pp. 75–90). Abingdon, Oxfordshire, UK and New York: Routledge.

Lu, Jiahuan, and Chengxin Xu. "Complementary or Supplementary? The Relationship between Government Size and Nonprofit Sector Size." *Voluntas* 29(3) (2018): 454–469.

Ma, Qiusha. "The Governance of NGOs in China Since 1978: How Much Autonomy?" *Nonprofit and Voluntary Sector Quarterly* 31 (2002): 305–328.

———. *Non-Governmental Organizations in Contemporary China: Paving the Way to Civil Society?* (London and New York: Routledge, 2006).

Mascarenhas, Michael. *New Humanitarianism and the Crisis of Charity: Good Intentions on the Road to Help* (Bloomington, IN: Indiana University Press, 2017).

McCabe, Helen, and Guosheng Deng. "So They'll Have Somewhere to Go: Establishing Non-governmental Organizations (NGOs) for Children with Autism in the People's Republic of China." *Voluntas* 29(5) (2019): 1019–1032.

Meeuwisse, Anna, and Roberto Scaramuzino. *Europeanization in Sweden: Opportunities and Challenges for Civil Society Organizations* (New York: Berghahn Books, 2019).

Mirabella, Roseanne M., Giuliana Gemelli, Margy-Jean Malcolm, and Gabriel Berger. "Nonprofit and Philanthropic Studies: International Overview of the Field in Africa, Canada, Latin America, Asia, the Pacific, and Europe." *Nonprofit and Voluntary Sector Quarterly* 36 (2007): 110S–135S.

Mirońska, Dominika, and Piotr Zaborek. "NGO-Business Collaboration: A Comparison of Organizational, Social, and Reputation Value from the NGO Perspective in Poland." *Nonprofit & Voluntary Sector Quarterly* 48(3) (2019): 532–551.

Musah-Surugu, Issah Justice. "The 'Third Sector' and Climate Change Adaptation Governance in Sub-Saharan Africa: Experience from Ghana." *Voluntas* 30(2) (2019): 312–326.

Nirello, Laura. *The French Nonprofit Sector* (Leiden, Netherlands: Brill Research Perspectives, 2019).

Okabe, Yasunobu, and Sakiko Shiraton. "What Motivates Japan's International Volunteers? Categorizing Japan Overseas Cooperation Volunteers." *Voluntas* 30(5) (2019): 1069–1089.

Othman, Radiah, and Norli Ali. "NPO, Internal Controls, and Supervision Mechanisms in a Developing Country." *International Society for Third-Sector Research (ITSR)* 25 (2014): 201–224.

Phillips, Susan D., and Steven Rathgeb Smith (Eds.). *Governance and Regulation in the Third Sector: International Perspectives* (New York: Routledge, 2011).

Read, Benjamin L., with Robert Pekkanen (Eds.). *Local Organizations and Urban Governance in East and Southeast Asia: Straddling State and Society* (London and New York: Routledge, 2009).

Salamon, Lester M., S. Wojciech Sokolowsi, and Megan A. Haddock. *Explaining Civil Society Development: A Social Origins Approach* (Baltimore, MD: Johns Hopkins University Press, 2017).

—— (Eds.). *Global Civil Society: Dimensions of the Nonprofit Sector* (Vol. 2, Bloomfield, CT: Kumarian Press, 2004).

——, and Regina List. "Global Civil Society: An Overview." In *Global Civil Society*, eds. Lester M. Salamon and S. Wojciech Sokolowski (Vol. 2, Bloomfield, CT: Kumarian Press, 2004): 3.

Schwartz, Jonathan, and Shawn Shieh (Eds.). *State and Society Responses to Social Welfare Needs in China: Serving the People* (London and New York: Routledge, 2009).

Smith, David Horton, Alisa V. Moldanova, and Svitlana Krasynska (Eds.). *The Nonprofit Sector in Eastern Europe, Russia, and Central Asia: Civil Society Advances and Challenges* (Leiden, Netherlands: Brill Research Perspectives, 2019).

Stroup, Sarah S. *Borders among Activists: International NGOs in the United States, Britain, and France* (Ithaca, NY: Cornell University Press, 2012).

Themudo, Nuno S. *Nonprofits in Crisis: Economic Development, Risk, and the Philanthropic Kuznets Curve* (Bloomington, IN: Indiana University Press, 2013).

Tocqueville, Alexis de. *Democracy in America* (Vol. 2, New York: Knopf, 1840).

Valero, Jesus N., Georgina Griffith Yates, Soo Stephanie Kim, Hyung Jun Park, Kyujin Jung, Min Jeong Kim, and Minhyuk Cho. "The Role of Nongovernmental Organizations in Refugee and Immigrant Integration: A Qualitative Exploratory Study of Seoul, South Korea." *International Journal of Public Administration* 43 (2020): 166–175.

United Nations. *ECOSOC Resolution 288[X]*, Article 71, 1950.

Wells-Dang, Andrew. *Civil Society Networks in China and Vietnam: Pathbreakers in Health and the Environment* (New York: Palgrave Macmillan, 2013).

William, E. DeMars. *NGOs and Transnational Networks: Wild Cards in World Politics* (London: Pluto Press, 2005).

CHAPTER 34

A Cross-National Philanthropic Puzzle

NUNO S. THEMUDO

Themudo, Nuno S. *Nonprofits in Crisis: Economic Development, Risk, and the Philanthropic Kuznets Curve* (Bloomington and Indianapolis: Indiana University Press, 2013).

"Sometimes things get worse before they get better"—Doña Mica reflected during an interview.[1] She was apologetic about the fact that her new initiative, which focused on building the capacity of indigenous youth to develop microenterprises, was rapidly losing money. Yet she remained confident that Fovaso—a small nonprofit organization in Central Mexico—would soon be financially viable again. Survival of small nonprofit organizations in Mexico is challenging in the best of times. But when I interviewed Doña Mica, Mexico was in the midst of the so-called Tequila Crisis, which "caused one of the worst recessions to hit an individual country since the 1930s" (Krugman 2008:32). The stock market had recently lost almost half of its value, unemployment was at record high levels, and Mexico's risk premium was the highest in the world.[2] At the time, no one knew how deep the crisis was going to be. Eventually the economy did improve, and Fovaso experienced some temporary financial relief. Over time, however, Fovaso's troubles returned. Ironically, the new social enterprise model alienated supporters of the previous model and failed to attract sufficient new support, leading to a reduction in social impact and financial decline. To witness the decline of this valuable organization, which at its peak had employed more than forty people, was devastating for its clients, already hard hit by the crisis.

The main argument proposed here is that the apparently simple notion of risk helps explain the fundamental and contradictory influence of economic development on the nonprofit sector. When economic development leads to increases in macroeconomic instability, nonprofits tend to face rising levels of economic risk, and nonprofit sector strength tends to decline. In contrast, the nonprofit sector tends to become stronger when economic development decreases macroeconomic instability and the risk nonprofits face. In other words, *risk resulting from the process of economic development is a major influence on nonprofit sector evolution*. Such risk is a powerful, yet largely neglected, influence on philanthropy and the sector.

The trajectory of nonprofits such as Fovaso over the past two decades provides a vivid example of the Mexican nonprofit sector's travails. Annually, Mexicans donate a smaller fraction of national income to the nonprofit sector than citizens in any other country, around half a billion purchasing power adjusted dollars. They also volunteer less than anyone else does.[3] Accordingly, Mexico has the weakest nonprofit

DOI: 10.4324/9780367696559-44

sector in the world, employing only 0.4% of its labor force (Salamon et al. 2004). Mexico's philanthropy and nonprofit sector are small, but what is astounding is that they are smaller even than in poor countries such as Tanzania, Kenya, and the Philippines as well as ex-communist countries such as Romania and Hungary.

Why does Mexico have the weakest nonprofit sector in the world? Mexico's nonprofit sector anemia is surprising because current theory predicts that a country with intermediate levels of economic development and welfare spending, significant protection of civil liberties and political rights, and a favorable legal framework for nonprofit organizations should encourage significant philanthropy and a medium-sized nonprofit sector.[4] Why are Mexicans less generous than others? Why are they less likely to make donations and volunteer for social causes? More generally, why do some countries have a vibrant nonprofit sector and others do not? The experience of countries with weaker nonprofit sectors, such as Mexico, is very relevant to general questions about the sector in other countries (see Hammack 2002). It offers a valuable opportunity for the study of the causes of nonprofit sector weakness and an important contrast to most existing research, which has focused on the much more developed nonprofit sector in rich countries. Research on Mexico's philanthropic anemia helps us understand the broader causes and consequences of nonprofit sector weakness in Mexico and elsewhere.

At stake is much more than an embarrassing ranking for Mexico. Since a robust nonprofit sector is generally associated with the healthy functioning of democracy and the market, the country's philanthropic anemia is likely to have political and economic ramifications. For example, a weak nonprofit sector might limit the opportunities for underrepresented groups to have a say in Mexico's incipient democracy, contributing to the country's low levels of civic participation. Nonprofit sector weakness helps to explain the paradoxical and troubling finding

that the majority of Mexicans were disappointed with democracy even as in the year 2000 the country held its first free presidential election in over seventy years.[5] Moreover, nonprofit sector weakness might contribute to low social trust and widespread corruption (Themudo 2013), which, in turn, is likely to hurt economic development and social stability (see Putnam 1993, 2000; Knack and Keefer 1997; Uslaner 2008).

An Enigma Wrapped in a Puzzle: Mexico and the Philanthropic Kuznets Curve

Mexican researchers have hypothesized that the country's undersized nonprofit sector is primarily due to the uniqueness of its political history (e.g., Verduzco 2003; Terrazas 2006; Layton 2009). This is a plausible explanation. Between 1929 and 1997, Mexico was a de facto single-party democracy. Throughout the duration of its rule, the Partido Revolucionario Institucional (PRI) was effective in co-opting and neutralizing (often through repression) any dissenting views (McAdam, Tarrow, and Tilly 2001). Such a political context, the argument goes, hampered the emergence of an independent nonprofit sector. However, while it is impossible to deny the importance of Mexico's idiosyncratic political history, a comparative outlook suggests other key factors may be at play. Several other countries, such as Brazil, Hungary, and South Korea, which have very different political histories, also display a weak nonprofit sector. We must contrast, therefore, explanations based on Mexico's unique political history against more general explanations of nonprofit sector weakness to assess their relative explanatory power and generate a more complete explanation for our puzzle.

A cross-national outlook also offers fresh doubts about the explanatory power of nonprofit theory. Current theories predict a linear relationship between nonprofit sector strength and the level of economic development. The

Mexican case, however, points to the intriguing possibility that this relationship might in fact be nonlinear. Surprisingly, cross-national evidence supports this supposition.[6] The predicted relationship is clearly nonlinear, with middle-income countries typically displaying the lowest levels of philanthropy.

Astonishingly, [a] U-shaped pattern can be found in every main operationalization of the nonprofit sector (such as nonprofit employment, expenditure, volunteering, and giving) and is also evident in every field of nonprofit sector activity for which we have comparative measures, namely culture, education, health, social services, environment, development, advocacy, foundations, international, professional associations, religion, and women's organizations.[7] To illustrate, Figure 34.1 depicts the relationship between prosperity and the two main measures of nonprofit sector size. It includes the scatter plot for the actual values of total nonprofit sector employment as well as predicted values for total nonprofit sector employment and expenditure.[8]

I label this nonlinear relationship between economic development and nonprofit sector strength the "philanthropic Kuznets curve" (PKC) because its U-shape resembles the "Kuznets curve." Half a century ago, Simon Kuznets argued that the relationship between social equality and economic development follows a U-shaped curve. He argued that at low levels, economic development leads to a decrease in economic equality, but at high levels, economic development contributes to an increase in economic equality (Kuznets 1955). More recently, researchers identified an analogous, nonlinear relationship between environmental conservation and prosperity, whereby environmental conservation first falls as the

FIGURE 34.1 Nonprofit Sector Size and Economic Development

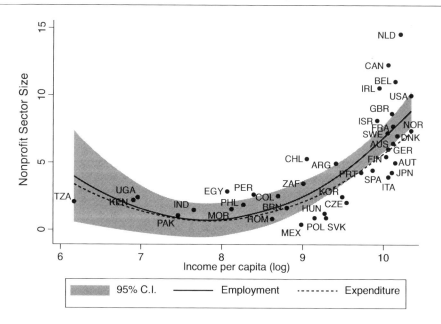

Notes: Author's analysis based on Johns Hopkins Comparative Nonprofit Sector data (ca. 1995–2000). Total employment includes both paid and full-time-equivalent volunteering as a proportion (%) of the labor force. The shaded area represents the 95% confidence interval for predicted total employment. Expenditure measured as a proportion (%) of GDP. Level of economic development is measured by the natural log of income per capita (in 1995) from the World Development Indicators dataset.

level of economic development rises, reaches a turning point, and then increases as the level of economic development continues to rise. Like the original Kuznets curve, this "environmental Kuznets curve" has quickly become a major area of research in economics (e.g., Binder and Neumayer 2005; Acemoglu 2009). The PKC has cross-sectional and longitudinal interpretations; that is, it describes a pattern of change in philanthropy and the nonprofit sector as countries develop economically over time, as well as a pattern of cross-sectional variation at any one time between countries at different levels of economic development.[9]

Evidence of a robust PKC is even more striking given the potential biases against the accurate measurement of nonprofit sector size in poor and non-Western countries. The comparative evidence presented here demonstrates that *the nonprofit sector can be as vibrant in poor countries as in rich ones*, even according to several indicators of the "real" (read "Western") nonprofit sector. Levels of nonprofit volunteering are much higher in Tanzania or Uganda than in some rich countries such as Portugal, Austria, or Japan and much higher than in middle-income countries such as Mexico, Brazil, or Poland. This fact is consistent with Musick and Wilson's (2008:343) finding that alongside the United States the highest levels of volunteering can be found in some of the poorest countries in the world, namely Bangladesh, Tanzania, Zimbabwe, and Uganda.[10] Moreover, levels of nonprofit expenditure as a proportion of national income in Tanzania and Kenya are on par with those in Italy and Austria, and much higher than those in most middle-income countries. Comparative nonprofit sector data lend support, therefore, to the minority view that civil society in poor countries is much more vibrant than generally acknowledged by academics and policy makers, who tend to view such contexts as the prototypical realms of "amoral familism," dominated by relationships based on patronage

and other forms of social coercion (Hann and Dunn 1996).

What accounts for the profound variation in philanthropy and nonprofit sector strength across countries manifested in the PKC? Mexico's experience suggests that we cannot take the nonprofit sector for granted and that these questions deserve careful study.

The PKC and Nonprofit Sector Theory

Increasing recognition of the nonprofit sector's social and economic contributions has made its study an important topic in the social sciences. A significant body of research, therefore, has sought to explain the emergence and development of the nonprofit sector. Familiar to many, for example, are studies on the impact of social diversity (e.g., Olson 1965; Weisbrod 1988; Chang and Tuckman 1996), religious competition (e.g., James 1989; Burger and Veldheer 2001), trust and asymmetric information (e.g., Hansmann 1987; Ben-Ner and van Hoomissen 1991), expanded civil liberties and political opportunities from democratization (e.g., Tarrow 1994; Hammack 2001), legal and regulatory frameworks (e.g., Galaskiewicz and Bielefeld 1998; Anheier and Salamon 1998; Salamon and Toepler 2000; Hammack 2001), modernization (Durkheim 1984 [1893]; Putnam 2000; Putnam and Goss 2002), economic growth and development (e.g., Hirschman 1982; Hammack 2001), higher social welfare spending and tax benefits for nonprofits (e.g., Salamon 1987; Smith and Lipsky 1993; Beito 2000; Steinberg 2003), nonmonetary values among entrepreneurs (e.g., Young 1983; James 1989; Rose-Ackerman 1996), globalization (e.g., Boli and Thomas 1999; Clark 2003; Ebrahim 2003; Lewis 2007), and "social origins" (Salamon and Anheier 1998). This extensive body of work, however, is unable to explain the PKC.

Economic Development and the Nonprofit Sector

Traditional approaches suggest that economic development has a detrimental effect on philanthropy and the nonprofit sector. They propose different mechanisms at both structural and individual levels for this effect, namely the rise of the welfare state, modernization, and increasing opportunity costs of labor that accompany economic development. Both government failure and welfare state approaches suggest that economic development typically leads to expansion of government social spending, which in turn weakens the demand for nonprofit sector provision (e.g., Weisbrod 1988; Salamon and Anheier 1998). Government failure theory proposes that the nonprofit sector is a response to failures of the state to provide the kinds of collective goods that people want but that the market is unable to provide. To the extent that the government increases its provision of such collective goods, reducing government failure, the need for nonprofit provision should decline. Like government failure theory, welfare state theory suggests that the emergence of the welfare state "crowds out" traditional welfare-related nonprofits, leading to an inverse relationship between the size of the nonprofit sector and the scale of governmental collective goods provision (Salamon and Anheier 1998; Skocpol 1992). Given that charitable organizations and welfare programs often seek to perform the same role, it is reasonable to suppose that, as welfare programs expand and their coverage becomes more universal, demand for nonprofit sector services should fall. A few scholars also believe that countries with strong welfare states not only have less need for volunteer services but also nurture a culture that stigmatizes volunteer work as charity (Ascoli and Cnaan 1997; Gaskin and Smith 1997). The decline of mutual-benefit societies and cooperatives since the 1940s (Beito 2000; Anheier 2004) would appear to lend support to this perspective.

An alternative approach, deriving from modernization theory and the earlier work of the illustrious sociologist Émile Durkheim (1984 [1893]), proposes that economic development leads to structural changes in the economy (such as division of labor, urbanization, and industrialization) that, in turn, weaken the social cohesion of traditional societies. Increasing division of labor and migration may undermine traditional social bonds, while the rise of the welfare state may contribute to the decline of traditional self-help associations as welfare state theory posits (Salamon and Anheier 1998). Recent analyses of the alleged decline of civic engagement in the United States point to technological change—a key element of modernization and economic development—in shaping social relationships. Famously, Putnam (2000) argues that the spread of television and the Internet is reducing face-to-face interactions, with detrimental consequences for philanthropy and the nonprofit sector. From a rational choice perspective, Olson (1965) argues that as the opportunity cost of participation increases, rational actors are less likely to participate in collective action (e.g., by volunteering). By increasing the opportunity cost of labor, then, economic development may reduce civic participation (see Acemoglu and Robinson 2006). In the same way, rising opportunity cost of labor can also weaken social entrepreneurship as the opportunity cost of the labor involved in starting a nonprofit rises. Therefore, we should expect that economic development would lead to a decrease in nonprofit entrepreneurship, volunteering, and other forms of collective action.[11]

A competing set of approaches predicts a symbiotic, or direct, relationship between economic development and both philanthropy and nonprofit sector size. The rapid expansion of the nonprofit sector in the United States has been partly due to the fact that, as service providers, nonprofits have benefited from the rapidly expanding share of services within the economy since the 1950s (see Hammack and

Young 1993; Weisbrod 1998; Hammack 2001). Another approach suggests that increases in social welfare spending, which typically accompany prosperity, may lead to nonprofit sector growth by increasing public funding for nonprofits (Anheier and Salamon 2006). Like social welfare theory, Salamon's (1987) "interdependence theory" argues that as national economies develop, citizens tend to demand more welfare provision. However, interdependence theory argues that the rise of states' welfare responsibilities actually encourages nonprofit sector development. The argument is that nonprofits can compensate for various types of government failure, while government can compensate for various types of "voluntary failure" inherent to the nonprofit sector. Both sectors can therefore establish partnerships to improve service provision. The high proportion of public funding as a percentage of total nonprofit revenues in rich countries is taken as evidence in support of interdependence arguments (Salamon 1987), as is the fact that governments in both sides of the North Atlantic have since the 1960s greatly increased their purchase of services provided by nonprofits (Hammack 2001:158–159). The welfare state, and especially universalistic systems, can also contribute to a reduction in social inequality and the strengthening of the social contract, which Uslaner (2002) and Rothstein (2005) argue is essential for social capital development. In turn, they argue, social capital promotes nonprofit sector expansion. High levels of social inequality, therefore, should be a key factor contributing to both low levels of social capital and nonprofit sector weakness.

Mancur Olson (1982) offers an alternative explanation for a direct relationship between level of economic development and nonprofit sector strength. He argues that economic development and the concomitant rise of government power and resources increase the incentives for citizens and corporations to create nonprofit organizations to influence the policy process. Lastly, while most scholars believe that

the cultural forces of modernization (e.g., rationalization, secularization, materialism, individualism) are eroding people's commitment to the public good, a few authors have suggested that modernization may promote nonprofit sector development by encouraging "post-material" values, such as environmental conservation and women's empowerment, which are directly associated with volunteering and broader participation (see Dekker and Van den Broek 1998; Themudo 2009). Ronald Inglehart (1997) argues that economic development is not necessarily conducive to decreasing rates of civic participation because although economic modernization means a shift from traditional to secular values that discourages volunteering in some nonprofit fields, the shift from survival to self-expression values encourages volunteering in all nonprofit fields.[12] Modernization, therefore, can have a positive impact on volunteering. Indeed, Pippa Norris (2003:157) found that purchasing power adjusted GDP per capita was positively associated with volunteering across forty-six countries. Various influential approaches, therefore, suggest a direct relationship between economic development and nonprofit sector strength.

The PKC contradicts both sides of this long-standing debate and offers an opportunity to break the stalemate. Welfare state, government failure, modernization, and collective action approaches predict that rich countries should have limited nonprofit sectors. The strength of the nonprofit sector in rich countries, however, denies their main prediction. In contrast, government-nonprofit interdependence, post-materialism, and human and social capital approaches predict that poor countries should have limited nonprofit sectors. The relative strength of the nonprofit sector in poor countries when compared to middle-income countries, however, contradicts their prediction. Moreover, while all approaches agree that the nonprofit sector in countries at intermediate levels of prosperity should be of intermediate size, the general weakness of the nonprofit sector in such contexts contradicts them. *By proposing that philanthropy and the nonprofit sector either always decline or always rise with economic development, available theories cannot account for the PKC.* Reliance on linear explanations has limited our ability to understand the nonprofit sector's nonlinear evolution.

Other Theories of the Nonprofit Sector

Nonprofit sector emergence and development are commonly explained by reference to government and market failure. Relating nonprofit sector development to government failure, Weisbrod (1975, 1988) argued that the higher the level of social heterogeneity the lower the ability of government to satisfy heterogeneous demands and the stronger the incentive for nonprofit sector development. Yet, social diversity cannot account for the PKC. Since social diversity is generally higher in poor countries (see, e.g., Knack and Keefer 1997), the theory would suggest that the nonprofit sector should be strongest in poor countries. The strength of the nonprofit sector in rich countries questions the theory's relevance as a main explanation for the PKC and for the cross-national variation of nonprofit sector strength in general. In addition, Mexico has a moderate level of social diversity, so social diversity cannot explain Mexican nonprofit sector frailty. Relating nonprofit sector development to market failure, Hansmann (1987) proposed that the nonprofit sector generates more trust than the business (for-profit) sector in fields where consumers are unable to evaluate the quality of service provision. In such environments, for-profits can exploit asymmetrical information to covertly lower service quality and maximize their profits. Nonprofits' nondistribution constraint reduces the pressure to generate profits for shareholders and, consequently, the pressure to lower service quality. All else being equal, therefore, consumers should generally prefer nonprofit providers in sectors characterized by asymmetrical information, such as health care, child and elderly care, and pure academic research. More generally, in cross-national perspective the nonprofit sector should be largest where trust in business is weakest (Anheier and Salamon 2006). However, while trust in business has a U-shaped relationship with national prosperity, it displays a direct relationship with nonprofit sector size—the opposite of what the theory predicted.

Another set of explanations emphasizes the influence of religion. For example, Estelle James (1989) argued that the degree of religious competition is a predictor of nonprofit sector size. The number and variety of churches in pluralistic religious systems sparks competition among them for members, which, in turn, leads to a proliferation of activities designed to keep members involved and committed (Woolley 2003:158). Indeed, religious competition tends to be lowest in middle-income countries, a fact that is broadly consistent with the PKC. However, religious competition is not a statistically significant predictor of variations in nonprofit sector size across nations, due to the large variance in religious competition at each level of economic development.[13] Intensity of religious values, that is, "religiousness" and "religiosity," is a different mechanism through which religion may influence the nonprofit sector. Based on their empirical investigation of volunteering at the cross-national level, Musick and Wilson (2008:359) claim that "The comparatively high rate of volunteering in the United States can be attributed to the religiosity of the American people." However, the United States is an exception among rich countries. Analysis of World Values Survey data shows that, generally, both religiousness and religiosity decline with economic development.[14] This explanation, then, cannot account for the PKC.

A different set of explanations focuses on political institutions. Many scholars have argued that the protection of civil liberties, such as freedom of association, expression, and worship, is a major determinant of civil society (Gutmann 1998; Inglehart 1997; Putnam 2000) and nonprofit sector strength (e.g., Wuthnow 1988; Hammack 2001; Brody 2006; Clemens 2006). Similarly, a competitive democratic system provides political opportunities that facilitate social movement emergence and activity (e.g., Tarrow 1994). Democratic regimes, then, are more likely to foster a vibrant nonprofit sector than autocracies, as the latter is typically inclined to limit freedom of association and to repress independent nongovernmental voices. Democratic governance can also contribute to nonprofit sector strength, because its traditional focus on majority interests encourages the emergence of the nonprofit sector to fulfill neglected needs of minority groups (Douglas 1987).

David Hammack (2001) argues that the increasing protection of civil liberties is a fundamental reason for the expansion of the nonprofit sector on both sides of the North Atlantic since the 1960s. He shows how, even in apparently strong democratic regimes such as the United States, minority groups have historically faced systematic restrictions to their civil liberties and considerable obstacles to creating nonprofit organizations. Restrictions on the civil liberties of minority groups should have a profound impact on philanthropy and nonprofit sector size, especially since the nonprofit sector commonly seeks to fulfill the unmet needs of such groups. On the other hand, however, the fact that democracy, civil liberties, and political rights have a direct, linear relationship with economic development questions their ability to independently explain the PKC or the Mexican puzzles. This apparent contradiction between the obvious importance of political regime and its inability to explain nonprofit sector weakness in middle-income countries suggests that the protection of civil liberties and political rights is a necessary but not sufficient condition for nonprofit sector development.

By facilitating or hindering the creation and operation of nonprofit organizations, the legal framework is another main influence on nonprofit sector development (Salamon and Toepler 2000; Archambault 2001; Hammack 2001; Layton 2009). Unfortunately, research on legal frameworks in developing countries is sorely missing. Salamon and Toepler (2000) is one of the few exceptions. They generated the Johns Hopkins Nonprofit Law Index by examining the legal framework governing nonprofits in several countries. Surprisingly, the authors find that Mexico is one of only four countries with a "high" index score (the other countries are the United States, the Netherlands, and Israel). This exceptionally favorable legal framework stands in stark contrast with Mexico's frail nonprofit sector. The only other middle-income country examined in Salamon and Toepler's (2000) study, Brazil, has a much less favorable legal framework, though it still was more favorable than Japan's framework and only slightly less favorable than Germany's. Thus, while it would be foolish to deny the importance of the legal framework, it seems unable to explain nonprofit sector weakness in middle-income countries.

A different approach focuses on the "social origins" of the nonprofit sector. Salamon and Anheier (1998) argued that the nonprofit sector is embedded in political and welfare regimes, which are a product of historical relationships between classes and social institutions. Political and welfare regimes reflect the balance of power between social classes as well as between state and society.

> Choices about whether to rely on market, nonprofit, or state provision of key services are not simply made freely by consumers in an open market as advocates of the economic theories seem to assume. Rather, these choices are heavily constrained by prior patterns of historical development that significantly shape the range of options available at a given time and place.

(226)

Such patterns of historical development generate various "nonprofit regimes," which according to Salamon and Anheier can be classified as corporatist, liberal, social democrat, and statist depending on the strength of government and nonprofit sector. With relatively weaker nonprofit and government sectors, the vast majority of poor and middle-income countries would be classified under a "statist" regime (Anheier 2005:136). This classification, therefore, is unable to capture the variation represented by the PKC.

As a pervasive social trend, globalization presents a final set of key influences on nonprofit sector development (Edwards and Hulme 1995; Lindenberg and Bryant 2001; Clark 2003; Anheier and Themudo 2004; Lewis 2007). Because international donor agencies are key funders of nonprofit organizations in developing countries, they have a direct influence on nonprofit sector development in those countries (Fowler 2000). Donors may also contribute to the spread of democratic values and privatization policies through the spread of neoliberal ideology among states, both of which can indirectly contribute to nonprofit sector development (Edwards and Hulme 1995; Lewis 2007). At the private level, through the diffusion of communications technologies and cheap travel, globalization decreases the costs of nonprofit action across borders and increases public awareness about social needs abroad (Clark and Themudo 2004). Existing accounts, however, suggest that these mechanisms have a linear, direct influence on the nonprofit sector, and since globalization processes are typically direct correlates of economic development, they cannot account for the PKC or the Mexican case.

To be sure, while current theories cannot explain the PKC independently, they may still help to explain cross-national variation in nonprofit sector strength collectively. Thus, to better assess their influence, I opted to hold those influences constant. I did so by focusing on the impact of an economic shock—the

"Tequila Crisis"—on the evolution of the Mexican nonprofit sector over a relatively short period. Important confounding influences, such as political regime, legal framework, social inequality, culture, and geography remained largely constant during the natural experiment, from mid to late 1990s. On the other hand, economic prosperity and stability varied widely, which permitted the systematic assessment of their influence on the sector.

Economic Instability, Risk, and the Nonprofit Sector

The PKC, then, provides a fundamental cross-national "stylized fact," which nonprofit sector research must seek to explain. Simply put, it argues that the nonprofit sector in middle-income countries faces an exceptionally high level of economic risk—understood as uncertainty or variation in the range of possible economic outcomes so that adverse outcomes are possible—which, in turn, generally depresses philanthropy and nonprofit sector size. Economic development, therefore, influences the level of economic risk nonprofits face and, consequently, nonprofit sector strength.

Economic crises offer a near ideal observation ground from which to examine the impact on the nonprofit sector of a sudden change in the level of risk within a relatively constant political, institutional, and social context. During crises, risk materializes in output losses, and new expectations about potential future losses are formed. Of course, risk does not affect the nonprofit sector only during economic crises. Thus, this study follows up several Mexican nonprofit case studies for over a decade and broader indicators of the nonprofit sector in Mexico since the 1980s.

On the cusp of the "Great Recession" (2008–2009), we are all painfully aware that economic crises have devastating social and economic costs. Aside from lost output, economic crises typically also entail large "rescue packages" for their resolution. Honohan and Klingebiel (2003) find, in a sample of forty banking crises, that governments spent an average of 6.2% of GDP on crisis resolution in developed countries and a whopping 14.7% of GDP in middle-income countries. The approximate resolution cost of the Tequila Crisis was between 20 and 24% of GDP (Halac and Schmukler 2004). Economics crises, then, have lasting impacts on economic agents' risk expectations. This is partly because resolution costs linger on after a crisis is officially over. Uncertainty about how governments will finance the costs of resolution and recovery as well as how the market will evolve more generally, then, increases economic risk long after the end of an economic crisis.

Mexico's economy has had a turbulent history and, unfortunately, Mexico is not alone. At least since the 1970s, middle-income countries have faced higher levels of macroeconomic volatility than either rich or poor countries (Wolf 2005; Perry 2009).

We know surprisingly little about the causes of economic volatility. Several explanations have been proposed—from John Maynard Keynes's "animal spirits" to technology shocks, political cycles, and "rational panics"—but there is little agreement about their relative merit (Acemoglu 2009). Accordingly, researchers have suggested different explanations for middle-income countries' exceptional levels of macroeconomic volatility. One explanation focuses on structural transformations within the economy, which may increase volatility and risk (Davis and North 1971; North 1990; Acemoglu 2009). Research on the original Kuznets curve suggests that economic development entails profound economic and social transformations as society transitions from a traditional, rural society to a modern, urban society (Kuznets 1955). Developing countries are experiencing such transformations at an unprecedented pace. Changes that took place over centuries in Western Europe currently take only a few decades in developing

countries (Kuznets 1973). That is especially true in middle-income countries, where rapid structural transformations have greatly contributed to their high levels of macroeconomic volatility (Agénor 2002; Lustig 1999). A second explanation focuses on the accelerated pace with which have middle-income countries liberalized their economies and opened up to international financial and trade flows (e.g., Krugman 2008; Perkins, Radelet, and Lindauer 2006). As Lustig (1999:14) put it, even as the Tequila Crisis "was unfolding, Mexico was hailed as a 'model reformer' by policymakers and investors alike." "Model reforms" therefore may lead to imbalances and volatility (Lustig 1999). A third explanation focuses on political instability. The fact that most middle-income countries are young democracies contributes to their political instability, which, in turn, leads to economic instability (see Williams 2001; Acemoglu and Robinson 2006).

Risk from macroeconomic instability, whether measured as volatility or inflation, does indeed peak in middle-income countries. Assuming, for the moment, economic volatility and risk have a negative impact on nonprofit sector strength, the inverted-U shaped relationship between level of economic development and macroeconomic risk is consistent with the puzzling U-shaped relationship between economic development and nonprofit sector strength. On one hand, because philanthropic giving depends directly on private income (e.g., Havens, O'Herlihy, and Schervish 2006), falling private income during recessions should depress philanthropic giving. On the other hand, falling investment returns and wages during recessions should encourage giving and volunteering. Falling opportunity cost of labor (real wages) lowers the cost of participation in collective action (Acemoglu and Robinson 2006), which should boost volunteering and civic participation. Also, falling opportunity cost of capital (i.e., investment returns) during recessions lowers the cost of giving, which should boost philanthropic giving. Moreover, in countries with a counter-cyclical fiscal policy, higher government spending during recessions could mean higher government funding to nonprofits. Also important is the fact that, while on balance recessions tend to depress nonprofit resource availability, macroeconomic volatility includes both good and bad years. As Olsson (2002:xiii) argues, "Operating in [middle-income countries] is riskier than doing so in the developed world. This is largely because they are often characterized by greater economic and political instability." Volatility, therefore, may also present significant opportunities for the nonprofit sector. If volatility weakens the nonprofit sector, why are nonprofits generally unable to take more advantage of the good years?

The influence of risk has received surprisingly little attention in the academic literature on nonprofits (Wedig 1994; Young 2006, 2007), perhaps because most research on the nonprofit sector emanates from environments with relatively low levels of risk. Thus, in my attempt to understand this influence I turn to broader social theory, particularly finance and game theory.

The main argument is simple, yet powerful. Risk influences philanthropy and other contributions to the nonprofit sector because resource providers are generally risk-averse. As such, risk influences the rate with which supporters discount future benefits to society and to themselves from nonprofit sector activity in relation to the cost of contributions in the present. As risk rises, the net present value of future nonprofit sector impact declines, discouraging voluntary contributions to the sector. In stable, low-risk environments, discounting of future benefits is small and the nonprofit sector can thrive. However, in unstable, high-risk environments, discounting of future nonprofit benefits relative to present contributions discourages contributions to the nonprofit sector. Rising risk levels typically attenuate most other incentives

for philanthropy, such as reputation effects and long-term access to nonprofit services.

A key implication from this approach is that the impact of risk on different nonprofits depends on the riskiness of their programs. Because short-term impacts are less discounted than long-term ones, support in high-risk environments should privilege nonprofit organizations and programs focusing on the short term. This is important because long-term problems, such as global warming, do not disappear during high-risk periods and in fact may actually worsen. However, supporters' willingness to contribute to addressing long-term problems may change. On the other hand, as risk falls, and long-term impacts become more appealing, support should swing back to programs and organizations with a more long-term focus.

Predicted risk impacts combine to generate an understanding of the impact of economic shocks that is distinct from their simple impact due to changes in supporters' and other stakeholders' income. Procyclicality of household income and company profits clearly plays a key part in explaining the procyclicality of philanthropic giving. Much of the influence of cross-national variation in the level of economic development must be understood from the perspective of its impact on risk and the subsequent impact of risk on the nonprofit sector.

Implications

Research on the PKC and on the impact of risk on nonprofit sector strength offers new opportunities for theoretical development and new policy insights. A major motivation for systematically examining the links between economic development, risk, and the nonprofit sector is the search for development paths that enhance nonprofit sector development in the future. Given the sector's contributions to welfare, public goods, democratization, and economic development itself, much is at stake. In the case of poor and middle-income countries, the PKC provides a convenient framework to guide policy makers' current efforts to "build" civil society. According to the PKC, the early to middle stages of prosperity could be quite detrimental for the nonprofit sector. The extent to which decision makers ought to devote their limited time and resources to designing and implementing policies for nonprofit sector development depends on the extent to which the driving forces underlying the PKC are susceptible to such policies. In other words, if nonprofit sector decline is an inevitable consequence of rising prosperity, attempts to avoid such damage in the early stages of development might be futile. Understanding the mechanics of virtuous and vicious cycles enables us to find an intervention point. The risk mechanism, which the present study identifies, suggests that some interventions, such as reducing macroeconomic risk, are structural and therefore difficult to implement, while others, such as decreasing nonprofit organizations' vulnerability, are more specific and feasible. From a policy perspective, therefore, the PKC

points to a historical tendency rather than a natural law. Indeed, the evidence suggests a proactive approach, whereby policy makers could learn from experience and adopt nonprofit sector–friendly development strategies that would permit the nonprofit sector to "bridge across" the PKC (Figure 34.2).

Economic development could lead to the lower path ABC. The adoption of corrective policies that reduce nonprofit vulnerability, and thereby reduce nonprofit sector decline, leads to an evolution represented by the bridge ABD. Avoiding the path of greater nonprofit sector vulnerability would help to prevent the costly-to-reverse nonprofit sector decline and, with a "double dividend," boost future economic growth prospects. In other words, the bridge would enable developing countries to short-circuit more conventional development paths (such as ABCE in the figure). In general, successful "bridging across" policy should be based on the awareness that, at early stages, economic development is accompanied by higher macroeconomic volatility and risk. Policy makers can

FIGURE 34.2 "Bridging Across" the Philanthropic Kuznets Curve

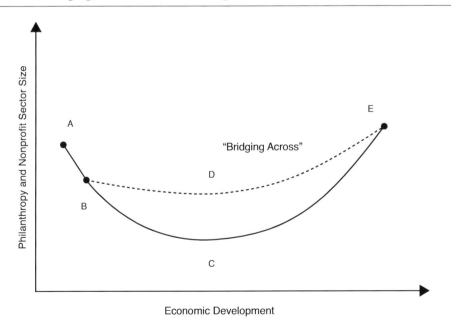

monitor harmful impacts on the nonprofit sector and address them through complementary measures.

The analysis presented here offers fresh insights into public policy aimed at nonprofit sector development in developing countries. Unfortunately, as this study shows, during crises government support for the nonprofit sector frequently gives way to other policy concerns such as rescuing the financial sector. Even during recovery periods, government support commonly shifts a disproportionate level of risk to the nonprofit sector through public-private contracting arrangements. International donor agencies, on the other hand, generally phase out their support to developing countries as their economies develop (Collier and Dehn 2001), without consideration of how the nonprofit sector is impacted by both economic development and the withdrawal of international aid (Suwannarat 2003). Currently, international donors' phasing-out policy is at odds with their stated interest in helping to build civil society in developing countries. Nonprofit leaders and supporters can also pursue several steps to increase nonprofit resilience and effectiveness as detailed in the conclusion.

A systematic examination of the links between economic development, risk, and the nonprofit sector is also relevant to the nonprofit sector in rich countries. Risk is intrinsic to the human experience and a key motivation for the evolution of social institutions (e.g., Acemoglu 2009; Beck 1992; Giddens 1999; North 1990; Shiller 2003). Thus, risk is increasingly central to contemporary social debates. As Giddens (1999) observed,

> the welfare state, whose development can be traced back to the Elizabethan poor laws in England, is essentially a risk management system. It is designed to protect against hazards that were once treated as at the disposition of the gods—sickness, disablement, job loss and old age.

Accordingly, political contests increasingly center on reducing risks such as social vulnerability, economic crises, terrorism, and environmental disaster.

A risk perspective encourages reinterpretation and reassessment of critical social debates, such as those surrounding appropriate roles for the state and society. For example, the welfare system is being reformed everywhere. According to Nicholas Barr (2001:262),

> under the old system, it was regarded as the duty of the state to look after people. A reformed system should encourage the idea that, though the state has an important role in promoting welfare, citizens—both individually and through various aspects of civil society—need to take responsibility.

This reform is partly dictated by fiscal constraints and partly by arguments that the private sector can manage most types of risk more effectively than government (Barr 2001; OECD 2008). As the nonprofit sector takes on renewed roles in social risk management and protection, understanding the relationship between risk and the nonprofit sector is imperative. Consideration of risk has also led to new calls for state involvement in the welfare system and the economy as the insurer of last resort (Moss 2002). The unprecedented involvement of governments across the world in rescuing their economies during the recent economic crisis (2008–2009) is a manifest example of how risk forces a reassessment of appropriate roles for the state and the market.

As a permanent social fixture, risk always merits careful study. However, on the cusp of the worst crisis since the Great Depression, understanding the impact of economic risk on the nonprofit sector is also urgent. In the United States, philanthropic giving suffered the worst decline, in current-dollars terms, since accurate records began in the 1950s (Center on Philanthropy at Indiana University 2010).

Reports of struggling nonprofits faced with a decline in revenue and a simultaneous increase in social need abounded in the media. Worse still, the recent crisis may be just the beginning of a new wave of global crises that are fuelled by global financial market integration and the globalization of systemic risk (De Nicolo and Kwast 2002; Alexander, Dhumale, and Eatwell 2006).

The risk explanation proposes that, by leading to profound changes in stakeholder preferences, the impact of economic crises goes far beyond a temporary reduction in disposable incomes. Risk has a particularly debilitating impact upon social support for capital formation and long term investments within the nonprofit sector, reducing the opportunities for financial, physical, human, and social capital development. This fact opens the door for policy makers, nonprofit leaders, and donors to play a role in reducing nonprofit sector vulnerability and, consequently, the impact of potentially unavoidable macroeconomic volatility in the future. How can nonprofit leaders promote nonprofit resilience and social impact? Noteworthy lessons from the evidence include the critical roles of volunteering, commercialization, and risk transfers between government and the nonprofit sector.

The stakes are high. Increased attention to the nonprofit sector has been partly fueled by growing doubts about the capacity of the state and the market to cope with today's challenges (see Anheier 2004; Clark 2003). Voluntary, nonprofit organizations have the knowledge, direct connections to society, flexibility, horizontal structures of decision-making, and expertise that the state lacks (Clark 1991; Hadenius and Uggla 1996; Hulme and Edwards 1997). Nonprofits, therefore, have become important actors in the provision of services that the state cannot or will not deliver as effectively.

Increasing attention to the nonprofit sector has also been fueled by the recognition that the nonprofit sector is essential for civil

society and social capital development (Anheier 2004), which are often directly associated with democratization and effective running of government (e.g., Fisher 1993; Putnam 1993) as well as the smooth functioning of markets and economic development (e.g., Knack and Keefer 1997; Narayan 1999; Putnam 1993; Woolcock 2001). Civil society has also been associated with many other socially desirable goals, such as the nonviolent transition from dictatorships to democracy (Acemoglu and Robinson 2006), a cleaner environment (Binder and Neumayer 2005), and lower levels of government corruption (Themudo 2013). By influencing nonprofit sector strength, therefore, economic development and risk have profound—and often detrimental—social impacts.

Notes

1. The name of Fovaso's officer was changed in line with my promise of anonymity.
2. As judged by the risk premium on public debt, which denotes market expectations of debt default.
3. Philanthropic giving is only 0.3% of national income, and total volunteered time is equivalent to only 0.1% of the labor force, both of which also correspond to the lowest levels in the world according to comparative nonprofit sector data collected by Salamon et al. (2004).
4. Since Mexico's level of social diversity is also intermediate, nonprofit theories emphasizing the role of social diversity would also predict an intermediate position for Mexico's nonprofit sector size.
5. Research on political participation in Mexico has produced the paradoxical and troubling finding that Mexicans were disappointed with democracy even as the country made steady progress toward increasing political competition, which culminated in the first free congressional election in 1997 and presidential election in 2000. In that year, according to World Values Survey data, the majority (58.9%) of respondents were not happy with the way democracy was developing. Despite steady institutional democratization in the late 1990s and early 2000s, the number of people who never discuss politics

increased from 26.1% in 1995 to 45.2% in 2000 (a 73% increase), the number of people who thought that democracy is bad for the economy increased from 47.3% to 55.5% (a 17% increase) in the same period, and the number of people who do not trust the government increased from 24.3% in 1990 to 29.9% in 2000 (a 23% increase). The 2003 midterm elections witnessed the lowest-ever voting participation in Mexico's history, 42% (Paras Garcia and Coleman 2006), and more recent elections have generated only marginal increases in participation.

6. Level of economic development is measured by GDP per capita.

7. Evidence from the Johns Hopkins CNP except for the last two fields, which is based on data on membership in religious and women's nonprofits from the World Values Survey, Fourth Wave (1999–2002).

8. The graph displays the predicted values of nonprofit expenditure as a proportion of national income, paid employment as a proportion of the labor force, volunteering as a proportion of the labor force, and total employment, which includes both paid and full-time equivalent volunteering, as a proportion of the labor force. While an assumption of linearity produces a familiar direct relationship between nonprofit sector strength and national income, the data actually displays a nonlinear relationship, more closely following a quadratic U-shaped curve. The adjusted R-squared for the quadratic model is 0.24, significantly higher than 0.09 for the linear model.

9. Of course, cross-sectional analyses of the relation between prosperity and the nonprofit sector can be misleading. The cross-section pattern may not have a longitudinal interpretation. The nonprofit sector could be weakening everywhere, even though the nonprofit sector is still stronger in poor and rich countries when compared to middle-income ones. A similar problem has plagued the (original) Kuznets curve. Even though cross-sectional data on social inequality and prosperity commonly support the Kuznets curve, longitudinal data typically don't.

10. Musick and Wilson (2008:ch. 16) looked at service, advocacy, and religious volunteering separately. Only advocacy volunteering was associated with gross national income, and, interestingly, it was more common in low-income countries.

This is surprising because we associate more developed countries with more vibrant civil societies and less developed countries with restricted political rights and opportunities (gross national income and scores on Freedom House measures of political rights are very highly correlated) and we would expect higher volunteer rates in the high-income countries for this reason. . . . The countries with few political rights are also poor countries. It would seem this negative effect is attributable to low income more than it is having few political rights. Since we are focusing here on advocacy volunteering, in which labor unions and professional associations are included, it would seem that poorer countries encourage more advocacy volunteering because people are trying to improve their economic conditions.

(Musick and Wilson 2008:353)

11. These competing views are sometimes reconciled by allusion to the different resource composition of social movements. Accordingly, nonprofits in poor countries should be primarily resourced by labor participation, while its counterparts in rich countries should be primarily resourced by financial contributions (the relative cost of giving decreases as wealth increases).

12. Inglehart (1997) finds a strong positive correlation between a country's score on survival/self-expressive values and its volunteer rate: the more a society values self-expression, the higher the volunteer rate in that country. This is true for all types of volunteer work. A country's score on the traditional/secular-rational dimension is related only to volunteering in church, youth, sports, professional, and cultural organizations. The more secular a society, the fewer people volunteer for these kinds of organizations.

13. The nature of religious values is also important since Protestantism is associated with stronger civic values and lower levels of corruption than other denominations.

14. World Values Survey data (1999–2002, N:77) show an inverse correlation (r = –0.624, p < 0.001) between national income per capita and the national average for respondents' reply to the question "How important is God in your life?" which was ranked from (1) not at all important to (10) very

important. Moreover, the relationship was close to linear. The same data also show an inverse correlation ($r = -0.472$, $p < 0.001$) between the national average on a "religiosity scale" and national level of income per capita.

Bibliography

Acemoglu, Daron. 2009. *Introduction to Modern Economic Growth*. Princeton, NJ: Princeton University Press.

Acemoglu, Daron, and James A. Robinson. 2006. *Economic Origins of Dictatorship and Democracy*. Cambridge: Cambridge University Press.

Agénor, Pierre-Richard. 2002. "Business Cycles, Economic Crises, and the Poor: Testing for Asymmetric Effects." *Journal of Policy Reform* 5:145–160.

Alexander, Kern, Rahul Dhumale, and John Eatwell. 2006. *Global Governance of Financial Systems: The International Regulation of Systemic Risk*. Oxford: Oxford University Press.

Anheier, Helmut K. 2004. *Civil Society: Measurement, Evaluation, Policy*. London: EarthScan.

———. 2005. *The Nonprofit Sector: Approaches, Management, Policy*. London: Routledge.

Anheier, Helmut K., and Lester M. Salamon. 1998. "Introduction: The Nonprofit Sector in the Developing World." In *The Nonprofit Sector in the Developing World*, ed. Helmut K. Anheier and Lester M. Salamon, 1–53. Manchester: Manchester University Press.

———. 2006. "The Nonprofit Sector in Comparative Perspective." In *The Nonprofit Sector: A Research Handbook*, ed. Walter W. Powell and Richard S. Steinberg, 89–117. New Haven, CT: Yale University Press.

Anheier, Helmut K., and Nuno Themudo. 2004. "The Internationalization of the Nonprofit Sector." In *The Jossey-Bass Handbook of Nonprofit Leadership and Management*, 2nd ed., ed. Robert D. Herman, 102–127. San Francisco: Jossey-Bass.

Archambault, Edith. 2001. "Historical Roots of the Nonprofit Sector in France." *Nonprofit and Voluntary Sector Quarterly* 30:204–220.

Ascoli, Ugo, and Ram Cnaan. 1997. "Volunteers for Human Service Provisions: Lessons from Italy and the USA." *Social Indicators Research* 40:299–327.

Barr, Nicholas. 2001. *The Welfare State as Piggy Bank: Information, Risk, Uncertainty, and the Role of the State*. Oxford: Oxford University Press.

Beck, Ulrich. 1992. *Risk Society: Towards a New Modernity*. London: Sage Publications.

Beito, David T. 2000. *From Mutual Aid to the Welfare State: Fraternal Societies and Social Services, 1890–1967*. Chapel Hill: University of North Carolina Press.

Ben-Ner, Avner, and Theresa van Hoomissen. 1991. "Nonprofit Organizations in the Mixed Economy: A Demand and Supply Analysis." *Annals of Public and Cooperative Economics* 62:519–550.

Binder, Seth, and Eric Neumayer. 2005. "Environmental Pressure Group Strength and Air Pollution: An Empirical Analysis." *Ecological Economics* 55:527–538.

Bob, Clifford. 2005. *The Marketing of Rebellion: Insurgents, Media, and International Activism*. New York: Cambridge University Press.

Boli, John, and George Thomas, eds. 1999. *Constructing World Culture: International Nongovernmental Organizations since 1875*. Stanford, CA: Stanford University Press.

Brody, Evelyn. 2006. "The Legal Framework for Nonprofit Organizations." In *The Nonprofit Sector: A Research Handbook*, ed. Walter Powell and Richard Steinberg, 243–266. New Haven, CT: Yale University Press.

Burger, Ary, and Vic Veldheer. 2001. "The Growth of the Nonprofit Sector in the Netherlands." *Nonprofit and Voluntary Sector Quarterly* 30:221–246.

Center on Philanthropy at Indiana University. 2010. *Giving USA 2010: The Annual Report on Philanthropy for the Year 2009*. Indianapolis: Giving USA Foundation.

Chang, Cyril, and Howard Tuckman. 1996. "The Goods Produced by Nonprofit Organizations." *Public Financial Quarterly* 24:25–43.

Clark, John. 1991. *Democratizing Development: The Role of Voluntary Agencies*. West Hartford, CT: Kumarian Press.

———. 2003. *Worlds Apart: Civil Society and the Battle for Ethical Globalization*. London: Earthscan.

Clark, John, and Nuno Themudo. 2004. "The Age of Protest: Internet Based 'Dot-Causes' and the 'Anti Globalization' Movement." In *Globalizing*

Civic Engagement: Civil Society and Transnational Action, ed. John Clark. London: Earthscan.

Clemens, Elisabeth S. 2006. "The Constitution of Citizens: Political Theories of Nonprofit Organizations." In *The Nonprofit Sector: A Research Handbook*, ed. Walter W. Powell and Richard Steinberg, 207–220. New Haven, CT: Yale University Press.

Collier, Paul, and Jan Dehn. 2001. "Aid, Shocks and Growth." *Policy Research Working Paper 2688*. World Bank, Washington, DC.

Davis, Lance E., and Douglass C. North. 1971. *Institutional Change and American Economic Growth*. New York: Cambridge University Press.

De Nicolo, Gianni, and Myron L. Kwast. 2002. "Systemic Risk and Financial Consolidation: Are They Related?" *Journal of Banking and Finance* 26:861–880.

Dekker, Paul, and Andries van den Broek. 1998. "Civil Society in Comparative Perspective: Involvement in Voluntary Associations in North America and Western Europe." *Voluntas* 8(1):11–38.

Douglas, James. 1987. "Political Theories of Nonprofit Organization." In *The Nonprofit Sector: A Research Handbook*, ed. Walter W. Powell, 43–54. New Haven, CT: Yale University Press.

Durkheim, Emile. 1984. *The Division of Labour in Society*. New York: Free Press. Originally published as *De la Division du Travail Social*. Paris: Presses Universitaires De France, 1893.

Ebrahim, Alnoor. 2002. "Information Struggles: The Role of Information in the Reproduction of NGO-Funder Relationships." *Nonprofit and Voluntary Sector Quarterly* 31:84–114.

———. 2003. *NGOs and Organizational Change: Discourse, Reporting and Learning*. Cambridge: Cambridge University Press.

Edwards, Michael, and David Hulme, eds. 1995. *Beyond the Magic Bullet: NGO Performance and Accountability in the Post-Cold War World*. London: Macmillan.

Fisher, Julie. 1993. *The Road from Rio: Sustainable Development and the Nongovernmental Movement in the Third World*. Westport, CT: Praeger.

Fowler, Alan. 2000. *The Virtuous Spiral: A Guide to Sustainability of NGOs in International Development*. London: Earthscan.

Galaskiewicz, Joseph, and Wolfgang Bielefeld. 1998. *Nonprofit Organizations in an Age of Uncertainty:*

A Study of Organizational Change. New York: A. de Gruyter.

Gaskin, Katharine, and Justin Smith. 1997. *A New Civic Europe? A Study of the Extent and Role of Volunteering*. London: National Centre for Volunteering.

Giddens, Anthony. 1999. "Runaway World." *BBC Reith Lectures 1999*. http://news.bbc.co.uk/hi/english/static/events/reith_99/week2/week2.htm.

Gutmann, Amy. 1998. "Freedom of Association: An Introductory Essay." In *Freedom of Association*, ed. Amy Gutmann, 3–32. Princeton, NJ: Princeton University Press.

Hadenius, Axel, and Fredrik Uggla. 1996. "Making Civil Society Work, Promoting Democratic Development: What States and Donors Can Do." *World Development* 24(10):621–639.

Halac, Marina, and Sergio L. Schmukler. 2004. "Distributional Effects of Crises: The Financial Channel." *Economia* 5:1–67.

Hammack, David C. 2001. "Introduction: Growth, Transformation, and Quiet Revolution in the Nonprofit Sector over Two Centuries." *Nonprofit and Voluntary Sector Quarterly* 30:157–173.

———. 2002. "Nonprofit Organizations in American History: Research Opportunities and Sources." *American Behavioral Scientist* 45:1638–1674.

Hammack, David C., and Dennis R. Young. 1993. *Nonprofit Organizations in a Market Economy: Understanding New Roles, Issues, and Trends*. San Francisco: Jossey-Bass.

Hann, Chris, and Elizabeth Dunn, eds. 1996. *Civil Society: Challenging Western Models*. London: Routledge.

Hansmann, Henry. 1987. "Economic Theories of Non-profit Organisations." In *The Nonprofit Sector: A Research Handbook*, ed. Walter W. Powell, 117–139. New Haven, CT: Yale University Press.

Havens, John J., Mary A. O'Herlihy, and Paul G. Schervish. 2006. "Charitable Giving: How Much, by Whom, to What, and Why." In *The Nonprofit Sector: A Research Handbook*, 2nd ed., ed. Walter W. Powell and Richard Steinberg. New Haven, CT: Yale University Press.

Hirschman, Alfred O. 1982. *Shifting Involvements: Private Interest and Public Action*. Princeton, NJ: Princeton University Press.

Honohan, Patrick, and Daniela Klingebiel. 2003. "The Fiscal Cost Implications of an Accommodating Approach to Banking Crises." *Journal of Banking and Finance* 27:1539–1560.

Hulme, David, and Michael Edwards. 1997. *NGOs, States, and Donors: Too Close for Comfort?* London: Macmillan in association with Save the Children.

Inglehart, Ronald. 1997. *Modernization and Postmodernization: Cultural, Economic, and Political Change in 43 Societies.* Princeton, NJ: Princeton University Press.

James, Estelle. 1989. *The Nonprofit Sector in International Perspective.* New York: Oxford University Press.

Knack, Stephen, and Philip Keefer. 1997. "Does Social Capital Have an Economic Payoff? A Cross-Country Investigation." *Quarterly Journal of Economics* 112(4):1251–1288.

Krugman, Paul. 2008. *The Return of Depression Economics and the Crisis of 2008.* New York: W. W. Norton.

Kuznets, Simon. 1955. "Economic Growth and Income Inequality." *American Economic Review* 49:1–28.

———. 1973. "Modern Economic Growth: Findings and Reflections." *American Economic Review* 63(3):247–258.

Layton, Michael D. 2009. "Philanthropy and the Third Sector in Mexico: The Enabling Environment and Its Limitations." *Norteamérica* 4(1):87–120.

Lewis, David 2007. *The Management of Non-governmental Development Organisations: An Introduction.* London: Routledge.

Lindenberg, Mark, and Coralie Bryant. 2001. *Going Global: Transforming Relief and Development NGOs.* Bloomfield, CT: Kumerian Press.

Lustig, Nora 1999. "Crises and the Poor: Socially Responsible Macroeconomics." *Presidential Address at the Fourth Annual Meeting of the Latin American and Caribbean Economic Association.* LACEA, Santiago, Chile, October 22.

McAdam, Doug, Sidney Tarrow, and Charles Tilly. 2001. *Dynamics of Contention.* Cambridge: Cambridge University Press.

Moss, David A. 2002. *When All Else Fails: Government as the Ultimate Risk Manager.* Cambridge, MA: Harvard University Press.

Musick, Marc A., and John Wilson. 2008. *Volunteers: A Social Profile.* Bloomington: Indiana University Press.

Narayan, Deepa. 1999. "Bonds and Bridges: Social Capital and Poverty." *Policy Research Working Paper 2167.* World Bank, Poverty Reduction and Economic Management Network, Washington, DC.

Norris, Pippa. 2003. *Democratic Phoenix Reinventing Political Activism.* Cambridge: Cambridge University Press.

North, Douglass C. 1990. *Institutions, Institutional Change and Economic Performance.* Cambridge: Cambridge University Press.

Organization for Economic Cooperation and Development (OECD). 2008. *Public-Private Partnerships: In Pursuit of Risk Sharing and Value for Money.* Paris, France: OECD.

Olson, Mancur. 1965. *The Logic of Collective Action.* Cambridge, MA: Harvard University Press.

———. 1982. *The Rise and Decline of Nations: Economic Growth, Stagflation, and Economic Rigidities.* New Haven, CT: Yale University Press.

Olsson, Carl. 2002. *Risk Management in Emerging Markets: How to Survive and Prosper.* New York: Pearson.

Paras Garcia, Pablo, and Ken Coleman. 2006. "The Political Culture of Democracy in Mexico 2006." Vanderbilt University. www.vanderbilt.edu/lapop/mexico.php.

Perkins, Dwight H., Steven Radelet, and David L. Lindauer. 2006. *Economics of Development*, 6th ed. New York: W. W. Norton.

Perry, Guillermo. 2009. *Beyond Lending: How Multilateral Banks Can Help Developing Countries Manage Volatility Center for Global Development.* Baltimore: Brookings Institution Press.

Putnam, Robert D. 1993. *Making Democracy Work: Civic Traditions in Modern Italy.* Princeton, NJ: Princeton University Press.

———. 2000. *Bowling Alone: The Collapse and Revival of American Community.* New York: Simon and Schuster.

Putnam, Robert D., and Kirstin Goss. 2002. "Introduction." In *Democracies in Flux*, ed. R. Putnam, 3–19. New York: Oxford University Press.

Rose-Ackerman, Susan. 1996. "Altruism, Nonprofits and Economic Theory." *Journal of Economic Literature* 34:701–728.

Rothstein, Bo. 2005. *Social Traps and the Problem of Trust*. New York: Cambridge University Press.

Salamon, Lester M. 1987. "Partners in Public Service: The Scope and Theory of Government-Nonprofit Sector Relations." In *The Nonprofit Sector: A Research Handbook*, ed. Walter Powell. New Haven, CT: Yale University Press.

Salamon, Lester M., and Helmut Anheier. 1998. "Social Origins of Civil Society: Explaining the Nonprofit Sector Cross-nationally." *Voluntas: International Journal of Voluntary and Nonprofit Organizations* 9:213–248.

Salamon, Lester M., Helmut Anheier, Regina List, Stefan Toepler, and Wojciech Sokolowski, eds. 2004. *Global Civil Society: Dimensions of the Nonprofit Sector, Volume 2*. Baltimore: Johns Hopkins Center for Civil Society Studies.

Salamon, Lester M., and Stefan Toepler. 2000. "The Influence of the Legal Environment on the Development of the Nonprofit Sector." *Working Paper 17*. Johns Hopkins Center for Civil Society Studies.

Shiller, Robert J. 2003. "From Efficient Markets Theory to Behavioral Finance." *Journal of Economic Perspectives* 17(1):83–104.

Skocpol, Theda. 1992. *Protecting Soldiers and Mothers: The Political Origins of Social Policy in the United States*. Cambridge, MA: Belknap Press of Harvard University Press.

Smith, Steven R., and Michael Lipsky. 1993. *Nonprofits for Hire: The Welfare State in the Age of Contracting*. Cambridge, MA: Harvard University Press.

Steinberg, Richard. 2003. "Economic Theories of Nonprofit Organizations: An Evaluation." In *The Study of the Nonprofit Enterprise*, ed. Helmut Anheier and Avner Ben-Ner, 272–308. New York: Kluwer Academic/Plenum.

Suwannarat, Gary. 2003. *Unfinished Business: ODA-Civil Society Partnerships in Thailand*. New York: Synergos Institute.

Tarrow, Sidney. 1994. *Power in Movement: Collective Action, Social Movements and Politics*. New York: Cambridge University Press.

Terrazas, Ireri Ablanedo. 2006. "De sociedad a sociedad civil Análisis de las causas del déficit de participación ciudadana en México." *VI Seminario Anual de Investigación sobre el Tercer Sector en México*, Centro Mexicano para la Filantropía, Mexico City, September 12–13, 2006. www.filantropia.itam.mx/documentos/documentos.html.

Themudo, Nuno S. 2009. "Gender and the Nonprofit Sector." *Nonprofit and Voluntary Sector Quarterly* 38:663–683.

———. 2013. "Reassessing the Impact of Civil Society: Nonprofit Sector, Press Freedom, and Corruption." *Governance: An International Journal of Policy, Administration, and Institution* 26(1):63–89.

Uslaner, Eric M. 2002. *The Moral Foundation of Trust*. New York: Cambridge University Press.

———. 2008. *Corruption, Inequality, and the Rule of Law: The Bulging Pocket Makes the Easy Life*. New York: Cambridge University Press.

Verduzco Igartúa, Gustavo. 2003. *Organizaciones no lucrativas: visión de su trayectoria en México*. Mexico City: El Colegio de México.

Wedig, Gerard J. 1994. "Risk, Leverage, Donations, and Dividends-in-Kind: A Theory of Nonprofit Financial Behavior." *International Review of Economics and Statistics* 3:257–278.

Weisbrod, Burton. 1988. *The Nonprofit Economy*. Cambridge, MA: Harvard University Press.

———. 1998. "The Nonprofit Mission and Its Financing: Growing Links between Nonprofits and the Rest of the Economy." In *To Profit or Not to Profit: The Commercial Transformation of the Nonprofit Sector*, ed. Burton A. Weisbrod, 1–24. New York: Cambridge University Press.

Williams, Heather L. 2001. *Social Movements and Economic Transition: Markets and Distributive Conflict in Mexico*. New York: Cambridge University Press.

Wolf, Holger. 2005. "Volatility: Definition and Consequences." In *Managing Economic Volatility and Crises: A Practitioner's Guide*, ed. Joshua Aizenman and Brian Pinto, 45–64. New York: Cambridge University Press.

Woolcock, Michael. 2001. "The Place of Social Capital in Understanding Social and Economic Outcomes." *Canadian Journal of Policy Research* 2:1–17.

Woolley, Frances. 2003. "Social Cohesion and Voluntary Activity: Making Connections." In *Economic Implications of Social Cohesion*, ed. L. Osberg, 150–182. Toronto: University of Toronto Press.

World Values Survey Association. 2006. *European and World Values Surveys Four-Wave Integrated Data File, 1981–2004*, v.20060423. www.icpsr. umich.edu/icpsrweb/ICPSR/studies/4531.

Wuthnow, Robert. 1988. *The Restructuring of American Religion: Society and Faith since World War II.* Princeton, NJ: Princeton University Press.

Young, Dennis R. 1983. *If Not for Profit, for What? A Behavioral Theory of the Nonprofit Sector Based on Entrepreneurship.* Lexington, MA: Lexington Books.

———. 2006. "How Nonprofit Organizations Manage Risk." *Paper Presented at the Biannual Conference of the International Society for Third Sector Research*, Bangkok, Thailand, July 11.

———, ed. 2007. *Financing Nonprofits: Putting Theory into Practice.* Lanham, MD: Alta Mira Press.

CHAPTER 35

Global Perspectives on the Legal Framework for Civil Society and Relational Governance

Douglas Rutzen

In Phillips, Susan D., and Steven Rathgeb Smith, (Eds.), *Governance and Regulation in the Third Sector: International Perspectives* (New York: Routledge, 2011).

Moscow, ahead of Washington, has come to comprehend a key fact: the world is becoming a polyarchy—an international system run by numerous and diverse actors with a shifting kaleidoscope of associations and dependencies.

—SERGEI LAVROV, RUSSIAN FOREIGN MINISTER, MARCH 2007, QUOTING THE *BOSTON GLOBE*

Introduction

Governments increasingly recognize the inter-connectedness of governance. Their response to civil society engagement, however, is starkly different. Some have embraced the "associational revolution" (Salamon 1994), while others have embarked on an "associational counter-revolution" (Rutzen & Shea 2006). The following sections examine the extent to which legislation enables—or disables—civil society participation in relational governance. (For purposes of this chapter, "relational governance" is an approach that focuses on interactions among the public sector, civil society, the business sector, concerned citizens, and other actors on issues of societal concern.) Specifically, this chapter expands the analysis to a diversity of other jurisdictions with less enabling environments for civil society to engage in relational governance. Through this analysis, it examines how specific legal provisions affect the ability of civil society to engage in relational governance. The chapter concludes with observations on current challenges and opportunities in the field of governance, providing a general synthesis as well as a look to the future.

The Role of Law

The legal framework for civil society 1) reflects governance theories, and 2) serves as an agent of change. In other words, the legal framework reflects views on the role of the state, the role of civil society, forms of engagement, and other societal norms. At the same time, the legal

DOI: 10.4324/9780367696559-45

framework helps determine whether civil society can influence these norms.

In 1998, President Jiang Jemin and President Bill Clinton participated in an internationally televised debate that addressed issues of democracy and governance. When asked about the status of Tiananmen Square dissidents, Jiang Jemin dismissed the issue, asserting: "Law-breaking activities must be dealt with according to law. I think this is true in any country of rule of law" ("Clinton in China," 1998). More recently, the President of Vietnam was asked if his country should improve its human rights record. He responded: "It's not a question of improving or not. Vietnam has its own legal framework, and those who violate the law will be handled" (Baker 2007). These are but a few examples of how countries have co-opted concepts, converting the "rule of law" into the "rule by law" (Lowenkron 2006).

The international community has become increasingly concerned about the use of law to constrict civil society. In November 2007, representatives from over 125 countries gathered in Bamako, Mali, under the auspices of the "Community of Democracies." They issued the *Bamako Ministerial Consensus*, which recognized the importance of civil society to democratic governance and which resolved to:

> Support and encourage non-governmental organizations by urging countries to adopt legislation aimed at strengthening civil society and to ensure that registration, formation, funding and operation of non-governmental organizations and their peaceful activities be carried out.
> (Community of Democracies 2007: para 44)

This concern is well warranted. In recent years, over fifty countries have introduced or enacted legislation limiting civil society and civic space (see ICNL 2006).

The Formation and Operation of Civil Society Organizations

Legal frameworks regulate the formation, operation, sustainability and other issues that impact the ability of CSOs to engage in relational governance. This section examines six specific themes:

- organizational forms and the blending of sectors;
- shared (or imposed) values;
- CSO registration and incorporation;
- the definition of charity;
- empowerment and advocacy; and
- transnational challenges.

Organizational Forms and Sectoral Blending

In the late nineteenth and early twentieth centuries, so-called progressive public administration sought to "keep the public sector sharply distinct from the private sector" (Hood 1995: 93–94). Subsequent privatization theories similarly depended on clear delineation between sectors. After all, the point was to transfer certain functions from one sector (the public sector) to another (the private sector). Under New Public Management (NPM), the sectors began to blend (Salamon 2001). This trend continued under relational governance (Skelcher 2004).

Prominent longstanding examples of hybridization include low income housing organizations, land trusts, and workforce development programs. Continuing this trend, in April 2008, Vermont introduced the "low-profit, limited liability company" or "L3C." A hybrid form, the L3C must have a charitable purpose but is permitted to distribute profits to owners and investors. Similarly, in the UK, social enterprises are commonly organized as Community Interest Companies (CICs). Also a hybrid form, a CIC must pass a community interest test, but it may sell shares and distribute profits to members under certain circumstances.

As these examples illustrate, some countries are clearly attempting to adjust their legal frameworks to reflect the blending of sectors. In other countries, however, sectoral distinctions are firmly entrenched in law. For example, Armenia, Ukraine, and Belarus prohibit public associations from directly engaging in economic activities, drawing a sharp distinction between the commercial and non-commercial sectors. Similarly, in neighboring Bulgaria, CSOs (but not commercial companies) have been prohibited from registering as health institutions, including hospitals.

Various policy motivations surround the blending of the nonprofit and public sectors. While this is an attribute of relational governance, interestingly it is also common in countries with authoritarian tendencies. For example, Syria has used "government organized NGOs" and "quasi-NGOs" as a tool to monopolize civic space, attack legitimate CSOs, and defend government policy under the cover of being independent (ICNL & World Movement 2008). Similar challenges have arisen in China, Russia, and Venezuela (National Endowment for Democracy 2006).

Shared (or Imposed) Values

Gaster and Deakin (1998) speak about the importance of "shared values" as an essential component of genuine partnership. Relational governance is consistent with this theme, as it reflects the movement away from the government as the "central source of the 'authoritative allocation of values' for the society" (Peters & Pierre 1998: 224). This notion is also implicit in the compacts of various countries and in the European Economic and Social Committee's (1999) *Opinion on The Role and Contribution of Civil Society Organisations in the Building of Europe*:

> In a pluralist society every member of the community determines his or her contribution, and the community tries to improve the conditions of co-existence. . . . What is remarkable is that this public is not purely factual, but that the parties involved also exchange value judgments.
>
> (5)

This view, of course, is not universally accepted. Putting aside broader discussions of pluralism, many governments use the law to limit the values advanced by civil society. For example, in Mali, CSOs cannot undermine "good morals": This provision was used to deny registration to a gay rights association. Morality provisions also appear in the laws of countries such as Algeria, Egypt, and Malaysia. Other countries rely on government officials to determine if a CSO's activities are, in their view, necessary. For example, in Bahrain, the government can deny registration to an organization if it decides that, in its opinion, society does not "need" the organization's services.

In countries trending toward relational governance, the concept of shared values is often reflected in compacts and policy documents, and the voluntary sector is given broad discretion to pursue pluralistic objectives. In other countries, we find that the CSO legal framework contains explicit provisions permitting the government to deny legal existence to organizations that contradict the government's view of morality or values.

CSO Registration and Incorporation

The foregoing discussion links to a broader issue—the extent to which countries facilitate or hinder the formation of civil society organizations. Recent legislation in England and Wales included a number of reforms of an enabling nature. The law also exempted more charities from registration and introduced other reforms to reduce administrative burdens on charities.

In sharp contrast, other countries have used the legal framework to erect barriers to entry. These barriers take myriad forms.[1] Sometimes restrictions impose high burdens on founders of new organizations. For example:

- In Turkmenistan, national-level associations require 500 members.
- In many countries, including Thailand, Malaysia, and Qatar, only citizens or nationals may found an association. This was also the rule in Bosnia-Herzegovina through the mid-1990s, which disenfranchised a number of refugees and stateless persons.
- In Kenya, founders of foreign organizations must prove they are of "outstanding character," supported by "satisfactory" references.

In other contexts, capitalization requirements serve as a key impediment. As one example, under Eritrea's Proclamation No. 145/2005, local NGOs must have access to the equivalent of $1 million US in order to engage in relief or rehabilitation work.

In other cases, the law contains vague criteria, vesting authorities with broad authority to determine whether to register or incorporate a CSO. A few illustrations include:

- The Ministry of Social Affairs and Labor in Oman has the right to prevent an association from registering if it finds that the services to be provided by the association are not needed, or if there are other associations that are meeting the need that would be filled by the new NGO. The Ministry may also reject an application for "any other reasons according to the decision of the Ministry."
- In Croatia a foundation can be denied registration if it is obviously lacking in "seriousness."
- In Uganda CSOs may not engage in any activity that is "prejudicial to the national interests" of the country.

A related issue relates to who interprets these provisions—in countries such as Egypt and Uzbekistan, members of the security service are formally or informally part of the vetting process.

Considering other aspects of an organization's lifecycle, the freedom of association would be largely theoretical and illusory if a government could arbitrarily disband an organization once formed. In many countries, however, governments retain broad discretion to terminate an organization's existence. For example, in Argentina, the government can terminate an organization if it finds that the organization's activities are no longer "necessary" or "in the best interests of the public." Oman has a similar provision.

In summary, in many countries, the law serves a gatekeeper function, keeping individuals from establishing CSOs as legal entities, thereby substantially diminishing the specter of relational governance.

Defining Charity

Significant challenges also arise when countries attempt to define and promote a class of charities (or public benefit organizations) distinct from the general voluntary and nonprofit sector. Until recently Scotland sought to promote the voluntary sector *writ large*, reflecting notions of partnership and relational governance. In 2005, however, Scotland adopted a new law that imported from England the more narrow concept of "charity." According to Ford, "[t]his legislative emphasis on a Scottish version of English charities regulation threatens to distort the effect of other measures aimed at developing relational governance for the third sector in Scotland."

The definition of charity has proved to be an issue in a number of other countries, including Canada. Illustrating this theme, a Supreme Court case involving the Vancouver Society of Immigrant and Visible Minority Women. The society was denied registration as a charity because the organization's life skills and job training did not qualify as the advancement of education under the common law. In addition, the class of beneficiaries (immigrants and visible minority women) was insufficiently broad to be considered beneficial to the community under the fourth head of charity. Moreover, it failed to satisfy the "relief of poverty" test because not all the beneficiaries were disadvantaged. The Supreme Court of Canada refused to expand the common law definition of charity; it did, however, invite the Parliament to address this issue legislatively, but neither the Parliament nor the government accepted this invitation.

Religious historians have come to the US to study traditional religious practices because practices, in some instances, have changed less quickly than in the country of origin. To a certain extent we witness a similar phenomenon with charity law. England and Wales passed a new charity law in 2006, but other Commonwealth countries are still burdened by antiquated concepts of charity.

This concept of charity is also an issue outside the Commonwealth. A number of other countries, including most of the countries of Central and Eastern Europe, have undertaken ambitious initiatives to define a class of public benefit organizations entitled to special tax/fiscal benefits. In addition, China has been working on a "charity law" for a number of years. A key issue is how to define charity. There seems to be pronounced interest in promoting organizations engaged in fields like health, education, and culture. But, as one might imagine, there are deep concerns about advocacy groups. The issue of advocacy—which is directly related to relational governance—is addressed more thoroughly in the next section.

Empowering Civil Society

Empowerment is a prerequisite for relational governance. In contrast to the view of 'cold charity' that emanated from Victorian England in which the main role of the voluntary sector was to help the less fortunate by providing services and support, the emerging approach emphasizes empowerment by which communities have resources, possess political voice, and are capable of representing and helping themselves. Raymond Atuguba (2007) echoes this theme when speaking about a partner organization in Ghana, noting that the group works:

to empower their partners to demand from duty-bearers (especially government) their rights and entitlements as full citizens of the Republic. This is a *political* process of building citizenship and has very little semblance to what charities traditionally do.

In democratic countries, a key issue often relates to the ability of tax-benefited organizations (e.g., charities) to engage in advocacy and the public policy debate. Unless greater latitude is provided, advocacy is chilled and relational governance is impeded. The point is well taken, and it also highlights the impediments to relational governance by countries with even more stark constraints on advocacy and empowerment. For example:

- In Equatorial Guinea, CSOs are prevented from promoting, monitoring, or engaging in any human rights activities.
- In the United Arab Emirates, the Law on Associations requires associations to follow government censorship guidelines and to receive prior government approval before publishing any material.
- In Belarus, the Criminal Code was amended to prohibit the dissemination of "dishonest" information about the political, economic, or social situation in the country, punishable by up to six months in prison.

In a theme addressed later in the chapter, governments often distinguish among CSOs. They tolerate—if not promote—organizations that support governmental policies or engage in service delivery. But if the organization seeks to challenge governmental policies, the law is often the tool of choice to clamp down on dissent.[2]

Enabling Transnational Operations

A cutting edge issue relates to transnational CSO operations. To engage effectively in many of the challenges of today—whether related to climate change, public health, the Millennium Development Goals, or the economic crisis—CSOs must engage across frontiers. This raises interesting legal issues because CSO issues are almost exclusively the province of country-level, domestic legislation. That said, there have been some important developments in this area.

There is renewed interest in reviving the Statute for a European Association. Similarly, the European Foundation Centre is actively promoting a European Foundation Statute. In January 2009, the European Court of Justice issued its judgment in the case of *Hein Persche v Finanzamt Ludenscheid*. In this case, the Court held that where donor incentives are available for donations to domestic recipients, they must also be available for donations to foreign recipients based in EU Member States or the European Economic Area, provided that the recipient is equivalent to a domestic public benefit organization.

In sum, while transnational activities by CSOs are an essential component of effective relational governance in contemporary society, the legal framework for civil society is deeply entrenched in country-level, domestic legislation. Absent regional integration or bilateral agreements, progress—particularly in terms of frameworks for international philanthropy—will likely be limited. Moreover, a number of countries are erecting barriers to the globalization of civil society, appealing to arguments of sovereignty, security, and aid effectiveness. Accordingly, transnational CSO operations will likely remain a source of friction and a cutting edge issue for future development.

Financial Resources

A related theme pertains to the importance of a sound financial base to support civil society's engagement in relational governance. For example, in the UK there was a concern over the declining trend in the levels of individual and corporate charitable giving, which led to a package of tax reforms in 2000. Some tools

are inconsistent with relational governance. In Australia, for example, two Commonwealth government departments employed a franchise model to structure their relationship with nonprofit organizations and other entities. Services were badged in the name of the Commonwealth program itself, and references to the nonprofit organization were expunged.

Extending the geographic scope of the analysis, Mexico further illustrates the way in which the legal framework can impede relational governance. To receive tax deductible donations in Mexico, an organization must seek accreditation from the ministry with jurisdiction over the organization's activities. Ministries have few incentives to grant this accreditation (particularly to advocacy groups which might use their benefits to advocate against the ministry), and few organizations in fact attain these tax benefits. Mexican organizations that overcome these barriers can only spend 5 percent of donations received on overhead. Because few organizations can survive on a 5 percent overhead rate, many people suspect that organizations engage in 'creative accounting.' As such, the rule, which is intended to promote public trust in organizations, actually ends up undermining public trust because of concerns over such creativity in accounting.

In some countries the legal framework is even more blunt, providing little or no incentive for private philanthropy. For example, in Nigeria, individuals receive no tax benefits for charitable giving, while in Russia, corporations receive no tax benefits for charitable giving. In Azerbaijan, neither individuals nor corporations receive tax benefits for charitable giving. In other countries, such as Ukraine, there are limitations on fee-for-service activities. As indicated earlier, a number of countries also impose significant restrictions on foreign funding. Continuing with this trend, under a recent proclamation in Ethiopia, an organization that receives more than 10 percent of its funding from abroad is prohibited from promoting the advancement of human and democratic rights, gender equality, the rights of children, disability rights, and other enumerated objectives.

Regulating Civil Society: Accountability and Transparency

Many of the initiatives seem to be based on the need to promote accountability and decrease prospects of abuse. The key issue, of course, is balance and proportionality. Balance and proportionality must also be determined in local context.

Perhaps not surprisingly, in some countries, the balance tilts strongly toward state regulation. As but a few examples:

- In Vietnam, the government has the right to intervene in all stages of an organization's activities; it may also veto new members of an organization and introduce members of its own choosing.
- Under the NGO Regulations of Uganda, an organization may not undertake direct contact with people in any part of the rural area of Uganda unless the organization provides seven days' notice in writing of its intention to do so to the Resistance Committee and the District Administrator of the area.
- Until 2009 in Russia a variety of CSOs, regardless of their size or tax status, were required to meet extensive programmatic and financial reporting requirements, which were premised on undefined terms, such as the requirement to report on all "events."

Some countries also apply what might be called the "Al Capone" approach to enforcement.[3] Instead of closing down organizations on substantive grounds, they establish a thick web of nearly impenetrable rules, regulations, and reporting requirements. They then sanction organizations on ancillary grounds, such as the failure to register a logo, to complete a form properly, or to meet some other technical requirement of law.

Synthesizing Themes

Are relational and authoritarian governance diametrically opposed in how they treat civil society? Table 35.1 presents the prototypical impact of relational governance and autocratic theories on the legal framework for civil society.

This table is merely an illustration. In reality, governance theories and the impact of these theories operate on a continuum rather than in a binary fashion. Moreover, the legal framework for civil society often reflects different objectives and policies. In part, this is because the framework reflects adaptation (new laws in response to changed circumstances) and layering (new laws imposed on top of existing legislation). Regardless of the process, these competing objectives have a significant impact on relational governance.

In addition, neither the government nor civil society is monolithic. Depending on the country, the "government" may include ministries, agencies, departments, offices, bureaus, and other entities. Depending on the structure of the state, there may also be various levels of national and local governments. Perspectives multiply as these levels are staffed by elected officials, political appointees, civil servants and others, with responsibilities ranging from health care to housing to "homeland security." Of course, civil society is also marked by tremendous diversity. As a result of the diversity of governmental entities, the perspectives of individual officials, substantive responsibilities, and the specific CSOs seeking to engage, there are often a panorama of approaches to civil society within a single state.

For example, NPM and relational governance had a "parallel presence" as a result of various challenges confronting post-communist

TABLE 35.1 Relational and Autocratic Governance Compared

Issue	Relational Governance	Autocratic Governance
Organizational Forms	Hybridization as a complement to independent civil society	Hybridization to undermine or co-opt independent civil society
Values	Shared values	Imposed values
Registration/ Incorporation	Low barriers to entry	High barriers to entry
Concept of Charity	Evolving concept that reflects emerging contexts and enables the engagement of civil society in governance	Focus on traditional notions of "charity" and/or instrumental approaches focused on service delivery
Empowerment/ Advocacy	Promoted	Restricted
Transnational Operations	Broadly permitted	Restrictions on cross-border programs and foreign funding
Resources	Broad range of instruments to enable a CSO sector engaged in governance	Broad restrictions on resources and/or more instrumental approaches focused on service delivery
Regulation	Marked by balance and proportionality, enabling the development of civil society	Marked by intrusive oversight and regulation, impeding the development of civil society

Hungary, including the modernization of public services and the challenge of democratization.

Moreover, exogenous factors continue to alter the legal landscape for civil society. For example, after September 11, a number of countries enacted counter-terrorism measures. Many of these measures were layered on top of existing CSO laws, imposing significant 'collateral damage' on legitimate CSO activities (ICNL & World Movement 2008; OMB Watch 2008; Sidel 2008). Indeed, it seems as though when conflict arises some governments ascribe to a *security-based governance* theory that prevails over relational governance and other theories. In turn, a security-based governance approach affects several layers of this framework. For example, a number of countries have enacted legislation affecting CSO financing as

a result of domestic pressures and international bodies, such as the Financial Action Task Force. Security-based governance objectives also impact registration and incorporation laws and the ability of organizations to associate with certain types of groups (ICNL & World Movement 2008; OMB Watch 2008; Sidel 2008).

Even more benign objectives, such as "aid effectiveness" and "donor coordination," can prove problematic. For example, in 2007, the Bolivian President issued a Decree on international cooperation that places new restrictions on the ability of civil society organizations to engage in development activities funded by foreign donors. The restrictions were based, in part, on the Paris Declaration on Aid Effectiveness. Similarly, in September 2008, a bill was proposed in the Mexican Senate that would have given a government body the ability to determine which Mexican entities are eligible to cooperate with foreign partners—whether the cooperation involved funding or even the exchange of information. Again, this bill was justified with reference to aid effectiveness.[4] These are only two examples: an increasing number of countries are attempting to convert 'host country' ownership into 'host government' ownership over development assistance with little room for independent civil society.

In summary, the framework depends on the legal framework for civil society [and] is not the product of a single, coherent theory.[5] Rather, the legal framework and its implementation are buffeted by competing objectives, leading to a degree of policy incoherence.[6]

Future Opportunities

A critical question is whether the financial crisis that began in late 2008 will serve as the kind of 'exogenous shock' that fundamentally alters governance models. For example, stagflation in the 1970s destroyed the faith of many Australians that governments could solve social and economic problems. In its place, a belief in markets emerged. Elsewhere, in the words of Salamon (2001), governance models were predicated upon "new-found faith in liberal economic theories."

Impacts continue to unfold, but it is likely that governance will be influenced by the financial crisis. Among other issues, new governance theories and institutions will emerge, particularly relating to the world's financial infrastructure. In addition, the blurring of the state and the market continues, following massive infusions of public money to bail out commercial enterprises. Moreover, deregulation and market-based solutions have become suspect concepts, at least for now. Tools employed in relational governance, like loan guarantees for low income housing, will also inevitably change.

Moving from the policy to the organizational level, CSOs have been seriously affected by these changes (Salamon, Geller, & Spence 2009). Private giving and foundation support have declined significantly (see Charities Aid Foundation & NCVO 2009; Prizeman & McGee 2009). Governmental authorities are also adopting budget tightening, which will impact the sustainability of a number of organizations. At the same time, new fields will develop, particularly as civil society grapples with how best to hold emerging economic and political powers to account.

In addition, there will likely be calls for change as governments have trouble 'delivering the goods' as a result of economic decline. These pressures will build on both democratic and authoritarian governments. Some new democracies are particularly at risk, in part, because of their existing precarious macroeconomic conditions and, in part, because of the fragility of their democracies. In addition, there is a concern that certain autocratic regimes will implement constraints with renewed vigor as they seek to cling to power and quash dissent.

At a minimum, we appear headed to a period of instability and an era when governance concepts will be challenged and changed. At the same time, one could argue that the fundamental principles of relational governance have been validated. Quite simply, the financial crisis has shown that issues are so complex and inter-connected that they are beyond the capacity of government (or even a collection of governments) to address on their own. Rather, it is necessary to engage key actors from various sectors to address contemporary challenges.

That said, some of the more extreme propositions of co-governance seem less tenable in the current environment. For example, in the late 1990s, some commentators argued that "governance without government" is becoming the dominant pattern of management for advanced industrial democracies (Peters & Pierre 1998, citing Rhodes 1997). Others cast governments as "hollow" states (Jessop 1998; Milward, Provan, & Else 1993; Peters & Pierre 1998; Rhodes 1994), and noted that "[s]tate agencies may place some imprimatur on the policy, so the argument goes, but the real action occurs within the private sector" (Peters & Pierre 1998: 225).

If anything, the importance of government, at least for civil society, has been highlighted in recent years. As a parallel trend, the power of the individual citizen has been strengthened as a result of the Internet and other participatory media. Indeed, we regularly hear that civil society organizations are essential because they give voice to the voiceless—that by joining together we are empowered. While this is certainly true, a college student sitting in her dorm room may well have more amplified voice than the CEO of a large nonprofit in a capital city—if the student has a popular blog. Borrowing from Putnam (2000), we are moving from "Bowling Alone" to "Blogging Alone," with significant implications for both governance and civil society.

In conclusion, the governance field seems to be on the cusp of a new era. It is an important time for the field, and new concepts and institutions will likely be born during this era. In the words of the political cartoonist Walt Kelly, "We are confronting a period of insurmountable opportunity."

Notes

1. The discussion of restrictions draws heavily on ICNL and World Movement for Democracy's Report (2008) entitled, "Defending Civil Society."

2. This chapter focuses on legal provisions. Of course, funding relationships can also reduce civil society's independence and tether organizations to the state. This is not just an issue in 'liberal democracies.' The governments of Uzbekistan and Azerbaijan recently announced new funding schemes for civil society. CSO representatives have expressed concern that these schemes may be used to compromise CSO independence and to co-opt key organizations.

3. Al Capone was a famous gangster in the US. After unsuccessful trials for racketeering, the US finally convicted Capone of tax evasion.

4. This bill is no longer active.

5. Moreover, problems arise even when countries attempt to engage in a more holistic review of government–civil society relations through compacts or other related initiatives.

6. Implementation is often key. Toward this end, some countries provide for the periodic review of laws and policy, as well as performance benchmarks and dispute resolution mechanisms.

References

Atuguba, R. (2007, April). "Legal Analysis of the Draft Trust Bill 2006 and the Draft NGO Policy Guidelines 2007." Paper prepared for the Parliamentary Advocacy Project of the Legal Resources Centre (LRC)-Ghana.

Baker, P. (2007, June 23). "Bush Prods Vietnamese President on Human Rights and Openness." *Washington Post*.

Charities Aid Foundation (CAF) and National Council of Voluntary Organisations (NCVO). (2009). *UK Giving 2009: An Overview of Charitable Giving in the UK, 2008/09*. London: CAF and NCVO.

Community of Democracies. (2007). *Bamako Ministerial Consensus, 'Democracy, Development, and Poverty Reduction'*. Online. Available at <www.bamako2007.gov.ml/PRODUCTION%20DE%20LA%204%E8me%20CONFERENCE%20MINISTERIELLE%20CD/CONSENSUS%20DE%20BAMAKO/MasterBamakoDocument.pdf> (accessed on 12 November 2009).

European Economic and Social Committee. (1999). *Opinion on the Role and Contribution of Civil Society Organisations in the Building of Europe*. Brussels. Online. Available at <http://eesc.europa.eu/sco/docs/ces851-1999_ac_en.PDF> (accessed on 15 February 2009).

Gaster, L., and Deakin, N. (1998). "Local Government and the Voluntary Sector: Who Needs Whom—Why and What for?" *Local Government*, 24(3): 169–194.

Hood, C. (1995). "The 'New Public Management' in the 1980s: Variations on a Theme." *Accounting, Organizations and Society*, 20(2/3): 93–109.

ICNL and World Movement for Democracy Secretariat at the National Endowment for Democracy. (2008). *Defending Civil Society: A Report of the World Movement for Democracy*. Online. Available at <www.icnl.org/KNOWLEDGE/pubs/ICNL-WMD_Defending_CS.pdf> (accessed on 15 April 2009).

The International Center for Not-for-Profit Law (ICNL). (2006, August). "Recent Laws and Legislative Proposals to restrict Civil Society and Civil Society Organizations." *International Journal of Not-for-Profit Law*, 8(4). Online. Available at <www.icnl.org/knowledge/ijnl/vol8iss4/art_1.htm> (accessed on 20 April 2009).

Jessop, B. (1998). "The Rise of Governance and the Risks of Failure: The Case of Economic Development." *International Social Science Journal*, 50(155): 29–45.

Lowenkron, B. (2006). *Number of Countries Fear a Tougher UN Human Rights Body*. Interview with the Council on Foreign Relations. Online. Available at <www.cfr.org/publication/10103/lowenkron.html?breadcrumb=%2Fbios%2F11891%2Frobert_mcmahon%3Fpage%3D10> (accessed on 20 April 2009).

Milward, H. B., Provan, K., and Else, B. (1993). "What Does the Hollow State Look Like?" In B. Bozeman (ed.), *Public Management Theory: The State of the Art*. San Francisco: Jossey Bass.

National Endowment for Democracy. (2006, June 8). *The Backlash Against Democracy Assistance: A Report Prepared by the National Endowment for Democracy for Senator Richard G. Lugar, Chairman*. Committee on Foreign Relations, United States Senate.

New York Times. (1998, June 28). "Clinton in China; The Leaders' Remarks: Hopes for a Lasting Friendship, Even If Imperfect."

OMB Watch and Grantmakers without Borders. (2008, July). *Collateral Damage, How the War on Terror Hurts Charities, Foundations and the People they Serve*. Online. Available at <www.ombwatch.org/npadv/PDF/collateral-damage.pdf> (accessed on 20 April 2009).

Peters, G., and Pierre, J. (1998). "Governance Without Government? Rethinking Public Administration." *Journal of Public Administration Research and Theory*, 8(2): 223–243.

Prizeman, G., and McGee, S. (2009). *Charitable Fundraising in an Economic Downturn: The First Annual Report on Income and Fundraising Activity in Irish Charities*. Dublin: Centre for Nonprofit Management, Trinity College Dublin.

Putnam, R. (2000). *Bowling Alone, the Collapse and Revival of American Community*. New York: Simon and Schuster.

Rhodes, R. A. W. (1994). "The Hollowing Out of the State: The Changing Nature of the Public Service in Britain." *Political Quarterly Review*, 65: 137–151.

Rhodes, R. A. W. (1997). *Understanding Governance: Policy Networks, Governance, Reflexivity and Accountability*. Buckingham: Open University Press.

Rutzen, D., and Shea, C. (2006, September). "The Associational Counter-revolution." *Alliance*, 11(3): 27–28.

Salamon, L. (1994, July/August). "The Rise of the Nonprofit Sector." *Foreign Affairs*, 74(3): 109–115.

Salamon, L. (2001). "The New Governance and the Tools of Public Action: An Introduction." *Fordham Urban Law Journal*, 28(5): 1611–1674.

Salamon, L., Geller, S. L., and Spence, K. L. (2009). "Impact of the 2007–09 Economic Recession on Nonprofit Organizations." *Communiqué No. 14, Listening Post Project, Center for Civil Society Studies*, Johns Hopkins University. Available at <www.ccss.jhu.edu/pdfs/LP_Communiques/LP_Communique_14.pdf> (accessed on 15 May 2009).

Sidel, M. (2008). "Counter-terrorism and the Enabling Legal and Political Environment for Civil Society: A Comparative Analysis of 'War on Terror' States." *International Journal for Not-for-Profit Law*, 10(3). Online. Available at <www.icnl.org/knowledge/ijnl/vol10iss3/special_2.htm> (accessed on 25 April 2009).

Skelcher, C. (2004). "The Public-private Partnerships and Hybridity." In E. Fairlie, L. E. Lynn, Jr., and C. Pollitt (eds.), *The Oxford Handbook of Public Management*. London: Oxford University Press.

CHAPTER 36

Organizations That Straddle the State-Society Divide: Illuminating Blind Spots of Existing Paradigms

Benjamin L. Read and Robert Pekkanen

This chapter is adapted from Benjamin L. Read and Robert Pekkanen's 2009 book *Local Organizations and Urban Governance in East and Southeast Asia: Straddling State and Society* (London and New York: Routledge).

The State and the Grassroots

The term "grassroots" refers to the local level of politics and society—indeed, the most local level of all: the realm of individuals within the communities where they live, of face-to-face relationships, of meetings so small that most people in the room know one another's names. Often, though, the term also implies a kind of authenticity or purity: ideas and demands and action coming directly from the people, without adulteration from outside forces or powerful institutions. Yet not all forms of local organization emerge in such a spontaneous and autonomous fashion. Indeed, in some parts of the world they are not even typical. Particularly in East and Southeast Asia, large swaths of the grassroots do not grow in unchecked profusion like a wild prairie but rather are cultivated and tended, better likened to a garden. Here governments actively shape their citizens' associational energies in ways that are unfamiliar to many Western readers.

The purpose of this chapter is to examine forms of grassroots organizations that embody some degree of state fostering and encouragement. We explore several cases of these organizations, which we loosely call "straddlers" for their spanning of the state-society divide.[1] These are groups that have extensive presence and that engage widespread participation yet are linked to the state rather than independent. Our focus is on a particular type of straddler: ultralocal groups that are anchored in particular localities such as neighborhoods or villages.[2] Importantly, such organizations exist in democracies and authoritarian systems alike, and range from those tightly tied to the state to those with a considerable degree of autonomy. The issues that we raise can be generalized to other kinds of groups as well, such as NGOs that strive for independence but are obliged (or perhaps choose) to partner with government. In places we refer the reader to recent work on empirical cases of that kind.

There are many ways in which associations can be said to straddle the realms of state and

DOI: 10.4324/9780367696559-46

society.[3] An extreme version has government officials actually running local organizations themselves. Much more commonly, of course, states provide funding for groups; even many organizations that are otherwise self-governing seek public monies, for instance by bidding on grants and contracts (Smith and Lipsky 1993). States also sometimes get associations to *do things* for them: collecting information, publicizing policies, distributing coupons for subsidized food, and so forth. In other settings, groups form a part of electoral-machine politics; they may receive special access to decision-making; or they may merely register with the government or otherwise obtain its imprimatur. While researchers are aware of these phenomena, there has been insufficient study of how the political and social properties of associations themselves change when they take on these functions.

Why do states invest in cultivating grassroots organizations? As it turns out, local organizations provide a tremendously convenient platform for administrative projects of just about every stripe. These include disseminating and collecting information, gathering input from constituents, and facilitating welfare, infrastructure, and public health programs. In many cases the groups in question obtain government resources such as stipends and office space, but they also receive less tangible support in the form of prestige, legitimation, and access to officialdom. States systematically propagate such organizations, greatly augmenting their numbers and magnifying their impact. At the same time, they typically provide a channel through which ordinary people can articulate demands, address local issues, and sometimes vote for representatives.

Researchers have published a scattering of English-language case studies on such groups, some of them deftly executed, painting their subjects in vivid colors (Guinness 1986; Bestor 1989). Yet the social sciences remain without a full conceptual understanding of them. This is perhaps even more true of nonprofit studies as a field than it is of political science and sociology.[4]

The attention of scholars steeped in the liberal tradition tends to be drawn to independent citizen initiatives, whether in the form of social movements or less contentious types of association. State-backed institutions, conversely, are often seen not only as deleterious but also as uninteresting and inherently stale.

Why then do straddlers deserve careful study? To begin with, the associations in question have a sprawling presence throughout this region. Japan boasts nearly 300,000 neighborhood and village groups that work closely with local government. Indonesia's network of community organizations was found by a World Bank study to figure prominently in the lives of the poor in particular, and is widely considered to be "a very important, effective, and trusted institution" (Mukherjee 1999, 94). In Taiwan, some 149,000 citizen volunteers serve as *linzhang*, or block captains, components of a finely grained system of ultralocal administration that blankets the island. While nonstate associations (whether religious, clan based, recreational, charitable, or oriented toward social change) also flourish in many parts of Asia, to ignore this quasi-public sector is to miss an immense part of the picture.

Their pervasiveness alone suggests that they ought to be understood, but they also deserve attention because of the practical uses to which many of these institutions are put. Some of these purposes, such as reporting information on dissidents to authoritarian regimes, many readers will find deeply troubling. Other institutions work to further policy goals rather than repression. For example, in both China and Indonesia, local women's associations are enlisted by the state to popularize family planning programs.[5] Straddlers form an essential component of the social security infrastructure in many cases, helping connect disadvantaged populations with government agencies whose purpose is to provide assistance. Whatever their flaws, these networks of organizations constitute a potential resource for just about any developmental or governance-related undertaking.

Theoretical Frameworks

There exist four broadly recognized frameworks within which associations are understood in political terms. The first is civil society theory, which focuses on citizens' groups that are autonomous from government. Second are theories of mass organizations as found in state socialist and fascist regimes. The third are accounts of corporatism, which can be defined broadly as state structuring of the representation of societal interests. Finally, the concept of state-society synergy offers a template for understanding cooperative partnerships between governments and communities. Each of these provides a salient framework for thinking about at least some of the straddlers found in Asia, yet each contains important lacunae that these hybrid organizations in some ways fill.

The civil society paradigm dominates current discussions about citizen associations in the world of politics. Contemporary theories within this long tradition isolate a specific class of organization—voluntary groups that stand independent of government—as distinct, possessing special properties.[6] They assert that civil society groups contribute to a host of salutary outcomes. Such groups are said to have internal effects on members, making them better citizens by encouraging political participation and providing practice in democratic self-governance, as well as external effects on the state, making it more accountable by asserting interests and exerting pressure.[7] Certain theories of social capital take these claims another step, arguing that dense interpersonal connections among people who join such associations serve to multiply and propagate these beneficial effects. The networks are said to undergird the commitment of community members to civic norms and drive them to more insistently demand responsiveness from the government (Putnam 1993). In short, civil society enhances politics by both enriching the practice of electoral democracy and also supplementing electoral mechanisms with direct forms of action.

If one were asked to think of the exact opposite of an independent civil society organization—the ultimate in government control—then theories of mass organizations would surely come to mind. Accounts of communism, fascism, and totalitarianism all highlight such organizations as a means through which ruling parties dominate specific sectors of society, with groups for youth, workers, women, neighborhoods, and so forth (Linz 1975; Linz and Stepan 1996). Many of the goals that regimes strive to accomplish through such "transmission belts" are fairly straightforward: spreading official beliefs, values, and doctrines; exercising surveillance over political threats or opposition; and drawing the population out of passivity and into active displays of loyalty. In his survey of what he terms "administered mass organizations" in dozens of authoritarian states, Gregory Kasza also points out several other functions: preempting autonomous groups, consuming members' time through countless diversions, and generating an illusion of mass democracy through "pseudopolitical" activities (1995).

At least one step removed from these stifling, wholly top-down institutions, corporatist arrangements constitute another fashion in which states intervene in the associational sphere. To paraphrase Philippe C. Schmitter's classic definition, the term refers to interest groups that accept constraints on the leadership they choose and the demands they make in exchange for receiving a representational monopoly in their category of activity (1979, 13).

While corporatist institutions are often imposed by the government, other institutional forms involve more equal partnerships between state and society. Scholars in the field of development such as Peter Evans, Elinor Ostrom, and others have delineated what they call "synergy," in which "active government and mobilized communities can enhance each other's developmental efforts" (Evans 1996b, 1119; see also Evans 1996a; Ostrom 1996; Warner 1999; Das Gupta, Grandvoinnet, and Romani 2000; World Bank 2004).

The synergy idea and related formulations assert that the resources, reach, and authority of the state are too important to neglect in development efforts, and that local networks and participation can extend these efforts while also holding them accountable. This embodies an optimistic perspective, in contrast with theories that highlight the dysfunctional aspects of public institutions. Yet it is also an ideal or felicitous condition that is difficult to bring about. In practice, many state agencies remain more prone to smother local initiatives than to engage them as partners. What about cases where governments actively shape communities rather than treating them as equal partners? What happens when the purposes of the collaboration are not merely developmental in nature but instead include broader programs of administration or policing?

Indeed, foundational though these frameworks are, the understanding that they provide of associations and their role in politics is highly incomplete. In the case of civil society theory, for example, although its close connection to democracy is often boldly asserted, much of the evidence concerning this relationship is mixed. Studies have found that civil society helps create or improve democratic governance only under certain conditions (Berman 1997; Bermeo and Nord 2000; Kaufman 2002; Alagappa 2004b; Sampson et al. 2005; Jamal 2007). We are only beginning to gather the kind of empirical data that can constitute real flesh on the bones of these bodies of theory.

Even more fundamentally, the existing paradigms are geared toward analyzing relatively clear-cut empirical phenomena rather than instances that blur the lines set by pat definitions. We may have sound intuitions and evidence concerning cases that *typify* concepts like civil society or mass organizations, such as Czechoslovakia's Charter 77 or the Soviet Union's Komsomol. But we are not well-equipped to understand cases, such as those considered here, that lie on the boundaries of these concepts, involving a great deal of nuance and profound tradeoffs.

In all of these concepts, the crucial element of stateness—or its opposite, nonstateness or autonomy—remains inadequately explored,

understood, or justified. A more complete understanding of the world's associational life would grapple with the full spectrum of configurations that relationships between (ostensibly) horizontal communities and vertical public authority can take. It would carefully unpack the multiple mechanisms involved. An organization whose direction is steered entirely by the state can hardly be expected to inculcate democratic practices through its internal operations, nor could the same group be expected to serve as a vehicle for bottom-up influence. All this may be true at extreme or heavy degrees of state control, but we do not know *what kind* of connections to the state prevent an organization from playing a healthy civic role, or *how extensive* state sponsorship can be before a deadening effect sets in. For example, partial funding from government sources may be enough to breathe life into an organization but not enough to declaw it. And what seem to be tame organizations embedded within powerful states, such as research institutions in late 1980s China, can in fact slip their moorings and undertake feisty activities that their sponsors never intended (Ding 1994; see also Kerkvliet, Heng, and Koh 2003).

Could there even be ways in which state involvement encourages rather than dampens organizations' civic qualities? At least in principle, yes. To begin with, there is no guarantee that non-state citizen organizations automatically adopt democratic modes of operation. In fact, doing so can be difficult and inconvenient. Associations' leaders or most active members, having invested a great deal of personal time and effort, may neglect to hold the kind of open meetings or internal votes that give rank-and-file members veto authority. Sometimes, factional strife within an organization can paralyze all participation and decision-making (see Read 2008 for one set of examples). But well-functioning democratic states have the knowledge, infrastructure, and authority to run fair elections and can extend this competency to associations outside the government proper.

Moreover, while state corporatism generally strives to minimize citizen pressure, other kinds of structured ties between public institutions and grassroots-level organizations can provide access to the halls of government. This is the fundamental claim of books like *The Rebirth of Urban Democracy*, which investigated U.S. cities like Dayton and St. Paul to understand how they "reach out to their neighborhoods and successfully incorporate the participation of average citizens into public policymaking" (Berry, Portney, and Thomson 1993, 1). For some, the aegis of the state even makes local organizations *more* attractive as an outlet for voluntary participation, adding prestige and cachet. Yet this effect varies across states, time, and contexts (being stronger in places like Japan than in the United States, for instance).

Questions

In short, a full understanding of the associational universe requires looking at phenomena that exist on or outside the fat, blurry margins of existing frameworks. In this chapter, we explore several puzzles posed by this ambiguous realm, thus bringing it into dialogue with the aforementioned theories while also transcending them. First, how do straddler groups interact with their members or constituents? Most basically, do people consider them helpful or oppressive? At a more abstract level, in what ways do these groups enhance civic engagement and citizen consciousness, and in what ways do they discourage or thwart popular initiative? How do vertical imperatives interact with horizontal solidarities? What is the impact of these associations on the type of interpersonal connections referred to as social capital? Do they stifle social interaction and reinforce patterns of dependence, clientelism, and distrust? Or is it possible that straddlers may contribute to thick community networks in spite of—or perhaps in part because of—links to the state?

Second, in what ways do these local organizations influence the broader political system?

What kinds of political participation do they encourage? Do they enhance the practice of democracy or detract from it? In authoritarian systems, do they serve as a force promoting greater openness and accountability or do they undermine pressures for change? Do they compete with independent civil society or encourage it?

Third, do straddler groups facilitate good governance, and if so in what ways? In what areas of policy implementation (for instance, in welfare, policing, and family planning) are such organizations most effective, and how precisely do they work?

Cases

This chapter examines a diverse array of cases across seven countries, selected in such a way that the precise relationship between state and grassroots organization varies among them. The reader might picture a spectrum of statism. On one end of this continuum we find heavily statist institutions, in which local associations come close to forming a part of the government itself. These elevate community leaders almost to the status of a permanent functionary, subject to higher-level supervision in nearly the same way that formal state employees would be. Farther down the continuum are organizations that cooperate with government and depend on its sponsorship but are free from direct control. The least statist end of the spectrum considered here comprises groups that are highly self-constituting yet undertake partnerships with government in order to further their aims.

The neighborhood organizations in urban China and Singapore lie at the most statist point on this continuum. Whether by coincidence or not, they are both called Residents' Committees (RCs) in English and exemplify a substantially government-dominated form of straddler institution (see Heberer and Göbel 2011; Read 2012). Their members are effectively chosen and directly managed by higher levels of city administration. In both cases, they also are subject to control through parallel systems running all the way up to the monistic parties that dominate political life: the Chinese Communist Party and the People's Action Party, respectively.

In both these cases the grassroots organization in question centers on a *committee* of people, essentially a team of staff who, though not formally employed by the government, must answer to it in something close to an employee relationship. In China these individuals receive stipends and are "elected" to their positions in what for the most part are heavily constrained procedures of vetting and balloting, designed so that the great majority of committee members are acceptable to the authorities and can be relied upon for support. In Singapore, as Ooi Giok Ling explains, they are more or less appointed from above (2009). As committees, these bodies differ from associations that recruit a broad base of members who populate the organization. Yet they have extensive associative functions, serving as an important nexus of neighborhood life.

Three other cases considered here—in Japan, Taiwan, and Indonesia—once looked substantially like their counterparts in Singapore and China and likewise served as grassroots buttresses for authoritarian systems. Since the democratization of each of these countries, however, they have evolved in ways that set them apart. Japan's neighborhood associations possess considerable autonomy; they are not subject to any formal levers of control by city governments. Their degree of independence is such that Pekkanen (2006, chapter 4) discusses them as a form of civil society, indeed as a characteristic and central form of civil society organization in Japan. Only a quarter of Japan's neighborhood groups (24 percent) report that cooperation with local authorities is one of their top priorities (Pekkanen, Tsujinaka, and Yamamoto 2014, 41). Yet almost all (81 percent) work hand-in-hand with local government, mainly in ways that oblige rather than resist or pressure it

(Pekkanen et al. 2014, 180). For example, they regularly circulate notices, distribute bulletins, collect fees, recommend citizens for various government or quasi-governmental committees, help with garbage collection, and even provide welfare services for the elderly. Quite a few also accept contracts to perform services for local governments (Pekkanen et al. 2014, chapter 7).

Taiwan's network of neighborhood heads and block captains was once intended to mobilize and incorporate the local citizenry under the externally imposed rule of Chiang Kai-shek's Nationalist Party. Yet in the past two decades it has evolved into what is in many ways the most democratic of the institutions considered in this book. Indeed, in terms of the rigor of the elections, the neighborhood wardens, or *lizhang*, may be the most democratically chosen leaders of their type in the world. Each comes to his or her position through formal processes of campaigns and balloting, often sharply competitive. As a result, these leaders face pressure to answer to their constituents, for instance, by lobbying for grants and services. Yet they are paid stipends by the state and, as in Japan, work closely with civil servants from municipal government (Read 2012, chapters 2–3).

In Indonesia the microlevel organization of society takes the form of the RT, or *rukun tetangga* (Guinness 1986, 2009; Sullivan 1992; Kurasawa 2009). In cities like Jakarta each RT corresponds to a small segment of a neighborhood, containing just a few hundred residents. Several RT, in turn, are clustered together to form larger units called RW. Once dominated by the Suharto regime, the RT/RW have become politically pluralized, much like Taiwan's neighborhood leaders. They remain, however, closely tied to the wards, the next-higher rung on the urban administrative ladder.

As discussed below, all five of the above cases have roots that extend back in time for generations if not centuries, whereas Thailand's Cooperative Community Groups (CCGs) were born only in the late 1980s. Chandra Mahakanjana

(2009) explains that although they do not cover every urban area, they nonetheless have a large footprint, numbering some 11,000 in total. Each is composed of a chairperson, officers, and as many as 15 committee members, all serving on an unpaid basis. As in the Japanese case, we see here wide variation in the degree to which leadership is constituted through democratic means. The CCGs emerged in a relatively liberal political context, and never had social control or surveillance functions. Thai bureaucrats had other motives for initiating them, such as reducing burdens arising from constituent demands. The author argues that they have nonetheless served as important new focal points for participation in an environment that previously did not encourage such involvement.

Why are these various kinds of institutions so prominent in East and Southeast Asia? No simple answer to this question will suffice. After all, state-sponsored organizations are hardly unique to this region. Corporatism as a concept was first theorized in Europe, and Latin America has provided many cases as well. China's and Vietnam's straddlers have counterparts in current and former state socialist regimes elsewhere, from Cuba to the former Soviet Union. And as noted above, the general questions of government's relationship to associational life are even relevant in liberal democracies like the United States.

Historical antecedents of today's arrangements can be found in institutions that the predecessors of modern-day states developed.[8] For purposes of social control and taxation, imperial China employed a strategy of organizing society on the ultralocal level into units known as *jia* (theoretically formed of ten households) and *bao* (formed of ten *jia*). A headman was appointed for each such collectivity, and he was held responsible for order and good behavior on the part of the whole group. Japan and Korea developed similar bodies, as well as their own organizational forms. Twentieth-century states then picked up on this historical model and propagated it. Thus, China's Nationalist Party set up *bao-jia* systems in city and countryside during the 1930s, and Japan employed them in places it colonized and occupied, notably Formosa, Korea and Java. Some of today's straddler organizations are at least loosely descended from these ancestors.

Moreover, the states under consideration here have certain general properties in common. The "East Asian model" is usually invoked to discuss patterns of industrialization and economic development or sometimes labor or human rights (Amsden 1989; Öniş 1991; Wade 1992; Kohli 1994; Evans 1995; Peerenboom 2007). Yet many of the qualities that underpinned the region's approach to economic development and civil liberties also influenced the evolution of local associations. Most of these states shared internal or external security concerns in the post–World War II era. Whether in socialist systems like China or Vietnam, fearing threats to the revolution, or under conservative regimes like Chiang's Republic of China or Suharto's Indonesia, wary of communist expansion, officials were driven to construct organizational networks capable of monitoring the populace and co-opting dissent. Moreover, the doctrines of liberalism found little resonance in the corridors of power here. Just as bureaucrats largely shunned the idea of a laissez-faire approach to building the economy, they also did not believe that societal organization should be left alone to grow haphazardly from the grassroots up. Instead, corporatist intervention, the active shaping of organizations, made just as much sense to them in overseeing urban and village governance as it did in guiding firms or labor groups.

These considerations speak to the "supply side," if you will, helping to explain why states in the region have persistently turned to such institutions. A further question concerns the "demand side"—whether publics in East and Southeast Asia are particularly receptive to the kind of state-society partnership that these organizations represent. Prominent Asia scholars have provided arguments in the affirmative. The late Benjamin I. Schwartz, in an essay titled "The Primacy of the Political Order in East Asian Societies," argued that "the conception of the supreme jurisdiction of the political order in all domains of social and political life" has been "a more or less enduring dominant cultural orientation" in China through the ages and in countries influenced by Chinese civilization, such as Japan, Korea, and Vietnam. He clarifies that this refers not to totalitarian control but rather to an assumption that the political order, or state, has such special "centrality and weight" that it appropriately claims jurisdiction over and intermingles with the religious, economic, intellectual, and social spheres rather than remaining clearly delineated from them (1996, 114–115).

As the cases discussed in this chapter show, there is considerable support for the possibility that political culture helps explain the prevalence of straddler institutions, but also reasons to refrain from overemphasizing this factor. We observe ample evidence of collectivist traditions and the embracing of state-society fusion. At the same time, we also see that citizens hold varying attitudes toward these institutions. By no means do they welcome just any form of government oversight and intermediation. In many cases it appears that in order to win whatever public acceptance they might enjoy, straddlers must continually prove their worth by providing services, leisure activities, or other benefits. This indicates that they cannot rely on any timeless cultural values for legitimation.

Engaging the Questions

What Do They Do and Whom Do They Benefit?

Governments give a wide range of tasks to grassroots associations: collecting information, disseminating information, resolving conflict locally, and promoting state-backed programs.

In authoritarian contexts such as China, Indonesia (pre-1998), Vietnam, and Singapore, a primary purpose of state-fostered organizations is to maintain the grip of a ruling party. They can do this by keeping a lookout for political dissent and reporting illicit behavior, for example. Or regime support can take more subtle forms, such as inculcating loyalty to Suharto's "New Order," building national unity, or identifying and recruiting leadership talent.

The cases of Japan, Taiwan, and Indonesia (post-Suharto) also teach us that these organizations can shed their more intrusive, control-oriented functions. In these countries democratic governments still find myriad uses for them that do not involve violations of civil liberties. But even here, the question arises: To what extent do these functions merely provide a tool for the convenience of the bureaucracy and to what extent do they genuinely benefit their constituents?[9]

The case of Thailand's Cooperative Community Groups addresses this issue. As Mahakanjana (2009) makes abundantly clear—and as is true of straddlers generally—these local groups, created at the behest of the Interior Ministry, unquestionably serve the interests of government authorities. They were founded as a means of encouraging communities to "depend on themselves in solving their own problems." Local politicians have pounced on them as means to winning the goodwill of voters and secure their own reelection. They also provide forums in which city governments can try to build cooperation for projects that they want to implement. Yet CCGs also serve their neighborhoods as well. The organizations do so, the author asserts, by building cohesion among residents; providing a channel for communication with authorities and thus enhancing their accountability; and promoting mutual aid.

Kurasawa's (2009) account of Indonesia's official neighborhood and village groups, the RT/RW, uses ethnographic techniques to show just how tightly such organizations can fuse with local society. The RT serves as a hub of neighborhood sociability and organization, not just convening its own meetings but also sponsoring the local branch of the women's association, the youth association, and the Koran-chanting association. Among their endeavors are mutual aid activities like rotating credit groups (*arisan*). The various associations engage the energies of roughly a third of the neighborhood, with long-time residents and homeowners particularly well represented. Clearly, at least in this locality, they are not a detested holdover from the authoritarian past but rather an integral part of the community. Kurasawa also points out, however, that residents whose lives intersect less regularly with their local surroundings (due to, for instance, transience or the pressures of work) remain marginal to the RT structure and may not be well-served by it. This underscores the fact that networks exclude as well as include, and systems of governance that rely upon networks may have strong built-in biases.[10]

Throughout East and Southeast Asia, states work together with societal organizations to provide services in many forms and settings, not just in neighborhoods and villages (Schwartz and Shieh 2009 surveys many such collaborations). Anthony Spires (2011) uses the term "contingent symbiosis" in explaining why China's authoritarian state tolerates some grassroots NGOs in exchange for the work they do addressing social needs and relieving the state of certain welfare burdens. Timothy Hildebrandt (2013) develops a related argument specifically concerning groups in the areas of the environment, HIV/AIDS, and gay and lesbian rights. In Japan, according to Mary Alice Haddad, "norms of civic responsibility encourage involvement in volunteer organizations that have close, embedded relationships with the government," such as volunteer firefighters and parent-teacher groups (2007, 6).

Straddlers thus carry out a highly diverse range of functions. In repressive contexts, state security and the prevention of unrest are usually central to the government's purposes. But states also use these organizational platforms for delivering services, gathering popular input, stimulating voluntary activity, and otherwise performing liaison work that is congruent, rather than at odds, with residents' interests and needs. Community networks often build themselves around the nucleus that is established by government structuring. It is characteristic of straddlers to meld together all these conceptually distinct functions, so that the boundaries between them are blurred.

Internal Democracy

Is it possible for such state-sponsored organizations to be run democratically, to choose their own leaders and be held accountable to constituents? The answer is a strong yes. Taiwan's neighborhood wardens seem to represent the high-water mark in this regard (Read 2012, chapter 3). Their elections are overseen by the same commissions that handle races for offices like mayoralties, legislatures, and the national presidency. Just about anyone can run for these positions, and in most Taipei neighborhoods the races are competitive. Candidates issue formal statements of their campaign platforms, which are circulated to each household in detailed brochures from the election commission. The counting of ballots in each polling place is conducted as rigorously as in contests for higher offices, under police guard with the scrutiny of election officials and the public alike. Indeed, the process of leadership selection is considerably more democratic than in many civil society organizations.

In sharp contrast with this, straddlers in urban China and Singapore remain firmly under the control of the dominant party (Read 2012, chapter 3; Ooi 2009). Although elections of a sort are held in China's RCs, they (at best) ratify staffing decisions made at higher levels, which brook no genuine contestation or pluralism. It should be noted as well that even some democracies, like South Korea, do not have elections for official grassroots organizations; for example, the part-time *tongjang* that serve as city governments' links to neighborhoods there are in no way chosen from below.[11] In other words, just because portions of the state are democratized does not imply that its local branches necessarily are.

Perhaps the most common pattern is one of partial democratization, whether through balloting or similar mechanisms, or in the form of informal constraints that promote some degree of consensus building and consultation. In Japan's neighborhood associations, for example, leadership selection processes vary by locale, and sometimes a small core of people appears to make the key decisions.[12] Similarly, Mahakanjana (2009) finds that only some of Thailand's CCGs hold elections, while the leaders of others are chosen by city officials. In Indonesia, neighborhood-level leaders during Suharto's rule were voted on by residents but hardly in a free and fair way, as candidates were subject to stringent screening on political criteria. Now, as Kurasawa (2009) reports, the elections have become much more open and RT leaders from any political background are eligible, though ward-level leaders may yet have room to influence the proceedings. She also documents contextual changes that enhance accountability; even poorly educated residents have become more demanding of their RT heads and insist on transparency in decision making.

Can They Make the State Listen?

Internal democracy is analytically distinct from external influence. It is possible to have fair and rigorous elections for local leaders who nonetheless have little substantive power to press demands upon higher levels. So to what extent are straddler organizations able to *represent* their constituencies, to speak to the powerful on their behalf? When the state embraces local associations, does it in fact open itself to influence or transformation in the process?

In many instances, such upward representation is limited. China's RCs, for example, are strongly geared toward carrying out duties and facilitating programs defined by the state and the Communist Party. They have very little standing to "talk back" to the branches of municipal government that oversee them. After all, committee members were essentially chosen for their positions by the state in the first place and can be summarily dismissed, thus illustrating an obvious connection between a lack of democratic accountability and a lack of representative voice. In cases like China and Singapore, upward influence takes the form of politely bending the ear of higher officials. They can call attention to individuals who need state assistance but are not receiving it, for instance. They can point out infrastructure that needs fixing or explain that a particular policy is not well received by residents and should be rethought. This is not negligible, but it falls far short of robust advocacy.

Even in democracies, grassroots representatives of this kind often confine themselves to a relatively subdued form of representation. Pekkanen and his coauthors (2006, 2014) argue that Japanese neighborhood associations do not evince much of an advocacy role regarding national policy issues. Several reasons seem to underlie this, in Japan and elsewhere. Association leaders may need government support, whether in order to keep their positions or to obtain resources. There are formal guidelines and informal norms that govern their behavior and that stipulate duties they owe to administrative higher-ups. They may also fall victim to "status seduction," as Jeffrey Broadbent posited in explaining neighborhood leaders who turn against their communities' wishes, swayed by the prestige that comes with playing a part in the great pageant of governance (1998, 190).

At the same time, we also see instances of straddler organizations prevailing on states in remarkable ways. In Hannah's (2009) study of NGOs in Vietnam that partner with the government, organizations appear engulfed by the bureaucracy but in fact push it to adopt practices imported from international models that are unprecedented for this single-party regime. He makes the case that by working closely with state agencies, these groups in some ways infiltrate it and sow progressive ideas about how to work with disadvantaged populations such as garbage collectors, homeless children, and trafficked girls. In Japan, fully 80 percent of neighborhood groups reported making frequent approaches to local government officials, and 62 percent reported success in their demands (Pekkanen et al. 2014, 154, 168). Relatedly, Susan McCarthy (2013) finds that by inflecting their charitable work with elements of faith, Buddhist and Catholic groups in China are able to "repurpose" the state, turning officially approved projects toward their own ends. And in his account of anti-dam struggles by Chinese environmentalists, Andrew Mertha shows that activists are sometimes able to make common cause with parts of the otherwise-hostile bureaucracy, such as tourism offices and media outlets.

In several of the cases local organizations can be seen lobbying the state to shunt construction or development money toward projects in their jurisdictions, such as building or repairing roads. This form of input into the budgeting process resembles the kind of access granted to city decision making found in Berry et al.'s (1993) study of U.S. cities. Taiwan's neighborhood wardens, like their counterparts in Indonesia and Thailand, may submit proposals for special allocations of public funds. They also obtain extra clout for such requests by dint of their ties to city council members and even mayors, who rely on their help during election campaigns.

Just as in the case of Japan, Taiwan's neighborhood leaders do not generally spearhead social movements. Indeed, NGOs there often see them as part of the forces aligned against the change they are working for, whether their efforts concern the environment, the preservation of historical sites, social equality, or others. The neighborhood heads can be perceived as stodgy or suspected of taking bribes from moneyed interests like property developers. But their reluctance to become caught up in single-issue causes also (perhaps ironically) reflects their *more extensive* democratic accountability relative to NGOs. These local leaders have to explain themselves to their entire electorate, or at least a majority of it, rather than just to those individuals who happen to care about a particular topic or grievance.

Thus, internal democracy is linked to external representation, but not always in straightforward or expected ways. There appear to be several channels through which straddler organizations can obtain influence at higher levels: through institutionalized processes designed to open up decision making to popular input, by informal connections to politicians at higher levels who need supporters at the grassroots; and by offering new ideas for solving problems in forms that are perceived as less suspicious precisely because they give the appearance of emerging from "within the system."

Participating in Straddler Organizations

In the economic realm government support for firms in the form of tax credits or trade subsidies can provide them with a decisive boost. So too with societal organizations, state sponsorship can confer tremendous advantages. Grassroots associations with official backing are propagated so extensively, in many of the cases considered here, that their geographic coverage is difficult or impossible for nonstate organizations to match. For better or for worse, this support brings them to people's doorsteps, as it were. But do people take part? Do they welcome these bodies or shun them? *Who* takes part?

In the neighborhood-based straddlers, we find remarkably common patterns. Even the most statist of these organizations engage a great deal of popular participation—though this participation often skews toward particular demographic groups.

High participation rates naturally raise the question of whether people have a choice about the matter. But in none of the cases under study, even in the authoritarian countries, are ordinary people threatened with state punishment for failing to join; rather, people's motivations for taking part are complex and varied. Social pressure and a sense of civic obligation appear to play a significant role in cases like Japan. In many others, factors like the pleasures of sociability and the psychological rewards to be gleaned from serving alongside others in an official auxiliary of the state seem to be important parts of groups' appeal. Whether in China, Singapore, or Indonesia, most citizens are proud of their country, and straddlers provide a way to serve the nation, even if only at the most humble of levels.

Evidence from Thailand, Indonesia, China, Taiwan, and elsewhere indicates that it is in poorer neighborhoods that participation is most concentrated. Kurasawa (2009) finds, for example, that in these areas residents more readily join activities like the rotating credit groups. Conversely, relatively wealthy households, living in more modern homes, tend to depend less on their communities and have less need for coordination with them. It also comes as no surprise that middle-aged and older individuals are most attracted to and available for this form of association, as is generally the case with community-based groups. Interestingly, though, whether the organization is internally democratic or not may have relatively little effect on participation. Neighborhood groups in Beijing and Taipei lie at opposite ends of the spectrum of formal accountability, yet they pull in roughly the same fraction of die-hard joiners to the activities that they sponsor, even though

in Taipei more people turn up for casual social activities (Read 2012, chapters 6 and 7). This highlights the centrality of sociability and camaraderie in the appeal of these groups.

Vertical and Horizontal Ties: Pulling Together or Apart?

Vertical connections involve state authority, demands, inducements, sometimes impositions. Horizontal ties are peer relationships or something like them, linking those who are close to equal in power. How should we understand the interaction between vertical and horizontal forces in the institutions in question? After all, interpersonal, face-to-face networks lie at the heart of how straddler organizations are intended to work. From the perspective of governments, their purpose is to reach into communities and borrow or co-opt some of the information, entrée, or persuasive power that inheres in the networks there, whether this is for purposes that are benign or crudely self-serving. One might well expect (and some theories predict) these two forces to conflict with one another. Vertical obligations could well kill off horizontal bonds. Alternatively, perhaps local communities might "capture" and subvert the efforts of the state (Migdal 1988).

A common theme found in research on such groups is one of politicians drawing on local state-linked organizations for the purpose of establishing contact with voters. This is especially pronounced in Japan, Thailand, and Taiwan. Does it amount to a form of clientelism?[13] And if so, how malignant is it? One way in which vertical ties can be harmful is when they are used to trade material goods and benefits for political support, thus substituting short-term payoffs for deeper forms of representation and undermining democratic accountability. This varies from place to place between and even within countries, and it changes over time. Pekkanen and his coauthors aim to debunk the idea that Japan's neighborhood associations are clientelist vehicles. While nearly four out of ten associations are involved in election campaigning, mainly for local offices, the groups are just one forum among many, providing gatherings where politicians have a chance to speak and appeal to voters but not to ensnare them in relationships of dependency (Pekkanen et al. 2014, 164, 152).

This might well be expected in a wealthy and well-established democracy, but what about in lower- or middle-income countries? Mahakanjana finds that in the poorer neighborhoods of Thailand's cities and towns, the ties that politicians form through the CCGs can indeed be clientelistic. Elsewhere, she argues, the communities are not passive subordinates but work with their city representatives on an equal footing. The evidence from Taiwan is also mixed and has evolved since the 1980s. Some neighborhood leaders there are classic examples of *tiau-a-ka*, party operatives who strive to get out the vote in legislative and presidential elections (Rigger 1999). These party "cornerstones" have been known to hand out cash payments before elections in trade for constituents' votes. While this practice continues in some parts of Taiwan, it is losing its effectiveness, and in cosmopolitan cities like Taipei it has all but disappeared. Voters' need and taste for such inducements seem to diminish with rising living standards and a greater sense of civic pride.

Clientelist ties are clearly at their most destructive when used deliberately to fragment a subordinate group and turn its members against one another. Such a situation, with clientelist links to Communist Party cadres shattering any possibility of shop-floor solidarity among workers, is depicted in Walder's account of Chinese state enterprises in the late Mao era (Walder 1986). The key factor creating abject dependency and polarization is the extent to which valuable material goods, opportunities, or discretionary power over the enforcement of rules are wielded by those who would be "patrons." A form of this kind of power can be seen here in Kurasawa's

(2009) description of New Order Jakarta, where one had to stay in the good graces of the RT head in order to receive letters of support needed to obtain various official documents. Most of this arbitrary authority seems to have vaporized with Indonesia's *reformasi*, however. What about China? In the Mao era, frequent political campaigns gave local officials a sometimes terrifying ability to tag a person as suspect and thus jeopardize his or her future. But today, this kind of discretionary power has greatly diminished in China, and certainly the lowly Residents' Committees do not have it (Read 2012, chapters 4 and 5). Some residents dislike the kind of monitoring that RCs engage in, while others see it as appropriate, yet few have much to fear from their neighborhood leaders or have a reason to curry favor with them. Nonetheless, given their advisory role to the government on decisions like welfare benefits, it is also true that they have some authority over subpopulations with special needs.

Vertical power need not actively smash horizontal solidarity; it can displace or preempt it in more subtle ways. It can cultivate bonds that center on political loyalists and are reinforced through activities geared toward serving the state rather than making demands on it. It can disrupt oppositional forms of solidarity by substituting for them. Thus, Singapore takes care to ensure that its grassroots organizations are run by individuals found reliable by the ruling People's Action Party, and discourages forms of community that sing an unorthodox tune. Yet we find this problem mitigated in settings where straddlers are open to competitive pressures. In Taiwan, for example, candidates from different parties (and in many cases, no party at all) vie for neighborhood leadership. Moreover, residents may form, at their own initiative, groups known as community development associations (*shequ fazhan xiehui*) that can apply independently for city support. This helps prevent vertical linkages being used exclusively for the benefit of any one political clique.

In some circumstances, government backing for grassroots organizations seems actually to promote horizontal connections in certain ways. Mahakanjana (2009) argues that Thai communities often lack preexisting associational foci, and thus state-fostered organizations create rather than supplant social capital. Moreover, government backing can give credibility to programs like cooperative burial insurance, which otherwise might be defeated by mutual distrust. And as Pekkanen (2006) insists, Japan's neighborhood groups could hardly have the astonishing extensiveness that they do without state support.

Synthesis

In the end, the phenomena considered here—which may strike some readers as quirky, yet in many ways are typical of the region—remind us how much more distance our theories must travel in order to cover the actual terrain of associational life around the world. Most of these groups fall between the ideal-typical poles of the oppressive Leninist mass organization, on the one hand, and the wholly self-initiated and independent citizens' group acting in civil society, on the other. Many have, in fact, moved during the course of their existence from one position on this spectrum to another. This calls attention to the possibilities for change and evolution inherent in these institutions, showing the malleability of associations with regard to their multiple connections to the state. Once established, these links contain the potential for either governors or governed to renegotiate and convert them to new purposes.

Broadly speaking, many of these entities could be said to constitute kinds of corporatist arrangements in that states use them in efforts to direct popular participation toward sanctioned channels. Yet the local or ultralocal scale and broad functional scope of these grassroots organizations distinguish them from the forms of corporatism that are most commonly known in the economic sphere.

With respect to "synergy" and related ideas, what we see here similarly constitutes a form of the phenomenon that puts existing theory into new light. The heart of the synergy idea is that states and communities each can possess valuable assets that the other requires: resources, reach, expertise, and authority on the one hand and micro-level networks, interpersonal trust, and credibility on the other. This is precisely the mix of ingredients that fuels an institution like Thailand's CCGs or Indonesia's RT/RW. While synergy was conceived to account for a relatively small set of exemplary developmental projects, its actual applicability is far wider. There are multiple forms of synergy, some producing wholly benign results and others with purposes that the theorists of this concept might find objectionable, such as surveillance and political mobilization.

In presenting a balanced appraisal of straddler organizations, we do not aim to deny the fundamental importance of independent civil society groups to good governance. We know how crucial civil society is in part by considering cases where it is absent or cowed into quiescence. Countries that deny their citizens the right to organize wholly autonomous associations through which to address public issues and make political demands are markedly different in important ways from those that respect this right. We also know this from cases around the world where citizen groups have led the way in bringing about sorely needed political change, whether at the regime level or in expanding rights and addressing injustices.

Moreover, this chapter does not follow the line of argument advanced by those critics who claim that civil society in its contemporary meaning is unsuitable for Asian societies. Some have argued that this concept is too beholden to the individualistic bent of the liberal tradition and thus unable to do justice to associations in non-Western societies (Wakeman 1993; Hann

1996). Yet this is far too strong an argument. We follow instead the reasoning of scholars like Frank Schwartz and Muthiah Alagappa, who point out that the existence of civil society in Asia is an undeniable fact, though it is much more highly developed in some countries than in others (F. J. Schwartz 2003; Alagappa 2004a).

The problem with civil society studies is that in seeking to establish a discrete concept, they have set rigid definitional lines that obscure important boundary phenomena. The idea of a white-and-black, binary distinction between groups inside and outside of civil society has impeded knowledge in many ways rather than advancing it, hindering our understanding of whole galaxies of actually existing organizations. We must develop much more fine-grained categories with which to comprehend the associational universe. This is, in fact, what some outstanding scholarship of recent years strives to do, whether we think of Mark Warren's (2001) categorizations; Verba, Schlozman, and Brady's (1995) analysis of the role of specific types of organizations (unions and churches) in building civic skills; or Lily Tsai's (2007) careful research on solidary groups in Chinese villages.

The hybrids here overlap with autonomous groups in certain crucial ways. From the point of view of participants, some straddlers offer opportunities similar to those available in other associational venues—for instance, companionship and a sense of contributing to useful purposes. In other cases, these groups may offer distinct types of rewards, whether in the form of influence on government, material incentives, or prestige. In some contexts they may in fact be better positioned than independent groups to achieve certain purposes, such as providing services to needy populations.

As we know from studies of mass organizations and state corporatism, crude top-down control of grassroots organizations unquestionably can kill them off as channels for meaningful political participation. Links to the state have both benefits and drawbacks with respect to the capacity of grassroots organizations to stimulate civic engagement. Their widely distributed nature ensures that they are readily at hand, and the government's seal of approval may enhance their appeal as an avenue for participation. Their connections to officialdom attract individuals seeking a way to communicate demands to the authorities, though they also constrain those who might use contentious tactics to bring visibility to a cause. Neighborhood structures in places like Taiwan and Indonesia suggest that even if state penetration of associations has negative effects, these can also be balanced with institutional features that reinforce popular accountability rather than undermine it. The key ingredients seem to be the inclusion of strong mechanisms to ensure democratic accountability and opening up rather than shutting off avenues by which ordinary people can meaningfully affect decision making within the state itself.

Cases where states sharply constrain the possible forms of citizen expression through local organizations and sometimes use them to help identify and silence nonconforming voices, like China's RCs, can hardly be recommended as a template for other countries to apply. Even the most constructive of the straddlers seem to have much to learn from institutions designed more specifically for empowering constituents to help, for instance, take the budgetary reins of local government, to participate in managing local schools, or to monitor the performance of the state (Abers 2000; Fung 2004; Cornwall and Coelho 2007; Fox 2007). Most of the cases presented in this book do too little to bring citizens together *across* the boundaries of small communities and may in fact perpetuate a form of social fragmentation. And whatever the merits or drawbacks of the organizations considered here, it is clear that not everything ought to "straddle." There are important forms of political action—such as transformative social movements, contentious calls for justice, and noisy demands for redress of official malfeasance—that are unlikely to emerge from state-society hybrids.

Yet associations sponsored by and plugged into local government contribute much to their societies and should not be rejected out of hand. Where immense networks of them exist, even as legacies from unsavory periods of authoritarianism, a strong argument can be made for reforming rather than discarding them. There can be no single answer to the question of the appropriate configuration of authority and autonomy, cultivation and spontaneity at the grassroots. What may be most functional and productive instead is an organizational ecology containing a multitude of creative answers.

Notes

1. To survey the ways in which scholars have questioned or explored the boundary between state and society is beyond the scope of this chapter, but see Mitchell (1991); Migdal, Kohli, and Shue (1994); and Rudolph and Jacobsen (2006).

2. The majority of our cases are urban associations, but many have rural counterparts.

3. Coston (1998) provides one framework for considering this issue.

4. Small, local organizations have been relatively little researched in nonprofit studies (David Horton Smith 2000).

5. Jeremy Shiffman (2002) highlights the significance of the Indonesian program's community-level embeddedness. On China's family planning program, see White (2006).

6. Larry Diamond defines civil society as "the realm of organized social life that is open, voluntary, self-generating, at least partially self-supporting, autonomous from the state, and bound by a legal order or set of shared rules" (1999, 221).

7. Scholars also advance many other claims about the possible benefits of associations; for example, that they can cross-cut and thus mitigate societal cleavages. More comprehensive statements of claimed effects can be found in Diamond (1999, chapter 6) and Warren (2001). Warren eschews the term "civil society," preferring a more open-ended approach to the study of associational life. See also Cohen and Rogers (1992); Walzer (1995); Anheier (2004); and Heinrich (2005).

8. See Read (2012, chapter 2) for a more detailed historical overview.

9. These are not necessarily mutually exclusive. To take one example, Pekkanen, Tsujinaka and Yamamoto show that local beautification projects are the top priority for Japan's neighborhood groups, and that often overlaps with local government priorities and projects (2014, 115).

10. Lussier and Fish (2012) also discuss the RT as an important site for civic engagement in Indonesia.

11. This draws on fieldwork by the first author in Seoul, July 2004.

12. The association's president is elected in 43 percent of neighborhoods and is chosen or recommended by the directors in 35 percent, while the position rotates among residents in 15 percent of the cases (Pekkanen et al. 2014, 49).

13. For recent reviews of the concept of clientelism, see Kitschelt and Wilkinson (2007) and Stokes (2007).

Bibliography

Abers, Rebecca N. 2000. *Inventing Local Democracy: Grassroots Politics in Brazil*. Boulder, CO: Lynne Rienner Publishers.

Alagappa, Muthiah. 2004a. "Introduction." In *Civil Society and Political Change in Asia: Expanding and Contracting Democratic Space*, edited by M. Alagappa. Stanford, CA: Stanford University Press.

———. 2004b. "Civil Society and Democratic Change: Indeterminate Connection, Transforming Relations." In *Civil Society and Political Change in Asia: Expanding and Contracting Democratic Space*, edited by M. Alagappa. Stanford, CA: Stanford University Press.

Amsden, Alice H. 1989. *Asia's Next Giant: South Korea and Late Industrialization*. New York: Oxford University Press.

Anheier, Helmut K. 2004. *Civil Society: Measurement, Evaluation, Policy*. London: Civicus.

Berman, Sheri. 1997. "Civil Society and the Collapse of the Weimar Republic." *World Politics* 49: 401–429.

Bermeo, Nancy and Philip Nord. 2000. *Civil Society before Democracy: Lessons from Nineteenth-century Europe*. Lanham, MD: Rowman and Littlefield.

Berry, Jeffrey M., Kent E. Portney, and Ken Thomson. 1993. *The Rebirth of Urban Democracy*. Washington, DC: The Brookings Institution.

Bestor, Theodore C. 1989. *Neighborhood Tokyo*. Stanford, CA: Stanford University Press.

Broadbent, Jeffrey. 1998. *Environmental Politics in Japan: Networks of Power and Protest*. Cambridge and New York: Cambridge University Press.

Cohen, Joshua and Joel Rogers. 1992. "Secondary Associations and Democratic Governance." *Politics and Society* 20: 393–472.

Cornwall, Andrea and Vera Schattan Coelho. 2007. *Spaces for Change? The Politics of Citizen Participation in New Democratic Arenas*. London: Zed Books.

Coston, Jennifer M. 1998. "A Model and Typology of Government-NGO Relationships." *Nonprofit and Voluntary Sector Quarterly* 27(3): 358–382.

Das Gupta, Monica, Helene Grandvoinnet, and Mattia Romani. 2000. "State-community Synergies in Development: Laying the Basis for Collective Action." World Bank Policy Research Working Papers 2439.

Diamond, Larry. 1999. *Developing Democracy: Toward Consolidation*. Baltimore, MD: Johns Hopkins University Press.

Ding, Xue-liang. 1994. "Institutional Amphibiousness and the Transition from Communism." *British Journal of Political Science* 24: 293–318.

Evans, Peter. 1995. *Embedded Autonomy: States and Industrial Transformation*. Princeton, NJ: Princeton University Press.

———. 1996a. "Introduction: Development Strategies Across the Public-private Divide." *World Development* 24: 1033–1037.

———. 1996b. "Government Action, Social Capital and Development: Reviewing the Evidence on Synergy." *World Development* 24: 1119–1132.

Fox, Jonathan. 2007. *Accountability Politics: Power and Voice in Rural Mexico*. Oxford: Oxford University Press.

Fung, Archon. 2004. *Empowered Participation: Reinventing Urban Democracy*. Princeton, NJ: Princeton University Press.

Guinness, Patrick. 1986. *Harmony and Hierarchy in a Javanese Kampung*. Singapore: Oxford University Press.

———. 2009. *Kampung, Islam and State in Urban Java*. Honolulu: University of Hawaii Press.

Haddad, Mary Alice. 2007. *Politics and Volunteering in Japan: A Global Perspective*. Cambridge: Cambridge University Press.

Hann, Chris. 1996. "Introduction: Political Society and Civil Anthropology." In *Civil Society: Challenging Western Models*, edited by C. Hann and E. Dunn. London: Routledge.

Hannah, Joseph. 2009. "The Mutual Colonization of State and Civil Society Organizations in Vietnam." In *Local Organizations and Urban Governance in East and Southeast Asia: Straddling State and Society*, edited by B. L. Read and R. Pekkanen. Milton Park, Abingdon, and Oxon: Routledge.

Heberer, Thomas and Christian Göbel. 2011. *The Politics of Community Building in Urban China*. New York: Routledge.

Heinrich, Volkhart F. 2005. "Studying Civil Society Across the World: Exploring the Thorny Issues of Conceptualization and Measurement." *Journal of Civil Society* 1: 211–228.

Hildebrandt, Timothy. 2013. *Social Organizations and the Authoritarian State in China*. Cambridge: Cambridge University Press.

Jamal, Amaney A. 2007. *Barriers to Democracy: The Other Side of Social Capital in Palestine and the Arab World*. Princeton: Princeton University Press.

Kasza, Gregory J. 1995. *The Conscription Society: Administered Mass Organizations*. New Haven, CT: Yale University Press.

Kaufman, Jason. 2002. *For the Common Good? American Civic Life and the Golden Age of Fraternity*. Oxford: Oxford University Press.

Kerkvliet, Benedict J. T., Russell H. K. Heng, and David W. H. Koh. 2003. *Getting Organized in Vietnam: Moving in and Around the Socialist State*. Singapore: Institute of Southeast Asian Studies.

Kitschelt, Herbert and Steven I. Wilkinson. 2007. *Patrons, Clients and Policies: Patterns of Democratic Accountability and Political Competition*. Cambridge: Cambridge University Press.

Kohli, Atul. 1994. "Where Do High Growth Political Economies Come From? The Japanese Lineage of Korea's 'Developmental State'." *World Development* 22: 1269–1293.

Kurasawa, Aiko. 2009. "Swaying Between State and Community: The Role of RT/RW in Post-Suharto Indonesia." In *Local Organizations and Urban Governance in East and Southeast Asia: Straddling State and Society*, edited by Benjamin L. Read and Robert Pekkanen, 58–83. Milton Park, Abingdon, and Oxon: Routledge.

Linz, Juan J. 1975. "Totalitarian and Authoritarian Regimes." In *Handbook of Political Science*, vol. 3, edited by F. I. Greenstein and N. W. Polsby. Reading, MA: Addison-Wesley.

Linz, Juan J. and Alfred Stepan. 1996. *Problems of Democratic Transition and Consolidation: Southern Europe, South America, and Post-communist Europe*. Baltimore, MD: Johns Hopkins University Press.

Lussier, Danielle N. and M. Steven Fish. 2012. "Indonesia: The Benefits of Civic Engagement." *Journal of Democracy* 23(1): 70–84.

Mahakanjana, Chandra. 2009. "Municipal Governments and the Role of Cooperative Community Groups in Thailand." In *Local Organizations and Urban Governance in East and Southeast Asia: Straddling State and Society*, edited by Benjamin L. Read and Robert Pekkanen, 101–120. Milton Park, Abingdon, and Oxon: Routledge.

McCarthy, Susan K. 2013. "Serving Society, Repurposing the State: Religious Charity and Resistance in China." *The China Journal* 70: 48–72.

Migdal, Joel S. 1988. *Strong Societies and Weak States: State-Society Relations and State Capabilities in the Third World*. Princeton, NJ: Princeton University Press.

Migdal, Joel S., A. Kohli, and V. Shue. 1994. *State Power and Social Forces: Domination and Transformation in the Third World*. Cambridge: Cambridge University Press.

Mitchell, Timothy. 1991. "The Limits of the State: Beyond Statist Approaches and Their Critics." *American Political Science Review* 85: 77–96.

Mukherjee, Nilanjana. 1999. "Consultations with the Poor in Indonesia." Report prepared for Poverty Reduction and Economic Management Network, The World Bank.

Öniş, Ziya. 1991. "The Logic of the Developmental State." *Comparative Politics* 24: 109–126.

Ooi, Giok Ling. 2009. "State Shaping of Community-Level Politics: Residents' Committees in Singapore." In *Local Organizations and Urban Governance in East and Southeast Asia: Straddling State and Society*, edited by Benjamin L. Read and Robert Pekkanen, 174–190. Milton Park, Abingdon, and Oxon: Routledge.

Ostrom, Elinor. 1996. "Crossing the Great Divide: Coproduction, Synergy, and Development." *World Development* 24: 1073–1087.

Peerenboom, Randy. 2007. *China Modernizes: Threat to the West or Model for the Rest?* Oxford: Oxford University Press.

Pekkanen, Robert. 2006. *Japan's Dual Civil Society: Members without Advocates*. Stanford: Stanford University Press.

Pekkanen, Robert, Yutaka Tsujinaka, and Hidehiro Yamamoto. 2014. *Neighborhood Associations and Local Governance in Japan*. Translated by Leslie Tkach-Kawasaki. Milton Park, Abingdon, and Oxon: Routledge.

Putnam, Robert D. 1993. *Making Democracy Work: Civic Traditions in Modern Italy*. Princeton, NJ: Princeton University Press.

Read, Benjamin L. 2008. "Assessing Variation in Civil Society Organizations: China's Homeowner Associations in Comparative Perspective." *Comparative Political Studies* 41: 1240–1260.

———. 2012. *Roots of the State: Neighborhood Organization and Social Networks in Beijing and Taipei*. Stanford: Stanford University Press.

Rigger, Shelley. 1999. *Politics in Taiwan: Voting for Democracy*. London: Routledge.

Rudolph, Lloyd I. and John Kurt Jacobsen. 2006. *Experiencing the State*. Oxford: Oxford University Press.

Sampson, Robert J., Doug McAdam, Heather MacIndoe, and Simón Weffer-Elizondo. 2005. "Civil Society Reconsidered: The Durable Nature and Community Structure of Collective Civic Action." *American Journal of Sociology* 111: 673–714.

Schmitter, Philippe C. 1979. "Still the Century of Corporatism?" In *Trends Toward Corporatist Intermediation*, edited by P. C. Schmitter and G. Lehmbruch. Beverly Hills, CA: Sage.

Schwartz, Benjamin I. 1996. "The Primacy of the Political Order in East Asian Societies." In *China and Other Matters*, edited by B. I. Schwartz. Cambridge, MA: Harvard University Press.

Schwartz, Frank J. 2003. "Introduction: Recognizing Civil Society in Japan." In *The State of Civil Society in Japan*, edited by S. J. Pharr and F. J. Schwartz. New York: Cambridge University Press.

Schwartz, Jonathan and Shawn Shieh. 2009. *State and Society Responses to Social Welfare Needs in China: Serving the People*. New York: Routledge.

Shiffman, Jeremy. 2002. "The Construction of Community Participation: Village Family Planning Groups and the Indonesian State." *Social Science and Medicine* 54: 1199–1214.

Smith, David Horton. 2000. *Grassroots Associations*. Thousand Oaks, CA: Sage.

Smith, Stephen Rathgeb and Michael Lipsky. 1993. *Nonprofits for Hire: The Welfare State in the Age of Contracting*. Cambridge, MA: Harvard University Press.

Stokes, Susan C. 2007. "Political Clientelism." In *The Oxford Handbook of Comparative Politics*, edited by C. Boix and S. C. Stokes. Oxford: Oxford University Press.

Sullivan, John. 1992. *Local Government and Community in Java: An Urban Case-study*. Singapore: Oxford University Press.

Tsai, Lily L. 2007. *Accountability without Democracy: How Solidarity Groups Provide Public Goods in Rural China*. Cambridge: Cambridge University Press.

Verba, Sidney, Kay L. Schlozman, and Henry E. Brady. 1995. *Voice and Equality: Civic Voluntarism in American Politics*. Cambridge, MA: Harvard University Press.

Wade, Robert. 1992. *Governing the Market: Economic Theory and the Role of Government in East Asian Industrialization*. Princeton, NJ: Princeton University Press.

Wakeman, Frederic, Jr. 1993. "The Civil Society and Public Sphere Debate: Western Reflections on Chinese Political Culture." *Modern China* 19: 108–138.

Walder, Andrew G. 1986. *Communist Neo-Traditionalism: Work and Authority in Chinese Industry*. Berkeley: University of California Press.

Walzer, Michael. 1995. "The Civil Society Argument." In *Theorizing Citizenship*, edited by R. Beiner. Albany: State University of New York.

Warner, Mildred. 1999. "Social Capital Construction and the Role of the Local State." *Rural Sociology* 64: 373–393.

Warren, Mark E. 2001. *Democracy and Association*. Princeton, NJ: Princeton University Press.

White, Tyrene. 2006. *China's Longest Campaign: Birth Planning in the People's Republic, 1949–2005*. Ithaca, NY: Cornell University Press.

World Bank. 2004. "State-society Synergy for Accountability: Lessons for the World Bank." Working Paper.

CHAPTER 37

Nonprofit Legislation in China

Peifeng Liu*

Legislation is not only used to affirm state power but also to form and regulate social relations according to the shared values of a people—particularly that of order. Order is imposed by the law, is influenced by the established social system, and ultimately responds to the demands of both. Therefore, both current legislation and cultural history are important factors in shaping civil rights and political order. The aim of this chapter is to analyze nonprofit legislation in China as part of a broader examination of the development of civil rights in the country.

Introduction

Nonprofit legislation in China has entered a new stage since the implementation of the Reform Era policies of 1978. Current legislation has fallen in step with historical trends. In the context of the sudden emergence, systematic reforms, and bourgeoning success of nonprofits, government legislation has at times actively regulated and at other times passively reacted to them. Modern nonprofit legislation was born out of various crises in the 1970s. These crises, which included waning government legitimacy, failure of centralized rule, and lack of democracy, nearly led to China's collapse after ten years of upheaval during the Cultural Revolution. During that time, the Chinese people, to their

benefit, realized the extent of corruption and the weaknesses of their political and economic systems. A highly centralized political and economic system would not lead to long-term social stability; instead, such a system would lead to social unrest and a paralyzed system of governance. Lingering civil strife and economic decline made social rehabilitation impossible and left the new government facing a crisis of legitimacy. These crises sparked the rise of civil society. The diverse nonprofit sector that emerged managed to rebuild social legitimacy, fill the gaps left by an ineffectual and corrupt central government, and encourage democratic participation. The emergence of nonprofits in the wake of these crises was, in many respects, a natural process. After the implementation of the Reform Era policies, people were able to manage their own resources independently, in a freer society. Thus, the development of a civil society to meet increasingly diverse needs should have been foreseeable. Many grassroots volunteer organizations were also established at this time.

The emergence of modern nonprofits occurred in response to both induced and spontaneous social changes. In some respects, the government effected change by taking a leading role in the evolution of nonprofits. Additionally, social vicissitudes contributed diversity and vitality to the sector. China's long history of statist rule and its efforts to develop a modern Chinese cultural identity have compelled the

 DOI: 10.4324/9780367696559-47

government to play a strong role in regulating the development of nonprofits. Vigorous government reforms have, at the same time, provided nonprofits a degree of autonomy and thereby influenced their development. Most nonprofits in China are corporatist (i.e., government-led) organizations. In the short term, Chinese nonprofits will not necessarily undermine government power but will more likely either contribute to or limit government power. Nonprofits exist at the secondary level of government, an intermediate sphere between government control and independence. Consequently, nonprofit reform can only take place within a framework of broader government reform. Social changes have given rise to new social problems and issues that have, in turn, determined nonprofits' path to reform. They have also determined the acceptance and normalization of democratic reforms. Only the rise of civil society and the subsequent emergence of political order and social participation can resolve the crises of waning legitimacy, the failure of centralized rule, and a lack of democracy. Only through this emerging civil society, can China establish a modern, integrated state and protect its people's civil rights.

Both induced and spontaneous social changes have influenced Chinese nonprofits to develop complex management models that most foreign nonprofits have never experienced. Government-affiliated nonprofits had to develop enough independence to become irreplaceable entities in the realm of public management. At the same time, private nonprofits needed to learn how to handle their position between the state and civil spheres. The most important aspect of nonprofit reform was to avoid being subsumed by the government. For grassroots organizations, which are a response to the lack of means for citizens to contribute to social and political endeavors, the most important goal was to achieve organized civil participation in social-reform movements. Only in this way could developing nonprofits

positively influence interactions between the nation and civil society and effect social change and integration. In this way, nonprofit legislation established an important balance between control and freedom.

A General Review of Current Nonprofit Legislation

The legislation that currently pertains to nonprofits in China was formulated in the context of the rise of China's Socialist regime and the Reform Era policies of 1978. Nonprofits have been managed unsustainably; in some cases, strict supervision has led to organizational collapse, whereas insufficient supervision has led to chaos. This situation is primarily a result of three circumstances. First, China's long tradition of nationalism has created an uninhabitable environment for nonprofits. Second, individuals' social participation and free expression are less feasible in a poorly organized system. Finally, the rigid administrative system leaves no space for conflict management, particularly at the level of administrative management. The government's recent crisis of legitimacy and low levels of public trust have left it no choice but to impose stricter means of social control. Compared to China's increasingly market-based economy, its social-governance system continues to embody strong characteristics of a socialist planned economy.

The centralization of political power and China's concurrent societal transformations have led the government to enact statist legislation pertaining to nonprofits, while at the same time approaching nonprofit management with a relatively hands-off approach. Article 5 of the People's Republic of China (PRC) Constitution, issued in 1982, reads, "Citizens of the People's Republic of China enjoy freedom of speech, of the press, of assembly, of association, of procession, and of demonstration." Article 5 reads, "All state bodies, the armed forces, all political parties and public organizations, and all enterprises and nonprofits must abide by the Constitution and the law. No organization or individual is above the Constitution or the law." These laws ensure the legal status of nonprofits and define principles by which they can operate. In the general principles of the Civil Law of the PRC, issued in 1986, nonprofit groups are considered individuals under the law.

The State Council commissioned the Ministry of Civil Affairs to draft a bill to regulate the registration of nonprofits. This piece of legislation went into effect on October 25, 1989, and was amended by the State Council in 1998. To bolster these regulations, the Ministry of Civil Affairs and other government departments issued additional guidelines that influenced the management and governance of nonprofits. Aside from minor adjustments, these regulations represented essentially no ideological shift from the 1950s.

Centralized Registration and Dual Oversight

China's centralized registration system requires nonprofit organizations to register with the Ministry of Civil Affairs and report to the local office of the government department related to their service area. In this system, nonprofits should enjoy the civil rights—and assume the responsibilities—of individual citizens. National organizations are registered by the Ministry of Civil Affairs and are governed by relevant departments within the State Council, whereas local organizations are registered by either the national or local Ministry of Civil Affairs, depending on their jurisdiction.

Each registration department has the following responsibilities: (a) perform all registrations and keep information filed for every registered, modified, or disbanded organization; (b) assess each registered organization annually; and (c) handle any breach of the law and administer penalties. Alternatively, the oversight departments are responsible for (a) performing

all registrations and keeping information filed for every application, registration, modification, and assessment; (b) ensuring that organizations comply with national laws and regulations and other applicable rules; (c) conducting intake assessments for new organizations; (d) supporting the institutions responsible for registration and any other entities involved in handling any breach of the law or regulations; and (e) cooperating with other institutions to guide organizations through the process of liquidation.

Once nonprofits register with the government, they acquire legal status. All nonprofits are deemed equal in terms of both status and rights; no nonprofit may subordinate or control another. This system of nonprofit oversight is characteristically Chinese, as it conforms to the planned economy. Although it is not perfect, this system is considered the best possible means for the government to oversee nonprofit operations.

The current systems of centralized registration and dual oversight create and maintain regional inequalities. The dual-oversight system also reflects the extent of state control in the nonprofit sector. Although the state encourages the development of nonprofits, it still attempts to control them and ensure that they do not overstep state-defined boundaries. In this way, these two systems conform to the patterns of the Socialist planned economy. In some ways, these types of oversight systems are appropriate in the Chinese context. Given China's insufficient administrative capacity, coupled with its vast territory, diverse cultures, and disparate levels of economic development across provinces, oversight at multiple levels of government is perhaps the most viable strategy. It is very important that dual oversight not be misinterpreted as doubly restrictive, as that would most likely prevent nonprofits from registering at all. Under such a restrictive system, competition among nonprofits would be limited, which in turn would obstruct the integration of a marketplace of free public goods, create divisions among organizations, and undermine the efficiency of resource allocation. At this early stage in their development, nonprofits are often plagued by disorganization and ineffective oversight. In light of these problems, registration and oversight by specialized departments may provide temporary sources of support. The Civil Affairs Department does not have the capacity to handle registration and oversight for all nonprofits; moreover, oversight by specialized departments allows nonprofits to serve as intermediaries. It is essential to employ the proper means to establish and sustain this system. As the present situation reveals, oversight has been too restrictive, and integration too rigid. Many regulatory agencies are operating far beyond their capacity.

Strict Registration Requirements, Lenient Oversight

Nonprofits must fulfill very strict qualifications to attain an official registration permit. Nonprofits that operate without this official permit do so illegally; their programs are not only unprotected by the law but are also at risk of being banned. China's registration process is more rigorous than in many other countries, where formal registration often only requires an initial, thorough assessment. In China, however, both the registration department and oversight department rigorously assess newly formed nonprofits. They impose strict measures to limit the development of the nonprofits in question. The dual-oversight system thereby acts as a means for the government to more tightly control civil society by eliminating antigovernment organizations. This results in red tape, wasted time, and potentially conflicting standards of assessment and censorship by the different authorities involved. The high costs of application and assessment are also burdensome for both the government and the nonprofits concerned. Another problem is that, at times, no relevant oversight departments are able to perform initial

assessments, which leaves some nonprofits no choice but to operate illegally.

In contrast with these tightly controlled registration processes, a more lenient approach is adopted to control nonpolitical, more loosely organized nonprofit groups, such as cultural and religious organizations, book clubs, and discussion forums. Although these groups do not technically qualify for legal registration, the government often treats them permissively and allows them to operate. This inconsistent application of the law often limits nonprofit programs to the short term. When circumstances become less politically stable, these groups are sometimes penalized or even outlawed. Registration standards are unjustifiably high, but there is little emphasis on overseeing their operations and implementation. Nonprofits, as members of China's civil society, must be transparent and develop solid internal management to grow; however, few regulations address these issues. Government officials place tremendous ideological importance on position; their perspective is that an individual or group's identity determines its behavior. As a result, most government efforts are focused on strictly regulating the registration process.

The government's strict registration requirements were intended to be a guide for the proper management of nonprofits. In reality, however, the inconsistent practices raise questions about the relationship between nonprofits and the government. Is the government capable of tightly regulating nonprofits, and if so, is such strict control necessary? How can we frame and understand the relationship between the government and nonprofits? Modern bureaucratic systems in China have allowed the government to control civil society. However, the complexities of China's pluralistic society are beginning to exceed the complexity of its governing structures. Given the state's limited resources and management capacity and the liberalization of Chinese society, achieving a totalitarian system will be impossible.

Nonprofits were established to meet the needs of the people; the diverse and pluralistic nature of these organizations reflects the diverse needs of society. When nonprofits are limited, human development is subsequently limited. Both the government and nonprofits are essentially social organizations, and both are absolutely necessary to achieve a highly organized, modern society. The government, from its position of authority, provides public services through enforcement, whereas nonprofits offer public services through volunteerism. They are complementary to some extent; nonprofits are able to address the problems that the government has neglected or failed to address. With respect to social management, both governmental and nongovernmental efforts are necessary. The government maintains social stability and prosperity by force, whereas nongovernmental actors play an important role in achieving social order by shaping public opinion. A complex modern society requires the integration of efforts from both civil society and individuals.

Limiting Competition and Constraining Development

Oversight structures tend to limit competition and restrain development. This is certainly true of the Chinese system, and is reflected in existing regulations. China's *Regulations for Registration and Management of Social Associations* (1998) is a 5,000-word document that contains the term *shall* in thirty-four instances; *must* in eighteen instances; and *cannot* in eight instances while barely mentioning strategies for development. Although this document is apparently aimed at protecting the civil and legal rights of nonprofits and improving the registration processes, in reality its only detailed content pertains to limitations and prohibitions. Notably, it lacks information about protection and development. Article 13 explains that multiple nonprofits with similar objectives and programs cannot exist in the same geographical area and that the

registration of any subsequent nonprofits in a given location must be rejected. Local authorities are also granted the power to "unregister" existing nonprofits or merge related nonprofits. This style of management assumes that competition is merely a cause of social instability. Additionally, an influx of nonprofits is considered undesirable, as it would potentially challenge the government's control over society. From the government's perspective, fierce competition among nonprofits could lead them to pursue resources at any cost, and in turn, deviate from their prescribed path. Article 19 describes regulations surrounding branches of large nonprofits, explaining that nonprofits do not have full legal status and that they, as well as nonprofit work units, are prohibited from establishing any additional branches. Nonprofits may only register in one location, and their operations are strictly limited to their registered location. Registration authorities oppose the establishment of multiple branches because they believe it would make the elimination of "unnecessary" nonprofits impossible. Moreover, authorities fear that, as nonprofits spread throughout provinces, counties, and towns and as new nonprofits follow suit, they will become uncontrollable.

These restrictive laws and regulations are technically effective; after all, the best way to solve a problem is to nip it in the bud. However, these regulations greatly inhibit the impact that nonprofits can make on society. Limited competition inevitably leads to abuses of power, and restricting the expansion of an organization undermines its potential effectiveness. In determining the legal status of a nonprofit, the Ministry of Civil Affairs requires that a nonprofit "meet the needs of society." This phrase is meaningless because the needs and the parties that determine those needs are not clearly defined. In theory, the government is a projection and representation of its people, so its standards and regulations should promote the needs of society. In reality, this is far from the truth—standards and regulations are designed to maintain government control over the services that nonprofits provide.

Inadequate Legislation and Outdated Ideas

In general, inadequate laws and outdated ideas are the key problems facing nonprofit legislation. Attributing problems only to inadequate laws and regulations would be an oversimplification. Legislation must be carried out in the context of broader political reforms, which shift the distribution of power and establish new systems of public management. Given the connection between power and vested interests, nonprofit legislation represents the reorganization and rearrangement of social benefits. Reforming management systems through legislation is essential to establishing a lawfully fair and open society.

When the government does not fully recognize social pluralism and lacks a sufficient understanding of and tolerance toward social organizations, the voice of civil society is silenced and its objectives are left unrealized. Currently, nonprofit legislation has three primary objectives: to protect citizens' right to free association, to control nonprofits' illegal activities and programs, and to ban and eliminate illegal nonprofits. As it stands now, the system has several problems, including overly restrictive control, a low level of legislative development, and ineffective channels for judicial solutions. The right to free association is a basic civil right that defines the relationship between the state and its citizens, as well as the relationship between state power and individual rights. The National People's Congress and its Standing Committee are responsible for producing legislation, which has the potential to guide and control this complicated web of relationships among stakeholders. In this way, legislation serves as a means to directly impose the government's will on the people. The guiding principles behind current legislation are

focused on maintaining social stability, limiting the development of nonprofits, and minimizing competition among them. This is owed to authorities placing great importance on their personal interests and convenience. In addition to simply expanding its scope and reach, this legislation will have to explicate civil rights as they pertain to associations. The most important of these are the rights to independently establish nonprofits and independently manage their internal affairs. Currently, these rights do not exist. Strict registration requirements have prevented many nonprofits from being established. Those that do obtain registration must deal with burdensome interventions and controlling measures imposed by administrative authorities. For instance, evaluation procedures and complex reporting systems limit the independence and social integration of nonprofits.

The result has been the widespread operation of illegal, unregistered nonprofits, and this has further complicated the legislative process. In its 2000 publication, *Interim Procedures for Unlawful Civil Organizations*, the Ministry of Civil Affairs classified illegal organizations into three categories: registered nonprofits that prepare programs or activities without first obtaining approval, unregistered nonprofits that operate illegally, and nonprofits whose registration has been revoked but continue to implement programs. Regardless of whether the aforementioned, unregistered organizations serve public needs, they are considered illegal. It is unreasonable to base the legitimacy of a nonprofit on its identity rather than its impact; certainly, many registered organizations conduct their affairs without scruple. Although the Chinese registration process simplifies the task of monitoring nonprofits, it also creates barriers to starting up an organization. In contrast, other countries have established simple, clear-cut codes to manage illegal organizations and have integrated those codes into criminal law. Government monitoring, to some extent, can also translate to social oversight by identifying violent and criminal organizations. The broad definition of "illegal organization" conflicts with the legitimacy of nonprofits and affects the legitimacy of the government and the public's recognition of government efficacy.

Another gap in legislation pertaining to nonprofits is the lack of legal recourse for the nonprofits themselves. Regulations do not specifically address any legal recourse for nonprofits in response to rejected applications for registration or sanctions. In the 1989 revision of the national Regulations for Registering Civil Associations, applicants may no longer appeal to higher civil affairs departments when their applications are rejected. Perhaps, the promulgation of the "administrative reconsideration" law will alleviate the problem. This law plans to make it possible for applicants and nonprofits to safeguard their rights by applying for administrative reconsideration and participating in administrative proceedings. These opportunities, however, will likely be limited within the current legal environment.

Additionally, current regulations surrounding nonprofit management are too rigidly principled and lack maneuverability. Legislators will need to develop provisions for intrabranch management, membership, performance reporting, and information disclosure, each of which is conducive to the independent management and oversight of nonprofits. To survive in a pluralistic society, nonprofits must demonstrate self-discipline and strong supervision. They must also be subject to regulations and standards. It is also very important to establish an effective performance-evaluation system. In turn, ineffective associations can be weeded out, which can prevent the waste of social resources.

Finally, nonprofits serve as intermediaries between the nation and society. For this reason, it is crucial for them to be governed by a fair and comprehensive set of laws. Currently China does not have a tax code specifically for nonprofits, and legislation relating to finances and government purchasing do not account for the recent development of civil society. In developed countries, the situation is quite different: over 50 percent of nonprofit funding comes from service fees and government support. In China, however, there is a great deal of skepticism surrounding the public services offered by nonprofits. As nonprofits have expanded and developed, there have been a number of public scandals involving abuses of power. For instance, price-fixing in the nonprofit sector is antithetical to the interests of the public and requires government intervention in the form of antitrust law. Continually amending the regulations pertaining to nonprofits is simply a delay tactic; instead, the legal environment must be fundamentally adapted.

Despite the significance of these issues, the core problem facing China's nonprofit legislation is its lack of guiding principles. First, current laws that regulate social management only focus on short-term social stability, rather than long-term peace and security. These regulations lack foresight and generally disregard the recent developments of civil society in this era of pluralism. This has led to misunderstandings about the status and role of nonprofits. Traditionally in China, nonprofits have been regarded as tools used by the government to implement policies and a bridge spanning public opinion and the CPC. It is often forgotten that nonprofits can be government affiliated, market focused, or nongovernmental and that each distinct form is a necessary mechanism for social integration and stable governance. These different types of nonprofits satisfy the range of needs at different levels of society. In most countries, with the exception of totalitarian states, the interplay of these different types of nonprofits is important, despite their distinct roles in social development, diverse cultures, and varying levels of autonomy. The balance among the market, government, and nongovernmental mechanisms is what guarantees prolonged social stability and peace.

Second, China's history of administrative management has been replaced by an unstable political system that features low administrative standards. Long-term social oppression and limited autonomy initially led to the broad failure of social management. Subsequently, the government became diffident about the capacity of civil society to manage itself. In the name of managing and educating nonprofits, the government imposed burdensome, controlling standards of oversight. In the absence of clear distinctions between political responsibility and administrative responsibility, short-term "stability" and financial indicators have become the only criteria for evaluating government programs. It is sometimes assumed that ignoring a problem may produce the desired outcome in the short run but will backfire in the long run. Similarly, based only on financial indicators, both the central and local governments support and foster the development of economic nonprofits, including trade associations, chambers of commerce, and agricultural collectives. This is the result of systemic change—the improvement of government functioning and the implementation of economic considerations. Many nonprofits perform unique functions. For instance, social service associations and fraternal associations, which certainly meet important social needs, also have the potential to act as agents of change for financial organizations, helping to expand their capability and reach.

Alexis de Tocqueville once suggested that civil associations contribute to the development of political associations, which in turn promote further development among civil associations. Given the diversity and interconnectedness of civil associations, their recent challenges will not necessarily lead to greater instability and conflict. The government maintains its monopoly on political mobilization by imposing restrictions on civil organizations and limiting their social integration. On the other hand, the government must face the public and take responsibility for social conflict. This will, in turn, affect the public's conception of the government's legitimacy and social stability. Sociologist Georg Simmel pointed out that

significant conflict could lead to the elimination of divisive elements in society and help to reunify the people. Conflicts could also stabilize opposition and thereby act as balancing forces. Loosely structured nonprofit groups are somewhat tolerant of conflict and can actually serve to clarify core values and minimize the risk of a societal schism. Interdependence and challenges among opposing groups help to stabilize society and prevent irreparable divisions. The government must take advantage of the current, stable social environment to learn how to cope with crises and govern civil society effectively. As nonprofits have developed and expanded in recent years, the government's ability to manage and regulate them has likewise expanded; however, the government's concerns about nonprofits are seemingly unwarranted.

As for the legal basis for nonprofits, the civil right of association enables people to meet their own needs through locally established organizations and provides opportunities for political involvement. Without nonprofits acting as protective barriers, individuals would not be able to withstand or confront government abuses or the harshest realities of the market system. The government is responsible for safeguarding the civil right to association and encouraging the development of nonprofits. In recent years, however, the government has made minimal efforts to implement its stated policies. In fact, it has resisted the establishment of nonprofits that serve vulnerable populations, including migrant workers and the unemployed, and has restricted the creation of fraternal associations. These vulnerable populations urgently need nonprofit organizations and associations to intervene on behalf of their rights.

Conclusion

A mature society is one that fosters tolerance and competition rather than oppression and monopoly. There are many ways, ranging in effectiveness, to deal with the existing challenges that face nonprofits in China. Some have adopted a passive attitude, choosing to ignore, deny, or downplay the importance of these issues. Others have suggested measures to wholly eliminate the problems, have attempted to relieve social pressure by overstating the problems and their consequences, have addressed the existing problems by proposing technological solutions, or have deceived themselves and others by pointing to problems that do not exist. In solving these problems, the most important steps will be to squarely face the issues and reasonably assess their gravity. In most cases, fear and hopelessness stem from misunderstanding. For this reason, problems can only be solved through direct confrontation. In a dynamic, pluralistic society, problem solving requires the implementation of both political wisdom and skilled governance.

According to this analysis, nonprofit legislation in China must address a number of important issues. These include political issues, such as the distribution of political power and delegation of authority, and technical issues, such as the establishment of effective mechanisms of governance and supervision. Political and social participation are also involved. Currently, social resources are available only to elites; this has become a serious problem. In such a polarized society and amid mounting conflicts, social crises are more likely than ever before. However, the systematization of social forces may be an effective means to address these conflicts. Systematization makes it possible to promote political reform through transitions in governance, even within an unchanged political system. This approach will also help to stabilize society and the political system over the long term. In other words, society is not only the source of problems but is also the solution to those problems. Regarding outcomes, an expanded civil sector has developed new ways to address social problems. This has set the stage for a multifaceted model of social governance. Nonprofit legislation relates to the civil right of association and to the rational arrangement of various social forces. Given that the Chinese Constitution entitles all people to freedom and to respectful and equal treatment under the law, the problem of governance is essentially a problem of how to govern. This problem can be solved by the rule of law. Although public management cannot take the place of public participation, it can be used as a means to promote pluralism, transparency, and eventually democracy. Public management also emphasizes the importance of public power and individual survival. Currently, the Chinese government does not sufficiently recognize civil society's pluralism, autonomy, and early development or the checks and balances that exist within society. In this regard, the right to association is obstructed by a lack of recognition and institutional barriers. It is, however, possible to resolve the right to association and strong social management through sound practices and institutions. As demonstrated earlier, a basic feature of social management is the coexistence of rigid control and leniency.

Currently, the government does not fully comprehend the level of societal pluralism or its impact on civil society in China. This lack of understanding, magnified by institutional barriers, inherently limits the people's right to association. There are ways to address these problems though. One possibility is to limit the government's role in oversight by requiring organizations to submit detailed strategic plans in lieu of registration. This would increase the number of organizations that are granted permits, which would thereby encourage organizations to form through legal means. Organizations would be held accountable to their initial plans, but the government would play a smaller role in regulation. Through this process, previously rejected organizations would have a second chance to gain legal status. It would also make it easier for the government to monitor nonprofits and would allow nonprofits to operate independently. Local governments are currently piloting this system, and many scholars have proposed using it to expand access to nonprofit registration. Second, the system of dual oversight, which is often criticized, could be reformed. The current system prevents some organizations from registering simply because they cannot locate an appropriate sponsoring department. In cases of nonprofits that are approved, these sponsoring departments interfere with their internal management, which restricts their development. In view of China's relatively poor management capacity, the system of dual oversight should be replaced by a centralized, integrated system. However, neither dual oversight nor a centralized system can fully address the nation's management capacity challenges. For instance, a centralized system would not be able to properly oversee all nonprofits. Because of this, the inevitable path would be toward the systematic management of nonprofits. Obligations to disclose information should be placed on political nonprofits, particularly those nongovernmental organizations that deal with foreign affairs, possess large funding bases, and raise funds publically. Regarding other nongovernmental organizations, the government should grant them some degree of autonomy as a means to promote their development. At the same time, the government should support regulatory organizations or individuals who can provide intermediary oversight. Certainly, the government must establish effective means to report offenses. Such technical approaches will help the country achieve a balance between nonprofit development and government administration and state power and state capacity.

As nonprofits mature, they will inevitably participate in the development of nonprofit legislation. In fact, there are two ways to deal with this: introduce competition or improve the quality of participation by instituting technical and procedural regulations. As civil society becomes more differentiated, the political system is becoming segmented, which obstructs competitive participation in the system. At present, it is important to systemically enhance competition. Political reforms since the 1980s have reflected strong efforts by the government to expand public participation and improve the quality of governance. These goals are reflected in the Constitution and the party constitution. As nonprofits mature and develop and structural reforms expand, the conditions for further progress are becoming ripe. Differentiation is common among interest groups, and current participation problems can be solved by gradually and systematically introducing new organizations. In addition, appropriate decentralization of authority, along with policy decisions being delegated to lower levels of government, will improve the relationship between the government and the nonprofit sector. It will be more practical to introduce new systems and policies at the provincial level. Other approaches to achieving improved participation include consultation programs and making government affairs more transparent. Social participation is a matter of governance, a realm that has matured with respect to integrating nonprofits into the legislative process. The current priorities should be to craft policies on public funding, diversify social services, and provide the opportunity for nonprofits to participate in policymaking. Expanded participation of nonprofits, along with diversified methods of social governance, will not only improve social management but will also enable the government to focus more on its own affairs. Subsequently, the government can transform from an all-powerful force to a limited force; in time, its traditional, controlling structures will give way to new modes of service provision. Moreover, authoritarian governance will be replaced by good governance.

Note

*   Translated by Juliann H. Vikse, Research Fellow, Huamin Research Center, School of Social Work, Rutgers University.

Index

Note: **Bold** page references indicate tables. *Italic* references indicate figures and boxed text.